COLONIZATION:
A GLOBAL HISTORY

'An extraordinarily adventurous work, in many respects almost a global history of the making of the modern world.'

Andrew Porter, *University of London*

'A lively and fascinating synthesis dealing with a major theme in the history of the world. Studiously avoiding the pitfalls of Eurocentrism, the author casts his net wide and his coverage is far more extensive than in any comparable work.'

Geoffrey Scammell, *University of Cambridge*

Marc Ferro's *Colonization: A Global History* is a wide-ranging comparative account of one of the most significant themes in recent history. Uniquely, Ferro considers European, Japanese, Turkish and Arab colonization. He emphasizes ex-colonial views, and does not subscribe to the orthodox view that the history of colonization is necessarily followed by the history of the struggle of the people for their independence. He examines the impact on decolonization of other factors, such as globalization.

Colonization: A Global History is also unusual in giving prominence to the social and cultural dimensions of colonialism. Ferro analyses the new types of societies and economies brought about by colonization. He considers, for example, the impact of colonization in areas such as education and medicine.

Ferro's richly textured overview offers a stimulating range of perspectives on a topic of considerable significance. It will be of interest to those researching and studying all aspects of colonization and decolonization.

COLONIZATION:
A GLOBAL HISTORY

Marc Ferro

London and New York

First published in English in 1997
by Routledge
11 New Fetter Lane, London EC4P 4EE

Original French edition
© 1994 Editions du Seuil
Histoire des colonisations

Translated by K.D. Prithipaul

Typeset in Baskerville by
Keystroke, Jacaranda Lodge, Wolverhampton

Printed and bound in Great Britain by
Redwood Books, Trowbridge, Wiltshire

British Library Cataloguing in Publication Data
A catalogue record for this book is available from the British Library

ISBN 0–415–14007–2 (hbk)
ISBN 0–415–14008–0 (pbk)

CONTENTS

PREFACE

During the time of the colonies we were given the rose-coloured view. Of course the colonist worked hard. Persecuted in his own country before setting forth, he had gone to settle down in a place to which he had been led by the Almighty. There he intended to cultivate the land, to grow and blossom, and there to multiply. However, to this end "he had to defend himself against aggressors, rebels and other such swine". How great was his glory! How meritorious it was to suffer in order to be a conqueror!

Today the tune has changed. A guilty conscience has taken over. Anti-colonialism, once confined to the extreme left in France and to old-fashioned liberals across the Channel, has become universal. There are very few false notes. History is called upon to judge, in turn, the terrible misdeeds of the slave trade, the tragic toll of forced labour and God knows what else besides! Drawing up a final balance sheet for the French, Dutch, or British presence, one cannot find a single orange that was not defiled, a single apple that was not rotten.

Thus, with unsurpassed intransigence and as the final prerogative of pride, the European historical memory has retained for itself one last privilege: that of painting its own misdeeds in dark colours and evaluating them on its own terms.

However this audacity raises some questions. For instance, when the anti-colonialist tradition claims that no rickshaw was shown at the Exhibition of 1931 "thanks to" the action of the League of the Rights of Man, one wonders. A few years earlier, at the Marseilles Fair, had not the Annamese vowed not to play the role of coolies and that, if forced to do so, they would set fire to the Exhibition Park?

In short these Annamese, these Blacks, these Arabs, played their part as well. It is advisable to let them have their say, for, if they remember the infamous crimes already mentioned, they also recall with gratitude their school teachers and their physicians, malaria and the White Fathers. For this too was colonization. Likewise the struggle for independence was not merely a "decolonization".

The histories of colonization have traditionally been told from the different points of view prevailing in the mother country. As Frantz Fanon puts it, "because colonization is the extension of this mother country, the history which the colonist writes is not that of the despoiled country, but the history of his own nation".

But here I intend to adopt a different plan. In the first instance, it is necessary to take into account the past history of colonized societies, because the relationship between the colonists and the colonized to a large extent depended on it. Nobody nowadays asserts, as they did till very recently, that these peoples have never had a history. We no longer speak of "dark centuries", but rather of "opaque centuries" (see Lucette Valensi), because they were unintelligible to those who came into contact with them.

These peoples were not similar, not uniform merely by the fact that they had not yet been colonized. Further, if it is true that one colonization was different from another, the response of the conquered societies was equally varied in terms of their respective pasts and of their own identities.

Moreover, it is difficult to understand why historical analysis should assume a vision of the past which Europeanizes the colonial phenomenon. Admittedly, for five centuries Europeans embodied it and thereby set their seal on the unification of the world. But other colonizations have also contributed to fashioning the present image of the planet.

Prior to Europe, there were the colonizations of the Greeks and the Romans. There were also those of the Arabs and the Turks, who conquered the coasts of the Mediterranean, part of black Africa and of West Asia, reaching as far as India, which had itself, at the beginning of the common era, colonized Sri Lanka (Ceylon), part of the Indonesian peninsula and the Sunda Islands. Nor should one forget the Chinese who, in the fifteenth century, explored the eastern seaboard of Africa and colonized Tibet. The Japanese, likewise, conquered and colonized Yeso shortly before the Russians reached Sakhalin and the French, Canada.

But my intention is not to draw up an inventory of all the phenomena of expansion, or of colonization, or even to make the European colonial enterprise seem commonplace. It is, rather, to compare and contrast that enterprise on occasions with others.

This bias in favour of a global perspective derives from a concern not to reproduce a Eurocentric view of history. It determines other points of view as well.

First, I shall be considering colonization as a phenomenon which cannot be dissociated from imperialism, that is, from forms of domination which may, or may not, have assumed the appearance of colonization. On the one hand, for populations who were subjugated without interruption from the sixteenth to the twentieth centuries – in India, in Angola, in the West Indies – there was continuity, and no break, in their state of dependency. This was so even if, during the age of imperialism, that is, from the end of the nineteenth century, their dependency assumed new forms. On the other hand, certain historical or geographical conglomerations which were not colonies – for example, the Ottoman Empire shortly before 1914, Iran, some Central or South American states – have lived their history as a struggle against the imperialist powers.

Secondly, I do not subscribe to the orthodox opinion that in every case there was first the history of colonization and then later the history of the people's struggle for their independence. In Benin or Burma or Vietnam, for example, these histories were synchronic. Moreover, although the colonial discourse may have clouded over the views of those who were vanquished, this does not mean that the latter had, while in subjection, lost the very idea of recovering control of their own history. Hence, in this book, the term decolonization has been used with prudence, for it still connotes to some extent the persistence of a Eurocentric view.

Lastly, in analysing these problems, I felt the urgent need to free the history of colonization from the ghetto to which it had been confined by tradition. It is indeed revealing that in the great works of reflection on memory or on the past – of France, for example – no mention is ever made of the colonial societies. Should one see this as an omission, a lost opportunity, or a taboo?

Undoubtedly, as far as European colonization is concerned, many studies have cogently analysed some of its reverse effects, especially the economic ones. One thinks of the work done on Seville, Bordeaux, Bristol, Nantes. However, the question has scarcely been raised as to whether the types of relationships established with the colonies were all specific, or whether they ought not to be compared with others.

So, first question: the case of the Russian Empire entitles one to ask whether the national problem and the colonial problem are different. Is it the particular status of subject peoples, the non-participation of elites in the central authority, that constitutes this difference?

And, above all, there is a second question that remains open: have not, in Europe itself, certain political regimes behaved towards subject populations in the same way as was done in the colonies? It has been noted that racism became more marked there as time went on. Did it not produce situations similar to those which the Nazis institutionalized? Is it worth asking such questions? One is prompted to do so by certain telltale signs.

One is struck by a sacrilegious analogy when looking at images of the British presence in India, especially the pictures of the Great Durbar of 1911, preserved in the National Film Archive of London: the march past, the helmets, the discipline, the theatrical space skilfully and aesthetically organized along a plunging perspective towards the Emperor George V, the public held at a distance by cordons of soldiers. One cannot resist the feeling that this coronation foreshadows Hitler's rallies of twenty years later.[1] Is this a fortuitous analogy?

Here is another parallel, an inverse one, established by Aimé Césaire, in 1955:

> What the very Christian bourgeois of the twentieth century cannot forgive Hitler for is not the crime in itself, the crime against humanity, not the humiliation of humanity itself, but the crime against the white man . . . ; it is the crime of having applied to Europe the colonialist actions as were borne up till now by the Arabs, the coolies of India and the negroes of Africa.
>
> (Césaire, 1955)

A final, and recent, sacrilegious analogy is found in the proposal made by the Prime Minister of Western Australia in 1993 to submit to a popular referendum a decision of the Supreme Court to restore part of the land of which the aborigines had been robbed in the last century. This led the Anglican Bishop of Perth to declare: "The State Government is adopting the methods of the Nazis." This recourse to the "democratic" will against the appeal to equity, to just right, is indeed one of the methods of totalitarianism, one of the problems of our time.

These premises account for the plan of this book. It deals with each problem from the time of its emergence in history, examining conquests, divisions or rivalries, from the twelfth and thirteenth centuries up to the present conflict in the Kurile Islands, as well as the views of those who were vanquished, their resistance, the pitch-black or rosy legends of colonization, the movements initiated by the colonists, the constitution of new societies.

Undoubtedly this plan diverges to some extent from traditional scholarship which examines first the discoveries, then colonial expansion up to the nineteenth century, then imperialism, and lastly "decolonization". But I believe it will help us to understand better the complexity of certain phenomena, especially the nature of certain nations, their appearance and disappearance in history, and the mentalities which have been developing slowly down to our own day.

In adopting the points of view of the various protagonists in this story, I am not suggesting that the intermingling of these different memories suffices in itself to explain the many problems posed by colonization and its consequences. But they do provide an essential piece of data, since imaginings are as much a part of history as historical fact and, even when it is mistaken, memory remains both an element and an agent of history.

That is why this work is a comparative one, organized in such a way as to explain situations and problems, rather than to follow the customary procedures of formal construction.

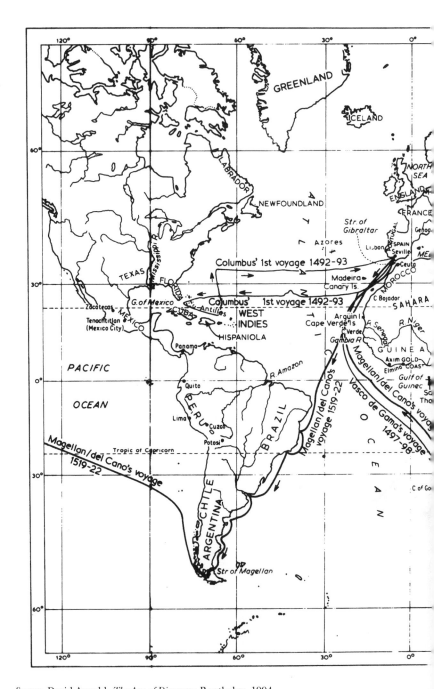

Source. David Arnold, *The Age of Discovery*, Routledge, 1994

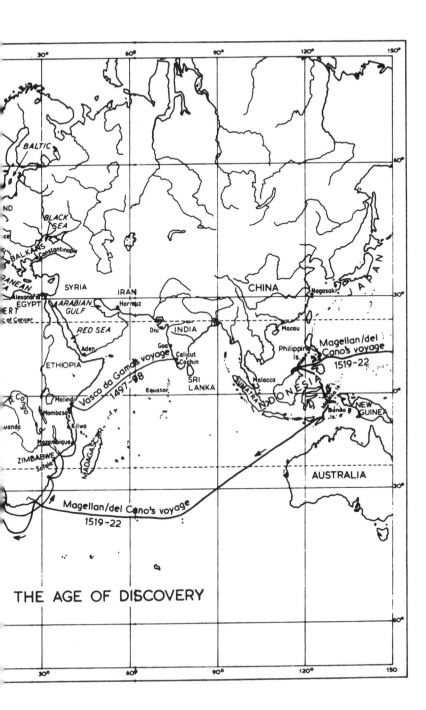

THE AGE OF DISCOVERY

1

COLONIZATION OR IMPERIALISM

Gold or Christ

Colonization is associated with the occupation of a foreign land, with its being brought under cultivation, with the settlement of colonists. If this definition of the term "colony" is used, the phenomenon dates from the Greek period. Likewise we speak of Athenian, then Roman "imperialism". Has there been any change in the meaning of this term?

Western historical tradition, however, places the date of the colonial phenomenon at the time of the Great Discoveries. For example, according to the *Histoire de la France coloniale*, published in 1991, the "real colonial adventure" began with the explorers of the fifteenth century, when Jean de Béthencourt received from Henry IV, King of Castile, the Canary Islands as fief. It goes on to say that the exploration and discoveries in America took place later: the Bay of Rio de Janeiro and the Florida coast were occupied towards the middle of the sixteenth century, prior to any interest being directed towards Canada, during the reign of Henri IV and thanks to Champlain. This way of looking at colonization is equally valid for Portugal, Spain and England. That is, historical tradition links the expansion of these countries to the discovery of distant lands in the West Indies, followed by the installation of trading-posts along the routes of Africa, India and Asia.

Thus terms such as "colonist" and "colonization" disappear from the vocabulary of the history covering the period from the Roman era to the fifteenth century. The exceptions, during these twelve centuries, are the colonies or trading-posts which Venice or Genoa established on the other side of the Mediterranean or on the Black Sea, but still a good way from home.

However the case of Russia needs to be thought about. "Colonization is the essential element in our history", wrote the historian M. Kluchevski in 1911. "Its development explains the growth as well as the changes experienced by the state and the society since the time of Rus, the Russia of the Dnieper." Beginning in the twelfth century, the incursions of Novgorod, then those of Suzdal in the direction of the Urals and beyond, ended in the submission of the Mordvins and other peoples. Interrupted by the Tartar invasion (1220), the incursions, following the expulsion of the Tartars after the victory of Kulikovo, were resumed in 1390.

But were these, in a strict sense, "colonial" expeditions? In any case, since the beginning of the eleventh century, Novgorod had been sending men up as far as the Pechora. This region, called the Zovoloche, to the east of the Dvina, was the habitat of foxes and sables for which a tribute had to be paid. The colonists lived in Matygory, Ukhto-Ostrov, and received their instructions from the officials and civil servants of the great city, the *posadniki.*

Up to the twelfth century the expansion proceeded without any noteworthy impediment. But the situation changed as soon as the principality of Suzdal-Rostov freed itself from its dependence on Kiev and intercepted the traffic between Novgorod and its colonies. In 1169 this principality provoked their secession and its colonists joined Suzdal. At the same time Suzdal-Rostov attacked the Bulgarians who were then grouped in the region of present-day Perm, in the Urals. The latter were themselves engaged in a struggle with the "natives", the "Yura" or "Yugia" of the chronicles of the period. Within a short time, the Russians completed the conquest of the territory of the Mordvin.

At this point the Tartars rose up. They reached Nijni-Novgorod, established in 1221, the former Mordvin territories and the countries of the Dvina. Novgorod in the west was the only city to resist them (1232).

Consequently the case of Russia would indicate that, between the territorial expansion in the direction of Siberia and the conquest of the Tartar and Turkish territories, there is certainly a gap, but there is also a similarity, except in the difficulty of conquest. Thus, territorial expansion and colonization are more or less synonymous. But, in the West, the distinction is carefully emphasized: sea space is supposed to constitute the difference between the former, which is part of the national question, and the colonial question as such.

The spice route: how much is this explanation worth?

How good a criterion is sea space? Here we are confronted with the problem of Spain and Portugal. In these countries the Americas are viewed as a land of conquest, of colonization. But can one not say the same about the furthest advances of the Reconquista? – beyond Granada, into the Riff and on to the Atlantic coast; from the Portuguese Algarve, that is the Al Gharb, as far as Tangiers and Mazagan, the conquered territories which were retaken by Don Sebastian, leading in 1578 to the disastrous defeat of Alcazarquivir, the battle of the Three Kings. This foray, like the Russian expansion beyond the Volga, is an example of continuity with former enterprises; there is no evidence of discontinuity.

2

It is now evident that the history of colonization cannot be made to start with the Great Discoveries overseas, that is, with the search for a route to India. The discoveries may have altered the dimensions of the phenomenon of colonization and perhaps its nature, but expansionism preceded it. The need to bypass the Turkish Empire, with all its consequences, does not by itself fully account for the different dimensions of the expansionist colonial phenomenon.

This is precisely what the Arab tradition holds. The Arabs believe that European expansion began with the Crusades, the first expression of "imperialism". The Western tradition, by contrast, views the Crusades as an attempt to reconquer the Holy Land from Islam which had seized a Christian country. In any event, a European history of colonization must of necessity take the perimeter of Christendom as its starting point.

From the seventh century on, Arab Islam had unified the greater part of that Mediterranean world which had been fragmented since the division of the Roman Empire and amputated by the penetration of the "Barbarians". In the east and west, Byzantium and the Carolingian Empire constituted, in the face of Islam and the Arabs, the two poles of Christian resistance. But, for the Muslims, the barbarian kingdoms of the West scarcely counted.[1] Only the Roman Empire stood as a real obstacle to the total reunification of the Mediterranean space. For the Muslims, Byzantium represented the survival of a state that was dominated by an outmoded religion, Christianity. The break-up of the Arab Empire began in the following centuries, under the pressure of internal, theological or dynastic conflicts between the Shiites and the Sunnis, but also as a result of the fragmentation of economic areas and of the difficulty of controlling such a vast territory, stretching from India to the far West.

As a result the Christian marches gradually succeeded in liberating themselves: in the West, beginning with the Asturias; in the East, thanks to the action of the Bagration dynasty which, for a while, "freed" Armenia and later Georgia. Was this a liberation? Was it a decolonization? Then, according to the Christian tradition, came the era of the Crusades, "for the reconquest of the tomb of Christ". This is how Ibn al-Athir, an Arab historian who lived in those times, refers to the earliest expeditions: "The first appearance of the *Empire* of the Franks (my italics), their invasion of the land of Islam occurred in 478 (A.D. 1086) when they captured Toledo . . . Then they attacked Sicily, Africa and finally, in 490, Syria." Even in the twentieth century the establishment of the Frankish States of Syria is thought of as a harbinger of the future "invasions", that of Israel being the latest. Moreover if the last crusade was indeed that of Saint Louis at Tunis, in 1270, it became possible subsequently to speak of a "thirteenth crusade" when, under the aegis of the Papacy and of Philip II of Spain, three centuries later, the Christian fleets defeated Islam at the battle of Lepanto

(1571). In the meantime the Turks had taken over from the Arabs, destroyed their empire and forced them into subjection. That was a dramatic upset which the Arabo-Islamic tradition conceals even today, as if the destroyers of the past greatness of the Arabs had been, not the Turks, but the Westerners who, during the period of imperialism, had renewed the attack.

When, after their victory over the Arabs, the Ottoman Turks replaced them, they did actually launch a new *jihad* which culminated with the fall, in 1453, of Byzantium, the Eastern Roman Empire, followed by the march upon Vienna, the capital of the Hapsburgs. Never had the Muslim Turkish Empire been as powerful as it was during the time of Soliman. The wars of Philip II and the battle of Lepanto constituted a halt to the second expansion of Islam. In the light of these events, should one speak of a conquest, or of a colonization?

The four routes

Christianity's counter-attack took place elsewhere and in a different manner. On one hand, in order to be able to trade with India and China, well known since the travels of Marco Polo, it was necessary to search for new routes to bypass the Ottoman Empire. However the expedition of Vasco da Gama had a religious connotation as well. When, after going round Africa, he arrived at Calicut the navigator declared "that he had come in search of Christians and spices". And, like the Portuguese, the Ottomans assimilated the trade associated with the Great Discoveries to one of the forms of holy war. "Let us dig a canal at Suez", they said at the time, "so that we may go to India and Sind, drive away the Infidels and bring back precious commodities."

Thus one ought not to overlook the context of the holy war in a search for the origins of the "discoveries" and of the history of colonization. As Fernand Braudel has shown, the main activities in trade and politics did indeed shift, around 1580, from the Mediterranean to the Atlantic. The legacy of the preceding conflicts was none the less still vivid in the memory of those who had not broken away from this past by transferring their attention to other worlds. Bernard Lewis has shown that, in the Islamic world, the remembrance of past greatness is the better preserved because Islam has a single dominant language, Arabic, which ensures the omnipresence of the Quran, while the "memory and the learning of the Infidels are dispersed in more than twenty-five languages". One comes across this manner of judging the other again, several centuries later, among the English colonizers in India, the French in black Africa, or the Russians in the Caucasus. As a result when the Christian reappears, in 1798 at Alexandria, and subsequently at Algiers in 1830, for the Muslim he remains the Infidel – still scorned and ignored. But if he establishes himself, takes command, colonizes, he very soon generates a trauma which is expressed with singular violence:

> We have humiliated emirs more powerful than you. They have
>   knelt down before our spears, their women have been our mats.
> The gallop of our horses made the mountains of Jemanah quake.
> We have pitched our tents in Voutoulou and in Damascus.
> We have chased from this land all the enemies who, like hyenas,
>   were harassing us.
> I have seen what happened yesterday, I know all that will happen
>   tomorrow.
>
> *Songs of war and of love of Islam*

This resentment provides a clue to understanding the violence of the events which were soon to follow.

The second route The nature of the efforts of exploration in the direction of the Americas is not without a connection with the preceding ones. Actually the writings of Columbus himself bear this out. He testifies that during his first voyage gold, or rather the search for gold, was omnipresent. On 15 October 1492 he wrote in his diary: "I do not want to stop, but to proceed further to visit many islands and to discover gold."

But Christopher Columbus was not out simply to enrich himself personally and his sailors. He also aimed to enrich his patrons, the Kings of Spain, "so that they should understand the importance of the enterprise". For him wealth was important first and foremost because it meant the recognition of his role as a discoverer. Furthermore, this thirst for money is justified by a religious vocation which is nothing less than the expansion of Christianity. On 26 December 1492 he wrote in his diary that he "hopes to find gold in such quantities that the kings will be able, within three years, to prepare for and undertake *the conquest of the Holy Land*".

The third route Christopher Columbus was obsessed by the idea of a crusade: the reconquest of Jerusalem was one of his aims. We may observe that the same applied to the third route which was supposed to lead to India by way of the interior of Africa, and whose very existence was questionable. As the work of Geneviève Bouchon has shown, the purpose of reaching India through the Kingdom of Prester John was an alliance with Ethiopia to take the Empire of the Moors in the rear. For her part Queen Eleni felt the need to loosen the grip of Islam which controlled all the accesses of her kingdom to the Red Sea and the Indian Ocean. The political worries of the queen converged with the religious preoccupations of the Coptic Metropolitan, whose nomination was in the control of the Egyptians. He wanted to have a closer relationship with Rome. So the decision was taken to send Mateus, the Metropolitan of the Ethiopian Church, on his famous mission from Ethiopia to Lisbon, *via* India.

Mateus met Albuquerque in India. The latter grasped the full import of the enterprise. At the same time he saw the illusory character of any relationships which the Negus might establish with the King of Portugal. The story of Mateus' secret departure from Ethiopia illustrates the ubiquity of the Egyptian agents and the fear which the Ethiopians had of the Arabs. According to the account related by Damiao de Gois, Queen Eleni gave Mateus and his young companion Ya'kob letters of recommendation for the *barnagas* (cf. Geneviève Bouchon), the viceroy of the maritime province, "in order that he might help them as secretly as possible in everything that would be necessary, by pretending that they were merchants who had come to him to do business solely on her behalf". "For a while (*aliquamdiu*) Mateus acted in full freedom, never confiding his schemes to anyone and revealing neither what he had to do nor where he had to go. He passed himself off as a pelt trader, the more safely to fulfil the task that had been entrusted to him. However, from time to time, he would buy pieces of Indian jewelery which he would send in secret to Queen Eleni. Under this pretext he travelled through various regions of various countries, doing all this in order that, protected from the ambushes of his enemies while crossing the kingdoms and states of the many adversaries to the Lusitanian name, he might reach the Portuguese and fulfil the duties of the mission he had undertaken. There was no other way of carrying out the task."

The fourth route The opening of a fourth route, the northern one, coincided with the beginning of the fifteenth century. Russians living under the Mongol yoke, who were sent to Peking as hunting guides or guards, discovered the riches of China, then those of India on returning from China by way of Samarkand. The information reached Tver where Afanasi Nikitin organized, as early as 1466, the first expedition to India. At that time, Astrakhan, together with Bukhara and Khiva, constituted the still tenuous point of contact between, on one hand, the products of China and India, and, on the other, the products of Russia or the Baltic countries. Subsequently Zotov would write to the Court of Russia that "these cities would be of great use to us, for there lie the riches of China and India".

This route is the only one which, at that time had no connection with a crusade. But later the situation changed. In the age of imperialism it was in the name of orthodoxy that the Tsar wanted to colonize the Far East.

A social cause: the decline of the nobility

The list of things which account for the discoveries and colonization is well known: religious zeal, love for adventure, thirst for wealth, revenge by conquest. Does this set of reasons account fully for the surging vigour that marked the fifteenth and sixteenth centuries?

Undoubtedly, yes, as regards the conscious or unconscious behaviour of individuals. But there are at the same time weightier causes which pre-determined the ability of some to act, while others did not.

The conflicts of the fourteenth and fifteenth centuries – the Hundred Years War among others – resulted in the displacement of the great trading routes. In part they had to abandon the land, particularly between Flanders and Italy, in favour of the sea, between Genoa, Barcelona, Lisbon, Bruges, Antwerp and Amsterdam. So it was that Ceuta became, at that time, a strategic point. This displacement resulted in the considerable enrichment of the ports of the Atlantic seaboard. This was particularly true of Lisbon, whose "nation" was established in Bruges as early as the fifteenth century. Thus it was that in Lisbon one could come across Italian merchants, especially from Genoa, who had an eye on the trade with the Orient, but they had no means of organizing expeditions on a large scale. Besides they ran the risk of being shut out by the Venitians, or even of being stopped, as we know, by the Ottomans.

Capital was available in the Iberian Peninsula. But the route to the far North lay through forests. To the south, however, the links with Islam remained active in spite of the wars. Besides sea traffic was easy as far as southern Morocco. Moreover, at that time, the States of Castile and Portugal were in the process of being strengthened, while France, Burgundy, and the Empire were tearing themselves apart. That is why the younger members of the Castilian and Portuguese nobility became interested in these wealth-promoting commercial enterprises. Not owning any land they felt the need for such enterprises so as not to suffer any loss of social status. They joined the merchants.

This social phenomenon operated in tandem with actual scientific or technical developments – related to the Renaissance – and the economic or religious situation. The Polish historian Marian Malowist wondered whether overseas colonization in the case of Portugal, Spain and Genoa, the wars in Italy in the case of France, and expansion to the north and the east in the case of the Germans, and of the Poles and the Russians, were not parallel phenomena having the same origin: the need felt by the nobility to regenerate itself following the decline brought about by the wars of the preceding decades.

It was in Portugal and Spain that the nobility demeaned itself by joining hands with the traders. Later, in the seventeenth century, European countries which had developed much earlier, took over from them. These countries – Holland in particular, England, followed by France – had political structures which were in the process of being firmly established. Consequently neither the Dutch, nor the English, expansion, nor even the weaker French expansion which followed, had the same system of causes as that which triggered off Portuguese and Spanish colonization, or the Polish and Russian colonizations to the east.

Demographic pressure also played its role. The increase in the Castilian population in the fifteenth and sixteenth centuries accelerated the movement for emigration, just as it did in Mazuria and in Russia. Moreover in the seventeenth century the easy victory which the Dutch won over the Portuguese was due in part to the Dutch having a surplus population: they could mobilize not only their own citizens, but a part of the German population as well.

Colonial expansion and imperialism: continuity or discontinuity

From the time of John the Navigator, the great enterprises in which the Portuguese monarchy had participated represented an alternative to the policy of reconquest and of crusade which had come to a tragic end, in 1571, at the battle of Alcazarquivir, the biggest disaster in the history of Portugal. In a magnificent film *Non, ou la vaine gloire de commander* ("No, or the vain glory of commanding") Manoel de Oliveira has correctly identified the link between the failure of the Portuguese attempts to unify the Peninsula or to establish settlements in Morocco, and the development and exploitation of those voyages. Serving as substitutes for the kings' previous objectives, these voyages pressed on at the same time, but elsewhere, with the task of evangelization and of conquest.

This explains how the glorification of the great Portuguese discoveries brought about Portugal's turning away from a frontal struggle with the Moors. It was an amnesia therapy which lasted several centuries, because a second humiliation took place later when the rivals of Portugal, the royal princes of Spain, avenged Alcazarquivir at the battle of Lepanto, before capturing Portugal itself, in 1580, in order to unify the Peninsula. Lucette Valensi has studied the forms and the extent of this amnesia therapy in *Fables de la mémoire.*

However its function as counterweight and transference was soon taken over by others: commercial development, evangelization, colonization, enslavement of peoples, to the point where the Western historical memory ended up by forgetting how vital a motive the struggle against the Infidel had been. In the eighteenth century, only the Abbé Raynal showed a keen awareness of what had been at stake. But the will to forget erased all trace of him.

One finds the same process at work again in France in the age of imperialism when, by a transference of the same sort, the Third Republic engaged in a policy of imperial conquest as a means of forgetting and erasing the defeat of Sedan, the failure of the European policy of the Empire and the loss of Alsace-Lorraine. Hansi's cartoon, aimed at Jules Ferry, the promoter of these imperial conquests in Indo-China and

Tunisia, expresses it correctly: "I have lost two children and you offer me two servants."

One can see the same game of alternatives being played in the Russian Empire where, in the nineteenth century, the Tsar, unable to impose his will upon Central Europe, transferred his will to domination to the Caucasus and later to the Far East. After the Crimean War, this expansionist stage was marked by the end of the conquest, and the "pacification", of the Caucasus, by the conquest of Tashkent (1865), Samarkand (1868), Khiva and Kokand (1876), and later by the conquest of the regions of Amur and Ossuri.

On a second occasion, when the conflicts in the Balkans had been brought to an end, in 1897, by means of an agreement with Francis Joseph, the Tsar wanted to "compensate" for the restraint imposed upon Panslavism by moving Russia's centre of interest towards the Far East and the Pacific. The intervention in China and the conflict with Japan were not viewed as presenting a "danger of war". They were represented as a colonial expedition (1904–05).

Another characteristic attributed to imperialism is the territorial greed of which the division of Africa, in 1885–90, was the most obvious expression. The concern of the main rival powers – France, Germany, England, Portugal, Belgium – lay in assuring for themselves, on the map, the most extensive territories possible in order to forestall any rival's attempt to seize territory at some unspecified time in the future. This is what became known as "the scramble for Africa".

Such behaviour was evident well before the period of imperialism. For example, during the occupation of Canada, Samuel de Champlain justified his ambition in a report of 1615, in which he wrote to the King: "If we do not settle in, either the English or the Dutch [that is, Protestants] will arrive in Quebec." This means that the first French colony was a "preventive" conquest, even though it had other purposes: the discovery of a passage to the west of the Pacific and to Japan, population and development, the conversion of the Indians.

This practice of occupying territories which belonged to no one before they could be seized by others, was both justified and criticized in colonial as well as in imperialist times, with the same arguments. From the time of Pufendorf and of Jean-Jacques Rousseau fictitious occupations were condemned. In the *Social Contract* the latter says: "In order to claim authority for a right of first occupation, one must acquire possession, not by means of an empty ceremony, but by work and culture." In 1805 the practice of annexation was abused by the United States which, in Louisiana, claimed that occupation of the mouth of a river entailed a right on the totality of the basin (John Quincy Adams). This *doctrine of continuity* applied equally to the occupation of territory situated in the hinterland of coasts.

Only differences of degree distinguished *continuity* and *hinterland*, from "spheres of influence". The law undertook to legalize them, the expression "spheres of influence" first appearing, so it would seem, in the Anglo-German agreement of 1885.

Diversion/substitution, alternative policy, lust for conquest: do the similarities among the different stages of expansion have the edge on the dissimilarities? An additional feature establishes a parallel between the period of the discoveries and that of imperialism. The same stages occur in the processes of domination. It is well known that in the nineteenth century the era of discoveries and the pioneers – Brazza, Stanley and others – preceded that of the governments which took over from them. Such was the case in the fifteenth and sixteenth centuries too. Dazzled by the final enterprises of Diego Cam, Christopher Columbus, Magellan, who, as is well known, were supported by kings, traditional historians have scarcely given heed to the pioneers who had preceded them. As much as either the outcome of a visionary project – the westward or eastward route to the Indies – or of the effect of a dynamic made possible by new technical resources, the expansion and the voyages were, as a matter of fact, the cumulative result of dozens of small attempts made by ordinary traders and adventurers like Luis Fernao Gomes, Eustache de La Fosse, and others. According to Joao de Barros, it was only when Portuguese sailors, while visiting Benin, learnt that the kingdom of Prester John could be reached through this country, that the Portuguese Monarchy decided to assume responsibility for Diego Cam's great enterprise to either penetrate Africa or to go round it (de Barros, quoted in Thornton, 1992, p. 35).

Christopher Columbus too had his predecessors, like Fernao Dulmo, who obtained from the King the privileges for any land found to the west of the Canary Islands and the Azores, the veritable crossroads of the discoveries and later of the conquests. But Dulmo did not meet with Columbus's success.

In summary, this two-stage expansion is as evident in the sixteenth as in the nineteenth century.

The market or the flag?

So, the imperialist period displays modes of behaviour which recall the era of the great colonial conquests. However, the general feeling is that 1870 marked the beginning of a new era. What were its characteristics?

In the first instance, it appears that, for a whole century up till then, colonial expansion had not gone through a solution of continuity. Whether it was a failure or a success, like France's ventures in Algeria or in Senegal, the growth of the colonial power of the different European states had not always been the result of an explicit political will. Rather it arose out of circumstances. Moreover, the new colonies, notably Algeria, Australia and New Caledonia, had been populated with rebellious individuals, delinquents and political prisoners – a fact which did not endear them to public opinion. But the same was true of the earliest Portuguese colonies.

In France the change becomes evident when the newly acquired territories start to have an identity. This occurred in Cochin-China, which the navy needed to counterbalance the influence of Great Britain and to have a good base in the west of the Pacific Ocean. Such was the case also with Algeria, after the "heroic" battles against Abd el Kader. The army identified itself with this country. In this connection Raoul Girardet writes: "At the same time as a section of the army 'colonized' itself, for a segment of public opinion, the colonial idea militarized itself" (Girardet, 1972: 13).

And if the colonial ideal and the missionary calling meshed with each other, just as they had done in the sixteenth and seventeenth centuries, there was a new development, which lay in a shift in meaning. Thenceforth conversion to Christianity became identified with the duty to civilize, for civilization could not be other than Christian. In *Les Missions catholiques*, Mgr. Miché, Apostolic Vicar in Saigon, denounces "those rebels who have long impeded the progress of conversions". Appointed Bishop of Algiers, Mgr. Lavigerie arrives "to help in the great task of Christian civilization . . . which must bring to light a new France freed from the darkness and chaos of an ancient barbarism". These then are the primary impulses of imperialism: to colonize, to civilize, to spread one's culture, to expand. And colonization was the "power" of a people to "reproduce" itself in different spaces.

For Prévost-Paradol imperialism was the ultimate resource of greatness, for Leroy-Beaulieu a generative force. Imperialism had roots in ideologies, but the ideologies were supported and sustained by more materialistic goals. In fact the latter are the source of the most widely spread formulation of the new-style colonial policy. Jules Ferry enunciated it on the occasion of the conquest of Tonkin: "Colonial policy is the daughter of industrial policy. For wealthy States . . . export is an essential component of public prosperity . . . Had the manufacturing nations established among themselves something like a division of industrial labour, a distribution based on aptitudes . . . , Europe could have resolved not to seek beyond its own frontiers for outlets for its products. But everybody wants to spin, to forge, to distill, to produce and export sugar." Consequently, with the emergence of new industrial powers – the United States, Russia, Germany – overseas expansion was dictated by necessity.

Jules Ferry adds two other reasons to the one referred to above. Actually we have already mentioned these two reasons: (a) the humanitarian argument whereby the "superior races" must fulfil their duty with regard to the "inferior races" who have not yet started on the road to progress; (b) the nationalist argument formulated in a dynamic expression: "Were France to withdraw from these enterprises, Spain and Germany would immediately replace us. A 'fireside' policy would lead us nowhere but along the path of decadence . . . To have influence without acting is to abdicate our responsibility."

Great Britain had to face similar problems, though it did so well before France. The victories of the Seven Years' War constituted the first major turning-point which altered its relationship with the colonies. Up till then the Empire had been small, relatively homogeneous, very English, Protestant, and *centred on trade*. Suddenly, after the treaties of 1763, it acquired Catholic Quebec, Florida, Tobago and still more territories, to such an extent that Great Britain became the mistress of an immense, and above all heterogeneous, empire, quite out of proportion to its means (see L. Colley).

The Empire had, up till that time, incurred little expense. It was manageable. It had very little bearing upon the manner in which the English governed themselves. Suddenly it became a burden, an essentially military burden. Above all its preservation became incompatible with the principles of English liberty – a cause for concern with Burke – since it ruled over hostile populations.

Was it by chance that Gibbon wrote his great work on the fall of the Roman Empire shortly after the Treaty of Paris?

However there was another cause of the rude awakening experienced by Great Britain: American independence. The War of Independence was a civil war which, in England as well as in the American colonies, pitted Englishmen against Englishmen, since opinions were divided on both sides. By way of compensation the English took note of the loyalty of Scotland, especially since Scottish pioneers, such as Warren Hastings, Charles Gordon and others, had played an important military role in the rest of the Empire. Consequently the *English* colonies gave place to the *British* Empire which, driven by a vindictive patriotism, culminated in a reaction against the latitudinarian attitude of earlier periods. The India Act of 1784, the Canada Act of 1791, the Act of Union with Ireland in 1800, are the expressions of this policy of recovery and domination, which is *one* of the characteristic features of imperialism.

The other, vying with the former but coming to harmonize with it, is evinced in the need, which Great Britain felt for the first time, to refurbish its vision of its economic relationship with the rest of the world in the aftermath of losing America and becoming an industrial power. More than the mercantilist monopoly of overseas trade, which had enabled it to accumulate wealth, England now needed markets and raw materials. It needed another America – Australia will fit the bill; another India – and the target is China. It needs an Africa different from the one that supplied the West Indies and North America with slaves.

It was certainly not by chance that, within a few years, Great Britain sent its first important ambassador, Mac Cartway, to Peking (1797); set up the

African Association; asked Mungo Park to explore Central Africa up to the source of the Niger; and established the North West Company in the North of Canada, while James Cook was installing himself in Botany Bay in Australia. This outburst of enterprise came after a long period of international conflicts. It heralded a colonial redeployment, that of imperialism – as it came to be called.

The example of Mungo Park is simple and lucid. He explains that he would receive his salary of fifteen shillings a day from his sponsors "only if he succeeded in making the geography of Africa better known, in making new sources of wealth available to their ambition, their trade and their labours".

The requirements of industrialization, the needs of the market henceforth rival the compulsion for domination. But very soon the latter prevails over the others.

Schumpeter or Hobson?

At the beginning of the nineteenth century, the will to dominate had acquired such primacy in Great Britain, that in 1919 Joseph Schumpeter, in his survey of British imperialism during that century, argued that imperialism manifests itself when "a state evinces a *purposeless* (my italics) propensity to expansion by force, beyond all definable limits", that is, when the warlike or conquering activity expresses itself "without being actually the means to some end other than what is implicit in its very exercise". That is what Max Weber called instrumental rationality. In this context Schumpeter gives the example of Disraeli – the eulogist and the incarnation of imperialist expansion from the time of his speech in 1872 at the Crystal Palace – who nevertheless had earlier referred to those "accursed colonies which are like an albatross around our neck". Disraeli now wanted to create an Imperial Federation by transforming the colonies into autonomous units within an Empire constituted as a single customs union. The available lands in the colonies would be reserved for the English. A central organization in London would be in charge of the coordination of these operations. A few years later Joseph Chamberlain would return to this plan of action. It is noteworthy that the expression "preservation" of the Empire, which was used in that context, actually meant territorial expansion. This turnaround of Disraeli's came about when the slogan of imperialism showed its effectiveness as a distraction for the citizens from their everyday worries, to which former conservative leaders had not known how to respond. Also at a time when they had no other political policy. The imperialist slogan was successful. It provided advantages to a whole range of vested interests, among others a custom rate that gave protection to all those industrialists who felt threatened by the dumping policy of German exporters.

Here we may note a contrast. On the one hand English public opinion had, at the beginning of the nineteenth century, turned more and more hostile to colonial expansion, which was identified with the slave trade[2] and with the humiliations associated with the formation of the United States. On the other, it was favourable to imperialism as it flattered and defended English interests, whether on the peripheries of India, against the "looters" and bandits, or in South Africa where, during the Boer War, "there was not one beggar who did not talk about our rebellious subjects". One comes across similar attitudes in France when the "bastards" (*salopards*) of the Moroccan borders "attack our colonists", at the beginning of the twentieth century.

In Russia, in an identical situation in the marches of the Caucasus or of Central Asia, one finds the Prince Chancellor Gorchakov, in 1864, echoing word for word, the arguments of the British and French imperialists.

> The situation of Russia, (he says) is that of all the civilized States which come into contact with nomads who have no well established state organization . . . To provide against their raids and their looting, we must subdue them and bring them under strict control . . . But there are others further away . . . consequently we too must proceed further still . . . This is what has befallen France in Africa, the United States in America, England in India. We march forward by necessity as much as by ambition.
>
> (quoted in Vernadsky, 1972, III, p. 610)

It was still a matter of "preservation of the Empire", as formulated by Disraeli.

Several incidents in the history of Great Britain illustrate how the symbolism of domination has weighed as much as concrete material interests: from the maintenance of the protectorate on the Ionian Isles from 1815 to 1863 – though in London the view prevailed that the possession of those indefensible islands was useless – to the military expedition for the defence of the Falkland Islands by Mrs Thatcher. In contrast, the loss of the whole of India, the Caribbean Islands and black Africa between 1947 and 1962, scarcely aroused any strong emotion. One comes across a similar paradox in Russia where, indifferent to the loss of the Empire in 1990–91, the citizens nevertheless mobilized for the defence of the Kurile Islands.

Popular support for expansion is one of the characteristic features of the imperialist age. It asserts itself despite opinions strongly opposed to it. This support goes hand in hand with a popular press which blossomed in the nineteenth century as a product of industrial development. In Great Britain the *Daily Mail*, in Germany the *Tägliche Rundschau*, in Russia the *Novoe Vremja*, in France *Le Petit Parisien* and *Le Matin* are the most widely known examples. Imperialism thus becomes a public phenomenon – which was not the case with expansion in the preceding centuries – even if certain operations are clandestinely carried out, in defiance of the prevailing opinion, such as, for example, the expeditions of Jules Ferry in Indo-China.

Economic interest is none the less one of the main pillars and mainsprings of imperialism. This has been well established by John Hobson in *Imperialism* (1902), followed by Rudolf Hilferding in *Das Finanz Kapital* (1910). Drawing upon these two texts, Lenin subsequently popularized these ideas in *Imperialism, the last stage of capitalism* (1916). His book was translated into German and in French in 1920.

However a difference separates the theses of Hobson from those of Lenin. In British imperialism Hobson saw "the will of well organized industrial and financial interests to control and develop – to the detriment of the population and through the use of the forces of the state – private markets in order to dump into them the surplus of their goods and to invest in them the surplus of their capital". In other words Hobson saw imperialism as a return to mercantilism, as its driving imperative was the need to accumulate a national capital in order to compete with the rival powers. In contrast, Lenin viewed imperialism as the final stage of monopolistic capitalist development. He carried out a debate with Kautsky who thought that at this final stage inter-imperialist conflicts would no longer be profitable. Lenin thought they were inevitable.

The important point is that, for Lenin, imperialism presented several faces and was the end result of a variety of phases in the historical development. Imperialism had existed before the era of capitalism (cf. the Roman Empire). But it had also existed during its development, for example during the constitution of the Austro-Hungarian and Russian empires. Consequently national struggles were merely part of the universal fight against imperialism: the struggle of the Baltic peoples against the Russians was equivalent to the struggle of the Irish or of the Indians against the British. For Lenin the First World War put an end to the distinction between colonial expansion and imperialism (1916).

Yet there was another more decisive divergence.

The imperialism of the late nineteenth and twentieth centuries was different. In one specific feature it differed both from the spirit of conquest and domination which marked earlier eras and from the colonial expansion of the preceding centuries. This imperialism was, more than the others, associated with financial capital, and colonization and conquest did not constitute the only expressions of its existence. Colonization and territorial conquest can be imperialistic. But, in the nineteenth century and up to the Great War, imperialism had means of action at its disposal which could be adapted to political independence. Such was the case of the penetration of financial capital into China, the Ottoman Empire and Russia.

At different times in history colonization assumed forms which may have been different, but which were superimposed one upon the other.

Domination over other peoples has indeed been the motor of expansion, whatever might have been the declared purpose of "imperialism": religious at the time of the Arabs, religious again in the Christian expeditions against the Infidels, still religious when Catholics and Protestants, in the sixteenth and seventeenth centuries, aimed to ensure the expansion of their faith.

Political interest may have been the adjunct of all these forms of crusades. It first evinces its autonomy, however, at the time of François I who concluded *Capitulations* with the Turk in order to fight against Charles V. Political interest becomes more and more prominent as from the time of the Thirty Years' War when Cardinal Richelieu formed an alliance with the Huguenot King of Sweden against the Holy Roman Empire.

Economic interest appears well before the so-called imperialist period. It asserts itself particularly when, with the Navigation Acts (1651), overseas expansion is held to be a monopoly of the English *nation as a whole*, and not merely in the interest of its traders. These Acts may be viewed as one of the sources of imperialism, because the latter claims to act in the name of the entire nation, of the nation-state.

Before the advent of imperialism the mercantilist doctrine – of which Bodin was the first theoretician, and which Colbert put into practice later – purported to associate the state with overseas enterprises in order to assure the monopoly of commercial exchanges and the maximum revenue in gold and in silver.

By prohibiting colonials from producing "so much as a nail", the mercantilists would soon provide them with a pretext to revolt, as occurred in the United States and in Spanish America. This type of relationship was brought to an end by these uprisings. Colonized indigenous peoples were ruined by the enforcement of mercantilist practices, as is shown by the example of the textile industry in India. Nonetheless these practices did persist to some extent and were even developed by force at the time of the Industrial Revolution. It is in this sense that Lenin could argue that imperialism was the ultimate stage of capitalism.

British colonization integrated these variables and variations. It ensured the fortune of a social group that knew how to associate the wealth of its soil and its sub-soil with financial and commercial applications which enabled it to accede to world dominion. But industrial capital remained for a long time disconnected from banking capital. In this way industry grew *by the side* of the Empire, rather than thanks to it, or for its sake, except when, after the 1929 crisis, the "imperial preference" became a veritable global policy (Cain and Hopkins).

High finance has almost always been the driving force of imperialist policy. For instance, in 1882 the Egyptian expedition was launched, not to acquire markets or annex territories, but to prevent the Egyptian rulers from not paying back their debt with impunity. That would have created a precedent. Likewise, for the sake of the City, the Boers in South Africa had to be prevented from helping the Germans to seize the gold reserves at a time when the gold standard stood surety for the preeminence of the pound sterling.

Comparison of results

In their *results*, the main difference between the colonial expansion of the sixteenth and seventeenth centuries and the imperialism which followed it, actually lies in the fact that the Industrial Revolution provided imperialism with the resources which enabled it to thoroughly alter the relationship between the mother countries and the colonies. In one way the colonial expansion of the first wave could be seen to be similar to the colonizations of the previous type (colonizations by the Turks, the Arabs, even by the Romans), in the sense that the economic, military, and technical gap between the colonizers and the colonized was narrow and trade was on a very small scale. At the outset the gap between the standard of living in Europe and in its colonies, at least in Asia, was of the order of 1 to 1.5, in so far as such an evaluation has any meaning. With imperialism and the effects of the Industrial Revolution deterioration set in, hitting the colonized peoples very hard. According to the computations of Paul Bairoch, the gap in the standard of living went from 1.9 to 1.0 in 1860, to 3.4 in 1914 and 5.2 in 1950. It may be noted that the gap has not stopped getting larger since the end of the colonial period. This perpetually increasing gap has been shown to be above all the result of structural changes brought about by colonization and also of the shift in power relationships. Until the eighteenth century, in fact, the consumption of extra-European products amounted to only between 2 and 10 percent of total European consumption. Lastly, with the exception of Spanish America, the first colonization merely grazed the surface of the structures of the conquered or dominated societies. Its foundations too were weak. In India, for instance, it mattered little whether goods were sold to the Portuguese or to the Arabs. The advantage the Portuguese had was that they provided new weapons.

But with the demands of the economic imperialism, the second colonization brought about profound structural transformations. Of these, two are important: de-industrialization and non-food-producing agricultural specialization.

The example of the textile industry in India illustrates the first change. In the seventeenth century light cotton fabrics represented from 60 to 70 percent of Indian exports. Industrialization enabled England to produce machines that were 350 times more productive than one Indian worker. And, owing to her dominant position, England could freely introduce her cotton fabric into India. The outcome was that in less than a century the

Indian cotton industry had almost disappeared. De-industralization took place in many other colonies. Together with excessive specialization in the non-food crops, de-industrialization constitutes the second aspect of the change which imperialism imposed upon the colonies, both the old-established and the new ones.

In black Africa, which provides an example of the second change, the colonial situation gave rise to an opposition between the subsistence economy, traditional mainstay of African societies, and the market economy. Henri Raulin has observed how the cultivation of cocoa, imposed by the colonial administration, provoked a strong opposition on the part of the Agni of the Ivory Coast. Every night they poured boiling water on the cocoa seedlings they had been compelled to plant. It was only later that they realized that this crop earned them some money which they could use. These same Agni were held to be unfit for manual labour, indeed for any work whatsoever. The truth was that they lived under a complicated set of rules, and that respect for this code did not allow them, especially those who belonged to the higher classes, to work in public. They were labelled as "lazy" though they showed that they were capable of being extremely active. The failure to adjust to "progress", as understood by the colonizer, could manifest itself in other forms of cultural "resistance". For instance, among the Masikoro, the Bara of Madagascar and the Peuls, trade in oxen had a special significance. Cattle had a social value; to sell cattle was viewed as a sign of degeneration, because that commodity formed part of a specific trade network outside the monetary economy. Likewise the Bété kept the amount of the future dowry which was usually considerable out of the monetary economy. Cotton cultivation failed among the Peuls and the Bambara, but succeeded among the Minyanka and the Senufo, because the former had established well structured historical societies which were undone by colonization, while the latter, less conscious of their identity, were more readily disposed to change their way of living.

Technical borrowings from the West were the issue in the conflict between the desire for progress and the resistance of tradition. Such was, for example, the case with the cultivation of yams. Some Senufo farmers of the Korhogo region had very early adopted the plough yoked to oxen. Instead of the tubers being planted in mounds made with a hoe, they were planted in ridges between the furrows formed by the plough. At first the saving in manpower was appreciated. But, as the new yams were less thick and more elongated, consumption decreased and the use of the plough was abandoned.

18

Between colonization and neo-colonialism

Several typical situations arose out of the domination of the colonizers and its consequences. Some of their features have managed to survive even after decolonization. Thus, in the first instance, we may distinguish:

1 *colonization of the old type*: it is of an expansionist nature, manifesting itself at a stage of free competition in capitalist development. Algeria, conquered in 1830, is one of its last examples;
2 *colonization of the new type*: it is linked to the Industrial Revolution and to financial capitalism. It is manifested in most of the post-1871 French conquests, of Morocco in particular, even though other considerations also applied. This form of colonization is also evident in the expansionist policy of Great Britain and Germany in East Africa and in South Africa;
3 *imperialism without colonization*: this occurred temporarily in the Ottoman Empire, for example, in the case of Egypt in 1881. It developed in a purer form – that is, without any disposition to settle colonists – in Latin America, where the City ruled in Argentina and in Peru, before yielding place to the United States. The practice of this imperialism without a flag has survived the independence movements of the latter half of the twentieth century.

Thus, the different forms of imperialism and of colonization overlap and penetrate one another.

The same applies to the phenomena know as decolonization and the independence of peoples, and to their liberation. Most of these peoples gained their freedom between 1945 and 1965. But if colonization, understood in its narrow definition, did indeed come to an end with the defeat of the French in Vietnam or Algeria, of the British in India, of the Dutch in Indonesia, it is none the less true that Western domination has survived, in one form or other, either as neo-colonialism or as imperialism without colonists.

Actually this phenomenon existed before the Europeans lost their overseas possessions. The United States, for example, created its colonies without hoisting a flag, particularly in Latin America, even if the marines had to be sent here and there whenever the "need" arose, as in Haiti in 1915. To some extent, after 1965, France has at times emulated this policy in black Africa.

However "decolonization" has often been limited to a change in sovereignty. There has indeed been a substitution of one political authority for another. But all manner of economic bonds have survived, and they have perpetuated the former dependence in another form, to the joint benefit of the mother countries and of the new local middle classes. Moreover the flows of human beings generated by this interruption have increased. In this way the old ties have been perpetuated, albeit in an altered form.

19

French consultants are active in Algeria and Algerian immigrants work in France. The same phenomenon can be seen operating between, on one hand, Great Britain and, on the other, the Caribbean Islands or India, between Germany and Turkey.

At the same time, since the 1960s, the evolution of the global economy has culminated in an interweaving and integration of national economies to such an extent that some of the formerly colonized countries find themselves in a situation of dependence or poverty worse than they had earlier experienced (cf. Ch. 11). In their turn the former colonizing powers themselves are realizing today that the dogma of liberalism, upon which they relied to give legitimacy to their domination, can be turned against them, to the advantage of new financial and industrial powers, like Japan or even former colonies like Taiwan, Singapore and Korea. And we need not limit the analysis of the processes linked to colonization to those effects which are the legacy of economic or technical domination. Its reverse effects have included such things as the increasing role of oil in the global economy, contacts between civilizations and the racism which such contacts have generated.

Civilization and racism

"I believe in this race . . . ", Joseph Chamberlain said in 1895. He was singing an imperialist hymn glorifying the British and praising a nation whose strivings had surpassed those of the French, Spanish and other rivals. The Englishman was engaged in bringing his superior know-how and his science to other "inferior" populations. The "white man's burden" was to civilize the world. The British were the torch-bearers.

This conviction and this task meant that the others were viewed as the representatives of an inferior culture. As the "vanguard" of the white race, it behoved the English to educate and train them – while keeping a proper distance. If the French too viewed the indigenous populations as children, and considered them to be inferior, their republican convictions led them to use a different language, at least in public, even though it was not necessarily in conformity with their deeds. Still what brought together the French, the English, and other colonizers, and imparted to them the consciousness of belonging to Europe, was the conviction that they represented Science and Technology and that this knowledge enabled the societies they subjugated to realize progress. And to accede to civilization.

But history and Western law had codified what civilization was and also what its connection was with Christianity. The American Henry Wheaton, the Briton Lass Oppenheim and the Russian De Malten had successively laid down the foundations of this law, on the occasion of the signing of the "unequal" treaties with China, Siam, Abyssinia, the Ottoman Empire.

That is how it came about that a cultural concept, civilization, and a value system came to have specific economic and political function. Not only did these countries have to safeguard the right of Europeans to define the meaning of civilization – which actually guaranteed their preeminence – but the protection of this right became, in addition, the moral raison d'être of the conquerors.

And those who did not conform to this requirement were looked upon as criminals, delinquents, and were consequently liable to being punished. In India, for example, the British designated entire social groups as "criminal tribes", though the latter were not necessarily tribes. Such a designation justified intervention aimed at substituting colonial legislation for traditional customs and the prevalent jurisprudence. Thus men and women who had in no way broken away from the social group to which they belonged were designated as "criminals". The Criminal Tribes Act of 1871, followed by the Criminal Castes and Tribes Act of 1911 mark the decisive turning point of this legal control which culminated in the condemnation of suttee (the suicide of widows) as well as the elimination of the Thugs and other "highwaymen". The chosen form of words, which lumps caste together with tribe, led to the exclusion of entire human groups, such as the Kuravar of the Madras region, who were designated as "hereditary thieves" (see M. Fourcade).

Does not this manner of repressing a population smack of racism to some degree?

In the nineteenth century, Darwin's ideas attracted a great deal of attention, as Marx shows in his works. The class struggle represents the human version of the struggle of the species analysed by Darwin. In this context colonization presents itself as the *third side* of this scientistic conviction. In his great goodness the white man does not destroy the inferior species. He educates them, unless they are deemed to be not "human", like the Bushmen or the aborigines of Australia who were not even given a name – in which case, he exterminates them.

The force of imperialist conviction arose from the fact that the movement brought together, on one hand, the eulogists of reason and of progress who, in history, believed in the inevitability of social development, and in its intelligibility, and, on the other hand, men who placed instinct above reason and saw in the need for action an essential component of life. Impelled, in England, by the neo-idealism of Oxford, those who belonged to the first category perceived the world as an organism animated by its moral strength and its will. The Empire – naturally the British Empire – was thus viewed as the highest stage of the social organization. Spencer Wilkinson was one of the main eulogists of this notion of the Empire. His pronouncements made their mark on men like Alfred Milner, Toynbee and Haldane in England, and the disciples of the historian Ranke in Germany.

If the British Empire is to fill its true place in the world it must first find its true place in the hearts of its own subjects; they must have a reason for the national faith that is in them. That reason will be given by an analysis of the laws of British power and of the conditions which justify its exercise. This final inquiry will set out not from the assumption that might is right, which is the creed of despotism and the argument of caprice, nor from the theory that right is might, which is the mistake of shallow enthusiasts, but from the conviction that the universe is the manifestation of an intelligible order inseparable from the order revealed in the processes of thought; that the laws of the material and of the moral world arise from the same source and are but different aspects of the same reality. We cannot but believe that in the end right must prevail over wrong, and the faith that this is the real and ultimate law of the world is the foundation of all that is best in human endeavour. . . .

(Spencer Wilkinson, *The Nation's Awakening*, 1896, pp. 267–8)

As a matter of course, British historians saw the British Empire as a historic fulfilment. Interestingly they set up against the Marxists, and especially against the German Franz Mehring, a parallel and different model of historical development. While the Marxists, in their analysis of historical development, defined the stages of slavery, feudalism and capitalism as the harbingers of socialism, the English imperialists – notably J. R. Seeley, but above all J. A. Cramb in *The Origin and Destiny of Imperial Britain* – emphasized other stages of historical development: the city-state, the feudal state, the class state, the national democratic state. The British state was thus the crowning achievement of a history in conformity with the ideals of freedom and of tolerance that were born during the Reformation.

To this trend of opinion was added a vision of man which tended to the glorification of exploits, of action, such as is found in the Lebensphilosophie eulogized by William Dilthey, Oswald Spengler and Max Scheler. All three were imperialists and, like Nietzsche, endorsed the idea of a form of social Darwinism directed against the outside world. In the wake of this biological trend followed scientists, sociologists, eugenists who returned to and took up the ideas of Gobineau. Like Gidding, they glorified the *Übermensch* of tomorrow. In this manner they brought about a fusion of predominantly British neo-idealism with predominantly German biologism. This process was stimulated by Houston Chamberlain – the Britisher who became a subject of Kaiser Wilhelm II – who acted as go-between.

This filiation enables one to understand better the relationship between imperialism and Nazi racism.

At the time of imperialism, the conquerors succeeded in establishing the primacy of the idea that expansion was the ultimate aim of politics. If only from the moment when subject peoples ceased to experience the same law as the conquerors, this oppression of others, in foreign lands, ran the risk of promoting a disposition towards tyranny in the mother country. A typical example of such an occurrence is provided by the case of Ireland, as Burke was the first to point out.

The British Empire was the equivalent of the Roman Empire only in its dominions, where an Englishman lived as a citizen in the same way he would have done if he had been in Lancashire. Elsewhere he acted as an overbearing ruler who could not survive and prosper without destroying the ways and customs of the subject peoples. The French Empire claimed to be different in the sense that it wanted the law to be the same for all. In fact, whether the territory was called a department, a protectorate, or a colony, this project came into conflict with the colonial settlers and with a whole range of vested interests. The overseas Frenchmen felt it was intolerable for them to be obliged to justify their preeminence over the natives in the eyes of the mother country.

The dichotomy between imperialism and the nation became apparent when the fate of the Bretons, the miners, the Welsh or the victims of war ceased to be at the centre of political life, which instead shifted to Fashoda or to Bechuanaland. Colonial expansion became the solution to all internal problems: poverty, class struggle, overpopulation. It was flaunted as representing the *common* interest, as being *above* parties. In the colonies, the administrator or colonist wanted above all, to be seen as a Frenchman or an Englishman, belonging neither to the Left nor to the Right. He defined himself by his race, not by his activity or by his social role. Race characterized the elite; it justified oppression.

Undoubtedly theories of race existed well before the period of colonization, or of imperialism. But they were confined to a few and were little known. Imperialism, however, infused life into them and disseminated them widely.

They found an application even in continental Europe where racist ideology generated a particular totalitarianism which legitimized the total power of an "elite", of a superior race, over other Europeans, and buttressed it with similar arguments.

2

THE INITIATIVES

First the Portuguese

"*E se mais mundo houvera, là chegara*" – and if the earth had been bigger, we would still have gone round it.

In praising Portugal's discoveries, this proud statement expresses well the nature of the voyages of those great explorers who are still glorified today by tradition. On land and on sea, from Vasco da Gama to Serpa Pinto, they went to the furthest limits and to the heart of the planet "bringing civilization".

In his *Chronicle of Guinea*, written in the middle of the fifteenth century, Gomes Eanes de Zurara already announced the "five and one reasons" for those expeditions. The Infante Henry, who organized them, "is driven by the service of God". He thinks that Christians are to be found in those lands. Goods can be brought back from there. And if none are to be found, the extent of the power of the Infidels can be assessed. Perhaps some foreign lord would like to help him in his war against the enemies of the faith, for great is his desire to spread the Holy Faith of Our Lord Jesus Christ.

It was King John of Portugal to whom Christopher Columbus appealed, about 1484, for supplies of all that was necessary for him to reach Cipangu (Japan) by way of the west, for indeed it was from Portugal that all the voyages started. The king consulted his cosmographers who advised him against that crazy scheme. As Fernand Braudel puts it, "the Portuguese have always preferred scientific certainties to idle fancies . . . That was how they lost America. When they discovered Brazil, it was too late."

As a matter of fact they were the first to go sailing south. They were equipped with all the available technical devices and, in particular, with those nautical maps with compass cards. The map of Pedro Reinel (1485) describes with great precision the coasts of Europe and of Atlantic Africa up to the furthest point reached by Diego Cam beyond the Gulf of Guinea. Following its development by the Italians, cartography became the Portuguese science par excellence, as Viscount Santarem described it. It gave birth in the sixteenth century to the first atlases with eight maps. Another secure advantage enjoyed by the Portuguese voyagers was the caravels which took over from the barcas with which Gil Eanes had rounded the cape of Bojador in 1434. Equipped with sails having an area double that of the ones used till then, the caravels could sail close to the wind, that is, they could constantly modify their sails to zigzag along their course, even against the wind if the need arose. With the advent of the galleons, which were larger and better adapted to sea warfare, Portugal became the ship-building centre of Europe.

For the blacks of the western coast of Africa the arrival of white sailors, especially the Portuguese and the Italians, was a discovery, as were their Lombard dialects and their tallow candles. The blacks' practice of eating while sitting on the ground and of living in straw huts, and so on, soon generated a feeling of superiority in the Portuguese. They noted that the fewer contacts they had with the Muslims, the darker was their skin. Many declared themselves to be vassals of the Emperor of Mali.

One of the first African kings whom the Portuguese came across, Battimansa, in Gambia, had declared himself to be the vassal of the Emperor of Mali. But this did not impress the Portuguese. On realizing the poverty of the Africans whom they encountered, the Portuguese did not think it worthwhile to penetrate or occupy the hinterland. They were already the ruling power in Madeira and in the Azores – the island of the goshawks – and had gone beyond the dark seas and Cape Bojador from where, until then nobody had returned, for the north-east trade winds drove the ships towards the Atlantic. The caravels enabled the Portuguese to reach Cape Verde in 1444, then the rivers of Guinea and in 1460 Sierra Leone. When John II ascended the throne the treaty of Alcaçovas had been signed two years earlier, in 1479. This treaty settled the succession of Castile and demarcated the zones of influence to the south of the Iberian peninsula. The Gulf of Guinea was allotted to Portugal. In 1483 Diego Cam reached Zaire and send messengers to the king of Kongo. In 1487–88 Bartholomeu Diaz rounded the Cape of Storms, henceforth called the Cape of Good Hope, and reached present-day Port Elizabeth, the bay of the Herdsmen, thus called because the Blacks used to raise cattle in that place. Then the Portuguese set out for India.

When Christopher Columbus arrived in the Bahamas, and just before Vasco da Gama reached India, Pope Alexander VI intervened to bring to an end the cut-throat competition that had arisen between the Portuguese and the Spanish. The bitter debates that arose in relation to the Treaty of Tordesillas (1494) to mark the boundaries of the Portuguese possessions, not at a hundred leagues to the west of the Azores, but at three hundred and seventy leagues to the west of Cape Verde – which brought Brazil within the area – present a problem. Was it on a matter of principle that the Portuguese obtained this shift to the west, or was it because they had a hint that a land existed in those zones – Brazil – "discovered" six years later in 1500? Several indications gave credence to this supposition as soon as Principe and San Tomé, in the Gulf of Guinea, had been reached: they had been "discovered" in 1471 and colonized as early as 1493 . . . by Jews and criminals. San Tomé was uninhabited. It was the first colony linked to the adventure of the Great Discoveries.

When Vasco da Gama reached Indian waters in 1498, a few local kings, like the Zamorins of Calicut and the Sultans of Gujarat, exercised their authority without however controlling the ocean which remained in the hands of the Arabs. When he reached Calicut Vasco da Gama claimed, in the name of his King, the sovereignty over the Indian seas. Naturally the Zamorins refused to accede to this demand. But their rivals in Cochin joined the newcomers whose fleet was quite impressive. The sultan of Egypt answered the call of the Zamorins but, after a naval battle, his admiral turned back. Then, returning in force, the Portuguese under Albuquerque occupied Goa, then the island of Socotra, Ormuz and Malacca. Thus the entire western part of the Indian Ocean came under their sway. Goa was the centrepiece of this scheme. It was heavily fortified and repeatedly strengthened. Albuquerque was the soul of this enterprise.

It was not land that the Portuguese wanted, but control of the sea trade. Dazzled by the wealth of India they intended to secure its traffic for themselves. Refusing to grant to others the right to sail in that part of the ocean, they henceforth confiscated the cargo of anyone who did not have their authorization. Any ship caught sailing without their permission, the *cartas*, was treated as a pirate and seized. Consequently the Portuguese flooded Europe, via Lisbon, with the calico of Calicut, with pepper and other spices.

The poet Luis de Camoens was the first to provide testimony to the sudden wealth of those rude sailors who were scarcely prepared for such a change in their way of living. Several centuries later, following the final departure of the Portuguese, an Indian writer has tried to relate the saga of the battles waged by Abbakka, Queen of the Ullal, who is supposed to have driven them out as early as 1623, a mythical date. In this story the Portuguese are described as burly, uncouth, scornful of women, unable to understand the refinements of art and culture, sensitive only to the language of force. With the exception of their corpulence, this representation differs markedly from the conception which the navigators had of themselves. But what is amazing is that, in enumerating these defects, the Indians left out the only one which the Portuguese admitted to – cupidity. It is easy to understand why: to recall their plunder would be tantamount to acknowledging that, instead of driving them away, the Indians had to submit to their law, however temporarily, and allow themselves to be despoiled. At the same time it would have exposed the degeneracy of the present, when the memory of opulence was all that remained.

Moreover it was Islam that the Portuguese encountered again on reaching India. The tragic end of the Infante Santa, who died in jail in 1443 in the city of Fez, the siege of Granada in which Portuguese soldiers had taken part – these events were still fresh in the memory when Vasco da Gama arrived in Calicut. Geneviève Bouchon has shown that, on the coast of Kerala, whatever was not Muslim did not count. The prohibitions relative to the sea actually affected the Hindu population, as Marco Polo had already observed. During the discussions held in 1500, at Calicut, Pedralvares Cabral had detained some notables on his ship as hostages, in exchange for the Portuguese left ashore. "As gentlemen, they could neither eat nor drink on those ships." Muslims were substituted for them. In Cochin too the Portuguese chroniclers refer to Hindu hostages who took it in turns to go on board their ships so that they could go ashore to purify and feed themselves. All that related to seafaring and, even more, to trade was viewed with suspicion by the Brahmans.

This explains how trade gradually passed into the hands of a new community called the Mappillas. They hailed from the poorest quarters of the ports of the Malabar coast. To escape from the caste system they had converted to Islam. They ranked lowest on the social ladder on account of their contact with foreigners and the sea, or because they were the off-spring of the temporary marriages (*muta*) which Islam tolerated – and still does. The statement – "When a Nayar woman strays into certain districts, she becomes a Muslim" – correctly affirms that when they were excluded from their caste the women had to convert to Islam.

Conversion elevated the untouchable or someone belonging to a low caste to a higher social status. This practice led to the enhancement of the power of the foreign community. Once they had put down roots and established themselves, the erstwhile transient Arab merchants soon occupied an honourable place in the society. In exchange they spared the Hindus of the higher castes the pollution of sea voyages while providing them with a share of the profits.

A century before the arrival of the Portuguese, the Arab geographer ibn Batuta observed that the Hindu majority evinced a condescending contempt for the temporal wealth of the Muslims. The Chinese, who were likewise active along the coasts of India, confirm that, when the Arab foreigners came, they were given seats outside the doorway and provided with lodgings in separate houses – as a protection against pollution. Food was served to them on banana leaves, and the leavings were eaten by dogs and birds. Ibn Batuta further notes: "The Infidels [that is, the Hindus] would turn aside from the path as soon as they saw us . . . "

However the situation changed when the Islamic invasions launched from Delhi brought about a Brahmanical reaction at the same time as the Islamization of a number of Indian princes, from Gujarat to Malacca, that is, all along the spice road. Gradually the Brahmanical community of

Dravidian India found itself hemmed in by Islam. In the north the Brahmins had to contend with a territorial power centred in Delhi. In the south they were surrounded by Islamic communities of traders and sailors who increasingly felt solidarity with their fellow believers. Among the latter, the Gujaratis had gained the upper hand over the Mappilas of Kerala. But, having become sailors or soldiers of the battle fleet, the latter became more and more integrated with Indian society. And when a conflict arose between Cochin and Calicut, they acted as intermediaries. For a while they continued to play this role with the Portuguese. It was with them that Vasco da Gama had to deal.

The Portuguese were eager for a fight with the *Mouros de Meca* – the Arabs – whom they wanted to eliminate in the Indian Ocean, even if that implied dealing with the *Mouros de Terra*, the Muslims in India, particularly of Kerala.

But when Albuquerque wanted to control all the routes and to exercise a monopoly by transforming Goa into the centre of his empire, the Muslims of Malabar immediately rose up against him.

Albuquerque and Mamal of Canador

An Indian adage says: "Princes are like crabs and they devour their parents." It explains partly the success which the Portuguese, Albuquerque in particular, won in taking advantage of their quarrels. The victories of Duarte Pachaco cleared the way for him. They culminated in the restoration of the kingdom of Cochin, which nevertheless remained under threat of an offensive by the Zamorin of Calicut, aided by the Sultan of Egypt and by Venice which joined this "shameful" alliance, because it did not view favourably the development of Portuguese enterprises.

According to Geneviève Bouchon's explanation, Francisco d'Almeida had, for a more effective control of the traffic, strengthened the fortress of San Angelo. From there it was easy to seize cargos, which greatly vexed the Indian merchants. In Cochin they murdered and burned the Feitor of Kollam and twelve of his companions who had taken refuge in a church. The reprisals were swift. The viceroy's son destroyed the entire flotilla of the merchants: twenty-seven ships went up in flames with their cargo of spices, precious stones, horses and elephants. The Portuguese crews dined by the light of the flames. The Muslims of Canador called for vengeance, the siege of the fortress speeding up the infernal cycle of attacks and war. The fleet of Calicut responded to the call, but the accuracy of the Portuguese gunners established the superiority of King Manuel's fleet (1505). On land they experienced greater difficulty in emerging victorious from the siege, for the Muslims protected themselves against artillery by means of huge bales of cotton which softened the impact of the cannon balls – until the day when the Portuguese came up with the idea of setting fire to the bales.

On the high seas the Portuguese still had to overcome the Mameluke fleet, anchored at Diu. This was accomplished in 1508: this victory assured for a long time the hegemony of Albuquerque's fleets. Indeed with the occupation of Diu, India was opened up to King Manuel.

But the Indian kings and the Muslim communities, inspired by Mamal of Canador, found the answer to the ambitions of Albuquerque. In fact the latter had realized earlier that there were leaks in the monitoring of the convoys of spices proceeding from Ceylon (Sri Lanka) and from the Far East. He wanted to control the route they took, working back to their point of departure. For this purpose he established control over the Strait of Malacca, conquering this position and installing his garrisons. But the Indian traders were using the Maldives route to bypass the controls and maintain their monopoly. In the Maldives lay the source of a conflict with Mamal of Canador who owned rights and interests there. In his fight with Albuquerque he had other cards available to him. Many Portuguese were calling into question Albuquerque's policy of belligerence and conquest. They regretted the time of Almeida when trade, and trade alone, formed the basis of relations between Christians and India, with war intervening only occasionally. On the other hand, with Albuquerque, the occupation of territories – Canador, Diu, Malacca – became the very raison d'être of his policy, the prerequisite for the creation of a sort of territorial empire. The repercussions of this policy were that the Portuguese got involved in the rivalries among the Indian princes, which gave Mamal cause for rejoicing for that weakened at the same time both his rivals and the Portuguese. Still Albuquerque proved to be the best at this game. However Mamal had not lost everything for, thanks to his relay outpost in the Maldives, he retained the monopoly of the trade in spices with the Arab world.

Once the trading-posts in India had been secured, Albuquerque hit upon the idea, after crushing the Mameluke fleet, of ruining Egypt by means of an army of stone-breakers. He would bore through the mountain and dry up the sources of the Nile, under the guidance of Ethiopian advisers. At the same time, from Aden, he would proceed to seize the body of the Prophet in Mecca and exchange it for the Holy Places.

It was a Crusade again, yet another Crusade.

The pride of the Spanish

As I have said before, the Spanish have discovered, explored and converted many lands in the span of sixty years of conquest. Never has a king or a nation explored and subdued so many things in so little time, as we have done. Neither have they done nor earned what our men have achieved and deserved by their use of arms, navigation, the preaching of the Holy Gospel and the conversion of idol-worshippers.

That is why the Spanish are most deserving of praise. Blessed be God who gave them this grace and this power. Great is the glory and honour of our Kings and of the Spanish for having made the Indians accept a single God, a single faith, a single baptism, and to have made them give up idolatry, human sacrifices, cannibalism, sodomy and still more serious and wicked sins, which our Good God abhors and punishes. Again they have had to give up polygamy, this old custom and source of pleasure to all sensual men. They have been taught the alphabet, without which men are like animals, and the use of iron which is so necessary to Man. Moreover they have been taught several good habits, the arts, civilized moral standards, to enable them to lead a better life. All this, indeed any one of these things, is worth more than the plumes, the pearls, the gold taken from them – the more so as they did not use this metal for currency, which is its proper use and the true way to profit from it. This holds true even though it would have been preferable to take nothing from them, and instead to content ourselves with what was obtained from the mines, from the rivers and from the burial places. Gold and silver – worth more than sixty million pesos – and the pearls and the emeralds they have extracted from the sea and from the land far outweigh the little gold and silver which the Indians already possessed. What was wrong in all that lies in their having been made to work too much in the mines, in the pearl fisheries and in the transports.

(Lopez de Gomora, Historia general de las Indias, quoted in Romano, 1972, pp. 112–13)

The encounter with the Indians

This glorious, though critical, review is undoubtedly one of the earliest theoretical texts which justify conquest and its violence. The itinerary of the encounters between the Spanish and the Indians sheds better light on the reality of these initial contacts, at least in so far as it was actually experienced. The first witness is Christopher Columbus who had preceded them.

"This king and all his subjects went naked, just as their mother had given birth to them; so did their women without any feeling of embarrassment. They all look like the inhabitants of the Canaries, they are neither white nor black . . . " Columbus is struck by that trait, and more so by the fact that they have no sense of property, nor of the value of objects. "They give all that they own in return for any trifle offered to them, to the point that they take in exchange even fragments of a bowl or of broken glass . . . For whatever one gives them, and without ever saying that it is too little, they will immediately give in exchange all that they own . . . " "They do not covet what belongs to others . . . They give gold as easily as they do a gourd . . . "

THE INDIAN TRIBES OF NORTH AMERICA BEFORE 1492

There were approximately one million Indians north of Mexico in 1492

Eskimo
Koyukon
Ingalik
Tanaina
Aleut
Kutchin
Han
Tanana
Nabesna
Tuchone
Ahtena
Kaska
Tahltan
Tlingit
Hare
Bear Lake
Dogrib
Yellowknife
Slave
Sekani
Beaver
Chipewyan
Eskimo

Tsimshian
Bella Coola
Haida
Bella Bella
Kwakiutl
Nootka
Salish
Makah Puyallup
Nisqually
Chehalis
Chinook
Cowlitz
Tillamook
Yakima
Klikitat
Molala
Kalapuya
Coos
Umpqua
Takelma
Karok
Yurok
Wiyot
Shasta
Hupa
Yana
Mattole
Maidu
Yuki
Pomo
Wintun
Miwok
Costanoan
Yokuts
Salinan
Chumash

Carrier
Chilcotin
Shuswap
Lillooet
Thompson
Okanagan
Sanpoil
Colville
Spokane
Palouse
Walla Walla
Klamath
Modoc
Chomawi
Tsugewi
Kawaiisu
Mono
Panamint

Kaigani
Piegan
Kutenai
Kalispel
Coeur D'Alene
Flathead
Crow
Nez Perce
Bannock
Shoshoni
Paviotso
Washo
Ute
Gosiute

Sarsi
Siksika (Blackfoot)
Cree

Atsina
Hidatsa
Mandan
Arikara
Teton
Dakota
Yankton
Dakota
Ponca
Pawnee
N.Cheyenne
Arapaho
S.Cheyenne
Jicarilla Apache
Kiowa
Kiowa Apache

Ojibwa (Chippewa)
Ottawa
Plains Cree
Assiniboin
Winnebago

Tobacco
Neutral

Santee Dakota

Iowa
Omaha
Oto
Kansa
Missouri
Osage
Quapaw

Fox
Kickapoo
Wea
Peoria

Sauk
Miami
Susquehanna
Pamunkey
Piankashaw
Illinois
Shawnee

Menomini
Potawatomie

Erie

Naskapi Montagnais
Micmac
Malecite
Passamaquoddy
Penobscot
Abnaki
Huron

Beothuk
Pennacook
Mahican
Mohawk
Nipmuc Oneida
Massachuset
Wampanoag
Narraganset
Pequot
Mohegan
Wappinger
Onondaga
Cayuga
Seneca
Delaware
Nanticoke
Powhatan
Chickahominy
Mattapony
Tutelo
Pamlico
Nottoway
Tuscarora
Catawba

Cayuse

Mohave
Serrano
Yavapai
Cahuilla
Yuma
Pima
Maricopa
Papago

Cochimi

Navaho
Pueblo
Mescalero Apache
Tawakoni
W.Apache
Lipan Apache
Opata

Zuni
Hopi
Kavasupai
Chemehuevi
Walapai

Comanche
Kichai
Waco
Tonkawa

Wichita

Caddo
Tunica

Natchez

Choctaw Creek
Alabama
Tuskegee
Cherokee
Chickasaw
Yuchi

Seri
Tarahumara
Cahita
Acaxee
Yaqui
Pericu
Waicuri

Concho
Coahuiltec
Tamaulipec
Huichol

Karankawa

Alakapa
Chitimacha
Biloxi
Mobile
Apalachee

Yamasee
Guale
Timucua

Calusa

Hichiti

Taino
Ciboney

Toltec
Tarascan
Otomi

Huastec
Totonac
Tlaxcalan
Aztec
Mixtec

Yucatan Maya

Zapotec

Lacandon
Maya
Quiche
Maya

Mosquito

Chontal

Rio Grande

Semole

0   600
Miles

Source: Martin Gilbert, *Atlas of American History*, Routledge, 1995

But woe betide them if they steal, for Columbus will have their nose or their ears chopped off! These good savages have suddenly all become thieves.

"They all believed that the Christians came from heaven and that the Kingdom of Castile was situated there", Christopher Columbus thinks. But in fact he is ascribing his own beliefs to them. "They come from heaven and are in search of gold", an Indian would have said to his king. But how much did Columbus understand since he did not know their language? He believed it because it was what he was doing: he brought his religion and took away gold in exchange.

The fact that he brought them religion means that he considered them as men, equal and identical with him, whom he was going to convert. But as soon as they resisted being despoiled any further, Columbus deemed it proper to subdue them – if need be, by the sword. "They are fit to be ordered." Those who were not yet Christians could only be slaves. Women shared the same condition, as can be seen from the story told by Michel de Cuneo, a companion of Columbus.

> While I was in the boat, I seized a very beautiful Caribbean woman. Having brought her to my cabin and as, according to their custom, she was naked, I got the idea of enjoying myself. I tried to put my desire into practice, but she did not want to oblige and belaboured me with her nails in such a fashion that I wished I had never started. But, on considering the situation, I took a rope and whipped her, as a result of which she gave vent to such unbelievable howls, that you would not have believed your ears. In the end we came to an agreement such that I can assure you she might have been raised in a school for whores.

The main interest of Tzvetan Todorov's book *The Conquest of America* lies in the fact that he shows, by referring to the texts of the earliest discoverers and conquistadors, that the essential features of the history of colonization were already present in them, in an embryonic state, and that they only had to grow and develop. We find examples of conversion, unequal exchange, sexual violence, and a vision of the other which either makes him a man like ourselves to be assimilated, that is, christianized, or makes him a slave.

In addition we find a tactic that was employed in most of the conquests from the sixteenth to the nineteenth centuries: a tactic used by the Spaniards in South America, by the Russians in Central Asia and in the Caucasus, by the French in the Maghreb, by the British in India. When a power of organized resistance arises to confront him, the conqueror negotiates with it in order to break it all the better later. This he achieves on many occasions by winning over to his cause some of the opponent's rivals, those notabilities who subsequently ensure his dominance over the rest of the population.

The conquistadores: Cortez, Pizarro, Valdivia

The establishment of the Spaniards began with the occupation of the island of San Domingo, Hispaniola. In 1509 the son of Christopher Columbus began the conquest of Cuba. Diego Velasquez completed it in 1514. It is from this island that expeditions were launched towards the *tierra firme* which was then believed to hold extraordinary wealth.

With 11 vessels, 100 sailors and 600 soldiers, 10 cannons and 16 horses, Hernan Cortez landed on the island of Cozumel on 18 February 1519. The tribes submitted, impressed by men who came from the sea and who, on their horses, resembled the Centaurs. Cortez founded Rica de Santa Cruz, a symbolic name, as in it gold comes side by side with the cross. Brushing aside the instructions of Diego Velazquez, Cortez thus created a settlement in the name of his king and, to show his resolve to be independent, burnt his own ships so as not to return to Cuba. Alerted by Diego Velazquez, Charles V despatched a fleet to fight him. But, in the meantime, Cortez had destroyed and conquered an empire.

First he triumphed over the Tlazcaltecs and used them as his allies against the Aztecs who had been oppressing them. To turn the conqueror away from the road to Mexico, Montezuma sent to the god from overseas the treasures of Quetzalcoatl and intimated that he would submit to Charles and pay tribute. When a plot was unearthed, Cortez in two hours had more than three thousand men executed. Finally he met Montezuma, asked him to destroy his idols, made him his prisoner and soon ruled in his name while holding him in chains. During these months, Cortez collected 600,000 pesos and sent a fifth to Charles V (the *Quinto*). He distributed the rest among the soldiers who, crazy with joy, destroyed all the idols. Following a revolt which broke out in spite of the vehement appeals of Montezuma, the Spaniards were forced to flee using a portable bridge, and the remnants of their army, assailed in their camps by flaming arrows, sought refuge with the Tlazcaltecs.

The second conquest too was a punitive expedition. Cortez systematically invested Mexico by building, piece by piece, a flotilla of thirteen boats which were drawn up on the lagoon of the city. Werner Herzog reconstituted this exploit in a film, but situated it elsewhere. Cortez cut off the aqueduct which supplied the city with water, destroyed 1,500 Aztec canoes, reduced the city to starvation and, as the report goes, had 67,000 men executed. More than 50,000 had already died of hunger or sickness. The conqueror's disappointment was immense when the booty he finally acquired proved to be very slim. But the spoils were substantial enough for Emperor Charles V to recognize him as Captain General of New Spain. Immediately afterwards Cortez transformed the Aztec Teocalli into a cathedral dedicated to Saint Francis.

What is the explanation for such an easy victory?

Cortez won thanks to his alliance with Xicotencatl, the chief of the Tlaxcaltecs and enemy of the Mexicans, who was thus reproved by the inhabitants of Cholvla: "Look at these vile, cowardly Tlaxcaltecs, worthy of being chastized. When they see themselves being defeated by the Mexicans, they run to seek strangers to defend them. How can you have, in such a short time, debased yourselves to such a degree? How can you have submitted yourselves to such faithless and barbarous people, to strangers unknown to anyone?" (quoted in Todorov, 1982).

Cortez had vanquished with the help of a handful of men who, very quickly, obtained allies against the Aztecs. A real coalition was formed, first with the Totouacs then, after the fall of Mexico, with the old warrior nation of the Tlaxcaltecs. The coalition supplied 6,000 warriors while Cortez had fewer than 500. His success in playing the game of alliances was, so the story goes, due to Dona Marina, whom the Aztecs had sold to the Mayas and who became Cortez's mistress. Eager to wreak vengeance on her own people who had dishonoured her, she knew, on account of her noble origin, the political disposition of the country and thus could provide her lover with the necessary information which led him to victory.

But the success of Cortez was also due – like that of the other con-quistadors, particularly Pizarro in Peru – to the long sword, the *espada*, to the horse, which the Mexicans tried to kill instead of men, and above all to firearms, though these often became rusty and the powder got wet. Lastly it was due also to the cross-bow which pierced enemy tunics, and to the *escaubil*, the lined tunic which the Indian arrows could not penetrate.

The technical or political details do not adequately explain why the Spaniards sometimes succeeded in winning even at odds of one to a hundred. One reason is that, faced with a series of prodigious events, the Mayas and the Aztecs were overcome by the feeling that the gods were no longer talking to them. "They asked the gods to be favourable to them and to grant them victory over the Spaniards and their other enemies. But it must have been too late for they could no longer get an answer from their oracles. They then held their gods to be either dumb or dead" (quoted by Todorov, 1982). The Aztec kings communicated only with the gods, through the intermediary of their soothsayer-priests, not with humans. The main message which Montezuma sent to the Spaniards was that he did not wish there to be any exchange of messages.

When Montezuma heard the tales of the arrival of the Spaniards, "he remained as if dead or dumb. He sent word that he was ready to grant the Spaniards all that they wanted, but they must give up their wish to come to see him, for kings must never appear in public . . . However the more gold and jewellry the Aztecs gave to induce the stranger to depart, the deeper the stranger, irresistibly drawn, penetrated into the country. And he wanted to seize their king . . . Accustomed to communicate with the gods, not with men, the king convened his priests and sorcerers, who could

34

not have failed to foresee this conquest, this defeat, since it was perceived as a supernatural event." In a sense, that was the only way to integrate the Aztec past with the present.

But the Spaniards did not approach the vanquished in a like spirit. By prevailing thanks to their material and technical superiority, by having learnt to communicate with allies, by catechizing them, they deprived themselves of the ability to integrate themselves with the world of those whom they called savages.

Peru presents a similar pattern. The great Quechua state, or Inca Empire, a veritable mosaic of displaced peoples, gathered these heterogeneous elements around a centre situated in Cuzco. This empire was undermined by internal conflicts, especially those between the two enemy brothers Huascar and Atahualpa, who were fighting over the claim to sovereignty. With his dream of emulating the exploits of Cortez, Francisco Pizarro acted in the same manner as his hero. Starting from Panama, together with Diego de Almagro, he hired two ships to explore the countries lying to the South which were rumoured to hold fabulous treasures. With about twelve men he reached the mouth of the Guayaquil. After gathering information about the state of the Inca Empire, he returned to Panama to get ready for the great expedition which he planned to carry out, once he had received the authorization of Charles V.

In 1532 the expedition set out, at the moment when Atahualpa triumphed over his brother Huascar. Francisco Pizarro encountered the Inca army at Cajamarca and initiated discussions with its chief. His idea was to take him prisoner by surprise, as Cortez had Montezuma. The trick worked and, aware of the invaders' greed for gold, Atahualpa, in his prison, offered to pay, as ransom, all the gold that the room where he was held would hold, up to the height of a man. Pizarro accepted and, once the ransom had been paid, had Atahualpa executed for the crime which he himself has committed in having his brother killed.

The death of Atahualpa, burnt alive in great pomp in front of the soldiers, was to brand itself into the memory of the people. Like Montezuma's, Atahualpa's death marked the transfer of power into the hands of the Spaniards. Pizarro had already laid hands on gold and silver equivalent in worth to fifty years of European production. He thought that the Inca Empire would continue to provide him with precious metals. To that end he had to control the entire country. But the Inca Empire did not collapse all of a sudden, as the Aztec Empire did, even after the fall of Cuzco (1533). At the head of the Inca Empire Pizarro placed Manco Inca, the half-brother of Atahualpa. But the latter took advantage of the dissensions between Pizarro and Almagro to attempt to make his people rise up against the Spaniards. Moreover, by setting up his capital at Lima, on the coast, Pizarro lost contact with the heart of the country, thus delaying the completion of the conquest. The Empire of the mountains was vanquished only in 1572. When Tupac Amaru, the last Inca, died in 1781, his memory was preserved by the Indians as vividly as that of the death of Atahualpa.

The centralized empires fell at one stroke. By seizing their head Cortez and Pizarro could gain mastery over the entire edifice, even though in Peru armed resistance lasted for half a century more. In Mexico, the resistance of the Yucatan of the Mayas lasted longer, undoubtedly because less effort was exerted to conquer it – it held less wealth. The same disenchantment, in addition to still greater difficulties, marked the enterprise of Diego de Almagro, who had parted company from Pizarro, and that of Pedro de Valdivia, when they tried to conquer the south of Peru, and afterwards Chile. They clashed with the Mapuchas, and later with the Araucans who, though they had not formed a centralized state, were none the less redoubtable warriors. The latter immediately knew how to seize the horses of the Spaniards and to make use of them to be at least the first to defeat Valdivia's army at Tucapel in 1553. Nevertheless, the conquerors little by little settled down. But gold and silver had become scarce. They became farmers, somewhat like the ranchers in the English colonies of the Far West. Their fortune lay in the fact that the strategic position of Chile, near the Cape Horn, was such that the king had constantly to send them the reinforcement which they needed.

The Rio de la Plata was the third anchorage point for the Spaniards. It was discovered by Juan Diaz de Solis who was looking for the mythic passage between the Atlantic and the Pacific. In 1527 Sebastian Cabot sailed up this immense mouth of fresh water and built the fort of Sancti Spiritus. He reached Paraguay, found that the silver used by the Indians came from the Potosi, in Peru. This estuary of the Parana and the Uruguay was named Rio de la Plata.

But when, in 1533, the Spanish monarch sent a large expedition of military conquest under the leadership of Pedro de Mendoza, who founded Nuestra Senora del Buenos Aires, it came up against the Guarani Indians further north, who also intended to conquer the heights of present-day Bolivia and Paraguay, around the coast of Asuncion which had been established during those years. The Guaranis were first-rate warriors, skilful in the use of the lasso, and they inflicted heavy losses upon the Spaniards. In their thrust forward the Guaranis had, coming from the east, repelled the Arawak tribes. After conquering one of the fragments of the former Inca Empire, they clashed with the Spaniards. Two conquerors found themselves face to face. In order to better resist the strangers, the alliances were turned around so that the Indian tribes united under the leadership of the Chiriguanos, the most active of the Guaranis. The Spaniards were compelled to launch difficult expeditions to triumph over those Indians.

Still it took more than a century for the road from Buenos Aires to Lima, through Paraguay, to be brought under complete control.

These immense conquered spaces (to which the Philippines were to be soon added) had been joined to the Spanish crown by a handful of men. These men were Andulusian and Basque sailors, conquistadores born of the gentry, penniless hidalgos, or soldiers of fortune who may have served in Italy and have thrown themselves into the adventure. The example of the conquest of Chile is significant. Pedro de Valdivia had 143 men at his disposal: they included 4 noblemen, 34 hidalgos, 6 metis, 1 slave, 9 men "of honour", and 86 individuals whose status is not known. The majority of them came from Estremadura, and the others mainly from Castile. When one contrasts this small number, which finally rose to between fifty and a hundred thousand a century after the conquest, with the millions of deaths caused by their arrival, to the demographic collapse of the indigenous population which seems to have fallen from eleven to less than one million, one cannot help observing that, never in history, have so few men have made so many victims, either voluntarily – by the massacres – or otherwise.

In these conditions, one can understand how Christian Spain was able to produce another race of adventurers: the missionaries and the martyrs.

The Church enters the stage: the missions in the Far East

The texts which denounced the cruel deeds of the conquerors had scarcely any influence on the attitude and behaviour of states or men. But with increasing intensity the Church took up a position against the abuses of colonization. Following Francisco de Vitoria and Las Casas, the Franciscan Juan Da Silva, himself influenced by the Dominican jurist-theologian Domingo de Soto, had sent several *Memorials* to Philip II, the King of Spain. In accordance with Pope Alexander VI's bull, the king had to undertake a spiritual mission in the New World. But no constraint was to be exerted in matters of faith. They must abide by the orders of Christ who had sent his apostles "like lambs into the midst of wolves". But, in Mexico, the Emperor Montezuma had been killed even before the Gospel had been proclaimed to the Indians. To act in that way was tantamount to "following the detestable example of Mahomet in spreading his iniquitous sect". True the Indians might massacre a few preachers if they were not accompanied by soldiers. "But, to be born, the Church needs martyrs." Juan da Silva advocated the use of "soft" methods, as in Florida and even in Peru.

An echo of these controversies was found in Rome where, as early as 1568, Pope Pius V set up commissions which were the origins of the *Congregation of Propaganda*. The concern was mainly to prevent acts of criminal violence, but also to coordinate, under the exclusive control of the

Holy See, the action of catholic missions in the world. In 1659 the *Instructions* of Alexander VI forbade all collusion between the bearers of the Gospel and the political authorities. They recommended respect for local traditions, and also prescribed the use of the local language.

The Jesuits, especially in the Far East, put these Instructions into practice more fully and to better effect than others. Francis Xavier (1506–52) was one of the first to enter Japan, which he believed to be an inviolate world. He was fascinated by the notion of honour as upheld by this nation. In the Moluccas he had walked in the jungle singing a Malay song to attract the attention of the natives. In Japan he trod the snow with bare feet, during a journey of several hundred kilometres which took him to Kyoto.

But in Japan, as in China, not all missionaries adopted the same attitude.

Extending the Kingdom of Christ

In order to propagate Christianity, the early missionaries – in China or in the other countries of the Far East – built hospitals, schools, etc. In short they penetrated society by means of their social work more than by their actual religious teaching, somewhat in the same fashion as Buddhism had done. Moreover technical novelties – mechanical clocks, optical or musical instruments – as well as the teaching of mathematics and astronomy contributed all the more to this penetration which, from the religious point of view, was soon to degenerate into a confrontation. Learned forms coexisted with popular forms of adaptation of Christianity. For instance, the educated class was interested in all that dealt with ethics and methods of self-discipline in the missionary teaching. This explains the interest shown in Diego de Pantoja's *The Seven Victories* (over the seven deadly sins) (1604). Matteo Ricci observes that, when he went to Nanking in 1599, "the practice was to form congregations where lectures on moral subjects were held". On the other hand, it was activities of a miraculous nature – in particular, the healings – performed by the missionaries which assured the implantation of Christianity among the common people.

The activity of the Jesuits reached its highest point during the first half of the seventeenth century. With the end of the Ming era began a period of instability which drew to a close with the installation of a new regime. It was increasingly distrustful of the foreign missionaries. The Jesuit order was to be suppressed in 1773 (Y. Ishizawa, in Forest, 1988, pp. 17–34, and J. Gernet, in Forest, 1988, pp. 34–46).

Were the persecutions the result of the missionaries' will to interfere in the internal affairs of the country, of an evangelizing zeal which provoked reprisals, or of a change which occurred in China at the time of the Ming Dynasty?

According to the Portuguese Jesuit Alvaro Semado who, in 1643, published in Rome a *Relazione della grande monarcha della Cina*, 54 persecutions can be listed between 1583, the date of Matteo Ricci's arrival in China, and the middle of the seventeenth century. This gives us a scale which is more or less valid for the eighteenth century.

For instance, in the province of Fu-Jian the persecution arose out of a conflict among the missionaries themselves. The first to settle, the Jesuits, held that the traditional rites of the Chinese, in honour of their ancestors, were totally secular and accordingly those who had been converted could take part in them. The Dominicans and the Franciscans, on the other hand, forbade the converted Chinese to participte in those rites, which were deemed by them to be "noisy" and bloody, and likened to super-stitions. Consequently the rumour spread that Christianity was ignorant of the cult of ancestors and showed no respect for Confucius. Soon after, a young convert broke the head of an idol to prove its impotence, where-upon an angry mob marched to storm the church, laid it waste and beat up the converted Chinese with bamboo sticks. The missionaries were forced to leave their settlements in Fuan, the converted to abjure their new faith and, in their turn, the Jesuits were forbidden to stay. A stubborn man, the Dominican Diez, went back to the Fuan square to tear up the inscription prohibiting Christianity. But martyrdom was reserved for one of his co-religionists, Capillar, who was accused by the authorities of fomenting agitation, opposing the cult of the ancestors, and above all of turning young girls away from marriage by setting up communities of nuns. Capillar was beheaded on 15 January 1648.

At the heart of the quarrels lay the problem of the Chinese rites. In 1704 Pope Clement XI had forbidden Chinese Christians to attend all traditional ceremonies. The Emperor of China thereupon decided to grant stay permits (*yinpiao*) only to those missionaries who would not be opposed to them. But the other grievances persisted. In particular Christianity was accused of turning people away from the requirements of filial devotion, since men and women refused to have children even though they were gathered in mixed communities. All that was contrary to prevailing moral standards, especially as, in order to build churches, the converted Chinese were actually throwing money down the drain. The persecutions increased. The missionaries went underground, hiding among the converted upon whom the authorities inflicted horrible tortures, among others the *zanzi* which fastened the fingers between five wooden sticks tied by a rope which was then pulled. The women often resisted this, while the men also had to suffer the *jiagun* which wedged the ankles with a board which was then struck with a hammer. People were encouraged to denounce the missionaries and those they converted. The courage displayed by the persecuted aroused admiration and brought about an increase in the number of adherents.

However, as time passed, the state was no longer concerned merely to control the activities of the missionaries. In 1746 the latter were regarded as rebels who were plotting with the foreigners. "Do you intend to lay hands on China in order to rule her?", Guohviren was asked before being hanged (1746). A premonitory question!

That was a question which was asked straight away in Japan. In this country the first encounter with Europe, the arrival of the Portuguese in 1543, was tantamount to the introduction of the firearms. This led to a drastic alteration of the conditions of the struggle for power during that period of ceaseless warfare. Oda Nobunaga, a warlord, made the most of it. Toyotomi Hideyoshi, his successor, was thus able to bring the period of warfare to a close. During those years, following the arrival of saint Francis Xavier in 1549, Christianity had developed as best it could. After supervising the missions as visitor of the General of the Company of Jesus, Father Valignano wrote a book designed to establish principles for the evangelization of the country: *Advertimentos e avisos acerca dos costumes y catangues de Jappâo* (sixteenth century). Valignano made recommendations covering salutations, table manners, contacts between persons living under the same roof. They were specific, meticulous orders which were based on the idea that attention ought to be paid to the interplay of social status, and even suggested following the example of the behaviour of the zen monks.

Father Valignano understood that the missionaries had to adapt to the way of life prevailing in the country. But the authorities held that, in a Shintoist society, Christianity was an "aberrant" religion. It was dangerous for the identity of the inhabitants and, in the long term, for their basic power structure (*kogi*), the supreme authority which was then under the supreme control of Hideyoshi. After his death, his successor Tokugawa Ieyasu was alerted by a sentence written by the Spaniards. On the occasion of an audience granted on 5 October 1604 to the envoys of the government of Manila, particular note was taken of the following text in the letter of the governor of Manila: "In Castile, our country, the Emperor and all the people adore God. The visit of our Fathers to your country is not motivated by the futile search for gold and jewels, but by the desire to spread the teaching of God for the salvation of souls."

A learned Japanese asked: "Was not all this meant to work for the decline of the country, for the overthrow of the regime?"

On 1 February 1614 an edict of the *Bakufu*, the shogunal system, decreed the expulsion of those missionories who had come under the pretext of indulging in trade, but were actually bent on destroying the Buddhist faith and on changing the political law of Japan.

Two decades later the country closed its door to the West (1639). Meanwhile, with the outbreak of troubles which might have been caused by groups of Christians, an alliance with the Dutch was envisaged with a view to launching a punitive expedition against the Philippines.

France: fishing or adventure?

More than the taste for adventure or the struggle against Islam it was cod fishing which, in France, was the origin of that country's first colonization of the Americas. It was fishing, likewise, which generated conflicts among sailors from Olonne, the Basque country, Brittany and Castile. As early as 1497 Christopher Columbus had to take shelter against them in Madeira. Besides Francis I of France demanded to see "the clause in Adam's will" which, according to the Pope, excluded him from the division of the world. In fact, for a long time, the French lacked the means to set up a strong commercial organization, and in the sixteenth century no one had really got around to thinking about such an enterprise. It was only during the period of the wars of the privateers that Saint Malo and Nantes, for example, were spurred to action. But they did so several decades after Portugal and Spain and with less determination than England. Above all the State had to be motivated by the desire to own colonies.

As a matter of fact, during the period of the wars of Religion and the struggle against Spain and England, the aims of the colonial war were strictly military. It is true that in Canada the first explorations, financed by Francis I, opened the way to Jacques Cartier who, in 1535, discovered the route of the St Lawrence, the pathway to Japan, as he believed and as testified by the name "La Chine" given to the waterfalls. This situation lasted until Champlain, in an anti-English spirit, paved the way for a genuine colonial settlement. Still it was fishing which fed the population, though the fur trade soon took its place.

In no time the English and the French were seeking support from the different Indian tribes – when they weren't fighting them while simultaneously trying to convert them. The scale of these settlements can be measured when one recalls that in the time of Richelieu – that is, of the struggles between the Iroquois, allied to the English, and the Hurons, allied to the French – Quebec boasted between 60 and 100 inhabitants, and Boston, 2,000.

Little is known of the first reactions of the Indians to the arrival of the French, except for an oral tradition which has gradually been eroded and which has been analysed by Bruce Trigger. Montagnais and Micmacs believed that the ships were floating islands, the discharge of their guns were lightning flashes. They were also struck by the white skin and the red clothes. But what really impressed them was the metal and the glass beads, as well as the clocks, knives and iron axes. In exchange the French asked for eels and especially beavers which proved to be an unexpected source of wealth. When the French were stricken with disease, with scurvy in particular, the Indians taught them to heal themselves by drinking a tea made with the bark of white cedar.

The voyages of Jacques Cartier were in fact a disappointment, since he and his companions believed that they could reach the other ocean by sailing up the St Lawrence and the lakes. They remained in the interior of the country, instead of reaching the Pacific. Moreover the Iroquois women they took back with them to France died during the course of the voyage (1536). On their return the disappearance of the women became one of the causes of the mistrust felt towards the white strangers, who besides brought diseases with them. Accordingly, from Indians who came to the Belle-Isle strait to exchange deer and wolf hides for axes and knives, a party of Spanish Basque fishermen learnt that more than 35 of Jacques Cartier's men had been massacred by the Iroquois of the St Lawrence.

These incidents, that disappointment, that painful legacy help to understand why, after the failure of this colonization, it took several decades for new schemes to be worked out in relation to a country where, instead of gold and diamonds, only quartz and pyrites were to be found.

From these regions part of the Iroquois disappeared, decimated either by the arrival of the French, or by conflicts with other Indian tribes.

The modus operandi of the French priests and administrators was different from that of the traders. The merchants got to know Indian customs in order to better appreciate what kind of trade they could set up with them. But, from Jacques Cartier down to Champlain, the administrators treated the Indians with haughtiness. The Indians became so embittered that in 1629 they helped the English to capture Quebec.

For a long time the traders did not look favourably upon the idea of a durable, long-lasting settlement, as it alienated the Indians from them. However they changed their mind when they realized that, as soon as their back was turned, or as soon as they set off on their way back to Europe, Dutch and English traders moved in.

In the Caribbean, Pierre Belain d'Esnambouc landed at St Christophe in 1625, after a battle with a Spanish galleon. Richelieu was responding to political imperatives when he helped in setting up the *Compagnie des Isles d'Amérique* for the purpose of conquering the lands occupied by the Caribs, but where the Spanish or English had already started to settle. In 1639 the Caribs of Guadeloupe were exterminated. Soon Martinique, Dominica – fourteen islands in all – were occupied. The settlement of San Domingo took place later.

According to Jean Meyer the French Monarchy did not, at the outset, have a genuine "colonial policy". Following the period of the expeditions, and when the search for wealth had tapered off, Canada remained a land of "religious prestige", a purely Catholic colony to counteract the heretical colonies. In 1609, Lescarbot addressed the future Louis XIII urging him to convert the Indians, an undertaking worthy of Alexander the Great and deserving of a crusade. And in other respects the monarchy favoured the missionaries.

If there had to be a colonial policy, it would only be for the purpose of conquering the Spanish Empire. At the time of Philip II such a policy was an empty dream. The lure of the tropical products was real enough, hence the interest shown in the West Indies which supplied tobacco and sugar, thus providing a way to motivate the monarchy financially. However too many obstacles stood in the way of any initiatives. Carib resistance, competition from buccaneers and other rivals, each of whom seized an "island" – all this put a damper on profit-making. From a mercantilist point of view these possessions counted for little. Nevertheless they had to be maintained for the "savages" must not be allowed to bring down the power of the Great King.

With the rise of Nantes and soon after of Bordeaux, the monarchy tried to bring colonial activities under a central administration, by giving the State Secretariat for the Navy responsibility for them. This became a dominant feature of French policy for it lasted up to the Third Republic. The turning point occurred during the time of Colbert when several basic directions for French policy were adopted and consolidated.

First there was the asiatic temptation which held the promise of more profits. It led to a whole series of failures, even of disasters, such as the loss of a fleet of nine ships with 2,500 men, of whom the 500 survivors were repatriated by the Dutch. This humiliation occurred in 1669. Still the first positive result was obtained when François Martin acquired the concession for the future outpost of Pondicherry (1674).

The second, which in a sense was the inverse of the first, was the preservation of Canada, less for the purpose of trade than for the perpetuation of a Royal Colony. In order to consolidate this agricultural colonization, the immigration of women was organized on a fairly large scale. However, the expeditions to new territories continued none the less. They were led by the *coureurs de bois* (trappers) of whom the most famous was the Cavelier de La Salle who extended the French presence as far as the Mississippi. When it started, French colonization in Canada was commercial. Very soon the French settlers became a landowning, Catholic presence, culminating in the constitution of a sort of small military empire. But Louisiana which, on the map, "hemmed in" the English colonies of the interior, gained importance only during the time of Law (1720).

The third and final direction lay in the development, in the West Indies, of a small essentially colonial imperialism sustained by the black slave trade from 1680. The local colonists encouraged this trade, in conjunction with the French ports and the monarchy helped and managed them, under the aegis of Seigneley.

At first France experienced a "double colonial failure" in the fifteenth and sixteenth centuries. In the fifteenth century the failure was due to its sailors not taking part in the great discoveries. In the sixteenth century the failure was due to the absence of France from the conquest of naval bases and the trade routes for the big profits being made in Asia and in America.

In fact, with its strong monarchy and a nobility, who were powerful but had no knowledge of business and commerce, the mass of French territory stood as a sort of negative pole in the west of Europe. The busy commercial routes had moved elsewhere and bypassed it: from Venice to Genoa and Barcelona by sea, from Lisbon to Antwerp and Amsterdam by the Atlantic. The great land routes which crossed France, the Champagne region in particular, between the Netherlands and Italy, henceforth fell into disuse. All these facts taken together contributed to the fact that the colonial expansion could not, in France, be anything but of a voluntarist character, with the monarchy as its source. With little support from society at large the French monarchy could act only with the help of its own resources, in its struggle for its existence against the Spanish hegemony; or, with its being Catholic, in its clash with the Protestant English.

And then the Dutch . . .

France boasts of being the eldest daughter of the Church. Holland claims to be the eldest son of the Ocean. As a matter of fact, of all the nations who founded colonies, the Hollanders and the Zeelanders were undoubtedly the ones most wedded to the sea. As a land floating on water, half flooded, Holland does indeed have water as its vital element: "Arising from the sea, the Republic of the United Provinces derives its power from it" (W. Temple, quoted in F. Braudel, 1979, Vol. 3). Herring fishing, salting and curing, the *Vlieboot* ("the Flute"), a ship with the bulging sides, manned by hardy and extremely frugal sailors, the unbeatable costs at the shipyards of Amsterdam due to the most advanced technology of the time: these were the factors which made the fortune of a fleet which soon enabled Holland to dominate the traffic on the seas all over the world. It owed little to the state, unlike the Portuguese and Spanish fleets. But the towns which contributed to its build-up could not avoid acting in common, as they were bound to one another by mutual interests.

Two events sparked off the spectacular expansion of Holland: first, the ruin of Antwerp during the crisis of 1576–1609 and the *Guerre des Gueux* (Beggars' War) which guaranteed the independence of the Netherlands; secondly, the occupation of Portugal by Spain accompanied by the union of the two kingdoms in 1580. As early as 1595 Van Houtman, of Gouda, received, from several merchants of Amsterdam who had formed a Company of Distant Countries, 4 ships, 60 cannons and 250 men. He sailed round the coasts of India and of the Far East and returned with his ships laden with cargo. His patrons were filled with enthusiasm. He set sail again and immediately afterwards several squadrons went round the world through the strait of Molucca. Olivier Van Noort and Van Neek were the heroes of these enterprises sponsored by individual companies which ended up by joining together, like the towns which had been helping them. Their competition resulted in the price of spices rising in India, and in prices coming down on their return home, when the spices were put on sale. Consequently, in 1602, they united to form the *Oost Indische Kompagnie*, a federation modelled on the federation of the United Provinces itself. The Dutch had a simple plan when they set out across the globe. It was to make money. Christ was absent from their preoccupations. They were not interested in evangelizing. They took advantage of the weakness of the Portuguese to replace them. Or rather to do business on better conditions, in their place. The Company became a genuine power which did not hesitate to use cannon fire against rivals who had to be eliminated, for profits jumped from 15 to 75 percent in 1606. The Portuguese, the English, the French from Dieppe were driven off the scene . . . But Jan Pieterszoon Coen, the Governor of the Company in the Indian Archipelago, very quickly grasped the fact that commerce based on trading-posts, in the Portuguese style, could not survive unless it was reinforced, in addition to the small forts at Java and Amboyna, by a permanent settlement. It became imperative to colonize.

In 1619 the foundation of Batavia marks the beginning of a genuine settlement of the Dutch in the Indian Archipelago. Jan Coen had discovered the location of Jakarta. The Dutch drove out the vassal of the Sultan of Banten, destroyed the local town and the mosque, founded a new city, then used the network of its relationships with the hinterland. As a counterweight to resist the "Javans" the Company populated the city with Chinese, Malays, Macassars, Balinese, Filipinos from Luzon. Some decades later the Dutch triumphed over the Sultan of Macassar and thenceforth held the south of the Celebes. Thus they replaced the Bugis who till then had been their main rivals in the trade with the Moluccas and beyond. Meanwhile the main goal – that is, the control of Java, acquired by means of a policy of hatching intrigues among the Princes – was attained towards the end of the seventeenth century. In 1681, Batavia had 2,188 Europeans in a population of 30,598 inhabitants.

It was not much, but it lasted. Java and the East Indies did not become a settlement colony. Unlike the Portuguese and the Spaniards, the Dutch thought only of returning home, once their fortune has been made. Moreover to be employed by the Company entailed a loss of one's freedom of action, since the Company acted as a large society. Once they left the Company the *Vrijburgers* – free members of the middle class – could engage only in inferior occupations, such as running a tavern, since all the profitable activities were controlled by the Company.

By contrast, in South Africa the Dutch seized the Cape and stayed there. Led by Jan Van Riebeeck, 200 Dutch citizens landed on 6 April 1652, the 6th of April being still celebrated as the national day. Protected by a fort,

Jan Van Riebeeck grew cereals and introduced the horse to the continent. Without doubt the Company asserted a strict monopoly on trade. Nevertheless the colonists were able to establish a patriarchal, biblical way of life, and gave themselves the name of a peasant population – the Boers – in order to shy away from mercantile civilization. They provide the first example of a settlement colony in Africa.

But their relationships with the Hottentots, Xhosas and Kafirs were bad as the latter did not obey the same laws regarding barter and property. The Hottentots, for example, did not believe that the land belonged to anyone. Accordingly there was no question of "defending" it by means of a fence. But it was cattle that became the bone of contention. Credo Mutwa has explained that the Boers did not know that, in barter with the Xhosas, a cow could not be exchanged for an inanimate object, even if this was a large amount of metal or of tobacco. The custom was to give back, in exchange, one of the calves of the female, the cow being considered as a pledge. When the Xhosas supplied them with cows, the Boers were surprised and angry when their cows disappeared as soon as they had calved. They treated the Xhosas as "thieves". As a result this ignorance of the Other became the cause of conflicts and of wars.

England: state piracy

In England too, towards the end of the fifteenth century, one finds a similar movement towards "nationalization" of economic forces. The state stimulated and controlled trade. For example, it decreed that imported French wines must be imported only in English ships. Again, following an edict issued by Henry VII, foreign ships could not be loaded unless no English freightage was available in the ports.

In the face of Castilian and Portuguese enterprises, all the efforts of Henry VII were geared towards opening up the Baltic sea. Nevertheless John Cabot depicted the wealth of the Atlantic to the English in glowing colours. In 1497, appointed admiral of England, master of 5 ships bearing the royal banner, he set sail in the search of a north-west passage. That is how he reached the Cape Breton and Labrador. His disappointment was galling when he found neither treasures nor spices.

In 1486, the creation of the Fellowship of Merchant Adventurers in London, responded to other needs. The aim was to obtain a dominant position in Antwerp in order to expand the market for wool and, in particular, for cloth. The latter had developed as a result of the tremendous growth of rural industries in England which guaranteed a cost price lower than that obtained in the cities. Immanuel Wallerstein has shown that the establishment of the Merchant Adventurers was both defensive and offensive, as its purpose was to protect the exportation of this fabric, the only product which England could sell abroad, to distant lands or those closer to home. We must also mention the north-east passage sought by Richard Chancellor when he landed in Archangelsk. In 1555 letters patent were granted to the Merchant Adventurers of England for the discovery of "regions, territories, islands, possessions and domains unknown and not frequently visited by sea or by navigation". This company, soon called the Muscovy Company, obtained the monopoly of the Russian trade and that of the border states. In 1557, after signing a treaty with the Tsar, Jenkinson sailed down the Volga, reached the Caspian Sea and, through Persia, discovered another route to India.

Up to the end of the sixteenth century England was concerned only with routes and commerce. But the period of Elizabeth marked a watershed, for it was then that Walter Raleigh became the theoretician of a sort of maritime imperialism: "Whoever rules the waves rules commerce; whoever rules commerce rules the wealth of the world, and consequently the world itself . . . "

Opportunity makes the thief. Francis Drake was conducting his war of piracy against Papist Spain when, together with the French pirate, Guillaume Le Testu, he seized a mule convoy carrying the gold of Peru to Panama. With the connivance of Queen Elizabeth he repeated his feat and plundered the coast of Chile and Peru before returning from there via the Pacific, and Indian Oceans. At Ternate he gave protection to a sultan who had revolted against the Portuguese. Thus was born the first overseas English settlement. As a reward for all his captures Drake was knighted by the Queen (1581).

These enterprises followed the directions taken from the very beginning – the West Indies, India, the North Atlantic, Russia – and were motivated by the lure of profit. They were henceforth buttressed by the idea of establishing English colonies, of "populating the pagan or barbarous countries which are not really possessed by any Prince or Christian people". That was the idea of Humphrey Gilbert, a gentleman educated at Eton and Oxford. He enunciated the doctrine, carried it into practice and helped in the settlement of the first colony in Newfoundland, to which England would send its unemployed citizens, sell its products and from which it would get its food supplies (1583). As a result *as early as the end of the sixteenth century the double identity of the English empire was already evident*: naval bases, or the settlement of the colonists. That is, on one hand, mercantile colonies; on the other hand, lands of settlement for the faith, for the establishment of those who have nothing – a colonization which, in its own way, resembled and perpetuated the English expansion into Ireland. After all, whether in Ireland or overseas, the same men were in charge of the operations.

In America, unlike the French who penetrated deep into the interior of the country, the English set up several coastal establishments from the Hudson to Virginia. James I granted concessions to two companies with respect to the American coast from latitude 34 to the 38 and latitude 41 to 45 north. Accordingly 104 colonists landed in Chesapeake Bay where the port was named Jamestown, in honour of the King. The beginnings were difficult, especially as regards relationships with the Indians. When a quarter of the colonists were massacred in 1622, the survivors wondered if they would be able to triumph over such ordeals. But the colony succeeded in overcoming these difficulties and in producing a crop which held great prospects of a bright future, tobacco, for which it obtained a monopoly of sales in England.

At the same time an expedition launched from Virginia towards the North discovered and described what henceforth came to be known as New England. The Pilgrim Fathers who arrived in 1620 had originally been aiming for Virginia. But the storms decided otherwise. The puritans, the actual Pilgrim Fathers, numbered only 35 out of the 200 immigrants who landed at Cape Cod and founded the port of Plymouth. They and particularly their descendants succeeded in making everyone believe that they were the founders of the future United States (1620). In a way they were, since they did sign a sort of agreement, the *Mayflower* Compact, which was the basis of a Calvinist democracy. That colony of Massachusetts, with its university at Cambridge, Harvard, founded by a clergyman from Boston, soon became a model of government emulated by the other colonies.

Till then plunder and privateering had been more profitable for England than the occupation of territories overseas. Besides it seemed apparent that the Spaniards had already grabbed all the big prizes. Following the disaster of the Invincible Armada, the decline of Spanish power and the rise of the Netherlands, the situation changed. It is soon altered in India too, where, after a naval victory over the Portuguese, Sir Thomas Roe, the ambassador of James I, was received by the Moghul Emperor.

There were several differences between the two empires. Managed from the centre by the Castilian Monarchy the Spanish lands overseas comprised distinct, separate entities. Coming after the Protestant Reformation the English empire was, for the time being, left to the initiative of individuals. In Maryland it was Catholic; in Massachusetts it was Puritan.

Russia: increasing the number of tax-payers for the Tsar

The Russians would like their "colonization" to be seen as totally different from that of the other western powers. From the twelfth century on, in the search for fur, the Russians of Novgorod and of Suzdal were sending colonists to settle beyond the Kama river in order to associate with the Mordvins, who were Finno-Ugrians. Even today the Mordvins, who are as numerous as the Estonians, form the most widespread non-Russian population in the entire interior of the former Empire. Only 28 percent of the Mordvins live in their autonomous Republic, around Saransk, on the Volga. This is a sign of complete assimilation.

The two centuries of Mongol domination interrupted this search. It was resumed as soon as the Golden Horde disintegrated, following the fall of Kazan to the Russians (1552).

The conquest of Kazan brought the Tartar State to an end. It also made it possible for the Russians to expand on both sides of the Urals and beyond, to a region which had an area of more than one million square kilometres. It was called Siberia, a term which subsequently covered the whole stretch up to the Pacific. The very first expansion, on the Kama, towards the north resumed the development that occurred before the Tartar period. But the main activity, in 1558, was due to the initiative of the Stroganov brothers who received from Tsar Ivan the Terrible a deed which made them real sovereigns, with the responsibility to defend their territory "against the Nogais and other hordes". "I, Ivan Vassilivitch, Tsar and Grand Prince of all of Russia, on the 4th of April 7066 (1558), have been presented with a petition stating that in our fatherland, on the river Kama, downstream from the great Perm . . . the country is a wilderness, that no tax reaches my treasury . . . that this has not yet been given to anybody . . . and as Grigori Strogonov has presented the petition and wishes to set up a new city, to clear, cultivate and there to settle people not subject to tallage to search for saltpans, I have hereby conceded to him this territory . . . " (quoted in Laran and Saussay, p. 208).

One of their first acts was to build the convent of Pyskor, on the bank of the river Kama, and to settle colonists in it. A century later, in 1647, 2,004 inhabitants lived in that region. But by that time they were paying tallage.

A few years later the ataman Ermak appeared with a band of 600 men. Stroganov provided him with arquebuses and cannon, powder and lead. Going up the Outka river, he took Tyumen . . . On seeing Ermak and his Cossacks arrive the Khan Khoutchoum said: "Let us march forward without fear. These pagans cannot do us any fatal harm since the gods are with us." On hearing these words the men dashed forward to fight as if rushing to take part in a feast and the ataman Ermak gave the order to open fire.

Then came the turn of the Samoyeds and the Ostiaks to submit and pay the *iassak*, a tax paid in sable, which was in very great demand at that time. Also to be had were elks, reindeer, bears, foxes, wolverines, otters, beavers, and countless fish, sturgeons, pikes, roaches. Thanks to his good fortune Ermak became a historical legend: the adventurous hero who soon brought to his Tsar the modest present of a territory of 6 million square kilometres.

In its own way, though in a lower key, the advance of the Russians was the equivalent of the Cape route for the Portuguese. It was a way of bypassing on the north the remnants of the Mongol Empire to reach the treasures of the Far East. Starting in about 1465, at the time when the Portuguese were crossing the Gulf of Guinea, the commercial progress of the Russians towards the east continued without interruption. It was, moreover, between 1466 and 1472 that the Russian Nikitin reached India.

The progressive advance proceeded from river to river where fortresses were built, even though the Tsars at first had expressed reservations. The Ob and the Irtysh were reached in 1585, the Yenisei in 1628, the Amur and the Kolyma in 1640. Irkutsk was built in 1632 – before Montreal – and in 1649 the Russians reached Kamchatka.

The Manchu Empire was the buffer that put a stop to this advance (Treaty of Nerchinsk, 1689). It must be emphasized that the integration of these immense spaces with the help of a few men preceded the expansion towards the Baltic and the Black Sea. Azov was occupied in 1701, Livonia in 1710. Hence one can understand the extreme sensitivity of the Russians to all border disputes with China and Japan.

Japan: colonization also begins in the sixteenth century

Japanese expansion and colonization occurred much earlier than is recorded by western historical tradition.

According to the Eurocentric view of history the arrival of Europeans in Japan – first the Portuguese, then the Spaniards, the Dutch, the English – marks the beginning of a phase in the broadening of the world. It dates this from 1543, the year of the first "navigational incidents". It then postulates the middle of the sixteenth century as the time of Francis Xavier's introduction of Christianity to Japan and of the emergence of problems in Japan related to the future and to the identity of the nation. Thereafter, still according to this view, Japan shuts the door on foreigners (*sakoku*) until, in the middle of the nineteenth century, it is subjected to a new invasion by Westerners; it modernizes itself, then displays the power of its conversion by emulating the West to the point of becoming, in its turn, an imperial power.

Stripped of this western view the history of Japan reveals that its first colonial venture dates back a very long way. It occurred at the same time as the attempts made by the West, in the sixteenth century, to gain a foothold in the Far East. While freeing itself from the Chinese yoke, Japan simultaneously established around itself a sort of colonial system. It did so first in the north where, from the Kamakura period (thirteenth century), the Shogun established official contacts with the Ainus of Yeso island (Hokkaido, since 1869). Organized into districts each having its chief officer, the Ainus had their own autonomous culture which they expressed in the *Yucar*, the epic poem of the nation. In the fourteenth and the fifteenth centuries the Japanese clans in the north of Hondo slowly extended their dominion over the isle of Yeso till Ieyasu, in 1604, from the capital, granted to the Matsumae family, a clan vassal to the Shogunate, the monopoly of the commerce to the north and recognized its right of control *both* over the Japanese merchants residing there and over the Ainus who lived in those regions (see A. Berque).

So it came about that the Ainus no longer had any control over their own way of life. They were not allowed to own rice fields. They were confined to their traditional activities. They paid tribute. Some of them were soon assimilated to vagrants, to pariahs. In 1669, in particular, they revolted. Their revolution was crushed.

At the same time, in the extreme south, the Japanese occupied the kingdom of the Ryu-Kyu islands. Already they were casting covetous eyes on Korea. Up to the beginning of the fifteenth century, both Korea and Japan were on a different footing in their relationship of dependence on China. Japan initiated the disengagement when in letters which it addressed to the King of Korea it adopted the Japanese, not the Chinese, system of dating. Subsequently, in the second half of the sixteenth century the new leaders of Japan withdrew from the tributary relationship with China and strove to place Korea under their domination. In 1592 the Minister Hideyoshi even despatched an expeditionary force to the Korean peninsula. His successor Ieyasu withdrew the force. But the reception given to the legate of the King of Korea in 1607 was viewed as an acknowledgement of vassalage.

Hence while the Portuguese were organizing a triangular traffic between Macao, Japan and Lisbon (see H. Ninomiya) which gave new vitality to Far Eastern trade, Japan for its part was embarking on a policy of territorial expansion and control of bases: Tshoushima, Ryu-Kyu. Three centuries later they still recall this past.

3

CONFLICTS FOR AN EMPIRE

Prefigurations

Even before the expression colonial empire existed, the city republics of the end of the Middle Ages did, in a real sense, possess one. It had strong points, it had the characteristics of modern capitalism, and all this well before the Great Discoveries. With regard to Genoa and Venice, Fernand Braudel has spoken of "European expansion" taking place as early as from the twelfth century. It was an enterprise realized by the new towns and cities. These aggressive little entities were oriented towards external trade and no longer lived in an exclusive relationship with the countryside around them.

Henceforth with economic life gaining the ascendancy over the agrarian, these clusters of city-states very quickly constituted two groups: the North and the South, Italy and the Netherlands, linked by trade routes which had their junction in Champagne. These two clusters complemented each other and competed with each other. But the North had the forests as its border and the South the treasures of Byzantium and the Arab world. Commercially stronger than the North as a result, it was the cities of the South, particularly Venice and Genoa, which at least for three centuries prevailed over this first micro world-economy with its boundaries marked by Lisbon, Fez, Damascus, Azov, in addition to Bruges and the Hanseatic League. After the elimination of Amalfi and Pisa, these two Italian cities owned trading outposts and possessions abroad, from the Barbary coast up to Caffa on the Black Sea. It was like a Portuguese empire before its time, but confined to the interior of the Mediterranean. During the time of the Crusades Venice came close to occupying the Byzantine Empire, but Genoa restored the Paleologue dynasty. Which of the two would prevail? Neither. For, divided amongst themselves, they came up against a wall: Islam, strongly entrenched in the Levant which, as early as 1282, the Vivaldis, from Genoa, had attempted to bypass by means of expeditions round Africa. Their enterprises failed because they were too large for such small states. But the idea lived on.

Portugal inherited it when the capture of Ceuta in 1415 set it on the routes of Africa. The country was spurred on by Henry the Navigator (1394–1460) and by the exploits of Bartholomeo Diaz who reached the Cape of the Storms in 1497. Besides trade was extensive between Genoa and Lisbon, Florence and Flanders. The transfer of sugar plantations, for example, just as certain nautical inventions belong to the credit of the Italians.

What provides Lisbon with an advantage is that, beside a recently developed middle class, it disposes of a landed nobility able to supply commanders for the fortified towns and the necessary cadres for the exploitation of the overseas concessions. Neither Genoa nor Venice disposed of a nobility to provide such service.

Hispano-Portuguese rivalry

From the onset of the first discoveries the rivalry between Portugal and Castile nearly degenerated into conflict. Portugal had reserved for herself the monopoly of trade with black Africa in the treaty of Alcaçovas signed with Spain in 1479. This monopoly was confirmed by the building, in 1481, of the Sao da Mina fort, the constituent elements of which had all been transported from Lisbon. But, after 1492, the success of the Castilians in America led to the restoration of another monopoly to the advantage of the Portuguese in the Atlantic, dating from 1456 when Calixtus III Borgia was Pope. *At that time the Papacy was the only state which possessed a "world-wide" authority.* Accordingly Alexander VI Borgia, the adopted nephew of Calixtus III, and of Spanish origin, defined, by means of the bull Inter Caetera, the zones of influence of each country and gave to Spain the lands lying 100 leagues to the west of the last of the Azores Islands, that is, "the mainland and islands discovered or to be discovered in the direction of India and any other direction". Forced by the demands of Portugal this line of demarcation was pushed further to the west by 170 leagues at the Treaty of Tordesillas (7 June 1494). Julius II confirmed the terms of this treaty in 1506.

As of that date, the Portuguese seemed to be the great winners in the struggle for the control of the trade routes, for they had reached India by going round the Cape of Good Hope and destroyed the domination of the Arab navigators in the Indian Ocean. Albuquerque's glory surpassed that of Christopher Columbus, as the spices and gold appeared to be more abundant in the East than in the West. In order to break up the Portuguese monopoly Charles, King of Castile (the future Charles V) signed a convention with Ferdinand Magellan which provided him with the means to reach India by a western route, that is, via Cape Horn and the Moluccas (1519).

But America had already offered up its treasures to Spain, and although the Portuguese had reached Brazil, the preeminence in the west of Spain, unified since 1492, was beyond question.

In America the rivalry between Spain and Portugal did not cease with the organization of their two empires, in the sixteenth and seventeenth centuries. Portugal managed to recover the territories of the Holy Sacrament in 1763. War raged in 1774 and, after the Treaties of St-Ildefonse (1777) and Pareto (1778) Portugal recovered St Catherine island, but lost Fernando Po, in Guinea, which Spain kept till the twentieth century. In the Americas Portugal again lost the territories of the Holy Sacrament, but she recovered the territories which the Papacy had appropriated from the states, the 7 *Redduciones* in Uruguay from which the Jesuits were soon driven out.

Proud of their past greatness, but diminished by Spain and later by the Netherlands, the Portuguese fell back on Brazil, Timor and Goa, in India, where their territory expanded, and later still on Africa.

The rivalry between Holland and Portugal

Hispano-Portuguese rivalry continued from 1580 to 1640, even though both countries had the same king. But Castile remained indifferent to the blows being dealt to the Portuguese dependencies. In alliance with an English squadron Abbas the Persian seized Ormuz from the Portuguese, while Oman the Arab deprived them of Muscat. Little remains of the great achievement of Albuquerque in the Gulf of Oman.

But it was the Dutch who posed the mortal threat to the Portuguese.

Actually their expansion lay within the ambit of the struggle in which the Dutch and the United Provinces were pitted against the Spain of Philip II. With Portugal losing its independence, Iberian unity presented a rare opportunity to attack Portuguese possessions. The Dutch Company only had trading outposts in Malacca and in Ceylon. But it established an empire in the Sunda Islands at the expense of the Portuguese. For the security of the route passing by the extreme southern tip of Africa, the Dutch seized the Cape from the Portuguese (1652). That was the starting point for Boer colonization in South Africa.

In the west the Company of the East Indies, founded in 1621, lets its buccaneers – Willekens, Piet Hein – plunder the coasts of Brazil, occupy Guyana and the region of Sergip and Maranhao. The heyday of Dutch Brazil coincides with the period of Maurice of Nassau who landed in Bahia in 1637 with a mission of town-planners and scholars. Endowed with a tolerant disposition he brought along a colony of Jews and Iberian Maranos who set up the sugar and tobacco trade. That was how the first synagogue in the Americas came to be opened in Curaçao.

Freed from the Spanish yoke in 1640, the Portuguese reacted by forcing the Dutch garrisons to leave. But the Dutch kept Curaçao and a portion of Guyana, around Surinam.

The Portuguese had not actually settled in the East Indies. They were based in Malacca, but could not hold on to Atjeh nor to the Island of Celebes. The year 1596 is a historical landmark. In that year the Dutch fleet of Cornelis and Houtman established in Celebes the East India Company (*Vereinigte Oost-Indische Kompagnie*) and gradually drove away the Portuguese. Their real difficulties had arisen from the Indonesian princes objecting to their presence and destroying the capitalist dynamics of the merchants of the Surabaya region.

Elimination left the Portuguese only with Timor. But the Dutch settled there too in 1613, close to Kupang, compelling the Portuguese to retreat to the north and east of the island. In 1642 a treaty demarcated the share of each party. Nevertheless for two centuries intermittent fighting opposed the one to the other. The definitive division came about in 1859 and was sealed in a treaty in 1904. Following the end of the Japanese occupation of the whole island independent Indonesia recovered the Dutch part of Timor, the western part remaining a "Portuguese province". Not for long.

England: a hue and cry against Holland

The rise to power and omnipresence of the United Provinces reached its highest point around 1625. With its hegemony lasting for the better part of half of a century, Amsterdam became the "Wall Street" of modern times. According to Immanuel Wallerstein the domination of the Dutch was characterized by a superiority in most aspects of economic life. Originally these were: fish salting and smoking on board ship, the production of lighting oil and soap from whale fat, a very intensive and technically modern agriculture due to the use of wind-mills, the ability to export horticultural products and to buy Swedish wheat cheaply. To these advantages must be added a renowned textile industry which benefited from the Flemish tradition and thenceforth had its centre in Leyden, the rival of East Anglia. Furthermore, on top of a flourishing Baltic commerce and the profitable textile trade with England, the Dutch engaged in intense ship-building activity, their shipyards then being the best in Europe, as well as in industries originating from the East, and from the East Indies in particular. In 1661 Amsterdam had 60 sugar refineries which worked for the export trade to France and England. The sugar and spice trade, maintained with the help of the largest fleet of that time, was carried out by the two giant companies which ensured the fortune of the country. These companies were the East India Company which had a determinedly pacifist outlook and was mainly preoccupied with commerce, and the West India Company which was more aggressive, more belligerent, and laid the foundations of New Amsterdam and the Dutch colonies of Brazil and Curaçao (1634).

The predicament in which the English, particularly, found themselves was that the Dutch were ruining them at home, for they could sell the products of the Baltic (wood for ship-building, wheat, linen) at prices lower than those of the English merchants themselves. Moreover the Dutch were omnipresent – in the Atlantic, in the Mediterranean, in the Indian Ocean, in the Baltic Sea – and could thus block the path to the enterprises initiated by the English merchants and navigators who were then also engaged in the full activity of expansion. They had to be driven off the scene.

This resolve began to take shape after the end of the Civil War in England when a semblance of national unity was restored with the aim of putting an end to the economic and maritime hegemony of the Dutch. Three Anglo-Dutch wars followed: in 1652–54, then in 1664–67, and again in 1672–74. France then took over from England, for the same reasons, from 1674 to 1678.

The hostilities were kicked off by Cromwell's promulgation of the Navigation Acts (1651) which stipulated that products entering England had to be transported by English ships or by ships belonging to the country of origin. This was a "provocation" to the Dutch who were maritime brokers and had cornered the market in transportation on account of their lower freightage. The tariffs – which Colbert promulgated a few years later – led, in France, to the same result.

The treaties which followed these wars resulted, at Breda, in the Dutch relinquishing New Amsterdam, which became New York. In return the Dutch got Surinam, but nevertheless this constituted a sharp check to Dutch power. It is true that Holland still held trading-posts at Mocha, Basra and on the Coromandel coast in India; it had twenty trading-posts or so in Bengal. The Dutch also maintained their presence in Bangkok and Malacca. But in the eighteenth century the dividends of the East India Company fell from 40 to 25 percent, and then lower. In the Atlantic the loss of North Brazil to Portugal was not compensated for by the preservation of Surinam.

The power of capital had been vanquished by the force of arms. In spite of its economic advantages, of its dynamics, Holland was constrained to surrender, as its fleets could not fight as well as did the English fleets. More correctly it may be said that the wealthy Dutch bourgeois ceased to ensure that their country was provided with the necessary services since the fleets were no longer as "profitable" as capital invested elsewhere or otherwise. Dutch decline was irreversible.

Weakened by England in the fourth war of 1780–84 Holland further lost Ceylon and the Cape as a result of the wars of the French Revolution and the Empire. Such losses were to the benefit of Great Britain, indeed to such an extent that, as early as the eighteenth century, it could be said that Holland had become a "rowboat hitched to one of the fleets of His Britannic Majesty".

Overseas England took over from the United Provinces, but in company with France. Conflicts lay at the heart of this change of guard. They started as soon as the Treaty of Utrecht was signed (1713). Moreover war was waged, not only on the high seas, but on the very territory of the colonies. It began in Canada but spread soon to India and later to Africa.

Designs on the Spanish colonies

Oriental commerce yielded a windfall. But the gold and the silver of America proved to be a temptation which the buccaneers and the rising powers – England and France – found it hard to resist. Drake had already set the example in the sixteenth century. Since the disaster of the Invincible Armada both Versailles and Westminster – as well as the shipowners and businessmen – were wondering how best to get their hands on the loot. Capturing it en route was only a temporary solution.

Louis XIV hoped to lay hands on the Spanish empire as a result of an association between the rising power of France and that of the Bourbons of Spain, Hapsburg Spain having been in decline since the reign of Charles II. As for the English, an illicit trade had sprung between Jamaica and the coasts of Mexico. In addition to this unlawful commerce they had managed to buy back the contracts of *asiento* which the King of Spain had conceded to the Portuguese. This leasing of the slave trade to the Iberian world yielded huge profits. As a result, by contraband and thanks to their extensive *asiento* contracts, the English hoped to penetrate the Spanish colonies in America rather than to conquer them. They were drawing considerable profits and running little risk of war.

The whole scheme was called into question when Charles II died and the Spanish succession was bequeathed to Louis XIV's grandson. Europe united against France (1701) and war began, in Italy, in Germany, in the Netherlands, on the seas, in the colonies. France was even invaded after the defeat of the Duke of Burgundy at Oudenarde and the fall of Lille (1708). The victory won by Villars at Denain improved Louis XIV's position. But already a compromise had been struck at Utrecht: Philip V, the grandson, would retain Spain, but he renounced his right to the throne of France (1713).

Independently of the power struggle between the Hapsburgs and the French monarchy – the emperor obtained Spain's possessions in Italy and the Low Countries – the real stakes in the war were the fate of the Spanish colonies in America. Under the terms of the Treaty of Utrecht they remained under the sovereignty of Philip V.

But England was expanding its sphere of influence in those regions.

In the first instance it obtained, on behalf of a private company, the monopoly of the *asiento* for thirty years, under a clause guaranteed by the two states. Then it got the right to send one ship which would be able to trade freely in America – and to indulge in illicit commerce. Soon the English improved upon and perfected these advantages by stationing the ship off Buenos Aires, while other ships shuttled to and from Bristol. The ship thus acted as a permanent base set up in the middle of the bay. As England had earlier, at Methuen, signed an agreement with Portugal, which would allow it to trade with Brazil, a route parallel to that of La Plata enabled it to traffic through the Paranagua, Asuncion, and Chaco. But the Jesuit missions stood in the way of the English. Meanwhile at the other end of the Spanish empire the English were settling in Honduras, using Jamaica as a base, whence they tried to control Panama by using the Mosquito coast as a springboard. Unlike the Spaniards the English had only one concern – commerce. They did not evangelize.

In this way the English, on one hand, assumed the right to indulge in contraband at all the entry points of the Spanish Empire while, on the other, Madrid dealt ruthlessly with them without declaring war. A crisis flared up when the merchants of Bristol and Liverpool started to protest against the way the Spaniards were settling the disputes provoked by their own abuses. They had dreamt of laying hands on a portion of the Spanish Empire during the negotiations at Utrecht and they deemed the concessions obtained to be insignificant. Robert Walpole was overwhelmed by this aggressive movement. War was declared in 1739, with Cardinal Fleury joining Spain.

The Anglo-Spanish war was distinguished by the renowned voyage of Admiral Anson, which has been glorified by Voltaire in his *Siècle de Louis XIV*. Under orders to land in Peru, with his fleet partly destroyed in a storm, he departed again, with his one remaining ship, in the direction of the Philippines in hot pursuit of the Manila galleon. He captured it, seized its cargo and returned to England in triumph. The peace concluded on the basis of the Treaty of Methuen allowed English products free entry to the Spanish peninsula.

What is new in the wars of the period of Walpole and of Newcastle is the intervention of public opinion aroused by the old anti-Spanish feelings, which evince a "jingoistic", vindictive and conquering mentality. Chauvinistic sentiments flared up against France too, because of her progress in Canada and in India, while it was actually the English colonists who, in North America, were pushing forward. Yet the capture of Cape Breton Island in 1745 was received with outbursts of jingoism quite in contrast to the numbness which prevailed in Spain and in France. "One of the most insuperable difficulties which I foresee in any negotiation with France", writes Lord Chesterfield, "is our new acquisition of Cape Breton which has become the possession closest to the heart of the nation and which is ten times more popular than Gibraltar ever was."

One encounters this anti-French and anti-Spanish bellicosity again in the Caribbean islands which lay at the cross-roads of the "triangular commerce".

Anglo-French rivalry

More than any other confrontation the Franco-British rivalry undoubtedly left a deep impression on the historical memory of the French nation. It was a conflict marked by painful experiences stretching over nearly two centuries, such as "the loss of India and of Canada", Fashoda, and so on. But this account might lead one to believe that from the very outset two well defined colonial policies collided with each other. Actually the Ancien Régime had a merely piecemeal approach to its colonial policy. It was only during the period of imperialism that in fact the two powers constantly confronted each other with a view to building an empire. A retrospective view of history later traced this antagonism back to the eighteenth century.

The period lasting from the seventeenth century to the fall of Napoleon witnessed the build-up of this rivalry in scattered conflicts, though, on the French side, there was no particular targeting of England. During the reign of Philip II it was the Spanish empire that was the object of envy to others. Then France joined in an alliance to prevent Spain from having her empire carved up by England. In India it was the Dutch possessions that were at first the object of rivals' designs. But the armed conflicts opposed the French and the English. When Holland began its dramatic decline around 1670, Louis XIV still considered England to be merely a weak ally of France. Obviously then, this underestimation of English power occurred very early.

Another feature of this rivalry needs to be pointed out. In Canada the conflict with England was characterized by papist, or in any case religious, overtones; it was a war of religion. On the other hand, in India, the goals were strictly commercial, before becoming territorial.

In the West Indies Franco-English rivalry came to an end, in the interest, let it be said, of their interests not being directly linked to those of their country of origin.

Another feature characterizes this historical rivalry. Immanuel Wallerstein has clearly shown that it arose at the very moment when the internal conflicts in each nation mattered less than conflicts with the foreigner. That is, the interest of the state took precedence over conflicts between the monarch and the feudal barons or the nobles, and over religious problems. This was a rivalry between nations. In the colonies the Companies which had been set up to exploit them gave way to their governments.

Thanks to its East India Company, Holland, in spite of its decline, still maintained a hold on the commerce of the Indian Ocean. But the Company had to contend with the British Chartered Companies. These often lent money to the state, and thus were well placed to receive help. Their development continued without interruption between 1720 and 1740, in spite of the financial corruption of the South Sea Company, of the upheavals that shook India after the death of Aurangzeb (1707) and the collapse of the Mughal empire. The rise of Maratha power threatened their trading-outposts in Bombay and in Calcutta: the Company was forced to enter into alliances with the Nawabs of the Deccan who had taken over from Aurangzeb. The French India Company was at that time more or less active in the same field: it founded Mahé in 1723 and Karikal in 1739. It operated under the control of the brother of the minister Philibert Orry, just as the British company depended on Robert Walpole. Soon, however, the agents of these Companies on the spot pursued a more active policy which went beyond the limits of commerce. It was the French who started it all.

The founder of Mahé, Lenoir, who had succeeded in saving the accounts of the Company at the time of Law's bankruptcy, had actually been an administrator and a consummate merchant. On the other hand, his successor, Dumas, behaved towards the Indians like a colonialist. He dealt with the nawabs, intervened in their conflicts. For instance, he had saved the son and the wife of Dost Ali Khan, when this prince was threatened by the Marathas. He thus initiated a purely political action which went beyond the mandate of the Company and asked for the ministers' help. His successor Dupleix followed in his footsteps. It was their policy which provoked the British into counter-attacking. From 1735 to 1741 Dumas' idea had been to organize the sepoys as a local militia officered by Frenchmen, to transform the trading-posts into fortresses all the while placing his troops at the disposal of the allied princes. He became very powerful and the title of Nawab was conferred upon him. Dupleix even went a step further. He believed that, instead of being satisfied with commerce and with the military occupation of one or more places, the Company should take the princes under its protection, the latter would in exchange concede to him either land to exploit or a share in the tax revenue. In short he was the *inventor of a concept of the protectorate* which was to be applied, a century later, in Egypt and in Morocco.

On the coast of the Sirkars (Yanaon, Masulipatam) and of Coromandel (Pondicherry, Karikal) Dupleix entered into an alliance with the Nawab of Carnatic. When, disturbed by this growing expansionism, the British besieged Pondicherry, the Nawab of Carnatic came to his rescue. A year later Mahé de La Bourdonnais – who had earlier transformed the Isle de France (now Mauritius) and Bourbon (now the Island of Reunion) into a large naval base on the route to India – sailed to besiege Madras and to capture it. But instead of handing it over to the Nawab of Carnatic, he gave it to the British in exchange of a ransom. Dupleix annulled the capitulation and had La Bourdonnais imprisoned in the Bastille. Dupleix was attacked by Admiral Boscawen; still he managed to have the siege of Pondicherry raised. But with the peace treaty of Aix-la-Chapelle he had to surrender Madras to the British.

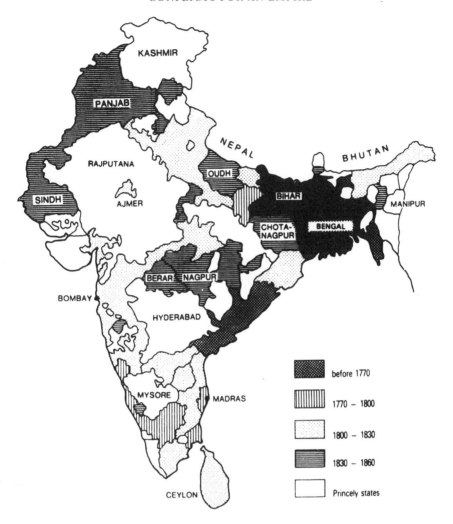

The British penetration of India (1750–1860)
Source: Hermann Kulke, *A History of India*, Routledge, 1994

However, by using the Indian princes as third parties, Dupleix once more intervened in the quarrels of succession in the Carnatic and in the Deccan, with the British emulating him. But Clive succeeded in triumphing over the successive condottieri of Dupleix. True, Dupleix still controlled vast territories, but his conquests were costly and, in Paris as well as in London, the Companies were looking for a compromise. The commissioner Godeheu came to the conclusion that Dupleix was guilty of imprudence: he was recalled (1754). The treaty which bears his name marks the end of the policy of conquest.

The war nevertheless was resumed, with the provocation coming from the Nawab of Bengal, Suraj ud-Daulah, who attacked Calcutta, forced it to capitulate and imprisoned 146 English people in the "black hole" where two-thirds of the prisoners died of asphyxiation (1756). With 900 Europeans and 1,900 Sepoys Clive retook Calcutta and Chandernagar and defeated Suraj ud-Daulah at the Battle of Plassey (1757). He then rolled back the army of the Great Moghul who had rushed to the rescue of the Nawab. Clive brought Bengal, Bihar and Orissa under the protectorate of the Company. That marks the beginning of the British establishing themselves in India.

Lally-Tollendal and Bussy tried to restore the French presence in India. But their attempt ended in failure and, at the Treaty of Paris, the French were left with only the five trading-posts: in a military sense it had actually lost them, but this seems to have been a diplomatic success on the part of Choiseul.

The defeat of the French arose from the fact that Dupleix, acting behind the back of his Company, had been constrained to ask only for limited help, to use "bluff" in order to emphasize his successes. Indeed these were real, since he had actually asserted a protectorate over the Carnatic and the Deccan had become a zone of French influence. Up to 1750 the British had let things sort themselves out, on the assumption that Dupleix would get himself embroiled in inter-Indian quarrels. But the march of Muzaffar and of Bussy on the capital of the Deccan induced the British governor Thomas Saunders to put an end to the prevailing situation. From then on Dupleix found him standing in his way, in the Deccan as well as in the Carnatic, which together constituted too large a prey for the French.

In his book on Dupleix Marc Vigié argues that he was the inventor of the colonial army and the promoter of a new policy. But Dupleix's blunder derived from his short-sightedness, coupled with his morbid anglophobia. This is how he records his perception of the situation: "In India England has led the Portuguese nation to slavery, the Dutch nation submits and will soon bear the yoke. England now wants to subjugate us too." To him the prudent realism of his superiors in Paris seemed like a sign of weakness, a lack of patriotism, a betrayal.

From this point of view too, Dupleix was a forerunner because it was as a result of his recall and of his failures that was born the myth of "the loss of India", which "the English have taken from us", though it was actually his actions which provoked their response especially as till then they did not really have any disposition to conquer. Approved by some, like Abbé Raynal, and criticized by others, like Voltaire, Dupleix was hailed as a hero when France tried to rebuild an Empire after 1870. His memory (like that of Montcalm) revived the hatred of the British. Between 1881 and 1931 fifteen books were published on Dupleix and on the French India Company.

In North America Franco-British rivalry set colonists against colonists. But the main difference between their respective situations consisted, in broad terms, in the fact that, on the French side, the mother country showed little interest in their fate, whereas London was very active in coming to the defence of the English-speaking people of America. What was the reason for this difference?

First, the exploitation of those regions had only a limited interest for French public opinion. "What is the worth of those few acres of snow?" asked Voltaire, while the minister Choiseul thought that a square league in the Netherlands was worth more than the whole of Canada. "The latitude in which this colony is situated", wrote Count Jean-Frédéric de Maurepas a little later, "cannot produce the same wealth as in the islands of America. The crops grown there are the same as those grown in the kingdom, with the exception of wine." De Maurepas was expressing the landholders' point of view. During the Seven Years' War when the Marquis de Montcalm appealed for help after the fall of Fort Frontenac, the Minister of the Navy, N. R. Berryer, responded by saying: "When the house is on fire, one does not worry about the stables."

The British had a different vision of North America. For them the colonists provided a supply of manpower and of customers who sent them cheap raw materials (especially wood) and furs, and to whom they sold manufactured goods. This "exclusive" system worked to the advantage of British entrepreneurs, but only on condition that the colonists of America did not themselves manufacture anything, "not so much as a nail", and that they purchased manufactured products in Great Britain.

The British government did not stop sending colonists overseas. Meanwhile the Bourbons of France had remained indifferent, ever since the religious aspect of the confrontation in Canada had become irrelevant. As a result, in 1740, while the British colonies could boast of almost one million inhabitants, the French colonists numbered only 80,000 at most, with a few thousand more in Louisiana.

In the eighteenth century religious persecutions were not the main cause of emigration. When, after the Revocation of the Edict of Nantes, the French Protestants wanted to leave for America, they were prohibited from doing so by the King. Still there is no evidence that they would have emigrated in large numbers. When people emigrated, they did so for economic reasons: the agricultural crisis in Ireland, the devastation of the Palatinate by wars. Emigration agencies looked after them: the agencies were British or Dutch, not French. That is why the migrants who flocked to America came from the Anglo-Saxon and Germanic countries, especially Scots-Irish, descendants of the Scots who had chosen Ulster as their homeland, and Swiss and Germans from the Rhine region.

These colonists moved deep into the interior of the country where they encountered the French settled on the Ohio whose lands barred the way to the west. This was the first cause of conflict. The second cause was that some of the French Canadians, particularly at the time of Governor Beauharnais, were prospecting all the routes which, from the Great Lakes or Hudson Bay, might have led to the Pacific. Certainly this "search for the Western sea" led men like La Varendrye to be the first to cross the prairies and reach the Rockies. But, though marked out and surveyed, this territory was not exploited. And the English Hudson Bay Company intended to seize it.

Finally, in Louisiana, where the India Company held sway, the conflicts between the British of Carolina-Georgia and the French deteriorated into an armed struggle with the use of the Indians as third parties. The British succeeded in having the Natchez and the Chicachas rise against the French. Following its inability to defend Louisiana the Company was compelled to cede it to the royal government in 1731.

Rather than the policy adopted by London it is this Anglo-Saxon penetration which lies at the source of the conflicts with the French. But Britain supported its colonists, public opinion spurred them on and unleashed its hatred of the French, while Versailles remained indifferent to the colonists. Following the Treaty of Aix-la-Chapelle (1748) the first offensive started from Halifax, in Nova Scotia, in the direction of Acadia, while the colonists of Massachusetts marched towards the St Lawrence river, reaching the ridge which demarcates the Laurentian and the Atlantic sides. At the same time other colonists, mostly Irish and German, spread towards Illinois, and founded Fort Pickawillany. The Virginians under George Washington clashed in a fight with the French who, led by Jumonville, capitulated at Fort Necessity, Jumonville having been killed under mysterious circumstances.

What galled the French most was the action taken by Governor Lawrence who, after the conquest of Acadia, proceeded with the dispersion of the Acadians. 7,000 (out of 10,000) of them were despatched to New England and the other British colonies in America.

When, during the Seven Years' War (1756–63), the hostilities resumed the British had a stronger fleet – 153 ships against approximately 60 – which immediately captured 300 other French ships, with the result that the French navy lost 6,000 sailors. The success in the sea war was such that, following Admiral Boscawen's victory over La Clue, at Lagos, the British contemplated the invasion of France and occupied Belle-Isle.

The French navy, incapable of defending the French coast, was powerless to go to the aid of the French Canadians who were already outnumbered. The military skills of the Marquis de Montcalm however stalled the successes of the Anglo-Americans. The latter first occupied Fort Duquesne and Fort Frontenac in order to cut Canada off from Louisiana, while in the east Boscawen's fleet occupied Louisburg, the fortress which symbolized the French presence in North America (1788). In a decisive battle fought by James Wolfe against Montcalm, both leaders died before Quebec fell to the British. Finally, in Montreal, the Governor, the Marquis de Vaudreuil, surrounded by English troops, was forced to capitulate (1760).

At the Treaty of Paris (1763) the government of Louis XV, obsessed with its continental preoccupations, abandoned the overseas territories. It lost Canada to Britain, retroceding Louisiana to its ally, Spain. Of all her immense possessions in America France retained, in preference to Canada, only a fraction of her possessions in the Caribbean. This is a choice to which we shall revert later.

During his lifetime the physiocrat Bourlamaque analysed the causes of the French defeat as follows: "bad distribution of powers between the Governor, the Intendant and the Commander of the troops, but also the denial of tolerance in favour of the Protestants, the absence of an immigration policy in favour of foreigners, the abuses of an expansion policy executed by the religious orders, the absence of an indigenous policy, and certainly the short-sightedness of the mother country".

With the hindsight of history 1763 marks the end of the French colonial empire, in its first phase. But the outlook of the contemporary players was different. First, France kept the West Indies, which then seemed to be of prime importance. Secondly, the French ministers hoped for a return to Canada. That is what Choiseul and Vergennes undertook to achieve.

Then began the War of Independence in the United States. The paradox is that, to take revenge on the British, Versailles entered into an alliance with those very colonists who had earlier been the main factor in the French defeat. One can accordingly understand why, in such conditions, the French in Canada chose to remain aloof and stay in the background.

Survivals and new grounds of rivalry

The rivalries which were spawned by the great discovery of the route to India did not end with the events in America in 1776, nor with the French Revolution, the Empire and the independence of the Spanish colonies down to 1821. But they lost part of their significance.

The collapse of the French colonial domain, with the loss of India, of Canada, of Haiti, is the most spectacular. But the collapse of the Spanish domain is no less impressive: Spain was left only with the Philippines, Cuba and a few small territories. Yet paradoxically enough it was Britain which seems to have been more seriously affected by the sequels of the Treaty of Paris (1763), the French Revolution and the Empire. She came out victorious from all the crises. Still she could not, after the independence of the United States of America, claim for herself one of the *raisons d'être* of her budding imperialism – the existence of British colonies all over the world – considering that the latter had only recently broken out in revolt. England needed to reexamine the policy of which she had become so enamoured, that is, of populating overseas territories with the British.

Moreover there was another threat facing colonies of a second type, particularly those, like the sugar islands, which had a high economic yield. Their profits had been substantial. For instance, on the French side, the colonies had never been so prosperous as after the loss of Canada and of India, between 1763 and 1789. However, after 1800, black revolts and the abolition of slavery and of the slave trade might have imperilled the future of these possessions. The question was raised and debated both in London and in Paris as to whether – even then – it would not be preferable to make these colonies independent and to trade profitably with them.

In this post-1815 context, when only India and the Indian Archipelago were bringing in increasing profits to the British and the Dutch, the old colonial rivalries did not have any immediate relevance. But they were kept alive in the memory. After all, when France reassumed its policy of conquest, it did so in places far removed from the areas of expansion of the old British rival: in Algeria, in Annam, in Senegal and soon in Tunisia. The British too took possession of distant lands: Australia, New Zealand. And the collision occurred in the Pacific.

A great turning-point: Egypt or Algeria

Freed from its legend, with all that signifies in terms of risks taken, of pitfalls avoided, of sheer irrationality, Bonaparte's expedition to Egypt represents the change from one type of expansion to another. The Consul appeared with his army in his capacity as a member of the Institute, accompanied by a group of scholars: 21 mathematicians, 3 astronomers, 17 engineers, 13 naturalists, 22 printers. Among them were such luminaries as Monge, Geoffroy Saint-Hilaire and Berthollet. Bonaparte wanted to show that he was landing with an army which represented *civilization*. It was a question neither of gold nor of Christ. Did not Bonaparte himself say "that he respects, more than do the Mamelukes, God, his prophet and the Alcoran", that is, the Quran.

The second feature is without doubt the entrenchment of this adventure in a longer perspective, which traditional historiography masks by dividing the narration of events in chronological sections: Ancien Régime, Revolution, Empire, Restoration. In fact, again at the Institute, Talleyrand had unearthed a project of Choiseul which claimed the transfer of Egypt to France. At that time Egypt was much in the news for, after Savary, Voltaire had described it in his *Voyage en Egypte et en Syrie*. The project envisaged the re-opening of the route to India, in order to join up with an ally Tipu Sahib, who had become Sultan of Mysore (1784) (see Y. Benot).

The novelty of the project lay in its association with an emerging idea, that of bringing down the Ottoman Empire, the impending collapse of which was foretold and for which Catherine II and Joseph II would like to have substituted a Greek Empire, apart from seizing a few portions of it in the process. Spain and France would have their share. Indeed France would receive Egypt and the Barbary coast. In 1802 Bonaparte planned an expedition against Algiers, "because its banditry is the shame of Europe and of modern times". In 1808, he thought of conquering Egypt again to prevent the British from keeping it. Thus was born the rivalry over this "sick man", the Ottoman Empire, which Napoleon could not touch, despite his early victories. But when, after defeating Napoleon's armies, the British wanted to settle in, Mehemet Ali forced them to leave and, with the French who remained on the scene, an alliance between France and Egypt was sealed.

Above all the Egyptian expedition and the Algiers plan mark a transition in the history of colonization. The promoters affirmed that they were inseparable from the struggle against the slave trade and against slavery. They thus initiated the argument that justified the conquerors of Africa in the nineteenth century.

A digression: the passing greatness of Egyptian imperialism (1820–85)

At the very time when France and Britain were setting their sights on it, Egypt had already begun to free itself from the Ottoman yoke and was discovering the ancient routes of Arab imperialism and colonization that led to the south, in the direction of the Sudan. Up to that date the Ottoman Empire's main source of white slaves had been shrinking, as a result of the Russian advance into the Causasus. Deprived of their Circassian and Georgian slaves, the Muslim states were forced to look for other sources of slaves. Hence arose a new upsurge of the slave trade along the Nile valley. This provided one of the first pretexts for Egyptian expansion in the direction of Ethiopia, whose male and especially female slaves were better appreciated than the *zanjs* (the blacks).

In order to utilize them in the Hedjaz, the Viceroy of Egypt, Mehemet Ali, nevertheless relied on recruiting blacks for his army, for the other soldiers of the Nizam al-Jadid (the name given to his army trained in the European style) found the heat of Arabia unbearable. Egypt wanted to retake the Holy Places from the Wahabis. And, master of Cairo, of the Sudan, of the Holy Places, Mehemet Ali would be able to rebuild the great Arab empire.

In the name of the viceroy the conquest of Sudan had begun at the time of Ottoman domination. Several decades elapsed before the conquest reached Darfur, near the source of the Nile. But the greater part of the country was conquered between 1820 and 1826. In 1824 the Egyptians founded Khartoum, set up a taxation system which was to provoke many a revolt, and imposed Ottoman Turkish as the administrative language. In harmony with the tradition obtaining in the Ottoman Empire, multi-ethnicity in the leadership was evident even in the colonization: of the 24 governors from 1821 to 1885 – the Ottoman followed by the strictly speaking Egyptian period – eight were Circassians (Tcherkessians), two Kurds, five Turks, two Greeks, one Albanian, one British (the future Gordon Pasha) and only one Egyptian. The land constituted the basis of the taxation: the unit was the number of large water wheels (*sagiya*) which had to pay from 15 to 132 piastres each year in proportion to the wealth produced. Non-irrigated lands had to pay a much lower tax. It was likewise with the date palms. As the black soldiers used to die of disease outside Sudan, they were employed to colonize their own lands. Nevertheless they soon constituted a militarily trained caste of mercenaries. They were called Nubi and, short of having a black army, the Khedive had at his disposal, in Sudan, efficient army corps which later acted as mercenaries for the Germans in Tanganyika and for the Belgians in the Congo. Idi Amin Dada is one of their descendants.

The expansion of the Egyptians resulted in the location of the sources of the White Nile. It proceeded easily downstream from Khartoum, considering the weakness of the black tribes. Elephants roamed in large numbers. Tourists and adventurers were drawn to the area and the "journey through the Sudan" became a sort of literary genre in the 1860s.

It is this European penetration that Abbas and Mohammed Saïd, the successors of Mehmet Ali, tried to oppose. Having become Khedive by hereditary right in 1867 Ismaïl strove to modernize the country. Like the other monarchs of that period he was fascinated by railways and steam-boats. He soon launched into the construction of the Suez canal, De Lesseps' masterwork.

Ismaïl presented the Suez Canal, the great event of the century, as an expression of the greatness of Egypt. He wanted to show his country as being from then on one of the "great modern powers". Princes, writers – Ibsen, Fromentin, Zola and others – and musicians attended its inauguration. In 1869 Empress Eugénie led the first procession of ships through the Canal. In Cairo, the Opera was inaugurated in 1871 with a representation of *Aïda* which Verdi wrote for the occasion. Egypt was yielding to the "temptation of the West".

Keenly aware of the imperialist designs of Europe, Ismaïl called upon American engineers and military advisers. He wanted to outstrip the French and the British who had their eyes set on Upper Sudan. At the Universal Exhibition of 1878 he announced that his country would present a map in which the African empire of Egypt extended up to the Lake Chad, with a project for opening a route to the Atlantic. Actually only the expeditions to the coast of Somalia produced any result, which was insignificant considering that Ethiopian troops defeated the Egyptians in 1875–76.

The Khedive had entrusted Gordon Pasha with the task of ending the slave trade. The governor of Khartoum transformed this activity into a real crusade. But the slave trade had been the lifeline of the country for nearly a thousand years and, without slaves, the caravans were ruined in their turn. However, expenditures necessitated by the modernization of Egypt culminated in a debt which soon proved to be fatal: the country slid under the sway of its creditors who took over entire sectors of the economy. The Khedive abdicated in 1879. Soon afterwards Arabi Pasha rose against the European ascendancy over Egypt. In 1882 the British occupied the country.

Having already been subject to Egyptian colonization and Ottoman administration, the Sudan became in its turn a British possession. These were the circumstances in which Gordon Pasha, at the head of a small force, returned to Khartoum to defend the city against the attacks of a Mahdi, Mohammed Ahmed. He was killed and Britain was convulsed by his death (1885).

Algeria-Tunisia: from one type of expansion to another

The conquest of Algeria was an answer to the political and commercial aims of, in particular, the Marseilles establishment. The colonization of the country belongs to an old, as it were pre-imperialist, type of expansion. However the nature of French domination changed to the extent that Algeria soon became the preserve of private capital, for the profits of which the state stood surety. That is why one can call into question the widespread opinion that colonies and the expansion entailed a huge budgetary loss, because it takes into account only one aspect of the problem. If the cost of the colonies to the state was high, they nevertheless yielded large profits to the private interests of the mother country.

There is one more point which is left unrecorded: the expenses incurred by the State contributed to the enrichment of the citizens turned colonists who, in the mother country, would not have enjoyed the same advantages and would not have increased their wealth in the same manner. Indeed it would be interesting to calculate how far the standard of living of the French citizens of Algeria, including the civil servants, had progressed a century after the total conquest of the country, and then to compare it with that of metropolitan citizens.

Besides to maintain Algeria in a pre-industrial state assured capital invested in the industries of metropolitan France of a safe outlet, given the protectionism reigning in those "departments". If the foreigner was kept out of the game in the Algerian enterprise, such was not the case in Tunisia where the European powers competed with one another to establish their influence through their respective consuls: Italy with Maccio, France with Roustan, Great Britain with Wood.

The method used consisted in obtaining concessions for the public works of the country, and allowing the Bey to borrow money which he would some day be unable to repay. This method was abundantly applied in Tunisia and in Egypt. In Tunisia Franco-Italian competition became quite sharp. It was evident when the Rabattino Company bought the concession for the Tunis-La Goulette railway from an English company, eliminating the French Bone-Guelma railways. Already these three countries had members sitting on the financial Commission of Debt. The three members exercised an authentic protectorate over the Regency with the Frenchman Victor Villet, as Vice-President, assuring the preeminence of France. In fine, having succeeded in having one of their clients, Kheredine, appointed as Prime Minister, French interests were able to acquire the 90,000 hectares of the *Enfida* domain. Thus was formed a financial consortium in which both those who speculated in land holdings and those who speculated on the Tunisian stock market took part. The members of this consortium, who constituted a nucleus of the colonial Party "often met at Gambetta's" and could not be unaware of what went on in political circles nor fail to collaborate with them. Jean Ganiage has brought out the connection linking these two groups.

A telling phrase of Lord Salisbury's had had an effect. "Carthage cannot be left in the hands of the Barbarians", he had said to Waddington at the very moment when Britain was about to seize Cyprus (1878). Disraeli had confirmed it and the difficulties which Wood outlined in Tunis could thus be overcome. Italy protested as soon as she sensed what the designs of the French were. She increased the shipment of colonists who soon numbered 10,000 as against 1,000 Frenchmen. She appealed to Bismarck and Gladstone, the successor to Lord Salisbury. The latter were not unhappy over the emergence of Franco-Italian rivalry. But Bismarck thought that, after the loss of Alsace and Lorraine, it would be inappropriate if France were to find Germany blocking her path in every circumstance. He told the French ambassador: "The pear is ripe, it is up to you to pluck it."

Since in theory it held sovereign sway, the Sublime Porte had never conceded, some decades earlier, that the loss of Algeria was irreversible. Since then, using Tunisia as a springboard, frequent incursions had been made into Algeria against the French colonists who were spreading themselves far and wide. From 1871 to 1881 no less than 2,379 such incursions took place. The 2,380th one was the last straw: it gave the French army the pretext to bring the "Khroumir danger" to an end. Everybody was surprised by the ease with which the operation succeeded. The Germans made a move to turn the Turks away from an intervention launched from Tripoli. Italy protested. The uprisings in the south of the country made a second expedition necessary. But the Treaty of Bardo signed by the Bey was, thanks to Jules Ferry, approved by the French Chamber, in spite of the opposition of Clemenceau.

The treaty was followed in 1883 by the Marsa convention which established the French protectorate over Tunisia, where the (French) Governor-General was to be the Minister of Foreign Affairs. This was carried out according to a new formula since it was a concession to the rival powers as well as to the Bey. Accordingly the protectorate reported, in the mother country, not to the Ministry of the Navy, but to the Quai d'Orsay. The fiction of Tunisia as a foreign and "sovereign" state was enhanced.

In the case of Tunisia the rivalries between the powers had not broken out into the open, because the French expansion took place in zones lying far beyond the designs of the English or Germans. Only Italy stood in the way. Great Britain chose to turn a blind eye. At the same time, France withdrew from Egypt, following the threat of a sharp outbreak of rivalry, especially as in that country Arab nationalism was in full swing.

The case of Morocco follows the same pattern as in the Tunisian situation, but with two differences. At first France was encouraged by Germany. But the situation changed when the Kaiser adopted a different posture as, between the 1880s and the turn of the century, his ambitions became all the more pressing as the division of Africa had left him dissatisfied. He tested the strength of the Entente Cordiale by threatening France. So, bringing Morocco under a protectorate took about thirty years. Another difference is that in France the economic and financial interests were able "in the last analysis to impose their will on the State, while in Tunisia they did not yet have the means to do so" (see J. Thobie).

Up to the end of 1906 the financial groups, especially Schneider and the Banque de Paris et des Pays-Bas, carried on as they had done in Tunisia: they lent money to the Sultan, assumed control of the finances of the country, opened markets for themselves, while the diplomats cleared the ground to make room for French intervention. Delcassé followed the financial situation closely. Thinking that the assets of Schneider were insufficient to satisfy the potential demands of the Sultan, he chose instead to bet on the Banque de Paris et des Pays-Bas. Financial capital was thus calling the tune. Accordingly the interests of the French banks seemed to coincide with the policies of the government. The banks imposed drastic conditions on the Sultan and some even believed that a military occupation would be the best guarantee of the approved loans. The *Comité de l'Afrique française* even subsidized General Lyautey, from Oran, to buy the collaboration of the chiefs of the oases on the other side of the frontier: Colomb-Béchar, Figuig, Berguent. "I move forward like a drill", observed Lyautey who, in Algeria, was supported by Governor Jonnart.

In 1844, in Algeria, we may recall that the intervention of the Sultan had

71

helped Abd el-Kader in his defence against France and that, despite a military defeat, it had circumscribed the expansion of the territory of Algeria to the west. But there the frontiers were not properly demarcated. What had been defined at the Treaty of Lalla Marnia was not a territorial line of division, but rather the obedience of the tribes – to Morocco, or to Algeria. Hence arose all the quarrels. These, after 1960, have survived the independence of the two countries.

However, the belief then was that in those regions rich phosphate mines lay under the ground.

Since 1880 France had had, at the Madrid conference, to accept the internationalization of the exploitation of Morocco, with the participation of Spain, Great Britain, Germany. Delcassé dissuaded England by allowing it a free hand in Egypt. Spain was let free to occupy the Rio del Oro. Only Germany was left out.

The conflict with Germany flared up before 1906, the year of the conference of Algesiras. It became worse in 1911 when Wilhelm II stationed a gunboat in front of the city of Agadir. For half a century the visit of Wilhelm to Tangiers won Germany the sympathy of the Arabs: the Kaiser represented the power without colonies which stood against the lust of the French and English imperialists.

Aggravation of the colonial rivalries during the imperialist period

Towards the end of the nineteenth century, mutual interference between, on the one hand, the financial and industrial groups which were in the process of development and, on the other hand, each state, sharpened the rivalries among the industrial nations desirous of investing their capital or selling their products. Colonization became one of the forms of this expansion. But it soon presented itself as the safest one because it meant the acquisition of territory. Yet it was not deemed to be the most advantageous in all the cases. For instance, in France between 1870 and 1914, the priority of economic and financial expansion asserted itself beyond the ambit of the colonial Empire, mainly in the Ottoman Empire prior to 1882, and, especially, in Russia after 1891. Such investment of capital did not exclude, in the long term, or if the opportunity arose, the idea of semi-colonial domination. This idea finds expression in the Egyptian crisis of 1881–82, the crisis of Tunisian finances in 1882, the division of the Ottoman Empire in 1918, and the plan for the division of Russia into "zones of influence" during the Russian civil war and foreign intervention (1918–20).

If there is not an absolute correlation between the political establishment of France overseas and the curve of French commerce, there exists at least an inverse correlation between the extent of the exports with the Empire and the fall in total exports. Hence just as, for France, expansion to the colonies became a compensation for its post-1871 failures, it served concurrently as an assurance of an economic nature and again acted as a compensation.

The division of black Africa

The Berlin Conference was organized by Bismarck with a view to settling the conflicts which arose out of the Congo becoming a bone of contention between King Leopold, in his capacity as a private citizen, Stanley, his agent, and Brazza in the name of France. Bismarck wanted to assert his role as arbiter of international conflicts. But he also wanted to have a share in the spoils.

France had obtained a preemptive or preference right on the Congo in case the *Association* of Leopold should surrender it. But Great Britain and Portugal protested against this extension of French claims, illustrated by the signing of the Treaty of Makoko which had been approved with great pomp by the Chamber of Deputies, thus establishing a precedent. Portugal invoked her "historical" rights. On the one hand, with their national pride bruised by the loss of Brazil, certain Portuguese circles deemed it necessary to rebuild an Empire which had been shrinking ever since. On the other hand, an economic recovery in Sao Tomé and in Angola, which was accompanied by a severe depression in Portugal, from 1873 to 1896, as in the whole of Europe, constituted a call for action which breathed new life into a sort of micro-imperialism. That was the start of a new rush for Africa. It was actually strongly in evidence at the Berlin Conference. It made it possible for Portugal to get a share of the spoils, largely as a result of the positions it had established in earlier times, but quite out of proportion with the strength of the country. Actually the British and the Germans preferred to see Portugal extend its possessions to the interior of the continent rather than allow France to expand indefinitely. That is what occurred in Angola and in Mozambique.

Fourteen countries took part in the Berlin conference (1884–85) which, in essence, established a sort of "gentlemen's agreement". Each of the European powers undertook not to proceed any longer with acquisitions of "savage" territory without informing the others to enable them to present their claims. The African populations or kings, considered as *res nullius* were neither consulted about, nor informed of, these decisions.

The net beneficiary was Leopold, whose title of sovereign owner of the Congo was recognized by all. He deemed this approval gave him the authority to integrate the Katanga. By virtue of its right of preference France did not intervene, hoping that later it would collect the prize, which actually was bequeathed to the Belgian State in 1908.

Subsequent to this conference, the main European powers which had designs on territories made a rush for them, even if it entailed concluding

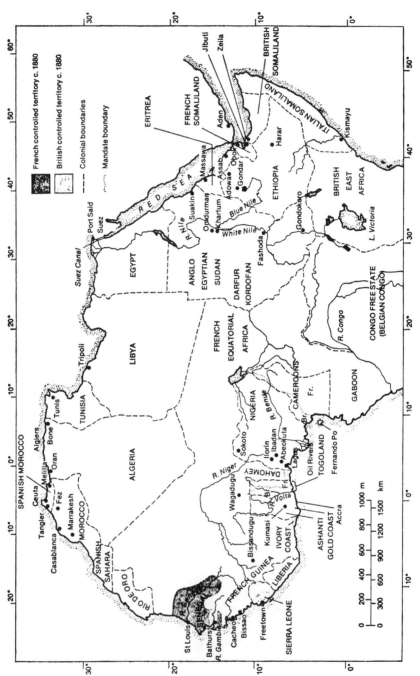

Northern Africa during the era of European expansion
Source: J. D. Fage, *A History of Africa*, Routledge, 1995

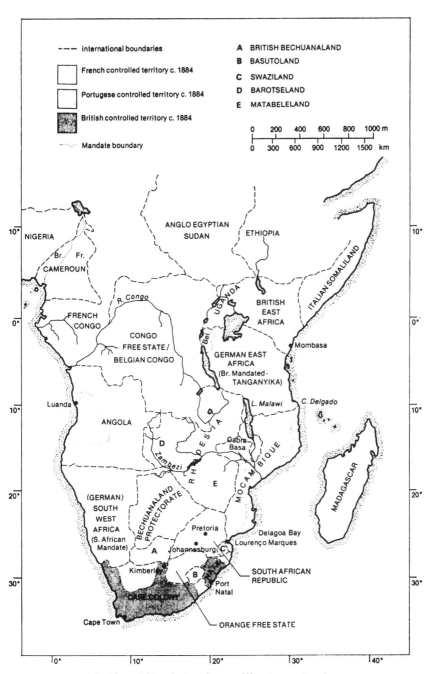

Legend:

- - - - international boundaries

French controlled territory c. 1884

Portugese controlled territory c. 1884

British controlled territory c. 1884

.... Mandate boundary

A   BRITISH BECHUANALAND
B   BASUTOLAND
C   SWAZILAND
D   BAROTSELAND
E   MATABELELAND

Scale:
0   200   400   600   800   1000 m
0   300   600   900   1200 1500 km

Map labels:

NIGERIA
Br. Fr.
CAMEROUN
FRENCH CONGO
R. Congo
CONGO FREE STATE / BELGIAN CONGO
ANGOLA
Luanda
ANGLO EGYPTIAN SUDAN
ETHIOPIA
UGANDA
Bel.
BRITISH EAST AFRICA
GERMAN EAST AFRICA (Br. Mandated - TANGANYIKA)
Mombasa
ITALIAN SOMALILAND
L. Malawi
C. Delgado
RHODESIA
Cabra Basa
MOCAMBIQUE
MADAGASCAR
Zambezi
D
E
(GERMAN) SOUTH WEST AFRICA (S. African Mandate)
BECHUANALAND PROTECTORATE
A
B
C
Pretoria
Johannesburg
Kimberley
Delagoa Bay
Lourenço Marques
SOUTH AFRICAN REPUBLIC
CAPE COLONY
Port Natal
Cape Town
ORANGE FREE STATE

Southern Africa during the era of European expansion
Source: J. D. Fage, *A History of Africa*, Routledge, 1995

– among Europeans – agreements demarcating the frontiers. These borders have survived till after the independence, a century later, of the African states. Great Britain signed about 30 such agreements with Portugal, 25 with Germany, 149 with France. As for "treaties" with the Africans, France concluded 118 of them from 1819 to 1880, and 126 more up to 1914. Stanley concluded 257 agreements.

Germany had already demarcated its zone of influence. South-west Africa where Luderitz, a merchant of Bremen, had landed in 1882, and to which a German fleet brought missionaries; the Kamerun (as it was then spelled) and Togo, where in 1884 Nachtingal had been active as an explorer; and finally East Africa, occupied thanks to Carl Peters, who had set out from Zanzibar with only a handful of men. Further to the West the Germans of the *Deutsche Ostafrikanische Gesellschaft* met the English of the *Imperial British East Africa*: the division took place between Tanganyika and Nyassaland, with the English settling alone in Uganda and annexing Zanzibar (1889–90).

Starting from Senegal the French rushed towards Lake Chad and the Niger river. Borgnis-Desbordes founded Bamako in 1882. As the British established themselves on the lower Niger the French moved to Lake Chad, at the centre of the African continent. And it was around this lake that France intended to knit all its possessions together: North Africa, Senegal and Niger, Gabon and Congo being united with the remaining French possessions.

The Berlin conference did not, as has been reported, actually lead to the carving-up of black Africa, not even to the recognition of the zones of influence in the hinterland. It only set forth the "rules of the game" which made possible this orgy of operations and annexations which people referred to as a "scramble", with each European power rushing to raise its flag on the largest number of territories possible. Nevertheless at Berlin the European powers did effectively take possession of Africa.

For, if at the Berlin conference the "division" was a myth, in Africa, on the other hand, the dreams of conquest became a reality.

Ruler of the waves, Britain wished above all to exert control over the coasts, from Freetown in Gambia to beyond Zanzibar going round the Cape. Subsequently, buoyed up by the action of Cecil Rhodes in South Africa and her recent occupation of Egypt, Britain dreamt of joining the Cape with Cairo via the Great Lakes.

Between Senegal and Niger France wanted to link the Sahara, North Africa and West Africa, around Lake Chad. Moreover it proposed to reach Djibouti, via the Upper Nile, through the Gabon which it hoped to enlarge by joining it to Leopold's Congo. It is at the intersection of this route with the English project of linking the Cape with Egypt that the Fashoda incident between Lord Kitchener and Captain Marchand took place (1898).

For its part Germany wanted to create an Empire of *Mittel Afrika* which would start from "Kamerun" and reach Tanganyika. Leopold's Congo constituted an obstacle between these two territories. Portugal dreamt of Angola and Mozambique but she encountered the opposition of the Boer republics and the English in their drive to the north.

Several treaties settled these conflicts, independently of the populations concerned who responded in their own specific ways to these encroachments.

The first of these treaties was concluded between Germany and Great Britain in 1886 to deal with the conflict occurring in the zone of Kilimanjaro and the sovereignty of Zanzibar. While the King Abushiri rose in Tanganyika against the Germans of Emin Pasha, actually Edward Schnitzer, the British and the Germans were divided on the question of sending help to the latter. In 1890 Germany signed a new treaty with England which granted it responsibility over the territories of the *Deutsche Ostafrikanische Gesellschaft*. At that time, the entire region that gave access to Uganda was under the control of the dervishes and it was demarcated in such a way that the agreements signed by Carl Peters did not pose a threat to the scheme of the British who, by way of the Sudan, intended to reach Kenya.

According to Henri Brunschwig this treaty of 1890 is quite typical of the agreements signed during this phase of colonial imperialism. Article I gave Britain the Mfumbiro Mountains (Rwanda), attested by Stanley. It was later discovered that these mountains did not exist. Likewise the Rio del Rey, which was to be the border between Nigeria and the Kamerun, was only an indentation of the coast. The spheres of influence were vaguely defined. In exchange for what it was giving up in Uganda and in Zanzibar, Germany got the small island of Heligoland in the North Sea, that is, it surrendered "three kingdoms in exchange for a bath tub" (Carl Peters). It must be conceded that in the eyes of Bismarck what mattered most was Europe. And in 1890 he wanted to conciliate Great Britain. Moreover, in evaluating his work, his successor Caprivi said: "the kingdoms had to be conquered and the bath tub had only to come into the bathroom". But the German nationalists were furious.

The first Franco-English agreement of 1890 on Chad bore the same hallmarks: absence of accuracy in border demarcations, indifference to the native authorities. "The two governments recognize that, in the future, it would be necessary to replace the ideal lines which have demarcated the frontier by a line which conforms to the natural lie of the land, and is marked by correctly identified points."

At the turn of the century Anglo-German rivalry was one of the aspects of the confrontation for the domination of the world. It was this rivalry which contributed to the solution of a Franco-British crisis, which arose out of the Marchand mission in the direction of Bahr el-Ghazal and the

Upper Nile. The operation had been conceived by Léonce Lagarde, the French Resident in Djibouti, with the connivance of Menelik, the Emperor of Ethiopia, who had, at the battle of Adoua (1896), just defeated the Italians who had come to occupy Abyssinia. Captain Marchand would set out from the Congo and would be met by Bonchamp, the explorer, who would move from Djibouti, in the east. But while Marchand did indeed reach Fashoda in 1898, Bonchamp, having arrived not far from there a little earlier, was exhausted and consequently forced to turn back. Meanwhile, alarmed by the commotion raised by the "from Sudan to Djibouti" project, the English announced their opposition to it. With 25,000 men Kitchener, after triumphing over the Mahdists of the Upper Nile, took Fashoda with the help of 3,200 men, "in the name of Egypt". Public opinion in Britain, as in France, was inflamed. Wilhem II found all this "interesting". Delcassé understood that "in the face of soldiers, he only had reasons". But an agreement was concluded as the British did not, for their part, wish to have any confrontation: on the contrary, it was necessary to oppose a common front to Germany. Marchand was ordered to retreat and France had to endure the humiliation. In fact, according to the 1904 agreement, it lost Bahr el-Ghazal, but in exchange got the Oubangui-Chari and the Sahara which Commandant Laperrine d'Hautpoul was to "pacify".

Africa had been divided. It remained to be conquered.

The new conquerors

Far from being sword-wielding sots, most of the new conquerors claimed to be the bearers of a grand design. However much they put entire populations to the sword – as Gallieni did at the beginning of his career – or burned them alive – as Bugeaud did in Algeria – these actions none the less stood in their eyes for the realization of a colonial scheme, that is, the civilizing mission which took over from the evangelization dear to the conquerors of the sixteenth century.

They saw themselves as the solitary heroes of a master work which distinguished them from the idle life they would have led in the mother country. One can better appreciate the nature of their ambition by observing that it did not answer to interested or inferior motives. Most of them come from well-to-do backgrounds: Faidherbe, the indigent officer, and Pavie, the postal worker, are exceptions. The others were men of noble stock; they were men of culture. Bugeaud, Brazza, Laperrine, Selkirk, Serpa Pinto belonged to titled families. Gallieni, Carl Peters, Lyautey, Wakefield, Milner were respectively sons of an officer, a pastor, an engineer, a lawyer, and a physician. They were not spurred on by need.

They constituted a sort of intelligentsia, like the Russian revolutionaries. Moreover they had all written or done research on the social sciences. Pavie was an ethnologist, Bugeaud a polemicist, George Grey a book-lover; Cecil Rhodes set out on his campaigns with Aristotle and Marcus Aurelius in his baggage; Saint Arnaud read *The Imitation of Christ*, Lyautey read as much as did Lenin, the avid reader of booklets and texts, but he read Baudelaire, Barrès and Bourget rather than military treatises. His motto was a verse by Shelley: "In action lies the joy of living".

In his *Voyage au Congo*, André Gide expresses astonishment over the contemptuous harshness with which the colonists spoke to the colonized inhabitants. Such harshness can be explained in terms of colour solidarity and of the lofty notion the colonists had of themselves, a view exclusive of any relationship with the other that could be construed as being egalitarian.

The difficulty lies in the fact that they planted their flag precisely in the name of human rights, of equality, of the *Habeas Corpus* and of liberty, without necessarily realizing that they were violating the very principles of their actions. However these considerations did not have a hold over all of them.

Bugeaud provides the best example. During his entire life he gave vent to his country gentleman's hatred for all social innovations and for all forms of freedom of speech. As an active monarchist he raved against the education of the people and made his views known to Thiers: "The nation can live only by means of hard toil which leaves the labourer in the fields or the mill-worker neither the time nor the strength for studies." Further he writes: "Send the ideologues to me in Africa, where I am, for them to get killed. In this way the country will be well served." According to him society stood on four pillars: work, family, fatherland, religion. Anyone who thought otherwise had to be eliminated.

In Algeria he defeated Abd el-Kader at the battle of Tafna. But, sure of himself, he did not check the text written in Arabic which accompanied the end of the hostilities. This text recognized the domination of the Emir over the whole of Algeria. The latter very graciously gave the general, who after all was opposed to the occupation of the entire country, the 100,000 boudjous (180,000 francs) which the latter requested as a bakhshish: for the by-roads of Dordogne and for his officers. The scandal helped to render him all the more popular among his men. He looked after their interests and the soldier's welfare was his first preoccupation. In exchange for an iron discipline he allowed them to plunder, rape, and have fun. In the battle he never lost sight of them. Hence arose the famous refrain: "The cap, have you seen the cap? Have you seen the cap of Father Bugeaud?" "Never has an army chief, by his kindness and his moral authority, been able to get from his soldiers as much as General Bugeaud did. He could have led them to the end of the world, he could have had them throw themselves into the fire" (C.-R. Julien).

From a military point of view he relied on strong fortresses and on the use of forays to bring the enemy to sue for *aman*, the forgiveness of submission. "In Europe we do not make war only on armies, but on interests . . . we lay hands on the commerce of the customs and these interests are forced to capitulate . . . In Africa we have to lay hands on only one interest, the agricultural interest . . . Here it is more difficult to seize than elsewhere, for there are no villages, no farms. I have thought about this for a long time, on waking up and before going to sleep. Well, I have found no other way to subdue the country than by laying hands on this interest."

So Bugeaud put the entire country to fire and sword. For instance, he had everything from Miliana to Cherchell burnt. "We are not fighting, we are setting the country on fire", wrote Saint Arnaud. "We are burning all the douars, all the villages, all the huts . . . How many women and children have died of cold and deprivation while taking refuge in the snows of the Atlas mountains . . . There is nothing but plunder and loot. Houses are destroyed . . . the still smouldering fires guide me along the march of the column . . . " Bugeaud used his authority to shield General Pélissier who killed a thousand Arabs by smoking them out in the caves of Dahra in 1845.

Bugeaud finally vanquished Abd el-Kader. He triumphed over the son of the Sultan of Morocco who had come to the latter's rescue (battle of Isly, 1844). Bugeaud wanted to hear nothing of the instructions received from the authorities in Paris who were alarmed by the reports of these ravages.

In fact Bugeaud is the originator of this tradition: that is, that a general serving overseas must act as he wishes, without paying any heed to his government. Nevertheless the French government made him Duke of Isly "for having given Algeria to France".

Faidherbe was different from Bugeaud. Though he was an army man, he did not want to be a warrior. He had been sent to Senegal at the request of the merchants of St Louis. Since that land had been retaken from the British in 1818, the merchants looked forward to the perpetuation of the metropolitan presence. Above all they wanted this presence to take root with the appointment of a governor for a long tenure of eighteen months, in order to enable the colony to play a role in a wider African context.

Faidherbe was the first governor. A graduate of the École Polytechnique, a poor officer, and a friend of Schoelcher, the liberator of the blacks, he remained a republican under the monarchy as well as under the Empire. Above all he felt himself to be endued with the mission to institutionalize freedom, in short, to transform the Senegalese into coloured Frenchmen, as the people of Martinique already were.

Unfortuntely two obstacles stood in his way. In the first instance, after he had ensured the safety of the merchants by means of the construction of a large number of small forts – a strategy which enabled him to defeat the Moors of Mohammed el-Habid – he had to confront the rival expansionism of El Haj Omar. Hailing from a large Toucouleur family Omar had been initiated into the Tidjanija fraternity. From Mecca and the Sudan he took a passion for holy war and breathed it into the struggle against the infidels. El Haj Omar personified Muslim Africa in its fight against both pagans and Christians. In the end he was defeated and killed (1864). But he lived on as a model for other African chiefs. Samory and Rabah took over from him.

The colonists themselves proved to be the second obstacle: they wanted to transform Senegal into a plantation colony. They thought their time had come for, with the termination of the slave trade, the West Indies, in their view, would of necessity be ruined. Their idea was to make the blacks work in the plantations: they would produce pistachio, gum, but above all peanuts, soon to become the main product of Senegal.

They had shown appreciation of Faidherbe when he put an end to the customs piracy practised by the Moors, or so long as he fought the Toucouleurs. But his assimilationist policy clashed with the resistance of these same colonists who were not inclined to accept that, with the effective enforcement of the Civil Code, blacks and whites would be equal in the eyes of the law. Faidherbe wanted to help the Senegalese to become producers and also intended to provide the blacks with education. In particular he did not subordinate their interests to those of the whites. Further he alienated the ministry by declaring that "as a rule the course of action must take into account the interest of the natives". The ministry called him a savage. The colonists nicknamed him "the dummy". For decades after him the Senegalese nationalists were still denouncing his paternalism.

Of all the conquerors, the founder of Dakar was undoubtedly the one who, in the context of the ideas of his time, strove with the greatest rectitude to conduct a policy in harmony with the ideals of the Republic.

Cecil Rhodes was, of all the empire builders, the one who conceived the most grandiose scheme: in order to bring about "the end of all wars" he proposed to "place the greater part of the world under our laws", that is, under British law. The first stage required the submission of Africa to Anglo-Saxon civilization. It would be followed by the occupation of South America, of the Holy Land, even of the United States which would be recast as an integral part of the British Empire with representation in the imperial Parliament.

Born in a large family, son of a clergyman, a cotton grower, Cecil Rhodes went to Kimberley at the age of seventeen, after learning of the discovery there of diamond deposits. He earnt enough money to go in search of gold. After making a fortune he went to study in England. He was then twenty. At Oxford he discovered the Darwinian theory and the teaching of Ruskin. Back in South Africa he increased his fortune and was soon the owner of 90 percent of the diamond mines of the world. It was with the help of this fortune that he would finalize his design of territorial conquest, for he spent little on himself. Money interested him only in regard to the power that it conferred. He was a cynic who believed that anything could be bought, especially consciences. Corruption became his favourite instrument. He believed that interest came before everything. To Parnell, the leader of the Irish Home Rule movement whom he admired and who was experiencing difficulties with the Catholic priests, he suggested that perhaps "the Pope could be bought".

But it was land that Cecil Rhodes wanted to accumulate. And the Cape needed land, not natives. "We cannot abandon Africa to the Pygmies while a superior race is multiplying itself . . . I have no scruples about taking the territory of Bechuanaland from Mankoarane . . . " "These natives are fated to fall under our domination . . . The native must be treated like a child and denied electoral franchise just as he is not allowed to take alcohol." Accordingly he supported the idea of the Strop Bill which gave magistrates the right to whip natives. Naturally enough, high-handed arrests, provocations meant to justify a war, the assassination of messengers and couriers, were methods used by the Chartered Gang, the nickname given to the *British South Africa Cy* or *Chartered.*

In the first instance his scheme consisted in the annexation of the Bechuanaland, the "Suez Canal" of the traffic of southern Africa, which was to lead to the Matabele by passing to the west of the Orange river and the Transvaal. The way of the Germans who had landed in the South-west Africa would thus be barred. Elected as the representative of the Cape, Rhodes succeeded in forming an alliance with the Dutch and got the upper hand over John Mackenzie who had been appointed Commissioner in Bechuanaland. Mackenzie belonged to the group of high "humanitarian" officers and tried to promote an imperial policy of, at least relative, protection of the natives exposed to the racism of the Boers. Thus strengthened and free to act as he wished, Cecil Rhodes used his customary *modus operandi* to dispossess the natives of the Bechuanaland of their land. In the Cape they were each allotted a demarcated, untransferable plot of land, with the result that their descendants were forced to work in the mines. Rhodes thus killed two birds with one stone.

The alliance with the Dutch was struck for the purpose of winning the confidence of the leaders of the Boer States, in order to "swipe" the region of the Matabele. That was a strategy which London could not but approve. But the British had no intention of getting entangled in so risky an enterprise. Cecil Rhodes succeeded in using the connivance of Sir

Hercoles Robinson, Governor of the Cape, and of his friend Sydney Shippard, the Commissioner in Bechuanaland, to acquire from King Lobenguela a sort of monopoly of mine prospecting in his territory (1888). That was the region between the Limpopo and the Zambezi, soon to be called Rhodesia, with Bulawayo as its capital. Foreigners flocked to the place in large numbers. Soon conflicts broke out on the matter of the contents of that charter. The men of Cecil Rhodes deemed themselves henceforth to be the owners of land on which they only had a right of prospecting. Lobenguela wrote a letter of protest to Queen Victoria. But his emissaries were murdered. It would have required much less for conflicts to arise, then war to break out, which Jameson, the representative of the Company, easily won, setting Lobenguela's kraal on fire.

In London, by an Order in Council, Lord Rosebery, the successor of Gladstone, gave to the Chartered all Lobenguela's territory (1894). It had cost the British Treasury so little.

Named "the Napoleon of the Cape" Cecil Rhodes made a triumphal tour of London. But his very successes had disturbed and irritated the Dutch of the Cape and the Boer leaders, especially President Kruger who did not look favourably on the conquest of the Matabele, on which he had nevertheless set his own eye. Actually the entire policy of Rhodes had the ultimate aim of forming an association with the Boer republics to constitute a South African Federation under British authority. With Cecil Rhodes sharing their ideas, particularly as regards the native question, this federation would show no hostility to the Boers. But, since diamond and gold had transformed life in the Transvaal, the number of foreigners, the Uitlanders, had increased and caused conflicts with the Boers. The Uitlanders became a sort of Trojan horse in Johannesburg, as soon as one of the brothers of Cecil, Frankie Rhodes, the administrator of Goldfields, became one of their leaders. Driven by impatience to see Kruger surrender to their wishes, the two Rhodes brothers and Jameson hatched a coup which proved to be a disastrous failure. It was the undoing of Cecil Rhodes.

However this spectacular failure did not dishearten him. He realized in part his scheme for a railway from the Cape to Cairo. At least it went as far as Bulawayo. Above all Rhodes made an about-turn in his position. To avenge himself on the Boers he assumed the role of defender of the rights of the blacks, claiming to be moved by the fate meted out to them ever since the great revolt of the Matabeles had been crushed.

In lieu of the formula "equality of rights for all white men south of the Zambezi", he proclaimed "the equality of rights for every civilized man . . . white or black, so long as he had a decent education, that he owned property or had a trade, in a word that he was no loafer".

"The purpose of colonization is, unscrupulously and with deliberation, to enrich our own people at the expense of other weaker peoples." By publicly flaunting its programme the *Deutsche Ostafrikanische Gesellschaft* of **Carl Peters** did not hide behind the pretence of a civilizing hypocrisy. Its dazzling beginning was belied by its dismal failure in the end. Nevertheless it gave Germany her most beautiful colony, the Tanganyika of yesterday, the Tanzania of today. Attracted by the power of the English, envious of their success, Peters thought, like Bismarck in 1848 speaking of the assembly of Frankfurt, that the German Colonial League, *Das Deutsche Kolonialverein*, was "nothing but an assembly of prattlers". Carl Peters wanted to found a colony – if needs be, all by himself. He was obsessed by the white patches of East Africa on his atlas. During a game of billiards with Felix Behr-Baudelin, the chamberlain of Wilhelm I, he confided to him that he intended to initiate an action and establish the *Gesellschaft für Deutsche Kolonization* with 24 subscribers (1884).

He was driven by one obsession: establishing a settlement before other States – Belgium, Britain, etc. – had located those immense spaces opposite Zanzibar. In these regions "the natives did not even know the name of Germany . . . If England had not settled there, it was only because it believed it was already there. The Suez Canal seemed to be an English undertaking, the Red Sea an English lake, the general commanding the troops of the Sultan of Zanzibar was an Englishman; English battle-ships had their guns trained on it" (M. Baumont, in *Les Techniciens de la colonisation*, 1946).

But England did not enter the continent on that side. Having himself appointed German Consul in Zanzibar, Carl Peters landed, one night, on the opposite coast with 4 Whites, 5 Blacks, one interpreter, one cook and 36 bearers. In his baggage he carried knick-knacks, fabrics and some old hussars' dolmans.

The main task consisted in evading the Sultan's vigilance so as to penetrate deep into the territory and to exchange a few dolmans for land. Peters offered 150,000 square kilometres to his Emperor, after signing twelve treaties with the native chiefs. "I know these agreements are a fiction", said Peters, "but have the others acted otherwise?"

A second, but this time a military, expedition followed as soon as the Sultan of Zanzibar made a show of protesting when he learnt what had happened. Bismarck had declared that the protection of German citizens was a sacred duty. Under Admiral Knorr 8 warships buttressed this statement which this time resulted in the transfer in due form of Dar-es-Salaam.

Meanwhile the number of the Germans dwindled to only three, then to no more than two, one being dead of fever, the other having been killed in the north.

Shortly afterwards Carl Peters rushed to the rescue of another German, Edward Schnitzer, who had given himself the title of Emin Pasha and was marching towards Lake Victoria. But in 1890, as we know, the English had concluded a treaty with the Kaiser according to which Zanzibar and Uganda were transferred in exchange for Heligoland. The State recovered from the *Deutsche Ostafrikanische Gesellschaft* all the administrative and customs rights.

The reason for this development is that, in the meantime, with the help of the English the extortions of the conqueror had become known. Besides the executions, misappropriations of funds, bloody whippings and beatings, Carl Peters was reported to have left his exhausted porters to the wild beasts. The scandal broke out when the catholic and socialist press denounced the criminal. Carl Peters was called back in 1897.

Twenty yeas later the national-socialists hailed him as a precursor. Moreover during the First World War the Wilhelm Solf Memorandum presented the broad perspective of a German domination of Central Africa. Meanwhile General von Epp adopted the "Peters pennant" and made it the symbol of the German colonial associations. In 1936, by the side of the black cross on a red background decked with five white stars, was added the swastika.

In contrast to the other colonizations, that of the Congo was not effected by the military, as in Senegal, or by businessmen ever ready to ask for the intervention of the army like Cecil Rhodes and Carl Peters. It was carried out by civilians motivated at first by the spirit of discovery and the imperative of civilization. This is what was original in the colonization of the Congo, even if subsequently the internationalization of the problem transformed the country into a territory that, like all the others, became the object of envy and of exploitation.

Those who took part in this colonization were explorers, like Brazza, journalists, like Stanley, ministers like Banning who helped Leopold, King of Belgium, to administer the enterprise and take charge of it. With a passion for geography, Leopold was also an enterprising man.

At first it was the discovery of the Congo River, which no one till then could sail up beyond the Ogooué, that set in motion the process of placing under supervision a country in which no one was interested. The main interest of the explorers, themselves more or less in league with their governments, was directed to the source of the Nile which Livingstone, physician and missionary, had tried to reach, whose death another explorer, Cameron, learnt of in 1873. Mystery surrounded this country of the "Loualaba". The press assigned to an Americanized Englishman, Henry Morgan Stanley, who had once met Livingstone, the task of rediscovering it. After leaving Zanzibar Stanley disappeared. But in October 1877 it was learnt that he had reached the Congo from the east, confirming the hypothesis of Banning, the adviser of Leopold, King of the Belgians. Banning had a passion for exploration and was an ardent supporter of the struggle against slavery. Nevertheless he was equally desirous of presenting his country and his king with a colony. However it was only as a private person that Leopold decided to act. "This King has a lot of spare time", Bismarck sarcastically observed.

At the same time a young French Navy officer of Italian origin, Savorgnan de Brazza, asked for a mission to explore the Ogooué, in Gabon. Without using any violence he managed to conciliate the local tribes, and afterwards to cross the Badeké plateau up to the Alima, a tributary of the Congo river. This was an indication that there was an access route from the Atlantic in the direction of the Stanley Pool. Brazza had scanty means at his disposal: 2 Europeans, 16 Africans and, according to Stanley, "he lacked everything, except red, white and blue flags, with which his luggage was stuffed". Yet, helped by his simplicity and his good nature, he signed treaties with the native princes, among whom was the Prince Makoko. During a second expedition Brazza set up 26 fortresses on a territory with an area larger than that of France. It was then that these conquests came into conflict with the enterprises of Leopold II.

In 1876 Leopold II had called a conference in Brussels where geographers and scholars met for the well-defined purpose: "To open to civilization the only part of the world where it had not reached." Each nation would act in the sphere corresponding to its political and colonial interests. An *Association* would be constituted of these nations in order to mutually support and expedite the penetration of their travellers and agents. A committee would be set up in which the emulation of each nation would come into play. It was not a matter of territorial acquisitions, but of "missions": the king knew that public opinion in his country was hostile to the idea of colonial expansion. The United States were impressed by the anti-slavery and humanitarian propaganda of the Association. They contributed their support to this sovereign who, in his private capacity, did not dispose of adequate means.

As the territories controlled by the Association overlapped those on which Brazza had hoisted his flags, it was agreed that, while retaining a preemptive right France would not hinder the work of the Association (1884). This alarmed the powers with the result that they decided to transform the Association into a sort of supranational state which would manage the affairs of the Congo. Already, however, Stanley was protesting, in his own name, against Brazza's holding on to his possessions, especially when under Malamine, a Senegalese corporal, the garrison refused to obey the orders of the representative of the Association. On his return to Europe Stanley did not disguise his bitterness. Leopold went a step further. As the President of the Association, the Executive Committee of which was international, he formed a Committee for the Studies of the Upper Congo which was entirely composed of Belgians.

Meanwhile the discovery had been made of a rich hinterland that held potential for development. Great Britain, Germany and Portugal claimed that they had the right to intervene. The turmoil over the Congo was to result in the actual division of black Africa. Even in the Congo, the time for initiatives was gone.

Curiously enough Stanley, the "explorer", then acted as if he was the soul of a sort of *anonymous imperialism*, expressed by means of symbolic actions. He became the subject of admiration on the part of some, and the butt of cruel criticisms on the part of others. One of D. J. Nicolls's cartoons shows him praying for a black African who has just been hanged, while the Angel of Capital, above his head, blesses Stanley. He offered his services equally to the English in East Africa and in the Sudan, to the Belgians in the Congo, and even to the Americans in Zanzibar. By following in his footsteps conquering imperialism certainly profited, for Stanley's energy was prodigious. But, as the Pall Mall Gazette asked: what civilization?

Of all the conquerors Lyautey, with Cecil Rhodes, was the one who was most fascinated by glory. More than any of the others, his name is associated with colonization and with nothing else but colonization. No one seemed to have noticed his time at the Ministry of War in 1916, while his great predecessors, Faidherbe and Gallieni, had equally been defenders of French territory, the former in 1870 and the latter in 1914. But such is not the case with Lyautey who is quintessentially the Colonial, and even more, the Moroccan, though he had at first served in Madagascar and in Indo-China.

Above all a man of action, Lyautey was a romantic who loved pomp and pageantry. The poet Shelley inspired his personal morality: "I felt I was born to create and I create, to command and I command." He was a staunch monarchist, a faithful believer. He was disappointed to discover that Pope Leo XIII was actually a republican, whereas, for his part, he welcomed the Republic only in so far as it gave France a colonial empire.

Like his mentor Gallieni he thought that a country must engage in the least fighting possible and show its power in order not to use it. Fostering a sense of security had been his obsession ever since he had experienced the unfortunate effects, especially in Madagascar, of the technique of "a blow with the lance", which consisted of setting fire to villages and taking stringent measures against the population. He advocates replacing this technique with that of the "oil slick", bringing to the natives a "bit of love", by "pressing his ear to their heart". In Indo-China he was moved by the gratitude of the peasants of Tonkin who, "liberated from the bandits, told him that for the first time in twenty years they had been able to reap their harvest in complete safety".

In helping to bring order back to Morocco he sought fulfilment of his need for adventure beyond his country, France – where he detested the red tape, and even more the infatuation with interminable speeches, those "vain discussions" – and of his desire to build, to some extent in emulation of a Roman emperor. Lyautey was a poet; he wrote; he was fascinated by the beauty of the rolling countryside. More than anything else he was urged on by the idea of his forthcoming creation of Casablanca. "I am so engrossed by this labour of creation, I live so much off my roads, off my fields, off my herds, off my nurseries . . . "

Lyautey's originality lies in that political mix in which he blends his own ideas as a traditional catholic with the imperatives of policy. A conservative, he believed in the necessity of strengthening the power of the Sultan and the Maghzen, the Moroccan State, in the face of the disorder of Siba: "I feel a profound revulsion at any disorder, at revolution." Accordingly he provided protection for Moroccan institutions and for Islam which attracted him as did the Buddhist ceremonies in Cambodia. He stated his desire to be buried in a white *kouba* with green tiles, like the mausoleums of the saints of the country, but with a bilingual inscription to recall that he was a sincere catholic though he respected the traditions of the people. He told the colonists that, on account of the treaties, the regime could not be swept away. But neither should it, even if no treaties stood in the way. On the contrary, he wanted to reinforce its prestige, and in particular that of the Sultan. This task of restoration, which he would have liked to accomplish in France, went hand in hand with aid to Islam and with an assurance given to the Berber tribes that their culture would be protected.

Naturally such a conservative policy made sense only insofar as it was implemented in conjunction with modernity. Lyautey wanted to develop medicine and education, and looked to the French administration to accomplish this modernization. He wanted this action to be the responsibility solely of the administration as such, not that of the colonists' representatives. He hated anything which smacked of parliamentary government. In his view the prosperity planned in this way ought to win the population over to accepting the principle of the protectorate, which could turn out to be a definitive solution.

But, in Paris, scandalized by his infatuation with pomp and by his homosexuality, the bureaucrats reined in the activities of this condotierre. "One cannot lay a brick (in Morocco) without its being studied for a year beforehand in Paris, and then controlled and paid for at great cost", Lyautey laments. He did not want Morocco to be, like our departments, "castrated by the prefects, and deprived of life". The Left, in the mother country, distrusted the proconsul; the Right thought that he was oppressing the colonists by protecting the Sultan, by proceeding against integration on the Algerian model. Indeed Lyautey was working for a duplication of the country, a Moroccan part and a French part, collaborating with one another.

In Morocco the Sultanate naturally appreciated the provision of this aid to its authority, this respect for Moroccan identity. But this reinforcement would one day help it to rid itself of the occupier. The revolt of Abd el Krim against Spain, the war in the Riff and its consequent spreading of the spirit of rebellion, backfired against both the Sultan and Lyautey. Though at first the latter saw in the revolt against Spain the vindication of the success of his own policy, the event soon turned out very differently and jeopardized the whole fabric of the work he had accomplished.

Russians and Englishmen: keeping watch over the Caucasus and Central Asia

The main preoccupation of the British was India which they controlled up to its "natural defences". But on the north-west side of the Himalayas the Russians were moving south. After the Crimean War in 1854, this movement posed a threat to Britain. While the British were keeping watch over Russian expansion, the Russians reciprocated by keeping watch over British expansion. This struggle, between "the whale and the elephant" as someone said, lasted for nearly a century, from 1829 to 1907. It had a few precedents: the conflicts in the Baltic, the fate of the English Muscovy Company. But it left its mark even after 1907, the date of the treaty for the division of Persia into zones of influence between the Russians and the British. The alliance against Germany in 1914 and again in 1941 did not erase its traces in Iran or in Afghanistan. The consequences of that struggle were apparent during the period 1950–90.

The Tsars' craving for land seemed to be insatiable. They had occupied the whole of Siberia and Alaska, yet in 1821 the Tsar issues a ukase "to assure to Russian ships the monopoly of commerce and navigation on the north-east coast of the Pacific to 51 degrees latitude North", in other words, as far as California. This ukase alarmed the President of the United States who, in 1823, issued a message known as the Monroe doctrine. It proclaimed that the European powers must not attempt to extend their influence to any part of the Americas: "The American continents, by the free and independent condition which they have assumed and maintain, are henceforth not to be considered as subject for future colonization by any European power."

At the same time Caucasia merged itself with Russia when the King of Georgia abdicated in favour of the Tsar rather than see his country taken over by the Muslim Persians. On two occasions the Persians reacted to this event. But General Paskievitch imposed the peace of Toukmandchaï (1828) which gave the Tsar a chunk of Persian Armenia. Under Paskievitch's command the Russians won big successes in the Tsar's war against the Turks. With the peace of Andrianople (1829) Turkish Armenia was annexed to the empire of the Tsars.

For a time the western powers did not perceive that these changes altered the balance of a whole sector of the East, the Ottoman Empire having lost Greece, and losing Egypt soon after. But, as the French Consul in Trebizond observed, the Tsar had recourse to beguiling manoeuvres to divert attention from his plans of conquest. For instance, in the Treaty of Andrianople, the name of Abkhazy was scarcely mentioned, even though Russia had been trying to annex this nation for about eight years, and in fact did annex it as well as a part of Circassia. It was only from 1830 on that the Russians came up against resistance from Imam Shamil, which lasted till 1859.

Imam Shamil's struggle in Daghestan recalls that of Abd el-Kader in Algeria, as was emphasized by the newspaper *Le National* in 1844, by the geographer Woiekov in 1914 and by the historian Gammer in 1991. Indeed the two situations do present similarities: the aggressors set out from the plains and run up against a continent of mountains. They then hesitate on what course of action to take. Like Desmichels in Algeria, von Klugenau, in the name of the Tsar, thought of negotiating. If you come to an agreement with the enemy, the latter at least loses the plains. But you strengthen him in his mountain retreats, and this may entail supporting him against his rivals. But total conquest costs lives and there is no need for it. Hence Shamil and the Russians could recover their breath before ending the "peace of the brave" which was concluded in the Caucasus, as in Algeria. It was a difficult Russian victory claimed by the St Petersburg autocracy, a victory which was enhanced by the legend honouring Shamil, recalling the legend which in Paris glorified the courage of Abd el-Kader.

Shamil's glory "which produced an electrifying effect on the people of those regions" (quoted in M. Lesure, 1978), alerted the West to the Russian conquests. "The European powers ought to intervene and not allow a power inimical to liberty to assert its strength by destroying it in Caucasia." For it was the autocratic Tsar who became the butt of criticism from those same liberals in Paris and in London who were occupying Algeria and Baluchistan. "It was feared in St Petersburg that liberalism would support the cause of the Circassians, as it had done that of the Greeks" (ibid.). Help was expected from Shamil and the Circassians during the Crimean War. But knowledge of those regions was so poor that no one knew how to join forces with him in order to mount a joint attack against the Russians. Better still, the Porte was asked for the relevant information, in spite of the fact that the Turks themselves looked forward to recovering the northern region of the Caucasus, which had been an Ottoman protectorate, and Abkhazia, which had been annexed by the Tsarist Empire.

Thus the Caucasus makes its first entrance on the international stage. David Urquhart, an English diplomat, had, in 1830, anonymously published a booklet in English and in French, entitled *England, France, Russia and Turkey*. It went through three editions in England. Urquhart warned public opinion by denouncing the "progressive invasion of the Black Sea coasts". After the straits, Russia would try to gain control over the whole of the Mediterranean, an action which would bring the freedom of the seas to an end. There was a need for unity in order to "provoke the explosion of the entire Caucasus . . . If only one thought that all the provinces of Georgia are waiting for a sign to shake off the Muscovite yoke, that in the Caucasus hundreds of thousands of brave and ever armed inhabitants live in conditions of feigned submission . . . and are ready to set upon the Russians who are within reach of them" (quoted in Lesure, 1978).

It is a paradox that the consequences of the Crimean War belied its goals. The war arose out of those anxieties. But it was due also to all sorts of other reasons, in particular, to the will of Russia, in the name of the Orthodox Christian religion, to dismantle the Ottoman Empire and to liberate the Slav populations. Neither Britain nor France were willing to let Russia act as she wished. Brushing aside Christian solidarity and the defence of the peoples' rights to liberate themselves, they sided with the Ottoman Empire – to save it and very likely in order to carve it up later. The Western powers were victorious, but once the Russian advance was stalled, they allowed the Turkish power in the Balkans to deteriorate, though they had joined the war in order to support it. At least the straits did not seem likely ever to fall into the hands of the Russians.

However bigger stakes henceforth opposed Great Britain to Russia: the domination of Central Asia and the borders of India. A two-fold push; an unavoidable clash. What were the aims of the Russian advance in Central Asia?

According to the Marxists the first phase of this imperialism (1865–85) was of a military-feudal nature. Subsequently the economic imperatives assumed a bigger and bigger role.

It is evident that the economic factors in the first push counted for little and they were only the result of an action initiated by the Tsarist State in order to create conditions favourable to Russian commerce in the khanates. Private interests did not endorse that action. This explains the fact that, while the agreements with the khanates were made in 1867 (Khodjent) and in 1873 (Khiva), the development of cotton cultivation *by the Russians* began only in or about 1890. What brought about this development was not so much the pressure exerted by the business circles as the Tsarist fear that those khanates would be too weak to assert themselves as independent states, and that the entire region would fall under the influence of a foreign power like, for example, the Ottomans. That was what justified the preemptive occupation of those territories. Thus it was the will to keep foreigners at arm's length, to maintain the isolation of those regions, that triggered the process of their being annexed. For very early it became apparent to the ministers Giers and Cherniaiev that the consequences of that occupation were economically counter-productive.

Keeping the foreigner at arm's length: this imperative explains of St Petersburg's maintenance of its veto, up to 1910, over the British project of building a railway in Persia. It also explains the refusal of a link between the Baghdad railway, another British project initially, and the Caucasus. Again it explains the Scott-Muraviev agreement of 1899, the terms of which stipulated that Britain would not build railways, nor assist in any project along the Russo-Chinese border.

Russia was attempting to settle itself economically in buffer zones, especially in Persia, and later in Manchuria. But its commerce made little progress, in comparison with that of the British in the first instance, with that of the Japanese in the second, because of poor follow-up on the part of Russian business. It made slightly better headway in the Ottoman Empire (Anatolia and Kurdistan), in Sinkiang, in Persia where Germany was also making its "entry", and in Afghanistan where Russian commerce increased three-fold, rising to 38 percent of Kabul's imports, in contrast to 62 percent for the British, in 1914. In was in relation to this country that the most intense Anglo-Russian conflicts broke out.

In 1872 and 1873 the Tsar had declared that Afghanistan was beyond Russia's "zone of influence". Then, "to keep the Russians at arm's length" the British, moving from India, occupied Baluchistan, and claimed to control the Afghan regime in Kabul. The British mission there was wiped out (1879) and Lord Roberts led an expedition which ended with the capture of Kabul. Thereupon the Russians occupied present-day Uzbekistan and Tajikistan, Merv, Panjeh and the Zulficar pass which opens on to Afghanistan. The crisis was then in full swing. The British sent a squadron to threaten Vladivostok. In 1885 a draft treaty gave Panjeh to the Russians, but handed the Zulficar pass to Afghanistan. Later the Simla Convention granted to Afghanistan such a strip of territory as would not allow the Russian Empire and India to have a common border (1895). A century later this territory lies at the heart of the conflict between Tajikistan, Uzbekistan, Afghanistan and Pakistan.

"Always think of India, but never speak about it", Alexander III advised his son Nicholas II before his death in 1894. But the Tsar also knew that an Anglo-Russian conflict would only benefit the Germans who had begun to expand in the Middle East and even beyond.

"To keep the Russians at arm's length" from the warm seas and partic-ularly from the Persian Gulf was equally one of the goals of the British policy. In 1892 Lord Curzon had written a book on Persia to demonstrate that the interests of both the Persians and the British would not be served by Persia falling into the same situation in which Bukhara and Khiva found themselves. Actually Tsarist Russia had won certain advantages in the north of the country, in which the revolutionary movement had already made inroads. The British wanted to have an equivalent zone of influence in the South near the Indian border. In the name of the Entente Cordiale, which was concluded in 1904, France intervened with a view to reconciling "the whale and the elephant". The outcome was the treaty of 1907 according to which Persia was divided into two zones of influence.

This is a situation which has survived the treaty. It has done so in spite of the historical changes which occurred between 1907 and 1918, and later. Further, despite the fact that Persia, under its new name of Iran, became formally independent, the British and the Russians more or less simultaneously occupied the country in 1942 and fraternized with each other on this first Oder-Neisse line, in the name of a rediscovered alliance.

The treaty of 1907 brought an end to a situation marked by mutual conflict and aggression. One of the early expressions of this mutual aggressivity had been the agreement which Britain made with Japan in 1902. It gave Japan a free hand to carry out in Manchuria and in China an offensive policy against Russia. A policy which culminated in the 1904–05 war.

The break-up of China
1. France in Indo-China

In the middle of the nineteenth century the British penetrated the Chinese market during the Opium War. Britain obtained the base of Hong Kong (1842), then the opening of the Chinese ports, which France also obtained. At about the same time, in the middle of the last century, Captain Nevelskoj, in the name of the Tsar, confronted Peking with a fait accompli by taking possession of the estuary of the Amur. This conquest was acknowledged by the Treaty of Aygun (1858). It marked the beginning of Russian expansion in the Far East. Before this the Treaty of Kolja (1759) had opened Sinkiang to Russian commerce. That was the first of the unequal treaties imposed on China by Russia.

At the same time the French navy, still smarting from the loss of India, manifested an interest in Indo-China where missionaries had been massacred "in spite of the treaties".

That was an old story. In the middle of the seventeenth century Alexandre de Rhodes, François Pallu and Bishop Lambert had set out, with the title of Apostolic Vicars so as to depend, not on the Portuguese primate of Goa, but directly on the Pope. The *Missions étrangères de France* ("French Foreign Missions") took charge of the operation. In Tonkin they established a trading-post, for the purpose of preparing for the evangelization. It was a failure, the Dutch, with their unalloyed commercial disposition, denouncing the fraud. A new attempt was made in the eighteenth century when, for a second time, Charles Thomas de Saint-Phalle deemed that "commerce will greatly aid the mission . . . and mitigate the severity of the decrees which slow down religious conversions".

After helping Nguyen-Ahan, the King of Annam, to regain his throne, Pigneau de Behaine, the Apostolic Vicar, expected France to become the protector of that country (1787). But events in Europe diverted the mother country from undertaking this task and the successors of Nguyen-Ahan gave vent to an intense hatred for "the religion of Jesus, . . . all the *European* priests of this religion must be thrown into the sea".

Nevertheless, as the British and the French, again in the name of religion, had intervened in China, Napoleon III asked Admiral Rigault de Genouilly to transfer his centre of activity to Indo-China. He bombarded Tourane, settled in a part of Cochin-China and in February 1859 occupied Saigon. But the French sailors had to endure a long siege. When Admiral Charner came back in full force, Emperor Tu Duc signed the treaty which ceded to France the three provinces of Saigon, My Tho and Bien Hoa (1863). Chasseloup-Laubat, the Minister of the Navy, declared: "We have no intention to make of Cochin-China a colony like the West Indies or Reunion." When the three provinces became the centre of the anti-French Annamese resistance, Admiral de La Grandière conquered them and Emperor Tu Duc had to surrender them. At the same time France offered Norodom, the King of Cambodia, protection against Annam and Siam. He accepted the offer, though not without hesitation.

In fact three forces impelled French intervention in Indo-China: first, evangelizing zeal which chronologically came first, but remained active during the whole of the nineteenth century; secondly, the anglophobia of the navy represented by the officer Francis Garnier who wanted to give France a colonial empire in the Far East on a par with that of Great Britain which, from Burma, was pushing forward towards Siam. The third force consisted of the racketeering on the part of the textile and arms dealers who, led by the businessman Jean Dupuis and the silk producers of Lyon, like Ulysse Rouge, wanted to occupy the Tonkin and better still control the Red River which they assumed to be the means of access to the Chinese market. That was the great myth of the nineteenth century. It was in this context that, as a result of certain incidents, Francis Garnier captured Hanoi (1873). He was then killed in a fight with the Black Flags. The treaty drawn up by Philastre, Garnier's successor, brought about Tu Duc's final recognition of the cession of Cochin-China, of a protectorate over Annam, of three forts in Haiphong and of the opening of the Red River. "Penetration in Tonkin is a matter of life or death for the future of our dominion in the Far East", opined the merchants and the admirals in Saigon. And in 1872 Gambetta considered the Red River to be another Suez Canal, "a road for the universal commerce of the world".

As a matter of fact, in the face of opposition to the colonial expansion, "this betrayal", the Third Republic wanted above all to prevent a conflict with China which remained the "protector" and suzerain of Annam. But the admirals and the missionaries incited to action. In particular Mgr. Puginier kept repeating that "the Tonkin is ready to throw itself into the arms of France". It was indeed through the missionaries and their Vietnamese followers, whose numbers had swollen in the meantime, that the French received information about the plans and the condition of the

Annamese state, its army, and the Black Flags, a sort of back-up army which was autonomous and at the same time subject to China. "Non-intervention would be an imprudence", said La Myre de Villers, governor of Cochin-China. In view of an escalation of incidents Captain Rivière was entrusted with a mission to occupy the whole of Tonkin. In Paris meanwhile the riches of Tonkin were detailed in a map distributed to the deputies by the friends of Jean Dupuis who had just set up the *Société des mines du Tonkin.* Captain Rivière died at the very spot where Garnier had fallen a few years earlier. He was then beheaded. In the words of Charles Fourniau: "The death of Rivière wrapped up Dupuis' large nuggets in a patriotic reaction."

"With the Chinese", wrote Jules Ferry, then the head of the government, "the real negotiators are good, old-fashioned cannon." But the government under-estimated the enemy. It was relying on the practice of sending small batches of reinforcements. Finally, Admiral Courbet, with 25,000 men, gained several successes and China signed the second treaty of Tien-tsin (1885) and promised to withdraw her troops from Tonkin.

But, in trying to occupy Lang-sön, the French troops were forced to withdraw. It was a failure, accompanied by panic and confusion. In Paris the crisis culminated with Clemenceau whipping up a hue and cry against Jules Ferry. Actually China had given in. But the agreement was still being kept secret, Jules Ferry had to resign (1885). Nevertheless the Indo-Chinese confederation was born: it comprised a colony, Cochin-China, and four protectorates, including Cambodia and Laos. As for the Vietnamese, their hour of resistance had come, though several decades more had to pass before they gave free expression to it.

The British reacted to the annexation of the Tonkin by the conquest of Upper Burma, where the sovereign had confiscated the assets of the *Bombay Burma Company.* In 1886, 10,000 men completed the conquest of the country and came close to Siam which, for its part, stood against the French penetration in Laos. It was a peaceful penetration thanks to Auguste Pavie, a postal employee, who had rediscovered the Khmer civilization. Once again Anglo-French rivalry was reactivated. But the treaty of 1896 brought it to an end, with Siam surrendering to Cambodia the province of Angkor.

The break-up of China
2. Russo-Japanese rivalry

China had to surrender to Europe concessions (Hong Kong, 11 ports) and domination of its vassal states (Annam, Burma, Siam). Simultaneously it clashed with Japan which, from 1894 on, was bidding to replace it, particularly in Korea. Military defeat forced China to give up all its influence in Korea, which became a Japanese protectorate. China further ceded

Formosa and the Lia-toung peninsula together with Port Arthur, which gave access to Manchuria (peace of Shimonoseki, 1895). The conditions of this peace worried the Russian government which, being at that time a privileged interlocutor at the Chinese court in Peking, had allowed England to act alone in the region so long as only commercial bases were concerned. But the territories occupied by Japan threatened the project of the Trans-Siberian Railway which needed to have its terminus in Port Arthur, in order to avoid Vladivostok which remains blocked under ice during four months in the year. The Tsar was ready to intervene for he did not like the Japanese, "those apes", and, in his eyes, to act against them was not tantamount to making war. But his minister Witte convinced him that the troops available on the ground were not sufficient, considering that the Trans-Siberian was not yet completed. Witte thought that a joint intervention by the European powers would be more decisive. Japan gave in, surrendering Port Arthur (1895), something which she would not forget.

The European powers profited from the weakness of China to acquire territorial advantages for the establishment of zones of influence. To Britain was ceded Wei-Hai-Wei, Germany got Kiao-cheou, France received Kouang-cheou-Wan. Russia obtained the right to construct the railway in Manchuria and in exchange committed herself to defend China against Japan. The Chinese reacted against this European penetration and following the Boxer rebellion (1900) an international expedition arrived to "punish" them. Nicholas II was forced to follow, if only to restrain and control his cousin Wilhelm II whose minister in Peking had been assassinated. Once the expedition was over, Nicholas II dreamt of realizing "his grand design" which General Kouropatkine had unveiled: to seize Manchuria, Korea and Tibet, then Persia, the Bosphorus and the Dardanelles, in sum, to become "the Emperor of the Pacific". But he believed that his ministers, especially Witte, were against the "vocation of Holy Russia" and chose to confide in "any Bezobrazov", a businessman and apologist of expansion to the Far East.

Following the Boxers' war Russia withdrew her fleet, as did everybody else. But she maintained her troops in Manchuria. And the French ambassador observed: "This is strongly reminiscent of a protectorate."

In 1902 when the Anglo-Japanese alliance was struck the Tsar understood that he must draw back and give up, at least for the time being, the intention of holding on to the totality of Manchuria. Russia evacuated a first zone. The Tsar's ministers thought his project to be dangerous and expensive. But Nicholas II was more determined than he was rumoured to be. He was resolved to give substance to this ambition and accordingly took responsibility for foreign affairs away from Count Lamsdorf, his minister, who opposed the plan. Thereupon Japan quickly realized that time was running against the Tsar. When she did not receive a satisfactory answer to a claim made upon the second zone, Japan made a surprise attack – without a declaration of war – upon the Russian fleet stationed in Port Arthur (1904). The Tsar, his generals and his admirals had underestimated the military strength of Japan. After suffering several defeats, they signed the peace of Portsmouth, thanks to the intercession of the United States. Russia acknowledged Japanese sovereignty over Korea, and Port Arthur once again became a Japanese base. Japan finally annexed the southern part of Sakhalin Island which the USSR recovered in 1945.

The dismembering of the Ottoman Empire

The idea of dismembering the Ottoman Empire goes back to the eighteenth century. Thanks to rivalries among the powers the Empire survived, in spite of the help provided by Russia to Serbia and to Bulgaria, by France to Egypt, by Britain to Greece, etc. To these one may add Britain's annexation of Cyprus ("in order to better help the Sultan to defend Constantinople"), France's annexation of Algeria and Tunisia, Italy's of Libya in 1911.

Since the time of Francesco Crispi, Italian imperialism, unable to seize Tunisia or Ethiopia, had been casting a covetous eye on Libya. In the west of this country, Tripolitania, despite the name of its capital, had been Punic, while to the east, Cyrenaica, had remained more hellenic in spite of the Roman, and later Arab, conquest. The *Banco di Roma* had placed deposits in those regions, which still recalled the Roman Empire. As it did in Tunisia the Banco acquired property for the colonists of the day, or for all those Tuscans or Sicilians who would arrive in the future, to settle in a land favourable to olive cultivation. The annexation of Morocco by France and the Agadir incident of 1911 provided Italy with the opportunity to act. It declared war on the Ottoman Empire and occupied Rhodes and the Libyan coast. But the conquest could not proceed very far as it encountered the resistance of the Senussis – the Sanusiyya – who were well entrenched in the oasis of Kufra and were consequently inaccessible. It was resumed only after the First World War, at the time of Mussolini. Given the difficulty of penetrating the desert it was a fierce and costly campaign of pacification. Nevertheless the Italian colonists of Tripolitania outnumbered the French in the south of Tunisia. That was so because the French government chose to promote large-scale economic colonization while the Italians were more in favour of the settlement of men as a solution to their demographic problem.

In 1911 when the Italians revealed their aims in Tripolitania, the Young Turk movement tried to react, for fear lest the loss of Libya would produce a chain reaction in the other provinces of the Empire. The Arabs had to be reassured against the belief that Istanbul was incapable of defending the Muslims against the West. Already, following the annexation of Bosnia-Herzegovina by the Austro-Hungarian Empire, of Crete by Greece, boycott movements had been organized against western products. After 1911 these boycotts were resumed with increased intensity, even against the Italians, in order to take the wind out of the sails of Arab nationalism. But it was a futile exercise. In fact it was indeed the Arab revolt which in 1914–18 delivered "a dagger thrust in the back" to the Ottoman Empire.

The Ottoman Empire remained a power threatened from within by the Armenian, Arab, Kurdish nationalisms, and from without by the joint appetites of the great powers. But the "imperialist" control began to act also within the empire. With the German initiative for the construction of the Baghdad railway, the B.B.B., the Kaiser got permission to regenerate the Sultan's army, while the customs remained more or less under the supervision of the British, and the French "helped" in the management of the finances. A sort of balance had set in among the powers. But it was not stable and the First World War brought it to an end.

The Allies openly planned to dismantle the Ottoman Empire in a way which would provide the Arabs with a sort of independence under their aegis. The agreements struck in 1916 (Sykes-Picot) and 1917 (Saint-Jean-de-Maurienne) made allowance for a "share" reserved for Italy. Further the Balfour Declaration of 2 November 1917 promised the Jews the establishment of a homeland in Palestine to which Hussein, the Shereef of Mecca, consented.

"We have all blithely divided Turkey", observed Colonel House, the adviser of President Wilson. Apart from Greece, Italy, the main beneficiaries were supposed to be the Arabs, with the blessing of France and Great Britain.

The soul of the Arab revival had been a descendant of the Prophet, Hussein Ben Ali, who had started the 1916 insurrection. But a double misunderstanding occurred with respect to the frontiers controlled by France and Britain and also to the Jewish homeland in Palestine. Till that date neither Shereef Hussein nor King Faisal could conceive that the Palestine would constitute a part of the future Arab Kingdom. An agreement was even signed between King Faisal and Dr. Weizmann, the representative of the Zionist organization, in which it was stipulated that the Muslim sacred places would remain under the protection of Islam.

But, at Lausanne, the carving up of the Turkish Empire provoked a reaction which culminated in the abandonment of the clauses of the Treaty of Sèvres. Following a war, the Turks under Ataturk recovered Smyrna and the independence of Armenia ceased to be on the order of the day. On the other hand the "Arab" territories – Syria, Lebanon, Iraq – which for the most part had been brought under the domination of France and of Great Britain, rose in revolt, as early as 1920, against the foreign armies of occupation. There, as in Saudi Arabia, the discovery of oil had sharpened appetites.

The French and the British in the Middle East

It is beyond doubt that in the Middle East French diplomacy was blinded by its rivalry with Great Britain and consequently erred in underestimating Arab nationalism.

During the Second World War the sympathy of the Arabs of the Middle East was for the Germans who, since Wilhelm II's journey to Tangiers in 1905, had been successful in posing as the upholders of freedom for the Arabs. In 1941 the German Wehrmacht was advancing from success to success and the Hitlerian regime in Berlin scarcely bothered Sayid Amil el-Husseini, the Grand Mufti of Jerusalem who declared: "We and the Germans have the same common enemies: the English, the Jews and the Communists." At that moment the French did not exist any more. They were not merely held in contempt, but scorned. The reason was that the Léon Blum Government had in 1936 signed an agreement which promised, during the following three years, the end of the mandate and independence for Syria and Lebanon, but that the agreement had never been ratified. With France defeated, the British Government resolved not to endorse the Arab claims in Syria and in Lebanon, and not to allow the Axis Powers to move in either. The French High Commissioner, Gabriel Puaux, at first seemed to go along with that line of conduct. But, on instructions received from the Vichy Government, he accused the British of hindering economic exchanges with Damascus and, particularly, of being in favour of a "coup" on the part of General Catroux's Gaullists, in order to bring Syria and Lebanon over to the side of Free France. Actually Catroux could do nothing. General Dentz, who replaced Puaux, showed his hostility towards the British. However the latter deemed it necessary to strike a bargain with the French of Syria and Lebanon – Gaullist or Vichyist – to forestall a movement arising from the Arab nationalists, a development which could have engulfed the whole region and in particular Iraq.

In fact Iraq was the first to rise when, with the occupation of Greece by the Germans and Italians, it seemed that the hour of liberation had come. A coup catapulted Rachid Ali to power. An associate of the Grand Mufti, Rachid Ali did not hide his feelings of hostility against Great Britain which had not been able to induce the Baghdad government, even before the coup, to break off diplomatic relations with Italy. Henceforth Germany worked for direct intervention, sending aircraft and military advisers to Alep, on the border with Turkey, and this with the approval of Darlan who signed the protocol of Paris (1941). In Syria General Dentz then began to offer resistance to the Gaullist forces of Legentilhomme who were supported by the British. The Allies seized Damascus after a last stand made by the forces of Vichy. In return for this show of good manners, the English treated Dentz with respect, excluded Charles de Gaulle from the Saint-Jean-d'Acre negotiation, and thereby substituted their authority for the sovereignty of France. There resulted a near break-down of the relationships between Churchill and de Gaulle. In August 1941 de Gaulle received assurances which he acknowledged in his letter to Lord Lyttleton, the British Minister of State in Cairo: "I am happy with these assurances which you have provided concerning the disinterestedness of Great Britain in Syria and in Lebanon and the fact that Great Britain acknowledges the preeminent privileged position of France when these countries shall be independent in conformity with the commitment France has made with regard to them."

In the Middle East the situation had turned around following the victory at El Alamein, which had been preceded by Iraq being brought to heel and the end of Rachid Ali and the exile of the Grand Mufti to Berlin. In January 1943 General Catroux, High Commissioner of Free France, announced the restoration of the republican order and elections in Syria and Lebanon. The nationalists triumphed and in Beirut they proposed a modification of the Constitution the terms of which were "incompatible with independence". Yves Helleu, the French representative, opposed this manoeuvre. The Chamber in Beirut disregarded his action and abolished the French mandate, whereupon Ambassador Helleu ordered the arrest of Bechara Khoury and Ryad Solh, respectively President and Prime Minister of Lebanon.

Immediately afterwards the Lebanese formed a "national" government in the mountains, with the support of Shoukri Kwaltly, the President of Syria. Moreover the Arabs were supported militarily by the English. Once again the region was in full crisis.

The French accused Spears and England, believing that they were the cause of the conflict. In fact Catroux and Masigli, as well as de Gaulle, did not want to concede that "independence" was irreconcilable with specific rights being granted to France and laid down in a constitution. The same men were to repeat their under-estimation of Arab claims in Tunisia, in Morocco and in Algeria, with the difference that instead of seeing the hand of Britain, which certainly was not a clean one, in those situations they saw the hands of the USSR and of the USA.

Japan: a "superior people" against the West

In Japan colonial expansion proceeded first from simple territorial extension with the settlement of colonists, towards the north, in Hokkaido-Yeso, and later in Karafuto, the southern part of Sakhalin Island. But from 1880 onward this movement changed direction. The political thinker Yamagata Aritomo came up with a justification for this new development with his theory of circles. According to this theory each sphere within the different circles which surround Japan must be first strengthened and then protected from without.

The change may have arisen from the new orientation sweeping over Japan since the start of the Meiji period, her departure from her traditional sino-centrism. But above all this change can be explained by Japan's felt need to imitate European development even in its colonial practice. To own an empire thus became a sort of imperative which, at its outset, did not answer to any economic demand. Japan struck wherever she sensed a weakness, a possibility, Ryu-Kyu, the Bonins, Korea, China. It was in Korea that for the first time economic interests overrode the demand for overseas dominions, as was evinced by the defence of the country against possible threats later by Japan's "mission" (1895 Treaty of Shimonoseki).

For some it was a civilizing mission mandated by Heaven: the colonies being viewed as external territories which were to be treated with paternalistic condescension. For others it was a matter, in view of the asiatic nature of Japan, of assimilating the populations, of japanizing them. The affinity of their roots made it appear as a possibility. The teachings of Confucius justified it, since Confucius insists that equality must reign under the same authority – in this case, that of the Emperor of Japan.

On the eve of the Second World War, however, a third notion took over from these earlier considerations: the colonial conquests – beyond Korea, Formosa, which were already occupied – were justified in the name of the superiority of the Japanese people. Such a vision carried along with it a strong whiff of racism.

Among the manifestos which define a colonial or expansionist policy – for instance, the speeches of Jules Ferry or of Joseph Chamberlain in the nineteenth century – one of the most explicit is a massive Japanese report entitled *Project for a global policy of which the Yamato race would be the nucleus*. It was written in 1942–43 by a team of about forty research scholars of the Ministry of Population and Health. It was indeed the translation of a project which was being put into practice in part. It was not to be shelved and allowed to gather dust. This project purported to give legitimacy to the Japanese colonization of a good part of Asia and of the Pacific Ocean, in the name of an idea of Asia, which Japan would modernize in the "sphere of co-prosperity".

The term race was not understood in a biological sense (*jinshu*), as the Nazis used it. It referred to something broader (*minzoku*), that is, a culture represented by a people, with Japan being placed at the summit of this cultural ladder and being accordingly destined to lead the others, as a result of the synthesis it had achieved between the East and the West. However in their colonization scheme these high officials advocated in their programme the establishment of groups of colonists around "Japanese cities" scattered nearly everywhere, mixed marriages being limited to a minimum, "not because people of mixed blood are inferior, but because mixed marriages would destroy the psychic solidarity of the

Yamato race". Twelve million of these Japanese would be settled in foreign lands, in Korea, in Indo-China, in the Philippines, with two million in Australia and in New Zealand. "Everyone had to stay in his place" in these territories, with the Japanese naturally occupying the dominant position. "They would plant their stock in these countries" and would thus help in solving the demographic problem. This is the main concern of the leaders for, at that time, that is, in 1942–43, Japan, with only 1 percent of the world's total land mass, had 5 percent of the world's population.

The slogan "eight directions for a single roof" accurately characterizes the Japanese notion of the colonization of others. The sphere of co-prosperity is indentified with a large family led by its eldest brother. In Japan this family hierarchy of rights and authority is one of the strictest foundations of social relationships. Moreover the role of the eldest brother is vindicated by his superiority over the other peoples, something which the Japanese learnt at school: "The Chinese are indolent or tricksters", says the report, "the Malays are lazy, the Filipinos may be superior to them, but they have no real civilization; the Koreans are capable of doing the hardest labour: they could be sent to New Guinea."

However, historically, the members of this large family had had to learn, since the beginning of the century, the manners of the eldest brother, which were fashioned, in the eyes of some, by the superior education of the Japanese, in the eyes of others, by their experience of isolation on an archipelago. That was after all how the superiority of the English was explained. The large circulation daily *Asahi* wrote on 3 August 1941: "However it may be, the purity of the Japanese has at last been established: only 6 percent of the inhabitants of this country suffer from mental or psychic troubles in contrast with 20 percent in the United States, Germany and in Great Britain."

It was this racial superiority that would allow Japan to maintain its hold on Asia and put an end to western domination. Actually the scheme went a little further. It was time to eclipse the Eurocentric view of history and geography and, by placing Japan in the centre of the planispheres, do away with the notion of Far East. Since 1911 the 0 degree of Greenwich had established itself as the symbolic representation of England as the centre of the world. But Professor Komaki Tsunekichi of Kyoto moots the idea of representing Africa and Europe as the western part of the Asian continent, America becoming the East-Asian continent and Australia the South-Asian continent. The oceans inter-connecting them would be called the "Grand Ocean of Japan". Japanization would assume other aspects. For example in the sphere of co-prosperity the year 1942 became, as in Japan, the year 2602 (according to the date system associated with the establishment of the imperial dynasty in 660 B.C.). The anniversary date of the Emperor became a festival of Asia (29 April), as did the date of the foundation of the imperial dynasty (11 February).

The problem of the Kurile Islands

Russo-Japanese rivalry remains alive at the end of the twentieth century. Its ultimate episode began in the nineteenth century when Japanese fishermen coming from Hokkaido, and Russian fishermen coming from Kamchatka, fought over the islands called Kurile in Russian and Chishima Rettao (the thousand isles) in Japanese. Actually these islands had been discovered by the Dutch in 1643 and the questions of rivalry had been settled once in 1855 by the Treaty of Shimoda. The large island of Sakhalin (Karafuto) had been declared to be jointly held by the two countries, with the frontier between the Russians and the Japanese passing, in the Kuriles, between Urup (Russian) and Etorofu (Japanese), that is, quite close to Kokkaido, a territory colonized by Japan.

The conflict arose out of a problem of definition: do the two islands of Habomai and Shikotan, attached to Yeso, constitute a part of Hokkaido, or are they the last of the southern Kuriles? By the administrative association of these two islands with the Kuriles the Tokyo authorities initiated a contentious dispute. It was settled, in favour of Alexander II, by the Treaty of St Petersburg, whereby Russia gave up the Kuriles in exchange of the totality of Sakhalin (1875).

Following its victory in the 1904–05 war, Japan annexed the southern part of Sakhalin, while holding on to the totality of the Kuriles. But, in 1945, Russia took back this territory and in addition annexed the Kuriles, which was confirmed by the Treaty of San Francisco (1951). The two islands Habomai and Shikotan became Soviet territory since, according to the Japanese definition, the expression "group of the Kuriles" included all the islands between Yeso-Hokkaido and the Kamchatka.

Today Russia under Yeltsin relies on the victory of 1945 and on the decrees of the Japanese administration of the previous century to keep all the islands up to Hokkaido. Japan would like to go back to the Treaty of St Petersburg, while giving up its rights on Sakhalin. Indeed wisdom would prompt a return to the old line of demarcation according to the Treaty of Shimoda. But if only nations conducted themselves according to the dictates of wisdom!

103

4

A NEW RACE OF SOCIETIES

In America, as in Africa and in Asia, colonization brought forth a new race of societies. At the same time it generated a form of economic and political relations which, though unprecedented, represented the consequences of the mutual encounters between civilizations. A number of new collective personalities thus made their entrance on the stage of history: the Creoles in the Americas, the "pieds-noirs" in the Maghreb. They either did or did not crossbreed with the populations of the territories which they occupied – except when they peopled those territories with blacks taken from Africa by force, as in the Americas. These slaves from beyond the Atlantic, and soon those runaways who escaped from their fate, are moreover new characters, as are the Eurasians, the mulattos. Is the racism which they experienced only the product of this encounter?

During the period of imperialism, which was marked by the increasing distance between the races, new symbolic characters take over from the buccaneer or accompany the missionary and the planter. They are the doctors and teachers. Were the apologists of colonialism right to take pride in them? Besides colonial practices were not everywhere alike. Angola is not South Africa which is so near. Nor is it Brazil, which is in the neighbourhood. North Africa is not similar to Turkestan.

Strangely enough, by dint of asking whether colonization was admirable or abominable, whether it earned profits or cost money, one fails to note that one of its functions was to rid the mother countries of people who were, or who were held to be, "dangerous". They were despatched to Guyana, or to Siberia, or to the other side of the world. "We were a Siberia, but in the sunshine", the Australians say today. The fate of the societies of "delinquent" people left to fend for themselves is as instructive a test for history as the fate of the societies of mixed race.

The mixed-race people of America

What wives for the conquerors?

The first colonization was achieved by a handful of men. From the very outset emigration in Spain was controlled by the *Casa de Contratacion*. As it was necessary to obtain a permit to settle in America, only subjects of the Crown of Castile could obtain one: the *conversos* of Jewish origin were excluded. According to official documents, during five decades (1509–59), a total of 15,480 persons left Spain. But these are not reliable figures, as stowaways were numerous. In fact in 1579 there were already 150,000 white men in the Americas. The number rose to between 400,000 and 500,000 by the end of the seventeenth century.

At first only the men left. But in Mexico Cortez agreed to settle 2,000 immigrants from Castile only on condition that their wives followed them within the following eighteen months. In 1604 an official text mentions the departure of 600 women, though the authorization had been given for only 50. Moreover on the spot the Spaniards had fallen for the charms of the Indian women. As early as 1514, in Hispaniola, 64 men out of 684 had already taken native wives. The *barrangana*, the practice of having concubines, had been tolerated till the advent of Isabel and Ferdinand. But it was common practice in the Americas, after a formal baptism of the most beautiful women offered to the conquerors by the Aztec or Inca princes. Cortez and Pizarro set the examples.

So this was the paradox. Hailing from the country which had invented *limpiezo de sangre* (purity of blood), and excluded all those who had Jewish or Muslim ancestors, which is actually a religious criterion, these same Castilians, in the Americas, imposed interbreeding in order to maintain themselves in those territories and not to experience the fate of Hispaniola where the entire native population had been massacred.

At that time it used to be said that "their children, the men and women 'of means', ought not to be called 'half-breeds', for it is the lifestyle which clearly distinguishes the white from the half-breed". The casual half-breeds, if this expression may be used, that is, the majority of the children, born of fleeting unions, were on the increase. They were the forsaken orphans, destitute wretches who enlisted in the army. Their numbers swelled rapidly: in Peru, about 100,000 to the 38,000 whites in 1570. They were forbidden training in European weapons, horses and admittance to the priesthood. They were cast out by both the Creoles and the Indians. In the sixteenth century the rate of illegitimate children had reached 40 percent and rose to 69 percent between 1640 and 1649, among the blacks and the mulattos.

The reaction in the mother country was harsh. Unmarried women were forbidden from sailing. Likewise men could not leave without their wives.

From the seventeenth century on, 60 percent of the Andalusians who set sail did so together with their families. Mexico attracted most people from Estremadura and from Andalusia: these regions supplied almost 90 percent of those leaving for the New World. Peru was the next most popular destination. Ties with relatives left in the home country remained, some were even perpetuated. Gradually these bonds were loosened, except where hope was kept alive of a possible bounty arriving from Peru. This is how the myth of the uncle from America survived.

In South America the most striking thing is the basic difference between the Spanish and the Portuguese colonizations. From the very beginning the Crown of Castile sponsored the emigration of Spanish women to the Americas. Thirty of them left on the third voyage of Christopher Columbus. Together with their servants they contributed to the expansion of Spanish civilization. The laws of succession gave them the right to their inheritance, which enhanced their authority when they happened to be only daughters. Consequently mixed marriages were rare, although liaisons between Spaniards and the Indian women were not infrequent. The concern for *limpia sangre* (pure blood) remained quite strong, if only to enable people to rise to the highest offices. The purity of blood was maintained as much as possible, wherever these high offices were available, especially in Lima and in Mexico.

In such a context the fear of rape by an Indian or by a black becomes an obsession, as it did later for the Europeans in North Africa. Yet the records of the cases that were brought in the eighteenth century before the Real Audiencia de Mexico testify to the aggressors being Indians in only half the cases, and Spaniards in more than a quarter of them. They do not provide substance to the stereotype. On the other hand the complaints relate mainly to aggressors and victims belonging to the lower classes, citizens of influence appearing rarely. Were they successful in warding off lawsuits? The ethnic pattern of the rapes sheds light on their true meaning. By far the most numerous attacks were those by Indian men on Indian women, while the Spaniards only very rarely attacked the women of their country. It may then be argued that it was the Indian woman who suffered under the double repression of Indian men. At the same time, the Spanish aggressor, whom the Indian men emulated was subject to the excesses of a conqueror's behaviour. Nevertheless in both cases rape was a challenge as much as a need, for half of the aggressors were married (Giraud, 1986).

The difference between the Spanish policy of emigration and that of the Portuguese was that the latter allowed single men to settle overseas. Large numbers of Portuguese women settled only in Morocco and in the Azores. As a result concubinage and inter-racial marriages in Brazil made it possible for half-breeds and subsequently mulattos to belong to the colonial society. A large proportion of the Portuguese of Brazil who were fascinated by the beauty of the Indian women, already had mixed blood. The black mistress soon took over from the Indian woman and accordingly incorporated many African cultural traits into the Portuguese customs. Through this "voluptuous" racial integration the Portuguese, it has been said, conquered the world, not with the sword and the cross, but with sex. This may be an exaggeration for the other two instruments of domination were never far away. With the passage of time cross-breeding also became a form of defence on the part of the founders of the country, the *Brasileiros de quatrocentos anos* (the Brazilians of four hundred years) – that is, the "true" Brazilians, as opposed to the purely white immigrants, the Italians, and especially the Germans – in order to distinguish better the identity of the nation.

The exclusively masculine nature of the emigration is also typical of the Portuguese settlement in India. Over two centuries, from 1549 to 1750, only one Viceroy's wife accompanied her husband. The same was true of the governors and other members of their retinues. The need was felt to adapt to the interdicts concerning unbaptized women because, in Kerala, where the Portuguese settled, they were said to be the most enterprising in all India. Don Francisco de Almeida, the Viceroy, thought that the simplest way out consisted in baptizing the most seductive of them. That was how several generations of mixed-race people came about, with the women accompanying their men to Macao and to the Moluccas.

In Brazil and in India, the practice of inter-racial marriages prevailed at all the levels of the population: it provided a means of social promotion, with illegitimate daughters benefiting from dowries and being quite often legitimatized. But, while these unions were tolerated at the beginning of the colonization they soon came to be frowned upon among the highest classes with the setting up of a whole apparatus of discrimination. It was better for a Portuguese to marry an Indian woman – either from Brazil or from India – than a converted Jewish or a mulatto woman. A reaction set in, coming from higher up and pressure was exerted on creole girls to perpetuate the purity of blood. We shall describe below a similar evolution in British India: this example further brings into question many stereotypes relating to different types of colonization.

In the history of Amerindian racial mixing the important point to note is that mixed-race people tended towards integration and assimilation only by breaking away from the pure Indians and from the pure Africans, that is, by forming a separate group. The policy of creating castes by the establishment of a "pigmentocratic" system (Mörner, 1967) proved to be a failure because the process that had been initiated continued to evolve to the point where the former Spanish/Indian opposition was replaced by that between cattle-breeder and peon. At this stage the mixed race and the pure white were lumped together in a group known as *ladinos*, hispanized Indians, in opposition to the Indians as such. Social considerations interfered with racial ones.

By contrast the mulattos in Brazil formed an intermediate stage. Despite any mixed-race people, however dark their skin, being able to climb up the social ladder, there emerged from the end of the nineteenth and in the twentieth century, a sclerosis, an obstruction generated by the resistance of the "integrated" metis.

The vocabulary of the pigmentocratic system defines all the forms of cross-breeding, all the variables of miscegenation: metis (Spanish male + Indian), castizo (metis + Spanish female), mulatto (Spanish female + Black), morisco (Spanish male + mulatto female), albino (morisca + Spanish male), torna atras (Spanish male + albina), lobo (Indian male + torna atra). The designations are not the same in Peru where they spoke of quadroon, quinteron or zambo (black male + Indian female). Of them all it was the black woman who suffered the greatest decline in status, in comparison with the distant time when she lived in Africa.

The fate of the black slave woman was worse than that of the men

The fate of black women became even worse than that of the male slaves.[1] The subject of black women's power in slavery is an echo of the jealousy felt by black males, or by the white women, when a white man abused a black woman or took her as a concubine. This is in sharp contrast with the fate of the white women, in so far as comparison has any meaning.

The emigrants of European stock to the French possessions in the Caribbean Islands were very small in number. Between 1695 and 1915 6,200 men embarked from La Rochelle and 1,900 from Dieppe, but only 90 women. The only women present on the spot were the wives and daughters of cabin owners, and afterwards the daughters born on the islands. Moreover the women lived more freely than they did in the mother country. For instance, they accompanied their husbands when the latter went visiting, a practice which rarely occurred in the France of the seventeenth century. To have white wives and black concubines was evidently a common practice, with the white women avenging themselves as best they could for a frequently experienced affront. With their husbands being often absent, they exercised their power with harshness. But apart from the fate of the concubines, and afterwards of the mulatto women, there was no interruption in the degradation of the condition of the majority of the black female slaves.

In Africa, among the Congos, the Yorubas, Ibos and Angolas – who constituted the vast majority of the slaves transported to the West Indies – the men and the women enjoyed a sexual freedom greater than obtained in the Christian or Islamic world. In wedlock the rights and duties of the men and of the women were clearly defined. The wives afterwards remained dependent, but, in the Bambara country, they participated in the men's conversation, even if men and women did not take their meals together (as in the Basque country) – the wives attended to their husbands and took their meals afterwards, standing. In a general sense travellers of the seventeenth and eighteenth centuries were struck by the independent spirit and behaviour of African women, even though they had to do their share of work in the fields in addition to the home tasks over which they often exercised sole authority. The dominant polyandry fostered a sense of solidarity among women which was absent in the Western world. That did not prevent the wife showing respect towards each of her husbands, a characteristic which, in the eighteenth century, surprised Father Labat.

In the Americas and especially in the Caribbean Islands, the problem is knowing if the owners were seeking to increase their human capital by means of the slave trade, or rather by encouraging births on the plantations. In *Masters and slaves* Gilberto Freyre in 1933 wrote that in Brazil economic interest drove masters and their sons to transform themselves into studs to increase their capital. In the main, however, except for short periods, only economic exchange and purchase prevailed. And the man was worth more than the woman, except as a sexual object.

The degradation of the condition of the women slaves derived from the fact that in the sugar refineries, for example, they were kept away from the specialized tasks. At first there was no difference in status between the man working at the furnace and the woman working at the mill, between the men digging the holes and the women who deposited the seeds in them. But qualified men were in greater number, and their value depended on their abilities. In contrast what determined the status of a woman was only her sexual value, which declined with age and maternity. Moreover women were given the use of traditional tools, such as the hoe, the thread, the needle, while the men learnt to build houses, casks, irons for the slaves. Thus the men soon acquired a monopoly of technical skills. According to Arlette Gautier, this division of abilities and labour maintained the subordination of women and even rendered it worse, with the result that slavery, far from levelling the condition of men and women, culminated on the contrary in an additional debasement of the woman in the white household, and subsequently in the black family for, in a disintegrated or fragmented black society, she no longer benefited from the protections and privileges which the black woman enjoyed in Africa.

Blacks and Indians

The double system of the *encomienda* and the *repartimiento* had been established in the Spanish colonies. By the encomienda the conquerors received a certain number of natives who paid tribute to them. By the repartimiento the land was divided among a number of beneficiaries. At first the main thing was the tribute. Soon labour came to be valued most. Manpower was needed to exploit the mines and build roads. Wars, assorted massacres and disease destroyed all or part of the Carib, Indian and Arawak populations. Therefore the arrival of the slaves provided the colonists with several advantages. The slaves knew how to raise cattle, ride on horseback, so that the first cowboys of Hispaniola (San Domingo, Haiti) were Wolofs and Mandingos. Further, the slaves from the Gold Coast and Angola were often skilful craftsmen, which enhanced their value in relation to the Indians who, in the end, became more marginalized than the Africans within the genuinely colonial economy.

As early as the end of the sixteenth century, on the sugar plantations of Bahia as in the mines of New Granada, the large majority of the workers were blacks, the Chibchan Indians having slowly died out. Moreover, like the Escorial, the Portuguese government encouraged this slow substitution of one type of workers with another, for the transportation and the sale of the slaves on the continent brought the Crown all sorts of fiscal advantages, at the expense of the colonists and independently of the *asiento* already levied during the voyage from Africa. The role played by the blacks in the local militias increasingly furthered their accession to a central position in these new societies. In Guyana the French used blacks against the Carib population. So did the Dutch, like Peter Stuyvesant in New Amsterdam, as well as the English of the Massachusetts who appealed to "the Scots and the blacks" to get rid of the Indians.

Europeans exploited the antagonism between the blacks and the Indians. In this way they diverted the aggressivity of the blacks, either against citizens of the mother country – for example, during the wars of independence in Latin America and in the United States – but above all against the Indians.

The antagonism existed *because the Indians were always held to be free, while the blacks were always slaves.* That is why the Indian despised the black. In New Granada, in the sixteenth century, when his daughter was betrothed to a black, an Indian lodged a complaint before a court of justice, "for, being distinct by the purity of blood, our race is equal to that of the nobles, and accordingly my daughter cannot be united to the class which is held to be most vile". This did not prevent the Indian women from going with Blacks. "She offers herself to the Indian out of matrimonial duty, to the white man for money, to the negro for pleasure" (Saint-Hilaire, 1821).

Gilberto Freyre says that in Brazil the three races collaborated each in its own way, at least in the sugar refineries of the Bahia region. The white woman owned the estate and managed it, the black toiled, the Indian protected the refinery from pirates and other Indians. During the time of the *bandeirantes*, in those expeditions carried out in the south towards the hinterland "the Indian walked in front clearing the path, followed by the whites and the metis, while the black closed the column at the rear, bearing the burdens, making arrangements for the rests".

Black fugitives and black resistance

The trauma of transportation was so severe that scarcely had they landed in the Caribbean Islands than the "new blacks" desired nothing but to escape. The colonists who understood the problem tried to soften the shock and acclimatize the slave before placing him in the workshop. But the despair of the blacks was such that they took to mutilating or strangling themselves, more than trying to kill their new master. One of them smashed his head against a stone. Even entire groups committed suicide, as did fugitives from the Danish island of Saint John when they were surrounded by the French troops in 1734. Similar behaviour was noticed among fugitives attacked by the British in the nineteenth century in St Vincent. "Thirty of them hanged themselves in a single house", Malenfant reports in his *Histoire de Saint-Domingue* published in 1814. "I know one owner who, the following day, out of four hundred negroes, found three hundred and eight hanging", Xavier Eyma records at about the same time. Some Ibos hanged themselves in order to return to their own country. At first one of the techniques used was to group the "Congos", or others, together with a view to reducing their despair. But suicide or escape thus became a form of resistance to the master. Above all for those who had become "accustomed", escape could help in gaining one's freedom, or in acquiring a certain measure of promotion. The gap grew between the blacks engaged in hoeing and cultivation and the "talented" or "day-worker" blacks, with the latter trying to merge with the class of freed slaves. "Claiming to speak French well, a little Spanish, and stating that he was free, a mulatto, a shoemaker by profession, came to the cabaret..." (quoted in Debasch, 1961). But the blacks working with the hoe also escaped. The insufficient diet and ill treatment, usually to save money, lay at the root of the fear which their discontent provoked in the hearts of the masters. Often the blacks forewarned their masters by means of a strike before disappearing. On many occasions the fugitive found a hiding place at a neighbouring owner's. The latter would remain silent, pretending not to see him. But what happened afterward?

External refuges were rare, practically non-existent in the small islands. Soon, however, networks were established which pointed to Dominique and St Vincent as regions of freedom. The only thing that mattered was to reach them. The fugitive also tried to take refuge with the Spanish because in the Spanish possessions administrative apathy made it possible for him to hope to be granted, or to be able to buy, his freedom. Indeed, despite several agreements, the risks of extradition were more theoretical than real. In Guyana it is known that the interior of the land can be reached where strong colonies of fugitives are constituted.

A latent war opposed slave society to its manpower. The fugitive was always an enemy who "had stolen the asset of the master" and weakened the established order. His desertion deserved punishment and the master wanted to get back in the workshop what he paid for him at the slave market. Sometimes, however, there was a need to offer an amnesty, with the promise of emancipation to come later. In other words, a need to negotiate a deal, as the English sometimes did in Jamaica. But public authority and domestic authority clashed on the matter of the real ownership of power and did not share the same goals. In 1750 a Guyanese police regulation laid down that "the masters have not considered the derelictions of their slaves as other than being personal with regard to themselves, as if the freedom which they have to own slaves, was not granted to them under the express condition that they should be responsible for their conduct with regard to the public". Consequently, when the Black Code was re-issued at the end of the eighteenth century for the benefit of the notables, it was found to be irrelevant to the prevailing situation, given the fact that slaves were running away. Thereupon the planters adopted another method: "When, by dint of caring, and by means of a few punishments, I succeed in offering one of my negroes the ownership of his earnings, I am then really his master. Pride, self-esteem hold sway over him; he becomes more careful, and rarely makes a mistake. The harshest punishment is to deprive him of the time to go to town. It is quite effective." Gardens were also handed over to the slaves, though the opportunity to work in them was meagrely doled out. In this way the owner profited because it cost him less to feed the slave's household.

The revolt of the "runaways"

Revolts by the blacks in America were extremely numerous. But since they failed to succeed, with the exception of Haiti, they have not earned the place in history that they deserve. Yet, as early as the sixteenth century there were 3 revolts in San Domingo and at least 10, between 1649 and 1759, in the different British West Indies; 6 in the seventeenth century and about 50 in the eighteenth century in the south of the future United States. In the French West Indies, in the north of Brazil and in Puerto Rico, the number of revolts increased following the independence of Haiti.

Admittedly, these revolts did not succeed. Nevertheless the runaways of Guyana gave birth to "republics of runaways". Even if these have not survived, they nevertheless existed, in Colombia, and above all in Guyana. The one which lasted longest was that of the Bonis of Guyana, who rose against the Dutch, with the encouragement of the French. When, in 1712, French sailors entered Surinam, the big owners fled and the slaves seized the opportunity to escape to the forests but not before ransacking the houses of their masters. Adoc, their chief, obtained independence in 1749, while another chief, Arabi, probably a Muslim, was granted the freedom to establish a republic provided he did not accept runaways. A third runaway republic was founded in 1762, with a Dutch adviser by the side of the black chief. But when the Bonis wanted to drive the whites away from the region, some of the blacks, apprehensive about their hegemony, joined forces with the Dutch. In their turn the Bonis were forced to sign an agreement with France and restrict themselves to the High-Maroni, where the Bosh, or Bush-Negroes, or black men of the forest have survived ever since. Their culture is a Fanti-Ashanti syncretism having its origin in Africa, especially as regards religion, blended with Indian dietary practices, and a language that consists of a mixture of African, Dutch, English and French words.

Two hundred years later, in 1991, Haiti still celebrates the uprising, in August 1791, of the slave Boukman, which in 1804 culminated in the first independence of a colonized people. Victory is always placed under the aegis of Voodoo which at the time of Toussaint Louverture gave the Blacks the power to fight and defeat the armies of Bonaparte and later of Napoleon. There followed other revolutions, inspired by the slogan "Freedom or Death". In 1848 in the Danish Virgin Islands the situation became so serious that independence was proclaimed even before the arrival of the decree from the mother country.

Accordingly, as the agents of liberty, the French Revolution and the Voodoo are viewed as having been equally effective, with the blessing of the Catholic Church which today, under the presidency of the Abbé Aristide, claims this heritage and the oath of the Caiman woods (cf. Najman's film, *Le serment du bois Caïmon*).

But did this first big victory by the slaves mean the "end of history" for the Haitians? Far from seizing the opportunity and using whatever good colonization had brought or created, they turned away from it and allowed instead those industries to die out so that they could rebuild elsewhere an African way of life. In a certain way they stood still in time, as if to perpetuate that unique moment on which the other Caribbean peoples looked with envy.

In the Americas, the forms of black resistance varied widely. At one end of the spectrum there was the revolt and the flight of the runaways, at the other, the sabotaging of work, a practice which gave rise to the myth of the lazy negro – a myth which one also encounters in South-East Asia regarding the "lazy native". All the varieties of cultural syncretism were present among the descendants of runaway slaves. They have been studied in Cujila, Mexico: the preservation of attitudes, such as carrying children on the back and packages on the head, the construction of round houses, the arrangements for wives, with the *queridas* (the beloved ones) living in different quarters. These attitudes wither away or get transformed through relations with other communities. But they continue to live thanks to the festivals and other "forms of freedom which constitute the institutional structure of the survival of the songs, dances and other artistic, particularly musical, expressions of Africa" (R. Bastide, *Les Amériques noires*). In New

England the organization of these festivals even becomes the core of a type of counter-power exercised by the "Governor" whose preeminece was recognized by the whites. Often he was a descendant of kings and negotiated with the master. The masters readily brought the delinquents before these "governors" for justice, thereby turning the anger of the slaves against members of their own community. Of a "religious" nature, such survivals were carefully preserved wherever the white man remained powerful. However those places where the white man disappeared, as in Haiti, they evolved. Here Voodoo transformed itself and became a sort of national peasant religion, while in Brazil or in Trinidad it has better preserved its African characteristics.

For their part the converted slaves preserved their African heritages better in Catholic countries where they gave rise to various forms of syncretism. This did not obtain in the Protestant countries where the black was welcomed as a member of the church only after acquiring a perfect instruction. Evangelization thus brought about the disappearance of African heritages. Has the black thereby acquired a white soul? Frantz Fanon has dealt with this question in *Peau noire, masques blancs* ("Black skin, white masks"). It has also become the object of a "scientific" debate between Herskovits and G. F. Frazier and raises the whole issue of racism and assimilation.

The birth of the Creole

In his will of 1547, Hernan Cortez asked that, if he died in Spain, his remains should be brought to Mexico and buried in the monastery of the Franciscan Nuns of the Conception, in *his* town of Cocoya. Cortez thus was the first of the Creoles to feel that Mexico was his real fatherland.

This identity with a land other than that of one's ancestors is the first indication of the widening gap which separated the metropolitan from the Creole. In Mexico, the Creoles of Spanish stock underwent, imperceptibly and without necessarily accepting the fact, an absorption by the pervasive environment, by the many facets of its culture. In *Les Espagnols dans le Mexique colonial* Solange Alberro has correctly observed that the colour of the Franciscan habit varies in Mexico. While beige continued to exist in tradition as the colour of the frock of the poor, the Franciscans adopted blue, the symbolic colour which the Mexicans associated with the warrior god of the sun, Huitzilopochtli. The ruined temple of this god provided the basis for the first Franciscan foundations. All sorts of borrowings mark the development of this inverted colonization: the wearing of the padded tunic, the *ichcahuipilli* hispanized as *escaubil*, such different, but now well known, foods as chocolate, tobacco, beans and especially the corn tortilla, as its harvesting, grinding and preparation required less labour than wheat bread. Moreover the consumption of the tortilla contributed to that

114

"idleness" to which the Spaniard effortlessly surrendered. To a greater extent in the isolated villages, though in the cities too, Indian customs "contaminated" the Spaniards: their children were brought up by Indian nannies and they were themselves served by the cooks of the country. The traditional use of time is thus assailed by all sorts of new customs. For instance, as early as the eighteenth century the Creole is seen as eating almost all day long. He drinks chocolate in the morning, has his breakfast at nine, eats something at eleven, has a meal soon after noon. He takes chocolate again following his siesta and later his dinner. This common custom of repeated consumption went hand in hand with conditions which, in a marked difference from what obtained in Europe, excluded the use of salted and smoked foods. The Creole lived on fruit, vegetables and fresh produce, not in the organization of a product meant for the future. He lived in a short present, not in the long present of his Spanish cousin.

Another feature distinguished the Creole: he was recognized by his dress, which betrayed his belonging to a particular ethnic and social group. While the Indians went about naked, with some of them trying to assimilate with the metis and accordingly wearing socks and shoes, and the blacks and the mulattos distinguished themselves by their sumptuous attire, the Spaniards strove to outdo them all by carrying arms and covering themselves with jewelery. This display of luxury contrasted sharply with the Indian simplicity. But it was also a necessary response to and emulation of the ancient Aztec or Inca courts. Moreover when the Creole returned to Cadiz he felt he had to show off the munificence of the Americas in relation to Spain.

Accordingly, in the Americas, the Creole increasingly enhanced his difference from his metropolitan cousin, both by the signs necessitated by his status and by conscious or unconscious borrowings from the civilization of those he had vanquished.

The Indians were undoubtedly really converted. But they not only persisted in their idolatry, they managed to contaminate the people of mixed race and sometimes even the Creoles and their priests. As a result the Indian succeeded in realizing a sort of *inverted colonization*. Is it then a mere coincidence that the fathers of the Creole identity, the ideologues of the independence movements, were sometimes priests, like Hidalgo and Morelos in Mexico who, more than others, felt greater affinity with the Indians and the Metis?

The Anglo-Indians

British India is one of the cases which provides early information on the problem of the relationships between the colonized and the colonizers and mixed marriages.

As early as 1793 Henry Dundas, the president of the Board of Control of the East India Company, drew attention to the danger of an excessive number of Englishmen in the country, "because this would alter the idea which the natives have of the superiority of the European man". This judgement was aimed at the Eurasians, of which the same company was, a century earlier, advocating the proliferation. But a complete break occurred when it was decided in 1791 to deny people of mixed race the right to serve in the Company. This sudden break completely altered the situation.

The reason given to justify it was that the Indians despised Eurasians and as a result the entire prestige of the Company stood to be adversely affected. Moreover, considering their aristocratic way of life, the directors did not look kindly on the accession of "half-castes" to the highest offices. Another non-acknowledged reason was that the London authorities had been struck by the fact that, during the French Revolution, the revolt in Haiti was brought about by the mulattos. That was something to be reckoned with.

This interdict drove the English to express their frustration, particularly in relation to Burmese women, who were considered to be endowed with all the charms and all the virtues. The clergy were at a loss as to how to react, for the Church frowned upon extra-marital relationships. These, however, developed and grew with impunity. During the Victorian years Lord Curzon tried to draw up new guidelines. Those who married native women had to realize that their careers would be hampered. The same for those who kept mistresses, whom they should no longer display in all circumstances. Otherwise the offender would be transferred. This resulted in a perverse effect: many military and civilian officers posted in the outlying regions began to sport Indian mistresses: by so doing they hoped to be transferred to a more central place, preferably Bombay or Delhi. "Such a regulation ought not to prevent a good official from marrying his mistress . . . ", commented a contemporary observer. But a real problem had emerged.

With the passage of time the number of Englishmen living with Indian women declined. And one knows very little – except through novels or films – of those rare Indian men who lived with an Englishwoman.

The 1951 census records 111,637 Eurasians. In 1926, in *Hostages to India*, H. A. Stark, himself a Eurasian, wrote: "If England is the land of our fathers, India is that of our mothers. England is a sacred souvenir, India a living truth . . . England is our traditions, India our daily life." An analysis, drawn from the *Anglo-Indian Review* (with a 3,000 circulation) and extended by an investigation bearing on the period 1926–59, gives an idea of what the situation was for an officially recognized community which had the right to have two representatives in the Indian parliament. At first they were known as *half-breed*, then *Chichi, East-Indian, Eurasian, Indo-Britons*, but in the end the term "Anglo-Indian" prevailed. They still bore the stigma of being despised by the British and by the Indians, which explains the status of inferiority in which the Anglo-Indians were held. The Englishman was more sympathetic to the views of an Indian than to those of an Anglo-Indian. This stigma weighed down heavily on the members of a community who very soon felt the need to acquire a legal status. They adopted western customs in their dress, in their eating habits, particularly at breakfast, above all in their education. The emancipation consequent upon modernity enabled young Anglo-Indians to join the administration, the postal services, or the railways where they monopolized the jobs. As a result very few of them pursued higher studies, which could have enabled them to fulfil the highest responsibilities.

Following the First World War, during the period of the great political struggles, the Anglo-Indians found themselves in a distressing situation. Having gradually adopted British customs, they feared that with independence the indianization process would jeopardize their situation and that, with the general decline in the standard of living, they would be the first to be affected, considering that they had been working in a world hitherto controlled by the British. Most of them were not practising Christians. Yet they feared the return of religious intolerance, on the part either of Muslims or Hindus. Above all they feared the revival of the prohibitions and obligations pertaining to the caste system from which they had succeeded in emancipating themselves.

The fate of the Anglo-Indians revealed to some extent the change that had occurred in the nature of the British presence in India.

In the eighteenth century, the British had been mostly merchants. Their number was small. The soldiers were still less numerous. But the situation changed, in 1746, with the Anglo-French conflicts. Thus, at that date, there were 200 soldiers in Fort St David at Madras; 589 in 1748; 1,758 in 1759 during the siege, and 2,590 in 1769. At that time there were only 253 civilians. One may add to the military the ever increasing number of the officials of the East India Company. The military presence was only temporary, with the soldiers living apart in their barracks or in camps. But the Company officials came into contact with the Indians, with the *nawabs* (governors) and the *zamindars* (landlords). Gradually they became indianized, they got richer and adopted the tastes of the nawabs. Consequently two tendencies seem to have functioned at cross purposes: on one hand the military people europeanized themselves, largely on account of the purely royal status of the army which represented tradition, on the other hand the civil servants grew more and more indianized. But under the Governorship of Lord Cornwallis the situation changed: the administration became increasingly scandalized by the methods used by all sorts of adventurers and others of the same ilk who took advantage of their wealth, of their power and of His Majesty's army. A report concluded that the harm arose out of a too large presence of the English in India. With the arrival of more English women who substituted dances and parties for performances by Indian Nautch girls and anglicized the homes, the process of disjoining the two societies became accelerated. As if henceforth India was to leave its mark on the Englishman simply by turning him into a caricature: "The major put on his pyjamas and his sandals, then he came out onto the verandah of his bungalow to sip a cup of tea." The gap between the two societies grew and that was how racism was born.

Besides, as the novelist Annie Steel explains, it became dangerous to try to probe the arcana of Indian life. It was indecent; worse – it was ridiculous. When one of her characters, the policeman Strickland, becomes a *sanyasi* (ascetic) in order better to approach his beloved, Miss Yughal, he becomes a comic figure:

> A strange man, this Strickland, from whom people would turn away. Did he not propound the absurd theory that a policeman must know as much of India as the natives themselves? He wallows in the stinking places which no self-respecting man would dream of exploring . . . Soon he is initiated into the Sat Bhai, in Allahabad, and learns the song of the lizzard of the Sansis, as well as the dance of the Hallihuk which is a rather surprising sort of religious cancan. But then people were wondering why did Strickland not stay in his office?

Anyway there was no need to try to understand India. The British thought – as Françoise Sagan would have said – that India was like a woman who does not want to be understood, but to be held.

Several decades later – as the writings of Annie Steel, Alice Perrin, or even Rudyard Kipling show – life in India seems to be marked more by dances and picnics than by suffering. India is divided into tigers, jungles, dances, cholera and the Sepoys. But for participation in the latter capacity, the Indian leaves the scene or appears only as the groom, until in the cinema he takes on the role of a traitor or of someone who cannot be trusted (cf. G. Stevens' film *Gunga Din*). Or rather, the Indian is represented as the opposite of what constitutes a genuine Englishman: discipline, physical prowess, organization, sense of honour. The abject shame of the heroine of one of Crooker's novels is that she gave herself, during the Indian Mutiny, to an Indian in order to save herself from the massacre. She has lost all sense of dignity . . .

Pieds-noirs and Arabs

The teacher used to say: "Children, love France, your new fatherland." In 1939 the 150th anniversary of the French Revolution was celebrated in Algiers with a march-past by young Arabs and Moors. The former paraded attired like the "sans-culottes", the latter with their brows wreathed with a tricolour crown. For "wherever it can France intends to spread its language, its customs, its flag, its genius", Jules Ferry used to say. But today in the Aurès, in the Atlas, one may ask: should not a century or so of French presence have had more of an effect than that of a tick on a camel's tail?

Obviously, large areas of social life in the Maghreb remained untouched and almost ignored by French colonization: the souks of Fez, the mosques and the madrasas hidden from the searching eye of the Christian. Indeed in the time of Lyautey the European city had its life apart, with its tarred roads, far from the native quarters, that is, the negro market, as they called it in Oran. Separated only by a police station, two cities lay one adjoining the other, while hating and ignoring each other. This is how Frantz Fanon describes them in his *Les damnés de la terre*.

The colonist's city is an expression of strength, built with stones and iron. It is a city with lights, with roads covered with asphalt, where the trash cans overflow with left-overs that have never been known, not even seen in dreams. No one ever sees the feet of the colonist, except on the beach. Their feet are protected by sturdy shoes, though the streets of their towns are smooth, without pot-holes, without gravel ... The native town is a disreputable place. It is a hungry town, starving for meat, for shoes, for light. It is a town of people squatting, a town full of Arab wogs ...

The colonized looks at the colonist's town with eyes filled with lust, with envy. His dreams of possession imagine him sitting at the colonist's table, sleeping in his bed, preferably with his wife. The colonist is not unaware of it: "They want to take our place." It is true. There is not a single colonized individual who does not dream at least once every day of sitting in the colonist's seat.

Apart from the school, the hospital, the army, the only exchanges between the colonizer and the colonized occur in the workplace.

The Arabs were good only for manual jobs or any kind of chore, or to work as dockers, or as porters ... One day the mayor of Algiers called and asked who had done that job. The head of the plant came up and said: "The Mayor is down below, he wants to congratulate you. Get dressed." I shrugged off this request and I kept my working clothes on. I came down. The Mayor was there. I can still see all those clots in front of me. The whole tribe was there. The commission, that is. Then he said: "You did this job? I want to congratulate you." "I have received so many congratulations that my pockets are full of them. They even overflow." He said: "What do you mean?" I answered: "We are poorly paid. You have here fathers of families who

119

earn only 40 Francs a day. To hell with your congratulations. What matters is the piece of steak."

("An Arab tells the story of his life", *Socialisme et barbarie*, 1959)

As the saying went: "Arab's wages."

In Morocco and in Algeria

At least in principle the spirit of the colony was not the same in Algeria and in the two protectorates. Algeria was conceived of as an extension of the mother country, with three departments, less – for the Arabs – the social advantages and the political rights. The protectorates had to set up a free association with France. Lyautey said: "The French contribute a more efficient administrative organization, the resources of a more advanced civilization, material means which make it possible to benefit from the resources of the country, and the power which guarantees safety against anarchy. Under this tutelary protection the Other maintains his status, his institutions, the free exercise of his religion, while exploiting his riches in an environment of order and peace."

However much the French have claimed it to their credit, this ideal of Lyautey did not last. Nevertheless it resulted in Morocco, and even Tunisia, creating relationships between the colonists and the colonized natives that were different from those which were established in Algeria.

In the first instance, the spirit of conquest spread to Morocco much later than elsewhere because, more than ten years after the war of the Riff, many zones in the Upper Atlas remained undefeated. The big companies called upon the army to provide better protection for their convoys. The "pacification" campaign flushed out warrior tribes, a relic of the Siba: the operations of "pacification" did not necessarily displease the Sultan, who thereby saw his own interests safeguarded, or even those populations who had fallen victim to the mountain tribes. This aspect of the "pacification" has been celebrated in the films based on the saga of colonialism: *La Bandera, Le Grand Jeu, Itto, Le Roman d'un spahi*.

The mass arrival of the colonizers who, in Algeria, occupied the best lands, or the lands that were reputed to be the best, and pushed the natives elsewhere, was the feature which has distinguished this country from the other two.

Behind the juridically contrived arguments this dispossession was acutely felt as an injustice, as a theft which "downgraded" the colonizer. As a result, especially in Algeria, the administration became, in the eyes of some, like Malek Benabi, synonymous with an "association of felons". Lyautey, in Morocco, tried to ward off such a reaction by limiting the number of the colonists. Instead he promoted the formation of large domains, held by companies, a practice which in the mother country fed the suspicion of the Left. But his successors – administrators or officers – did not know how, or did not want, to resist the pressure of the newcomers and the colonists who were insisting on having more land. Here too, as elsewhere, the European believed that "he does not deserve to own the land who does not make it fertile and in depriving the natives of their land they were actually serving their best interests". That is, the exploitation of the land by the colonists made it possible for the standard of living to rise. Nevertheless the small colonists in Morocco were less numerous than in Tunisia or in Algeria. But the big companies benefited from greater advantages, especially financially, than they did elsewhere.

Tradition and europeanization

The third problem relates to the fate of the traditions and customs of the natives. As a general rule these were not called into question insofar as they did not constitute an obstacle to European penetration and to the exploitation of the country. Otherwise they were forced to adjust.

Attachment to Islam and to Arab civilization formed the hard core of this confrontation.

In Morocco as in Algeria the French deliberately set the Kabyles and the Berbers against the more arabized populations of the big cities. Mistrust of Islam was always a corollary of this policy, even if, for tactical and strategic reasons, the religious leaders were always protected and made to serve as the power relays and representatives: from the Sultan of Morocco, a descendant of the Prophet, to the Ulemas, theologians respected by the French authorities. Being less arabized and less islamized, the Kabyles and the Berbers seemed likely to become good Christians in the near future. It must not be forgotten that in the Maghreb colonization was always a little reminiscent of the Crusade. One of the strong features of this policy was the segregation of the two religions, as if it was necessary to set Islam within limits before reducing it. This explains why Arabic, the language of the Quran, was held in little esteem. Certainly during the colonial period the Arabic language was recognized in education, but only as a foreign language, for example, as the first language in the baccalaureate pro- gramme. Students saw this limitation as a painful handicap. Indeed it provides substance to one of the most telling grievances on the part of the educated Arabs, especially in Algeria. They saw in it a political will. Lyautey was right – but in a different sense. He had strongly opposed all missionary activities; he refrained from entering a mosque in order to better express his respect for religion. In this way he openly upheld the rights of Islam and of the Sultan, its representative, in order to safeguard the "provincial" characteristic of Morocco, far from the heartland of Islam. For a long time it was possible to prevent all the books written in Arabic and published in Egypt and in Syria, even those published in Tunisia, from entering the Moroccan kingdom. He trusted in the religious autonomy of the country and accordingly preferred good students in theology to be trained in Fez rather than in Egypt or in Bagdad.

Another problem lay in the process of europeanization, of assimilation, that is, in the interpenetration of societies. "We are progressing", said the colonists, "but they neither move forward nor regress." Such an opinion was heard at the beginning of the century. Fifty years later it remained unchanged.

Indeed the improvement in the standard of living of the natives at the time of colonization has been evaluated only in terms of the criteria which the colonizers themselves selected. This improvement has even been denied and rejected by some non-Arab observers (for instance, A. Nouschi, for the period 1871–1919 in relation to the Constantinois). Nevertheless large collective benefits to a large extent accrued mainly to the colonists, while the natives had to content themselves with the scraps. The railways, the roads, the mines, the ports served mainly the interests of the colonizer. In 1958, the *Plan de Constantine* represented a great effort intended to benefit mainly the natives. But, late as it was, this project was only launched after the irreparable damage had been done.

Still the European example was an inspiration to the fellahs, in Morocco, as well as in Tunisia and in Algeria. In the early fifties they had started to equip themselves and to take part in the market economy. Interpenetration was no longer a one-way traffic.

Naturally, as institutions, the hospitals and the schools were the most appreciated. First in the order of approval came the schools, for they offered the right to be admitted to a better world: they were associated with the idea of progress. Even then a governor observed: "These schools enable the Arabs to go to the station, but then they do not have the right to take the train." In fact, in 1952, out of 706 doctors only 11 were Moroccans; and only 1 architect against more than 200 Europeans. The ratio was higher in Algeria and in Tunisia. Still these figures provide a measure of the situation. One fourth of the civil servants were Muslims, but they remained confined to the lower ranks. The Director of the Grande Poste of Oran said: "I could not bear to have an Arab *under* my orders, that is, as the head of a department." It was out of the question to obey an Arab. In 1954, a corps of several hundreds of officers had one, and only one, Arab "sous-préfet" (sub-prefect).

That posed a major problem. For a large number of Arabs had gone through the French schools: after their academic success, they faced rejection despite the hopes engendered by obtaining a genuine diploma. National education provided the only outlet; there were large numbers of Muslim instructors and teachers in the public institutions, at least in the lay schools and lycées. But the great majority of those who were not cut out for the teaching profession felt the disillusion most painfully, for at school, the teachers were most of the time friendly and understanding, as shown in Mohammed Lakhdar Hamina's film *La dernière image*. The teachers willingly gave a little push to gifted pupils who had difficulty in speaking French.

Only the Jews totally welcomed French civilization which they identified with progress and enlightenment. They were the first to be assimilated, at the outset in Algeria thanks to the Crémieux decree, but also in Tunisia and in Morocco. With the exception of those who wanted to remain Jewish at all costs, they also benefited by integration with the other "pieds-noirs", with the Spaniards, Italians and with the French of metropolitan stock. Those who stayed in the *mellah*, the Jewish quarter, have today gone to Israel, although many remain in Morocco where the King protects them. On the other hand those who left the mellah, crossed the avenue or the street, have become completely westernized and live, in France, like the other ordinary citizens. Above all young Jewish women were able to emancipate themselves, as a consequence of colonization. But what of the other women?

Frustration felt by the elites and ordinary racism

The question of the unsatisfied elites was raised in exactly the terms that the great colonizers had feared. Conflicts arose as soon as power became an issue. "You took charge of a young child. That was in 1912. He was wearing a dress of a size that fitted him. The child has grown and he still wears the same dress." In Algeria, where the myth of French departments survived, the establishment of a political regime based on inequality was all the more resented since, during the two wars, the Muslims did their duty and placed their trust in the words of the statesmen who, in the mother country, promised them equality and integration. As, during the time of its conquest, Algeria did not have structures as strong as those of Morocco or of Tunisia, resistance was channelled through the political parties, and to an equal degree even by the unions. It further asserted itself within more limited circles, that is, in households that remained adamantly rebellious as demonstrated in their rejection of mixed marriages.

Families remained as the inviolate refuges of self-identity and of Islam and accordingly offered the stiffest resistance to the politics of inequality. It is true that families sent their children to school for them to have an education, to be aware of technological progress, to flow with the stream of modernity. Some wished to be westernized and to become French, like Ferhat Abbas in Algeria. But in the face of the intransigence of their counterparts and of colonial rejection, most of them turned away from this project and explored other ways to emancipate themselves.

The Europeans wished History to stop in its course. With the sweat of their brow, with the help of "their" Arabs, they had had to, and had known how to, reconstruct their life there. This land was theirs. "Before us, it was the Middle Ages." They evinced no hatred for the Arabs so long as the latter asked only for a rise in wages. On the farms, for example in Oranie, the Europeans and the Arabs lived together, ate the same couscous, participated in each other's festivities, in the celebrations of births, of anniversaries. But mixed marriages did not exist, or if they did, they did so in small numbers.

One must not go beyond certain limits, as is illustrated by an incident involving Gandhi in South Africa, but which could have occurred in the North as well. It shows how racism works. Having purchased a ticket for the train leaving Durban for Johannesburg, Gandhi found that he could not ride in it as "a coolie travels only outside". In Pretoria Gandhi carefully scrutinized the regulations of the railways, insisted on having a first class ticket, thus provoking the ire of the clerk, for the latter had already refused to sell him a third class ticket. Meanwhile Gandhi had acquired a well tailored suit of a European cut and a tie.

The story brings out one of the salient features of the prevailing racism. The native most often is unaware that his greatest crime is an image cobbled together, "like false currency which is still legal tender" (Jean Cohen, *Les temps modernes*, 1955). In the mother country the worker owes his condition to chance, not to his essence. Overseas the colonized are at the same time both a class and a race. In other words they are not people, citizens like the others. Sometimes ordinary language bears witness to this distinction. On one occasion a European was testifying in court. The judge asked: "Were other witnesses there?" – "Yes, five, two men and three Arabs." Moreover they do not have names. In addition to being addressed as "tu" or "toi", the Arab was always called Mohamed, if a man, and Fatma, if a woman. In Algeria the natives gradually lost all their attributes. By 1950 there were only a few rare newspapers or publications written in Arabic, which had regressed to the status of an oral language, like a patois. The natives did not count any more, or they only half counted. "Does this doctor have many patients?" – "Yes, *but* they are only Arabs."

Hatred and all sorts of delusions burst forth as soon as the natives made their demands known and started to press them. What do people in the mother country know about the situation? What are the reforms worth, that they mean to implement in a society whose customs are a closed book to them? On the ground all the "pieds-noirs" turned into ultras. Though they were racist, they denied it, claiming allegiance to the ideas of the Left, of the Republic. Are they not the descendants of the outlaws of the historic days of June 48, of the communards of 1871? They are struggling against the obscuratism of Islam, promoting the civilization of progress, even "leading the Arabs up to the voting booths". Up to 30 percent of the pieds-noirs in the Oranie, by 1952, were voting for the Left. They were not even conscious of their racism, as was revealed when a communist leader in

Oran confided to Marc Ferro: "Even my Moorish maid would understand that." The author may record another piece of evidence of this racism when, in 1948, in his first history lesson, he told the 8th grade pupils of the Lycée Lamoricière that after the fall of the Roman Empire and the rise of Christianity he would be dealing with Arab civilization. At this he was interrupted by a loud burst of laughter. Two years later he came across a girl who did not attend school. "It is out of the question", her father said, "there are only Arabs in the school."

There is thus no need for an explanation of why the colonists fought tooth and nail to oppose the reforms proposed by the mother country. After all the "pied-noir" did not ask the metropolitans to understand him, simply to love him (Nora, 1961).

Symbolic figures

The societies constituted within the framework of colonization started new activities which grafted themselves on to the traditional forms of life. The plantations were the first establishments of an economic nature. They were one of the first distinguishing features of colonial society. In addition to the new cities which were built, with their distinctive architecture – particularly the churches – the colonies were subsequently criss-crossed with railways and dotted with hospitals and schools. All of these were signs of progress in the eyes of the conqueror.

The planter and his plantation

After the period of plunder or of the exploitation of mines, such as the Potosi, the plantation became, at first in the Americas, the centre of the colonial enterprise. Actually it was an original creation, the distinguishing feature of Europe and its conquests. Whether called *hacienda* or *estancia*, the *casa grande, great house* or *grande case* is the centre of the property. It has well defined characteristic features: control over natural resources like water and land, control over the labour force and over local and regional trade. Besides the property has the second characteristic of breaking away from the landscape and from the natural products of the country: the plants which are grown there have been brought from other continents. For examples: the Asian sugar-cane and the African coffee tree were brought to America, the American cocoa-tree, the hevea and tobacco were transported to Africa. A third characteristic consists in meeting the demands of consumers living in distant countries, either in Europe or in the temperate zones of America. Above all the landscape of the property is well ordered, dominated by the main residence of the Master, the Casagrande and by the *engerros, engins, engehos de assucar* for sugar in Brazil. Further away stand the workers' shacks, *senzalas* in Brazil. In a separate plot are cultivated potatoes, yams, bananas which provide food for the slaves who themselves have been brought from far away places.

The plantations represent an aggressive form of European intervention in the tropical countries. They have given rise to entirely new human situations which the slaves or those who were reduced to forced labour had to endure.

Especially in the Caribbean Islands the slave was the central character on the plantation – together with the Master's family: he had been brought over from Africa, on the understanding that America provided the land and Africa the workers. At the outset, naturally, the white man came to raise a fortune, not to work. But very soon he observed that, once he became accustomed, the black man worked less or poorly, so he preferred to buy "new" more docile ones. Moreover the slave who had been raised on the spot cost more than the imported slave. For instance, Jamaica went from 45,000 slaves in 1703 to 205,000 in 1778, though during the same period it had imported 359,000 Africans. However the slave soon escaped, as we have seen earlier, and "runaways" became one of the first signs of the slaves' reaction against their fate. Still their departure confronted the plantation owners with their first problem.

By the time the termination of the slave trade was rightly honoured in practice – first by the English – a large number of slaves had already disappeared into the hinterland, at least wherever it was possible – in Jamaica, in San Domingo, and elsewhere. Consequently the colonists had to rely on another source of manpower which they expected to be more docile. From India it was sent to Trinidad, but also to Reunion Island and to Mauritius. By 1950, in British Guyana, there were 190,000 workers of African descent and 270,000 of Asian descent on the plantations. This ratio obtained also in Trinidad.

A second change set in. In the eighteenth century the typical plantation could be found in the West Indies or in Brazil. By the nineteenth century the plantations in these regions had been impoverished and suffered regression and decay, with the absenteeism of the masters acting as a major cause of this process of decline. The plantation henceforth prospered in Ceylon (Sri Lanka), in India, in Indonesia or in Indo-China – before they were hit by decolonization. In the ancient spice island that was Ceylon, British capital covered about a million hectares of land with tea, coconut and rubber plantations. The plantations were set up on uncultivated land and they became enclaves that made minimal use of the local economic channels and exported their profits. The same situation obtained in French Indo-China. Soon the Ceylonese discovered that the lands into which, from time to time, they would make a foray, were being taken away from them. Accordingly they refused to share in their maintenance. The reasons were different from those which confronted the West Indian owners. But the effects were similar. The British relied on Tamil workers brought from the continent. Soon the latter numbered about a million on the island, a situation which has spawned severe problems, especially since the independence of Sri Lanka in 1947.

With the juxtaposition of the plantations – or of other industrial enterprises – and the traditional forms of production, an economic reversal came about, with frustrations and conflicts following in its wake. French Indo-China is a typical example.

The Indo-Chinese reversal

On the eve of the Second World War, the French considered that, together with Morocco, Indo-China was one of the finest jewels in their colonial crown. In only half a century the French had accomplished this work in Indo-China with their own resources, in contrast with Morocco where the local society had earlier experienced other contacts with Christian powers and the contribution of the Republic was less well defined.

At the time of the heyday of glory Indo-China was traditionally represented as two bags of rice – Tonkin and Cochin-China – linked by a staff, Annam. What is striking about this image is that it corresponds to what colonization had made of Vietnam, to the way in which the country had been transformed, for before the arrival of the French the prevailing situation was just the opposite: it was Annam that provided the basic resources. A reversal had set in. While it did not fail to benefit the colonizers, it impelled the population to rise against them.

As a matter of fact the practice in Vietnam had been to develop colonial interests in those regions that had been little exploited earlier, in the empty spaces, if this term may be used. Such, for example, were the coalmines of Hongay and Dong Trieu in Tonkin, with their harbour of Campha, created *ex nihilo*; the rubber plantations on the scarcely inhabited plateaus of the Terres Rouges of Cochin-China; and the coffee plantations that were intensively cultivated in the half empty zones in the middle region of Tonkin. When the French first landed the harbour of Haiphong was merely a small village. There were other more active ports in the region. But Haiphong was created to serve the cement factories set up in the region and because it was the terminus of the railway which went up as far as Kunming in the Yunan (see H. Pia, quoted in Chesneaux, 1965).

Far fewer were the activities of the colonial period which, with French initiative and support, maintained continuity with the earlier activities, like the mines of non-ferrous metals in Tonkin, renewed with modern technology, and certain capitalist companies, particularly those concerned with zinc. Continuity is also evident in the case of Saigon harbour which was active before the arrival of the French who developed it still further.

127

On the other hand discontinuity prevailed in the centre of Vietnam. The pre-colonial activities there declined, such as the zone of Bindiah with its wealth of sugar-cane, silk, tobacco; the ports of Qui-nhon and Faïfo too which were active before the coming of the French and went downhill. This decline was linked to changes in the trade pattern of Vietnam, but it was felt to be a result of the French presence, as was the decay of craftsmanship in north Tonkin. Again the decline of the peasantry and of tree cultivation impoverished local business. Further the interruption of the economic relations with China dried up a traditional market (Chesneaux, 1965).

Priority given to commerce with the mother country led to the neglect of all production meant for the internal market and resulted in the disloca-tion of erstwhile complementary regions. For example, the north-south link was taken care of by the railway only late. But in 1920 two-thirds of its revenue came from passengers, not from the movement of goods. Benefiting the French companies, the exploitation of the country disturbed a social equilibrium, and generated movements of migration, thus bringing about an impoverishment felt and resented as a degeneration. Between 1890 and 1937 the rice fields belonging to French companies increased from 11,000 to 800,000 hectares, with the result that 45 percent of rice production was held in the hands of the colonizers (who numbered scarcely 80,000 out of 20 million inhabitants). The production of rubber was outstanding. The output of the mines was satisfactory. The consortium which, in 1898, was set up under the leadership of the Banque d'Indochine, grouped together all the big French banks (Société Générale, Comptoir National d'Escompte) as well as the Société de Batignolles, the Régie Générale des Chemins de fer. The balance sheet represents 16 percent of the capital absorbed by the Empire. Public investments amounted to nearly double the private investments (426 to 230), according to Jacque Marseille.

But, on the unhealthy building sites of Tonkin, out of 100 workers who arrived from healthy regions driven by the above-mentioned economic imbalances, 25 were eliminated by death or evacuation by the end of a six month period. The working ability of the group diminished by 44 percent. The commentary on this in colonial language reads: "In India [also], from 1901 to 1931, malaria directly killed thirty million persons. It indirectly [i.e. in furthering the action of other diseases] killed more men still. But perhaps *the most serious* fact is that one death by malaria corresponds to at least 2,000 days of sickness, that is, of unavailability" (*sic*).

In Vietnam the first grave incidents were directed against the recruiting agents. Soon the Yen Bai garrison rose in revolt (1930), followed by the great peasant march in Nghe An, Ha Tinh, and Quang Ngai, that is, between the two bags, along the staff – in Annam.

The administrator and forced labour

Especially in Equatorial Africa complex techniques of exchange replaced the original "barter", in the wake of the deeper penetration of the Europeans in their conquests during the nineteenth century. The use of currency became widespread. As a source of profit and moreover for the payment of taxes, the use of forced labour was developed, under the supervision of Africans as much as that of the administration. Forced labour was thus split in two: one part was put to use for the development of the country, the other part benefited the merchants. The outcome was that slowly taxation, forced labour and compulsory cultivations replaced the slave trade which civilization claimed to have eliminated.

Without doubt it was in the kingdom of the Congo that the harshest system of exploitation was established, for the sake of ivory and rubber. Over long decades forced labour was perpetuated for the profit of African chiefs and their business partners. Its practice culminated in the depopulation of entire provinces, if not in an endemic depopulation. For example, in the 13 villages of the district of the Lake Mantouba the population went from 9,450 persons in 1893 to 1,750 in 1913. Many perished after being taken far from their homes to work. The number of villages lost or transformed into deserts defies computation. E. D. Morel's *King Leopold's Rule in Africa* (1904) reprinted in Elikia M'Bokolo's book, takes stock of those zones and villages that became the victims of a depopulation brought about by taxation, by forced labour, by ill treatment, by the persistent pressure exerted by the colonial administration or by those private companies that acted with impunity, like the *Compagnie du Congo pour le commerce et l'industrie*, established in 1889, the *Anversoise*, established in 1892. Impressed by the profits which these societies were accumulating, the French wanted to emulate the Belgians in "their" Congo: in 1898 the Ministry of Colonies received 119 applications for concessions, described as "colonial enterprises", such as, for instance, the *Compagnie des sultanats du Haut-Oubangui* which got a concession of 140,900 square kilometres. According to the specifications the state would receive a fixed government royalty and 15 percent of the profits. Even though the abuses had earlier been denounced, particularly in Charles Péguy's *Cahiers de la Quinzaine*, yet the injustices persisted none the less.

In 1929, thirty years later, the Grimshew report, submitted to the International Labour Office in Geneva, gave an account of the forced labour prevailing in black Africa as described in an investigation conducted with the collaboration of the Christian missions who "had succeeded in freeing their consciences by revealing the odious excesses to which their parishioners were victims". Compulsory work was not the issue, it was forced labour, imposed under such threats as, for example, military draft of an entire village, for a variable duration of two to eighteen months. Moreover this labour was remunerated with minimal wages, paid to the workers or to their boss who afterwards might or might not distribute the sum handed over to him. As a rule the workers could be sent hundreds of kilometres away from their place of residence without any compensation in case of injury, sickness or death. According to the texts of the decrees of the governors of the colonies those workers could be considered as having been employed in works of general or local interest. The traditional tasks were portage, public works, maintenance of the concessions. These demands were at times combined with an obligation to cultivate cotton, the castor oil plant or coffee.

The report observes: "Often women and children are employed in road repairs." While the administration was not directly linked to the origin of these abuses, it nevertheless demanded of the local chief that he make the men of his village take part. When he lacked the authority and the disciplinary means at his disposal, he relies on weaker and more docile individuals. The administration obliged by turning a blind eye (extracts from the report, in F. Auplais, "Le travail forcé" (Forced labour), *Revue apologétique*, No. 527, 1929).

The administrator L. Sanmarco who considered himself to be a "liberal and a little romantic" writes that during the thirties when the official doctrine advocated assimilation, the order of the day actually consisted of constraint in the form of protective paternalism, or of pure and simple exploitation. "For many, for even the most humane, it was with zero speed that the passage was made from constraint to equality of rights." As a former administrator in the Cameroun he gives this explanation: "On the contrary I do not blush for having taken part in this ambiguous undertaking. Though the system lends itself to criticism, it at least provided the opportunity to fight against and to improve it." He explains how he contrasted his experience with that of Jeffreys, his colleague in the British part of the country. He points out how he managed as best he could to increase the wages of his porters. Still he remained trapped within a system of finicky regulations, sending "statements of expenses" which were shot through with false claims and totally inappropriate as he had to have them signed by illiterate porters. He finds that in the British outpost the judge is an African, and at the Treasury there is an African who handles the funds: an African for this, an African for that. "Like me Jeffreys goes on his rounds on foot with the porters, and back in his office he records 'Out of my pocket, so much'. And he is refunded without any explanation. He is held to be a gentleman; no one checks up on him, which saves on the cost of such control. He will be dismissed the day he is no longer held to be a gentleman" (see L. Sanmarco, *Souvenirs de colonisation*, manuscript).

Wealthier, more diversified, more progressive also, the Cameroun differed to a large extent from the rest of Equatorial Africa. There the administration was proud of its achievements: banana plantations in

N'Kongsamba, heveas in Disanga, medical teams from Ayos, etc. The elites sprang up quickly, with those of the private sector impatiently demonstrating their desire and their ambition to take charge of the management of their country. "Legitimate ambition", writes Pierre Messmer to Gaston Deferre in 1956. However the first obstacle consisted in the election of a truly representative assembly. But in the maquis of 1948 Um Nyobé, the popular orator, had already stirred up the population to revolt. For while the local elites were speaking of "independence" the administrators were speaking of "better management".

The physician and the hospital

Together with the teacher, the doctor has always contributed to legitimizing the colonist's presence. To broach the subject of his role, his successes, his practice, his limitations is to pose not only a human or demographic problem, but also a political one, something which the medical profession denies, as it claims to be a purely scientific practice.

Before tending to the medical needs of the natives, the doctor first served as an instrument of the Empire. This is indicated at the very outset by the British setting up the *Indian Medical Service* in 1714. Its purpose was to nurse the British soldiers and colonists, in the same way as the health services were meant to serve the troops of the Royal Navy, or of the Imperial or Republican Navy. The medical struggle transformed itself into a sort of crusade against sickness to the extent that at the zenith of the colonial era, at the beginning of the twentieth century, the question was put bluntly: which of the two will win, the mosquito or man? During the twenties of this century the future of imperialism was linked to the success of the microscope. For instance, man's fight against the tse-tse fly became "the fight for Africa".

Actually, by slow degrees, medicine began to look after the natives as well, starting, naturally, with those who worked for the colonists. Then the medical effort was extended to the entire population and assumed epic proportions. The medical undertaking of the followers of Louis Pasteur and the publicity given to it in the mother country are a pretty representative embodiment of the manner in which the colonizers appreciated their task overseas.

The extent of the benefits of western medicine must also be evaluated from two other points of view: first, from that of the native patients; secondly, by taking into account the fact that while the colonisers brought with them a learned medical science, they also brought diseases hitherto unknown to the indigenous populations.[2]

Algeria: resistance to vaccination

Up to the time of Louis Pasteur's discoveries, European medicine had won only limited successes and had encountered indigenous mistrust. In Algeria it claimed to be the vehicle of civilization, capable of transforming man and his mentalities. It was hoped then that science would resolve all health problems and that the Arab population would be won over by its successes. In sum, the doctor would succeed where it was possible for the soldier or the priest to fail. Indeed some of the remedies were effective, particularly quinine, which eliminated many types of fever, and sometimes even malaria. It had a definite success amongst the Arab populations, as did, for example, the drops used against the different ophthalmological ailments which were a widespread threat to the health of the country. The local populations also welcomed the lessons in hygiene.

But the Arabs resisted the anti-smallpox vaccination. At first, like rural populations in the mother country, the Arabs mistrusted injection as a new-fangled technique which ran counter to the practice of bleeding. But whereas in France there was apprehension about the adverse effects which animal matter extracted from a cow could bring about, the Arabs did not want European "blood" to mingle with theirs. Further the vaccination represented a form of assimilation of the Arabs to the French since it was viewed as integral with the collective steps taken to place both parties under the aegis of the same law. The acceptance of vaccination came about only during the Second Empire with the appearance on the scene of Arab doctors trained in it (see Marcovich, 1988).

Till then the French medical profession believed it had a civilizing mission, and though its successes were limited, they were equally limited for the Europeans. Its range of activity was restricted. The natives continued to rely on their traditional doctor who was scarcely less effective in the treatment of common diseases. Often his competence went beyond the therapy of the particular disease since he could also "treat" depressions and other disturbances resulting from family or business conflicts.

However, with the triumph of Pasteur's disciples, beginning at the end of the last century, European medicine in the colonies went through a sea change. Up to then it had been believed that contagious diseases resulted from all sorts of hygienic or cultural causes. But henceforth, thanks to the bacteriological discoveries of Koch, Pasteur or Yersin, the battle was to be waged against nature alone. And the victory that seemed certain would be a victory for civilization. It was believed – naively – that the resolution of a medical problem is followed by the easy solution of a social problem. It is against the background of such beliefs that one can understand the rivalries between the Institut Pasteur, the Lister Institutes and other scientific institutions which duplicated imperialist rivalries.

The purpose of that type of medicine was to protect society from invisible agents, the microbes and the viruses. Only the specialists could fight these characters when they were finally identified. More, it is the diseases as such, isolated one from the other, that constitute the objects of medicine in the hospital. The latter took over from the cathedral or from the barracks as a symbol of the alien power. Acceptance of European civilization was at its height when it succeeded in wiping out malaria or sleeping sickness.

Congo: protection of human capital

The eradication of sleeping sickness in the Congo provides a good example of the interplay and interference between colonization, the health of the natives and the effort made to cure the sick and to put an end to epidemics. Linked to the tse-tse fly, trypanosomiasis appeared in 1898, in the Niari, between Brazzaville and the ocean; it was triggered by the repeated coming and going of Loango porters. It spread to Gabon, went up the Congo river and, in 1901, struck a mortal blow around Lake Victoria and in Uganda. In five years (1900–05) 250,000 Africans died in the British protectorate. At the same time the Belgian Congo was affected, or rather the Congo of King Leopold which became a colony in 1908. The King's image suffered a blow by the revelation of this disaster. For if there was an Institut Pasteur in Paris, a school of tropical medicine in London and in Liverpool, an Institut für Schiffs und Tropenkrankheiten in Hamburg, nothing had been anticipated by the owner-king who appealed to the British and to John Todd. The latter says: "After we had explained to the King how we would restore health to the Congo, he made us – Boyce, Ross and myself – officers of the Order of Leopold II . . . The opposition newspapers are bound to write that the funds allocated to the Liverpool researchers were a form of corruption, the price paid to our Institute and to myself to keep silent on the atrocities committed earlier in the Congo and to cover up what is happening there" (quoted in Lyons, 1988).

The British doctors were not the last to come to the conclusion that an entire sanitary system was being set up also for the purpose of protecting the value of this precious capital, that is, the workers exposed to the danger of disease. Nevertheless its development continued till it reached its highest level in 1930 with the result that the entire country was brought under medical care. Later the Belgians would boast that the Congo was the best equipped country of all the African colonies. However this situation is indeed the result of a very ambiguous process in which the intentions and the results must be fairly evaluated and compared.

It has already been mentioned that in Busoga (Uganda) more than 200,000 fell victim between 1900 and 1905 and that the ravages recalled those of the plague in earlier times in Europe. Did the epidemic have an

133

African origin, preceding the arrival of the Europeans? Or did it arise with the seizure of the Congo? It is worth noting that, in contrast with AIDS as it occurs today, the sleeping sickness did not travel, neither to America, neither, via Nepal, into India. One may also note that it accompanied the change in the way of life of the inhabitants, their impoverishment – and spread in those regions affected by famine. It has also been said that there are no tropical diseases as such and that some of them, or some of those understood as tropical diseases, have also been present in temperate zones, like leprosy, for instance, or cholera. In short they are diseases, even epidemics, of poverty, which strike only the most vulnerable individuals.

Moreover, smallpox absolutely did not exist in America, before the contamination of the Indians by the Europeans.

South Africa: segregation

In countries which had a large white population, the leaders, for a long time, wondered whether epidemics recognized social barriers. Actually it was the social barriers that would spare the most affluent the experience of the effects of the epidemics. This is clear in the case of cholera which strikes the lower classes who have no running water. Nevertheless, as microbes travel fast, the health officers in South Africa were very active in advocating the segregation of the black quarters. A proper *cordon sanitaire* was established to protect the whites from bubonic plague which earlier had spread from Durban in Natal province. In 1917 a scandal blew up when the authorities evacuated the trains bringing the blacks to the mines, in order to protect the Rand from a possible extension of typhus fever. At the Sterkstroom railway station, in the Cape Province, the black passengers were stripped and all of them, men and women, were made to move from hall to hall – A, B, C – and with inhuman brutality were shaved and showered. Deaths occurred (see Marks and Andersson 1988).

Under such conditions, it is not surprising that South Africa became the first country to have a rigorous sanitary policy. This was mainly for the benefit of the whites, since the disease afflicted only the Blacks, because they were poor. When the smallpox epidemic broke out its very name was not uttered in order not to reduce the flow of the black workers who already knew what its outcome was. The constraint was less severe for typhus fever, because this anti-racist microbe could also affect the white man.

Reversal: the Indian doctors in Great Britain

It so happens that it was in British India that colonial practice ultimately ended up by conforming to the language of "civilization": it did so by a paradoxical interplay of astonishing causes and effects.

At first it was a question, as in the other imperial possessions, of protecting the soldiers of His Majesty. In the first half of the nineteenth century only 6 percent of the dead in the army lost their lives in actual combat. The others succumbed to disease: first, the fevers which accounted for three quarters of the admissions to military hospitals, then dysentery and, above all, cholera, when the troops were in constant movement. These endemic diseases struck at the Indians, but the Indian troops were neither more nor less vulnerable than the British, which proved that the problem of health must be viewed in its totality. This proved to be an insuperable difficulty in a country with a dense population where tens of millions of believers flocked together when they went on pilgrimages. The politics of segregation thus had a legitimate foundation. It could even be practised with a good conscience since it concerned both the British and the Indians, in the cantonments as well as in the administration. Consequently there arose a double quarantine network: one protected the British armed forces and the administration, the other isolated the pilgrims from any contact with the rest of the population. These quarantine precautions were more or less put into practice except in the neighbourhood of the military quarters.

After the great plague epidemic of 1896–1918 which caused more than 10 million deaths, and several cholera epidemics, it became evident that the laisser-faire policy of leaving health care in the hands of the Indians themselves had to be ended. The Indian princes appealed to Waldemar Haffkine, a Russian emigré, a member of the Pasteur Institute of Paris, who in 1893 had managed to eradicate a cholera epidemic in Bengal. At a time when imperialist rivalries were so intense, this appeal to the Russian was viewed as a provocation. In spite of the protests of the famous doctor Ross, the Indian government suspended Haffkine, under pressure from the military authorities who felt humiliated by this Franco-Russian success. Furthermore anti-plague inoculation like anti-smallpox vaccination was expensive for those 300 million Indians.

The population complained. The government in London and Delhi understood that there was an urgent need to face this monumental challenge. In a Declaration made in 1900 the Secretary of State for India affirmed the need to create, in the interest of the Indian people, an independent medical corps, by sponsoring the development of the profession. Only such a corps of Indian physicians could answer to the demands of the situation. That is what was done. Fifty years later, when India became independent, the Royal Laboratory of Bombay was renamed the Haffkine Institute by the Indians.

Fifty years after independence, in a paradoxical reversal of history, these same Indian doctors are today treating the British in Great Britain. In fact, the decline of the medical profession in Britain, especially in the 1960s, led to a drain of doctors to the United States and Canada. Those who stayed behind did so by occupying positions, conforming to their expectations, in private luxury clinics. Consequently, as a paradoxical effect of the Welfare State, it was the Indian – together with, though in lesser numbers, the Caribbean – doctors who replaced them and filled the hospitals of Her Majesty.

In Claude de Givray's film made in 1980, *Une histoire de la médecine* (A History of Medicine), no scene is more arresting than the suspicious and furious look of that old, typically British lady listening to the orders of a doctor with the swarthy complexion hailing from Madras.

The school and the problem of schooling

In the mother country schools were presented as one of the major achievements of colonization. Certainly schooling developed, but it did so late and in conditions such that here and there it acted as an anchorage point for a challenge to the French presence. Within the French Empire the case of Indo-China presents a striking contrast with that of Algeria.

In no other place was schooling so highly developed as in Indo-China where "France could not be satisfied with the destruction of the traditional system of education, by means of successive repressive measures; in the face of societies with well tried intellectual traditions, the need was to innovate" (see Catherine Coquery-Vidrovitch, 1992). The Vietnamese, Cambodian and Laotian languages were recognized as the exclusive vehicles of education at the elementary level. That is why in Cochin-China, in 1932, only 115 out of 1,419 districts did not have a school. After learning French, 4,800 students went on to secondary school, being distributed among 21 institutions, 3 of which were reserved for girls. The colonial conservatives criticized this educational system which nevertheless became an instrument for the modernization of the society.

In contrast the school system established in Algeria did nothing but widen the cultural gap between the natives and the Europeans. The debate rested on two problems: that of the private education in association with that of the status of the Arabic language; the problem of the extension and the significance of such schooling.

At first the problems were mixed. "The native schools train rebels and misfits", declared an administrator as early as in 1895. "Considering that the education of the natives poses a genuine danger to Algeria, from both the economic point of view and the point of view of the French population, the Assembly proposes that the primary education of the natives be abolished." Nevertheless up to 1944 the number of schools did increase, however slowly: 36 Franco-Arabic schools in 1870, 221 in 1900, 468 in 1913. There were 1,205 classes of this type in 1930. This means that a hundred years after the conquest only 5.4 percent of the Muslims were educated. Concomittantly there existed a private education in the Arabic language – the instruction given in the Koranic schools and the *zaouias*, boarding schools and rest homes, tolerated by the administration. There were 6,000 of these establishments in all which were teaching 100,000 Muslims to recite the Koran. On the other hand, the administration viewed with mistrust the 150 *madrasas* which provided a genuine education in Arabic to 45,000 children. Most of the teachers possessed diplomas mostly obtained in the Zitouna in Tunis. They taught the same subjects as were taught in the French schools, but in books brought from Lebanon or from Egypt. In 1947 secondary education was provided at the Ben Badis Institute in Constantine. To pursue higher education in Arabic young Algerians had to go to the universities of Tunis, Cairo, Damascus, or Kuwait which was in 1950 held to be the most modern of all of them. But the administration balked at granting a passport to those young students. It balked all the more at subsidizing the *madrasas* while the same deputies from Algeria voted, in France, for the Barangé law which approved of aid to private Roman Catholic schools. Moreover those who taught Arabic "unlawfully" were often prosecuted, like the President of the Board of Education of the Ulemas who was caught, in El Oued, writing Arabic on the blackboard and condemned to two years in jail and seven years under house arrest.

Yet the retrograde nature of the *zaouias*, or authorized Koranic schools, brought the colonizing role of France into a sharper focus. Accordingly one can observe, after a span of a century, the paradoxical process of a regression in education: in 1847 "education in Arabic was nearly universal, at least in so far as it concerned reading, writing and counting", whereas in 1944, 8 out of 9 Arabs were illiterate. Only a minority attended school. While, in the French schools, the Arabs attended the primary level classes in large numbers, their number was much smaller at the secondary level. For example, in Oran, with a population of 119,000 Muslims and 173,000 Europeans in 1953, the statistics are as follows:

	Non-Muslim	Muslim
Boys' lycées (high schools)	2,162	62
Girls' lycées	1,136	17
Modern college for boys	1,221	160
Modern college for girls	1,317	43
Total	5,836	282

It was the teaching of the Arabic language, more than a rise in the number of pupils, that constituted the main demand of the nationalist organizations and the political parties. Proclaimed "a foreign language" by order of the Council of State in 1933 and by the decree of 8 March 1938, Arabic did not even have the personnel capable of teaching it. The Arabic classes admitted the least academically inclined pupils. Arabic was considered as a second-rank language, coming after English, German and Spanish. As late as 1954 the departmental inspectors of primary education in Algeria were reporting: "Neither spoken Arabic, which has as much worth as a patois, nor literary Arabic, which is a dead language, nor modern Arabic which is a foreign language, can be entertained as a compulsory subject of primary education."

Fanny Colonna has written a harsh indictment of the role of the French school in the colonial enterprise, with special reference to Algeria. According to her, the primary school was the source of a socialization of life. It fostered a political awareness which fed the elites with ideas, more particularly the Arab or Kabyle teachers. These, like Ferhat Abbas, soon came to be known as the *Young Algerians* characterized by their infatuation with assimilation. Thus the school formed the liberated Arabs who soon became liberators. On the other hand, it is evident that while the school ought to have shrunk inequalities, it did not enable the deprived to rise. Actually it deepened the inequalities within traditional society. Though it recruited 70 percent of the native teachers whose parents were illiterate, it is till true that their pupils could rarely improve their condition. An adolescent testifies to the gap between the idea generally held of the school as a means to open up possibilities and the harsh realities of colonization:

> At school no one helped me. My mother did not know how to read or write in French. I did not have a good position in class. I did not learn. Well, I had no one to urge me on. So I had to leave school and go to work . . .
>
> When an Arab tried to get a job, to look after himself, he was soon eliminated. The colonel had advised my first boss against letting me learn to work. "He will leave you afterwards", he had told him (1958, testimony).

Yet in his film *La dernière image*, made in 1986, Mohammed Lakhdar Hamina affectionately recalls the love which his young childhood friends felt for their French teacher, as well as for their school, which provided them with a space of freedom and of happiness where they could fulfil themselves. Fifty years after independence one is struck by this still prevailing impression. Thanks to this film it will not get blurred with time.

Colonial experiments

Is there a Portuguese exception?

Before all others we *alone* have brought to Africa the idea of the rights of man and of racial equality. We are the *only* ones to have practised "multiracialism", the perfect expression of the brotherhood of peoples. No one in the world challenges the validity of this principle.

But there is still some hesitation to acknowledge that this is a Portuguese invention. To do so would enhance our authority in the world.

(Franco Nogueiro, Minister of Foreign Affairs, 1967)

Against the backdrop of active guerilla operations in Guinea-Bissau, in Angola and in Mozambique, the Minister's proud words do not constitute an improvised statement. The idea at the core of his pronouncement was well entrenched in the historical conscience of the Portuguese leadership. Its echo even reverberates beyond the Lusitanian world. After all, as early as the seventeenth century, Portugal designated "overseas provinces" what the other mother countries called colonies. In 1576 the historian Joao de Barros used to refer to "our province of Brazil". Even if the term colonies was sometimes used, the fact is that it was officially abolished in 1822 on the occasion of the drafting of the constitution which established the principle of the indivisibility of Portuguese territory and of the citizenship of all its inhabitants. The term came back at the end of the 1926 Republic, before Salazar again forced it out of circulation in 1951. This simple enumeration is enough to indicate that the double problem of the status of the conquests and of their inhabitants was part of the mental heritage of Portuguese leaders.

As regards the Lusitanian world, what strikes one as genuinely original is that this concern and these ideas were also expressed outside the mother country, especially in Brazil, where they were popularized by the famous writer Gilberto Freyre. Actually his book *Caça grande e senzala* (1933), translated into French under the title *Maîtres et esclaves*, coincided with the trend towards a revival of Brazilian culture, a trend linked to the crisis of the twenties which brought Getulio Vargas to power and to the integration of a large number of German and Italian immigrants.

Up till then a racist ideology had prevailed in Brazil. But Gilberto Freyre reemphasized the contribution of the blacks to Brazilian culture, and concluded that interbreeding between whites and blacks had been a great opportunity for the country. Far from being a shame, this interbreeding foretold a fusion of races, the sole agent capable of insuring the future of humanity. In its own way, the Portugal of Salazar adopted this diagnosis to its own advantage and claimed the credit for this process, thus giving a new polish to its whole colonial past at a time when overseas possessions had little interest for anyone, in view of their decline and their economic failure. In 1935 *O mundo Portuguez* wrote in an editorial: "We must keep alive our pride in having established an Empire . . . Africa is not merely an agricultural land, it is more than that. As far as we are concerned, Africa is a moral justification and makes us a power. Without Africa we should be a small country. Thanks to it we are a great nation."

But the influence of Gilberto Freyre went beyond the ambit of the world of politics. It pervaded the cultural and university ambience of the entire

West, expanding the area of the Brazilian "miracle" to the whole Portuguese world. When, in 1940, he published *O mundo que o Portuguez criou* (The world which Portugual creates), he argued that it was not only in Brazil that the Portuguese had succeeded in creating a new civilization, but they had done so wherever they had gone – in India, in Timor, in Africa.

As early as 1955, Mario Pinto de Andrade was vigorously criticizing this luso-tropicalism, calling it a myth. It was not easy to substantiate the charge, for it so happens that myths often carry a stronger flavour of truth than does reality.

Angola: the first penal colony

For many, leaving for the Americas, for India, for Africa was an adventure. At the end of the voyage lay fortune and, at the least, another existence – or death.

But this emigration was not in all circumstances free and spontaneous. The overseas voyage was often an exile, a semi-voluntary exile when necessity was its genesis. In the case of the British one recalls the Pilgrim Fathers, the Irish Catholics, who started to leave as early as the seventeenth century. Yet this exile was also penal servitude, worse than being sent to the galleys.

The Portuguese were the first to get rid of their criminals and their delinquent offenders by sending them away to serve their sentence elsewhere. The British followed this example and applied it on a gigantic scale by sending their "convicts" to populate Australia as from 1797.

The Portuguese were the first to come up with this idea, well before Bartolomeu Diaz reached the Cape of Good Hope. From 1415 on, following the first conquest of Ceuta, every ship which left to explore the coasts of Africa carried its quota of *degredados*. In fact the first law related to this practice was passed in 1434. As early as 1484 the first permanent establishments – Principe, Sao Tomé and Sao Martinho – were accordingly populated with delinquents and Jews. The practice of transportation became systematic in the settlements of Angola. In precise terms, as from the seventeenth century, the country was almost exclusively populated with delinquents, a practice which had an influence on the exploitation of the colony as well as on relationships with the natives.

At the time of the Marquis of Pombal, about 1750, the Jesuits were also deported to Angola. But on account of their small number they had little influence on the life of the colony. As a result the reputation of the colony was such that it was difficult, and took a long time, to induce free immigrants to go there. It was widely reported that the city of Luanda was full of gangsters and crooks for, in contrast with the convicts sent by the British to Australia, the *degredados* were indeed real, hardened criminals whom the Governor did not want to arm, in case a war broke out with the natives. He preferred to rely on African troops both to fight the rebellious tribes and, in due course, to keep at bay the *degredados*. In any case, scarcely had the latter been armed than they would desert.

Consequently, acting as a colonizing colony, Brazil sent Angola the largest groups of white immigrants. The latter came from Pernambouc where, since the time of the 1847–48 uprising, security had ceased to exist. The new immigrants therefore chose to go to Angola where they developed the sugar-cane, the cultivation of which had been ruined in the north-east of Brazil. In any event for a long time Angola had depended economically on Brazil. Actually as early as 1781 Minister Martinho de Melo e Castro complained that commerce and navigation had completely freed themselves from Portugal, "for what the Brazilians do not control is in the hands of the foreigners", that is, the slave trade which had drained the country.

But at the end of the eighteenth century the delinquent *degredados* still held the high ground. "It is scarcely possible to keep here, or in the interior of the country, the smallest group of colonists, and still less so to settle the *degredados* . . . It would be necessary to raise an indigenous armed force, but with sufficient strength for it to be worthy of respect."

Under such conditions, with the elimination of the slave trade, colonization became possible and the Africans, at least, felt that the Portuguese were not indeed "the expression of civilization", as official propaganda had started to reiterate. Between 1902 and 1914, 57 percent of the criminals of the colony had committed crimes of violence in the mother country.

With the beginning, in the nineteenth century, of the colonization of the land on a large scale, one of the features which characterize the status of the blacks in Angola is that at that time there were no laws to regulate racial segregation. The Angolan situation was different from what obtained in the neighbouring South Africa. It was somewhat similar to the situation in the United States where the North differed from the South for cognate reasons.

However the absence of racial laws did not suggest that the slightest integration of the blacks in a unified society had occurred. For whatever racial mixture may have existed, it had been of a "descending" rather than an "ascending" nature: that is, those who had been excluded from white society retreated to the *musseques* (shanty towns) where they ran some shop or other. But in 1970 during the riots which broke out when the Caetano government was toppled the Portuguese and the Cape Verde islanders abandoned the "negro quarter".

Mixed marriages had been rare in Angola as they were in the rest of Portuguese Africa. Yet the idea has persisted in the mind of the Portuguese as in that of many black Africans that the practice of racism was alien to Portuguese colonization. For example, when about 20,000 to 30,000 Cape Verde islanders emigrated to the United States, they considered themselves as Africans, as did the 40,000 Cape Verde islanders who lived in Angola.

With the exception of Cape Verde, and of Sao Tomé and Principe, following the abolition of the slave trade, Portugal had been unable to populate these dependences. Consequently the number of the Whites remained small: in Angola, 20,700 in 1920, that is, 0.5 percent of the population, the rest being mainly black. Mulattos were rare: 7,500, or 0.2 percent. This proportion of whites increased only after Salazar's reforms when the flow of the *degredados* was stopped, unless jails were built for them in Angola. The number of Whites rose to 5.1 percent of the total population. The number of the mulattos too had increased to 53,392 at about the very time when there were 172,529 Whites and 4,604,362 Blacks.

Evidently Angolan society had nothing in common with the society that was being formed in Cape Verde or in Brazil where up to 42 percent of the population was mixed race.

Boers, Blacks and the English in South Africa

It is a fact that in South Africa racism did not obey the same laws and follow the same customs as in North Africa. It stands comparison with the *Solid South* of the United States. The comparison may only be apparent, for the two societies have developed in different ways.

First the Dutch encountered the Hottentots who have almost disappeared as a tribe, but whose blood still flows in the veins of the mulattos and the blacks of the Cape Province. At the time of the Great Trek in 1836, the exodus undertaken to escape from the mercantile civilization of the British settled in the Cape since 1815, the Dutch, having become the Boers, clashed with the Xhosas, the Swazi and especially the Zulus of Shaka. The latter, after the death of their King, were crushed by Andries Pretorius at the battle of Blood River. But it was the British who, coming from Natal, picked up the stakes. The Boers retreat to the interior of the country and created the Orange and Transvaal republics. For long decades more they clashed with the Xhosas while the British definitively triumphed over the Zulus in 1879.

At the end of the nineteenth century three of these peoples, on being driven back by the Boers, sought the protection of the British who provided them with stability and territories: the Swazi, the Sothos, the Tswana. The situation soon became stable apart from the Boers, as well as the British, attempting to lay hands on the still autonomous tribes, or rather on their lands. This rivalry culminated in the 1901 war in which, by common agreement, the adversaries resolved to rule out the use of black troops. Once peace was concluded and the Union of South Africa was formed, the Native Act of 1913 allotted the share of land reserved to each community. The blacks receive 8 percent of the totality of the land. Elsewhere, even when the population was in its majority African, the land was white, with some rare exceptions. Thus the blacks lost the plots of land which they used to cultivate. Nearly one million of them were expelled. It was not until 1936 that the tribal lands of the blacks increased from 8 percent to 13 percent of the area of the Union.

Expelled from their land the blacks went to work in the mines. Nevertheless the Colour Bar of 1911 prevent them from seeking employment as skilled workers. The pass system assigned them to particular areas.

Till then the status of the coloured population differed markedly from one region to the other. In the Cape Province still survived a liberal tradition whereby the blacks and the mulattos enjoyed political rights so long as they fulfilled the conditions required by the voting system based on the poll tax. In fact few of them benefited from these rights. But even then the "poor whites" were also excluded. In Natal and in the Orange and Transvaal Republics, the blacks and people of mixed race were deprived of all political rights. The Indians were prohibited from staying in the former Boer Republics. Indeed it is the Indians who led a largely successful campaign against the Colour Bar. That is where Gandhi learnt about racism.

In a general sense one may observe that there were only differences of degree between the racist legislations of the English and Boer territories. Still the principle was different: the Cape Province remained the more tolerant, while the gap widened between its practices which the Dutch, with General Smuts among them, endorsed and those of the Boers who were more and more frequently called the Afrikaners.

The antecedents of apartheid

The great event in the history of the Afrikaners was the Great Trek. The Boers did not want to live under the foreigner's law, especially in their relationships with the blacks. They wanted to preserve their language, their traditional way of life. "To give the blacks a status equal to that of the whites is contrary to the law of God. It is opposed to the natural difference of race and religion. Such a humiliation is intolerable to the Christian." In 1858 the first Constitution of the Transvaal stipulated: "There shall be no question of equality between the whites and the non-whites, neither in the Church nor in the State." The Great Trek, an anabasis which lasted several years (see Marianne Cornevin, 1979), was viewed as the equivalent of the exodus of Moses: its itinerary was sacred. It still is, a century later.

For the purposes of teaching the principle of apartheid a 1948 text of the *Institut vor Christelike-nasionale Onderwys* offers the following formula: "The education of the children of white parents must be conducted on the basis of the conceptions of the parents, that is, it must be based on the Holy Scriptures . . . We believe that God has willed nations to be separate, peoples to be separate, and has given to each its vocation, its tasks, its talents." Interbreeding between races and their equality went against the will of God, of which the Boers were the only interpreters. A combination of the Bible and the Gun.

Yet, under the pressure exerted by the English, the Afrikaners had been, since 1901, forced to modify their practices. But the victory of Dr. Malan, an Afrikaner, in the elections of 1948, was felt as a revenge against the English. It steeled the determination of the victors, who lived "as if entrenched in their language and in their religion", to set up a strict racial segregation, or apartheid. In 1949 mixed marriages between Europeans and non-Europeans were prohibited. This prohibition included the Indians. Residential segregation was particularly enforced. Racial classification was rendered harsher: in the case of people of mixed race, it defined which group they belonged to. The comb test was one of the humiliating measures adopted by the special commissions: the comb remained stuck if the hair was a little frizzy. Segregation was applied to public places, to public transport, to the universities, to sports. Even the representation of the Africans by Europeans was abolished in 1959. At the same time it was decided that the black reservations, henceforth called *national homelands*, would constitute states, Bantustans.

This policy, under the rubric of separate development, naturally provoked violent reactions among the Indian and black populations. They organized themselves and established the African National Congress (ANC) and the Coloured People's Organization. Their leaders were arrested, beaten, imprisoned, killed, after every campaign of civil disobedience. More than one million Africans were arrested in 1968 for violations, while the majority of the black leaders, with the Marxists in front, were, like Nelson Mandela, imprisoned. The struggle continued.

The complete change in the practice of South African racism between the Boer period and that of the rule of the Afrikaners, that is, between the end of the nineteenth century and the second half of the twentieth century, was undoubtedly due to the transformations experienced by the white South African society, in particular by the Boers. They were constrained to adopt a market economy and industrialization, while earlier they had lived under a traditionally pastoral order, the violence of which was different from that which the economic boom brought about.

In fact, for a long time, in Boer country, whites and blacks lived on the land, with the former lording it over the latter by overcoming their resistance "with fisticuffs, whip lashings, and fire-arms". Still this violence was tempered by forms of paternalism. "The violence ran like an undertow and strengthened the dynamism of the patriarcate" for, as whipping was a ritualized practice, the patriarch used it with his children also.

As regards the Blacks, any act of violence inflicted on a tenant farmer had to be duly compensated, by gifts and concessions in order to preserve the stability of the system. If the blacks were not invited to his home, the owner would let them in for prayers. Likewise he attended the funerals of old servants, gave the permission to slaughter one of the farm animals on the occasion of certain festivals, and so on.

In such a system the white owner perpetuated a childhood status in the blacks: he conferred Christian names on them with the addition of a diminutive to them. Respect for the elders fostered a particular form of connivance both among the whites and the blacks. The very young children played together; the separation occurred with the first signs of puberty. Charles Van Onselen reports an oral testimony which shows how everything changed when the British replaced the Boers, in the Schweitzer-Reneke district, in the highveld. The monetary economy had taken over and perhaps the liberal ideas of the new owners had little impact on the reality. "The Afrikaner owners gave us curd, or fresh milk and good food; the British stopped everything. Instead they gave us a few cups of milk every day . . . They counted them. The Afrikaners did not sell their belongings. They gave us their trousers, shoes and other objects. But the British sold their clothes. They would have never given us a pair of trousers without asking to be paid for it" (Van Onselen, 1992).

Among the Boers also these traditional relationships dwindled as soon as machines deprived the use of the blacks' livestock of its logic, with the consequence that black manpower, deprived of its plots of land, got fragmented; it was forced to seek employment in the mines. The changes were initiated by the white man who from then on no longer had any interest in perpetuating a paternalistic order. For the violence which he used to moderate, he now substituted the absolute racism of apartheid.

It would be unfair to compare the racism which may have been practised in Algeria with racist practices in South Africa. Undoubtedly the segregation may have existed in a few sectors of social life: there were no Arab tennis players, but only ballboys, there were "reserved" quarters, very few mixed marriages. But Islam generated its own exclusivisms: with the exception of a few dignitaries few metropolitan French or pieds-noirs could cross the threshold of an Arab's home.

What exacerbated the ire of the blacks in South Africa was indeed the fact that religion did not act to protect them, as Islam did the Arabs. As W. G. L. Randles has shown, during the eighteenth and nineteenth centuries, many Bantus had given up their myths to adopt the Christian god of the missionaries. Simultaneously the Europeans had surrendered their own principles to adopt those of reciprocity and of barter which, before their arrival, had been practised by the Bantus. Up till then the Kings of the Bantus and they alone fixed the value of things. Henceforth the prices fluctuated with the laws of the market, which appeared to the Bantus as a trick whenever the value of their products went down, while the Europeans saw no evil in it since they were earning profits. As a form of compensation the Bantus, who had no idea of a supreme Deity, soon discovered its merits which they used as a weapon against the European intruders. An example is provided by the Xhosa Makanna who awaits "the great day of resurrection when the dead shall rise at the last sunset". This millenarian vision lies at the root of the uprising of 10,000 Xhosas against the town of Grahamstown, at the beginning of the twentieth century. But, in spite of the many millenarian movements, the Bantus could not take advantage of the transformation of their founding ancestors into Biblical divinities. They lost everything, on the level of symbols as well as on that of trade. They lost even their history, for the South Africans refused to acknowledge that the Bantus had been on the veld before them, in spite of the proofs accumulated by the archaeologists. Nor did the South Africans accept the idea that, further to the north, the blacks could have been able to build the monuments of Zimbabwe: their rancour, their suffering and their anger were extreme.

Australia: where the "criminals" wished to set up a just law

Australia is different from other territories in that it was not occupied in 1787 to prevent its being seized by the "frog eaters" or by the "herring smokers", but actually for the purpose of getting rid of the "criminal class". "An experiment", said Jeremy Bentham: a first experiment which the French subsequently emulated in Guyana, later in New Caledonia, but in a different context.

But how should one get rid of criminals? Such was the problem posed to Parliament under George III. In London alone there were then 115,000 criminals. And, in the name of their liberties, the British refused to have a police. Peel established one only in 1830. The criminals were listed in a hundred categories, from the *drag sneaks* who robbed travellers, the *snoozers* who stole luggage from hotels, the *skinners* who deprived children of their clothes. Delinquency increased with the growth of the large cities: Fielding, Dickens, afterwards Karl Marx described the misery and the cruelty which accompanied it. In those days the real class struggle did not oppose the employers to the workers, but the delinquents to the workers.

Anyhow, according to the elegant expression of Robert Hughes, "crime was still a cottage industry". Really organized gangs did not exist. That is why the army or the navy were sufficient to round up the delinquents who were handed over to them. And they were penned up in their thousands. The law was very harsh: for the slightest offence or for any prejudice to private property the offender was punished with a death sentence. Such was the fate of the girl of thirteen who stole a shirt.

But, with the rise of humanitarian sensitivities – it was the time of Wilberforce – the abolitionist movement gathered momentum. It opposed surgical experiments carried out on dogs; it likewise hesitated to execute those sentenced to death. From 1749 to 1758, 365 executions were carried out in public out of 527 death sentences. From 1799 to 1808 not more than

126 were executed out of 804 sentenced to die. The percentage thus went from 69 percent to 15 percent.

But, with the jails being full, what was to be done with the criminals entrusted to the army?

The authorities had already sent some to America. But after their independence the United States did not want to have any more. Then the idea came up to send them to the end of the world, to that Australia which Cook had more or less touched on, and which was populated with strange beings – kangaroos, koalas – and even human beings who "were so little human". The criminals would not return from that country. Of the first 733 who left, embarked in dreadful conditions, there were 431 who had been condemned for "minor thefts, 44 sheep rustlers, 9 who had committed gross larceny, and in all 31 who had committed violence on a person"; nearly half of them were under twenty-five. In short, as "criminals" they were mostly very young and petty delinquents. Forty-eight of them died during a very difficult journey which lasted 252 days: scurvy proved to be particularly deadly. In Britain 25,000 "criminals" were on the waiting list.

Such were the "convicts", whom tradition has described as fearsome "criminals". Even today the inhabitants of Adelaide who arrived later and of their own free will, are wont to recall that Southern Australia "is not a convict country". But if they were not criminal at the outset, they became criminal without realizing it, that is, by the massacre of the aborigines. Sensitive only to what had been their own misfortune they strove to transform New South Wales into that land of justice which their motherland failed to be for them. A large number of their descendants hate England.

The first encounters between the British and an aborigine were recorded, around 1798, by John White, the surgeon of the expedition.

> He then, by signs and gestures, seemed to ask if the pistol would make a hole through him, and on being made sensible that it would, he showed not the smallest sign of fear, on the contrary he endeavoured ... to impress us with an idea of the superiority of his own arms, which he applied to his breast, and by staggering and a show of falling seemed to wish us to understand that the force and effect of them was mortal and not to be resisted.
>
> (R. Hughes, 1986, p. 15)

As a matter of fact the massacre began quite early. Some of the indigenous customs – to beat the women till blood was spilled, to crush the skulls of the soldiers seized in an ambush – gave cause for a good conscience to all those who deemed "that they were not human beings but apes".

For a long time the official history has blotted out the memory of these actions. Ethnology helped in this history. In his classic work on the aborigines (1938) A. P. Elkin gives an entire paragraph to demographic growth since 1930, but not a single sentence to the demographic collapse

147

that occurred in the preceding century. Assuredly the disappearance of three quarters of the indigenous population is of no concern to any department of science.

Indigenous memory has retained the remembrance of the arrival of "Captain Cook", the eponymous hero of the invasion of the Whites. The young hear it from the elders who themselves heard it from their ancestors: "You will be killed, do not fight, run. He will gouge your eye, cut your nose. Do not meddle with him, run . . . Because in those days they would shoot you in the back like a dog . . . The Whifellows shoot the Ngumpin."

Children have recorded in little note books what they have heard from their ancestors. In Marika Wandjuk's anthology of *The aboriginal children's history of Australia* one can read the story of the beginning of that genocide.

> One day we saw a ship with strange men. The aborigines were afraid and they hid behind the bushes. Then they climbed up to the top of the hill and when the strange men came near, they caused big rocks to hurtle down on them. The aborigines thought they were dead. But that was not so. They then fired their guns. The aborigines hid themselves again. Then they threw their javelins. The strange men managed to dodge them, went back to their ships and disappeared . . . Captain Cook came back, got wounded and left . . . Then came the army . . . We did not kill them because we were friends. They were fifty, we were two thousand and we did not fear their guns. In the bush we were invincible; they were incapable hunters and they caught fever as soon as it became damp . . . But as one of those men had taken a woman, then another, the oldest aborigines organized themselves to kill him. He had his throat cut with an axe. The white men rounded up a large number of aborigines and killed them all . . .

Naturally there is a good deal of myth in this testimony provided by a child (1975). Still it bears a grain of truth, especially as regards that "peace" which was indeed concluded off the Botany Bay, in those times when the soldiers kept watch over the convicts working on the construction of roads and villages. A sort of serialized comic strip (1828), preserved at the Hobart Museum, illustrates the policy of Governor Arthur: 1. a white nurse breast-feeds a black baby, a black nurse breast-feeds a white baby; 2. In full red, white and blue uniform the general welcomes an aboriginal delegation; they shake each other's hand; 3. an aborigine kills a civilian; 4. soldiers hang him; 5. a civilian shoots an aborigine; 6. soldiers hang him. These scenes suggest a certain measure of illusion. Nevertheless they evoke the ambiguity of the rather brief period when the pure and simple extermination had been discarded.

When Governor Philips arrived in 1797 the number of aborigines ranged from 300,000 to 400,000. Less than a century later they had been, on ten occasions, pushed back to the territories of the North and the West. Independently of the cruelty exercised by racism, at least two particularly telling examples testify to the reality of the extermination. The first governors did not bother to "civilize" the aborigines in order to make them work, for it was the convicts that had to be made to work. Further the introduction of black slaves from abroad had itself been prohibited in Australia. Consequently the aborigines were deemed to be virtually "useless", and it was "useless" to try to assimilate them. The process of "taming" them appeared on the scene only much later.

One has to wait for the 1980s to witness the moment of remorse, with its cluster of rehabilitation remedies: museums, oral investigations, Centre of Aboriginal Studies in Canberra. In imitation of America – as, for instance, in the United States where, during the 1960s, it became fashionable to take pride in proclaiming that one had Indian blood coursing in one's veins – today in Sydney it is good taste for someone to claim to have "abo" blood. In fact there are about 50,000 mixed-race people of aboriginal descent in Australia.

At the beginning Australia was a land of convicts. But it did not remain one for long, for the penal colonization was called into question by, among others, Edward Gibbon Wakefield in his writings. In *A letter from Sydney* (1830) he proposed the substitution of a systematic colonization to the anarchy of the present situation, with the sale of concessions, subsidized and controlled emigration. His influence led to the establishment of the settlements first organized by the New Zealand Company, followed by the South Australian Committee. Wakefield was a disciple of Adam Smith whose basic premises consisted of viewing land, capital and labour as the fundamental constituents of production and of maintaining a reasonable balance among them. But, in Australia, there was a surfeit of land, an absence of capital, and manpower was hard to obtain as it disappeared as soon as it arrived, a fortiori in the case of the convicts as soon as there was no one to watch over them. People in England ridiculed Robert Peel who had obtained a concession of 300,000 acres in western Australia, and brought 300 individuals with him. But six months after his arrival he was reduced to drawing his own water and making his own bed, for everybody had left and gone away. Others too had gone through the same mill, with each trying to acquire too much land both for himself and for his own folks and proving unable to make any profit out of it. Wakefield's idea was to have land sold at a fair price to the colonists hailing from the mother country, to subsidize the transportation of the volunteers and the settlement of those who, in Australia itself, like the sons of the convicts themselves, were too poor to buy land (Siegfried, 1946, pp. 175–94). His project was feasible only if the prospective emigrants could be persuaded that leaving for the antipodes was no longer a form of punishment, but indeed an opportunity for them to seek their happiness. The number of

149

those leaving Great Britain for Australia and New Zealand rose from 68,000 during the decade of 1830–40 to double that number, reaching subsequently a maximum of 378,000 during the decade 1880–90. German emigration to Australia after 1871 proceeded at the rate of about 2,000 to 5,000 persons per decade (Gollwitzer, 1969).

On the road to the legal state

Who deserves punishment, for what crime, and how should they be punished? Such was the problem that confronted Governor Philips when in 1788 he had to decide the fate of both the convicts, who were the workers, and the soldiers placed in the charge of watching over them and who themselves had to abide by a stringent discipline. Such discipline was actually necessary for neither of them for, off the coast of Sydney, no escape was possible. Some tried to escape, with the fond belief that China or Japan were not too far away. Their bones were later discovered, unless they had been devoured by the dingo dogs. The first clashes occurred when the soldiers thought that the convicts were better off than they were. Indeed the convicts worked hard, they got whipped till blood flowed: one of them received more than 2,000 lashes during his lifetime. But they had the opportunity to take a mate, for as many women as men joined the convoys. The governor realized that there was no need to use so much violence as punishment for indiscipline, as otherwise the works would not progress. That is why the news spread in England that it was a good thing to be a convict in Australia.

In fact, while they were grouped together with the first colonists, the sons and grandsons of the convicts continued to be treated as criminals and experienced the law of the whip. They appealed to the judicial system which provided them with the only recourse against the authorities representing the Crown – the military, who were bitter to see the sons of convicts emancipating themselves, while they had to endure the unchanging, iron discipline of the army. Accordingly, in the name of English liberty the descendants of the convicts sought the help of lawyers to defend them. As a result the earliest political men of the country were lawyers and judges.

Undoubtedly the important point to note is that, gradually, *juridical language became the language of politics.* Consequently the judicial power took over from the executive and the legislative, as the jurists had the last word in the enactment of the decisions taken, first by the governors and later, after 1901, by the political representatives. As early as in the middle of the nineteenth century one witness reports that the Australians matched the Americans in arrogance and deemed all the governments of the world, except theirs, to be bad. Every Australian would protect his petty interests with a selfishness the like of which could not be seen anywhere else. Thus,

150

by a sort of "perverse" effect, the Australians established in their country a judicial order in order to break away from the situation which had been bequeathed to them. What they thought was incumbent upon them – their parents having experienced the abuses of the law – was a return to the norm. In *The invisible state* Alastair Davidson has demonstrated that, in Australia, juridical jargon and the spirit of pettifoggery slowly reduced to nought the grandiose options of political or union leaders, whether the latter were socialists, or liberals, or whatever they chose to call themselves. In this country the people constantly *appeal to the law, and deem themselves betrayed by ideas.*

In consequence, by a revenge of history, the aborigines have been able to claim their rights on the Murray Islands, north of the Great Barrier Reef. The Supreme Court thus extinguished the doctrine of *terra nullius* according to which Australia was unoccupied before the arrival of the British: it created a new title deed, the *Native Title.* This 1992 decision calls again into question the status of large tracts of land, in particular in western Australia. In Queensland the Wil tribe has taken on an economic giant, the CRA Company, and its aluminium production.[3]

Richard Court, the Prime Minister of Western Australia has proposed that the Supreme Court decision be submitted to a referendum. This is one more example of the clash between right and the democratic will. Where does equity lie?

Absorbed nations, conquered nations: Russian and Soviet originality

We have seen that the policy of the Portuguese Empire and that of the French Empire tended towards assimilation or integration. French colonization, it is true, evinced a few specific, but nevertheless rare, exceptions. At the same time the British policy tended towards the constitution of the Commonwealth ever since the secession of the United States unveiled the dangers of adopting any other policy, even though there occurred a tightening of the Empire during the period 1783–1830. But up to 1917 Russian imperial policy obeyed a supranational logic as soon as the problem of annexations and the need to solve it emerged. The first characteristic of the empire was actually not to have an ethnic basis (*Russkaja imperija*), but to be a state where different peoples lived under the rule of a single monarch (*Rossiskaja imperija*). It was a policy that tried to neutralize those who could have, in the name of a national ideal, challenged the power of the Tsar.

But all that was not realized without any upheaval as, for example, the Tsar's being confronted with the problem of the absorption of the Tartars (not excluding the threat posed by Poland and Sweden). This absorption occurred in two main stages. The first began in the sixteenth century and was marked by the Tsars extending their activities to the regions of the

Volga, where the Tartars, the Bashkirs and the Cheremis lived together or as neighbours. This stage ended in 1774, during the reign of Catherine II. The second stage was undertaken in Crimea in 1783. In both cases the policy followed was the same, even if, with the benefit of experience, the promises made on the occasion of the conquest were more explicit in Crimea than in Kazan, though nevertheless they were subsequently kept more in the breach than in practice.

Still several changes influenced and transformed the attitude of the Tsarist power towards the peoples that had been annexed. In the first instance, the acquisition of pre-existing states of Christian persuasion: Georgia, Poland, the Baltic States. Then came the policy of the complete break whereby non-natives were russified. Finally, after the 1917 Revolution, Soviet Russia reevaluated its policy concerning the nationalities.

Several Tartar states arose out of the disintegration of the Golden Horde in the fifteenth century. They were Turkish-Mongol. "A wicked branch, Kazan, separated from the evil tree that was the Golden Horde and produced a bitter fruit. A second state then arose under another Prince of the Horde." Thus Kazan posed the greatest threat to the Muscovite state. Its territory grouped, together with the Tartars, the Chuvashes and the Bashkirs who were Turks, and Cheremis or Mari, Mordvins, Votiaks, who were Finno-Ugrians. Despite the denials of the Russian historians of the nineteenth century, Moscow did indeed pay tribute to Kazan, as to the successors of the Golden Horde. But Ivan III understood the advantage which he could derive from the quarrels dividing the family of Gengis Khan. He made it a point to have under his control in Moscow Tartar Tsarevitches who could count on the support of part of the Kazan oligarchy. Such a combination inspired a first attempt to seize Kazan in 1468. It failed. It resumed when a Kazan prince allied himself to the Tsar of Moscow against the Tartars of Crimea, that other branch of the former Golden Horde. The situation was reversed when the Khan of Crimea claimed to rule over Kazan. Henceforth Moscow set out to look for more trustworthy allies, who this time happened to be the Cheremis. Ivan IV made use of their timely help, as they had asked. Soon the decision was taken to march on Kazan to settle once for all this conflict with those "blasphemous Saracens". But the latter knew "their country" very well, as Kurbski says. They called for help from the Lithuanians to attack Moscow in the rear. But the Russians triumphed over the latter and the collapse of Kazan caused a sensation among all the peoples that had had to suffer from the harsh rule of the Tartars.

For all that the *Pax Rossica* was not to last: there were uprisings of the Tartars, afterwards those of the Cheremis and of the Chuvashes, and subsequently the recurrence of those of the Mordvins until the time of Stenka Razine (1667–71) and of Pugachev (1742–75). The Russians had decapitated the Tartar aristocracy of Kazan and levied on all the *iassak* a land tax. A "register of grievances", presented in 1767 to the legislative Commission set up by Catherine II describes, two centuries later, the service records of the Tartars, and summarizes in a way their adhesion to the government of the Russians. "We have served the Sovereign Emperor Peter the Great, of blessed and glorious memory, beloved grandfather of Her Majesty, and we have taken part in many a war and battle, for instance, in 7112 [1614], against defrocked Grishka the traitor, in 7120 [1612] against the rebellious Tartars of the province of Kazan, in 7197 [1639] to defend Samara against the Kalmuks of Astrakhan; in 7162 [1654] to defend Smolensk against the Poles; in 7166 on the occasion of the Bashkir revolt . . . " Around 1660 the number of the non-natives thus at the service of the Tsar was about 2,000. It had grown twenty-fold half a century later (see B. Nolde, 1952–53).

At the same time a large-scale expropriation had dispossessed the former sovereign and the Tartar oligarchy which was nearly exterminated in its last struggles for independence. The Tsar, the orthodox clergy and the Boyar cadets, that is, the men in the active service of the Muscovite state, helped themselves to the land and the loot, with the soldiers and military officers and their families constituting the majority of the colonists. The military colonization opened the way. Others followed in its wake. But the assets of the non-natives were protected. The Code of Tsar Alexis (1649) prohibited the Boyars, gentlemen and Russians of all ranks, from buying, exchanging, mortgaging, and even renting lands belonging to the Tartars, Mordvins, Chuvashes, Cheremis, Kotiaks and Bashkirs. This measure provided a sort of balance which few conquerors have instituted. Everybody had to stay at home. But this situation did not last. Peter the Great demolished this structure while an intense evangelization effort was subsequently and unceremoniously undertaken. The evangelization culminated, in the eighteenth century, with the more or less theoretical conversion of the Chuvashes, Cheremis, the Mordvins. But the Tartars resisted and demonstrated their intention to be able to continue to build mosques freely and to receive a passport to make it possible for them to go to Mecca. By degrees, the Orthodox Church used against them the methods of which the West had had prior experience: seizure of children, forced christenings in lieu of conscription, and schools for "Mohammedans" run by the Russian clergy, which soon became centres of rebellion.

In the nineteenth century the persistence of Islam took over from the Tartar patriotism. With its 2.3 million inhabitants in 1897 the Tartar community, after having offered a stiff resistance to the politics of russification, had gradually transformed itself into a varied society. It owned a third of the industrial establishments of the province and controlled the commerce with Central Asia. The Tartars of Kazan were thus the first community in the entire Muslim world to have had a powerful, well educated middle class which provided the leadership of the national movement within the

Russian Empire. Further, in 1917, it generated the first feminist movement in the Islamic world.

On both sides of the Urals and around the Ufa outpost the colonization of the Bashkirs took a different course as there was no unity in this semi-nomadic environment and it consequently lent itself to having Russian law imposed upon it. The Russians collected the *iassak* in furs and reconciled themselves with the aristocracy by conferring upon it the status of *tarkhan* (exempted from *iassak*). Thus protected, its members welcomed Chuvash, Votiak, Tartar refugees who developed their land. Up to the middle of the seventeenth century the number of Russians was small. But the occupying Russians very soon clashed with the Bashkirs. Endemic troubles persisted until a charter, drawn in 1728, defined the rights and duties of the three parties at odds one with the other: the state, the Bashkir tribes and the colonists. That was the first expression of the awareness which manifested itself by the establishment of a Muslim national movement inspired by Abdullah Miagsaldin, actually a Tartar, who wanted to "drive away the Russians with the help of God".

"Do not collaborate with these dirty Russians, shed their blood, loot their wealth, reduce them to captivity." The repression was awesome, to the point that a large number of Bashkirs resolved to become the slaves of the Kirghiz (to the south) for fear of being massacred. Those who stayed behind and survived took part in the uprising led by Pugachev. At the end of 1774, "the rebels and the Bashkirs are once more subjects of Your Majesty", wrote Pierre Panin in his report to Catherine II.

The disappearance of the other branch of the former Golden Horde came later, in 1783. It was not a mere Russo-Tartar conflict, for it had international repercussions. Actually the Tartars of Crimea had become the vassals of the Turkish Empire. In order to free themselves from this tutelage they had called upon Persia for help. Together making war against the Turks, they crossed the steppes to the north of the Sea of Azov to reach Daghestan. Now the Russians had been settled in Azov since the time of Peter the Great: these circumstances enabled them to intervene in these regions, and afterward to annex the Crimea during the reign of Catherine II. Meanwhile, to escape from the persecution inflicted upon the Christians, the Greeks and the Armenians had left the country for the Government of Azov.

A *Manifesto* and a decree accompanied the annexation of the Crimea:

> On our behalf and that of our successors, we make the irrefragable promise, to the inhabitants of Crimea, to hold them equal to our hereditary subjects, to preserve and defend their persons, their property, temples, their ancestral faith which shall remain sacred.
>
> We further promise that each class [*sostojanie*] shall have the same rights and privileges as are enjoyed by the equivalent classes in Russia.

In exchange for the peace that we guarantee them, we ask for their loyalty and we expect them to be as loyal as our subjects, to be as full of zeal, and also to deserve the imperial favour.

(Vernadsky, 1972, vol. 2)

The Manifesto was supplemented with a decree which Catherine sent to Prince Potemkine, Governor General of New Russia. It dealt with the collection of taxes – customs, salt, etc. – by stressing that "care be taken to avoid their being too heavy for the population . . . And, together with these revenues, it is necessary to assure the upkeep of the mosques, schools, and charity. It is fitting that a monument be erected to the glory of the annexation of Crimea and of the Tartar territories to the Russian Empire. Lastly, none of our subjects must do military service against his will or wish."

The annexation of the "provinces" of the Northern Caucasus, in particular of Georgia, was the pretext for a discussion, in St Petersburg, on the status of the new territorial acquisitions. This debate took place in 1820 and it dealt with the question: "Is it a question of colonies or not?"

These colonies can be said to be our colonies, and this not without foundation . . . for they bring us the products coming from the South . . .

We call them colonies because the government does not try to include these territories in the state system; it does not want to make them into a part of Russia, to russify the population; but merely to keep them as an Asian, but better governed, province.

Thus, at the time of Alexander I, a colony was for the Russians what the French called a protectorate, while the central lands, be they Tartar or other, formed part of the Empire and their inhabitants witnessed the gradual loss of the guarantees offered to them during the reigns of Ivan and Peter the Great.

The same fate was to befall the new territories acquired at the beginning of the revolutionary period and the Napoleonic era: Georgia, Finland, Poland.

In January 1801 the Manifesto of the annexation of Georgia recalled the circumstances which had led the Tsar George Ira Klievich to call for the protection of the Russians and the fact that the latter recognized that annexation as being "for ever". Georgia would keep the territories which it controlled and its populations would enjoy, according to their rank, the same status as the Russians. The Manifesto dealing with the annexation of Finland, which had been Swedish till then, proclaimed in 1809 the "preservation of the laws and customs, and the religion of the country [*Grundlagar*]" and guaranteed the freedoms and rights of each order. This meant that the Tsar acknowledged that "the oath of allegiance to Russia had been freely given" (Vernadski, ibid.). In other words, an autocratic Tsar in Russia, Alexander I recognized that in Finland he was only an elected Tsar.

But he went much further in Poland. In 1815, on receiving the main part of the territory of this country at the conclusion of the Conference of Vienna, he expressed his liberal tendencies by granting Poland the status of a state, indissolubly linked to his person, and without an independent foreign policy, but nevertheless enjoying the advantages of a constitutional charter. Article 16 of this charter guaranteed the freedom of the press; according to Article 156 the army would retain its own uniform and the insignia which indicated its nationality; the Orders of the White Eagle and of Saint Stanislas would be maintained (Article 160).

The Poles thus had the advantage of a genuine constitutional system, something which the Russians themselves did not have. "By putting into practice these liberal institutions", in a charter written in Russian and in French too, in order to offer the Poles this guarantee, Alexander I was perfectly aware that that example would have an impact on his own subjects. Indeed such was his wish.

But the period of grace ushered in by the 1815 Charter and the Speech to the Polish parliament of 1818 lasted only a few years.

The nationalities policy of the Soviet system

From 1917 onward, the nationalities policy of the Soviet Union tried, in a first movement, to take back the territories which had become independent during the civil war, Georgia, Ukraine, Armenia. With the conclusion of the military occupation, the operation was carried out in two phases: first, a bilateral alliance; secondly, the loss for these nations of their independent diplomacy, of their autonomous military forces – the process was completed in 1923–24, therefore before the Stalinist period – and afterwards for other nationalities. Stalin had recourse to a violent liquidation of the structures hostile to a reunification within the framework of the USSR: for example, the panislamic socialism of Sultan Galiev, Poale-Zion.

In fact, in 1917, the Bolsheviks had not imagined that nations, which had obtained their freedom thanks to the Revolution, could be reborn as entities and would be reunited to the Republic of Soviets only under violent constraint. Lenin called the high-Russian chauvinism into question. Actually those responsible for the failure of this ideal policy were rarely Russians, but authoritarian and centralizing neo-jacobins. They made use of several methods: either the right to self-determination surreptitiously passed from the nation to the working class (e.g. Ukraine, Finland), or to the "party of the working class" (for the recapture of Bukhara); or Moscow would provoke the emergence of more or less real nationalisms which made it possible to organize and defend Byelorussia in the west at the expense of Poland, or to balkanize Turkestan. Otherwise the reconquest was carried out to "prevent foreign intervention", that of Ataturk, of the Japanese; with the exception that in Georgia the intervention in 1919 occurred after the departure of the Germans, and that country had to sign an alliance treaty.

Anyhow for the reconquered Republics as for the others, the action of the Soviet power expressed itself by a whole series of measures, these being the same in all cases.

- The derussification of the authorities entrusted with the task of deciding the status of the non-Russian territories, for example, the Kav-kom (committee of the Caucasus), the Muskom (Muslim committee), the committee of the publication *Life of the Nationalities*. At first the *Narkomnats*, the Nationalities Committee, was composed only of non-Russsians, although it was difficult to find Bolsheviks in every nationality.
- The regeneration of the national cultures, which had fallen victim to the russification practised during the Tsarist period. This regeneration could go as far as being a genuine resurrection, for example in Armenia, if not even a self-revelation in the case of some of the peoples of the Caucasus. In this way, some explicit or latent frustrations came to an end. It may be said that no political system has done so much for the cultures of minorities, by using them in the interests of the Soviet State, as is illustrated by the case of the Kalmuks. On the other hand this policy later also served to set the peoples of Turkestan one against the other: Uzbeks, Kazaks, Tajiks.

   In its embryonic stage a contradiction existed between the Marxist vision of the development of societies which was represented by the Soviet system, and a Lenino-Stalinist practice related to the ethnic groups and the nations. This came out into the open a century later.
- The constitution of an entire constellation of entities – national, federal, state, all fitting into one another like Russian dolls (Federal Republics, Autonomous Republics, Regions, Territories) – made it possible to develop a non-Russian intelligentsia and to entrust it locally with para-state functions at least on the representative level, if not even with the effective exercise of power. With time these functions grew and got more varied. The effects could be felt during the short period of perestroika: in Baku, in Azerbaijan, the police were Azeri, opposed to the Armenians; in Erevana the police were Armenian.
- The policy of inducting an increasing number of non-Russian cadres into the federal constitutional system, on the pansoviet scale, was con-tinuously followed. Krushchev, Shevernadze, and others continued the practices of Stalin and Mikoyan. Such a penetration was slow, but it was irreversible and uninterrupted. However at the summit of the Soviet

157

State the tendency is reversed: from the middle of the twenties on, the Russians become proportionally more and more numerous in the Central Committee of the party.

The contrast with the preceding characteristic explains some of the facts of the disintegration of the USSR in 1989. There were no longer any non-Slavs at the head of the Soviet State. Neither were there any Russians in control of the Republics of the Caucasus or of Central Asia.

- The creation of the double nationality, federal and national, considered by the majority of non-Russians as a political promotion, was viewed as a humiliating step by those citizens – in particular, the Jews – whose nationality did not refer to a territorial status. The freedom granted to each to choose his own nationality proved to be a fiction. If those citizens wanted to be considered as Jews, they had the option of relinquishing. If they wanted to be Soviet citizens, their choice of nationality encountered the hostility or the racist reaction of the officials belonging to the nationality in question, in Ukraine and especially in Russia. That situation entailed the creation of the Republic of Birobijan, meant for the Jews, in eastern Siberia, a district which became autonomous in 1934, where no more than 100,000 Jews were still living on the eve of perestroika.

- By means of legislation sovietization of the Russians and non-Russians culminated in the equalization of status, in the standardization of political culture, from one end of the USSR to the other. However with the Stalinist reaction and the violence that accompanied it, particularly in relation to the nations which during the Second World War sided with the Germans (the Tartars of the Crimea, the Ingushes, the Germans of the Volga), sovietization was, after the war, felt, in Ukraine as well as in the Baltic states and in Moldavia, as a resumption of the russification process to the extent that the higher echelons of the hierarchy continued to be filled by Russians. The proliferation of laws common to the entire USSR, without bearing the seal of Russia, was nevertheless felt as such, considering that the standardization of the status of each nationality could have been seen as the subversion of its specific traits. The relative decline in the number of mixed marriages in Islamic countries, as well as the refusal to speak Russian in the Baltic countries, are signs of that resistance which in Ukraine became more cultural, political and religious – as it did in Georgia.

- For its part national Russian feeling ended up in its turn by reacting to the slow colonization of, with the exception of the highest institution of the State, some soviet bureaucracies (for example, the radio and the television) by the nationalities, by Georgians, Armenians, especially by Jews. The awakening of the high-Russian national sentiment must be seen as the obverse of the resistance offered by the nationalities. In any case, during the eighties, it is one of the forms of the latent opposition to the regime.

Consequently one can find nothing in common between the status of persons and that of the institutions, in the former Republics of the USSR, and the situation obtaining in Algeria. The only formal similarity was that while, during the fifties, in Algeria, in relation to the French, the "natives" wanted to assert themselves as Muslims, or as Arabs, or as Algerians, likewise in Central Asia, they wanted to see themselves either as Muslims, or as Turks, or Persians, or Uzbeks, or Tajiks. By actually claiming theirs as the real home of the Persian nation the latter provide the unique example of an expansion conducted by third parties.

The colonized: instruments of colonization
The Tajik example

Within the Soviet mind-set there existed no difference between those annexations which the West defined as the conquest of a nation – for instance, Russian then Soviet expansion in the Baltic countries – and those which the West views as colonies, for instance, Central Asia. The status of the Soviet Republics developed according to different criteria which "Marxist" ideology crafted to suit the demands of the moment. Moreover, in its relationship with its non-Soviet neighbours, Moscow elaborated a pattern of relations which was designed to favour the insertion of the still non-integrated nationalities. By so doing this set of relations opened the way to a limitless expansionism. The existence of the communist parties provided strength and justification to a new practice of annexations led by those very societies which, as submissive entities lying within the Empire, acted as the agents of this expansionism.

The expansionist process was carried out in several stages and in different ways. It culminated in the case of Tajikistan.

The earliest characters in this political drama appeared on the occasion of the recognition of the independence of Finland, in accordance with the right to self-determination. "It was enforced against our will", Stalin explained, "for it was granted not to the people, but to the bourgeoisie, and this by the hands of a socialist government" (December 1917). Moscow also recognized the counter-government which the Finnish Bolsheviks established in Tammersford. The first shift in the movement had occurred: the right to self-determination passed from the nation to the working class. The next example is offered by Ukraine where the government of Kharkov was recognized instead of the Rada of Kiev. A second shift developed when Moscow substituted, as legitimate representatives, "the party of the working class" for the restive working-class as such – as was the case in Bukhara.

Expansion had another avatar: the creation in the interior of the USSR of a national movement on the borders of a neighbouring country part of the territory of which was claimed by the Soviet government. This practice was invented in (Russian) Karelia with designs on (Finnish) Karelia. It was applied afterwards in Byelorussia, where an independence movement was active in the period prior to 1917, though the socialists refused to acknowledge its legitimacy. After 1920 Stalin urged the Byelorussians to claim portions of Lithuania and of Poland.

These two methods of expansion converged more or less in Soviet and Iranian Azerbaijan, but more so in Tajikistan, and by so doing exposed infinite horizons to the expansionist imagination of Stalin.

The centre of a civilization honoured by Avicenna and Firdausi, the Tajik country corresponded more or less to the ancient Sogdiana and had for long been the stakes in the rivalry between Bukhara and Khokand. The population spoke Persian and lived under the domination of the Uzbeks who spoke Turkish. When it became an autonomous region within the Soviet republic of Uzbekistan, this Tajik country rebuilt its identity, largely as a result of the teachers' fulfilling their tasks. The Tajiks opposed the carving-up of the ancient Russian Turkestan which led to the annexation to Uzbekistan of Bukhara and Samarkand, centres of Tajik civilization. Deprived of their cities the Tajiks first had to discover their identity, which they achieved by modernizing their language. They promoted it by delinking it from the Uzbek language and by substituting Latin for arab characters. "Latinization formed part of the project for national affirmation" (G. Jahangiri). Stalin supported the movement to weaken the Uzbeks, doing so all the more because the Tajiks represented the poorest of the rural populations. Above all, making Tajikistan an independent Soviet Republic presented vast opportunities to expansionism.

The creation of the Republic of Tajikistan, the "7th Republic", was initiated from the eastern regions of the ancient emirate of Bukhara. It was just a simple republic in 1925. It was promoted to the rank of Soviet Republic four years later, once the wounds of the struggle against the Basmashis were healed and the adventure of Enver Pasha, who had set up his headquarters in Dushambe, was forgotten. This promotion was in response to the fall of King Amamullah of Afghanistan, an ally. To enable it to have a wider foundation, Moscow allotted to Tajikistan the eastern part of Gorno-Badakshan – the roof of the Pamir – which was actually populated by the Kirgizes and should have remained federated to that other political entity. Indeed it was for the sake of the Persian identity of Tajikistan that the creation of this state had been initiated and given legitimacy: it was developed in opposition to the other autonomous republics who were members of the Turkish world.

Furthermore the Soviet view of the history of the Tajiks considered this territory as the very centre of the entire Persian civilization. Bobozdhan G. Gafurov, a young historian and also First Secretary of the Tajik Communist Party, recalled that Spitanem who, twenty-three centuries earlier, had driven Alexander the Great from these regions, was a Tajik. According to him the Tajiks were the first to oppose the Mongol invasion. As the fatherland of the great poet Firdausi Tajikistan would help the Persians recover their true identity and culture which had been subverted by the reactionary regime of Teheran. Moscow made a contemporary Persian revolutionary, Abulkasim Lakhuti, the national poet of Tajikistan. In his writings he prophesied that Iran would soon cease to be defiled, would become free, "a Soviet land". Naturally this "blemish" was the oil concession of the Anglo-Iranian Company.

In addition to its being the centre of a regenerated Persia, Tajikistan was also meant to serve as the starting point for a resumption of Russian influence in Afghanistan. This was an old story, with its ultimate fallout happening in 1979. The idea of annexing Afghanistan had been kept alive on account of the intervention of this country in the Soviet civil war, since it was used as a base for the Basmashis and it provided shelter to their leaders. According to the Soviet encyclopaedia, the peoples of Afghanistan are Tajiks, Uzbeks, Turkomans, all and each of these constituting real nations in the USSR. The number of Tajiks was evaluated at between two and three million, thus comprising 24 percent of the population of Herat province, 48 percent of that of Kabul, and so on. Soviet ethno-historians recalled that in the eighteenth century the Afghan tribes of Ahmed Khan carved out the southern part of the khanate of Bukhara, in which operation the Tajiks lost the Bakh region, thus bringing about the break-up of that state, which had actually been multinational. These historical reminders became helpful in the subsequent process of recovering a part of Afghanistan, and at least in preventing a repetition of Kabul's interfering into the affairs of ancient Turkestan.

By creating the autonomous Republic of Tajikistan in 1925, Stalin had sent this message to its leaders: "Salutations to Tajikistan, to the new Republic of workers at the gate of Hindustan . . . may it serve as a model and as an examplar for the peoples of the East." This tendency lost its meaning and its scope when India became independent in 1947. But that did not prevent Tursun Zade, the Stalin Prize of 1948, from inviting the Indians, at the time of glory for the triumphant USSR, to join Tajikistan, the capital of which, Dyshambe (Stalinabad), had gone from 5,000 to 82,000 inhabitants in less than twenty years.

These grandiose expansionist projects – in the direction of Iran, Afghanistan, even India – collided with the reality of the situation in Tajikistan and with the mentalities of its populations. The local leaders, poorly versed in the strategic vision of the Supreme Leader, did indeed exert themselves, but to reach goals which were more familiar, more accessible and more popular. The purpose was to drive away the Russians, to constitute a great Tajikistan, *but* at the expense of the neighbouring Uzbekistan. How could something which did not materialize in 1931–33 succeed in 1994?

5

ROSE-COLOURED LEGEND AND PITCH-BLACK LEGEND

In the mother countries, the rose-coloured legend assumed a multiplicity of forms, wherever it may have been found in the "colonial party", in the make-believe world of the writers and artists. The pitch-black legend likewise from its very origin arose from several centres and expressed itself in different forms. In the twentieth century both made use of the cinema.

In the West colonization has been certainly presented as an essentially economic fact. It was also a proselytizing enterprise which assumed it had a mission to christianize and civilize peoples deemed to be or defined as inferior. Still at the very outset this representation of colonization was challenged. Without doubt the colonized peoples did not fail to manifest their sensitivity to the different aspects of the phenomenon. But the racist aspect of colonization provoked their anger and incited them to offer the most dogged resistance because they felt that their identity was at stake. It is a moot question whether the colonizers were aware of the problem. Those who called into question the principle of colonization certainly were, but to the point that they did not perceive that racism prevailed also among the colonized peoples, at least among some of them, and well before the Europeans laid their hands on them.

The eulogists of the colonial saga saw things from a different perspective. A sophisticated structure of propaganda had been built, channelled by newspapers, illustrated magazines, post cards, school text-books, and colonial exhibitions like, among others, that of 1931 in Paris. Such a system was more or less organized by what came to be known as the "colonial party", with its lobbies. Long before the effective elaboration of an imperialist policy, men like Thomas Carlyle in Great Britain, Chomyakov and Tiouttchev in Russia, proclaimed the superiority of the British, of the Slav. These movements spawned *leagues* which were set up in every country: the Round Table circle in Great Britain, the *Deutscher Nationalverein* in Germany, the *Società nazionale* in Italy. In France men like Eugène Etienne before 1914 and Paul Doumer, especially after the First World War, were the foremost champions of this colonial party.

However this influence descending from on high merged with another one which deeply affected the western society. It did so incidentally, indirectly. It was a legend that arose spontaneously and it won the adherence of the public. It did not set out to reach political or economic goals; it did not intend to glorify the greatness of empire. Its actors only meant to stimulate the imagination, to send out an invitation to dream.

From travel literature to Jules Verne

At the outset such was indeed the role played by the travel literature of which *Robinson Crusoe* was the prototype. This has been brought out by Octave Mannoni in *Psychologie de la colonisation*. After *Robinson Crusoe* Europe came into contact with the natives by means of the collection of exotic literature the earliest heroes of which are encountered in America. This literary fashion is illustrated by Chamfort with his *La jeune Indienne* (1748), by Colman in *Inkle and Yarico* (1787), well before Chateaubriand, Fenimore Cooper or Bernardin de St Pierre. From these symbolic characters emerges for the first time a romantic structure: a story of the love between a European and a young native girl which represents purity in contrast to the rottenness that prevails in the mother country. In the writings of Pierre Loti, Joseph Conrad the exotic societies – Tahiti, Turkey – are always more just than those of the European. They incite people to leave for the far-off lands.

A second category of books – the adventure story – reinforces this tendency. It transforms the difficulties encountered in Europe into a chain of heroic deeds which transfigures the reader who identifies himself with the adventurer. Independently of those who, like Rudyard Kipling, by this artifice praise the greatness of the Empire, others consolidate the representation of these new "elites" of technical and industrial civilization. Jules Verne invented these new adventurers whose actions take place in the colonies.

Located at the very edge of racism his works present an ambiguous standpoint – still in the tradition of the *Supplément au voyage de Bougainville* – reminiscent of the idealist view which, in the eighteenth century, while extolling the superiority of the natural state, nevertheless insisted on the movement to a genuinely civilized world. That is, a world of progress, of technology, of hygiene: arguments which repeatedly provided justification for the colonial enterprises together with all their abuses.

In *Enfants du capitaine Grant* (1868) Thalcave, the Araucanian guide is the ideal representative of the Good Savage. He is "grave and motionless, full of a natural grace, with his proud casualness, his discretion, his devotion, his innate closeness with the natural world". The other types can be met with on the borders of the Americas and of Siberia, in deserts, in short, in those places where they have not instituted a genuine state. On the other hand the "Bad Savage", those "wild beasts with a human face" are to be found in black Africa and in the land of the "Tartars". They are more often leaders than subjects. In a subtle sense they represent those who oppose the enterprises of France and of Russia, its ally. Captain Nemo is the avatar of the revolt against the masters of the world. Defining himself as an Indian, from India, he stands as an opponent to the British. So are the heroes of the *La maison à vapeur* (1880), or the Maoris of New Zealand, those "proud men who offer a stubborn resistance to the invaders".

Criticism of the British system of colonization lies at the root of Jules Verne's works. This is how he evokes their behaviour in Australia: "Where the major maintains that they are monkeys." The colonizers believed that the blacks were wild animals. They hunted them and killed them with their guns. The opinions of the jurists were sought after to prove that the Australian was beyond natural law. The newspapers of Sydney even went so far as to propose the use of the efficient means of wholesale poisoning to get rid of them. "The killings went on on a massive scale and entire tribes disappeared." About Tasmania and Australia Jules Verne writes in *Mrs. Branican* (1891): "If the annihilation of a race is the last word in colonial progress, the English may boast of having succeeded in their task."

Jules Verne relied on principles derived from the ideology of the 1848 Revolution for his defence of the victims of British colonialism. Still what strikes one in Jules Verne is that the idea of progress – the progress of civilization based on technology – overrides all other considerations. The right of peoples has reality only in so far as they adhere to this civilization. For example, in *Mathias Sandorf* (1885) he reserves his sympathy for the Hungarians and the Poles, but not for those who refuse to accept progress. "Certainly right gives in to force, but civilization never retreats and it seems that it draws all rights from necessity." "It is the law of progress – the Indians will disappear. In the face of the Anglo-Saxon race the Australians and the Tasmanians have vanished. Perhaps one day the Arabs will be annihilated by the French colonization" (*La Janganda*, quoted in Jean Chesneaux, 1971).

As a matter of fact Jules Verne lends to the English sentiments which are shared by Frenchmen too – among others, the idea that the blacks are beasts. On 19 September 1887 the critic Jules Lemaître writes:

No particular event to report this week. I can only see Ashantis at the Zoological Garden. This garden is indeed charming . . . , the little children experience the joy of watching the mysterious animals they read about in the travel stories: they can imagine themselves riding an ostrich, or perched on a camel. Moreover, that nothing be lacking in the festive atmosphere, savages parade before their eyes. These exhibitions do not present a glorious image of humanity . . . But surely someone will ask me what have these folks come to the world for? – Well, let us face it, the Ashantis of the Gold Coast and other savages do exist to serve us one day.

The cinema takes over: "The Charge of the Light Brigade"

The cinema took over from the novel or the newspaper to entrench this "colonialist" mentality. Some of the leading directors who have contributed to foster this attitude have done their best to forget it. For example, soon after having directed his "leftist" films *La Vie est à nous* and *La Marseillaise*, and while recalling his "souvenirs" in *Le Point* (1938), Jean Renoir simply leaves out a reference to *Le Bled* (1929). One can guess the reason for this omission. That film was financed by the Governor General to commemorate the centenary of the capture of Algiers: it opens with a glorification of the conquest and is considered to be "a work of useful colonial propaganda" (*Afrique française*, May 1929). What is striking in this representation of French Algeria is that one scarcely sees any Arabs in it. Nor do they exist in *Le Grand jeu* which Jacques Feyder directed in 1934. This characteristic threads through a whole succession of films made during those years of imperial glory. Of course, the Kasbah is present, very much so in *Pépé le Moko*. But it provides the stifling backdrop to the action more than it represents a refuge from colonization. Elsewhere the Maghreb does indeed appear as the background, in the same way as the ancient Rome does in Shakespeare: that is, this background has no historical consistency, even when the film, like *La Bandera*, is shot entirely outdoors.

Like the Other, the "native" does not exist. Moreover his role is played by a European.[1] If he still wants to express himself, he would not know how to do it except by westernizing himself. Pierre Sorlin is right in pointing out that in *Pépé*, the Arab is identified with the Jew, in keeping with the anti-semitic atmosphere which prevailed in the thirties: cunning deportment, elusive look. If the native crosses the limit and if the Moorish woman falls in love with a colonist, the stage is set for a major sensation. Pierre Billon's *Bourrasque* (1935) shows for the first time a native woman as the heroine of a story, with the action set in Algeria. The French cinema would never again take up this taboo subject.

Whatever the background of the story, be it the hot sand, the kasbah or the dives, the heroes are invariably military men, from *Roman d'un spahi* of M. Bernheim to *La Bandera* of Julien Divivier. In this film the Arab is indeed present, but he is seen at a minimum, and even then as the "bastard" who disturbs the order established by the colonist. The action takes place in Spanish Morocco: it bespeaks only the glory of the Foreign Legion. The men who have joined the Legion cleanse themselves of their criminal past by insuring the continuation of this pacification, and by dying for it.

In 1934 a Pathé newsreel describes the operation of the French troops in Morocco. By a sort of "lapsus" which commonly occurs in the history of the cinema the commentary lucidly explains the role of the troops. This is what the soundtrack says, against the background of a convoy of trucks making its way in the Moroccan mountains:

166

Together with these troop movements there is an uninterrupted movement of civilian transport, and we may now utter the word conquest, for it is a matter of a peaceful conquest. Observe the line of trucks beside the military machines: they are civilian trucks; they are already there; they follow the army; they resupply the troops and the pacified ksours. They have come by road, by trails, and sometimes without the advantage of a road or a trail, "in the middle of nature" as they say it here. The civilian drivers of these trucks, the true knights of the Moroccan adventure, have seen many of their comrades killed at the steering wheel. That is why they are now accompanied by a fast and vigilant guard, the armoured car. *Observe that these armoured cars are not military vehicles* (my italics). They belong to industrialists mindful of the protection of their staff against the rebels, the dissidents, the pirates. The drivers are civilian, but the army, won over by these methods, supply them with a crew under the leadership of a non-commissioned officer. These armoured cars have made such a good impression upon the minds of the bandits that, since their introduction, none has failed in the fulfilment of its mission, which is to resupply the ksours, even those that can only be reached with the utmost difficulty.

A convoy of trucks in this Pathé documentary, a convoy of horses in *The Charge of the Light Brigade*: the action takes place a century or so earlier, on the confines of India, but who cares? However, the difference between those films celebrating the glory of the British Empire and the others is that, with the exception of *Four Feathers* (1929) in which the action takes place in the Sudan, they do not show outcasts who strive to redeem themselves in the colony. On the contrary they show the flower of the youth educated at Oxford, or at Cambridge. The joints and brothels, the favourite locations of Julien Duvivier and of Jacques Feyder, are replaced by the governor's dance parties, the clubs, the hunting parties filmed by Henry Hathaway (1935), or by Michel Curtiz (1936). It is true that the latter films are American. But they are inspired by the same ethos and above all they display the same stereotypes which have been competently analysed by Jeffrey Richards in *Visions of Yesterday*. The exercise of power rests on the consent of subjects who assent to the code established by the British, whereas native despots, greedy for power, oppress those who are under their control. The gap between the two systems – Indian and British – is stressed by exaggerating the essentially British characteristics – for example, humour, calmness, love for sports – and the characteristics attributed to the Indian. There are several archetypal natives: the faithful one is the most highly valued, frequently a child, as in *Gunga Din* for example, where he climbs to the tower and sounds the bugle to save Cutter, captive of the Thugs (Cary Grant), then dies, leaving behind an undying memory.

The valiant adversary is another character who brightens the British vision of the Empire. In *Khartoum* (1966) the Mahdi who fights against the British is so sympathetic – it is true that he is played by Laurence Olivier – that, even with the British dying in large numbers, he wins the affection of the spectator. Another type emphasizes the racist nature of these films: it is the native who would like to westernize himself and to be accepted by the English. But he does not succeed. Such is Surat Khan in *The Charge of the Light Brigade*: he has studied at Oxford and is a good cricketer. But deep within himself he is perverse. Of necessity he is a traitor, or he commits perjury. The educated native is almost always a wicked man.[2]

This trait reveals the fear which the British have of seeing the natives getting educated and hence to see their dominion losing its legitimacy. We can see therein the transfer of the old phantasm of the ruling classes of the mother country – who were always hostile to free, public education – to the colony, with this difference that here the rising class belongs also to a race which has been defined and actually perceived as being inferior.

Bartolomé de Las Casas and the defence of the colonized

Bartolomé de Las Casas, famous for his defence of the Indians, still stands as the greatest opponent of colonial violence. Admittedly he was preceded by the appeals of Francisco de Vitoria who, as early as 1534, called into question the war prosecuted against the Incas. But at that time he was challenging the principle of the Pope's donation, as the latter was not the temporal leader of the world. In contrast, the appeal of Bartolomé de Las Casas was essentially humanitarian in nature. When he writes the *Brevísima relación de la destrucción de las Indias* (1552), he justifies this accusation in terms of his compassion for *his* fatherland, Castile, for fear lest God destroy it on account of its heinous sins. "The cry of human blood now rises to Heaven." As an eye witness of the crimes perpetrated in the Bahamas, and later in Hispaniola, he quotes his sources whenever it is possible and collects reports (*probanzas*) submitted to him by priests who share his ideas. He deems that it is proper for the message of the Gospel to spread to the Indies. But war and violence visited upon peoples who are free by natural right jeopardize and sully the colonizing mission of which the message is a part. On the spot he was able to arrange for the peaceful access of his Dominican brothers to the Tezulutlan, that land of war which soon became a land of peace, the Vera Paz.

The defence of the Indians lies in showing that they are human beings, without any difference from those who were colonizing them. The barbarism which gives legitimacy to the violence of the Castilians occurs only on rare occasions. Accordingly no one ought to give them any other lesson than conversion to Christianity, but with their own free adhesion, after presentation of the Gospel to them. Las Casas makes known his first argument in the *Tratado comprobatorio* (middle of the sixteenth century), written for the sake of Charles V, to confirm his rights on the New World. "To those who claim that the Indians are barbarians, we reply that these people own villages, towns, cities, kings, lords, and a political system which, in some of the kingdoms, is better than ours. Likewise we can prove to them that if, in some part of the Indies, human flesh has been consumed and innocent persons sacrificed . . . there are nevertheless thousands of leagues of territories where none of these actions has been committed, neither in the large Spanish island, nor in Cuba, nor in Jamaica, Yucatan, Florida, Peru, and in many other places."

His *Apologetica historia* described the nature of their customs. This text is written in Castilian in order to give it a circulation larger than his theses, to popularize his fight. After describing the Inca Empire and the Aztec Empire this monumental work of 263 chapters ends characteristically with the conviction that human societies can evolve. It was an act of faith shared by no one in those times.

> These nations were equal to, if they did not surpass, the many nations of the world known to be well ordered and reasonable and were inferior to none of them. They were thus the equal of the Greeks and the Romans and, in regard to some of their customs, even surpassed them . . . They were superior to England, France and some of our regions of Spain . . . It is therefore a matter of fact that, on the whole, they are well disposed to receive not only moral doctrine, but also our Christian religion, even if in some particular region some may have not yet reached the political perfection of a well governed republic and still maintain certain corrupt customs. There is no reason for us to be surprised by the defects, the barbarous and loose customs which may be observed in the Indian nations, nor to hold them in contempt . . . However much it may be mired in vices no nation is excluded from full participation in the Gospel . . . Most of the nations of the world, if not all of them, were indeed more perverted, irrational and depraved . . . We were ourselves much worse at the time of our pagan ancestors, over the whole expanse of our Spain, in terms of the barbarism of our way of life and the depravity of our customs.

The power of Las Casas derives from his having been a tireless propagandist of his humanitarian idea. It provoked the hostility of the powerful eulogists and beneficiaries of the conquest, those captains and soldiers, as well as the *encomenderos*, who had enriched themselves with the loot. Las Casas first clashed squarely with them when he was appointed Bishop of Chiapa, in Mexico, before having to face a threatening coalition which succeeded in recruiting in Spain itself a talented lawyer, the learned de Sepulveda, of the University of Salamanca.

The "Great Polemic" between Las Casas and Sepulveda became the subject of an open controversy in August 1550, in the chapel of the San Gregorio convent, in the presence of fourteen participants. The learned Sepulveda replied to the arguments of Las Casas by contending that:

> the war waged against the Indians was not only legal, but was to be recommended for it was a legitimate war in regard to four points: 1. The seriousness of the offences of the Indians, above all their idolatry and their unnatural sins. 2. The vulgarity of their intelligence which makes them a servile, barbarous nation, destined to be the obedient subjects of more advanced men, such as the Spaniards. 3. The requirements of the faith, as their subjection will make preaching to them easier and more expeditious. 4. The sufferings which they inflict upon one another, killing innocent men as offerings in their sacrifice.

The controversy ended in favour of Las Casas, for the learned Doctor did not obtain the right of imprimatur. It is true that his arguments went against the interests of the King who hoped to deprive the conquerors of their power to treat the Indians as they wished. He wanted to bring the Indians, as much as possible, directly under his rule, in the name of the Church. Henceforth the Kings of Spain did not want the discoveries to be called "conquests". At the head of the Council for the Indies they appointed men who must lead the populations "peacefully and charitably". "The Indians must be pacified and indoctrinated, but in no way harmed." The ambition and the intention of the monarchy was indeed to subject the lands and the peoples to the Crown, but in a different way.

The controversy had unveiled two conceptions of colonization. Sepulveda's emphasized the differences between the Indians and the Spaniards, to justify the dominion of those who deemed themselves to be superior. Accordingly he defended the principles of a hierarchical society, as Aristotle advocated, in terms of the recognition of differences invariably associated with inferiorities. The view of Las Casas is egalitarian: it emphasizes the Indians' similitude to the Christians, and even attributes the virtues of the faithful to the faithless, since everybody can become Christian. He stresses that no time must be lost to broaden the kingdom of Christ. According to Las Casas, the real dregs of humanity are those who cannot become Christian, that is, "the Turks and the Moors, the Muslims".

The appeals of Las Casas had no effect on the behaviour of the Spanish conquistadores, in fact, not more than those of the poet Camoens (1524–80) on his Portuguese fellow-citizens:

> Glory of empire! Most unfruitful lust
> After the vanity that men call fame!
> It kindles still, the hypocritical gust,
> By rumor, which as honor men acclaim . . .

Thou who now into pleasant vanity
Art swept away by fantasy so light
Thou who to cruelty and savagery
Now giv'st the names of courage and of might,
Thou who dost value in such high degree
Contempt of life, which should in all men's sight
Still be esteemed, for One in time gone by,
Who gave us life, was yet afraid to die;

Hast thou not ever near thee Ishmael's breed,
With whom to carry on perpetual war?
Does he not cleave to the false Arab creed,
If it be but Christ's faith thou fightest for?
If further lands and treasures be thy need,
Of towns and fields, has he not thousands more?
And is he not in arms courageous still,
If praise for triumph earned be all thy will?

Wilt thou raise up the foeman in the gate,
While seeking out another worlds away,
Whereby unpeopled is the ancient state,
Weakened afar, and falling to decay?
Will thou rush on unknown ill and dubious fate,
That Fate may flatter thee and great things say . . .
(The Lusiads, translated by Leonard Bacon,
Canto IV, 95, 100, 101)

Against the black slave trade: reasons and sentiments

One observes that no less than two centuries separate the first appeals for the defence of the colonized peoples and the second wave of the humanitarian movement. Was it regenerated by the travel literature which thrived around 1700 and later? One recalls Louis Bougainville, Father Lafitan, Walter Raleigh . . .

It was the priests who, in the sixteenth century, led the first movement. It is a moot question if their aim was to defend the Indians or to call into question the Princes who were exercising their domination over them, unless it was a matter of their contributing to the expansion of Christianity. For the Church did not evince the same concern when the soldiers of Charles V or of Philip II were submitting the Infidels to fire and sword.

However two centuries later the struggles between the Church and the Empire had ended with the result that the Church was reduced to impotence in the face of the great enterprises of the large states. Its humanitarian appeal lost its power and also one of its raisons d'être. The Church limited the application of its principles to its own limited sphere, with its funds reserved for the missions, those of Florida and of Paraguay in particular.

In the eighteenth century one encounters the same ambiguity in the humanitarian appeals in favour of the Indians and the Blacks, as is evident in Afra Behn's best-seller *Oroonoko* (1688), which relates sympathetically the story of a rebellious black of Surinam. But the action against slavery proceeds from the fact that it is the slaves who henceforth bring forth surges of pity, especially on the part of priests, particularly those Methodist and Quaker sects who soon in England finally succeeded in bringing about the end of the slave trade and the abolition of slavery. The ambiguity lies in the criticism coming from the philosophers on the continent – today they would be called the intellectuals. Such criticism was aimed at the "despotic" governments which condoned that colonial policy more than those who benefited from it, that is, the colonists and the merchants. The contradiction shows up during the French Revolution.

From this point of view, and even though they were initiated by Louis XV the Instructions sent in 1760 to Clugny, the Administrator of the Leeward Isles, testify to this ambiguity: "See to it that masters treat the slaves with humanity . . . it is the surest means to prevent the slaves from running away, as this is not only ruinous for the inhabitants, but dangerous for the colony." The Governor of the Martinique, Count Ennery, receives these Instructions: "Informed that the majority of the inhabitants of the islands fail in doing their essential duty of feeding their negroes, His Majesty recommends . . . that the greatest attention be paid to those abuses which are so contrary to humanity and to the very interests of the inhabitants" (Duchet, 1971).

Abbé Raynal's *Histoire philosophique et politique des établissements et du commerce des Européens dans les deux Indes* (1770) may be considered – together with Las Casas' *Mémoires* (1542) and the several writings of Frantz Fanon (1960) – as one of the main manifestos of anti-colonialism. Father Raynal's work became a best-seller. Most of his successors drew their examples and arguments from it, just as he himself had borrowed from the writings of Las Casas and other priests as well as from the reports of his contemporaries on the situation obtaining in the islands, particularly those of Baron Bessner, of René-Victor Malouet, and a few others. The tone of his book is polemical. He castigates the colonists, the policy of the Kings.

Beyond the equator, man is no longer English, nor Dutch, nor French, nor Spaniard, nor Portuguese. From his country he retains the principles and the prejudices which sanction or condone his behaviour. Crawling when he is weak, violent when he is strong, urged on to acquire, under pressure to enjoy, capable of committing all the crimes that will all the more quickly enable him to attain his ends. He is a domestic tiger in the forest. The thirst for blood wells up again in him. That is how all the Europeans, all of them, without any distinction, have revealed themselves in the regions of the New World, to which they have brought a common fury, the lust for gold.

In the thirteenth book of his work Raynal shows to what extent the King holds those men in contempt:

> Let the fury of a storm bury thousands of these colonists under the ruins of their dwellings, and it shall concern us less than does a duel taking place at our gate . . . Let the horrors of famine drive the inhabitants of San Domingo or of Martinique to devour one another, and we shall commiserate with them less than with the disaster of a hailstorm spoiling the harvests in some of our villages . . . It is quite natural that such an indifference be an expression of distance . . . That is so because the Kings do not recognize the colonists as their own subjects . . . I say it emphatically because this is what I think: the invasion of that part of their estate by the sea would move them to a lesser degree than if they lost it by its being invaded by a rival power. It does not matter that these men die or live so long as they do not belong to somebody else . . .

Well before Raynal, Fénelon had been one of the first to denounce the spirit of conquest, wherever it was practised. But his censure remained on a moral level. Voltaire's innovation, however, consisted in pragmatically approaching the problem of the colonies, with an evaluation of the pros and the cons from the point of view of the interests of the state. Spain, he observes, has acquired an immense fortune, but it has thereby depopulated itself. "It remains to be seen if the worth of the cochineal or the quinquina is sufficient to compensate for the loss of so many men." Such a reasoning was to persist and develop for centuries, down to Gladstone in England, later to Raymond Cartier in France, with each of them providing his own specific computations.

In the eighteenth century the anti-colonialist arguments clash with those of the liberals and merchants who praise the advantages and the profits generated by colonial commerce and colonization. That is why they were confronted with dangers of another kind: above all that of the depopulation of the mother countries criticized by Boulain-villiers, Mirabeau and Montesquieu. Men must stay where they find themselves. Otherwise they fall sick and die and the nation dissipates its strength.

But soon questions arose about the economic interest of the colonies itself. The new argument was propounded by William Petty who, in *The political arithmetic* (1690) was the first to make an account of the expenses and revenue to put to the credit and the debit of the English colonies.

François Quesnay prepared a similar assessment for France by squarely asking the question which became an obsession during the following centuries: are the colonies profitable?

The criticism of the slave trade culminated in its limitation, and subsequently in its prohibition. Nevertheless the practice persisted.

As is often the case, it is Montesquieu who comes up with the clearest and most explicit diagnosis: "Having exterminated the peoples of America, the Europeans have had to enslave the peoples of Africa in order to use them to clear all those lands." This observation does not in the least imply any commiseration with regard to the blacks: "It is impossible for us to assume that these folks are men; for if we supposed that they were men, we would begin to believe that we are not ourselves Christians." Voltaire provides us with realistic and moral description of their cruel fate: "We go to buy those negroes on the Guinea Coast . . . Thirty years ago one could buy a negro for fifty pounds; about five times less than a fat ox. This human stock today in 1772 costs fifteen hundred pounds. We tell them that they are men, like us, that they have been redeemed by the blood of a God who died for them, and then we make them work like beasts of burden. We feed them poorly. If they want to escape we cut off one of their legs and we make them use their hands to turn the sugar mills, after they have received a wooden leg. And after all that we still embolden ourselves to speak of the law of nations!"

The ambiguity which pervades these positions derives from the prevailing conceptions of the time: the blacks must first become men before one can speak to them of their freedom. Such indeed is the intention of the *Société des Amis des Noirs* led by Jean-Pierre Brissot who wished to see "the end of this loathsome trade" (in slaves), but in the meantime advocated that they be submitted to a softer treatment. "The enemies of the blacks take delight in spreading false rumours about this *Société*, which it is our duty to dispel. They insinuate that the aim of the *Société* is to destroy slavery at one stroke, something which would ruin the colonies . . . It only asks for the abolition of the slave trade because, as a consequence, the planters . . . would provide better treatment to their own slaves. Not only does the *Société des Amis des Noirs* not call for the abolition of slavery at this moment, but it would see it as a cause for sadness if it had to entertain such a proposal. The blacks are not yet ripe for their freedom; we must prepare them for it . . . "

However the interest in Brissot's movement lies in his being the first to have tried to internationalize the humanitarian campaign. The partner of the *Société* (whose members included Condorcet and Abbé Sieyès) was, naturally, the Society for the Abolition of Slavery established in London by Thomas Clarkson and Grenville Sharp. It possessed a unique forum, as soon as its representative, William Wilberforce, was elected to the House of Commons. The membership of this committee was not comprised of philosophers, as was Brissot's. But it was anchored in the popular imagination. Actually it was an offshoot of the Methodist Church, which made abolitionism a humanitarian cause, and a justification for living as far as its followers were concerned. It won its first victory in winning a case in 1772 in London. By referring to natural right and to the absence in England of any law or custom which sanctioned the practice of slavery, a judge freed a Black slave who had run away and had been recaptured by his master on English soil.

The first stage may be defined thus: if, as from that date, slavery and the slave trade continued to exist in the British overseas territories, it nevertheless disappeared in the mother country where blacks and whites coexisted in full possession of the same rights. Accordingly the 20,000 black slaves then living in Great Britain were freed. The second stage occurred in 1787 when Granville Sharp, who had established a Committee for Help to the Poor Black, settled 411 "black" colonists on the coast of Sierra Leone in order to create a Christian society similar to English society. As a matter of fact these blacks had learnt the lesson of their past experiences: instead of cultivating the land and displaying the Christian virtues, they did not hesitate to indulge in the slave trade themselves, which they discovered to be more profitable, and did so while singing hymns to their glory. It was a dismal failure. Still neither Wilberforce, nor the Baptist Missionary Society, nor the Church Missionary Society gave up the struggle against the slave trade which was officially prohibited by the British Parliament in 1807.

In the meantime, after being conquered by Napoleon, then retaken by the English, Sierra Leone became in 1808 the first Crown colony in Black Africa.

The eighteenth century movement had been of a humanitarian nature. It did not arise as the result of a reduced need for slaves. The evidence lies in the slave trade being as active after 1807 as earlier. The culmination of the trade coincided with the peak of the sugar plantation economy, between 1740 and 1830. It is not a mere coincidence that the receiving ports happened to be successively those of Jamaica, Martinique and Cuba. Around 1830 the rate of departures from Africa was still 60,000 each year. The trade slowed down only when it became more profitable to keep the blacks in Africa for their use in the production of palm oil. This transformation became important during the latter half of the nineteenth century.

Nevertheless the movement had been initiated. It was indeed the English sphere of influence that witnessed the first symbolic acts. The disillusion arising from the experience of Freetown, in Sierra Leone, bore the seed that was to grow later: to put an end to slave trade it was first necessary to civilize Africa.

After all, up till then, the slave trade had been a legal operation, at least south of the Equator, that is, to Brazil. Other movements, spawned by the after-effects of the French Revolution, finally called into question the old system of slave trade, of slavery, and of labour in the colonies. Victor Schoelcher took up this cause with uncompromising passion.

Socialists and the colonial question

After the Church in the sixteenth century, then the philosophers in the eighteenth century, it was the socialists who, at the beginning of the twentieth century, provided the impetus for an in-depth examination of colonial conquests and imperialism. With the International having been still-born in 1871, it was the Second International which, after its appearance in 1889, dealt with it, but even then in a lateral sense. The socialists were concerned with the interests of the working class and they approached the colonial problems only in relation to these interests. For instance, when Jules Guesde, in France, manifested his opposition to the conquest of Tunisia in 1881, it was only because he viewed such an enterprise as benefiting only the bourgeoisie. Inversely when Turati in Italy or Kautsky explained that the conquests were carried out by the backward and parasitic classes – the dynastic circles, the military elite – the struggle against expansion then became tantamount to fighting for the real interests of the rising classes, the industrialists and the workers.

The first socialist to confront these problems directly was the Dutchman Van Kol who had lived in Java. "I spent there the sixteen happiest years of my life, in the midst of the natives whom I learned to love, among people so sweet-natured and peaceful, always enslaved, always abandoned, always martyrs." He believed that the French colonization in Tunisia was a model of humanity, in comparison with the Dutch colonization, because the French had preserved in that country the traditional institutions. Together with Edward Bernstein in Germany, Vandervelde in Belgium and Jaurès in France, the socialist movement was in favour of a "positive colonial policy", which would cease to be the colonial policy of the bourgeoisie. The British socialist Hyndman went a step further: he denounced the colonial exploitation of India: "We deliberately create famines in order to feed the greed of our prosperous classes."

Van Kol stressed the necessity of the colonial reality, on account of the vital interests of the bourgeois class in full expansion, as well as of the necessity of civilizing the populations that had not yet reached the technological level of Europe. At the same time radical thinkers, such as Karski in Poland, directed their denunciations specially against imperialism of which Hobson calls into account the economic raison d'être in a demonstration which Lenin later used in writing *Imperialism*. However there were no natives among all those critics. The exception was one of the spiritual fathers of Gandhi, Dadabhai Naoroji, who was the first Indian to take part in the debates with Van Kol. Naoroji was a moving, moderate old man of eighty-four who pleaded with the British to grant, under their sovereignty, self-government to India, in the best form applicable to the Indians themselves.

Even in such a context, instead of paying heed to one specific voice, that of the colonized, the socialists felt that their ideas had spilled over the borders of Europe: they congratulated themselves on establishing new parties rather than taking cognizance of the particular nature of the demands made by the colonized peoples.

It was at the Stuttgart conference, in 1907, that, following the conflicts that had wracked the Far East, the incidents of the Congo, the famine of the Hereros in German South-west Africa, that the colonial problems and "colonialism" were taken up with real earnestness in the debates. For the Germans in particular "the socialist movement strives after the universal goal of civilizations of which the colonizing idea is an integral part". E. David, Noske, Hildebrand support this imperialist trend. "Without the colonies, we would be assimilated with the Chinese." It is true that the imperialist modes of operation come in for criticism. But it is soft criticism, because it is for the sake of civilization that the needs of the state are held to be of prime importance. Van Kol, Jaurès, Vandervelde, as spokesmen for the second trend, lean more or less towards an international management of the colonies: they deem that colonization is a historical fact, it exists, and therefore it would be foolish to oppose it. They emphasize their censure of colonial barbarism and they adopt the attitude of a benevolent father towards his young children. They consider that it would be preposterous to grant those peoples independence. Bernstein avers: "That would be like giving the United States back to the Indians . . . Our opposition to the colonial policy blinds us to the fact that it represents a movement which, in its promotion of civilization, is unrelated to any of the forms of capitalism and of militarism."

Lastly, on the left, Kautsky and Jules Guesde deny that colonialism was a factor of progress. To condemn it was not tantamount to an opposition to the dialectic of history. After all democracy is possible in the colonies as it is elsewhere. At that time the proponents of a socialist colonialist policy were tirelessly parroting that they stood against capitalist colonial policy. Kautsky says: "If we are against all forms of capitalist colonial policy, we are accordingly the opponents of any possible, if not imaginable, colonial policy . . . The civilizing mission must not be a pretext to condone practices of domination. The victorious proletariat will not constitute a dominant class, even in the countries that are at present colonized: it will, on the contrary, renounce all sovereignty over a foreign country." These ideas found an echo, particularly among the Muslims of Russia.

In a general sense the idea of a socialist colonial policy won the day in the International: it was entrusted in each country to its specific socialist party. Accordingly the debate proceeded in Belgium and in France. But the

International was more concerned with the risks of war, clouds of which had begun to gather on the horizon. And as the colonial question did not seem to be a major cause of conflict – as it had been during the period 1895–1905 – it receded to the background and was put on the back-burner.

Yet the accession to power of the Young Turks in 1908, the Iranian revolution of 1906 and the Chinese revolution of 1911 indicated that a liberation movement among the peoples of the East was still active. Consequently it incited the European socialists to broaden their approach to a global vision of the crisis of that time. Those who emphasized the necessity of this vision were, on one side, the "soapbox" Dutch socialists Pannekoek and Gorter, and Lenin, on the other.

At the same time independence movements were launched in Batavia, a powerful trade union movement was born in India, a large number of revolutionary organizations arose in Baku: all of these indicated an "awakening" on the part of Asia which linked the colonial problem with national demands. At the centre of these problems, the Russian socialists were better placed to understand the situation than were the British or the Germans.

After the First World War the war in the Riff provoked an anti-colonialist furore in France, sustained by the French Communist Party under the direction of Jacques Doriot. However, in a general sense, the idea which had gained ascendancy was that, in view of the sacrifices made by the colonial peoples during the World War, colonialism had something going for it. It had produced "good and strong soldiers", as well as Annamese workers. The anti-colonialist discourse had lost its power, as it did in Britain, where the Labour Party nevertheless took it over and adopted it as its own in its defence of India's progress towards self-government.

In France, following the Second World War, and independently of the action led, especially by the Communists, against the war in Indo-China,[3] one of the forms of the revival of anti-colonialism is associated, according to the felicitous classification of Vidal-Naquet, with the tradition which had its beginnings in the defence of Dreyfus. That particular anti-colonialism claims to safeguard the principles and observances which constitute the foundation of the Republic and of democracy. It opposes all that brings it into ill repute. One of the earliest expressions of the post-war anti-colonialism is *Justice pour les Malgaches* by Pierre Stibbe. It deals with the "events" of 29 March 1947: that is, a revolt and its repression, the court cases which came afterwards, and the manner in which the judiciary con-demned 17 men "in the name of the French people". Those men had risen in revolt for the very reasons which the *Esprit* quarterly had described in reference to Algeria: "Violence lies on the side of the French. It is the racial hatred of the Arab, the rigging of elections, the poverty of the slums, emigration and hunger; violence is constantly present in the hypocritical

use of the democratic principles for the purposes of an oppression practised in fact . . . This violence has been unveiled, one must admit, only by
the recourse to armed rebellion."

Indeed it was for the sake of fidelity to a radiant image of the influence
of France that some tried to give legitimacy to, and defend, dialogue and
negotiate with the movements of colonial emancipation. In 1953 Louis
Massignon sets up the *France-Maghreb* committee. By striving to reconcile
Christianity with Islam, he thus provides an example of the obverse side of
humanist and Christian anti-colonialism.

Other socialists evinced similar attitudes. They included Alain Savary,
the founders of the Parti Socialiste Unifié and, till the moment of
the explosion of the Algerian war, reformers like Jacques Soustelle, whose
position shortly afterwards underwent a radical change. A widening and an
intensification of the anti-colonialist movement followed in the wake of the
war in Algeria.

But was it actually favourable to the independence of the colonies and
is there not some misunderstanding as to its role and its orientation?

The intellectuals and the war in Algeria: after the battle?

When one reads the texts written after the "events" of Algeria, one cannot
escape the feeling that the intellectual class was in the main mobilized
against the war. An entire generation claims to have been marked by
this involvement which was more or less attributed to the action of the
intellectuals: whether it was the *Manifeste des 121*, Jean-Paul Sartre's action
– some have even referred to "his" war – or the role of the important
organs of the press, such as the *Nouvel Observateur, L'Express, Témoignage
Chrétien, Le Monde*, and other reviews like *Esprit* or *Preuves*. Indeed this war
was fought as much on political ground as on the battlefields. That was so
even if it was actually the forms of the armed struggle – torture, terrorism
– that have spurred the most passionate controversies, the publications
that elicited the most comments, the most illustrious writings, for example
those of François Mauriac. Even new publishing houses like Maspero,
Editions de Minuit acted as the purveyors of this war of words.

Still one observes that the action of these intellectuals showed itself,
if one may say so, *only after the battle*. That is, after the political battle to
solve the Algerian problem, and once the war had started. Since then the
leaders of the National Liberation Front have succeeded in establishing
their own chronology of the struggle for independence by reckoning
the date when the revolt started, that is, November 1954, as the date of
the Algerian revolution. In fact if in reality the war started only during the
middle of 1955, the political problem of the future of the country
had already been posed a long time before. It goes back at least to the
bombardment of Sétif in 1945, indeed to the violent calling into question

of the status of Algeria, instituted in 1947, which culminated in the rigging of the elections of April 1948. But one notes that the intellectual class woke up to the issues of the day *only in 1955*. Till then, with very few exceptions, the intellectuals had displayed no concern for Arab demands; they were totally ignorant of the Algerian question. It is only during the years 1956–62 and more so at the end of this period that the intellectuals' interventions become more frequent, to such an extent that, after 1958, one can scarcely discern whether they are motivated by the Algerian problem, or by De Gaulle and his policies, or by the government and its institutions. It is worthy of note that the famous *Manifeste des 121* dates only from the autumn of 1960.

Before the intellectuals appeared on the scene, the lawyers had had their day: an occurrence which has been more or less ignored. It was through their contacts with the nationalists that lawyers like Pierre Stibbe, Yves Dechezelles, Renée Plasson, Jacques Vergès and others, gained a more realistic vision of the nature of the conflict and of its stakes. At the same time a first wave of intellectuals had already taken a position on the Algerian problem: Robert Darrat, Claude Bourdet, Germaine Tillion, and others, and the reports of Jean Daniel. But their views were suppressed in France and were later driven to the background by the noisy hullabaloo made by the popular press which was then totally engrossed with its own political struggles: for or against Mendès France, for or against Guy Mollet, for or against De Gaulle. Yet there had been earlier intellectuals who had been writing in Algeria, living in close contact with the country. But their voice was not heard. Among them one must mention André Mandouze and François Châtelet, who in 1950 established *Consciences algériennes*, a review magazine on the committee of which sat two Arabs, Abd el-Kader Mahdad and Abd el-Kader Mimouni, as well as Jean Cohen, a Jewish pied-noir. In its *Appel* the review defined its stand as being "against colonization and against racism, for a free, social democracy". Such a liberal programme could not but provoke a ban on the publication of this review which nevertheless observed – and for the first time – that in the normal course of events "anti-colonialism emerges only from the statements of its metropolitan proponents". In contrast the review advocated a process of associating all Algerians in the search for a solution to their problems. "We do not share the dangerous mistake of those who think that a solution of French problems would entail, as a consequence, the solution of Algerian problems."

Such an analysis was undoubtedly the most advanced of all that had till then been offered. It ran counter to that of the Algerian or French Communists who wanted the future of Algeria to be tied to that of the mother country and, in 1950, still believed in the possibility of the Communist Party acceding to power. Nevertheless the analysis of *Consciences algériennes* was set in a Marxist context, to the extent that François Châtelet believed that the problem of the liquidation of the colonial system "disturbed the *normal* function of the class struggle". He further argued that Islam was assuming the role of a founding principle of the "nationalist struggle". He advocated the need for a formula to progressively unite the PCA (Algerian Communist Party), the PSU (Unified Socialist Party), the MTLD (Movement of the Workers for Democratic Liberties), the UDMA (Democratic Union of the Algerian Manifesto). He rejected as impossible or unthinkable a political process in two stages: national liberation followed by democracy.

The French Communists, for their part, held a variety of positions. In 1939 Maurice Thorez remarked that "the Algerian nation is on the road to constituting itself as a historical fact". He deemed that this evolution could be made easier or could be helped by the efforts of the French Republic. He reiterated this idea in 1945 at a time when the minister Charles Tillon, a Communist, approved the bombing of Setif.

However, in a "global sense" Communist anti-colonialism moved on a different level. As late as 1958 Jacques Arnault was writing, in the *Editions de la Nouvelle Critique*: "An Algerian problem does not exist. There is only an Algerian aspect of a problem of our time."

There was also another trend, characterized by its concern for the Third World, and represented in the fifties by Jacques Berque. According to him colonization had "distorted history" by interrupting the free development of the extra-European civilizations. He claims that colonization was an enterprise which had subverted the nature of other cultures. It seized the nature of the Other in order to exploit him, to supplant him in all the domains of social life – political, artistic, linguistic – and casts over the Other a veil of "opacity". The Other is cut off from his history, he loses his heritage and is constrained to seek the reconstruction of his identity in terms of the model imposed upon him by his ruler.

In a sense this Third World ideology, appearing in advance of its time, borrows some of its features from the cries of the colonized peoples themselves, whether they are those of the two West Indians, Aimé Césaire and Frantz Fanon. "They speak to me of progress", says Césaire, "of realizations, of diseases wiped out, of improvements in the standard of living . . . As for me, I speak of societies emptied of themselves, of lands stolen, of religions assassinated, of artistic glories annihilated . . . " This Third World ideology also borrows a few of its features from Albert Memmi's analysis *Portrait d'un colonisé*. The difference lies in Jacques Berque's building this analysis into his vision of History.

The silences of anti-colonialist discourse

Nor is the anti-colonialist discourse entirely free from a certain blindness, a refusal to see things as they are. It is easy to point out some of its taboos.

181

The emancipation of women

For example anti-colonialism disregards, in the context of the Maghreb in Black Africa, the fact that colonization helped in the emancipation of women. This evidence is provided in the story of the three generations of Tunisian Jewish women as described by Annie Goldmann in *Les filles de Mardochée*. In the first generation that she describes, that is, before the arrival of the French, Elise weds a pioneer of the emanciption of women. At that time she lives in the Hara ghetto close to the sea. The Jews wore black pants, the Arabs wore red. Whenever an Arab met a Jew, he gave him three mild pats on the head with these words: "In remembrance of the enslavement of your father and of your grandfather." The women did not go to the market; the men did. The Jewish women wore the shafshari, a rectangular piece of cloth wrapped around the entire body of the woman. But their faces were not veiled. When the French arrived in 1881, Elise was frightened for the rumour was current that the Arabs were about to revolt. A boat was hired to escape to a distant place. Only Arabic was spoken to, and around, little Ziza. No education, no school was available. The boys went to the Hebrew school to study the Mosaic law and religion. Ziza knew nothing about dolls which were viewed as idols. But the director of the Jewish Alliance resolved to create a school for the girls to learn French and to sew. Then Mardochée sent Ziza to school, in spite of the Rabbis. And Ziza wore an apron; she was clothed in the "European fashion". Accordingly it was through French that Elise learned to read. She was married dressed as an Arab; but her trousseau was European. Juliet – of the second generation – was the glory of the family. Born in 1890, trained by her father, she became the first woman lawyer in Tunisia, in 1920. But very soon, after her marriage, she reintegrated the traditional role of the woman. In the third generation the Jewish woman has been emancipated: she marries a metropolitan Frenchman.

In fact many young Jewish women experienced this symbolic story – in Tunis, as well as in Oran and in Casablanca.

On the other hand the emancipation of young Muslim women ran into obstacles and failed to swell into a mass movement. Even then it associated itself with the colonization, though in an ambiguous fashion, as a result of a perverse effect. Arab families offered stiff resistance to the influence of europeanization, for the sake of Arab identity and of its defence. At the Stéphane-Gsell Lycée, in Oran, one could, between 1948 and 1956, count on the fingers of both hands the number of the young Muslim girls authorized by their parents to pursue studies up to the baccalaureate.

In Algeria a pseudo-emancipation had been initiated, when the time came for the freedom struggle, as demonstrated in the speeches of the FLN (National Liberation Front) on what the future of women would be once independence has been obtained. However, after independence, Assia

182

Djebar was the first woman to have powerfully expressed her disillusion, her despair, her anger in *Les femmes du mont Chenoua*.[4] The fact remains that anti-colonialist discourse, with its current third-world sensitivity, is circumspect in regard to this problem.

In Black Africa, it is likewise thanks to colonization that, in Dahomey, for example, the women preserved the status of equality which they already had in the social activities of the traditional society. In that country the administration opened the schools to girls, thus enabling them to partici-pate in activities of responsibility. These were certainly limited, but they were as much for the men. Female teachers, nurses, all sorts of employees provided for themselves a counterweight to their subservient status in the tribal or family set-up, which ultimately led to their emancipation.

The racism of the non-Europeans

The anti-colonial tradition which, during the last decades, has adopted a pro-third-world stance, remained for a long time silent on the role and the responsibilities of the Arabs in the slave trade and in slavery, as well as in their racism.[5] To the extent that the struggle against the scourge of slavery served as an argument favourable to colonial imperialism, some have claimed that it has been "magnified", exaggerated, that the statements of Livingstone on the 21 million slaves who were channelled through Zanzibar represent an "inordinately high" figure. That is so, no doubt, since the figure has been established as being of the order of 3.5 million. Nevertheless one may wonder if it is indeed fortuitous that, for the most part, the studies and symposia on the slave trade and on slavery refer to the Atlantic.

In the matter of racism, one may observe that no other civilization has, with such meticulous precision, defined the classification of races, supplemented with such evaluations as are described in *Dix conseils pour acheter des hommes et des femmes esclaves* ("Ten pieces of advice for the purchase of slave men and women") and, in literature, the *Thousand and One Nights*. "The Zanj women have many defects. The darker they are, the uglier are their faces, the sharper are their teeth . . . Dance and rhythm come naturally to them. Music and dance compensate for the obscurity of their speech. It is said that if a Zanji were to fall from paradise to the earth, he would be beating time during the fall . . . One cannot enjoy their women because of their bad smell and the coarseness of their body . . . The Ethiopian women have graceful, smooth and weak bodies; they are prone to consumption . . . If the young *bujjas* are imported and they have a golden skin, beautiful faces, smooth bodies they are spared the mutilation and they can still be used for enjoyment." In 1802, a (French) witness reports: "In Cairo their sale recalls that of domestic animals in Europe. The buyer goes round the slave and selects . . . If the negro man or woman

183

snores much or pees in bed, they can be returned, and exchanged within twenty days of their having been bought" (quoted in Lewis, 1971). As of that date a boy is worth 50 to 100 Spanish piastres, a young eunuch 160 to 200.

In the East slavery and the slave trade have no more obligation towards Islam than they had to Christianity in the West. Arab expansion, conquest and colonization widened the scope of their practice. At the outset it was in practice the same thing to be an Arab and a Muslim. But as conversion to Islam increased, most of the time by means of violence, there emerged a new category of Muslims, that is, non-Arabs converted to Islam. Though in principle they were equal, yet they were subjugated: "they clean our streets, they mend our shoes, they weave our clothes". The problem of people of mixed race soon arose: they came across more or less "advanced" peoples in Africa and in South-East Asia with whom they could interbreed. It is because of this that the Arabs began to associate a light skin with civilization. That did not prevent them from having light-skinned slaves, such as the Circassians, and other white, even Christian, slaves. Since the enslavement of Muslims who were born free and of non-Muslims living under the protection of a Muslim state was prohibited, the result was a proliferation, starting from the tenth and the twelfth centuries, of the importation of slaves, from Eurasia in the north and from Black Africa in the south.

The outside, "non-civilized" world was thus a source of slaves for the Arabs, and later of the Ottomans. This lasted down to the nineteenth century, when in 1846 Tunisia became the first state to abolish slavery, an operation undertaken under "French occupation". The anti-slavery process in Turkey started around 1830: at first it affected the whites – Georgians and Circassians – then the Blacks in Hejaj (1857). Nevertheless slavery persisted in some parts of the Arab world: Saudi Arabia abolished it in 1962, and Mauritania in 1980.

What may perhaps explain the near absence of traces left by slavery in the East is that there were a large number of eunuchs among the black males brought into the Muslim world. The black merchants and the Arab merchants took charge of the operation, considering that the value of the merchandise increased after castration. The history of black anti-colonialism makes scant reference to this aspect of the slave trade.

Today the pitch-black legend and the rose-coloured legend have lost their arrogance. There are Africans who, on pondering over the fate of their country, opine that the effects of colonial domination were not as bad as had been made out to be. Thirty years on, they argue that colonialism cannot be held to be responsible for all the failures that followed independence. Actually many expectations were ruined by the constriction of independence brought about by the unification of a global economy (see Ch. 11). On the other hand a Cameroon writer dared to ask if indeed in Africa development has not been rejected (Axelle Kabou). Besides the age-old tribal structure may have been, from early on, a fact that made dependence possible. Likewise in the Maghreb the situation is not due only to colonialism and to its effects, nor can it be said that colonialism is alone responsible for the deterioration of the Arabo-Islamic personality. "At the time when Europe was entering the period of the Enlightenment, the Maghreb was fragmenting itself into regions, into linguistic and ethno-cultural islands administered by brotherhood leaders and local holy men" (Mohamed Arkoun).

Japan offers a counter-example: from the seventeenth to the nineteenth century it was scarcely better armed than Africa to resist the West. Yet it succeeded in doing so.

Conversely the eulogists of the colonial endeavour must not forget that there were only two baccalaureates in the whole of the Belgian Congo in 1960, that 95 per cent illiteracy was bequeathed by France to the Niger and to Mali, that colonialism was "a patchwork of crimes and of good intentions", and lastly that neo-colonialism is only an interested form of aid.

But, as we shall see, the problems are actually more complex.

6

THE VISION OF THE VANQUISHED

The trauma of occupation struck all those peoples who, in order not to be exterminated, were forced to submit. Still the shock has not been equally felt everywhere. It has been more violent in the Americas because, due to their isolation from the rest of the world for thousands of years, the Indians were not aware of the existence of other peoples. They were terrified by those beings with a "human bearing, riding unknown monsters". They did not know how to comport themselves in regard to those invaders, whether to form an alliance with them, or to fraternize with them, or to show them hostility. But it was the vision of fright that prevailed over all experiments that were attempted.

The trauma caused by the invaders in the Americas

The prophecies which had anticipated such a catastrophe were recalled both in Mexico and in Peru. For example, a prophecy, the *Shilam Balam*, had foretold the Mayans of the arrival of the White men: "The Earth will be in flames, and great white circles will be formed in the sky. Bitterness will appear while the abundance shall leave the land. The Earth will be in flames and the war of oppression will break out. The times will be immersed in painful works. There is no doubt, it will be seen. It will be a time for suffering, of tears, or misery. This is what will happen."

In Peru too strange events are supposed to have occurred before the arrival of the white men: recurring earthquakes, pillars of fire appearing over the horizon, temples toppled by lightning, comets coursing in the sky. In all these cases the important point was that, in the Andes as in Mexico, the invaders were, if not expected, at least foreseeable. Montezuma welcomed the Spaniards as if they were gods whom everybody was expecting. He told Cortez: "My Lord, this is your home." At the same time the *Chronicle* of Titu Cusi relates that in the Andes, when the Spaniards arrived, they were taken for the *Viracochas*, the sons of God.

In *Histoire de Lynx*, Claude Lévi-Strauss explains that the two-party polarity, which obtains in Indian myths and opposes water to fire, the heaven to the earth, favours the predisposition to deem it normal that a non-Indian correspond to the Indian. And in the absence of a belief in perfect twinning, some must be strong and others weak. He says: "This bipartism may perhaps provide an explanation to the question: how is it that at the moment of the conquest of the New World the Indians behaved as if they were waiting for the white men, or rather, as if they recognized them." Once the Demiurge had created the Indians something symmetrical and contrary had also to be created: this explains why the Aztecs bowed before Cortez and 20,000 Incas remained as if paralyzed in the face of 160 Spaniards.

Even today some of the people of the First Nations in Canada do not complain of the arrival or of the presence of white men, but only of the fact that the white men excluded them.

In Mexico and in Peru, though the prevailing prophecies foretold the arrival of the invading strangers, agents of a disaster, yet belief in the divinity of the Spaniards very quickly came to an end, even though the invasion retained a religious or even cosmic significance. Actually it was this very belief which accounted for the behaviour of the Incas and the Aztecs. One incident confirms this opinion. On his way to Cuzco Pizarro intercepted a message sent by Callcuchima to Quizquiz. Callcuchima was sending this important information: the Spaniards were mortal.

It was the cruelty of the conquistadores which shook the native's initial beliefs: their frenzy at the sight of gold, their brutality, their cruelty in fighting, their behaviour after the battle. The Mexicans' description of a siege confirms all the cruelty of the Spaniards, especially their capacity to infect their enemies with diseases.

The exchange of diseases

"During those times there were no diseases, no fevers, no bone or head diseases . . . During those times everything was in order. The strangers changed everything when they arrived." However much nostalgia runs through this complaint, it certainly seems that the diseases of the Old World were more often deadly in the Americas than in Europe. At the very end of the seventeenth century a German missionary wrote that "the Indians die so easily that the mere sight or smell of a Spaniard causes their death" (A. W. Crosby Jr., 1972, pp. 36–7). A dozen epidemics decimated the population of Mexico and of Peru. Yet it seemed that the Spaniards were not affected by those same epidemics. "Enraged, some Indians injected contaminated blood into the cakes meant for the Spaniards: with no visible effect." The same phenomenon was observed by Thomas Hariot in Florida where the Indians died after the passage of the Europeans, as they did in New England, and in French Canada. The Europeans brought measles, the flu, smallpox, the typhus fever also. But they were less vulnerable than the natives. One may even ask if the Arawaks of the Greater Antilles did not disappear as a result of these diseases as much as of the massacres wreaked on them following the arrival of the Spaniards. Unless one takes into account that ill treatment also rendered them more vulnerable to diseases. But this argument does not apply to Mexico where smallpox prevailed over the small folk as much as over the Aztec princes and, in Peru, over the military chiefs.

More than the disease itself, it was the invulnerability of the victor that awed the imagination. The gods had given the Spaniards "another shield than the one they were wearing . . . They had arrived on those ships, those horses and evidently, they were indeed those men who could not die." And the Mayans were destined to die . . . "this stench that the vultures wait for". They were destined to die (Crosby, 1972).

Conversely scarcely had he returned from the Americas than one of the companions of Christopher Columbus, Martin Alonzo Pinzon died of syphilis. Through Seville and Italy – "the Naples disease" – the disease spread all over Europe. Up to 1526 this disease proved to be deadly; then its effects became weaker, from as early as the middle of the sixteenth century. It was an indigenous epidemic to which the Indians were already accustomed. It developed apparently from the contact of the Europeans with the American women and nature. It was transmitted by the sailors in their varied and numerous sexual activities. The contamination reached as far as Ceylon.

In America the trauma of conquest was accompanied by massacres which might be described as genocide, even if it was not premeditated, especially in the islands, some of which were totally depopulated. But the evidence is more in favour of the microbial shock having been the main cause of this "demographic disaster", at least in the low-lying areas, before the coming into play of the forces of inurement. For example, in Mexico, only 2 million Indians were living on the plateaux, in contrast to about 20 million in 1519. But this tendency was subsequently reversed (Benassar, 1991, 246ff.).

Destructuring and forms of resistance

According to a questionnaire formulated between 1582 and 1585, the document at the basis of the *Relaciones geográficas de Indias*, testifies, by means of its answers, that the Indians were perfectly aware of the demographic disaster they were experiencing. They listed the following causes of the catastrophe, in this order: the war, the epidemics, the migrations, the mortality due to excessive labours. Nathan Wachtel wonders if it is out of fear, or out of a desire to please, that they also gave such strange answers as: formerly they used to eat less; they now have more freedom than ever before; in the olden days there was no alcoholism. For the pulque in

Mexico and the chicha in the Andes were ingested only on festive occasions. Henceforth the Spaniards set the example and the old taboos disappear, like the cultivation of the coca "which was developed as soon as the Spaniards arrived".

In this way, Indian society was to a great extent destructured by the conquest. Among the Incas, near Cuzco for example, the base of the ethnic groups was called *ayllu* (similar to the Calpullis of Mexico). The *ayllu* formed a sort of endogamous nucleus unifying a certain number of lineages that collectively possessed a complex of lands which were most of the time unrelated among themselves. Several of these nuclei constituted a whole. The state was the summit of these wholes: at each level of this pyramidal structure, it assured the periodical distribution of the different types of land (for maize, for potatoes, for pasture). Each family was entitled to a complex of lands, and the exchange of services among themselves was well regulated. This system constituted the structural foundation of the organization, in which each *ayllu* had, in addition, to provide the service of the *mita*, the compulsory work on the lands of the Inca and on those of the Sun. The Spaniards ruined this complex structure built from bottom to the top like a "vertical archipelago" by carving it into their *encomiendas*, thus bringing about a displacement of populations. Moreover the introduction of a monetary economy and of new forms of tribute – that is, forced labour in the mines – completed the disintegration of the system. In 1562 a study conducted by Cortiz de Zuniga showed that, before the arrival of the Spaniards, the Chupachos paid a tribute in textiles and the Inca supplied them with the raw matter, wool, the *encomendero* insisted on being paid with cotton textiles, and on the Indian himself growing the cotton. These types of tribute rose to the extent that, even at that early time, the Indians complained that they no longer had any time left to cultivate their own fields to survive.

The Spaniards used the old system of power and trade to their own advantage, by substituting themselves for the Inca. They did so without the working principle of reciprocity which was the foundation of the exchange. The monetary tribute was an addition and it did not stop growing. But, for nearly thirty years, in the mines of Potosi, the Indians knew how to assert their own ways of extraction, known only to them, and which the Spaniards failed to control. It was only in 1574, when an amalgam technique was introduced, that the Spaniards succeeded in undoing the control which the Indians had till then exerted on the production of silver. A new era began: it spelled the acceleration of their decline.

The transportation of silver, the wars between Pizarro and Almagro had speeded up the process of the social decomposition, as many Indians found themselves thrown beyond the pale of the traditional production network. Those *forasteros* (free strangers), with their higher status since

189

they were not tied by any bond to the land and were accordingly free, would soon pose a problem during the following centuries, for the *hacendados* (landholders) could no longer lay claim to the land. The members of the old nobility too lost their rank: they were forced to act as intermediaries between the Spaniards and the other Indians who had to pay tribute.

Revolts soon broke out, especially in 1536, when Manco, who had at first collaborated with the Spaniards, realized "that they were not the sons of God, but rather of the Devil". Other revolts followed – in 1560, in 1571 and above all in 1781 when the last Inca Tupac Amaru was hanged in Cuzco in the presence of the entire population that had been assembled there. In 1980, a great film, with his name as its title, reconstructed the event. As an expression of the vision of the vanquished the film was shown in Peru in theatres filled to capacity with Indians.

In their submission to the victor the Indians naturally had to produce a few cultivations meant for him, wherever the climatic conditions made it possible – orange-trees, fig-trees, above all wheat – but they retained their subsistence economy for themselves.

The Indians' fidelity to their religious traditions and to their language remained stronger in the Andes, where they could live in greater isolation from the conqueror, than in Mexico. In the latter country they even seemed to evince some enthusiasm for Christianity, at least in the early days of colonization. But never did this obtain in Peru where fidelity to the local deities was the result of social fragmentation and disintegration. For example, they exhumed their dead from the cemeteries built by the conquerors to have them cremated according to their rites. Viewed from outside they seemed to conform to Christian customs. But they preserved their own customs by raising, if the need arose, a cross on their own sacred places. "While the Spaniards viewed the local deities as a manifestation of the Devil, the Indians looked on Christianity as a form of idolatry" (Nathan Wachtel). Actually the Indians of Peru integrated Christianity to their culture, but preserved the latter. They continued to indulge in social practices established on the principle of reciprocity. Further they continued to represent space in ways specific to their culture, for example, in drawing the map of the universe in the form of two oblique axes which intersect at a centre which is not the sun but the kingdom of Castile.

In Mexico resistance to the Spaniard and to his religion assumed other forms.

In Mexico

Must one speak here of colonization or of the westernization of an imaginary world? At any rate imagery and the pictographic mode of expression acted as the substratum of the oral memory preserved among the nobles. Serge Gruzinski has shown that the "paintings" had an irreducible specificity, because within the same setting they crammed together the wars, the prodigies, the deities, the taxation system, the tranfer of goods. In its own way the image was designed to be an instrument of power. Now, space was the first thing which was transfigured by the Spanish-style sketches, accompanied by a chromatic impoverishment. Soon the "illustrations" were reduced to a subordinate position in relation to writing and to the rules of Western narrative which, with its linear continuity, gained the ascendancy.

To the westernization of the representation of space there also corresponds a transfiguration of the past time. Its re-reading tended to give to the pueblo a Christian and Spanish legitimacy, that is, the foundation of a community identity. But the repetition of similar episodes represents the survival of a cyclic view of time as corroborated by redundancies in speech; the mingled prehispanic and colonial periods intermingle.

More than any other practice, idolatry resisted colonization and in Mexico it was rather Christianity which became indianized. However idolatry borrowed from the Church such formulas as the trinitarian invocation as well as such gestures as the signing of the cross. Gradually, however, idolatry yielded to the indigenous Christianity which, under the direction of men-gods, assumed the radical form of messianic movements against colonial domination by foretelling the elimination of the unbelievers, that is, the Spaniards. Thus witchcraft acted as the connecting link between colonial idolatry and indigenous Christianity.

In Sao Tomé, as in Peru, folklore denounces the invader

The survival of an irreducible part of the imaginary world testifies to the last form of resistance to the conquest. It shows itself in the *Dance of the conquest*, in Peru as in Guatemala, and in the *Tchiloli*, or *Tragedy of the Emperor Charles the Great*, in Sao Tomé, the oldest Portuguese colony in Black Africa.

Nathan Wachtel has given us the first structural analysis of the death of Atahualpa and the dance of the conquest, which is a poetic and choreographic theme so widely known among the Indians of the Andes: the play, written in archaic Quechua, has been staged since the sixteenth century. The actors are divided into two groups: on one side are the Indians and the Spaniards on the other. The chorus of Indian princesses wears white embroidered robes. Nowadays they wear sunglasses to enhance their prestige. The Inca's attribute consists of a sceptre decorated with red woollen braids with which he strikes a metal plate. The soothsayer is accompanied by an actor dressed in a bear skin. Facing them the Indians playing the roles of the Spaniards wear helmets similar to those worn at the time of the Conquest, breastplates of the time of independence, or uniforms of the army of the day.

The action begins with a threat: Atahualpa, the last Inca, relates to the princesses the dream which has disturbed him. He has seen the Sun, his father, veiled by black smoke. And soon he is informed of the arrival of the bearded warriors, clad in metal, who have come to destroy his kingdom.

Following this, preliminary encounters are held between the servants and the lieutenants. The central episode sets the Indian chief against the Spaniard chief. The Inca dies, lamentations are heard in all places and the King of Spain appears, like the Commendatore, to punish Pizarro.

Throughout the tragedy, the Indians and the Spaniards, despite their communication, do not understand one another. When a Spaniard opens his mouth, no sound is uttered, and Pizarro's anger arises from this lack of understanding. At the same time, without Atahualpa, his subjects are lost and the Earth does not communicate with the Sun.

The tragedy of Atahualpa is one example. The *Dance of the conquest* is another. But their structure is similar: they distort the historical facts, it is true, but they do so in abiding by a certain logic which reproduces the feelings of those who lived at the time of the Conquest.

Violence is at the heart of that logic. In the Gulf of Guinea, in Sao Tomé, it is rather injustice. But, in both cases, the multiplicity of the actors' apparel which represents, from scene to scene, the different centuries that have gone by since the Conquest, testifies that, except for the costumes, nothing has changed in the behaviour of the conqueror.

In Africa too, resistance to colonization started together with the colonization process itself, as soon as the latter was felt as an aggression and as an oppression,

At the very outset the expression of this resistance can be found in what was, in a way, the first Portuguese colony, Sao Tomé, a small island in the Gulf of Guinea. It is represented in the play, the *Tchiloli*, in which all the black inhabitants take part. This play is called the *Tragedy of the Emperor Charles the Great*. It dates from the sixteenth century. Of course, Charles the Great never set foot in Sao Tomé. But, for the inhabitants of the island, he personifies the King of Portugal who took them to that place by force. And Charles the Great must judge his son who has committed a crime, and his son is necessarily a Portuguese.

What is interesting in this play, which has been staged every year for centuries, is that the number of episodes in it increases with time. To the initial crime is added a whole series of later misdeeds. This is evident in the costumes worn by the "complainants": they represent all periods – a soldier of the sixteenth century, a bishop of the seventeenth century, a policeman of the time of Salazar. For, in every century, the sons of the Master have committed new crimes, new injustices. This play is also the trial of all colonization.

The counter-history of the African resistance: Samori, Shaka

The histories of colonization readily contrast the case of Portugal, with its commercial trading-posts, with that of Spain and its genuine territorial empire. Certainly there is a contrast, an opposition between the two. But the right explanation is lacking. For, in Brazil, the Portuguese did indeed build a territorial empire.

The truth is that in Brazil the conquerors came up against scattered tribes, while in black Africa the peoples of Mali and of the Congo prevented them from settling down in the depths of the hinterland. This the Portuguese succeeded in doing two centuries later in Angola and in Mozambique, like the other Europeans in the several regions of Africa.

Consequently we must take into account the African resistance which European historiography has blotted out, in order to explain what could have, in the sixteenth century, reined the conquerors in, even if Africa did not offer the same commercial advantages as did India or Brazil, since it had neither pepper nor cocoa, nor tobacco, but only the malaguetta pepper, a spice which had no success.

But Black Africa had the slaves who were worth all the spices put together.

Consequently it was not lack of interest in Africa which stopped the progress of all the colonizers from the fifteenth to the nineteenth centuries, or even their commercial choices, it was Africa's ability to defend itself. Otherwise the Europeans would have established their dominion over whole territories, as they did previously in the Canary Islands, and later in Brazil.

The truth is that while the Portuguese and the other Europeans were masters of the seas, they were quite vulnerable on land and on the rivers.

Easy to manoeuvre, the African canoes and other ships were both fast and capable of carrying up to a hundred warriors. A first alarm was given in 1446. It warned the Portuguese of Nuno Tristao of the danger posed by the flotillas of Senegambia. His expedition met with a tragic fate. Others had the same experience until the King of Portugal sent Diego Gomez to negotiate the conditions of a settlement on the coast. However Mali and its neighbours controlled an entire network of rivers around the Niger, Senegal, Gambia and it was the concerted action of these armed flotillas that stopped the invaders. Again it was this military resistance that compelled the Europeans to negotiate the manner in which the traffic with the populations was conducted. For example, the King of Kongo informed Joao Alfonso, a Portuguese merchant in the service of François I, of the conditions on which he could penetrate the Zaire. A duly negotiated treaty initiated the first settlement of the Portuguese in Angola (1571), which became the hub from which their commerce would be controlled in those regions, in particular the slave trade.

Africa: history without Europe

The black slave trade was tragic and cruel: it has left its mark on the imagery of the societies – certainly that of the Africans transplanted to the Americas, but also that of the Europeans who, long after the event, have nurtured a guilt which, while coming indeed a little late, manifested itself, as we have shown, from the eighteenth century on.

The immorality of this mass deportation has often overlaid the study of the real conditions of those departures for the Americas. These are facts which in no way mitigate the horror of that trade – it should be pointed out immediately – but which must not be discarded by strict historical analysis.

In the first instance, it must be recalled that the slave trade directed to the Americas was grafted on to a slave trade which existed before the arrival of the Europeans in Africa and supplied the Arab world and the Maghreb. Avelino de Teixeira da Mota observed this diversion on the way through Arguim, as early as the fifteenth century, before the discovery of America, of slaves intended for the Portuguese trading posts and islands of the Atlantic (Sao Tomé, the Azores). The Atlantic trade culminated in a huge increase of the trade which went, on an average, from 5,000 souls per year around 1500 to 9,500 around 1600, with still higher figures for the eighteenth century.

Thus slavery and the slave trade were practised well before the arrival of the Europeans. This trade was not due *only* to the action of the Arabs, or later of the Portuguese, the French, the English. Slavery and the slave trade were part of the working structures of African societies and states. As the private ownership of land did not exist or had no legitimacy in the tradition, only the ownership of slaves and of the produce of the land enabled merchants or monarchs to increase their power. Accordingly African monarchs could wage war in order to plunder and acquire slaves intended for sale or for their own domains. The status of the slaves varied and their worth depended on their origin and on the conditions of their acquisition. It is only with the Arab, and later the European, trade that the fate of the slaves becomes standardized, and in a tragic way (John Thornton, 1992).

If it is true that in the nineteenth century the Europeans used military means to conquer vast territories and exert their dominion over them, to introduce forced labour, it was nevertheless not so at the beginning. For example, in Senegambia, the slave trade began in earnest, with a departure of 700 to 1,000 individuals per year, only from the moment when the Portuguese ended their raids and started to negotiate the purchase of slaves. That is, the African states were the beneficiaries of this trade and they spontaneously developed it. It is even possible to argue that the wars among the kingdoms became more frequent from the moment when the slave trade got a boost generated by the Atlantic demand. Such a development can be verified by the events in the Congo. Such was the situation as it was observed by Mungo Park in 1797 (Mungo Park, 1815). What the Europeans, and only they, brought about is the deterioration of the victims' lot. In the Atlantic African societies the slaves were not particularly forced to do repulsive and inhuman tasks. Undoubtedly, when they were captured, or even bought, they were, as "strangers", subjected to a discriminatory treatment. Subsequently, however, their descendants lived like the serfs of the Western Middle Ages, on the land of their lords. For instance, on the Gold Coast, they had one day free every ten days or every week in order to cultivate a plot of land allotted to them, while the rest of the time was taken up with the harvests of the master or of the state. In fact, at the very beginning, the Portuguese applied the same system to the first black slaves transferred to Sao Tomé-Principe. The worsening of the slaves' lot happened later, in stages, inexorably. After the horror of the Atlantic crossing and the ill-treatment experienced in the Americas, Africa remained engraved in the memory as a Paradise lost.

In black Africa, as in Mexico or in the Andes, the existence of organized states provided the source of a resistance to foreign occupation. This resistance found its expressions in wars which in the end proved to be disastrous. But it is noteworthy that it was the least developed, the least centralized of the state formations which, in the long term, showed the most sustained continuity in their opposition to the Europeans. This would indicate that genuine states did exist, if not at least structures which fulfilled this role of resisting: this is something which the colonial tradition has tried to ignore.

From this point of view the state which Samory was able to build in the Sudan, in the nineteenth century, offers a typical example: it was brought about by the conjunction of an extraordinary individual and the Dyula, a social group of merchants whose development is linked to an Islamic revival. A military chief, exploiting the advantages of his kinship, of commerce and of Islam, Samory assumed the leadership of a society and carved out an empire covering an area of 400,000 square kilometres. He managed to reorganize the army by establishing a hierarchy between the professionals who constituted the permanent core loyal to its chief, and the temporary soldiers and back-up troops. Above all he succeeded in making the craftsmen produce fire-arms, and knew how to tighten up the state administration by making use of Islam and of its marabouts to ensure its unity, and in so doing established a theocratic, hierarchical system of government. He had a chance encounter with Gallieni's French troops. He concluded a treaty with him and got ready for the English alliance. In 1890, in his confrontation with the French he practised a scorched earth policy after a revolt rocked his states and forced him to move his empire to the east, in order to escape from the Europeans. Such an action established the proof of the strength of the structures of that state. But in 1898 Samory was finally taken prisoner by General Gouraud and his state disappeared with him.

Yves Person and the materials which he has gathered make it possible to analyse the history of Samory and establish how different it is from the traditional view. He was a "gang leader" who dominated the situation for seventeen years. Together with him the Mandingos constituted a *sort* of nomadic empire against which Joffre, Archinard, Gallieni, Gouraud had to fight. As a champion of Islam, resourceful, coldly ferocious, Samory appeared and disappeared. He was taken prisoner by Gouraud in 1898 and died in exile (Maurice Baumont, 1949, p. 267).

The historical legend which embraces the official history of colonization thus echoes the point of view of the conquerors. It is "drawn from the archives"; it is accordingly considered as being sacred and passes for "scientific" analysis. "Starting from Dahomey it traces the race to the Chad, the race to the Niger, towards the bank of the river, towards the land of the Kong, towards the Mossis country – and then the race to the Nile." It totally ignores the other points of view. The reliance on geographical classifications culminates in a reduction of the historical knowledge. These countries do not have written archives, and have accordingly no "true" state. Therefore they have no history.

In fact, beside Samory's State, other state formations existed, and had their own specific structures. One such state was the Ashanti or Asante Kingdom, a military and conqueror state. Kumasi, the capital of the Kingdom, boasted of an administrative structure more sophisticated than what obtained elsewhere. The state managed to integrate, around Asante properly speaking, the mother country, incorporated provinces, internal provinces, external provinces. This unification brought in its wake internal conflicts between centralists and federalists, and soon between modernists and traditionalists. Foreign intervention in Asante followed a classic pattern: a friendship treaty (1817), the passage of the British possessions of the Gold Coast under the control of Sierra Leone which had already been annexed (1821), the campaigns of the Ashantis against the Wasas, the Fantis. In 1873 the Fantis ask for British protection. The latter oblige by making war and insure the defeat of the Asante vanquished by the coalition of the English and the peoples who had risen in revolt. Twenty-three years later the British occupy Kumasi and proclaim their protectorate (1896).

Hence it is only when genuine states existed – which historical tradition has chosen to ignore – that their fall led to a collapse and to the end of all military resistance. But that did not snuff out the idea of independence which lived on in Alucca in the west as in Madagascar or in Kenya. Per contra one may say that the popular or scholarly legend has transformed those defeated chiefs into real heroes: Benhanzin, Samory, Msiri in Katanga; Rabah, or Mapondera, the honourable bandit in "Rhodesia". On the other hand peasant resistance, spontaneous and scarcely lasting, has not been associated with the memory of a similar legend.

The King of the Zulus, Shaka, is the most illustrious of these heroes. He is the first of the great founders of warrior kingdoms over which the white men triumphed (1816–28). But the legend arose after his death. He had modernized the military art and reorganized the army to which he gave a spartan training. At first he altered the length of the assegais which had till then been fabricated long and were thrown by the Zulus at a distance. Shaka replaced them with shorter assegais which could accordingly be used in hand to hand combat. He increased physical exercises to strengthen the muscles of his soldiers. He provided them with an enhanced meat diet. He stimulated his soldiers by tests of endurance: the winners were entitled to virgin girls, young and among the most beautiful in the King's concession, trained in wrestling and in fighting. Shaka saw to the training of these girls under the supervision of his warriors. The latter were however forbidden to have the least contact with them, on pain of death. Hence "the sexual impulse was diverted from its reproductive function to be transmuted into a battle drive" (W. Randles). Shaka's tyranny transformed his kingdom into a power which the whites dared not challenge. But fed up with twelve years of his tyranny a section of his army rose up in revolt and Shaka was murdered (1828). After his death the empire weakened and the Boers defeated the Zulus at Blood River. The British destroyed their army in 1879. This denouement is well known in Europe mainly on account of the death of the Imperial Prince, the son of Napoleon III. And that was the end of the "Men of Heaven".

With his transformation into a mythical and legendary hero, Shaka has become a black Christ for some, and the symbol of negritude for others. His eventful career has been transfigured first by the oral, and afterward by the written, tradition. This tradition has its origins in Thomas Mofolo's *Shaka*, written in the Sosotho language, which remained for a long time buried in the archives of the *Missionnaires de la Société Évangélique de Paris*. His hero is triumphant. But, with the devil's help, he commits a thousand crimes and extortions before falling victim of a plot hatched by his brothers. In another version he kills a leopard when he is only nineteen years old, and imprisons an enemy queen in a hut together with a hungry hyena. In yet another version he transforms an invicible nucleus of 500 men into an army of 40,000 men destined to rule the world.

In a way Shaka had created a Zulu nation. Soon he personifies the revolt of the entire "African nation", and survives death in the play by Badian and A. A. Ka. In the Christian Mofolo's piece, while Shaka's death represents the defeat of Evil, it does subsequently recall the heroic sacrifice of the founding father of a genuine African state. With Shaka dead, the whites were able to enslave Africa without any hindrance: "We shall become the slaves of their compasses and of their squares. And our priests will let that happen. In the cafés, our intellectuals shall whisper to one another over a bottle. And our priests shall let all this happen. And our brothers shall smite us for a handful of rice . . . We shall have known more martyrs than the plains of Judea" (*Les Amazoulous*, Act III).

It may be noted that the Black cinema of Africa has shown scant concern for the treatment of historical themes which recall its slavery. It has not glorified its heroes, even if plans for a *Samory* are afoot. On the other hand, popular revolts have inspired genuine masterpieces. For instance, proceeding against the grain of official history of the present time, Ousmane Sembéné shows how, in the nineteenth century, islamization was accompanied by tyranny and abuses. That is the theme of the *Ceddos*, those men who, among the Wolofs, refused to yield to the Council of Imams who, in the name of the Quran, claim to have the right to legislate over the whole of society. To demonstrate their refusal of this heavy-handedness, the Ceddos kidnapped their princess. They were defeated. The princess was recovered and delivered to the Imam. But, at the very moment of the marriage, she seized his weapon and executed him in the presence of the people that had been forcibly converted and now showed its solidarity with her. In this magnificent drama, the Muslim elite felt itself to be under attack. But so did the French colonizer, for the white man in Sembéné's film appears as a priest, whose only concern is the ideal of a black Church for all. In the pursuit of his chimera he is absolutely indifferent to the fate of the Ceddos, to their destruction, to their will to survive.

But films on anti-colonial resistance are rare. An exception is Bakabé Mahamane's *Si, les cavaliers* (1982), a film which recalls the resistance and the failed plot of a local sultan against the French occupation in the Niger, at the beginning of this century. The greater number of African films deal with the decline of the Africans as victims of "neo-colonialism", that is, *after* the colonization.

The colonial past in the eyes of Algerian cinema

Algerian cinema offers a striking contrast with African cinema. More than the others, in the Maghreb and in Africa, it recalls the colonial past, the humiliations suffered at the time of the French. During two long decades it was the cinema of resentment. Then a change occurred in the way in which the French period was viewed.

This is how Ferid Boughedir in *Cinéaction* defines the three cinemas of the Maghreb:

In Morocco, it is the silent complaint, I suffocate, I suffocate, these are the Middle Ages; how can I remove these walls, decode what I have to say. That cinema speaks of the present. In Tunisia, it is the search for truth: tourism – let's speak of it, emigration – let's see, the feminine condition – it must be explored. This cinema too speaks of the present. It claims to be a political sociologist. The Algerian cinema speaks of the future, but more of the past. We were a great people . . . Let us have trust in ourselves. This cinema expresses the dignity of the humiliated.

A favourite subject of Algerian cinema was, first, the expropriation brought about by the action of the French administration – in Mohammed Lakhdar-Hamina's *Chronique des années de braise* (1975), in Lamine Merbah's *Les Déracinés* which analyses the dispossession of the fellahs in the Ouargenis, in Mustapha Badie's *La Nuit a peur du Soleil*. Another recurrent theme in the cinema as well as on the television is the collaboration of some local potentates with the authorities. Another, that of the exploitation of miners, as in *Sueur noire*. But what is best remembered is the Algerian people's resistance, starting with Temfik Farès's *Les Hors-la-loi* (1969) which shows how the first colonial administration cannot substitute the Napoleonic Code for the code of honour in force in Algeria. Accordingly those who remain faithful to this code of honour become bandits; they are called outlaws; they personify the repudiation of the colonial order. Above all, with Temfik Farès and Mohammed Lakhdar-Hamima, Algerian cinema produces in 1966 a masterpiece: *Le Vent des Aurès* is the tragic story of a family that is destroyed by the war. After the death of his father, the son undertakes to supply the underground resistance. He is arrested. Tirelessly the mother sets out looking for him. She goes from barracks to barracks, all the time holding a hen in the hand in order, in exchange for this offering, to be able at least to see her son. She dies, electrocuted on the barbed wire of the camp where he is interned.

Such a presentation brings forth three features of the colonization which are viewed as being particularly intolerable: dispossession, cultural subversion, exploitation. It perpetuates the notion that at no time did the Arabs and the Kabyles of Algeria agree to accept the foreigner's yoke. Thus are forgotten the time of the "Arab kingdom", of the collaboration which was partly accepted in the same way as the idea of integration, as conceived by Napoleon III, was accepted by many, and the uprisings are emphasized. The most important of these uprisings was that of 1871, called the "uprising of Kabylia" in the chronicle of colonial tradition, though only 250 tribes revolted, that is, a total of only a third of the Algerian population. Actually the majority of the djouad chiefs had been restless ever since the administration had deprived them of their power. In addition to this restlessness the "lower classes too rebelled", an event which has been brought to light by the calls of the conference of the Darquawa, which bespoke a fierce hatred of the French (1864). The progress of the colonists, the weakening of the officers – they understood better the feelings of the Arab aristocracy, the announcement of the generalization of the civil system threw into a turmoil the "natives" who still looked upon Napoleon III as a protector. He had after all declared that he was as much "the Emperor of the Arabs as that of the French". His fall and the French defeat in 1870 seemed to presage a massive revolt. In *Les Politiques coloniales au Maghreb* Charles-Robert Ageron has shown that in that context the Crémieux edict that granted French citizenship to the Jews played only a minor role, not even that of the detonator, in that explosion. That was so even if one of the leaders of the insurrection, the Sheikh Mokrani, declared: "I shall never obey a Jew ... I would rather place myself under a sword, but never under a Jew." What is striking is undoubtedly that, as a member of the General Council of Constantine a few years earlier, he had voted for the naturalization of the Jews. The rationale was that he did not want such a naturalization for his fellow believers. He did not believe that a citizen could rank above the believer, the proof being that the Jew was being naturalized. The decree meant that the Jew was being compelled to give up his faith. That is something a Muslim would never do.

Another factor in the revolt was the Commune of Algiers in 1871, which had witnessed the French fighting among themselves, between Republicans and Bonapartists, and declaring themselves in favour of Algeria becoming independent all by itself. Republican "separatism" – this typically French defeat would be repeated in a different form in 1954–62, after Dien Bien Phu and the Organization of the Secret Army – provided an impulse to the insurrection. The many-sided revolt was harshly suppressed, according to the "Algerian rule". It was followed by a large-scale expropriation. After that the Kabyle ballads said: "1871 was our ruin, 1871 was the year when we became beggars."

The revolt of Abd el Krim: a suppressed memory

When the colonized peoples were struggling for independence it was asked whether the War of the Riff (1921–26) had been the last death throes of their defence, or, on the contrary, the forerunner of a movement which subsequently culminated in independence. In 1923, after the victory of Anoual, Abd el Krim proclaimed the "Republic of the Riff", he was actually throwing down a challenge to the imperialist powers. The proclamation was in response not only to Spanish penetration but also to the will of the French, of Lyautey among others, to associate the colonial presence to the Moroccan monarchy.

The insurrection called into question the relationship which the Riff maintained with the Moroccan State. It was a relationship which, as a result of imperialist penetration, was actually causing the disintegration of the country. It was ruined and was forced to fall back on precarious local political balances. Such a situation was the outcome of the loss of the ancient bonds which the Riff had established with the rest of Morocco and it had been brought about by colonial investments. Consequently it is within the interplay of these networks of authority – and certainly not in an isolated Riff – that Abd el Krim undertook his action, through the mediacy of the Quranic law which he represented and by means of his duties as a judge which gave him control over the whole society. He maintained himself in the area of Fez, in spite of his being a dissident. But Abd el Krim did so by conforming to Islam which he hoped to reform and separate from the state, as Ataturk had done.

Accordingly there is no justification for establishing a parallel with Abd el-Kader, even if both were elected chiefs, with the title of Emir, who resorted to arms and to European techniques. Both envisaged, by referring it to the Quran, a state which parted company with the cadres and the customs of the brotherhood, and which promoted democratic consultation. Actually both were successful in fostering a readiness for war in a country and in a population facing an enemy bent on occupation – for without it colonization would not be complete. But the difference between Abd el-Kader and Abd el Krim lies in the latter's going further in the collective organization of the resistance, and above all in the political transformation of the preceding social organization. Abd el Krim took his first steps in the religious domain but he was aiming at a more drastic political transformation, not necessarily in league with the Sultan. He may have thus given rise to the notion of "revolutionary war" which may have inspired Ho Chi Minh in 1946.

Abd el Krim explained his defeat as being due to religious fanaticism, that *ta'assub* being the fragmentation of the Moroccan communities into mutually opposing groups attached to contradictory loyalties. And, of course, he explained it also as being due to the technical and numerical superiority of the French who marshalled up to 325,000 regular troops, in addition to the 100,000 Spaniards, arrayed against 75,000 partisans. He had chosen the rubric "Republic of the Riff" in order to express the fact that "we were a state consisting of federate, independent tribes and not a representative state endowed with an elected parliament."

Abd el Krim's experiment was hailed by the revolutionaries of all countries. It won the support of the Comintern and of the French Communist Party then under the influence of Jacques Doriot. Yet it failed to win acknowledgement, either in Morocco or among the reformist groups within the Egyptian Wafd or within the Tunisian Destour. They maintained a certain mistrust towards Abd el Krim because they conceived their own opposition in parliamentary terms, and not in the form of a popular uprising. Likewise the nationalist reformer Allal el-Fassi, in

Morocco, observed that in five years Abd el Krim, in his own insurrectional zone, "had not built even one school". Everything points to Abd el Krim's being the subject of interest more in Lebanon or in Moscow than in Morocco itself. Abdallah Laroui has noted that as late as in 1971, when a Moroccan describes the battle of Anoual where the Spanish army was defeated in July 1921, the facts are presented from the Spanish point of view. This provides the evidence that in Morocco the counter-history has not been written (see *Abd el Krim et la République du Riff*). Again, Allal el-Fassi's *Les Mouvements d'indépendance en Afrique du Nord* contains only brief remarks on Abd el Krim. This shows that, between 1925 and 1954, those who were directing the Moroccan nationalist movement showed no real political interest in the riffan experiment, because they interpreted it through the prism of the liberal democratic movement and of the Salafi movement of resistance, which posited that, in the final analysis, Abd el Krim would have surrendered his powers to the Sultan. As a matter of fact Abd el Krim went much further than that, for he deemed that if he had had the possibility and the time "we, Moroccans, would have become a great nation of free men".

In such a context it is easily understood that the organizations linked to the Sultan, and afterwards to the King, would have to some extent drawn a veil on the Riff insurrection, even if this entailed conferring upon it a touch of glory which would henceforth bear no risk for the powers that be.

"From our mountains free men raise their voice, calling for independence" : these words sung by the men of Abd el Krim seem to have, in their time and up to the 1950s, been heard in Tunisia, in Algeria or in Turkey, more than in Morocco.

In Vietnam, moral armament in opposition to the French

In 1922 Lord Northcliffe, editor of the *Times* and of the *Daily Mail* told André Tudesq of the *Journal* how much he admired the French presence in Indo-China. "You earn there the dividends of three hundred years of colonial experience . . . You have been able to discover and move the heart of the native. Your colonial action is tactful. In these regions the politics of friendship prevail" (quoted in Chauvelot, 1931).

Without doubt, the Vietnamese themselves did not all share this analysis.

At first, from 1885 onwards, the Vietnamese felt that they had "lost their country". They gave vent to their feelings in an anti-French idiom: "these hairy men, with their foul smell and long noses". However, soon enough, they became more anti-colonialist than anti-French, for they thought that there were "good Frenchmen", such as Montesquieu, Voltaire, Rousseau and Napoleon. At first they did actually envisage the French invasion as on a par with the preceding ones, like the Mongol invasion, for instance. As a matter of fact as early as 1842, they were expecting a French invasion.

They were divided between those who wanted to "lock all the doors shut" and those who wanted to "know the bread and the milk", that is, to learn from the West its recipes – not only its gastronomic recipes – in order better to resist it. It was the defeat of Ki-hon (1861) which convinced them the latter course was better, with the French artillery having already demonstrated its supremacy.

A second turning point occurred in the Vietnamese reaction when, under the leadership of their intellectuals, they challenged the attitude of the Hué Court "which sought to make cautious arrangements with the 'Barbarians'". It did not call the monarchy into question, but only the person of the King, who was no longer worthy of his calling. The intellectuals compared the behaviour of China with that of Japan which had been able to complete its Meiji reform, while Vietnam, like China, chose to stagnate. The severed head of Captain Rivière proved that it was possible to offer resistance. The head was exposed in village after village, in order to rouse the spirit of resistance.

> We are fallen, hope lies in our sons;
> We own our life, but we must learn to sacrifice it,
> Were we to remain silent, we would be treated as cowards.
> We shall read the proclamation of our victories on the Wu,
> We shall act like those who have exterminated the Mongols . . .
> (Quoted in David Marr, 1971)

In 1885 the flight of Emperor Ham Nghi marked the end of any illusions about the ability of the Hué Court to defend the country and the beginning of a resistance led by the Can Vuong movement of those intellectuals who, in their pamphlets and writings, denounced the invader. One of the leaders of this movement was Phan Boi Chau who was asked to surrender in order to save his brother who had been taken prisoner. He told his close associates: "Ever since I joined our movement, I have forgotten all about the problems of my family, or of my village. Because I have only one tomb, a very big tomb, to defend: it is the tomb of my country, the land of Vietnam. And my brother in danger, that is the twenty million of my fellow citizens. If I save my brother, who then will save the others?"

But this moral armament was inadequate to drive away the French. It galvanized only a small number of intellectuals. Still they won the adherence of the entire population around them. They never gave an explicit expression to their rigorous behaviour. But everyone understood what they wanted to signify. That understanding was a prefiguration of the attitude of the French under the occupation, in the face of the Germans, as evinced in *Le Silence de la mer*.

This explains why, in 1900, the French administration believed that, from an administrative point of view, patriotism no longer had any means of expression. Paul Doumer organized the systematic protection of the country. At the same time by organizing the exploitation of the country Doumer unwittingly sowed the seeds of the future uprising of the peasantry.

The dramatic change in the mentality of the Vietnamese was that they felt that they not only had lost the material substance of their territory, but that, with the colonial administration persisting in stretching its tentacles over the country "they ran the risk of losing their soul". The degradation of some, that is, the mandarin-collaborators who had become the servants of the French occupier, provided the spectacle of a degeneration which justified their worsening treatment at the hands of the French.

Phan Boi Chau's book *Vietnam Vong Quoc Su* (History of the Loss of Vietnam), written after a visit to Japan, had a great success. The book was written in Chinese, in order to warn both the Chinese and the Vietnamese. If China did not pay heed, it would soon experience the fate of Vietnam. Its translation in about fifty copies reached the most distant villages of Vietnam, because it was written in a simple prose. It denounced the ineffectiveness of the Hué Court in not having educated the people to warn it against the dangers that threatened the nation. It also denounced the policy of the occupier who attacked the intellectuals in order to keep the people still more ignorant. It took stock of the taxes and contributions which the Vietnamese were forced to pay: for instance, 4 on salt, the plot of land, weighing, transportation, sale; 6 on tobacco, and so on. In the villages he narrated the popular story about the miserliness and the harshness of the Frenchmen: "A family had been ruined because of all the taxes it had had to pay. It went to see the official. 'We own nothing at all, except the sky above our heads . . .' 'Sign this paper', answered the official . . . When the family wanted to return to their village, a group of soldiers blocked their way. 'You cannot go back to your village', they said. 'You are going there to breathe the air which, according to the paper you have signed, does not belong to you.'"

It goes without saying that Japan's victory over Russia spurred the movement of resistance which was still confined to the intellectuals. Phan Boi Chau's second book *Tan Vietnam* (The New Vietnam) listed the ten great paths of life, in short, a complete political programme: that the Vietnam does not "need" to be protected, that the mandarins must no longer exploit the people, that no unjust taxes be levied, that the educational system needs to be revised, that the industries must not be in the hands of the foreigners. The manifestation of moral qualities was necessary for the fulfilment of these marvels, not to speak of independence: the spirit of initiative, the love for one's neighbour, the concern for modernization, the affirmation of patriotism without unduly speaking of one's country.

This moral movement was in response to the measures taken by Paul

Doumer around 1908, measures which soon began to pervade all the activities in the society: taxes and forced labour were enforced more stringently in order to "build the country". That "transformation of Indo-China" provoked the first great revolts of the peasants and later of the workers. Naturally the movements of resistance had not provided a structure to this response of the Vietnamese society to the new burdens which were weighing so heavily on it.

They had provided it with a moral weapon.

History revisited: the vision of K. M. Panikkar in India

The vision of the vanquished, for Asia and for India in particular, has been the subject of a genuine synthesis,[1] apparently the first of its kind. It is the work of the Indian historian K. M. Panikkar, *Asia and Western Domination*. This work was started in the thirties, that is, before Independence, and was completed in 1953.

In a manner little different from the Western historical vision he divides into distinct periods the four hundred and fifty years that span the interval from the arrival in India of Vasco da Gama in 1498 to the departure of the British from India and from China in 1947–49. His important themes are not always the same: the Battle of Lepanto in 1571 is, according to him, the first great turning point. Up till then the mainspring of the action of the Europeans had been the idea of a crusade against Islam and a strategic outflanking of the Muslim power. But this motivation disappeared with the defeat of the Ottoman fleet, which brought the Muslim threat to an end. The European drive to gain the monopoly of the commerce in spices gave place, within a span of a hundred years, to a drive to import textiles and tea. For its part, after its Industrial Revolution, Britain was driven by the need to find outlets for its manufactured goods or places favourable to its investments. First religious, European interests had become commercial and political. In the process the supremacy changed hands and passed from the Portuguese to the Dutch, then to the French and the British.

The "Vasco da Gama" period was characterized by the ascendancy of the maritime powers over the continental powers, by the imposition of economic trading upon communities whose main activity had till then been based essentially on agricultural production and on internal trade. But then it was the mastery of the Atlantic which had begun to govern the world. Spain may well have lost it with the defeat of the Invincible Armada, but the other powers took over from it. What is true in the explanation of what befell India or Indonesia is equally so in explaining the fate of China or of Japan, which lost the freedom of their trade with Malaysia, Formosa and the Philippines. In fact, from the sixteenth century on, China was submitted to a genuine blockade – in turn Portuguese, then Dutch, and later British.

205

The second intermediate period, according to K. M. Panikkar's scheme, began when the Europeans ceased being crusaders to become missionaries. That was the era of the Counter-Reformation which roused the spirit of the mystics like Francis Xavier. It was a short period. But its features were fixed by the missionary endeavour of the Protestants at the end of the eighteenth century. The connections between Europe and Asia henceforth gave rise to a system of relations between independent countries, in a sort of face to face relationship.

The third period which began with the middle of the nineteenth century, "the Augustan century of the European empires of Asia", was marked by Russia and the United States joining the Far-Eastern scramble for economic spoils. K. M. Panikkar adopts the theses of R. H. Tawney's *Religion and the Rise of Capitalism* and accordingly considers that "drawing upon the wealth of the East through the narrow opening of the Levant" was, for Europe, an imposition of fateful limitations upon itself and condemning itself to a slow death "like a giant who could not take his food but through the cracks in a wall". Western domination had perforce to be more deeply entrenched and this too over a wide territory in order to survive. In its wake followed the structural changes in the societies which had been reduced to submission. Hence the reason of their revolt.

These considerations of K. M. Panikkar overlap or correct the Western vision of history. To his critical analysis he appends original observations on the missionary activities. It is worth noting that these comments prompt the reservations expressed in the preface to the French version by Albert Béguin, the Editor of *Esprit*, in 1957.

Panikkar emphasizes the arrogance and the self-sufficiency of the missionaries, especially of the Catholic missionaries, while other Indian historians stress the cupidity of the Portuguese conquerors. The missionaries acted as if India was not aware of what had occurred in the West.

For the fact is that India knew Christianity long before the arrival of these missionaries. The Church in Malabar even claims to have been established by the apostle Thomas. In any case it has been in existence since A.D. 182. It was during the Mongol invasion, in the middle of the thirteenth century, after the meeting of the Council of Lyon in 1245 that the Pope resolved to send the first legates to the Khans of the regions bordering Europe and even to the Great Khan himself.

Giovanni de Plano Carpini, of Perugia, a companion of Francis of Assisi, had been designated to convert him. Even at that early time he thought that it was enough to expound the principles of Christianity to the Khan for the latter to resolve to be baptized. Later other missionaries showed the same attitude towards Emperor Akbar, who had ascended the throne in 1582. Akbar was educated and loved to engage in free discussions of religious subjects and he used to invite to his court the representatives of all the religions then known. The Jesuits were welcomed at Agra. But the debates indulged in proved to be deeply shocking on account of "their intolerance, their dogmatism, their pretence to be the sole possessors of divine Truth and their scorn for their adversaries could not but be viewed as shocking". Half a century later the same Jesuits kidnapped two of the Great Moghul's women servants and converted them by means which were "anything but orthodox". Panikkar explains it as "the normal behaviour of the missionaries". As early as the thirteenth century Giovanni de Monte Corvino, sent by the Pope to China, "had bought forty slaves and given them baptism . . . That was an original, but costly, method of spreading the faith."

Persecution was, at that time, another method of proselytizing, as is shown, for example, in the action initiated by John III of Portugal in India where the Church, in Goa, had the Hindu temples destroyed and their wealth distributed to the Christian religious orders (1540). The ecclesiastical courts showed intense earnestness in condemning the heretics, even before the Inquisition was officially established in 1560. Despite his generosity, the passage of Francis Xavier did not change the situation. The revival became effective only after the arrival of another Jesuit, Roberto de Nobili (1577–1656), who studied Hinduism in order to improve his discourse with the Brahmans. In Madura he wore the ascetic's garb, learned Sanskrit and transposed the Christian dogmas into the language of the *Upanishads*. He became popular at the court of the King of Madura. But his success proved to be his ruin. He was recalled to Rome. Finally the establishment of the Inquisition in Goa, the first auto-da-fés (1563 and later) deprived the missionaries of all the sympathy which they had till then received.

During the British period the failure of the Protestants was all the more rapid, because the Baptists of William Carey, who had settled near Calcutta, encountered nothing but the hostility of the other British who had settled in the country. These were for the most part the agents of the East India Company. They thought that the social disorder that the missions could provoke could not but precipitate the deterioration of the commercial trade. The contempt in which the missions held the Hindus was such that "they believed that the presence of a bishop, of something splendid, regal, would be sufficient to impress them, to convert them . . . "

Besides this self-sufficiency coincided with the aggression of the Europeans, "those imperialists". The missionaries identified themselves with the victors: they taught the natives Europe, its greatness, its glory, its primacy. At the same time they quarrelled among themselves, among nationals, among denominations, among sects. "What a farce, for an Asian who does not believe in the unity of Truth."

Panikkar's theses represent not only a Westernization of the historical approach to the past of India, but also an attention to historical discipline, which was almost absent in the classical tradition. At first the past of India had been analysed by politicians, journalists, but not by the historians. The shock which humiliated the Indians and sparked the initiative for a nationalist construction of history was due to the publication of James Mill's *History of India* in 1817, which was written with the purpose of establishing the rank of India on the scale of civilizations. India was ranked lowest because "by the combination of despotism and of priest-hood, the Hindus are physically and morally the most enslaved part of humanity". As a reaction Surendranath Banerjea initiated the development of a historical school. According to him the past deserves to be known if the country is to regenerate itself. This entails a criticism of the occidentalists like Bankim Chandra Chatterjee, according to whom the subjection of India was due to the "weak" and "effeminate" character of its inhabitants who were devoid of any national pride, due to the lack of historical knowledge. The reaction went on to oppose even those, like G. K. Gokhale, who adopted as their point of reference the British political tradition.

The first theme to be promoted is the ancientness of Indian civilization, of its history, which existed before the Islamic invasions. Beside it the one hundred and fifty years of British domination appear like a relatively "insignificant" episode. The originality of the *Ramayana* and of the *Bhagavad Gita* is an absolute sign of ancientness, much earlier than the European civilization. Moreover this ancientness goes hand in hand with a cultural permanence and continuity. It is true that this continuity had been interrupted by the Muslim invasion. Nevertheless the cultural continuity has persisted despite the vicissitudes of history. Bipin Chandra Pal brings out the landmarks of this tradition: a way to govern oneself without despotism and without submission to a military power; kings whose will did not have force of law; a spontaneous separation of the executive and the legislative powers represented by the king and the councils of Brahmins. "The political nature of the political system preserved it from conflicts between the king and the people": "in short, a contractual conception of the monarchy".

The impoverishment of India under British domination naturally constitutes the central argument which explains the decline of India. But, in the final analysis, this impoverishment is not as traumatic as the Muslim conquest which the Maratha revolt strives to limit and which, for the first time, testifies to the renaissance of the country and to the active formation of the Indian nationality. The existence of an Indian nation is henceforth taken for granted, as a reaction to the British tradition which emphasizes the heterogeneity of the country and claims for the English the credit of having unified a territory as vast as it is diverse.

Muslim domination, British domination

Successively vanquished and dominated by the Muslims – Arabs, Persians, Afghans – and by the British, the Hindus, at the beginning of the twentieth century, drew a parallel between these two "occupations". This contrast is not to the advantage of the British. B. C. Pal writes: "Even in the darkest days of Muslim domination, the people continued to manage their own business . . . and enjoyed a measure of freedom greater than what is allowed to them under the highly praised system of representative local government, introduced by the British." Further, the Islamic domination was characterized by "the absence of social and political discrimination against the Hindus, the right granted to the population to bear arms, the respect of the economic interests of the natives". The difference lies in the theory of the "drain", the politics of sucking the blood out of the wealth of India. At the worst, the Afghan and Moghul emperors deposited in the national treasury the heavy taxes they levied. They had to maintain their palaces, their armies, which enabled Indian craftsmen to earn a living and feed themselves. The revenue from the taxes benefited the country, even when magnificent works testified to the vanity of the kings. But the arrival of the East India Company put an end to this system. It was England that derived profit from the country. Not India any more.

All this undoubtedly is an idealization of the Muslim past and of the pre-Muslim institutions, like the village community. Such a double diversion masks the existence of a hierarchy at all social levels; remains silent over the existence of the caste system, which the Indian historians reduce to its being only a division of labour; observes that a part of the population went over to Islam precisely because of the social order which it was promoting. At the beginning of the twentieth century this "forgetting" of the importance of the caste system promoted the interest of the high castes who then dominated the national movement. For caste could not be integrated with the historical Western model which was imitated and sought after as a means to achieve independence. To brush aside the role of the castes did in practice assure the predominance of the highest castes; it reduced differences with the Muslims, and favoured the unification of the country under the aegis of the Hindus, identified, as a consequence, with the whole of India.

History and counter-history

In this way, one finds that history and counter-history contain silences and taboos which have contributed to substituting a partially imaginary representation for the reality of historical analysis. In *L'Histoire sous surveillance* (pp. 71–135) I have tried to establish a typology of them, beginning with their written forms which the American blacks initiated in 1794, up to their various expressions in the cinema from the sixties of the twentieth century. In this field, the colonized peoples have played the role of pioneers.

7

THE MOVEMENTS FOR COLONIST-INDEPENDENCE

I use the expression "movements for colonist-independence" to designate those actions, whether successful or not, undertaken on the initiative of the colonists, that is, by white men. In this manner this first "decolonization" marked the highest level attained by expansion. On the other hand the other independence movements, that is, those of the colonized peoples, actually marked a reflux from expansion.

Actually one may observe that, from its beginnings up to almost the end of the twentieth century, the relationship which the colonists maintained with their mother country was of a rather ambiguous nature. As is well known, most of the time the mother country supported them against rivals, against the natives. But the conflicts in which they become involved may have nevertheless worsened to such an extent that, in order to give to themselves greater freedom of action, the colonists chose to break away from the mother country.

It is in this sense that one may view this series of struggles for independence as the most advanced stage of white colonial expansion.

Conflicts of this nature broke out from the very outset of colonization. An example is provided by the Pizarrist movement against Charles V (in 1544–48): it evinced characteristics which one observes in other contexts. Indeed one encounters a host of such movements during the entire period down to the end of colonization. The stakes were varied, and one must refrain from assimilating the aims of the "American Revolution" (1783) to those of the Spanish colonies between 1819 and 1825, or let alone to those of South Rhodesia, later Zimbabwe, which claimed affinity with the principles of the American Revolution. Likewise one ought not to confuse what was at stake in the revolt of the colonists of Algiers in 1871 with what was at stake in 1958. The facts and the contexts are quite different. From one extremity of the history of colonization to the other, the movements of the colonists each had its respective logic and its specific configuration.

In the Spanish possessions the colonists rose up against the movement initiated by Bartolomeo de Las Casas, that is, they rose up in protest against the protection granted by the mother country to the natives. One finds such features elsewhere.

A precedent: the Pizarrist movement in Spanish America (1544–48)

When Don Antonio de Mendoza, the first Viceroy of Mexico, handed over his office to his successor, he clearly explained how incompatible was the Crown's desire to protect the natives with its expectation of an increase in the revenue derived from the Indies. As is well known, the Crown wanted to preserve what was then called the "Republic of the Indians" which lay under the threat of the excesses and depredations of the conquerors and the newly arrived colonists. The numbers of the Indians had declined as a result of the violence and the diseases to which they had been subjected. Consequently they had to endure the increasingly overbearing pressure exerted upon them by the colonists. The latter were masters of the place. But, from the mother country, they were receiving instructions which, on paper, were issued by the Council of the Indies whose 249 members – from its inception down to 1700 – were *Letrados*, jurists mostly, among whom only 7 had set foot in America. Caught between, on one hand, this mass of instructions and, on the other, the colonists, the viceroys and the 35 provincial governors acquitted themselves of their duties, by more or less putting into practice the decisions of the Escorial.

What was at stake in the war declared on Blasco Nunez Vela, the Viceroy of Peru, was apparently the application of the laws of 1542 which stripped the conquerors of their privileges. Marcel Bataillon wonders whether the Viceroy was, or not, in favour of the ideas of Las Casas. Still, ever since the laws of Burgos (1542), the conquerors had got used to evading the legal constraints upon the exploitation of the Indians, forced labour, and sharing out. It was in Mexico that the colonists first started to protest against the *audiencia*, an institution set up to watch over them. But it was clear to all that it would be difficult to bring to heel men who would stop at nothing in their opposition to justice: they were "like men guilty of a crime waiting to be arrested". But, whether the Viceroy really wanted to protect the Indians or not, the equivocations and betrayals on the part of those whose duty was to collaborate with him prevented him from fulfilling his mission. Besides the magistrates despatched by the mother country had, on their arrival, no other preoccupation but to enrich themselves and lost no time in conniving with the colonists. These law officers shared in the latter's aversion to the new law which considered the colonists unfit to have Indians in *encomienda*.

Gonzalo Pizarro rose in revolt against this law. A relative of the conquistador, he described to the colonists the adverse effects which that law had on the rights and privileges of the conquerors, "without in any way evoking the slightest suspicion that the Indians too could have rights". As the *procurador* of Cuzco he had himself elected *capitan general*, then *justicia mayor*, and subsequently as the acting Governor. When war with the legal power broke out, Pizarro asked his assistants "not to cause the remaining Indians to die because without them the country would be worth nothing". What was at stake was to prevent an expedition despatched against him from Chile with the purpose of carrying off the Indians, for then there would be none left for work. The conquistadores were served notice to choose between Gonzalo Pizarro and the King who was the "provider of Indians" and of other favours: they hesitated and yielded. Finally they rallied to the side of the King, for often the bonds of solidarity are frail among men of prey. The Church intervened in order to ensure the granting of a pardon and a re-examination of the application of the "accursed laws".

Another cause for the anger of the colonists was the establishment of the Jesuits who "deprived them of Indians".

The challenge of the Jesuits in Paraguay

One of the achievements of the Jesuits was the constitution of the *redduciones*, a genuine alternative to the usual methods of colonization and of evangelization which the Church had hitherto practised in Indian America. The daring of the Jesuits consisted in proclaiming their resolve to organize a parallel society beside that of the colonists, a society which would be free from any interference on the part of the central authority or of that of the local civil administrators. These *reduciones* would not be used as a pool of manpower for the colonists. Their purpose was to raise the Indians, to develop their individual and collective personality.

For example, the Guaranis of the Jesuit *reducion* created in 1607 in Paraguay had their own militia and actually constituted a state within the state. In the eighteenth century, it comprised about 40 centres with a population numbering between 96,000 and 130,000 Guaranis. The authorities did not take kindly to the principle according to which "the Indians were to be made men before being made into Christians". In 1767, Charles III followed the example of the King of Portugal and decided upon the expulsion of the Jesuits from the Americas. Their independence and their obedience to the Pope were intolerable.

1776 – The American colonies: independence or revolution?

In contrast with the independence movements of the second half of the twentieth century, the first decolonization was carried out by the initiative of the Europeans themselves, that is, of the colonists who lived overseas. The independence of the United States in 1783, of the Spanish colonies and subsequently of Brazil owed little to the indigenous populations subjugated by those same colonists. Only in Haiti the enslaved Blacks of Africa won their freedom on their own, both against the mother country and against the colonists.

Such indeed is the main difference between the first decolonization and the later movements that occurred especially in Asia and in Africa, where the vanquished peoples rose in revolt in order to gain their independence and to bring the rule of the colonists to an end.

Another feature calls for scrutiny. Depending on the historical period and the standpoint of the observers, the events that occurred in America between 1774 and 1783 have been at times described as the Independence of the United States, at other times as the American Revolution. This ambiguity has had a great influence, since it raises the question of the agents of history, of their intentions, of the manner in which they contemplate their action. The same ambiguity can be seen in the representation of the events in Algeria, following 1954, in the context of which the literature of the FLN (National Liberation Front) speaks of the Algerian Revolution as much as of the struggle for independence, even after the latter has been achieved. This means that after the example of the Pizarrist movement, the case of America does indeed serve as a model for the political and national problems of the two centuries that were to follow.

It is a paradox that it was the victory of the British during the Seven Years' War, which ended in 1763, that initiated the process that led to American Independence. In fact, up to that time, and before the elimination of French Power in North America by the Treaty of Paris, the British colonists stuck to His Britannic Majesty in order to be able to dispose of his fleet and of his armies. "In the absence of this threat, the Americans would sever the bonds which unite them to Great Britain", wrote a contemporary observer as early as 1749.

The British colonists were increasingly asserting their American indentity. As a result they actually expressed their grievances with an intensity corresponding to the rise of their economic power and the development of their ability to use the law for their defence.

Ever since the Navigation Acts the American colonies had depended on the Board of Trade, on the Admiralty, on the Privy Council. Foreign vessels were not allowed to have access to them. Imports and exports were regulated in the interest of the mother country. The Southern colonies – Virginia, Carolina – were better treated because they supplied tropical produce in exchange of British manufactured goods. For example, they were authorized to export rice directly to Spain and they had even managed to have the cultivation of tobacco prohibited in Great Britain. But the colonies of the Centre and, above all, of the North were under observation because their produce (wood, salted fish) had little interest for the mother country which was disturbed by the development of their fleet of 1500 vessels. They were not allowed to trade directly with the other colonies, especially the Caribbean colonies. And of course that prohibition extended to the relations they had with Spain, Portugal and with France.

The first act of an irreparable conflict was the Molasses Act of 1733 which imposed prohibitive duties on the entry of molasses from the French West Indies. This act was in response to a complaint on the part of the sugar manufacturing colonies which desired to have the monopoly on the production of rum.

In 1750 the second act came about with the prohibition imposed upon the colonists of New York and of Pennsylvania against setting up ironworks in order not to place the English industry at risk. A certain deliberate negligence, particularly during the wars, prevented the growing antagonism from developing into a genuine conflict. This compromise would last as long as the French posed a threat to other colonists who were in search of more land lying in the west.

But the feeling of a budding and irreparable rivalry was emerging and this process started as soon as the Treaty of Paris was signed and France had to cede Canada to Britain. London wanted the Americans to share at least partly the costs of this security as they were the beneficiaries of the peace. But the latter showed their teeth and dared to organize a boycott of English goods. "New England is more to be feared than the Old", wrote Accarias de Serionne in *Intérêts des nations de l'Europe développée relativement au commerce* (1766).

Undoubtedly the important point to bear in mind is that, at the very moment when the British wanted to tighten their control over commerce in America and the Atlantic, their colonies in New England were eager to free themselves from it. They even wanted to bring it to an end, but this not so much for economic reasons, for they had earlier earned large profits from the illicit trade that had been carried out for several decades. *The real reasons were political.* The Yankees wanted to have full freedom of movement. Accordingly they realized that they had never paid any taxes except those to which they had themselves consented. On the other hand they understood that in the mother country the subjects of His Majesty were represented in Parliament, while they were not. They were vexed that, without having consulted them, Lord Shelburne would have prohibited the settlement of colonists beyond the Alleghenies, on the lands conquered and won from the French, undoubtedly due to his desire to avoid any war with the Indians. But this prohibition was detrimental to the interests of the capitalists and speculative promoters like the planter George Washington or even Benjamin Franklin.

The second important point is that in Britain itself some people upheld the cause of the colonists, in the name of liberty, by arguing that the

Crown was letting its victories go to its head and manifesting a growing arrogance towards the rights of its citizens. If the colonies allowed laws and decisions to be applied to them without voicing any protest, would this not spell the end of British liberties in the very near future? Actually it was to prevent the consequent separation of the colonies that concessions had to be made to their mostly British inhabitants.

In the face of this pressure Lord Grenville withdrew his Stamp Act: this was an internal tax which was opposed by the delegates of the nine colonies of North America. But that Act was replaced by a Declaratory Bill which stated that Parliament had the right to legislate on all matters relative to the colonies and therefore to tax them. At that stage the swords were not drawn. But gradually the tension grew on either side of the Atlantic, even if on either side radicals ready to do battle coexisted with loyalists ready to submit. Pitt and Burke in Great Britain, as well as George Washington in Virginia and Dickinson in Philadelphia, were among those who stood out against the ministers bent on imposing sanctions.

Accordingly the conflict took a revolutionary turn. But, with the exception of a few American radicals, secession was certainly not at issue in the conflict. Besides, in Britain, where a few individuals could see that the authorities were driving the Americans to secede, rare indeed were those who actually uttered the word "independence" or even imagined that it could happen.

Yet incidents kept recurring in which Americans and Englishmen faced one another. British soldiers exacted reprisals on the citizens opposed to their presence (the Boston massacres). The famous Tea Party is well known: disguised as Indians, Americans threw into the sea the cargo of tea brought by the East India Company. The low price of the tea brought ruin to the American merchants who were receiving their supplies from other sources.

At the same time the Americans increasingly met in meetings and in frequent assemblies of the representatives of several colonies. The continental Congress held its first sitting in 1774, thereby welding in some way the colonies together: "I am not a Virginian, but an American", said Patrick Henry who asked that voting by states be replaced by voting by individuals. Everybody was ready for the war, though it was still understood as an economic war. Further, if one was a member of the Association, a permanent institution set up by the Congress, one threatened with a boycott, not only the British, this was taken for granted, but also those Americans who did not put the boycott into practice.

In addition this "terrorism" explains the irritation provoked by the Quebec Act. Enacted in London this act assigned to the left bank of the St Lawrence river – that is, to the Catholics – the lands populated by the Indians which were the object of desire of the colonists living in the distant West.

It was in this state of turmoil that, after an incident in Lexington between an armed militia and the troops of General Gage, that John Adams asked for the constitution of a genuine army to serve under the orders of George Washington. At the same time Thomas Paine published his *Common Sense* (1776), a stirring call for the independence of the Americans. It must be added that, in the meantime, to avenge 1763, the King of France had promised his support.

Thomas Paine's call was heard. Within a few weeks 120,000 copies were sold. He wrote: "The blood of the dead, the voice of nature weep and call: the time for separation has arrived." The proponents of independence continued to gain ground. In spite of the reservations of those who, in the South, like Edward Rutledge, were apprehensive of the demagogy of the "levellers", and of the loyalists scattered over the entire region, the colonies, one after the other, recommended their delegations to vote for independence. The task of writing the text was entrusted to Thomas Jefferson, delegate of Virginia. It was voted on 4 July 1776.

From the time of its proclamation in 1776, this text has been the source of inspiration for a large number of independence movements, whatever may have been the substance of the particular independence, whether sought by native or by colonist, such as Rhodesia in the 1960s. That is why I consider this foundational text to be important enough to be included here in its totality.

The unanimous Declaration of the thirteen United States of America

When in the Course of human events it becomes necessary for one people to dissolve the political bands which have connected them with another, and to assume among the powers of the earth, the separate and equal station to which the Laws of Nature and Nature's God entitle them, a decent respect of the opinions of mankind requires that they should declare the causes which impel them to the separation.

We hold these truths to be self-evident, that all men are created equal, that they are endowed by their Creator with certain unalienable Rights, that among these are Life, Liberty, and the pursuit of Happiness; that to secure these rights, Governments are instituted among Men, deriving their just powers from the consent of the governed; that whenever any Form of Government becomes destructive of these ends, it is the Right of the People to alter or to abolish it, and to institute new Government, laying its foundation on such principles and organizing its powers in such form, as to them shall seem most likely to effect their Safety and Happiness. Prudence, indeed, will dictate that Governments long established should not be changed for light and transient causes; and accordingly all experience hath shewn that mankind are more disposed to suffer, while evils are sufferable, than to right themselves by abolishing the forms to which they are accustomed. But when a long train of abuses and usurpations, pursuing invariably the same Object, evinces a design to reduce them under abolute Despotism, it is their right, it is their duty, to throw off such Government, and to provide new Guards for their future security. Such has been the patient sufferance of these Colonies; and such is now the necessity which constrains them to alter their former Systems of Government. The history of the present King of Great Britain is a history of repeated injuries and usurpations, all having in direct object the establishment of an absolute Tyranny over these States. To prove this, let Facts be submitted to a candid world.

He has refused his Assent to Laws, the most wholesome and necessary for the public good.

He has forbidden his Governors to pass Laws of immediate and pressing importance, unless suspended in their operation till his Assent should be obtained; and when so suspended, he has utterly neglected to attend to them.

He has refused to pass other Laws for the accommodation of large districts of people, unless those people would relinquish the right of Representation in the Legislature, a right inestimable to them and formidable to tyrants only.

He has called together legislative bodies at places unusual, uncomfortable, and distant from the depository of their public Records, for the sole purpose of fatiguing them into compliance with his measures.

He has dissolved Representative Houses repeatedly, for opposing with manly firmness his invasions on the rights of the people.

He has refused for a long time, after such dissolutions, to cause others to be elected; whereby the Legislative powers, incapable of Annihilation, have returned to the People at large for their exercise; the State remaining in the mean time exposed to all the dangers of invasion from without, and convulsions within.

He has endeavoured to prevent the population of these States; for that purpose obstructing the Laws of Naturalization of Foreigners; refusing to pass others to encourage their migrations hither, and raising the conditions of new Appropriations of Lands.

He has obstructed the Administration of Justice, by refusing his Assent to Laws for establishing Judiciary powers.

He has made Judges dependent on his Will alone, for the tenure of their offices, and the amount and payment of their salaries.

He has erected a multitude of New Offices, and sent hither swarms of Officers to harass our people, and eat out their substance.

He has kept among us, in times of peace, Standing Armies without the Consent of our legislatures.

He has affected to render the Military independent of and superior to the Civil power.

He has combined with others to subject us to a jurisdiction foreign to our constitution, and unacknowledged by our laws; giving his Assent to their Acts of pretended Legislation:

– For quartering large bodies of armed troops among us;

– For protecting them, by a mock Trial, from punishment for any Murders which they should commit on the Inhabitants of these States;

– For cutting off our Trade with all parts of the world;

– For imposing Taxes on us without our Consent;

– For depriving us in many cases, of the benefits of Trial by Jury;

– For transporting us beyond seas to be tried for pretended offences;

– For abolishing the free System of English Laws in a neighbouring Province, establishing therein an Arbitrary government, and enlarging its Boundaries so as to render it at once an example and fit instrument for introducing the same absolute rule into these Colonies;

– For taking away our Charters, abolishing our most valuable Laws and altering fundamentally the Forms of our Governments;

– For suspending our own Legislatures, and declaring themselves invested with power to legislate for us in all cases whatsoever.

He has abdicated Government here, by declaring us out of his Protection and waging War against us.

He has plundered our seas, ravaged our Coasts, burnt our towns, and destroyed the lives of our people.

He is at this time transporting large Armies of foreign Mercenaries to compleat the works of death, desolation and tyranny, already begun with circumstances of Cruelty and perfidy scarcely paralleled in the most barbarous ages, and totally unworthy the Head of a civilized nation.

He has constrained our fellow Citizens taken Captive on the high Seas to bear Arms against their country, to become the executioners of their friends and Brethren, or to fall themselves by their Hands.

He has excited domestic insurrections amongst us, and has endeavoured to bring on the inhabitants of our frontiers, the merciless Indian Savages, whose known rule of warfare, is an undistinguished destruction of all ages, sexes and conditions.

In every stage of these Oppressions We have Petitioned for Redress in the most humble terms: Our repeated Petitions have been answered only by repeated injury. A Prince, whose character is thus marked by every act which may define a Tyrant, is unfit to be the ruler of a free people.

Nor have We been wanting in attentions to our British brethren. We have warned them from time to time of attempts by their legislature to extend an unwarrantable jurisdiction over us. We have reminded them of the circumstances of our emigration and settlement here. We have appealed to their native justice and magnanimity, and we have conjured them by the ties of our common kindred to disavow these usurpations, which would inevitably interrupt our connections and correspondence. They too have been deaf to the voice of justice and of consanguinity. We must, therefore, acquiesce in the necessity, which denounces our Separation, and hold them, as we hold the rest of mankind, Enemies in War, in Peace Friends.

WE, THEREFORE, the REPRESENTATIVES of the UNITED STATES OF AMERICA, in General Congress, Assembled, appealing to the Supreme Judge of the world for the rectitude of our intentions, do, in the Name, and by Authority of the good People of these Colonies, solemnly publish and declare, That these United Colonies are, and of Right ought to be FREE AND INDEPENDENT STATES; that they are Absolved from all Allegiance to the British Crown, and that all political connection between them and the State of Great Britain, is and ought to be totally dissolved; and that as Free and Independent States, they have full Power to levy War, conclude Peace, contract Alliances, establish Commerce, and to do all other Acts and Things which Independent States may of right do. And for the support of this Declaration, with a firm reliance on the protection of divine Providence, we mutually pledge to each other our Lives, our Fortunes and our Sacred Honor.

Between 1763 and 1776, one of the features which characterize the events in America is actually the rather extraordinary gap between the material, but essentially minor, grievances of the colonists against the Government in London, and the magnitude of the movement which leads to independence and to war. Moreover the list of the grievances marshalled by the Declaration of Independence is undoubtedly important. But, for the most part, they apply equally to the condition of the English, the Scots or the Irish of old Europe.

Again it has been established that the direct or indirect taxes levied on the colonists had not in the least affected their growing prosperity, that London turned a blind eye to illicit trade, and the centres of British power changed according to the economic pressures of each group of trading partners, in London, in Boston, in Jamaica. Indeed the Americans were not victims of a deliberate policy.

The tidal wave which swept the relations between the British and the Americans rose up from another shore. More than the removal of the King or the affirmation of the right to elect one's representatives, it was the moral significance of the event that mattered. At stake was the affirmation of the right of the totality of the population to participate in the government of the body politic. Opposed to it were, by their very existence, the King, a badly elected Parliament (cf. the "rotten boroughs"), an inadequate representation. Thus what was needed was a project for the *building of a new political order*. It aroused the entire population stirred by the economic and institutional conflicts. It infused a terrific energy into the people, as witness the number and the contents of the booklets, lampoons, newspapers published in the British colonies of America between 1763 and 1783. Above all the situation is characterized by the high moral tone of the Declaration of Independence.

Because they were foremost in the struggle against tyranny and corruption the members of the left wing of the Whigs, called the Radicals, ultimately won. As Burke wrote in 1775: "They guessed from afar the vices of the government and sensed the approach of tyranny in the wafting of the slightest deleterious breeze" (G. S. Wood, 1969, p. 38).

The conflict with the King or with the Parliament unveiled a deeper insubordination. It was not a question of justifying one's opposition to taxes imposed without the consent of the population. The real issue was to give to oneself one's own laws, in short, to *subject those who were governing to those who were governed*, to set up a genuine democracy in which the general interest would prevail over particular interests and in which each individual would be incorporated into the community.

In such a context the question of the relation with London was pushed into the background, for the entire system should have collapsed. The Radicals were animated by an almost religious faith which had its roots in the Scriptures as well as in the classics of the Enlightenment philosophy, such as Rousseau, Blackstone, Locke. They saw themselves as the bearers of a universal mission: they were the "heirs of Israel, the new Chosen People", they were a "new Christian Sparta", in the words of Samuel Adams. Actually these classics had contributed to their intellectual formation. But the American citizens could henceforth think for themselves. It is for this reason that it is now accepted that Jefferson and the Americans were indeed the authors of the Declaration of Independence – and there is no need to refer to Locke or anybody else.

Accordingly, independence, viewed from this angle, was but a first step to the creation of a Republic, that is, the fulfilment of a genuine revolution.

The American example fascinated the colonists in other British dependencies. In the nineteenth century, while the United Kingdom was experiencing a period of economic prosperity, London slackened its hold on its dependencies populated by whites. Gradually, in successive stages, they benefited from a representative, and sometimes from a parliamentary, system of government. In 1867, together with its four provinces of Québec, Ontario, New Brunswick, Nova Scotia, Canada was the first colony to benefit from Dominion Status. Soon the colonies and territories that wished to join were added to it: British Columbia in 1871, Prince Edward Island in 1873, territories arising from the breaking up of the Hudson Bay Company in 1870.

At first the Dominions (Canada, Australia, New Zealand) enjoyed a simple internal autonomy, which could be limited by the Governor's veto. Soon they acquired external autonomy, of which Canada offered the first example by concluding a trade agreement with Germany in 1907, without paying deference to Great Britain. This freedom was stretched further when, in 1914 and then in 1939, South Africa declared war on Germany independently of the mother country. At that time the King was the sole permanent link with London considering that the imperial conferences, at which the members of the Commonwealth gathered, had become irregular and informal. Increasingly these conferences evinced the separateness of each party's economic interests, with British solidarity coming into play only in the case of an external threat. Particularly from this point of view, the preference shown by Churchill, in 1942, for the defence of India over that of Australia, initiated the process of this Dominion's divorce from the motherland.

The Creole movement in Latino-Indian America

In South America the movement of the colonists responded to motivations similar to those of the North American colonists, with this difference, that racial domination played an important role. For wherever the Indians posed the greatest threat the eulogists of independence got the least following, as occurred in Peru. But the main drive for a trial of strength with the mother country took place in those places where there were hardly any Indians, in Rio de la Plata and in Venezuela.

The colonists had been used to getting round the laws. "*Obedezco pero no cumplo*" ("I obey, but I do not act"). Under Charles III the Bourbons of Spain wanted to change the situation, to make the state more efficient, to take advantage of the overseas colonies. As we have seen, the stakes in North America were economic as England was committed to monopolizing the market for the protection of her industries. But the stakes in South America were to a large extent fiscal, in view of the similarity between the metropolitan economy and that of the colony: identical export of minerals, commercial dependence on foreign navies, aristocratic elities little inclined towards business. The only difference lay in the production by South America of precious metals, from which little profit accrued to the mother country. To change this Charles III and the Bourbons intended to regain control of the administration of the country, by means of a "modernization" implemented by officials or dignitaries coming from the mother country. Up till then this administration maintained a balance with the Church which lay under the persistent suspicion of defending the interests of the natives, and with the local elites whose prosperity was on the rise. But even the steps taken against the Jesuits, at least in Mexico and in Chile, seemed to be arbitrary for it was an issue that concerned the local population. *This means that the Lascasian spirit had ceased to be dreaded,* and it had become possible to stand in direct opposition to the royal administration. Above all, while the army obstructed the rise of the Creoles in the hierarchy, the elites realized that taxation was beginning to affect them in so far as the administrative mechanism of control was being developed. At the same time the Creoles were, in their numerical proportion, less and less able to purchase *audiencias* (offices): they had only 23 percent of the total, while the rest went to metropolitans. *At bottom, the Creoles felt that Spain was colonizing them.* In 1781 they rose in revolt against the taxes in New Granada.

The hostility between the Creoles and the *peninsulares* (metropolitans) became more and more intense and antagonism began to grow between the patrician land-owners and the industrious officials who had come to enforce the law upon them.

Yet the Creoles kept watch over their servants. Most of the latter were Indians; also some were Metis. They still preferred Spain to anarchy, in the face of such revolts as Peru had experienced from 1742 to 1782. There is no doubt that the Indian revolt was a consequence of the difficulties brought about by the decline in the prices of agricultural produce: its project of a return to a utopian past was more hostile to the Spaniards than to the Church. Certainly about twenty chiefs chose to side with the Spaniards and the Creoles. But the latter had a keen awareness of this latent threat which existed under different forms in New Granada, for example, where the mulatto Galan had marched on Bogota. And, to some extent, these colonists wanted to be able to act freely. Moreover for Spanish America the revolt in Haiti had the force of an example: by no means should it be allowed to reproduce itself. It served as a warning. Of course, the Creoles who were impatient to govern their own country on their own thought less of the perverse effects of the French Revolution than of the advantages brought by the American Independence to the rebels. Moreover they too relied on the Enlightenment literature – Locke, Rousseau, Adam Smith – not to defend the rights of the metis or of the Indians, but to fight against the despotism of the Bourbons of Spain.

The weakness of Spain is what determined men like Francisco de Miranda, or Simon Bolivar who was himself part metis, to decide on a radical solution. While Madrid intended to demonstrate its efficiency, the means used by the mother country were ridiculously inadequate, as was demonstrated by the British taking Buenos Aires in 1806. No Spanish fleet was available to intercept them. But the invaders had under-estimated the will of the inhabitants of the capital to defend themselves. It was the Creole militia, led by Saavedra, that drove the British away. Accordingly Spain had been humiliated, and the credit went to the inhabitants of La Plata who had undertaken the defence of *their* colony. They had thus felt their power, they had discovered their strength, they never forgot it.

The situation was quite different in Mexico. With the failure of the Spanish monarchy from 1808 to 1815, the first movement for independence was initiated by a little downgraded priest, of Creole stock, but indeed close to the Indians. As much as an anti-Spanish movement, it was a sort of social, even ethnic, but vague revolution: Hidalgo the priest, and subsequently Father Morelos need not be viewed as the ancestors of Emiliano Zapata. The former called for an insurrection in favour of "the King, religion, the Indian Virgin of Guadalupe, and against the Spaniards". The latter set against himself not only the Spanish, but also the Creoles and the clergy, whose lands he wanted to share out. Hidalgo was executed in 1811 and Morelos in 1815.

However, when liberal movements burst forth in Spain which might threaten the hegemony of the colonists, the latter reacted and rallied quite naturally behind Agustin de Iturbide, a Creole officer who had crushed Morelos. He proclaimed the Plan of Iguala, the so-called Three Guarantees: independence, unity in the Catholic faith, equality between the *peninsulares* and the Creoles. It was indeed a colonist-independence movement.

On the ground its latent purpose was the containment of the Indian community's rise in power. In Mexico the application of the colonial plan of the hacienda was far from universal. This was an immense and unproductive estate belonging to big families who put to work peons weighed down by debts; it dominated the villages of the Indians who had been despoiled of their fertile lands and forced to retreat to the mountains. But there existed regions, for instance the Bishopric of Oaxaca, in the South of the country, where the majority of the Indian communities retained their integrity. The aristocracy might have lost its political power, but it managed to increase its landed properties, and the villages had been able on their own to defend their rights. In 1800 Indian property extended over two-thirds of the cultivated land in the valleys. On the other hand, Creole property was quite varied, small and dispersed, unstable (during the colonial period the 8 main haciendas changed ownership 89 times), while the clergy had the lion's share, with mainly the Dominicans controlling the mortgages and the financial life of the region. Here power belonged, not to those who own land, but to the merchants and to the political.

Here, more than elsewhere, the 1821 revolution had as its goal the restoration of the respect which the Indians had forgotten. Brian R. Hamnett convinces one that the second independence was actually a reaction.

To a certain extent, the independence of the Indian American countries opened the way to a new colonial order, which soon placed these countries under the economic influence of new mother countries: the United States and Great Britain. The indebtedness of the newly created states *foreshadows the neo-colonialism* of the twentieth century. The case of Brazil is similar, even if its independence was associated with different circumstances, but also with a failure of the monarchy (1822).

A situation similar to what obtained in Spanish America occurred in Portuguese Angola where the separatism of the white minority came to life somewhat at the time of the independence of Brazil, of which Angola was in some way a colony. In the face of the *assimilados* who posed a threat to their supremacy, the colonists – who were often individuals in exile – expressed vague intimations of republicanism by envisaging a union with Brazil. In 1910 the establishment of the Republic in Portugal did not change the situation. On the contrary, the new laws against forced labour ran counter to the interests of the colonists. Strong men arriving from Lisbon then proclaimed the installation of the *Estado Novo* in 1926. Thereupon those vague impulses for independence disappeared and the "understanding" colonists were given the assurance of rule by Lisbon and of its police, the PIDE.

Rhodesia: colonist-independence, the ultimate stage of imperialism

What strikes one as original in the situation obtaining in South Africa is that the colonists themselves initiated the resumption of imperialism during the period 1877–1901 and the international conflicts which arose from within the local antagonisms. In contrast, in other places, imperialist expansion usually had its roots in the mother country.

At first British South Africa abutted the Boer Republics – Orange and Transvaal – and African communities. That was a situation which compounded the difficulties experienced in Canada with the presence of "foreigners", the French, in New Zealand with the Maori resistance and in Ireland with the conflict between two religious faiths.

Essentially that South Africa comprised two colonies, the Cape and Natal, which did not enjoy the same degree of autonomy. The former held sway over the Sothos of Basotoland as well as over the Nguni of the Transkei. Natal did not enjoy such a semi-imperial advantage, a situation which did not prevent its colonists from being interested in the arable lands of the Zulus, the Swazis and of the Tongas.

At that time these black communities were in full possession of their freedom, even if they depended more or less formally on the British authority.

At the same time the two Boer States coexisted together. However, while Orange, since 1852, had been an independent State within British South Africa, only Transvaal had enjoyed a *de facto* independence, at least since the 1881 convention. Like the Cape it exerted control over black communities in Stellaland and among the Zulus.

In London the British presence was viewed as an unavoidable necessity, considering the importance of the route round the Cape, which remained vital despite the opening of the Suez Canal and which "must be preserved at all costs" (Charles Dilke, *Greater Britain*). These costs were the control of the hinterland, for "we could hold the Cape unless we held the rest". What was otherwise at stake was the defence of the interests of the British community. These interests suddenly multiplied with the discovery, in 1867, of diamond mines in the Transvaal, of gold in the Rand in 1881, then of copper in Rhodesia. Without doubt these riches lay in Boer territory. Nevertheless, since the Dutch of the Cape, who at that time were in a majority, had integrated themselves into the British Empire – in the same way as the French had done in Canada and rather better than had the Irish – it seemed possible, seen from London, to build a South African Union under the British flag. Besides in several conflicts between the Boers and the Zulus, the English thought that the Afrikaners were helping them to maintain law and order.

From the point of view of London, such indeed was the "line" of the imperial policy. But the Cape also had its own views on the situation: in its own fashion, "colonialism", as it was called in Cape Town, opposed itself to "imperialism", understood as the policy of the British government.

Above all the colonists wanted to settle the native issue. The wars between the Kafirs and the Zulus, the incursions of both into lands which "had been conquered by civilization", brought forth a situation which could not be tolerated, especially in the light of the certainty of a mind-boggling future emerging from the discovery of the diamond and gold mines. In fact their resistance and the insecurity that they were perpetuating had delayed the development of the country, increased the costs of its defence, and had affected the standard of living of the colonists. "Either we have to clean up the country or make ourselves respected; for, wherever we go we come into contact with barbarian tribes . . . The only solution lies in their being submitted to our control. It will be difficult, but it is inevitable. We must gain the upper hand over the tribes", wrote Governor Brownlee, when revolts broke out in Transkei in 1870.

At any rate the colonists thought that, in the face of civilization, the fate of barbarism was to surrender. The blacks must be brought along the path of progress and the first step to success would be to make them work. "It is work that civilizes", wrote Anthony Trollope. "If you came to see these men who, ten years ago, lived in a state of complete barbarism, you would learn how they work. They arrive at 6 in the morning, leave at 6 in the evening. They take their meals here, learn how to use their wages. When I see three to four thousand of them working here in the Kimberley mines, I feel that 3 or 4,000 new Christians are being born." And Trollope wished for more Kimberleys to arise all over the continent. The construction of the railways taught the Bantu how to use the pick and the spade; with the use of the railway they learnt the notion of time. "Above all, they understand that work is the first principle of civilization."

Accordingly the war against the Zulus in 1879 was viewed as a struggle for civilization, for "these people cannot be left apart, on their own".

Soon Cecil Rhodes' penetration into the Zambezi took place as a result of this colonist expansionism, rather than following an initiative taken by the mother country. Simultaneously, in the Cape as well as in Natal, the general feeling was that, among the natives in the Zulu country as well as in Transkei, indications of a sort of common will were emerging, aimed at beating back the white invaders. "We deceive the Kafirs, we want them to work and we seize their lands", Trollope observed. But the blacks were aware of it: "At the beginning the whites came and they took a part of our lands . . . then they developed and advanced further, with their cattle. Thus established, they built and have erected missions in order to subjugate us by means of magic . . . First a fortress, then the land, then again the missions, in order to push us back still further." A Xhosa chief had this comment: "The government does not speak to me as a man to a man; it does not tell me 'I am taking this and that' . . . It robs me of my rights in the darkness . . . the government is a wolf" (quoted in Schreuder, 1980).

The situation of the Boers was different. So were their relationships with the Africans. Numbering little more than 30,000 in Transvaal as well as in Orange, they had, despite their small number, strong family ties, and their training in fighting in commandos enabled them to resist infiltrations by the African tribes, with whom they actually entered into agreements of good neighbourliness. What has to be borne in mind is that, as they were exclusively cattle breeders like the Africans, they had a better understanding of the problems of coexistence. Further, marking their difference from the English of Natal or of the Cape, they knew that they were not strong enough to subjugate the main African communities. The dynamism of their expansion was linked to the development of extensive cattle breeding which required more and more land as the population and the cattle grew and increased. President M. W. Pretorius contemplated pushing the frontiers further to the west, in the Tswana territory, or to the north, in the Ndebele territory. Kruger considered Swaziland as it also provided an access to the sea. For his part Joubert supported Boer intrusions in Zululand. More than his rivals he represented this expansionist policy, in his efforts to sow division among the natives, whose territories were being little by little eroded by the Boers. But the weakness of their political organization prevented them from achieving more, at least up to the first annexation of Transvaal in 1877. The situation changed after the revenge of Majuba and the departure of the English. Then the old resentment against perfidious Albion which had recently seized Basutoland flared up. It excited the Boer nation which had not stopped asserting its identity.

By their resistance the African political communities determined the places where the colonists could establish their settlements. For an entire century the Xhosa of Transkei stood against the European encroachment. And for a long time so did the Zulus of Natal, the Sokho of the central plains, the Bapedi of Transvaal, the Ndebele of the Zambezi. But these Africans never knew how to set up a common front against the Boers or the British. The latter knew how to set one against the other and even fomented conflicts within these communities. But it was not before the 1870s that a black intelligentsia began to emerge and to formulate a global vision of the situation. The missions gave birth to this intelligentsia. The foundation in 1884 of a Thembu National Church by the Wesleyan Nehemiah Tile serves as a point of reference, preceding the pioneering activity of Tengo Jabavu, the first westernized black, who, in his own way, appealed to Great Britain to fulfil its duties with regard to the abuses committed by the colonists. Disillusionment was the lot of those who adopted this position.

As matter of fact, neither among the Africans, nor among the Boers, nor even among the British where the people of the Cape and those of Natal were frequently at odds with one another, did the least expression of unity of view or of action prevail. Moreover the different communities had not actually regrouped, except on each side of a very few segments of the frontier lines. People were scattered in isolated places, like the spots on a leopard skin.

In such a situation any kind of conflict could break out. In fact it was the pressure of the Cape colonists who, from 1877 onward, set into motion a chain of conflicts which then proceeded without interruption. It set the Xhosa against the culturally integrated blacks, the Tshembu of Transkei: this led to a chain of uprisings in which 60 white women perished, the number of black women going uncounted. This is how the King of the Swazis, Mbandzeni, justified his conciliatory attitude: "I have whites all around me. They have by force taken the lands and the territories of my neighbours. If I do not grant them rights here, they will claim them. Therefore I give them these rights when they pay for them. Why could we not eat before dying?" But others did not have a similar reaction. The contagion of war spread to Zululand where King Cetshwayo had thought he could join in the little game of alliances – with Natal against the Boers – while he was himself the victim of interfactional struggles. He became a sort of puppet king, who was welcomed in Britain with full honours. Meanwhile in the place of this small kingdom the British set up 13 smaller kingdoms, an action which accelerated the fragmentation of the ancient monarchy of Shaka.

In 1884, the intervention of Germany and her occupation of South-west Africa, in particular the threat of her settlement in the Bay of St Lucia, on the eastern coast, just north of Natal, in Zululand, did not fail to complicate matters in the game of the inter-South-African rivalries, with London feeling it had to join in. Needless to say, it was the gold and diamond revolution in the Witwatersrand, together with Kruger's resistance, which sharpened appetites and soon transformed the region into an arena of international rivalries. The production of gold went from 10,000 pounds sterling in 1884 to 8,603,821 pounds sterling in 1896. In the same year the export of diamonds rose to 4,247,000 pounds sterling, thus exceeding all other exports, with the exception of the export of gold which represented 51 percent of the totality of exports. This rush was accompanied by the arrival of thousands and thousands of immigrants. At the time the number of the young men migrating from foreign countries soon exceeded that of the local whites, that is, the Boers.

In such a context the whites more than ever wished to create a colonial order solely favourable to their own interests. This became evident when the British South Africa Co. of Cecil Rhodes occupied the region of the Zambezi despite the opposition of the government in London. "The time for a peaceful and gradual absorption of the region is gone", wrote Leander Jameson to the brother of Cecil Rhodes. Even though the government in London disapproved of the methods used to provoke conflicts in order to keep pushing forward, the progress of the B.S.A. proceeded apace. At the same time the British in London hesitated to take over from an occupation which would have brought ruin to the Treasury. Without giving his approval to this method, Lord Milner, the High Commissioner in South Africa, formulated the following analysis: Cecil Rhodes is striving to make the Company's territory into a separate colony, which will later be self-governing. He would like to unite it to the Cape and to Natal, and with these three colonies exerting a powerful pressure on the Boer Republics, the latter would be forced to join in a Federation.

Only the second part of this strategy has been remembered on account of the wars that ensued. But the first part has transcended and survived all the vicissitudes: *national-colonialism survived British imperialism*, at least in Rhodesia, if not in the whole of South Africa.

Following the 1901 Boer War the main worry of the British consisted of ensuring the loyalty of the Union of South Africa which, though a member of the Commonwealth, needed to be kept under watch. But, under the leadership of General Smuts, himself of Boer stock, the Union did not fail in 1914, as it did in 1940, to answer to the call of the King, despite the existence of strong pro-German groups among the Boers. Nevertheless South Africa did not cease to resist the orders emanating from London for the application of the stages – obtaining in other dependencies – which more or less satisfied the demands of the coloured peoples for self-government. For example, in 1951, it denounced the movement of the Gold Coast (Ghana) towards self-government. A few years later, avoiding being driven out of the Commonwealth, it thought of *leaving* it, and even of forming a government in exile.

Simultaneously, while South Africa was in the process of separation from Great Britain, another similar movement rose above the horizon. It was the separatist movement in Southern Rhodesia, the national-colonialism of which had triggered a crisis which nearly caused a break-up, if not war with the rest of the Empire.

The antecedents had come to light in Northern Rhodesia during the negotiations on the constitution of a Central African Federation which was meant to comprise, among others, Nyasaland, Northern and Southern Rhodesia. That was a manoeuvre engineered by London for the purpose of detaching Northern and Southern Rhodesia from South Africa. However, with a large number of states obtaining their independence, the 1960s were really the years of Africa. Black leaders, like Kenneth Kaunda, had decided to play the game, since some of their demands would be met; such as, for instance, that the status of the Africans in the totality of the country to be federated had to be reconsidered. *The Times* of 14 February 1961 wrote that one had to go forward, coolly and without flinching along the path of wisdom in that period of revolutionary upheavals. It under-estimated the strength of colonialism in both Rhodesias. In his weekly letter to the Queen, Harold Macmillan wrote that if he leaned more in favour of the Europeans, the confidence of the Africans in Her Majesty would be weakened. Serious disorders would break out in Northern Rhodesia and would spread into Southern Rhodesia and Nyasaland. Ministers would resign; the government and the party would be divided. That would also happen if preference were shown towards the Africans, even without giving them full satisfaction. The Europeans would no longer have any faith in Her Majesty, the Federation would declare its independence and a civil war would break out in which the officials, the troops and Africans would oppose the Europeans. The proposals put forward by the Colonial Secretary provoked riots resulting in the jailing of 2,500 blacks. Nevertheless the negotiations which followed did offer some guarantees to the Africans and, in 1964, at the cost of abandoning the scheme of Federation, Northern Rhodesia, or Zambia, became independent.

What Roy Welenski had not achieved on a large scale, that is, a Federation, was what Ian Smith dared accomplish in Southern Rhodesia. By availing himself of the armed forces of Northern Rhodesia, he unilaterally declared independence in Southern Rhodesia on 11 November 1965. This Unilateral Declaration of Independence raised a hue and cry: Ian Smith ignored it by taking a step further and proclaiming a Republic.

The British government, now led by Harold Wilson who had replaced Harold Macmillan as Prime Minister, was thus presented with a fait accompli. It toyed with the idea of appealing to the United Nations. But it was evident that metropolitan opinion was hostile to the idea of the British shooting at other British, in order to defend the rights of the blacks. That would have been another Algiers 61, with the difference that this time it would have been British and sparked off by the Labour Party. True, the British had already fired at insurgents, but in Kenya, against the Mau-Mau, or in Aden, not on white colonists. The Commonwealth Conference extracted a promise from the British government that it recognize that independence only on condition that the rights of the African majority were guaranteed. As the Bulawayo government was then supported by South Africa, Julius Nyerere, African President of Tanganyika, warned the British government that he would withdraw from the Commonwealth if South Africa remained in it as a member. Under pressure from the other states of the Empire the British government opted to stand by black Africa.

Nonetheless in South Africa national-colonialism had given birth to independence, the ultimate stage of imperialism. Many years went by before the blacks witnessed the genuine recognition of their rights and Rhodesia regained possession of the name of the ancient kingdom which had preceded the arrival of the Europeans and of Cecil Rhodes: Zimbabwe.

This independence movement which Jorge Jardim thought of emulating on behalf of the whites of Mozambique, aptly expresses the ambiguity of the feelings of fidelity towards the mother country, which was the true motherland only for as long as it allowed colonial racism to assert itself without the slightest hindrance. Thas was, *a fortiori*, true of South Africa.

Algeria in 1958: a colonist movement captured by Gaullism

There are similarities between the colonist movements in South America at the beginning of the nineteenth century and the movement of the colonists in the Maghreb, particularly in Algeria, in the middle of the twentieth century. They are essentially of a structural nature.

At the time of the conquest the colonists had stretched to the maximum their control of territorial possessions, a characteristic feature of South African colonization too. Then when the resistance of the native populations began to pose a threat, the colonists attributed it to the weakness of metropolitan officials, those *gapuchines* (metropolitans). They relied on the latter to repress – here the Indians, there the Arabs – but they demurred when the Escorial or Paris formulated a native policy of which they did not approve.

When the tension became intolerable and the mother country appeared incapable of taking any action, the colonists of South America proclaimed their independence. In the Maghreb they felt that the weakness of the Fourth Republic would allow them to impose their point of view.

Rather than one colonial party of the old type, of which there survived, after the war, about fifty publications and associations – including *La Ligue maritime et coloniale* and *Marchés tropicaux* – the colonists now possessed a sort of informal lobby. This lobby comprised members of Parliament, such as Borgeaud, the President of the Rassemblement Gauche Républicaine and one of the wealthiest landowners in Algeria, Rogier, Vice-President of the Independent Republicans, and a lawyer in Algiers, such distinguished figures as Antoine Colonna and Gabriel Puaux of Tunis and very powerful high officials like Philippe Boniface in Rabat; but the dominant figures in the group were René Mayer, deputy for Constantine, Léon Martinaud-Deplat, who served several times as a minister, and Emile Roche, Vice-President of the Economic Council of the Radical Party. During the period 1950–54 they controlled a part of the Council of the Republic and, in the Chamber of Deputies, they availed themselves of the support of the Gaullists who, without the explicit backing of General de Gaulle, believed, as Georges Pompidou said, that "if attacks by the deputies can help in bringing about the disappearance of the regime, what do their contents matter?" Lastly, the governors were sometimes "colonials", like Marshal Juin, the Resident-General who, in Morocco, intended to perpetuate the domination of France over the country.

The colonists knew, at least in Morocco and in Tunisia, that they were living in protectorates which might come to an end and also that, as a result, the authority of the Sultan and of the Bey, as recognized by the treaties, was a reality which could threaten their position in the country. Accordingly a situation had to be created so that the protectorate would last. To this end the colonists deemed it a good policy to bring the Sultan and the traditional powers into disrepute and to render themselves indispensable. The task appeared to be relatively easy to accomplish, so great was the ignorance, in the mother country, of the problems of the country and, worse still, of the nationalist movements which might be active. For example, in 1954, Pierre Mendès France knew little of the specific nature of the Algerian problem. Three years earlier, Maurice Schumann was talking, without proper judgement, of autonomy, independence, sovereignty thus causing an incident with Tunisia.

When a coalition, relative to Morocco, was formed in Paris and in Rabat, with a view to the deposition of the Sultan who was deemed to be too intractable, no one knew the rules which could be used to select a replacement for him. The colonists strongly endorsed the operation which, with the help of the *glawi* of Marrakesh, concluded with the forcible exile of

Mohammed Ben Youssef. Their rationale was quite simple: anyone who deals with the Sultan or with the Bey is a traitor and must be held up to public obloquy like, for instance, General Périllier, in Tunis. Martinaud-Deplat told him: "You are following a dangerous policy, it can only weaken France." The colonists further accused the necessarily foreign "occult powers" which supported the nationalists: Communism, as in Vietnam, and the Arab League, "the Soviet agent". These views prevailed during the period of the Cold War. On the other hand the reverse argument was strongly voiced in equal measure: the situation was getting worse because of the Americans or because of the United Nations. But because of the Cold War this argument placed the governments in an awkward position and set limits to the action of the colonists. As result both in Morocco and in Tunisia the action of the colonists served, at best, only as a goad. For the decisions came down from Paris where the power rested in good hands, even if they were weak.

Accordingly in Morocco and in Tunisia the colonists' movement acted merely as a delaying device. But in Algeria it was an all-or-nothing game – "the suitcase or the coffin" – and the softness of the Republic could be fatal. The colonists knew it; they decided to act.

As long as speaking of the nationalists was a taboo subject in Algeria, the problem was kept out of the political agenda. But, following 1952, the "retreats" or the failures of the Republic in Tunisia and in Morocco and the rise of the Algerian national movement spread anxiety among the pieds-noirs. In Paris, the deputies representing the latter, knew very well that, after Dien Bien Phu, French defeats provided an encouragement to the nationalists. Slowly the idea grew and matured that there was a need in Paris for a strong government, not a compromise government. That was the direction taken by events which, in Algiers, led to 6 February 1956, then to May 1958, when the colonists succeeded in getting the army to join them, and General de Gaulle came to power.

But the colonists made a wrong diagnosis when De Gaulle came to power. They took some time to gauge its seriousness, especially after the famous "Je vous ai compris" ("I have understood you"). Their resentment was in proportion to what they deemed to have been a hoax. They never forgave him for it.

In 1958, General Salan said: "The difference between Vietnam and Algeria is that, in Vietnam, it was the Viets who were shooting at me, while in Algeria I am being shot at by the French." This remark illustrates well the hostility which the metropolitan authority encountered – even the army – when the colonists suspected it of making a deal with the "revolt", of not being concerned to maintain order. It is true that General Salan was accused of having sent to the *Express* the generals' report which concluded, before Dien Bien Phu, that the Indo-China war could not be won. He was also criticised for having "sold it off", then accused of trying to "sell off"

Algeria at a discount. Actually he knew General Giap, he admired his talents, he understood how the timid Annamese had been transformed by nationalism and Communism. Salan understood the nature of revolutionary war and he strove to "hold" the ground, in Algeria as in Vietnam, while "waiting for the definition of a national policy, which never came". He was called the Mandarin.

But the colonists did not like this kind of language. They saw in it a sign of weakness. They felt their situation was getting worse, even if they did not surmise that it was being threatened. They persisted in thinking that if their contribution to the prosperity of the country did not earn the gratitude of the Muslims, it was because of leaders who dissuaded them from making a healthy analysis of their situation.

They could not understand the meaning of the words which Ferhat Abbas said to me: "It matters little to me that my house is supplied with electricity, if the house does not belong to me."

As a matter of fact, since the "à la Naegelen" elections, the colonists still believed they could rig the ballots. The administration still called all those who denounced such methods delinquents, who "disturb public order". Despite the awareness of the nationalist danger which had been emerging since 1952 and even more so after 1954, it was still taboo to speak in public of the future status of Algeria.

When the uprising broke out in November 1954 the Europeans of Algeria persisted in seeing it as only a series of terrorist attacks, the perpetrators of which "represented nothing". At that time, it is true, only a very small Muslim minority was ready to join the FLN or the MLTD, and to take up arms. The Muslim deputies hesitated. But the Europeans remained blind to this opportunity to negotiate a modification of the status of Algeria with genuine elected representatives. The Algerian population then consisted of 1 million Europeans and 9 million Muslims. In view of their minority status the Europeans deemed that granting a status of genuine equality to the Arabs was tantamount to surrendering the country to them. "The Arab is always at it, and the Moorish woman is a female rabbit", Ferhat Abbas added, laughing. But the Europeans were not laughing at all.

When the war spread to a part of the country, the colonists tried to ignore it while at the same time appealing to the mother country. The FLN had initiated the war because it deemed that, after Dien Bien Phu and the opening of negotiations with Tunisia, the moment was favourable and would never come again.

The Mendès France government was then preoccupied with the peace problems in Indo-China, the negotiations in Tunisia, the Moroccan question. "I have not had time to open the Algerian file, I do not know it", Mendès France confided to Ferhat Abbas who had called to inform him about it. "Algeria is not my department, see Mitterrand", he told Roger

234

Stéphane, one of his personal friends, the co-founder of *L'Observateur*. This is the confirmation: Pierre-René Wolf, director of *Paris-Normandie*, informed Marc Ferro, then a teacher at the Oran secondary school, that the Prime Minister lacked information about Algeria and asked him to send a few analyses for subsequent publication in the Normandy daily. In the archives of Mendès France, Georgette Elgey discovered the sub-file: "Pelabon Notes: Why Algeria is calm. Can it so remain?" It recalls that the Algerians are not only Muslims, but also Frenchmen, that they are not in the least colonized, "having received full French citizenship with all the prerogatives that go with it" (sic); and, in the fall of 1954, Mendès France received Ferhat Abbas, "something which none of my predecessors had done" (sic). "Contrary to what has been said, calm prevails in Algeria", said Mendès France; he did not want to seem to be selling anything off. Moreover, people said: "there are no valid representatives to negotiate with".

Thanks to Georges Dayan, François Mitterrand knew Algeria better, in particular its main European personalities. His purpose was to secure the application of the Statute of 1947, or at least a limitation of the electoral frauds which culminated in the Europeans outnumbering the near totality of the Muslim representatives. "The Algerian assembly ought to be dissolved", he was told confidentially. "Roger Stéphane is certainly an extremist", Mitterrand replied. To the metropolitan Jean Vaujour, the Director of General Security in Algeria, Henri Borgeaud stated: "Algerian political cooking is prepared in an Algerian pot, by Algerian cooks. Of course, by Algerian Europeans." "Honest elections? Lay off, there will not be a political problem, unless you create one", someone told Pierre Nicolaï, the Permanent Secretary to François Mitterrand. In the interior of the country, the administrators wanted a loyal consultation. But Paris decided to ignore them too and appointed General Catroux as the resident minister in charge of supervising the ceasefire. This provoked an outburst of anger, of rage: the man who had brought the Sultan of Morocco back from exile was now going to sell Algeria off. The mood was such in Algiers that, within a few hours, Guy Mollet cancelled the appointment: that was his first capitulation. The second capitulation occurred on 6 February when, on being welcomed by an enraged crowd, he changed his plan of negotiation – which was nevertheless proceeded with, though in secret – and appointed Robert Lacoste in place of Catroux. Very quickly Lacoste took action, set about fighting only on the terrorist front which became the war front, despite having pledged himself to Guy Mollet – who wanted to avenge himself on the colonists – to fight also against the pieds-noirs who intended to scuttle his policy, defined by the triptych: ceasefire, elections, negotiations. The colonists let him carry on for Lacoste was waging war. Further he had trapped himself within dogmatic formulas which forced him to call for more and more troops since, according to Lacoste, the "last quarter hour" had arrived.

Another policy was gradually being applied, and simultaneously those pillars of Algeria, those big feudal personalities who, with the backing of the small colonists, had laid down the law were disappearing from the scene: senator Borgeaud, the owner of the large domain of La Trappe, master of the valley of the Chelif; Schiaffino, senator and ship-owner; Blachette, former deputy and proprietor of the *Journal* of Algiers, and king of Esparto paper. Only Alain de Serigny, director of *L'Echo d'Alger* and mayor of the city, and Jacques Chevallier who had relatively progressive ideas were left to play an active political role. But Chevallier was rejected. He had said: "With or without the chechia, I shall remain in Algeria." What did those words mean?

All this began to excite those who wanted neither to see nor to listen. They still had enough common sense to understand that the "bigwigs", when the going got rough, would have their bases to go to in France, but not the small pieds-noirs, those represented in *La Famille Hernandez* – Spaniards, Jews or Frenchmen. But the Algerian notables raised a hue and cry as soon as Paris spoke of reforms. They even opposed a rise in the minimum wages and overwhelmed Paris with telegrams, with delegations to the Chamber of Commerce. "We were going to ruin the Algerian economy", they said.

Henri Borgeaud intimated to Pierre Mendès France that it would be imprudent to initiate administrative reforms at the "present" time. René Mayer, former deputy of Constantine, thought likewise and he controlled many votes in the Chamber. "From the highest to the lowest rung of the ladder, all the institutional organizations in Algeria were united against any attempt at reform initiated by Paris" (Pierre Nicolaï, Georgette Elgey, 23 February 1968). It was a correct diagnosis.

Since that time, thanks to Franz-Olivier Giesbert and Benjamin Stora, history has done justice on one point to the action of François Mitterrand who, on 5 November 1954, shortly after the insurrection,[1] told the Internal Commission of the National Assembly that "the action of the fellaghas makes it impossible to entertain, in any form whatsoever, the notion of a negotiation. It can only lead to war as its final form." That is the expression which the polemicists have enshrined in a terse formula: "the only negotiation is war". Better still, in circular No. 333, François Mitterrand clarified his instructions concerning vigilance over the militant Algerian nationalists, and indicated that those measures "must not produce the errors which, in the past, may have led people to believe that the law protects, to a lesser degree, Muslim French citizens".

History acknowledges his action. History nevertheless records that, following the attacks carried out in November 1954, the main action then taken by the Minister in charge of Algeria was to dissolve the great nationalist party, the MTLD.

Subsequently Pierre Mendès France appointed Jacques Soustelle, a close collaborator of De Gaulle, as the Governor of Algeria. It was consequently a bad omen for the colonists. A guarded welcome greeted the new governor whose mandate was nevertheless confirmed by Edgar Faure after the fall of Mendès France. Soustelle succeeded in turning the colonists' opinion around, first by vigorously condemning the attacks and the crimes committed by the FLN, and then by making them understand that to integrate Algeria with France would amount to submerging the 9 million Arabs among the 45 million Frenchmen – not the inverse process, which they feared. Thereupon the colonists assented to Soustelle's reforms, which were favourable to the Muslims and included a single Algerian electoral college. It was at the very moment when he was becoming popular that Soustelle had to leave, for new elections had brought a Guy Mollet government to power (February 1956). A hundred thousand citizens of Algiers accompany Soustelle to the harbour. Public enthusiasm is such that a tank had to be pressed into action to enable him to embark without being suffocated.

It was an apotheosis followed by a shout of anger, when the Government declared its intention to negotiate – with the FLN. The colonists had their backs to the sea, at Bab el-Oued as at Choupot or at Kebir. They resolved not to yield. In Paris, the Chamber refused Robert Lacoste his blueprint law, but in Algiers the pieds-noirs paid no heed to it. Even with the army getting more and more involved, the colonists knew that the regime could not "set fire to the kasbah" or, in Suez, beat Nasser (summer 1956). The sole success was the interception of Ben Bella's plane. But the debit side was that the suburbs would stop at nothing to ensure that the army could make use of all means necessary for the suppression of the revolt.

Robert Lacoste had already shelved the triptych of Guy Mollet, his Prime Minister: ceasefire, elections, negotiations. He replaced it with a diptych: reform and the capitulation of the FLN. But, with the failure of the Suez expedition, the pied-noir activists deemed it necessary to act again. Emboldened by their success of 6 February they reactivated plans for demonstrations and action: against the FLN and against the regime. A counter-terrorism was set up against the former. Against the latter, new organizations rose from the earth: the *Organisation de Résistance de l'Algérie Française* (the Organization of the Resistance of French Algeria), led by Dr. Kovacs, former swimming champion; the *Union Française Nord-Africaine* (French North-African Union). The president of the latter organization was Boyer-Banse, who claimed to have 15,000 adherents: he was succeeded by Robert Martel, a wine grower of Chebli who was an associate of Dr. Martin, formerly of the the secret extreme-right society, the Cagoule. But the military too – like General Faure, a follower of Poujade – were plotting and even contemplated a double coup against Algiers and against Paris. Others were informed of the move.

Accordingly the new situation that emerged was that the colonists wanted to impose their law on Paris, with the difference that it was no longer the notables who were leading the way, but the pied-noir activists, who were trying to drag the military into a conspiracy. The movement was becoming plebeianized and militarized.

There is no doubt that the army harboured a latent revolt, as the result of the concatenation of the defeats it had had to endure, from Dien Bien Phu to Rabat, from Rabat to Suez. As the Mandarin Salan was (wrongly) suspected – "that republican, freemason, seller-out" – it became a patriotic duty to get rid of him, according to Dr. Kovacs who fired a bazooka at him.

The plan was to place at the head of the army General Cogny, known to be a Gaullist, then to seize power in Paris by installing Soustelle and Debré, who never ceased to attack the government. Mitterrand saw in these activities a plot against the regime, but nothing tending towards a secession between France and Algeria! What had to be done was to gain control of the government in order to perpetuate French Algeria, to algerianize France, if needs be. One of the Parisian plotters, Biaggi, the lawyer, said: "Let's repeat Brumaire." Soustelle answered: "No, for that would lead to secession. We must bring about integration."

As the leader of the agitation against the regime in the mother country, Biaggi played the Soustelle card. Soustelle was in favour of De Gaulle, but the people of Algiers were mistrustful. In his *Révolution du 13 mai* Serigny records that both his intentions and his determination lay under a cloud of doubt and suspicion. As regards Soustelle, he repeated that while he was the idol of the pieds-noirs, he was Antichrist in the eyes of the deputies. The entire operation of the 13th of May resulted in bringing the army round – thus giving Paris a fright – to call for De Gaulle, since Parliament chose to ignore his existence. The coordinating role played by Soustelle in Algiers was played by Michel Debré in Paris where, after the fall of the Gaillard Government, René Coty had appointed Pierre Pflimlin. The activists appealed to Lacoste urging him to refuse to obey. But Lacoste shied away. Thereupon Algiers mobilized and the activists pressed the military leaders to declare their position; Massu came forward, then Salan who finally shouted: "Long live De Gaulle."

The Thirteen Plots of the 13th of May culminated in De Gaulle being recalled. With the exception of Serigny, the Algerian leaders had little to do with it. But would there have been a coup without the pieds-noirs who had mobilized?

8

LEAVEN AND LEVERS

"We had become strangers in our own country." Word for word this expression has been repeated several times in the course of history. It was first uttered by Gandhi, later by Pham Quynh, one of Bao Dai's advisers, in 1945, when the Japanese proclaimed that they had themselves replaced the French administration. In 1952 the Arabs of Algiers too used the expression. Like the Vietnamese they were denied their fundamental rights. The words found an echo among the Mexican-Americans of New Mexico and of Arizona, when they were treated like immigrant foreigners by Washington, despite the fact that they were at home on either side of the frontier fixed in 1848 when the Yankees annexed the three former Mexican provinces. The expression is heard today in Central America.

One of the more typical situations was actually that of the people of India, who were gradually dissociated from their mode of organization by the British administration.

Within the caste system where, involved in a network of relationships of variable reach, the status of individuals matters more than their functions within a defined field, the part played by kings and state hierarchies was different from that of their own counterparts in the West. There was no functional relationship between the political and the social. Consequently small territorial entities could be confined within the caste system which included the monarch as well as the village community. Jacques Pouchepadass has correctly shown how the practice of conferring on rulers the title of *zamindars*, responsible for the levying of income part of which was paid back to the colonial government, transformed them into owners in the western sense of the expression. This practice transplanted the rules of Western private law onto the customs of the Indians. Nonetheless the *zamindars* continued to levy customary dues and accordingly perpetuated the relationship of authority which existed before the arrival of the British. Nevertheless some traditional social practices did become "illegal", following the enactment of the Criminal Castes and Tribes Act, which dispossessed the individuals of their true social identity.

One encounters an equally violent dispossession in black Africa where the English and French colonizations substituted their liberal and state form of organization for systems described as "all-encompassing", in which it was not "political" power that ensured the unity of the entire society any more than it was in India.

Foreign presence was still more violently resented in the settlement colonies where the large-scale establishment of people from the mother country intensified the impression of dependence even if, within the French space, official policy claimed to stand for assimilation. Indeed, more than once, especially under the "arabophile" Emperor Napoleon III, the army and the mother country did help the natives of Algeria to defend themselves against the abuses of the colonists. The idea of an Arab kingdom included the protection of a certain number of originally Berber or Islamic institutions and customs. But the economic interests had the last word: they acted more or less with the assumption that the populations would on their own become integrated with the European civilization.

The colonized inhabitants did indeed feel themselves to be strangers in their own country but with the difference that the policies of the mother countries varied from time to time. Sometimes they exterminated the natives; or they forced them back; or destroyed their way of life and their institutions; or more or less integrated them within their space, that of the Republic in the French case. But after the lapse of a century or two, still in the case of French colonization, the dispossession was real and integration, except for a minority, was a myth.

These were intolerable situations which acted like leaven in the anti-European movements. But, other correlative facts contributed to the development of movements towards independence.

New elites and popular movements

A few general or specific features have predetermined the liberation movements and directed their action.

In the first instance, new elites emerged. Some of these belonged to the business movements and to economic activities associated with colonization. This occurred above all in India where a genuine capitalist class, arising between 1890 and 1930, succeeded in penetrating the most advanced international business environment. So did the dynasties of the Tatas or of the Birlas in Bombay. They granted subsidies to the Congress Party to promote the cause of independence. Their only fear was that an excess of disorder would have unfortunate consequences for discipline at work. Viewed in this light their nationalism was not merely a hostility against the Europeans. They did not reject the established order. For them independence was not linked to change. Such was, in Malaysia and in the Dutch East Indies, the attitude of the mercantile bourgeoisie which, prior to 1940, relied on the imperial power to protect it against Chinese competition. To a lesser degree, one finds a westernized mercantile bourgeoisie also in Ghana, and in the French possessions of Tunisia and of Indo-China.

But elsewhere, before 1914, the new elites belonged to intellectual or militant circles who had learnt their lessons in colleges and universities, or in seminaries, or even in the authorized unions and organizations. The first pro-independence leaders appeared on the scene in the Philippines, at first the Spanish Philippines and later the American, like Osmena and Quezon; in Vietnam, like Phan Boi Chau; in Burma, like U Ba Pe; in India, like Tilak and Gokhale; but also in Cairo. Subsequently their numbers increased: in India, clustering around the Congress Party of Gandhi, around the National Congress in Ceylon (Sri Lanka); around the Destour in Tunisia; later, with the formation of the Communist parties, in Indonesia from 1920 on, in China, in Vietnam, in India.

In French Africa these elites were particularly active in Senegal, where the policy of assimilation had been put into practice very early, as a large number of Africans had become French citizens from the time of the enactment of the Diagne law in 1915. The four communes of Senegal – St-Louis, Gorée, Rufisque, Dakar – became the breeding ground of the assimilated blacks of whom Lamine-Gueye is the prototype: they initiated a process which produced men like Houphouët-Boigny and Apithy. But it would be wrong to mistake the "assimilated" for the elites: the tradition of Sheikh Anto Diop and of Léopold Sédar Senghor represents a search for an African identity in association with belief in progress, especially as the latter plays a vital role in the awakening of the African political movements. Quite often the Church and community movements stimulated them, when assimilation depended on conversion.

However, in many parts of Africa, a gap grew up between these generally urban elites and the peasant masses whose revolt drew its inspiration from sources which were alive before the colonization, with which new grievances coalesced. Their rebelliousness sometimes assumed the form of a repeated insubordination like that of the Hollis in Benin.

In contrast with the colonial myth, there were countless centres of revolt in black Africa in the twentieth century. In equatorial Africa the first large-scale uprising occurred on the porterage route, between Brazzaville and the coast: it gave vent to the exasperation of the exhausted Loangos, while, on account of ill treatment, a murderous explosion gave rise to widespread guerilla activities among the Manjas, in Upper Chari. These countries were ravaged by a harsh exploitation, as described by André Gide in his *Voyage au Congo* (1925). The recruiting of soldiers during the First World War was a second cause of ill-feeling, especially in Upper Volta. It generated rebellions as much among the tribal territories as against the French. The introduction of a market economy was a third cause: the crash of 1932

241

brought in its wake the ruin of whole communities who accordingly rose in revolt, as did the peasants of Burundi in 1934.

Coming into being between 1908 and 1920 the Mau-Mau rebellion in Kenya was one of the most violent. It unleashed its fury against "black collaborators", before attacking the whites. Lastly, the largest African revolt broke out in Zaïre, *after* independence, with Patrice Lumumba asking for a "new independence" from the "corrupt regime" set up by the new administrators.

Accordingly the elites had to confront a movement rising from below. It could assume a religious dimension when its most basic aspects were to be found along the millenarist and messianic groups. These were movements which awaited a collective, imminent, total salvation expressing a radical need for social change by means of the advent of a supernatural man or power, in Nyasaland, with John Chilembwe, as well as in Belgian Congo where the syncretistic rhakist or mpadist movement appeared which set the African values against those of the Europeans: "You shall no more listen to the prayers of the white men." In Brazzaville, in 1946, lassysm appeared, a movement having its roots in the Catholic church. But the most important of the African movements was the Mau-Mau: it arose as early as 1920 in Kenya and had Jomo Kenyatta as its substitute for Christ. In the 1950s the movement became more radical as a result of the loss of lands which had been seized by the colonists.

Christianity, Buddhism, Islam

To a greater degree than others, the case of Africa raises the question of the role of the Church and of Christianity as agents and instruments of decolonization, after their having been associated with European expansion. Indeed from the time, in the fifteenth century, of Francisco de Vitoria, the great theologian of Salamanca, the Church had actually referred to the natives of America as "the legitimate owners of their land, having full freedom to refuse a religion which was being presented to them in an unacceptable manner". Likewise, in the twentieth century, the Polynesians retorted: "You came with the Bible in your hand; we had the land; today you have the land and we are left with the Bible." Linked to religion in the mind of the natives, such a dispossession plunged the missionaries into a state of utter confusion, particularly in Africa. As a matter of fact the Popes, up to the nineteenth century, had not given up their efforts to dissociate the missionary movement from colonial expansion, as had been attested by the existence of the territory of the missions in Paraguay. A similar situation obtained among the Protestant churches. But in reality, on the ground, and for the natives, the situation was different.

On many occasions the missionaries had been led to believe that a government was to come "to the help of the populations" and, by standing surety for peace, would ensure their evangelization. Such a belief was not necessarily a form of disguised nationalism. Evidence for this fact is provided by Cardinal Lavigerie, the French founder of the order of the White Fathers, who tried to get the Germans to be interested in Uganda; and by Coillard, the French Protestant missionary, who thought of serving the interests of the native population of Rhodesia by calling upon the British to ensure the maintenance of order in the country.

For decades in the nineteenth and at the beginning of the twentieth century, missionaries and colonizers remained relatively independent, even if the mother country was often led to strengthen the hold of the former or of the latter. But for the colonized populations they all constituted a single totality.

However, evangelization, especially in Africa, resulted in a certain number of individuals moving out of their group. Consequently, with its foundations shaken, traditional society became destabilized. Conversely, colonization relied on the former structures, which made it easy for the administrators to fulfil their task.

Moreover the education provided by the Christian missions in colonial territories sustained the political emancipation of adolescents, then their nationalism, with the chaplains and priests standing by the aspirations of their flocks. They still do so in Guatemala and Nicaragua.

This explains why one often finds members of the Church in the forefront of the struggle of the colonized populations.

In Algeria, even though the colonized populations had not been christianized, the lower clergy often stood by their aspirations and, in 1957, could be seen among the "carriers of suitcases". It is true, the latter could be reckoned only among the lower clergy. But the attitude of the Pope, at the other end of the hieararchy, did foster the belief in a "plot" hatched against France by the Vatican.

It is true that the Popes had warned the mostly French missionaries that they ought not to work "for their fatherland, but for *the common good*". Now was not France a secular republic, which had separated the Church from the state and not abided by that principle?

At the time of decolonization, against the background of the ambiguous attitude of the Papacy in the face of Nazism, its sympathy for Franco and for the Vichy government, its opaque silence in the presence of the tragic fate of the Jews, questions were raised about the meaning of the solidarity evinced by the Church with the fate of the colonized, even of the Muslim, populations; about the Pope's hostile attitude towards Israel, but favourable attitude to the grand Mufti. In *Le Vatican contre la France* and *Le Vatican contre la France d'outre-mer*, Edmond Paris and François Méjan provide a study of the Pope and the Catholic clergy. Actually the latter were quite critical of the former. Moreover there is no doubt that there was absolutely no collusion between the action of the "suitcase-carrying" priests and that of the Papacy.

As far as black Africa was concerned, the situation was different, for the stakes were much higher, with the black clergy playing an increasingly bigger role within the Church.

Of all the religious movements, during the period of the "second" decolonization, it was first the Buddhist renaissance which offered resistance to Europe. In Burma, where the monks educated 50 percent of the children, Buddhism had equally to combat Islam, as is evident in the double fight of U Ottama who, at the beginning of this century, visited India, met Tagore, moved to Japan and was overwhelmed by the self-assurance of the Japanese and by the glorification of their race.

Thanks to these monks, Burma was one of the best educated countries of Asia at the beginning of the twentieth century. It gave rise to powerful xenophobic associations, like the *Young Men's Buddhist Association* (1906) and soon to a number of anti-British, semi-Buddhist, semi-socialist parties, and publications like *Our Burma* which appeared in English. These movements were based among the peasant communities who often rose in rebellion before the arrival of the British. In particular, in the delta of the Irrawaddy, the revolts had the support of the budding workers' movement.

As in the Sudan and in a part of the Maghreb it was Islam which, in Indonesia, became the harbinger of the nationalist mass movements. Moreover in Indonesia Islam was anti-Chinese. Above all, by means of its network of merchants, Islam was the source of a modernity which preceded the arrival of the Westerners: the sultanates represented the equivalents of the former merchant cities of the Mediterranean (Lombard, 1990, vol. III, p. 152). At the beginning of the twentieth century the *Sarekat Islam* proclaimed the imminent coming of the Mahdi, the Islamic saviour, the "just king" for whom 2 million believers were waiting. Around 1920 Tjoroaminoto became the object of a popular cult which soon benefited his son-in-law Soekarno. He looked up to a modernist Islam, or rather to such an Islamic modernity as seemed to be arising in Cairo. One of the branches of the movement adopted the ideology of social-democracy, then established the Communist Party in 1921. It regrouped the *Abengan*, of which Islam was the principle, while the faithful followers, or the *Santri*, remained in the *Sarekat Islam*. Soekarno vacillated between these currents: "Neither a messenger of Moscow nor a caliph of Islam will bring independence."

The search for an organizational model

Nationalism arose from a crystallization of feelings provoked by a foreign presence within groups artificially organized by the occupier, as, for example, the Dutch in Indonesia, the French or the British in black Africa. On the other hand, nationalism also persisted as a matter of course in such countries as Morocco which had an ancient common existence, even if for a long time it went through recurring conflicts, between "Berbers" and "Arabs", between "Maghzen" and "Siba". The onset of genuine nationalism, or *salafism*, came from a combination of the rejection of an adjustment with the foreigner and a complete break with the past.

The example of North Africa demonstrates that sometimes it was Islam, at other times it was the feeling of belonging to the Arab world, or patriotism more closely linked to the land of one's birth, that provided the leaven for the popular uprising. Indonesia displays the same backward and forward swings: in 1926 Soekarno writes *Nationalism, Islam, Marxism*, in his effort to unite these three forces which constitute the levers of liberty. But it was Islam which acted as the forerunner of freedom.

Nationalism was also taken for granted in Vietnam, an old nation-state the identity of which had been forged in the struggle against the Chinese determination to dominate it. Nevertheless, in Vietnam, as in Korea, the national movement followed the Chinese example, borrowing its slogans from Sun Yat Sen and Chen Du Xiu.

> Be indulgent, not servile,
> Be progressive, not conservative,
> Be aggressive, do not be on the defensive,
> Be cosmopolitan, do not isolate yourselves from the world,
> Be utilitarian, do not be conformists.

These instructions, repeated by the Chinese communities, mainly of students, between the revolution of 1911 and the movement of 4 May 1919, and echoed by the Vietnamese, clearly indicate how China and its nationalism had been transplanted into the soil of Western ideas. But the nationalism of South-East Asia also borrowed its passion and its strength from Japan. For this country offered the triple example of closing its door to the world, of modernization, of the humiliation inflicted upon European imperialism. It had succeeded in putting into practice the Chinese principle: "oriental morality as the foundation, western science as the instrument". It was in China and in Japan that the nationalists of Korea, Vietnam, like Phan Boi Chau, received their training.

Accordingly, in East Asia, Chinese and Japanese nationalism nurtured and inspired anti-colonialist movements which emerged in the wake of Islam (Indonesia) and of Buddhism (Burma), while it infused, in no lesser degree, new life into the peasant and religious movements (the caodaists in Vietnam) that built on an already well tested tradition.

But these movements did not culminate in the expulsion of the foreigners, with the result that it was left to other, especially Western organizational, ideas to make possible their transformation by means of the establishment of political parties, the levers of which the *Kuo-min-tang* was the first example.

They drew their inspiration from the models which fascinated them, not so much by the contents of their programme, as by the political techniques which revealed their efficiency. Such models were provided by the English and French political parties of the end of the nineteenth century and the beginning of the twentieth century. In the Muslim world the *Young Turk* party or movement also served as a model. So did the social-democratic parties, though this did not necessarily imply an adhesion to their socialist programme. Later the Bolshevik organizational model was emulated by a whole spectrum of political parties, some of which were Communist and accordingly adhered to the Comintern, while others were not, such as the *Étoile Nord-Africaine*, of Messali Hadj.

The second variable was the freedom or the ability to organize in that fashion. But, prior to 1914, this possibility was available only in some English, French or Russian possessions – though not in all of them. A few organizations thus managed to develop.

In the British Empire it was the Congress Party, established in Bombay in 1895 by an Englishman and a Scot, which inherited from a number of Indian organizations, for the most part inspired by Hindu *and* Muslim jurists. It did not start as a religious movement and therefore did not enjoy the same popularity as did other organizations. But, thanks to its efficiency, its fame grew rapidly accompanied by an overwhelming influence. In the Empire the other example was the *Wat'ani*, the Egyptian nationalist party which gave rise later to the *Wafd* in 1918, a "delegation" of several political groups. The *Destour* in Tunisia was a spin-off from this model, due to the action of Abd el-Aziz Taalbi, a preacher at the Zitouna mosque, who called upon the elite to reject the French colonization (1908).

Again it was the political parties, especially in Russia, which impressed upon Islam its most efficient organizational form. As in Tunisia, the fascinating influence of the Turkish renaissance was the factor which triggered the formation of the first Muslim political organization, the *Al-Hidad al-Mislimim*, with its style of operation imitating that of the Russian K. D. Party (constitutional-democratic). As a movement led by reformists it was soon overtaken by the *Young Tartars* (1906) which was set up with the initiative of the *Young Turks* who combined a religious with a socialist ideology. In 1905, the Vaïssite sect of Kazan offers a striking example of a political party in which religious ideology, nationalism and socialism blend together. The Vaïssites were a dissident group of a Sufi brotherhood: they were at the same time conservative and allied to the Bolsheviks. The *Hümmet* Party, established in Baku, is more important, as it was the only organization having a national base, sponsored by the Russian Social-Democratic Party, even though the latter did not, in the name of internationalism, tolerate such groups. Actually it tolerated it, in the same way as it tolerated the existence of the Jewish *Bund*.

Henceforth Asia saw the triumph of the social-democratic model, from Japan to the Philippines, where it competed with other models. But the Russian Revolution of 1917, the Arab national movement and Pan-africanism breathed new life into these movements and imparted to them a global vision of history which they had until then been lacking. Each in its own way, they greatly contributed to the emancipation of the colonized peoples.

The Arab independence movements

One of the paradoxes within the rise of the independence movements in the Arab countries, both before and after the occupation of some of them by Europeans, was that the affirmation of their will and of their rights was accompanied by an examination of their own identity. During the Ottoman occupation the emergence of a national feeling, especially in Egypt, and later in Syria, went hand in hand with a de facto autonomism with, as its condition, the union of all against the Sultan, that is, the abrogation of all differences between Christians and Muslims. The feeling for the place of one's birth, for the fatherland (*watan*) prevailed over Islam, while the Arabic language and culture fostered an active solidarity among the diverse constituents of the same country. The reason is that, during the centuries of Ottoman rule, a sort of deconstruction had been slowly at work: it was visible in the Christian territories of the Empire, that is, in the Balkans, more than in the Muslim territories. It became a moot question whether in the nineteenth century Islam had been or would become the protector of Oriental power, of its defence against the West, and the very essence of the Arab world. But, under Ottoman rule, perhaps the teaching of the Quran had strayed from its right course. Would not a return to the origins of Islam restore to the Arabs their true freedom? Such was the alternative which rejected the nation-state as the context of a genuine renaissance.

The intrusion of the West first in Algeria (1830) and later in Egypt (1882) did not eliminate this ambiguity or this incongruity. The contradiction between these two paths was heightened by the fall of the Ottoman Empire in 1918. But the debate which was engaged during the time of Nasser, of Mossadeq, and which still rages today, had its beginnings in the nineteenth century, since its roots lay in the very history of the Ottoman Empire.

The claims of the Arabs were expressed in different ways and took different forms: in the East, where countries had passed under Ottoman rule, and in the West where the Ottoman conquest, as early as in the sixteenth century, had stopped the enterprise of European colonization as it stretched from Morocco to the Tripolitan area.

It was in 1516 that Sultan Selim I defeated the army of Al Ghuri at Mardj Dabik, near Alep. This defeat marked the beginning of the collapse of the Mameluk Empire which had dominated the Near East for the previous two hundred and fifty years. The conquest of Syria, of Palestine and of Egypt followed. Shortly after the Turkish pirate Khayr al-Din, called Barbarossa, swore allegiance to Selim and brought Algiers, Constantine and Tunis under Ottoman rule. At the two ends of the Arab world, only two countries – Yemen and Morocco – remained beyond the reach of the Sultan.

The independence of peoples under Ottoman rule

All these countries remained for nearly four centuries under Ottoman rule, with the exception of Algeria which was conquered by France as early as 1830. The administrative divisions which were then instituted have survived till today – for earlier, a Berber dynasty, the Hafsids of Tunisia, had imposed its authority on Constantine and on Tripoli. Further to the east Tlemcen preserved an independence which became a bone of contention for the Merinids of Morocco.

As early as the sixteenth century the Sultanate carried out, for fiscal purposes, a sort of inventory of property (*tahrir*): it gathered a wealth of documentation which enables one to have, as do the rules (*kanunname*), an accurate idea of the resources and of the trade of each part of the Empire. The responsibility for the administration of the Arab provinces rested, in addition to the financial services, with three main departments: the pashas or the governors, the cadis or the judges, and the janissary militia. But one can observe that the duration of the pashas' mandate diminished with time as their rotation was due to their abuses and to the conflicts generated by them. There were 110 pashas in Cairo from 1517 to 1789, 75 pashas in Damascus in the seventeenth century. The practice of rotation resulted in the strengthening of the counterweights to their authority. Consequently the military or the local forces little by little gained the ascendancy over the representatives of the central authority. This process became further entrenched as the local military institutions acquired more and more control over the janissaries. For instance, in the Tunisian army fighting against the people of Constantine in 1807, there were only 1,500 Turks among the 20,000 soldiers who took part in the battle of the Sarrat Wadi. Such a situation obtained wherever a State had been in existence before the Ottoman conquest, as in Egypt or in Tunisia. But in Algeria the recruiting of soldiers remained in Anatolian hands, for the Turkish minority was isolated and wanted to be strong enough to keep the local elements away from the instruments of power.

While there undoubtedly existed forces which contributed to the independence of certain provinces, other factors of cohesion were also active, particularly solidarity with the Empire buttressed by the help provided to the Muslims driven out of Christian Europe, especially in the sixteenth century. This cohesiveness drew its substance also from people taking pride in having a Sultan who was fighting at the same time in Vienna, in Iraq, in Crete, in the Crimea, while remaining in control of a part of the Mediterranean. In the eighteenth century the decline of the Empire affected the non-Arab regions. But the latter considered themselves to be nevertheless protected against any external danger. In 1830 the shock felt in Algiers was all the more intense. A few decades later, in Tunis, it was thought that a great Ottoman army would soon arrive to free Algeria.

However the dynamics of deconstruction in the imperial structure were stronger, in spite of Islam and the economic bonds. Besides genuine local Arab dynasties were governing Palestine in the eighteenth century and the province of Damascus at the turn of the eighteenth and nineteenth centuries. At the same time, in Iraq, the conflicts between Ottomans and Persians, which went back several centuries in time, promoted the emergence of a sort of independence, particularly in Mossul, where the dynasty of the Jalilis ruled over the region from 1726 to 1834. In this way a large number of provinces enjoyed a *de facto* independence, while acknowledging allegiance to the Empire. Such a situation culminated in many an internal armed conflict, particularly between the Dey of Algiers, Morocco, and Tunisia the Bey of which in the end supplanted the Dey.

The Ottoman Empire was a colonization without colonists, without a genuine, other than fiscal, central administration, without a turkizing policy. It was only protected by troops drawn in part from the "nations" or provinces which constituted its fabric. That being the case the Empire gradually lost its authority, except on those occasions when it displayed it by means of warnings and intimidation.

Arab identity: its contradictions

The following is the first contradiction:

On one hand the Arab peoples of the East, lying beyond the reach of the West, claimed a *de jure* independence which Egypt, more than any other Arab country, had won at the time of Mehemet Ali. But, to achieve its purpose Egypt did not hesitate to seek the help of the West. On the other hand, these Arab countries of the East rose in rebellion against the Ottoman Empire particularly because the "Sick Man" offered a weak defence against the West which was in the process of colonizing it. In this context the Arab nation took off, understanding that unity could not be realized without of necessity a de-islamization of the movement, in order to win the support of the Christians of Syria and of Lebanon, as well as of the Copts of Egypt.

The "nationalitarian" movement found itself confronting a major difficulty (see Abdel-Malek). The identification of Islam with the Arab world and of the Arab world with Islam had to be doubly consigned to oblivion for this tactical reason and because the Sultan was still the Commander of the Faithful.

As a result Arab political thought of the nineteenth and twentieth centuries was forced to face up to this contradiction: if it opted for modernity in order to be able to better resist encroachment by the Western world, thus making Arab identity depend solely on the Arabic language and attachment to the territorial fatherland, this choice would generate a backlash in the form of the revival of a fundamentalist Islam, opposed to the idea of the nation thus conceived and seeking to rediscover the sources of the true faith.

It is thus evident that the search for an identity lies at the heart of Arab aspirations as they expressed themselves in Egypt, in Syria or elsewhere. Published in Cairo in 1869, a text by Rifa'a Rafi el-Tah Tawi advocates the separation of politics from religion, the notion of work as the spring of all values, the demand for equality for all citizens whatever their religion within the confines of the fatherland. These ideas call to mind the views of Saint-Simon and the Englightenment writers. "The fatherland must be the place of our common happiness, built by liberty, thought and history." Associated with the *Young Egypt* movement, Abdallah Al-Nadim became the official spokesman of the country following the revolution of 1882: he deemed that "the union of the Muslims and the Copts has acted as the bulwark which has protected Egypt from the propaganda of the West. We must adapt ourselves to the other nations" (quoted in Abdel-Malek, 1970). After the defeat, he was arrested, but he ended up by being pardoned. London kept him under surveillance, while the Sultan wanted to neutralize him.

Watan

Taha Hussein took a step further along the road to modernity. Educated at the Al-Azhar University and the first Doctor in Literature of the Arab world, he brought in a new historical dimension to this search for identity with an examination of the true role of a Mediterranean and Oriental Egypt. It became clear to him that belonging to the East had a meaning only in the context of religious unity, or of temporary political exchanges. "However History has established that the unity of religion or of language cannot serve as a valid foundation for political unity, nor a basis for the constitution of states. For a long time already the Muslims themselves have given up the assumption of religious or linguistic unity as the foundation of the monarchy, or of the state ... From the second century of the Hegira on they have strictly based their policy only on practical advantages.

Consequently, from the ninth century of the Hegira on, the Muslim world replaced the Muslim state. Nationalities came into being, and the states began to proliferate . . . Egypt was quickest in recovering its ancient personality which it had actually never forgotten . . . We learn from history that, after the conquest, its acceptance of Arab domination was not free from resentment and from rebelliousness . . . " (quoted in Abdel-Malek, 1970). Some decades later Antoun Sa'adah made the same diagnosis and observed that at one time Syria had been the mother of nations, under the appellation of Canaanite Phoenicians.

Thus was developed the idea of fatherland, *watan*, which up till then conveyed a feeling of affection, of nostalgia, but not of loyalty, since loyalty expressed itself in relation to a dynasty or to a religion, but not to a territory. It was the Egyptian poet Rifa'a Rafi el-Tah Tawi who, in 1855, published the patriotic ode *Qasida wataniya misriyya* in Arabic and popularized the patriotic notion of *watan*. The patriotism of Sheikh Rifa'a owed no loyalty to the Ottoman Sultan, for he evinces little interest in him. It was not Islamic, for he claimed allegiance to the glory of ancient pre-Islamic pagan and Christian Egypt. His patriotism was not Arabic because the other Arab countries did not concern him. The idea of a great Arab fatherland came later (see Bernard Lewis).

While up to now the histories of Egypt had begun with the advent of Islam, Sheikh Rifa'a's ended with the Arab conquest. The novelty in this for the Muslim world, what had been hitherto unknown was the idea of a country and of its people, of their continuity, despite the changes occurring in the language, the political regime, the religion, the civilization.

A reaction set in. At the end of the nineteenth century a virulent Muslim fundamentalism arose against these "nationalist" trends. It was led by Mohammed Abdo who advocated a return to the origins of Islam in conjunction with common sense. He writes: "Only a just despot will be able to assure the renaissance of the East. Fifteen years are sufficient to enable men to nourish themselves with the fruit of freedom . . . " The enterprise was to begin with the municipal councils, followed by the higher levels of the State. But first "we shall have forced the great ones and their kin to submit . . . and all the defects of their nature shall be corrected by the most efficient methods, up to and including excision and the red hot iron, if needs be; and the souls of the small folk shall be raised in the direction of the will, and we shall act on souls as does the horticulturist when he sticks props in straight lines in order to straighten the growing plants." Later, these ideas were echoed by Hassan al-Bauna, the founder and guide of the Muslim Brotherhood (1928).

During the period of the emancipation from Ottoman rule and from the Caliphate, the legitimacy of which was contested by Ali Abd Alrazeq, Egypt had been at the forefront of the modernist movement. But, suddenly, it shifted from a nationalism established on sovereignty, on patriotism, to a nationalism which straight away took on the features of expansionism – though, it must be added, it did so only for a short period.

The Arab League

At the outbreak of the Second World War the Arabs expressed their sympathy for the Axis powers whose enemies were the same as theirs: the English, French, Jews. For a while the British managed to forestall an Arab uprising by stopping Jewish immigration to Palestine, by supporting the independence movements in Lebanon and in Syria against France, by stating their approval of Arab unity, and even by promoting the formation of the Arab League, consequent upon the fear of Rashid Ali's uprising in 1941. The scheme was developed by Noury Said, the Prime Minister of Iraq and made public in 1942. He envisaged the formation of a Greater Syria comprising of a federation of Syria, Lebanon, Transjordan and Palestine. In that plan the Jews of Palestine would have their autonomy, as would the Maronites in Lebanon. In fine, an Arab League would unite the federation with Iraq. Greater Syria would be placed under the aegis of King Abdallah, Iraq would head the League and the whole federation would be placed under Hashemite rule. Thus would be reconstituted, apart from the Hejaz, the great kingdom dreamt of by Colonel Lawrence and King Hussein in 1916.

Early in 1943 Anthony Eden approved of the project. But he came up against the reservations of Saudi Arabia, of a fraction of the Lebanese, of Egypt in particular. But Nahas Pasha stole a march on Noury Said and, at the Alexandria conference, proclaimed the creation of an Arab League which Iraq and Transjordan had to accept. In fact, the purpose of the pact, signed on 25 May 1945, was to protect the independence of the extant Arab States. It ran counter to the project of an Arab unity based on the Fertile Crescent.

This victory of Egypt over Iraq, together with the 6 member states, also implied the exclusion of Iran which, though actually Muslim, but was not an Arab country. Further it implied the promise of help available to any Arab national movement, from one end to the other of the Arab world. Such help soon extended to North Africa and to war against Israel. But the League could not function smoothly on account of the large number of political entities which constituted it, especially as it had to cope with limited means. It tried to give itself a new lease of life by means of more revolutionary organizations, such as the Syrian Ba'th Party, but it was events in Egypt and the coup staged by Neguib and Nasser in 1952 that transformed the League into a new instrument, leaven and lever of the uprising of the colonized peoples. Moreover they disposed of the powerful transmitter, *The Voice of the Arabs* which, broadcasting from Cairo extended over North Africa.

In the East the International had been another such instrument. It came into being in 1919 and exerted a greater influence in the East, among the Turks, the Persians, the Indians.

The Communist International and the colonial peoples

The Second International had indeed denounced colonialism, but only to replace it by a socialist policy. In a 1914 booklet, *Of the Right of Nations to Self-determination*, Lenin was one of the earliest theoreticians who emphasized the "progressive" role of national demands, considering that colonial policy made it possible to improve the condition of the European workers and accordingly to delay the social revolution in Europe. The national struggle against imperialism thus became an essential element in the struggle of the proletariat. It was a more radical action than those advocated by the other leaders of the International, *but* it persisted in not taking the national demands of the colonized peoples as a goal to be attained on its own merit.

One can judge to what extent the outlook of the colonized peoples and that of the revolutionaries could be foreign to one another by an examination of the composition of the delegates at the Lausanne Conference which met in 1916 while the war was still on. Attending the conference were sympathisers of the oppressed minorities of Austro-Hungary, particularly the Swiss Eugène Privat who had organized it, representatives of these minorities from Russia, Egyptians, Armenians and Tunisians. But, with the exception of the Finn Kuusinen, not a single socialist attended the conference. Most of the Russian exiles – Bolsheviks, Mensheviks, or revolutionary socialists – were then in Switzerland. But neither Lenin, nor Martov, nor anyone else showed the slightest interest in that conference of nationalities. On the other hand, in France, Jacques Banville, then a journalist, and a future nationalist historian, observed that the national problem and the colonial problem were only two variables of comparable situations: he urged the Ribot government not to raise the issue of the national problem in Austro-Hungary, if they wanted to keep it from having an effect on the future of the French colonies.

During the 1917 Revolution, most of the Russian nationalities viewed the fall of the Tsarist regime and then of the provisional government as an opportunity to regain their freedom. They could observe that the right to self-determination, as proclaimed by Lenin, had only been an instrument meant to hasten the collapse of the former regime. But, for the sake of revolutionary solidarity Moscow deemed that to put it immediately into application would imply a weakening of the camp of world revolution. Its future was broached at the Second Comintern in 1920 where, in spite of the victories of the Russian army in Poland, it appeared that world revolution would not become a reality, at least in the immediate future.

Under such circumstances the Indian M. N. Roy argued that the outcome of this European revolution depended entirely on the revolution in the East. But he also opined that this movement "had nothing in common with the movement of national liberation", promoted by the bourgeoisie and which, especially in India, would be counter-revolutionary. Lenin opposed these theses, for his main concern, as head of the Soviet government, was to seek out allies capable of undermining the rearguard of the powers which were fighting him: he therefore opted for the powerful and sophisticated Congress Party in lieu of the Indian Communist Party which was still in its infancy.

The interest generated by this debate lies in its having foretold the conflict between the interests specific to the USSR and the ambitions of the revolutionaries of the colonial or semi-colonial countries like India, Turkey, Egypt. It became more intense at the Baku conference where the colonial problem was placed at the centre of the agenda: its vehemence, to a large extent, especially as regards the Asian countries, went far beyond what was heard at the Comintern conference. The representatives of the East were mainly Muslims of Central Asia for, out of 1,891 delegates, there were 235 Turks, 192 Persians, 8 Chinese, 8 Kurds, 3 Arabs, the others hailing from the non-Russian parts of the USSR. They had responded to this call sent out by Karl Radek and Grigori Zinoviev:

> There was a time when you used to cross the desert to reach the Holy Places. Now you cross the deserts and the mountains and the rivers in order to come together to discuss the ways of freeing yourselves from your chains and to unite yourselves in a brotherly union for the purpose of living a life of equality, liberty and fraternity.
>
> (July 1920)

Zinoviev's declarations were greeted by the raising of swords and revolvers and with cries of "Jihad", "Long live the resurrection of the East". Extant photographs still testify to the reality of these gestures. But once the enthusiasm produced by Zinoviev's words had died down, the Muslims expressed their reservations about the way they had been treated by Moscow. "We had to bear the scorn shown by the former leading classes towards the indigenous masses. Such is the attitude of the Communists, who still retain the mentality of the rulers and look down on the Muslims as their subjects." The delegate of Vladimir Lenin, Georgi Safarov, confirmed the harmfulness of that attitude: "In Turkestan the proletarian dictatorship takes a characteristically colonialist turn." Accordingly one finds, among the Communists, the behaviour of the Mensheviks and of the SR who had cried: "Reaction!" when the non-Russians of the Caucasus had claimed their right to exist outside the pale of the socialist parties. Consequently, at Turkestan, the Third Conference of the Muslim Communist organizations demanded the Turkestani organization of the Russian Communist

Party be transformed into a Turkish Communist Party. In Baku the argument had been put forth that the concept of class solidarity had no meaning in a colonial environment. The Muslims insisted on the necessity of national revolutions, which alone could assure the emancipation of the East. It was actually the only means of recovering their identity: the question of the leadership of the movement – entrusted to the bourgeoisie or to the national Communist Party, as raised by Mananbendra N. Roy – seemed of secondary importance to them.

This conflict lasted till 1923 when "national deviations" were condemned by the Soviet leaders: Lenin, Stalin and Zinoviev. This led to the split with Sultan Galiev, the most prominent of the Tartar communists, and former assistant of Stalin at the Commission of Nationalities. He declared that the proletariat of the West and of the East were fundamentally different and actually "irreconcilable". He added: "The Muslim nations are proletarian nations . . . their national movement has the characteristic of a socialist revolution." That was a sacrilegious statement. By inventing this concept of "proletarian nation" Sultan Galiev was distinguishing between the West, where the proletariat was a social class, and the East where there were entirely proletarian nations. He added that, in the West, the substitution of the proletariat for the bourgeoisie did not, or would not, bring any change in the relationships between the Western proletariat and the oppressed nations of the East, for that class had inherited the national attitude of the class which it had replaced.

It was then imperative *to replace the dictatorship of the Western mother countries by that of the proletarian nations over the mother countries of the West* . . . To that end, Sultan Galiev proposed the constitution of a Communist Colonial International, but independent of the Comintern. The first stage would consist of the establishment of a great Turkish national State, the Turan. With the help of Hanafi Muzzafar, Sultan Galiev next tried to construct a theoretical fusion of Communism with Islam by introducing into it cultural features specific to the peoples of the East, while, on the other hand, at the fourth Conference of the Communist Party in 1923, Kalinin argued that "the policy of the Soviets ought to have as its goal the teaching of the Leningrad worker's ideals to the peoples of the Kirghiz steppe, to the Uzbeks and to the Turkmens".

Sultan Galiev was violently liquidated. Following the "normalization" of the situation in Turkestan, the Comintern resumed its policy of using national movements as instruments. As an illustration of this policy the commercial treaty signed between London and Moscow in 1921 stipulated that Moscow would desist from carrying out any propaganda that could incite the Asian peoples to act against England. The Eurocentrism of the Soviets asserted itself with increasing arrogance, with the Russian communists henceforth resolved to determine the nature of the national movements, or to select those that had to be supported, and not others.

Such an attitude provoked the ire of the delegates at the third and fourth Conferences, especially the Malay Tan Malaka, the Vietnamese Ho Chi Minh and the Indian M. N. Roy.

By refusing to see in the Oriental revolution a possibility other than that of a national revolution – because for these leaders it was only a phase – the Comintern was saying, without clearly enunciating it, that only the West could carry out a social revolution. That clearly meant that only the USSR could be in a position to determine which nation was able, and therefore had the right, to carry out a revolution.

This policy was vindicated by the Chinese example in 1927. The failure of the Chinese Communists in 1928 and the part played in it by the policy of the Comintern in its preferential relationship with Chiang Kai-shek are factors which – following Stalin's action with regard to the Muslim Communists – could lead to a very negative understanding of the role played by the USSR and the Comintern in the struggle of the colonized peoples. Such a diagnosis would be partly wrong for this evaluation would not take into account the fact that the beginnings of the Comintern may have played the role of "inflammable materials" which lit the fire of revolt among colonial nationalists. If it is true that M. N. Roy or Tan Malaka – after Sultan Galiev – despaired of the actions of the USSR, Ho Chi Minh remained faithful to it. In 1935 when, for the slogan "class against class", the Comintern substituted the struggle of "nation against nation" he rejoined it and like the Filipino Communists, he led the struggle, by the side of the democracies, against Japanese fascism and its allies.[1]

Further the theses of those who opposed the leadership of the Comintern, the debates that they provoked, did not wither away by being condemned by Moscow. Their subterranean survival brought them to the knowledge of the Malays, the Indians, and of Mao Tse Tung. Soon after, in the 1960s, Boumedienne and Gadaffi adopted the views of Sultan Galiev on the "proletarian nations". At the outset these views were held by Tartars or Turks. Now they are held by the Arabs.

In fact it is the theory of Galiev which has historically been effective. Once they acceded to independence Libya, Algeria and later Iran adopted the idea of substituting the dictatorship of the Western nations with that of Third World nations.

Whether direct or indirect, the action of the Comintern had especially affected, in the East, the peoples of Turkish or Muslim origin, as well as the Persians, Indians, Vietnamese, Malays, Indonesians and, of course, the Chinese. It had little effect on the Arabs before the Second World War, the only organized Communist parties which had some following in those countries were those of Syria and of Lebanon.

Comintern action had little effect on black Africa either, with the exception of South Africa which had its Communist Party, with the contacts with Moscow being limited to sending a few Africans to the University of the Workers of the East and to take part in the Brussels conference against imperialism (1927), organized by Willy Münzenberg. But the "negro question" was scarcely granted more importance than the colonial problem at the first Comintern conferences, despite the presence of Senghor and of two South African representatives and many black Africans. In the spotlight were Jawarharlal Nehru, Mohammed Hatta (Indonesia), Sun Yat Sen, Albert Einstein, Victor Haya della Torro (Peru) and Messali Hadj (Algeria).

The earlier progress of Panafricanism

Panafricanism, or the Panafrican movement, has played a dynamic role in the freedom of the populations of the dark continent. It provided the substance to the ideology of decolonization in black, especially British, Africa. In its larger context – African unity – it owed its beginning to the Accra conference in 1958. But, in a more profound sense, it goes back to the very beginning of the twentieth century, to the London conference of 1900. Indeed this conference was also a culmination of the black liberation movement, the prehistory of which dated from the eighteenth century.

It was a boomerang effect of the slave trade and of slavery. The movement had its roots in the three corners of the triangular trade: first, West Africa, more specifically the Gold Coast (Ghana) which was one of the most active suppliers of slaves. The first African who denounced the slave trade was Ottobah Cugoano, a Fanti of Ghana, who has left us with: *Thoughts and Sentiments on the Evil and Wicked Traffic of Slavery and Commerce of the Human Species, Humbly Submitted to the Inhabitants of Great Britain*, (1787). Subsequently, together with Ghana, Sierra Leone and Nigeria became the breeding ground of the black nationalist movements.

The second side of the triangle was located in Britain, where the Methodist movement inspired the struggle against the slave trade and brought about the abolition of slavery at the time of Wilberforce.

The third side of the triangle ran between the Caribbean Islands and the English colonies of North America, the future United States. As early as the sixteenth century blacks had revolted, from Guyana to the Caribbean, and in 1688, in Barbados, the institution of the first Black Code came into being. Again the West Indies were in the frontline of the fight for the liberty of the blacks at the time of the French Revolution and of the Empire. Led by Toussaint Louverture Haiti became effectively independent in 1804. Since then the Afro-Americans of the Caribbean Islands supplied the main leaders of the Panafrican movement, such as Marcus Garvey, George Padmore, Father Dubois; and on the French side, Aimé Césaire, Frantz Fanon, and then again other eulogists of negritude. Moreover on the British side the first movements benefited, at least in

257

London, from freedom of expression, as well as from the rudiments of partial representation.

However, in Britain, the creation of the Sierro Leone Company was a signal failure. Yet this colony was destined to become a sort of laboratory for the modernizing process in West Africa, with its college at Fourah Bay in Freetown and its first missionary cadres. The latter proliferated in Nigeria and in Gold Coast where appeared the first Christian king, Joseph Aggrey, who did not fail to demand independence for his country. For this he was temporarily deported to Sierra Leone, but the progress of the notion of self-government had already become a reality (1865).

By declaring themselves independent in the name of liberty, in 1783, the Americans did not expect to be burdened with the claims of the blacks who had fought by their side. This explains why a large number of blacks did, out of disappointment, support the British. In *Notes on the State of Virginia* (1787) Thomas Jefferson, himself a slave owner, examined the question of the condition of the blacks. He summed up his statements with this formula: "What further is to be done with them?" The idea of sending a large number of them back to Africa was considered and, in 1816, the American Colonization Society managed, in a few years, either by persuasion or by threat, to reembark from 12,000 to 20,000 who founded Liberia in Africa. Naturally this action provoked the indignation of American blacks who intended to take their return to Africa into their own hands. This led, a few decades later, to the formation of the Back to Africa Movement, led by Marcus Garvey.

When the Panafrican conference opened in London in 1900, the general condition of the blacks had, over the span of a century, deteriorated, as much in the United States, despite the War of Secession, as in South Africa and in the rest of the continent. While there was no let up in the domination by the white man the slogan "Africa for the Africans" was vindicated by only one single "historical" confirmation: the victory of the Abyssinians over Italian troops at Adoua in 1896. It infused hope and vigour into the Panafrican myth which had designated Ethiopia as the original site of the African civilization. As a matter of fact, the defeat of the Russians in 1905 revived the coloured peoples' hopes for freedom. In Madagascar, in 1913, the pastor Ravelojaona published *Le Japon et les Japonais* ("Japan and the Japanese"). He had established the Vy Voto Sakelika, or VVS, Iron-Stone-Network, under an anti-colonialist impulse. However, within the French colonies, the attractiveness of assimilation continued to hold sway: this explains why the Panafrican movement remained confined to the anglophone colonies.

The second feature of the Panafrican movement is its relationship with the churches, especially Methodist, which, first in the Gold Coast, and elsewhere in West Africa, contributed to the emergence of a mulatto or black europeanized elite, described by the British as "educated natives".

258

Little by little members of this elite took over the positions of the traditional leaders, for instance when the Fantis elected J. R. Ghartney, a trader
in Anomabu, King of Winneba, under the name of J. R. Ghartney IV. The
Methodists could not play the same role in the Caribbean Islands or in the
English American colonies because there they encountered the hostility
of the colonists.

As a reaction the movement had its most vigorous development in the
Americas. Led by W. E. B. Du Bois it demanded the return of the blacks
to Africa and the independence of their country of origin.

It is a paradox that in the American exile, the blacks of diverse ethnic
groups joined together to elaborate a very active, though undoubtedly
fictitious, image of Africa. On the other hand, in Africa itself, the old
divisions of the kingdoms, the fragmentation of the territories, followed by
the colonial divisions, had never fostered an African consciousness. Again
one observes that in the Caribbean Islands as in America the mulattos were
less inclined to sing the praise of African negritude than were the pure
blacks, men like Martin R. Delany and Garvey, who also advocated the
return to Africa.

Just like the abolitionist project, of which the Quakers were the proponents in Massachusetts, the action of the Afro-Americans, in the United
States, became evident in 1787. There came into being, particularly in
Philadelphia, societies and schools for blacks, led by the Huguenot
Anthony Benezet of Saint Quentin, whose family had been driven out by
the Edict of Nantes. In these schools the Constitution of the United States
was the subject of discussions which terminated with the rejection of slavery
in the states which were then in the process of being formed: those of the
mid-west. In the same year the blacks established the Free African Society in
a Methodist church. Others set up the first Masonic lodge in the United
States, the Free African Lodge, independent of the African Lodge of
London. Also in that year the demand for equal opportunities in education
was formulated by Prince Hall, a Barbados mulatto who sent a petition to
that effect to the Parliament of Massachusetts (1787).

Less than a century later, at the opening of the first Panafrican conference,
its 30 participants in the London conference came mainly from the
Caribbean Islands (10) and from North America (11), 4 from Africa and
5 from Great Britain. But, at the preliminary conference, the number of the
Africans was larger. The Reverend Bishop Alexander Walters presided and
opened the conference with these words: "For the first time in the history
of humanity, the blacks of the whole world have met to improve the fate
of their race." The orators denounced the policy of the British in
their Empire, especially in South Africa, the policy of segregation which
prevailed in the United States; they hailed the great ancestors, above all
Wilberforce. They also thanked the Quakers for their struggle against

slavery, still practised in Zanzibar and in East Africa. In an appeal to "the nations of the world", W. E. B. Du Bois (1868–1963) announced that "racism will be the number one problem of the dawning twentieth century, and the colour of the skin or the texture of the hair are in the process of becoming the criteria of inequalities, of the right to privileges". A Panafrican Association was set up to defend the rights of the blacks. The countries that were represented in it were the United States (W. E. B. Du Bois), Haiti, Abyssinia, Liberia, Natal, Sierra Leone, Lagos and Jamaica.

But Du Bois was soon overtaken by Marcus A. Garvey, a Jamaican living in the United States, who broke away from the demanding attitude of the Panafrican Association. Turning the situation upside down, he valorized the black race and proclaimed the idea of the reconstruction of a Panafrican Empire, as the heritage of the great kingdoms of pre-colonization times. He stood for the birth of a black racism, described by Léopold S. Senghor as the anti-racism of negritude. More than Du Bois he stirred Africa and better than the latter he appreciated that neither Europe nor the whites would ever in fact come to the help of the blacks. He saw clearly that without violence Africa would come to nothing.

Du Bois remained within a humanist framework: he admired France for decorating the black deputy Blaise Diagne with the Legion of Honour. He dreamt of a collaboration among the races, which would be realized by means of radical demands and not by following the path of a soft adaptation as advocated in the United States by B. T. Washington, a slave who, by dint of perseverence, became the director of an institute. At the other extremity, Garvey conceived of an African renaissance based on knowledge and strength, of which Japan provided the example. But, at the Fifth Panafrican Conference held in Manchester, shortly after the end of the Second World War, the arguments of George Padmore prevailed. They were deemed to be more realistic and at the same time demonstrated that the different opposing visions did at least all converge to claim first in favour of the blacks their independence in the country where they were living: "All those whom we call Communists are nationalists . . . They must first be free before we define the political system of their choice." He violently denounced those who looked kindly on French colonial rule, by arguing that assimilation and integration were only myths. For proof of his thesis, he referred to the freedom experienced by the Africans under British rule, their participation in the government, compared to the repression which was common in the French Empire. On this point, Padmore was supported by the blacks of the West Indies, in particular, by Frantz Fanon.

Accordingly the Panafricanism which preceded independences played the same role as the Comintern in the East: Sultan Galiev and Marcus Garvey walked along the same path from Communism to the nation, while awaiting the revolution. However, Panafricanism was different from the Comintern in one aspect: it had no centre and was indeed quite modest in its activities since no state endorsed it. But with its disorganized activity and its minority status, it too scattered "inflammable materials". These gave a direction to the African nationalists, like Nkrumah, who attended those debates. They hastened the access to self-government, then to independence of a large number of West African and of the Caribbean countries.[2]

It has been said that Panafricanism was mainly an anglophone movement. However, in its final phase, a fair number of francophones took part in it. Iba der Thiam observes that in West Africa, particularly in Senegal, the history of the demand for independence went through several phases: the demand for equality before 1914, the rebellious protest shortly after the end of the First World War, then passionate and violent recriminations. Represented by Garvey, the junction of the International and Panafricanism occurred during the 1920s. The future flag of the African nation would be "red like the blood spilled throughout the course of history; black like the colour of the skin, as a source of pride, not of shame; green, like hope".

To this concept has been often added "a need for independence" which has been in existence since very early, and even from the time of the conquest, in the West as well as in Kenya or in Madagascar.

In Madagascar, in 1947, as in Sétif in 1945, or in Haiphong in 1946, the administration or the army responded by a massacre.

9

INDEPENDENCE OR
REVOLUTION

Was the end of colonization brought about solely by the struggle for the liberation of the subject and vanquished populations? Or was it the result of the decline of the mother countries rendered incapable of managing the huge capital which they had accumulated? Or was it caused by the external pressures of the world, in conjunction with the other factors?

At any rate each independence did not draw all its strength solely from within its specific territory, whatever might have been the reaction and the vision of the vanquished. The example of the North African countries testifies that it was, at one time, Islam, at another time, the feeling of belonging to the Arab world, and at other times still, a patriotism more directly linked to the motherland, which served as the leaven, or even as the lever of the popular uprising. If the national sentiment in Vietnam and in Indonesia provoked the reaction of the populations in their opposition to the French and the Dutch, it is equally true that proletarian internalism also exerted its influence, in the same manner as did Panafricanism, especially in anglophone Africa.

With their affirmation of ideologies of liberty or of revolution these movements may have emerged and developed in harmony with others or not, or even in anticipation of them.

Which goals?

The liberation movements benefited from the support of Churches, or of parties which sometimes rivalled one another, with one common objective: independence. They were distinguished by the variables in the tactics used, by the variations in the contents of this independence.

Some claimed to be more revolutionary than nationalistic. Such was the case of the Vietminh which triumphed all the more as no religious power – neither the Caodaists, nor the Christians – could compete against it. Moreover, after 1949, it was backed by Communist China.

On the other hand, when religion played a dominant role, as in India or in Burma, or even in the Philippines and in the Maghreb, the revolutionaries found themselves with little or no hope of succeeding. This was so especially where Hinduism prevailed, as it hid its colours behind the mask of patriotism and democracy.

Between these two extremes one finds those countries, like Indonesia, where Communism and Islam were powerful and in conflict one with the other. Conversely, in Angola, it was the political parties, including the Communist Party, which were the 'instruments' serving the good of the nation, that is, creating one (Cahen, 1989).

Lastly, certain movements have till today failed in carrying out their purpose. Such is the case of the *Sendero luminoso* (Shining Path) of Peru. They need to be studied, for history is also the analysis of what has failed to attain its end.

Indeed though the liberation movements may have been borne and sustained over a long period in history, in the Arab as well as in the black or Afro-American world, it is nonetheless true that they have been co-ordinated and stimulated by other forces, which they were able to join, such as the Comintern and the Tricontinental. They also benefited from some actions which did not have their freedom as their end. The Japanese victory over the Russians in 1905 had psychological and political effects on all the coloured peoples, even in such faraway places as Madagascar.

The decisive consequences of the Japanese expansion during the Second World War are unparalleled. There can be no doubt that it dealt a death blow to European dreams in South-East Asia, even if the cause and effect relationship did not appear to be that simple. For instance, one could plainly see that during those years the colonists in French Indo-China did not entertain many illusions about their future. At the same time other colonists, for example in Algeria, still believed, in 1945–50, they were living a hundred light years away from what was happening in South-East Asia. This applies equally to the English or Dutch colonists in South Africa.

A second effect of the Japanese occupation may be noted. Before 1941 British domination was the only one to experience difficulties, for instance in Egypt, and particularly in India since 1919. But at the end of the war the Dutch and the French were the ones confronting the most violent ordeals in Asia. On the other hand the British had already prepared the ground for their withdrawal. Nevertheless they all lost part of the control they had exercised over the rubber and oil markets.

The shock of the Japanese victories

The humiliation inflicted upon the West by the Japanese victories exerted a strong influence on the colonial populations and emboldened them in subsequently undertaking their struggles. In the Philippines they witnessed the horrible Death March (1941) which the Japanese military imposed on the American prisoners. The latter perished of exhaustion in the presence of spectators moved by pity for them. In the end that incident proved to be counter-productive against the Japanese army of occupation. In Indo-China Frenchmen were imprisoned by the Japanese police, the Kempetai, in cages smaller than a cubic metre: the worst torture inflicted in the presence of powerless witnesses. In this case too compassion overcame the feelings of the Vietnamese, in spite of their resentment against the French. Nevertheless, in the Philippines as well as in Indo-China and in Indonesia, the colonial power lost for ever all its authority and prestige.

In principle, on account of the policy of collaboration adopted by the Vichy Government, the French administration continued to be in operation, at least up to 9 March 1945, when the Japanese authorities brought this fiction to an end and seized all French assets. Already occupied at least partially by the military, Indo-China henceforth experienced the common fate of the other European possessions in East Asia.

At that time two features characterized the Japanese colonial policy which claimed to act in the name of "this sacred mission", the sphere of "co-prosperity" and of the liberation of the peoples subjugated by the West. First, it brought these populations within such a system as to serve the purposes of the war, that is, the exclusive interests of the Japanese economy. Secondly, it promoted the politics of military and economic integration which ran counter to the hope for independence which the colonized peoples might have entertained, especially those Indonesians who had welcomed the Japanese as liberators. Unlike the Westerners the Japanese were very meticulous in the administration of all the possessions they had occupied. It is possible that this was so because their occupation was more military than civilian. They did not abandon to their fate those regions which did not bring them any profit. As a result of this attentiveness the people warmed to them, especially in Indonesia, at least in 1942, and sometimes in Indo-China too.

When the Japanese had intimations of their impending defeat, they proclaimed the independence of the former European possessions, but neither that of Taiwan nor that of Korea. They even got together the representatives of all the "liberated" nations in a big conference held in Tokyo at the end of 1943.

That was indeed a time bomb which exploded a few years later. Actually when the English landed in Java and in Sumatra, before the Dutch did in 1945, the Indonesians resented this return as a new occupation. On the other hand, the Filipinos had become very hostile to the Japanese and the puppet governments they had installed: they welcomed the Americans as liberators.

The situation was much more complex in Indo-China.

Vietnam: independence and revolution

In Vietnam the Japanese victories had infused a new spirit into the independence movements which, in view of the repression which had marked the 1930s, were inspired most often by sources located in places outside the country. The *Vietnam Quoc Dan Nang*, or National Vietnamese Party, emulated the Kuo min tang and endorsed the slogans of Sun Yat-sen: nationalism, democracy, socialism. It had great success in Tonkin. Another group had been formed in Kwantung, under the leadership of Ho Chi Minh who was a member of the Krestintern, a peasant International linked to the Comintern. After it had been active in France and taken part in the Tours Conference, this party set up the first Vietnamese group at the Communist University of the Workers of the East. The organization which it had established included the patriots who had been disappointed by the strictly moral action of Phan Boi Chau. Gravitating around Bao Dai – heir to the throne, whom the French administration had recalled to Hué following the incidents of 1930–31 – were reformers, for instance the Catholic Ngo Dinh Diem, who clashed with the uncompromising colonial authority. Bao Dai used to say: "My only power consisted in granting certificates to the villages."

Another political movement arose in Cochin-China: the Cao Dai. It was a Buddhist, religious movement which drew, like others, its inspiration from Japan, beginning with the Meiji restoration up to the 1905. It functioned in association with anti-French sects, like the Hoa Hoa. Lastly an Indochinese Democratic Front led by Pham Van Dong and Vo Nguyen Giap constituted the legal façade of a prohibited Communist Party. Soon Ho Chi Minh was to join it. By the 1930s Trotskyist groups were equally active.

Decoux's administration strove to delay the rise of the nationalist or revolutionary upsurge by a display of good management. It was none the less repressive in regard to these movements and still more so in regard to the Gaullists who after all were few in number. For the latter had declared war against Japan. For its part Japan encouraged these independence movements, in particular the Caodaists. But the entry of the USSR into the war caused a split between the organizations which were waiting for liberation by Tokyo and those who were betting on Chiang Kai-shek or the Allies. Under the leadership of Ho Chi Minh, the Vietminh was committed to fight "the Fascism of the French and of the Japanese", and thus went against the main trend of the balance of forces obtaining in 1942. Accordingly, on one side, was the Vietminh–United States–China front which, with the collaboration of the Free French Forces opposed, on the other side, the Caodaist allies of Japan, supported by Bao Dai. They all fought among themselves and for independence.

In such an environment the French presence was not destined to be swept aside by an outbreak of hatred, but it was to be "blasted away by history" (Mus, 1952). After all that was what F. D. Roosevelt too thought when he rallied to Stalin's view on France relinquishing Indo-China, while Churchill wanted the British and the French empires to survive. "Come on, Winston, you are beaten by 2 to 1", Roosevelt told Churchill.

Ho Chi Minh's tactic corresponded with the instructions given by the Comintern. The Front which had been constituted tended towards the union of all the social strata and hid its revolutionary colours. The goal of the Vietminh's programme actually was to drive out the French Fascists (Vichy, then Admiral Decoux) and the Japanese, to return Vietnam to independence, to enter into an alliance with the democracies which were struggling against the fascist and the Japanese aggressions, to build a democratic Republic.

In fact Bourguiba in Tunisia, Gandhi in India, had made the same tactical choice, respectively against Salah Ben Youssef and Subhas Chandra Bose. But, in Vietnam, the Japanese were actually on the soil, with their promise of independence to Burma, as they have already acknowledged it for the Philippines. Consequently the Vietminh ran a greater risk, and the stakes of a republican government were still higher. The alliance with the Gaullists could equally be illusory, the more so as Ho Chi Minh had denounced De Gaulle's attitude in Brazzaville, in such terms as had also been used against him in Syria and in Lebanon.

9 March 1945: the Japanese ultimatum, an unexpected bombshell, even though, following the fall of the Vichy government, in August 1944, France, not merely Free France, was officially at war with Japan. From the time of the difficult battle of the Philippines, Tokyo had demanded from Admiral Decoux, who was still in office, that the French Forces be placed under a joint command. Faced with his refusal the Japanese seized all the garrisons, interned the French, and, on 11 March 1945, on the initiative of the Japanese occupiers, Bao Dai, Emperor of Annam, proclaimed the end of the French protectorate and the independence. From his hiding place in the mountains, Ho Chi Minh established contact with the small number of De Gaulle's men, represented by Sainteny. Hardly had the atom bomb fallen on Hiroshima that Ho Chi Minh gave the signal for a general uprising. With the capitulation of Japan, Bao Dai abdicated his throne "asking France to recognize the independence of Vietnam . . . For the sake of its interest and its influence." But, on 25 August 1945, a large demonstration marked the success of the Vietminh which, as if emerging from the earth, displayed its strength in the streets of Hanoi. The other nationalist parties rallied to it, for they deemed it to be in a better position to have the independence of the country recognized by the Allies. Bao Dai was appointed supreme adviser to the provisional government which was formed with the participation of many Communists. Independence – once more – and the democratic republic were successively proclaimed. The text was placed under the aegis of the American independence and of the

Declaration of the Rights of Man of 1789. There was no question of Communism in it; it did not even refer to the USSR. But the Communist Party assumed alone the direction of the Vietminh Front.

But that independence and that power still remained to be conquered from France, which was soon back on the scene.

Ho Chi Minh was indeed the master craftsman of this first revolution in the war. His qualities as a negotiator and as a tactician had worked wonders. As his biographer Jean Lacouture has shown, Ho Chi Minh had earlier evinced the other aspects of his identity: the peasant, the migrant, the militant, the unifier, the prisoner. Soon he was to become the guerilla.

What strikes one about this revolutionary patriot is the absolute distinction which he established between the French and their colonization. He did not spare the harshest words for the latter and its abuses; he was equally unsparing in his expressions of gratitude for the former and the values which they represented. The story goes that, on landing in Marseilles and being addressed as "Vous", he immediately understood the difference between the France which liberates and the France which oppresses. So he had French friends, he spoke French, he was active in French organizations. In Hanoi, on the day of independence which was proclaimed in September 1945, he spoke to the Vietnamese and to the French, in French, to express his friendship, his trust in the France of the Revolution and of the Paris commune. That speech was taped live and has been preserved.

According to Dang Xuan Khu (Truang Chinh) the decision for the 13 August 1945 general uprising was taken at the Tan Trao meeting to disarm the Japanese before the arrival of the Allies and thus to place them before a "deserving" fait accompli. In such a perspective France did not count for much. France counted for still less than the Vietnamese themselves imagined for, at Potsdam, the decision had been taken to entrust the North of Indo-China to the armies of Chiang Kai-shek and the South to the British. The limit separating the two armies would be the 16th parallel. What could the 2,500 French soldiers in Indo-China do in the face of 25 Chinese divisions? But, for its part, the Vietminh did not want to see the Allied project carried out, and Ho Chi Minh sent word to the French representatives of the GPRF (Sainteny, Pignon, General Alessandri) to inform them of the Vietminh demands: independence in less than five years, not after ten years.

But in Paris the Indo-Chinese question was viewed as if there had been neither war, nor defeat, nor Japanese occupation, not the double proclamation of independence, nor the general uprising. De Gaulle wanted to send troops. He appointed Admiral d'Argenlieu as High Commissioner. But the Americans did not have "the ships for that". Meanwhile Paris had restored the Indo-Chinese Federation, comprising its five former territories, with a High Commissioner at its head. These decisions even represented a retreat from the concessions made a year earlier by Admiral Decoux to the Vietnamese nationalists. They simply denied the existence of Vietnam.

But the Vietnamese most feared the Chinese who had one man in the Ho Chi Minh government: the Vice-president Nguyen Hai Than. During the negotiations that ensued, the stumbling block was the *doc lap* which had been proclaimed on 2 September in Hanoi: freedom, according to the French; independence, according to the Vietnamese. Finally the latter gave in and the agreement of 6 March, backed by Leclerc, involved the Vietnam, the "Free State", joining the Indo-Chinese Federation, but without the three Ky – without Cochin-China. Ho Chi Minh and Giap justified these important concessions by recalling the experience of Brest-Litovsk: "Thanks to this truce we shall be able to strengthen our army . . ." And Ho Chi Minh told his people, with his voice broken by sobs: "I swear to you that I have not betrayed you."

While, under the command of Leclerc, the first French troops were landing at Hanoi, and others at Saigon, with the discreet help of the British, Admiral d'Argenlieu, it is reported, referred to "A new Munich" before his meeting with Ho Chi Minh.

It may be observed that neither one side nor the other was ready to abide by and honour the agreement of 6 March 1946.[1] The negotiations were resumed with Marius Moutet, at the Dalat meeting. But they stumbled against the question of Cochin-China, with Ho Chi Minh also refusing to budge. He was relying on the support of the French Communists who, in 1946, obtained 26 percent of the votes.

The proclamation by France of the creation of an autonomous Republic of Cochin-China caused a chain reaction. In the South the Vietminh resorted to terrorism against the Vietnamese who were in favour of this agreement with France. In the North General Valluy seized the opportunity to bombard Haiphong. Twelve hundred French men and women were attacked; 40 were massacred. In full flight, the Ho Chi Minh government, on 21 December 1946, gave the order for a general uprising.

The war was on.

The specific character of the national movement in India

In India, the emergence of a big business bourgeoisie and the elaboration of a historical memory and of an identity brought about partly by the colonizer and partly by the colonized contributed to the building up and development of a freedom movement which was not necessarily anti-capitalist – in contrast with other movements – nor unanimously anti-British, even though independence (*svaraj*) remained one of its goals and the hostility to the ruling occcupier was widespread.

One of the most remarkable features of English domination in India is that the worst wrongs inflicted upon this people outwardly seem like benefits bestowed by Heaven: the railway, the telegraph, the telephone, the radio, and others were welcome. They were necessary and we owe a great debt of gratitude to England for having brought these to us. But we must never forget that their first aim was to reinforce the British imperialism on our soil by making it possible to tighten the grip of the administration and to conquer new markets for the products of English industry. However, despite my resentment for the presence and the behaviour of foreign masters, I never felt any animosity towards Englishmen as individuals. In the depths of my soul, I rather admired this race.

(J. Nehru)

Other expressions go a step further: "Totally loyal to His Britannic Majesty we felt we were unworthy of undoing the laces of his shoes."

No Vietnamese or Arab ever used such expressions in regard to the French in the colonies. But that did not preclude an equally powerful determination, a critical and, in its way,[2] condescending attitude towards the Englishman "who normally always meets the same little group of Indians, those who belong to officialdom . . . This class reeks of boredom and narrow-mindedness. Even a young and intelligent Englishman, on reaching our shores, did not take long in succumbing to a sort of intellectual and cultural torpor. On leaving his office at the end of the day, he would indulge in some exercise, after which he would join his colleagues at the Club, drink his whisky and read the illustrated magazines of his country . . . He rendered India responsible for this deterioration of his mind, . . . while the real cause of this decline in him was but the consequence of his bureaucrat's existence" (Nehru).

A third feature of the Indian national movement as represented by B. G. Tilak, M. K. Gandhi and J. Nehru was the "perverse" effect of the interest which the English showed for the past of India and for its society. By means of a reconstruction of the most ancient traits, to the point of fossilizing the description of the caste system – in order to better administer the Indian society – the English revived an essentially Hindu past and history. This flattered the self-esteem of the Hindus and resulted in erasing the memory of the Muslim past. Tilak immediately understood the advantage which the Hindus could take from the extant situation by establishing "Societies for the protection of the cow", by glorifying Shivaji, the Maratha King who triumphed over Afzal Khan by strangling him with steel claws and then attacking the army of the Great Mughul. Under cover of a veneration of this past and of this culture, Tilak was actually infusing new vigour into Hindu India, not the India that had become a part of Islam. Likewise Gandhi made use later of non-violent practices which he presented as means of fighting the British occupant. But these means had their roots in the Hindu tradition. They were not Indian.

In this manner, thanks to the British, the Muslims had been ousted from their position of power, first by losing their position of suzerainty and of sovereignty, then by being deprived of any form of preeminence by means of this revaluation of the tradition. Finally their loss was compounded by Hindus joining the big business movements and constituting that capitalistic bourgeoisie, whose wealth, which had hitherto rested on shaky foundations, was growing into a genuine economic and political power. Of course, the Hindus could not proclaim it from the rooftops. But it could be plainly seen because the priests were taking over the authority formerly claimed by the state. Moreover the difference between the two communities was becoming more and more pronounced. This showed that, under cover of independence, the great leaders were striving to give back to the Hindus their dominant status by means of an apparently innocent endorsement of the democratic methods used by the British who, in the context of the numerical superiority of the Hindus in India, would ensure that in a unified India the non-Muslims would hold sway. With independence, the minority which once ruled the country would see itself inevitably in possession of an inferior status, even if the leaders of the independence party took all precaution to help the Muslims save their face, mainly by accepting the principle of separate electoral colleges. One can understand that, after having used the Hindus to demolish the former Moghul state, the English subsequently supported the Muslims in order to slow down India's march towards independence. One also understands that the leitmotiv of the "unity of India" would have impelled such a political process in the service of the Hindu majority.

"A Muslim college is worth four army corps", a high British official said, in 1883, at the time when preparations were afoot for the meeting of the Indian National Congress in 1885. The Indian Empire had become a Crown possession after the outbreak of the Indian mutiny. This revolt was the outcome of the greed of the agents of the East India Company as well as of the ruin of the craft industry, of the exclusion of the Indians from the management of their affairs, of the impoverishment of a part of the population. These were the barrels of gunpowder which were lit by that question of bullets. This was the clearest proof of the scornful ignorance in which the officers held the Indians, refusing to see that they were making the Indians violate a taboo: the cartridges were greased with pork fat and had to be torn with the teeth.

Drawing the lesson from the Sepoy Mutiny, the reform of 1858 transferred power to a Secretary of State for India. He prescribed policy to the Viceroy. Queen Victoria was proclaimed Empress of India instead of the Great Moghul (1876). But a great part of India, called the India of the Princes, did not come under the Crown. Subsequently the restoration of Mysore to its dynasty, after half a century of British administration, was an indication of the new attitude of London towards the princes. At the same time the British made it possible for Indians to join the legislative councils without going through the Indian Civil Service examination which was held in Britain. The Morley-Minto reforms of 1909 enabled organizations or certain categories of citizens – Muslims, Parsis, Sikhs – to take part in the different legislative bodies set up in Calcutta, Bombay. Thus the embryo of a parliamentary regime came about, while regional councils set in motion a process of decentralization. In a general sense the British were engaged in strengthening the political muscles in the higher levels of the social body while being particularly worried over the peasants' indebtedness which they sought to alleviate.

It was through this narrow gate that the Indian national movement entered the scene. Side by side with it the *svaraj* movement joined the struggle and gave birth to the Congress Party. It was only after the First World War that the Congress Party included elected peasants in its ranks.

The individuals who had first joined the Congress Party were the tycoons who, in order to resist the growing encroachment of the colonial government on local affairs, supported the agitation launched by the intelligentsia of Calcutta and Bombay in favour of a more representative form of government. The integration of these local tycoons within a provincial, and later a national, system, culminated in a unification of the different views of the struggle. This led, in 1917, to a massive confrontation between the colonial authorities and the nationalist movement.

There was a relationship of dependence between those small and big magnates and the politicians or professional publicists who appeared at the turn of the century. The politicians served the cause of the former who did not want to jump into the political arena. As a result the nationalists did not constitute an independent body: they were merely the spokesmen of the dominant groups. The characteristic example is provided by the patron-client relationship which, in Allahabad, united Pandit Malaviya, one of the leading politicians of the Congress in North India, with the family of the richest banker of the city, Ram Charan Das. It was the formation, in Allahabad, of separate electorates for the Muslims which generated the Hindu-Muslim opposition. Till that time this opposition had not been so evident. But it became an important feature of local political life, as the source of "communalism" (struggle between the communities).

From 1930 on, with strategic retreat becoming a component of the policy of the English, the Congress began to play an increasingly greater role. It adapted itself to a new situation and gradually gave up mass agitation and chose instead to take part in elections and in parliamentary functions. The Congress became a part of the partially parallel government, ready to take over power on the day of independence, or waiting for the transformation of India into a dominion.

"There is no need of revolutionaries to make a revolution; let the leaders act . . .", Lenin used to say. This opinion may be relevant to the attitude adopted by the British in India, in view of the analysis which Gandhi made of it. Certainly, like Lenin, Gandhi thought that the state, in its present form, and still more so the colonialist state, was an instrument of exploitation. He also thought that the plutocrats had the peasants held by the throat. But his humanism and his beliefs imparted to him a more optimistic vision of social relationships: his faith taught him that neither the Marxists, nor the Buddhists, nor the Muslims could be the Just. Nor were the Christians because their churches were "in the service of those who have, not of those who have nothing". Nor were the Communists who, instead of reconciliation, advocated the class struggle. His model was Leo Tolstoy (and more particularly the formula: "The Kingdom of God is within us") who taught that, to resist evil, a total renunciation of violence is indispensable. As the state, the Churches which glorify it, and the class struggle are evil, the just man must detach himself as much as possible from an iniquitous society; he must be non-violent; he must strive to convert the leading classes.

Consequently he put into practice this principle, non-violent action (*satyagraha*), in its ancient Hindu form: *ahimsa* ("thou shall not kill"). "In its dynamic form non-violence means: lucid and voluntary suffering. Not a docile submission to the will of the evil-doer, but a total mobilization of the soul against this will of the tyrant. By applying this law of our being to the task, it is possible for a single individual to dare the brute force of an unjust domination, thereby to save one's honour, one's religion, one's soul and to prepare the fall or the regeneration of the oppressive Empire." "I therefore do not call on India to practise non-violence out of weakness, but in full awareness of its strength and of its power . . ." Gandhi himself gave many examples by means of his many planned hunger strikes. One had to be powerfully calm even in the face of a regiment of mounted police. The documentary films of 1931 still preserve the images resulting from this instruction: when the mounted police arrived, escorted by other police detachments, the protesting Indians lay down on the ground, motionless, actively passive: two or three policemen were needed to remove them, one by one, from the place where they were lying. But, carried away in this way, they fell down as if they were lifeless. These are unique, incredible scenes of the historical memory.

The non-violent manifestations were provoked, as Lenin saw, by an action committed by the rulers, for example, by an insult to the sentiments of the Hindu, as at an earlier time the cartridges had been.

The first provocation was the arrest of Annie Besant in 1919. She was an Irish-American lady, leader of the Theosophical Society which had the vocation of reviving Hindu ideals and institutions. Further she had become one of the leaders of the *svaraj* movement. Her arrest was justified by the

Rowlatt laws: by carrying in her pocket a nationalist tract she had committed an offence punishable with two years' imprisonment. These measures spoiled the Montagu scheme of India's progressive development towards Independence, which came into being with the *Government of India Act* which propounded a diarchic administration of the country.

The second provocation was the meeting, in 1927, of the Simon Commission on the future of the Anglo-Indian diarchy. The Viceroy Lord Irwin showed the conclusions to Gandhi. According to the anecdote of the time, Gandhi read the conclusions and remarked: "A post card would have been sufficient." In reality the Indians had not been consulted and they could not accept even such a procedure.

The third provocation was Viceroy Lord Linlithgow's declaration in 1939: in the name of India, by virtue of his vice-regal powers he declared war on Germany, without having consulted a single Indian.

These snubs testified to the inadequacy of British behaviour towards the cultural and political realities of India. "The British are like travellers in a strange land, but they must not stop moving forward", observed R. A. Butler who thereby meant that firmness must be combined with reforms, "something which only Minto had managed to balance". For the reforms, produced by initiatives taken in New Delhi, but elaborated in London, could – the evidence is available – be reduced to nought by these "blunders" arising out of the contempt felt for India.

Gandhi responded to the three affronts by launching three campaigns: the non-cooperation movement of 1920–22; the civil disobedience of 1930–31, marked by the strike against the salt tax; and lastly the "Quit India" campaign during the Second World War.

During these two decades the Congress Party of Gandhi had established and tightened the bonds with the peasant masses whose specific difficulties were well known. It was the indigo crisis in one place; stern repressive measures in another. Gandhi had a way of being everywhere, "inflaming the peasant minds with millenarist visions". But he assured the British that he could rein in all excesses, which, most of the time, was true. Nehru observed that "he was imperious and his magnetism worked wonders". Actually Gandhi knew how to ward off revolts in the rural areas, for he knew that the British would repress them, as they had done with the Moplahs in 1921, with the Red Shirts in the 1930s.

The effects of Gandhi's strategy were quite plain. The British could not do anything without the support of the Congress Party, which was fast becoming a counter-power and a parallel power. The British had the advantage of dealing with a "valid representative". The Congress membership had grown: it reckoned 3 million adherents in 1937.

The rise of the Congress implied the relative decline of the India of the Princes and of the Muslim community. Armed with this certainty, those British who were hostile to the independence of India could envisage their remaining masters of the situation for at least a decade. They could not then imagine how correct this forecast was.

The Japanese aggression at Pearl Harbor, followed by the disasters that befell Great Britain, with the fall of Singapore at the beginning of 1942, caused a schism in the ranks of the Indian national movement. Some of the proponents of *purna svaraj* (complete independence) judged that the opportunity should be seized to link up with the Japanese, who had already reached close to Burma, and drive out the British.

That movement was led by Subhas Chandra Bose. Indeed he had led that movement ever since he published *The Indian Struggle*, in 1934, in which he criticised the inadequacy of the results of non-violence, arguing that the goals were ill defined, even though the techniques used by Gandhi were worthy of the highest praise. Above all Bose criticised Gandhi for cosying up to the powerful, of not being revolutionary enough, and even of flirting too much with the British, even of fraternizing with them, in London. In this regard Bose was in agreement with the Communists. He led the radical wing, while Nehru stood for the policy of moderation. In 1939, Bose was elected the President of the Congress, beating the candidate proposed by Gandhi.

Gandhi displayed an ambiguous attitude when the hostilities started. He wrote to Hitler appealing to him for peace, especially for the peace of the soul, and advised the Jews to adopt non-violence. In case of an invasion (13 April 1940, before Japan and the United States entered the war) he proposed "non-cooperation with the aggressor if Nero occupied India – or non-violent resistance, to offer himself as a victim, and a people in chains waiting for death". But the Congress rejected both the revolution advocated by Bose and non-violence. Vinoba Bhave, disciple of Gandhi, made a speech against war. He was arrested, as were Nehru, Vallabhbhai Patel and 400 members of the different state institutions, following Gandhi's pronouncement in favour of civil disobedience. A British mission, led by Sir Stafford Cripps, had indeed proposed to Nehru the transformation of India into a dominion at the end of the war, but at a time when Japan had never been so close to the frontiers of India. Nehru observed: "By promising us dominion status at the end of the war, the English are signing a post-dated cheque on a failed bank." The discussions were deadlocked.

Thereupon Bose took the decisive step. He resolutely engaged himself in a cooperation with Germany and Japan. Soon he formed a free Indian government, in Singapore, and, in 1943, was received with great pomp first by Hitler and later by the government in Tokyo.

In Burma Bose raised an army from prisoners of war taken by the Japanese. Still even if his uprising took on the characteristics of a myth, and the Congress honoured him after his – accidental – death, very few followed his lead. That was because, with the USSR joining the war, the Indian Communists had broken away from his movement. Further the words of F. D. Roosevelt on the application of the Atlantic Charter to all the nations subject to foreign domination had raised the hopes of the Indians. Following the riots that broke out after Gandhi was arrested in 1942 the Congress, led by Nehru, took India into the war, at least on the economic level. Only the reward remained to be collected.

The outstanding issues were the Muslim question and the attitude of London.

From the time of Lord Curzon, the colonizers relied on the hatred which opposed the Hindus to the Muslims. Of course, there had been, in the past, moments of reconciliation, even attempts at syncretism. But the differences were too powerful ... The credit goes to Gandhi for his understanding that this antagonism was a stumbling block to *svaraj*: after the Rowlatt laws he organized, with the help of Swami Shraddhanand, a strike of religious solidarity in conjunction with the Great Mosque. Five Hindus and four Muslims died as a result, an incident which worried the British authorities, for the *hartal* movement – general interreligious strike – developed on a large scale. The government in Delhi then decided to help in the development of the *Muslim League* under the stewardship of M. A. Jinnah: the incidents became more frequent, especially on those occasions when elections were held. The hunger strikes, led by Gandhi to prevent an escalation of the violence, had no effect on the conflict. Actually the Muslim League was concerned with the growing strength of the Congress party and its tendency to dominate the dialogue with the British.

The idea of a separate Muslim nation was mooted in 1933: it gave birth to the expression Pakistan which meant "Land of Purity".

Gandhi thought that the notion of a Muslim nation in India was absurd. He wondered why there should not also be a Sikh nation, or a Parsi nation, for "we all belong to the same race". But this was not a merely innocent ignorance, for the Muslims deemed that they counted for nothing in a state governed by the Congress. If non-violence was an effective technique, the attainment of its aims, the adoption of a Western form of parliamentary democracy, resulted in ruining those who felt they had their own specific identity.

But Gandhi did not want to recognize it, and the rise of Muslim India left him nonplussed. He was shattered by it: the nature of the problem was beyond him.

For its part the League had neither the wealth, nor the power, nor the organization, nor the rootedness of the Congress Party. It was flatly beaten in any contest having an institutional characteristic. That is why Jinnah chose to do battle only on the dimensions and the frontiers of that state. He was uncompromising, and avoided all talk on the future control of the army and of taxation.

The population exchanges and the grave disturbances caused by the partition took place, *after* partition had been decided, and 200,000 victims perished. In 1947 Viceroy Mountbatten presided over the negotiations by fixing *deadlines*, thus compelling the League and the Congress to form governments, to get ready for the management of "their" country, etc.: independence in June 1948 and transfer of power in August.

The Sikhs were sacrificed. So were the Princes, the Untouchables whom the different partners abandoned to their fate, whatever might have been the debt owed to them. The Princes were compensated for the loss of their sovereignty. But what of the others? In its turn, French decolonization would soon evince the same ingratitude towards the *harkis*.

In this story the opportunities for a Communist revolution, of the Vietnamese type or any other, were never considered. That was due mainly to the strategy of the Indian Communist Party which, from 1930 to 1947, piled up error after error.

The first mistake, in view of the situation and of the make-up of Indian society, consisted in relying on the principle of the class struggle, by favouring the working class which, for decades, was not capable of giving life to the national struggle. In the Indian context the Marxists were close to the trade unionists: they defended a few social groups, not the others, while Gandhi claimed or asserted that he represented all Indians.

The second strategic "mistake" was their sudden turnaround in 1941 when the USSR entered the war: instead of continuing to ask for independence, they opposed the Quit India resolution of the Congress Party. Accordingly they lent themselves to being called the agents of a foreign ruler. Lastly, in 1946, in their defence of nationalities, they supported the Muslim League point of view in favour of a separate State and, on that account, totally alienated themselves from Hindu opinion and from all those who held the unity of India to be sacred.

Indo-China – Maghreb: French policy paralysed

"It will be a war between a tiger and an elephant. If ever the tiger stops, the elephant will gore it with his powerful tusks. But the tiger will not stop. He crouches in the jungle during the day only to prowl at night. He will leap on the elephant and will tear off large morsels from his back, then he shall disappear and the elephant shall slowly die of exhaustion and loss of blood" (V. N. Giap). That is how the Vietminh, at its beginning, imagined the war would be fought. And it happened that way. It ended in the same way as Giap described it to the Australian journalist Wilfrid Burdett: "Had the French command chosen another place than the basin of Dien Bien Phu and if a leader other than Navarre had commanded the French forces, the end of the war in Indo-China would have been the same."

"Ineluctable advance", that was the expression used by General Morlière to whom, at the end of 1946, General Valluy had said: "To maintain your hold, do not hesitate to strike hard with artillery and bombs." He deemed that the Haiphong incident had activated the detonator. Following that incident all the bridges to the Ho Chi Minh government had been blown up – "It is evident that we have opted for a policy of strength."

Haiphong was the detonator. But, during the summer of 1946, the first decisive step had been taken when France proclaimed the existence of a Republic of Cochin-China, as confirmed at the negotiations in Fontainebleau. When the war resumed, France recalled Bao Dai, "because the thinking French are convinced that a movement supplied with automatic weapons and supported by the greater part of the population cannot be defeated by a foreign army" – which comprised 200,000 men. "The only way out is to fight fire with fire. That is why the French have just granted to Bao Dai an independence broader than Ho Chi Minh was claiming." This analysis by the American journalist Alsop conformed exactly with what had taken place in Paris: it was a technique which was applied again in Morocco, with the call to Ben Arafa in 1953. But it does not take into account the other aspects of the problem.

Before the war, the Vietminh had adopted a policy which took into account the presence of French Communists in the government, or in circles close to it. Besides Ho Chi Minh himself had established close links with trade unionists and with the extreme left during the period between the two world wars. "All my life I have fought against French colonialism, but I have always loved and admired the French people who are sensitive and generous, being the first to have raised the flag of another principle of liberty, equality and of fraternity . . ." Ho Chi Minh uttered these words on the Hanoi radio in 1946, in the presence of General Leclerc and of Jean Sainteny. He repeated them at the meeting in Fontainebleau: "We want collaboration between our two countries to be free, loyal and fraternal. We want to have collaborators, friends, even advisers; not masters who exploit us and oppress us as they used to do."

But, with France granting to Bao-Dai – who, as we have seen, had been restored to the throne – more concessions than to it, the Vietminh decided not only that a part of the French left could not be trusted – in this case the socialists, such as Marius Moutet – but also that the social revolution it wanted to bring about was being jeopardized. Indeed the return of Bao Dai encouraged the colonial establishment and the military to express openly their opposition to any progress towards an association with the "Annamese" on the basis on equal rights.

In the middle of the war, Léo Figuères, the representative of the French Communist Party, went via Moscow, Peking and Hankow to meet Ho Chi Minh who was then hiding in the jungle. Ho explained that the situation "has turned around completely". "Up till then we were besieged, clinging to the mountain slopes, striving doggedly to create a state out of a maquis having no links with the outside world. Henceforth, we have a common frontier with the socialist world" (1949).

Mao Tse-tung's victory in China had in fact "completely turned the situation around" in the Far East.

But with the war in Korea about to start and the presence of Bao Dai supported by the Americans who were determined to oppose Communism, the colonial conflict clashed with the imperatives of the cold war, thus altering the particulars of the problem.

On the French side, the colonial conflict was saddled with administrative sluggishness. For instance, Bao Dai was deprived of the means to act, even though he had been set up in opposition to Ho Chi Minh. President Ngo Dinh Diem complained: there was no national army, no budget, no control of the currency, no totally liberated administration. "It is not possible to rely on the Vietnamese army and at the same time deny its existence. . . . A national army can exist only if it has a flag, its own victories and its own defeats, its own chiefs. . . . Vietnamese soldiers integrated as auxiliary units of the French army scarcely constitute a Vietnamese army." In the fighting more than 27,000 Vietnamese died, together with 17,000 from the Federated States, 15,000 Africans and North Africans, 11,000 legionnaires, and 21,000 "French", out of a total of nearly 100,000 deaths. And this was, after all, a typically colonial way of counting. Moreover, the military chiefs were Valluy, de Lattre, Salan, Navarre; no Vietnamese.

The struggle against Communism proceeds inside the country, and indirectly on the international stage. Even in France, from 3 May 1947 on, the Communist Party launched a strong campaign against the "dirty war". It recovered the strong voice heard at the time of the war in the Riff. This campaign was supported by the intellectuals – Jean-Paul Sartre in the forefront, and the Catholics of *Témoignage chrétien* – who took part in the public demonstrations. The hidden war was denounced, the "shameful" war the scope of which dawned on "public opinion" only gradually, for the government did not call up the conscripts.

It was in such a situation that the governments declared the connivance of the Communist Party with Ho Chi Minh to be contrary to national interests. At that time there was little understanding or scarcely any concern for the prospect that the "revolutionary war" waged by the Vietminh could end with the establishment of a "totalitarian" State. On the contrary what was certain was that, by refusing to show confidence in the Ramadier government the Communists were playing with fire. They denounced French policy in Madagascar and in Indo-China, the government's social programme, and especially its German policy. The Ramadier government seized the opportunity, as did Spaak in Belgium, and Gasperi in Italy at that very moment. It heeded the speech by Truman who spelled out that

American aid was predicated on the assumption that the governments of countries which appealed for it were free of Communists. Accordingly the war in Indo-China became a by-product of France's need for American loans to replace its equipment, and for German coal, then under American control, to increase its industrial production. The struggle against the Vietminh, together with the support of Bao Dai, was financed with this aid. It was under the government of René Mayer (January 1953) that the army became even further transformed into an expansion industry. The war in Indo-China was a double operation: due to the flow of American dollars the economy ceased to be burdened with military expenditure. This made it possible to purchase goods abroad, which was all the more fortunate considering that it coincided with the termination of the Marshall Plan. The war drove the economy forward and proved to be a godsend for profits, such as from currency trading.

Viewed against such a background the uncertainties and the powerlessness of the French administrators can be easily understood. When China started helping Vietnam, General Salan asked for instructions, which failed to reach him.

It is possible that these administrators, from the very beginning, believed that the war was already lost, considering the distances, the vastness of the country, the ambiguity of American policy in regard to a "colonial reconquest". That is what de Lattre was very quickly led to think; so too was Salan who was fascinated by the intellectual brightness of Giap with whom he was acquainted. Nor did René Mayer believe in a military solution. Nor René Pleven, Prime Minister in 1951–52, who, as Minister of Defence in 1954 declared, two months before the defeat of Dien Bien Phu, that "the enemy has not, till now, been able to reach any of his essential goals". But, till then, the negotiations could not proceed to any conclusion because the Vietminh was not prepared to make any concessions. "How do you negotiate with an enemy who wants your capitulation?" René Pleven wondered, ten years later.

The pressure upon those who were for peace but prevented from acting was very great. To begin with there were the military who were bent on avenging the defeat of 1940 and opined that the glory of the Empire alone could bring about the recovery of France. Next came the colonist lobby. Moreover there was the burden of the American alliance which was the price that had to be paid, if only to secure the advantage of the United States not opting for Germany against France, for fear of the rearmament of a country which had just been occupied, with the pretext that the USSR had to be contained.

The German question lay at the heart of French preoccupations, among the rulers and among everyone else. To make peace would mean losing the American aid, seeing Germany prosper, helping in the victory of Communism. That was the point that Georges Bidault, René Mayer and others who took part in most of the governments from 1950 to 1954 laboured in their speeches. And Robert Schuman succeeded best in making the American forget that the war in Indo-China was a colonial reconquest.

But then what weighed most heavily on the minds of the leaders was actually what *was not said.* That is, it was not so much the complete independence of Vietnam which gave the French leaders pause, but the conviction that subsequently all the countries of the French Union would follow this example and become free on their own.

Following Dien Bien Phu, Pierre Mendès France had the courage to confront the problem squarely by publicly declaring that the end of the war was a condition for French recovery. It is true that on 7 April 1954 De Gaulle had urged negotiation. Though he was out of power at that time, his statement created a breach and covered Mendès France. The latter was joined by Marshal Juin whose intervention, at his side, in Tunisia, created the conditions for the success of that negotiation (1954).

Meanwhile, during the Geneva conference, Pierre Mendès France led the negotiation with resolve, by fixing deadlines for himself – as Lord Mountbatten had done in India. But he did so by running much greater risks, for his government had been weakened by the disaster of Dien Bien Phu and by the events in Tunisia and in Morocco. Some thought a military coup was in the offing; others speculated about the role which General de Gaulle would play.

The Chinese, the Vietnamese, the Americans and the French were present in Geneva. The agreement which was signed stipulated that the 17th parallel would be the line of provisional demarcation between North and South Vietnam, with each part remaining under the control of their respective civil administrations. Given the state of the war map, this meant the independence of North Vietnam. Elections were to be held in the whole country before 1956. These elections never took place.

On the French TV, this is how Pierre Mendès France commented on this agreement:

> From the beginning the Americans have said that they did not want to sign a document which bore the signature of the Chinese since they do not recognize China. Accordingly the minutes were kept of the points on which agreement had been arrived at and the General Secretary of the conference read it at the general meeting. Then each delegation made a unilateral statement to record its comments ... but also to commit itself not to break, not to call into question what had just been proclaimed and, after all its reservations with respect to China, to the Vietminh, the American delegation, solemnly made two commitments: first, we shall never call into question what had just been agreed upon, by means of force; secondly, we shall

consider as an aggressor any country which would use force or the threat of force to destroy it. Consequently, though they had not signed, the Americans have quite scrupulously made the commitments which we expected of them, and which were precisely the ones to which we ourselves had agreed. That is why the Geneva conventions were never signed by the Americans, nor by the others.

Once the war in Korea was over, they did not abide by their promises, nor did North and South Vietnam. The French political leaders had a premonition that the events in Indo-China were to have repercussions on the future of the French Union. They were paralysed by it.

When, in 1952, well before Dien Bien Phu, the High Council of the French Union met, under the chairmanship of Vincent Auriol, in the presence of Prime Minister Antoine Pinay and of the representatives of Vietnam, Laos, and Cambodia, one of the delegates of the latter country, Nhiek Tioulong, proposed that the sovereigns of Tunisia and of Morocco be invited to take part in the meetings of the High Council. President Auriol gave a sudden start. In the government Pinay was not opposed to an idea which was so simple, so plain, so ordinary. But Martinaud-Deplat, Brune, René Mayer were keeping watch. The plan was shelved.

For many years the French political leaders did not want to know anything, did not want to understand anything.

> Many people entertain the naive belief that the defeat of France is a punishment meted out by God, that her domination is over and that our independence will follow from an Axis victory deemed to be certain. That is understandable. But I say that it is a mistake, a grave, unforgivable mistake . . .

Habib Bourguiba was taking a serious risk in uttering those words in 1943. He was reckoning with a victory of the democratic nations. It was possible, even probable, but still not certain at that date. Above all, any one who, at the end of 1942, had not seen the *Deutsche Wochenschau* that showed young Tunisians giving an enthusiastic welcome to the soldiers of the Wehrmacht, would have had no conception of the extent to which the leader of the Neo-Destour was taking positions that were against the tide of opinion among his fellow citizens.

Those words strike one all the more by their boldness considering that the Italians had just freed Bourguiba who was rotting in a French jail and that the Fascist regime had given him an honourable welcome. However, on Italian radio he again warned his fellow citizens against yielding to their basic sentiments, for "that would be taking the risk of subjection to another foreign domination".

The Tunisians rejoicing at the arrival of the Germans could be explained as the result of the disenchantment and the anger provoked by the French policy in the protectorate for the previous thirty years.

In fact, nothing had changed since the publication in Lausanne, in 1917, of *Tunisie et Algérie, protestation contre le despotisme français*, following the Conference of Nationalities. The Destour had tried to associate the Bey with the demands of the nationalists for the election, solely by Tunisians, of an assembly with a government responsible to it. The Bey was forced to disown his Prime Minister who had conveyed the message (1922). Ten years later "rogue laws" suppressed the Tunisian press and Marcel Peyrouton began his authoritarian proconsulate. The Destour not seeming equal to the ordeals endured by the Tunisians, a schism resulted in the creation of the Neo-Destour of Habib Bourguiba. The Neo-Destour was less committed to Islam, but it put forward stronger claims. Thus began the war between the two Destours, between the old and the new. Several events marked the beginning of the rise of Bourguiba: a strike in Monastir in 1934; a riot in Tunis which culminated in the proclamation of martial law in 1938; taking the leaders of the Neo-Destour into custody and the dissolution of the party. However, in the meantime the Neo-Destour had become strongly entrenched, with more than 400 cells, a youth organization, and so on. But the Neo-Destour felt the blow all the harder especially as the Destour chose that very moment to bear down on it. Then, in 1943, the Bey was dismissed by General Giraud, on charges of "collaboration", while in fact he was being blamed for having chosen his ministers without any consultation with the President.

In Morocco the situation was similar to that in Tunisia: the Governors and the Residents took a summary view of the development of nationalism in the country. "Morocco, the unity of which has been formed by France, must turn its back on oriental plots", declared General Juin, the new resident at the end of the war. He meant to denounce Morocco's involvement in the Arab Islamic world which, at least in the east, under the leadership of the Grand Mufti of Jerusalem, had evinced its Germanism and stirred up nationalist sentiments in the countries still dependent on Britain and France. As a matter of fact, ever since the speech of Kaiser Wilhem II in Tangiers in 1905, a certain Germanism had always prevailed in Morocco where the people felt an intense pleasure at the defeat of France in 1940. But this infatuation for Germany could not, as in Tunisia, be expressed openly in the presence of German troops. The Sultan actually relied on the Americans to recover his independence: F. D. Roosevelt had paid him a visit during the conference of Anfa-Casablanca (January 1943) and Mohammed V remembered the terms of the North Atlantic Charter.

But the French authorities decided to overlook the loyalty of the Sultan as they ignored that of Bourguiba. The "oriental plots" referred to by

General Juin were actually the demands made by the Sultan in conformity with the 1912 treaty of the protectorate.

As in India, the calculated blunders of the French administration had been feeding, over a period of thirty years, the anger of the Moroccans. The war in the Riff had raised the hopes of the nationalists and it was just over when the Resident replaced a *dahir* (decree) issued in 1914 under the influence of Lyautey with a more radical one. While the earlier *dahir* laid down the obligation to respect Berber customs, the later *dahir* of 1930 acknowledged the competence of the *djemaas* and set up customary tribunals. French jurisdiction thus extended its competence to the punishment of crimes committed in the Berber country, irrespective of the author of the crime. The Sultan was forced to sign the *dahir* which extinguished the competence of the Moroccan High Court. Both a juridical abuse and a political blunder, this action was intended to remove the Berbers from the jurisdiction of the Arab Sultan. It raised to a high pitch the nationalist passion roused by Shekib Arslan, a Lebanese feudal chief trained in Jamal Ed Din el-Afghani's school of thought, and an Arab "prince of eloquence". "Christendom was posing a threat to Islam, it was depriving it of its rights by trying to convert the Muslims by force . . ."

This was one of the first campaigns which testified to a sort of an Islamic community which, including the Arabs, stretched as far as Indonesia. The French language Moroccan press remained silent over this campaign which reached the League of Nations. But, in France, one publication, *L'Afrique française*, which voiced the views of the large economic associations and of the colonists, denounced "the gang of a few hooligans who, equipped with phoney academic diplomas, wish to act in Morocco like Gandhis and Zaghlouls" (1934).

The Resident was compelled to postpone the application of the Berber *dahir*, and later to modify it. But the attempt to win the Berbers over, like the Kabyles in Algeria, failed to achieve its purpose.

Encouraged by this turn of events, the Moroccan nationalists voiced their claims in a lengthy text: the *Plan de réformes marocaines* ("Plan for Moroccan reforms"). They asked for the strict observance of the treaty of the protectorate and the abolition of all direct administration, the participation of Moroccans in the exercise of power in the different branches of the administration, the creation of elected municipalities and the access of all Moroccans to education.

Though it was supported by politicians like Gaston Bergery, César Campinchi, Georges Monnet, this scheme was turned down by the Quai d'Orsay and by the Residence. It was an action which sparked street demonstrations in Fez, Kenitra, etc. in November 1936 and in 1937. As in Tunisia it also provoked a split within the *Comité d'action marocaine* between a populist wing, led by Allal el-Fassi, which was to become the Istiqlal, and a wing which, under the direction of Mohammed Hassan Ouazzani, was more open to contacts with the French Left. Both leaders were arrested, interned or exiled; their organizations were dissolved.

Morocco was calm when General Noguès was succeeded by General Juin in May 1947. In the meantime the nationalist leaders had been freed.

From the time of the war in Indo-China, the nationalist leaders of Tunisia and of Morocco were aware of the powerlessness of French governments, their ignorance of North African problems, with the exception of the core of the colonist party. They also knew the reluctance of the Quai d'Orsay to promote the evolution of the internal autonomy of the two protectorates. The Bey of Tunis had expressed the right to breathe the air of freedom. The Resident Périllier, who had expressed the view that it would be necessary to "open the safety valves", was replaced by Jean de Hauteclocque who decided to travel to Tunis on board a warship (1952).

In Morocco, at the same time, General Juin had tried to win over the Sultan to the idea of a co-sovereignty: Mohammed Ben Youssef refused, for he expected to see the application of the protectorate treaty. Juin's successor, General Guillaume, arrived in August 1951. Regarding the Sultan he summed up the broad lines of his policy with these words: "I am used to a good fight, for that is my job; I am going to make him eat grass."

Tunis was racked by strikes. Violent riots broke out in Casablanca. On 5 December 1951 the second-in-command of the nationalists after Bourguiba, Ferhat Hached, the union chief, had been assassinated in Tunis. The Association of Moroccan Unions responded with a general strike. Tanks fired on the crowd. Juin and Guillaume found themselves managing a crisis, which culminated in the dismissal of the Sultan. Boniface, the "Prefect" said: "He is a nuisance, he ought to stay with his wives, his menagerie, his monkeys and all the rest. He takes himself for the Führer" (quoted in Werth, 1956, p. 619). It was at that moment that the "Glawi operation" was carried out, and the Sultan was replaced by Ben Arafa.

Such words, such actions, clearly indicated to the leaders of the Istiqlal and of the Destour that a genuine dialogue had become impossible. Yet, neither the one nor the other were revolutionary leaders like Ho Chi Minh. Nor were they extremists, like the leaders of the FLN – as subsequent events confirmed. Neither the Bey nor the Sultan were extremists. From the moment when the French leaders obstinately refused to see that, in the global context, the peoples of the Maghreb were irresistibly being driven by the national clamour for independence, the leaders of Morocco and Tunisia, for their part, made use of the international forum as a means to attain their goals. The slow internationalization of the Indo-Chinese problem had showed them the way.

As means to stop this internationalization all that the French could muster was the argument that the Istiqlal and the Destour were favourable to Communism. On the other hand the Americans viewed nationalism as an antidote to Communism. But they proved to be a disappointment in not willing to interfere openly as the King of Morocco had expected. In order to forestall any attempt at interference on their part, the Americans were offered bases in Morocco by the French government. Then, in 1951, the crisis came and Eisenhower refused to commit himself not to be involved in the affairs of the Maghreb. However he did not side with the Tunisian leaders, Bourguiba and Ferhat Hached, who had asked for a more decisive gesture.

It was in 1952 that the great turning point occurred. With the help of the States of the Arab League, the United States included the Tunisian question on the agenda of the United Nations. But, in order to keep their bases, they refrained from any action when the Sultan was dismissed. Nevertheless the United Nations passed resolutions, rather moderate resolutions, "recommending the development of free institutions in the two protectorates".

That French setback proved to be the springboard which provided the nationalists with their last leap forward. In the meantime Dien Bien Phu and the Geneva negotiations enabled Pierre Mendès France, to overcome the obstacle in order to negotiate the independence of Tunisia; and Edgar Faure, to ensure the return of the "genuine" Sultan.

Accordingly, by their opposition to the initiatives asked for by the Sultan, by yielding to the colonists' movement, by playing one power-hungry group against another in Morocco, and all this without perceiving that the U.N. stood by nations moving towards independence, the French leaders in Paris and in Rabat had hastened the inevitable.

The paths of the Algerian "revolution"

"We declare ourselves to be a revolutionary party . . . in terms of the goals of our action, by its forms . . . or quite simply because we take all the risks, while the patriotism of the UDMA and of the Ulemas keeps well back from them."

The opening statement of this Manifesto was written in 1948, by Ait Ahmed, member of the political bureau of the PPA (Parti Populaire Algérien). Its wording is charged with meaning: it says straight away that the revolution in question marks a break with timid, crawling patriotism . . . But the word will stay: a national, patriotic movement wearing an ill-fitting mask: revolution. And it retained it. The revolution did indeed concern the forms which the struggle for freedom would take. But was that all?

In this founding document Hocine Ait Ahmed explains that the liberation could not be a mass uprising, for the lessons of 1871 must not be forgotten. That insurrection failed "less because it was geographically limited than on account of its improvised nature". The struggle for liberation "should not involve a widespread use of terrorism either". "Eliminating the wicked and the traitors" is a popular notion, but it does not take into account the conditions necessary to bring about the conclusion of the enterprise. By referring to Lenin's *What is to be done?* Ait Ahmed shows that terrorism leads to a dead end. But he does not completely reject it: "We must reject terrorist action as the *main* vehicle of the fight for freedom." Ahmed further points out that there is a danger in trying to set up a free zone. Despite the existence of precedents – Yugoslavia during the war, Communist China in its early years – "we must not compare the incomparable". The final hypothesis, the leader of the PPA goes on to explain, consists in "technically re-enacting the French Revolution of 1789"; compelling the Algerian assembly to declare itself a Constituent Assembly. That strategy came from the Communist André Marty who had suggested it to Lamine Debaghine: it foresaw progress towards the co-existence of two sister Republics. Ait Ahmed rejected this hypothesis because "the French Revolution opposed classes and not an oppressed people to a colonial power".

But, emulating Mao Tse-tung, Ait Ahmed considered that the struggle for independence must be a revolutionary war. It must bring together different forms of action, using the advantage of being on favourable ground for strategic defence, and making guerilla operations the main form of war.

All other forms of struggle, as advocated by Abbas, must be rejected, for "legalism died with the congenital illegality as the foundation of colonialism". However, for the time being, "our movement is weak as an instrument of this war of liberation". What is needed is to sharpen the revolutionary consciousness of the masses, replace the cadres, procure arms and money, unify the North African struggle; further, to use the Arab world as the stage and catalyst and Islam as the mobilizing force. Finally, Ahmed proposes the undermining of the enemy by subversive actions in France, by taking advantage of the contradictions of the French Left which tends to side with national imperialism in opposition to the American imperialism. Regarding the Algerian workers in France, "in exchange for their participation in the workers' struggles, they must denounce the refusal on the part of the French parties and unions, to recognize the existence of an Algerian nation".

This text is interesting in the sense that it offers an analysis of the scope of the liberation struggle, a definition of the fundamentals as perceived by the nationalist movement and the lessons it learnt from them in view of attaining its goals. In that sense Ahmed's text contains an entire programme. It was, more or less, carried out in practice, though without any reference to him.

To steer clear of a premature mass uprising – as in 1871 in Kabylia where, by confining the natives to prescribed districts, the colonial regime provoked a revolt against the first colonists, those low-status urban plebeians. Already the Arabs had lost their laws and customs. Shortly after a Mokrani, lord of the Medjana, would be forced to submit to a civil mayor, and a profiteer at that. It was quite evident to the Arabs that the disappearance of Emperor Napoleon III entailed the extinction of any charismatic bond between the Arab notables and "the Sultan". Uprisings broke out in Souk Ahras, El-Miliah, then in the whole of the Kabylia. The colonists in Constantine did not believe it, they saw the French situation in an Algerian setting, and viewed the despatching of soldiers as an action to restore the power of the army. They deemed the Muslim brotherhoods to be responsible. Consequently Cardinal Lavigerie felt justified in settling his Pères Blancs in the heart of the country in revolt. But the revolt had made no provisions for extending itself to the whole country. And, sending people from Alsace and Lorraine to Algeria, France simply thought that it had not striven hard enough to bring the inhabitants out of a state of "savagery". The repression was very harsh. The nationalists reckoned it necessary to draw the same lesson from the failure of the premature uprising of 1945.

The Muslim soldiers had taken a heavy toll during the Italian campaign and in their share of the victory at Mount Cassino where Ben Bella earned his Military Cross. The anger of those soldiers and all sorts of other reasons fed the dissatisfaction of the people. The expected order granting them French citizenship failed to materialize. With the men returning to the country to experience a new poverty and the humiliation of the colonial yoke, the independence movement relied on the promises made by the Americans to Ferhat Abbas and to the Sultan of Morocco. But in the interior of the country, especially in Constantinois ravaged by famine and death, the tendency towards independence was vigorously affirmed. Messali Hadj had been arrested and deported to Brazzaville. On 1 May 1945 the demonstrations became more numerous (independently of those organized by the unions). The police fired on the crowd in Algiers, Bougie and Oran and the fury burst forth a week later on the occasion of the Victory celebrations. In Sétif and in Guelma huge processions demanded the release of Messali and a sovereign Constituent Assembly. These demonstrations provided the starting point for an uprising which extended from the Constantinois to the Kabylia: it was sponsored by the AML (Amis du Manifeste et de la Liberté) which included all the nationalist tendencies, from Ferhat Abbas to Messali. The centres of La Fayette, Chevreul and Ain Abessa were surrounded, farms were attacked. The number of the French victims rose to about a hundred. Completed by the air force, the repression causes from 1,500 to 40,000 native victims, the number varying according to different estimates. Several *douars* were levelled to the ground, 44 *mechtas* were destroyed. For the nationalists the "Sétif massacres" remained a burning memory. But neither the Europeans of Algeria, nor the metropolitan French had a real clue as to what was happening because the repression, directed at the time of De Gaulle and on his order, was put into practice while the Air Minister, Charles Tillon, a Communist, neither intervened, nor subsequently resigned. In the midst of the jubilation of the Victory celebrations French opinion was not properly informed of the events in Algeria; nor was it able later to gauge their extent and weigh their consequences.

No generalized terrorism, Ait Ahmed's report declares. In actuality, terrorism spread in the folowing years, when the mother country's response to Algerian aspirations proved to be a disappointment for the militants who were convinced they had been deceived and betrayed (rigged elections, arrests, repression). A few armed attacks – like the hold-up of the main takings of the PTT (Post, Telecommunications and Telediffusion) in Oran, in 1949 – were presented to the Europeans as the activities of delinquent youths. But for the PPA they were the means of acquiring money (and weapons). With the acquisition of the first arms, terrorism became more systematic, for by now the means available to the PPA and to the OS, its military organization, had increased. According to Boudiaf, the first consignment of 300 arms came from Libya, the second consisted of 200 sub-machine guns, 30 colts, 5 military rifles and 2 crates of attack grenades.

However there was no let-up in terrorist activity either before or after the insurrection of November 1954. It had several functions. In its first form – assault on public buildings, for example – it demonstrated hostility to the colonial system, and to those who represented it. In its second form – the attack on a motor-car in the passes of Tighnimine during which Monnerot, a French teacher, was assassinated – it stated that in Algeria there are no "good" or "bad" Frenchmen. All of them had to be driven out: they had to choose between the suitcase or the coffin. The third aspect of terrorism was anti-Arab, that is, it aimed at the purification of the militant community: "traitors" do not belong in it. This radicalization of terrorism, which led to real carnage, was perpetrated mainly by activists on messalists, following the schism within the ranks of the MTLD (Movement of the Workers for Democratic Liberties). According to Harbi, "Messalism occupied, in the Algerian world, the place which Trotskyism did in the Stalinist world". The fourth form of terrorism, the "blind" type, struck at buses and markets, at an anonymous, Muslim as well as European, population, in order to demonstrate the omnipresence of nationalist activists and to create a climate of insecurity. The last form of terrorism, directed solely against the Arabs, fostered a climate of terror as its main purpose, in order to show that the FLN (National Liberation Front) risen from the ashes of the MTLD, had become the true counter-power to the French administration, that it was taking over from it. The FLN had become the embryo of a new state. In it lay the Algerian revolution.

With the start of the war, the terrorists struck all the harder, independently of the armed struggle undertaken since the beginning of 1955. The most cruel acts occurred on 20 and 21 August, in Collo and in Philippeville, with the executions of pieds-noirs as well as of metropolitan Frenchmen and of Muslims like, for example, Abbas Alloua, the nephew of Ferhat Abbas. The aim of the FLN was to eliminate anyone who might possibly establish contacts with Jacques Soustelle, the new head of the French administration, and especially the beneficiaries of the land distribution scheme set up by the government.

It was the massacres of 20 August that forced the moderate nationalist leaders to rally to the uncompromising position of the FLN. These massacres also induced Jacques Soustelle to turn around the position he had adopted. He denounced the "mental confusion" of metropolitan French opinion: "Pacifists who condemn violence in our midst and worship it in others; Christians who do not shed a single tear over the massacre of their fellow believers just because they are Christians; progressives deriving comfort from the sight of Algeria sinking in chaos; internationalists who genuflect before the African and Oriental nationalists; strong minds who recoil from the bar of the Legion of Honour but bow before the Guennour" (J. Soustelle, 1963, p. 132).

Viewed against the political landscape immediately after the end of the war, the complexity of the *relationships* which were established *between* the *Communists and the national movement* extends across the relationships which the Algerians maintained with the liberal Europeans.

It seems that early in the fifties the Algerian Communist Party provided massive support for most of the demands formulated by the Algerian national organizations. It also appears that communist and non-communist militants fraternized with one another, through the UGTA (General Union of Algerian Workers). But this agreement is related only to social problems, to work in the rural areas or on the docks. While claiming to be closer to the MTLD than to the UDMA (Democratic Union of the Algerian Manifesto) of Ferhat Abbas, the extreme leftist organizations were, in actuality, more favourable to the essentially democratic claims of the Arabs than to their aspirations for recognition of their collective identity, the "Algerian personality".

During the period 1947–52 the Algerian Communists showed greater sensitivity to the development of the international situation, to the context of the Cold War, to the struggle for peace promoted by the Appeal of Stockholm, than to the claims of the strictly nationalist movement. For instance, the UDMA's demand for the teaching of Arabic was not seriously taken into consideration. Moreover, at a time when the Communists' return to power did not seem to have become a permanent improbability, the Communists of Algeria deemed the independence of their country to be somewhat "counter-revolutionary". Against the background of the Cold

War they denounced in strong terms "the pseudo-independence which could not but reinforce the American imperialism". They thought instead that their country could become a sort of French Uzbekistan, "Algeristan", if the Communists, once in power in Paris, brought about the reforms which would lead to an integration: the federation of the associated Republics of France and of Algeria. But, at that time, the PCA (Algerian Communist Party) was running tours to "Turkestan" and the pilgrims, on their return from Tashkent, did not fail to sing the praises of the Muslim policy of the USSR. In fact during those years the great concern of the Algerian Communists was to rally the Arabs to the struggle for peace. In such a perspective the struggle of the Arabs for their specific demands retreated to the background.

The Arabs were, for their part, quite cautious. Those who were active within the UGTA followed the orders of priority proposed by the Bureau, though the majority of them were rather reluctant to do so. It was clear that they mistrusted the PCA and recalled that, in order to justify the repression exercised in 1945, in Sétif, by the government of which they were a part, the French and the Algerian communists had talked of a "fascist plot". However the UGTA had relatively a certain edge to the extent that it was organically bound not to the PCA, but to the trade union groups in the mother country. Still the Arabs kept repeating that they were not Marxists. With hindsight one is struck by this political feature because the Communists only on rare occasions broached the problem of their own doctrinal identity. But, in the context of that time, such a declaration meant only that the Arabs, the majority of whom belonged to the MTLD, wanted to be Muslims, "not materialists". Only the UDMA, the friends of Ferhat Abbas and of Dr. Francis, used a more secular, arabizing language. But as they were held to be more "moderate", "bourgeois", the Movement for Peace and the PCA attached little importance to their joining them. Besides, as they passed as representatives of the bourgeoisie, the adherents of the UDMA were deemed to have no future and were viewed with mistrust. But, while being so vigilant with regard to the UDMA's drift towards the bourgeoisie, the Communists winked at the MTLD's adhesion to Islam. On the other hand the French and Arab socialists held on to their genuinely secular views. They remained faithful to their convictions even though the number of the former rose with the arrival of the Spanish Republican refugees, while the number of the latter remained smaller. Nevertheless within the Socialist Party as well as in the MTLD and in the UDMA, there were *strong groups of Arab activists who were motivated by a secular outlook.* Their attachment to Islam related more to those features of its practice which tended to the defence of Arab identity, than to a truly Muslim ideology.

As of that date then, the Algerian Communists were associated with the struggles then being waged in France. To enable their organizations to grow and to exert a greater influence on Algerian society, they tried to strike an alliance with the Arabs, either overlooking their adherence to Islam, or offering resistance to their specific demands. Judging by appearances one might suppose that the Communists were completely hostile to those aspirations inasmuch as they threatened to jeopardize the maintenance of the links of the departments to the French Republic.

A few incidents illustrate this fundamental disagreement. In 1949 the MTLD proposed to the PCA that they should undertake a common action on the basis of a declaration spelling out the rights of the Algerian people and stating that "all the colonial peoples are in a state of war" against "colonialism". The PCA refused to associate itself with the MTLD even though a statement on the rights of the Algerian people had been read at the Conference of Peoples for Peace. However, in Oran, the PCA and the MTLD signed a common text, but it was not published. The Communists and the "centralists" of the MTLD joined together only to fight against the repression which jailed 195 militants during the trials of July 1951. Though it is true that the elections "à la Naegelen" resulted in a common front against the socialists who, in France also, joined in the repression.

This situation arose out of the fact that the *Communist electorate was European*, given the existence of two distinct electoral colleges. In such a context, even with Arabs as members of its bureau, the PCA had only European representatives. The number of the latter was large, considering that the Communists won up to one fifth of the votes in Oran. The paradox is that *the PCA was dominated by Europeans while the UGTA, by statute a French union, had a large majority of Arabs* who could also be members of other Arab political parties: the MTLD, UDMA. In an attempt to algerianize itself the PCA finally modified the composition of its leadership: the Muslim delegates at the sixth Congress of 1952 were in a majority. Subsequently the same change occured among party members, *but not among the voters*.

The PCA thus began to reverse its stance and wanted to form an anti-imperialist front for independence – which the Muslim parties rejected – and rallied to the slogan of a democratic Algerian republic which did not even contain a reference to the Union with France. Yet, at that very moment, the mass of the pied-noir electorate manifested a total hostility to any emancipation of the Arabs that would compromise the monopoly which the Europeans had on the polical life, or more precisely on its representative or parliamentary forms. The exceptions were a few intellectuals or members of the liberal professions who were members of the PCA: they were aware of the fundamental aspirations of the nationalist organizations. Accordingly they found themselves to be standing on shaky ground. However such was not the case with the leftist Catholics who shared the same opinion, but without having any "electoral ambition".

In 1952–54 a succession of resounding echoes from national movements in Iran (Mossadeq), in Egypt (Nasser), in Tunisia (Salah Ben Youssef and Bourguiba), in Morocco (the return of Mohammed V) provided a powerful impulse to the Algerian national movement which had till then been wanting self-assurance. A large number of Algerians were still attracted by the values of integration, despite the many violations and vexations wrought upon the Muslim populations by the administration (rigged elections, repression). The French defeat at Dien Bien Phu prompted a certain number of the militants of the MTLD to break away from a political party which, despite its extremism, had no future. The grafting of the struggle of the Arabs of Algeria onto the Islamo-Arab cause acted like a leaven, like a lever which raised up the CRUA (Comité Révolutionnaire pour l'Unité et l'Action), and soon roused the masses to extraordinary passion. Such was the Algerian revolution which culminated in 1954 with the formation of the FLN and the insurrection of November. The secessionists of the MTLD, won over to the CRUA, then to the FLN constituted, in some way, the *embryo of a future Algerian state* with the prerogatives and function of a government, though without the name: it issued demands for obedience, backed by terror, if necessary; it held a monopoly on decision-making, with terrorism again as a concrete consolidation of its own power; and lastly it internationalized the problem with the help of Nasser and of the Islamo-Arab block.

In this context the PCA was convincingly outmanoeuvred, despite its rallying to the principle of the democratic Algerian Republic. Further the FLN's loyalty to the Islamo-Arab block kept it confined within its former hesitations: it was pointless talking of the resistance that its followers would offer to an apparatus which felt the ground collapsing under its feet, because its troops were mainly Europeans. Moreover, at the same time, the FLN pressed for its dissolution, as it did for that of the other parties.

Still, with hindsight, it would be sheer self-delusion for anyone to imagine that the "revolution" of 2 November 1954 was felt and lived as such in the country. Undoubtedly this date has been consecrated as historic and legitimately so. But it was the FLN party apparatus which made it so. At the time the majority of the European and the Arab populations did not yet know of the FLN: the 2nd of November went unperceived, once the attacks which started the armed struggle became known. At first the terrorist acts occurred only in the djebel and for a year the state of war was not seen as such, except in the Kabylia and in the Aurès. Given, on the other hand, that national organizations maintained a discreet silence on their real aims, the city-dwelling Europeans were living light years away from the emerging tragedy, and persisted in ignoring everything, at all costs. Neither could most of the Muslims clearly discern the way things were going.

The Oran region was spared most of the violence. In the eyes of the majority of the population a political solution seemed to be still possible, even while the troops sent by the mother country were in the process of landing at Algiers. That optimism prevailed even though the leadership of the FLN – as is now known – intended to carry on the struggle up to independence, accompanied, for a few, by the idea of the expulsion of the French. By the end of 1955, however, very few could conceive of such a conclusion of the Algerian problem. The political climate was getting worse. Yet the majority of the Europeans still persisted in their thinking based on the assumption that Algeria was a French department and that many Arabs were simply hoping for a real integration, though without believing firmly in it. The moderates of the UDMA stood at the cross-roads.

The victory of the Republican Front seemed to usher in a genuine change. But everything suddenly collapsed on 6 February 1956 when Guy Mollet capitulated in the face of the uprising of the colonists.

A few months earlier, in Oran, where the Communist Party had lost a major part of its following, a small group of "liberals" attempted to bring about a reconciliation between the two communities. To that end these liberals set up the *Fraternité Algérienne*. At that time the term "liberal" meant anyone who, as in Algiers, was trying to seek out ways to a negotiated solution between the Europeans and Muslims. Arab union leaders, nationalist militants of the FLN, European and Muslim Communists, an assortment of individuals belonging to the fragments of the former MLTD, responded to the call of the "liberals". About two hundred individuals in all, teachers, merchants, members of liberal professions, signed the manifesto, two-thirds of the names being European and one-third, Muslim. That was in a city with an identical proportion of inhabitants from the two communities. Sensing the military solution looming above the horizon, the *Appel* hoped to act to end that war: it asked the French government to engage in a dialogue with *all* the representatives of the Algerian people. For a while the Appeal offered a genuine hope: it was signed in the climate of the Night of 4 August (17 December 1955).

The *Oran républicain* simultaneously published a series of proposals on the future of Algeria which advocated a solution by means of co-sovereignty. The author had written those proposals after consultation with the representatives of all the Algerian organizations.

At the beginning of 1956 *Fraternité algérienne* had resolved to ask the Prefect for an interview with Guy Mollet who was due to arrive soon in Algiers. The delegation that rode to Algiers by train was composed of 5 members, including one CGTA and one official representative of the FLN. Whether it was due to the turn taken by the events on 6 February, or to the previous hardening of the FLN's stance, the fact is that the FLN member did not attend the interview which had been fixed for the 8th.[3] On the occasion of this meeting Guy Mollet assured the delegation that "genuinely free elections" would be held in Algeria. The delegates were dumbfounded at such an abysmal ignorance of the facts of the Algerian problem.

With the retreat of the government on 6 February 1956, any attempt to bring together the Europeans and the Arabs was doomed to failure.

Besides, from the moment of this defeat and of the reversal of Guy Mollet's policy, the FLN contemplated only one solution: the armed struggle up to independence. Still, prior to 6 February, other solutions were still being entertained, in particular the formula of independence which did not imply the massive exodus of the French from Algeria. By forcing Guy Mollet to capitulate, the latter sealed their own defeat.

"*All the forms of struggle à la Abbas must be denounced*": this last feature of the report by Ait Ahmed shows clearly that the leaders of the MTLD movement had taken their cue from Leninist practices. It also takes into account the policy of extermination directed against his Muslim rivals or enemies. The nationalist leaders affirmed and reiterated that they were not "materialists", that is, that they wanted to remain Muslims, not Marxists. But emulating most of the Muslim national movements of the former Russia, they took from Lenin their organizational form – a party established on the principles defined in *What is to be done?* – and later from Mao Tse-tung the idea of a prolonged war. But, prior to 1917, Leninist praxis involved not only the project of a group of avant-garde militants, but also the principle of a single party. His tactics were a product of the circumstances.

In Algeria the first conflict broke out between the leader of the Party, Messali Hadj, supported by Moulay Merbah – who was exiled to Chantilly and later to Niort – and the Central Committee. The former criticized the Committee for relying too much on the United States, and not enough on Morocco and on Tunisia. Above all they objected to the Party's being led by the reformist movements. Ait Ahmed and Ben Khedda were asked to get ready for the armed struggle (1951) and the Central Committee agreed to reconstruct a special organization (OS) under the direction of Abdelmalek Ramdane. But the principle of a request for an authorization from Mesali was soon questioned by some activists who, with a few centralists, constituted the CRUA, with Boudiaf. Borrowing a Soviet expression, they denounced Messali's "personality cult". Mohammed Harbi has unveiled the whole chain of tactical reversals and turnarounds which recall with startling similarity the internal history of the Bolshevik Party during the period 1903–14.

On the eve of the insurrection, two tendencies dominated the situation. The first was that of the messalists: mistrustful of any arrangement with the French government or foreign intermediaries, they wanted to steer close to Islam and showed a marked populist hostility towards the intellectuals. The centralists constituted the second tendency: they comprised a large number of "middle-class intellectuals", such as the druggist Ben Khedda and the journalist Salah Louanchi. They differed from the messalists by their stress on the need to have competent leaders and institutions, to tolerate pluralism, to maintain some distance from tradition, to be fundamentally hostile to the Communists.

Constituted on 23 October 1954, the founder group of the FLN included both activists and centralists of the external delegation, such as Ben Bella and Khider, etc. What, in the final analysis, led them to break off from the messalists and the centralists was that the latter wanted to resolve their political differences before any engagement in the armed struggle. They parted company also with the centralists who deemed the insurrection to be premature. The FLN programme was simply: action first. Taking over from the CRUA they fix as their first goal: "to regroup by using *all means* the forces of the country" (Khider, 7 February 1955).

The overriding idea was that independence could be won only by war. Yet the group that dedicated itself to this end still lacked confidence. That is why it had to prove its existence, and then embark upon the task of explaining. Following this, would come the second phase in which the group would make insecurity general and constitute itself as a counter-power. Finally it would set up free zones, seized from the enemy. The general concept was the sum total of many meetings in which Boudiaf had played a dominant role. But it was Abbane Ramdane who transformed the FLN into a large national mobilization. He had succeeded in imposing himself by his fighting spirit and his courage, not yielding under torture.

The rallying of the other politicians was the consequence of the attitude of the French government, to which, in February 1955, Abbas again appealed for the application of the Statute of Algeria. The rigging of the elections in April convinced the moderates that there was nothing more to be expected of the Government-general or from Paris. The Muslims saw clearly that the reforms of Soustelle were designed to isolate the MTLD or the FLN. They asked what could be done when leaders, like Ferhat Abbas, had ceaselessly asked for simple reforms and indeed for integration, while the colonists obstinately refused to make the slightest genuine concession.

In the attacks of 2 November 1954 the UDMA had seen nothing but "despair, chaos, adventure". But the reactions of the government in Paris and in Algiers were manoeuvres; they laid the ground for the repression; and there was no longer any question of allowing the "terrorists" to be crushed. Ferhat Abbas met with Abbane Ramdane and they agreed to fight each on his side on two parallel lines: the armed struggle and the political front. However this "pact" did not stand in the way of the FLN organizations of Constantine which killed several of the local leaders of the UDMA, among whom was the nephew of Ferhat Abbas. Soon the violence of the repression, of the war, of terrorism, exerted such pressure on the UDMA as to convince it of the futility of following the political path. "Things are getting out of our hands", said Ahmed Francis and Ferhat Abbas who joined the FLN in April 1956. The centralists followed suit.

"The political parties had to disappear." Even the Communists yielded to that necessity. Only violence would force the recalcitrant ones to rally

– if the violence of the colonizer did not do the trick, as the leaders of the FLN thought. As Krim Belkacem put it: "Otherwise it is war."

However, for Messali Hadj, the integration of the reformists to the FLN provided clear proof of their betrayal, for they were "all members excluded from the MTLD". Moreover the MNA (Algerian National Movement: the new name of Messali's MTLD following a schism) believed that the FLN was totally under the control of Nasser who was supplying it with money and arms. This was echoed repeatedly by Jacques Soustelle. The MNA too intended to have recourse to direct action, but not without international-izing the Algerian problem, in order to place it before the United Nations for consideration. The leaders of both the FLN and the MNA were equally uncompromising and equally determined to have independence. But, on the ground, the FLN had a marked superiority while the MNA was taken by surprise by the insurrection of November 1954, which broke out without its having any knowledge of it. It was also taken unawares when the FLN eliminated its local cadres, repeating its actions against the UDMA in the Constantinois. In Marnia and later in Oujda the militants of the MNA fell into a trap and were murdered.

From then on the internal war that divided the Algerians exceeded in violence anything that had been experienced hitherto. Taking into account only what happened abroad, where there were about 10,000 to 15,000 members of the FLN and as many of the MNA, 12,000 attacks, 4,000 dead and 9,000 wounded were recorded. In Algeria itself the numbers were far higher than this. Slowly the FLN gained the upper hand in this fratricidal war, which recalled the struggles between the Bolsheviks and the other revolutionaries in 1918–19. The FLN's need to be the only party, to hold undivided sway over power, drove it to exterminate the hesitant. As a result some of the latter turned against the FLN, "betrayed" it: the Bellounis case is a typical example. By 1958 all the historical leaders of the MNA had been assassinated and an attempt on Messali's life failed.

In this war within the war, the "error" of the MNA had been to seek to subordinate the armed groups to it, in the context of its "historical" priority, instead of building its own armed force. Further its uncompromising nationalism had antagonized the Arab world, particularly Nasser, who had Mezerna arrested in Cairo and supported Ben Bella, a member of the external delegation of the former MLTD. Its relative Islamism deprived it of the support of Nehru and Soekarno, though ironically it was banking on the consequences of internationalization in its dealings with France.

The Algerian conflict was different from the Indo-Chinese in that it began with a war without the name, with faceless terrorism and repression. Such a situation generated a confused environment, characterized by the refusal to acknowledge that an irreversible trial of strength had been engaged. The November 1954 explosion became a real war only after the massacres of August 1955. The war became total, with its trail of cruel acts, during the battle of Algiers where 8,000 parachutists enter the town, with the mandate of carrying out a police action (7 January–24 September 1957). The bombing of the "Otomatic", an Algerian café, of the "Coq hardi", the lynching of Arabs in reprisal, that infernal round of "blood and shit" ("du sang et de la merde") as Marcel Bigeard put it. It ended with the success of General Massu who arrested Larbi Ben M'Hidi, who soon commited "suicide", Yassef Saadi and forced Abbane Ramdane to leave the capital.

But on the French side a moral crisis accompanied this military victory: General de la Bollardière and Paul Teitgen, General Secretary of the Algiers police, resigned to protest against the methods used by General Massu.

In the interior of the country the FLN's army of national liberation was reinforced despite the Morice line, which was raised at the frontiers to prevent the arming of the fellaghas. With the help of 250,000 Muslim back-up troops – the harkis – General Salan scored a number of successes, to such an extent that in 1958 Robert Lacoste reiterated that the victory would belong to the one who held out "till the last quarter hour". In actuality, the Algerian nationalists were engaged in a veritable fratricidal war as evinced by the massacre in Melouza of 374 villagers who were considered to be loyal to Messali Hadj (May 1957). Meanwhile, subsequent to the meeting of the conference of Soummam, a new schism had divided the nationalists: it opposed Abbane Ramdane and the representatives of the combatants to the Khider-Ben Bella group which challenged the "counter-state" instituted by the conference from which the Aurès, the external delegation, Oranie and the Federation of France were absent. Khider and Ben Bella further denounced the objection to the Islamist nature of future Algerian institutions; they rejected the secularity of the State and refused to consider the feasibility of a place reserved for the European minority.

The prolongation of the war and of the military operations produced the "13 May 1958" in Algiers.[4] During the same period the French forces under the command of General Challe, 500,000 men strong, scored successes against the armed groups (*katibas*) of the different regions (*willayas*) of the FLN State. The "pacification" of "a thousand villages" was carried out by repressive steps or by "forced regroupings" which affected close to two million Algerians. On the battlefield "victory" seemed to be within reach.

At the beginning of 1960 General Massu stated that, in such conditions, he did not understand General de Gaulle's policy any more. The latter had actually denounced the "Algeria of nostalgia" ("l'Algérie de papa") and incurred the anger of the pieds-noirs who did not want to hear any talk about the "peace of the brave". In such a climate the "week of the barricades" was a foretaste of the generals' putsch and the reign of the OAS.

In Angola: the political parties as instruments

The liberation of the Portuguese colonies grew out of events which recall the situations in Indo-China and in Algeria. That is so in regards to the project for independence, the reaction of the mother country, the beginning of the war. Actually the war broke out suddenly, in Angola as in Algeria, by a number of simultaneous attacks on the military outposts of Luanda on 4 February 1961. Leadership was provided by one of the nationalist movements, the Movement for the Liberation of Angola (MPLA). Though the MPLA was actually outflanked by its troops, yet its leadership remained firmly in the hands of Agostino Neto and Mario de Andrado, two assimilados, as well as of Amilcar Cabral, the leader of the African Party for the Independence of Portuguese Guinea and of Cape Verde (PAIGC). The leaders borrowed from the strategies already adopted by Ho Chi Minh and by Mao Tse-tung for "prolonged war" and guerilla activity. Theirs was a revolutionary project. But, as in Vietnam, it proceeded through phases towards sovereignty. It had similarities with the Franco-Vietnamese situation in the sense that this independence movement – inspired by the independence of French Guyana and traumatized by the events occurring in Rhodesia-Zimbabwe, and by the murder of Patrice Lumumba – was resisted by a mother country which decides to re-invest in its colonial possessions. At that time the Portuguese population amounted to more than 250,000 in Angola, 130,000 in Mozambique.

The events of 1961 exploded the myth of racial harmony, triggering the war, in which Portuguese Guyana – Cabral was murdered in 1973 – also joined. Led by Samora Machel, the Frelimo of Mozambique in its turn launched itself into a struggle for independence, more or less in conjunction with the Africans of Zimbabwe. They had no support in the mother country.

Several other features bring to mind the events which happened in North Africa. The first is the impatience of the nationalist leaders of the former Portuguese colonies. They saw the entire African continent liberated, with themselves as the only exception, lagging far behind. This recalls the case of the Algerians who witnessed the independence of Libya, Tunisia and Morocco. Above all, in Angola particularly, several liberation movements engaged in a merciless fratricidal war, again recalling the feuds between the FLN and the MNA, with the difference that in Angola the struggles for power and the ideological differences interfered with ethnic conflicts. Such a situation lent credence to the opinion that, instead of one, there were actually several nationalisms, with their antagonisms and divergences coinciding with those of the society. However, in Angola, as in the other Portuguese possessions, there was no racial divide of the kind that existed elsewhere, the split was between the *assimilados* and the *indigenos*. The former did not necessarily lead the latter's revolt or involve themselves with it. Such was at the least the case of the urban, revolutionary MPLA, the leaders of which were well acquainted with Lisbon and the jails of the PIDE. It was quite different from the UPNA (Union of the Populations of the North of Angola), an exclusively Bakongo movement led by Holden Roberto. He transformed the movement into the UPA (Union of the Peoples of Angola) which gave it an expansionist colour though, in actuality, it commanded the support of only 15 percent of the population of Angola. It was a homogeneous movement, without a revolutionary ideology. It relied on the other Bakongos of the Belgian Congo where it found a haven. The conflict between the UPA and the MPLA made it possible for the Portuguese to go through the year 1961, which was marked by a reciprocal social massacre with from 8,000 to 50,000 African dead and at least 1,800 whites massacred first. The northern movement was crushed and an entire section of the Bakongo population took refuge in Congo-Léopoldville. Still Holden Roberto created a pan-Angolan government in exile (1963). The FLNA was recognized by several African States. In the meantime, one of the dissidents, Jonas Savimbi, rallied the Ovimbundu, an important ethnic group on which the MPLA was training its sights.

What makes the difference between the anti-Portuguese independence movements and all the others, including the Indo-Chinese, is the double internationalization which was the goal of their struggle. The UPA-FLNA was, *via* Congo-Léopoldville, supported by the United States; the MPLA received financial and military help from the USSR and Cuba. In fact Castro, in 1966, said: "The people understood its duties, because it knew that there was only one enemy, the one who was attacking our shores and our lands. It was the same enemy who was attacking the others. That is why we proclaim that, in all places, the revolutionary movements can rely on Cuban combatants." Indeed the latter arrived in Angola, to fight alongside the MPLA. But, in the context of the Sino-Soviet conflict, the Chinese came to the aid of UNITA, which was already receiving the support of South Africa, geographically so close to it. As a result Angola became the micro-cosm where the three camps which were vying for world hegemony clashed, while, simultaneously, the United Nations, on the occasion of its 25th anniversary in 1970, condemned Portugal, South Africa and Rhodesia.

In Guinea-Bissau, at the same time, the PAIGC completed the organiza-tion of the "liberated zones". The commander of the Portuguese forces General Spinola understood that a military solution was henceforth impossible, despite the efforts exerted by the mother country which allocated half of its national budget to the colonial conflicts. Produced by the convergence of the military forces and popular sentiment, the "carna-tion revolution" of 1974 brought to an end the Salazar regime which had lasted too long.

General Spinola, the chief of the military junta, had repudiated the idea of a colonial war which could not be won. He wanted to build a reformed

Portugal and associate it with Europe. Negotiations had taken place with the independence movements. But it was the army which, in control of the situation on the ground, dealt with them. As in Algeria, the colonists left (fewer quitted Mozambique, fewer still Cape Verde where the *assimilados* seized power). But here it was the army which brought democracy and, in the colonies, after the longest war (1961–74) was able to make peace.

The "Shining Path" of Peru: a syncretistic movement

Abimael Guzman was arrested by the army in 1992, and President Fujimori had him jailed in a barred cage to enable the population to see him and realize that he was no longer a public danger. Nevertheless the "Shining Path" (*Sendero Luminoso*) has resumed its activities, because it has its roots in several traditions. Its localization also reveals its significance.

If Ho Chi Minh and Mao Tse-tung were the successors of Lenin, a third generation of nationalist revolutionaries has since come to the fore. It adopts arguments and the techniques from both the former European model and from the anti-colonial model. Pol Pot represented it in Cambodia. But at the present moment it is most intensely active in Andean America. Central America follows the Cuban model, while Peru especially, Columbia, Bolivia, display a syncretism made up, on one hand, of the Marxist theory advocated by José Mariategui who views Peruvian society as a colonial society, and, on the other hand, of the terrorist practices which, in Peru, recall those of the Algerian FLN, backed by a Leninist rationale. In Columbia guerilla activity is the dominant feature.

The Sendero proclaims itself to be Maoist, hardline Maoist, in solidarity with the "Gang of Four". In the heart of the Andes the Sendero spews its hatred against the "traitor" Deng Hsiao-ping by displaying dogs hanging from trees and thereby at the same time giving a warning to all those of his ilk. The Sendero is equally hostile to the "Albanian renegades" and certainly to Moscow which has betrayed the cause of the world revolution. Its only foreign associates, which together with it constitute the "International of the Sendero", or the Fourth Sword after Marx, Lenin and Mao, are the Maoist Communist Party of Columbia, and about a dozen of revolutionary groups from various countries.

The Sendero originated in an environment of poor students, especially the sons of peasants. It derives its theory and practice from a variety of revolutionary sources as much as from Maoism. From Maoism it takes the central concept of a "prolonged war" (a peasant war, at least in its earliest stage, though urban guerilla activity can take over from it or join it). In addition it makes use of the technique of the "fish in the water": the movement adopts it, as Mao did in Yenan, by collaborating in the works and days of the peasants. It expels with jeers the inoffensive, or otherwise, state officials or agents; it even executes them so that the population can develop the consciousness that the government and the state do not count any more since "they have disappeared". The peasants and the Sendero have taken over.

Trotskyism has contributed a few militants to one of the branches of the Sendero. It provides the movement with a tendency towards militarization, towards a permanent need for action with the aim of fostering a constant, obsessive tension.

But the Sendero takes its essential doctrine from Jose Mariategui, the father of Latin-American Marxism. This is based on the identification of Peruvian (or Columbian) society with *a semi-colonial, semi-feudal society which, in the absence of a bourgeoisie, needs a state bureaucracy.* That is the core of Sendero's ideology. For, even if the transfer to Peru of the practices and slogans of thirties China provides the movement with its roots and with a model, the analogy with China nevertheless remains a little deceptive. In many of its features, Sendero has greater similarity with the nationalist organizations which led the struggle for independence. Though it claims allegiance to Marxism, yet it has an affinity less with the Vietminh, than with the Algerian FLN and with Pol Pot in Cambodia, above all in its combined use of terrorism and of terror.

Like the FLN in its first phase, Sendero terrorism strikes at targets which define its action: it destroys ballot boxes, it attacks government institutions – police stations, law courts, it executes big land-owners, it sabotages multinational firms. Subsequently, in a second phase, the Sendero completes its action by striking at government agents of *subordinate* rank: the latter are, in one way or the other, eliminated in order to create "a liberated zone". In its third phase, the movement takes over a territory – for instance, the Ayacucho region. In these poor, traditionally under-administered regions the Sendero establishes a counter-power which, in the name of the armed insurrection, now exercises its authority from on high, by means of "state terror". Terrorism and state terror thus complement each other: the reciprocal action ensures the extension of the movement as well as its internal consolidation. But the Sendero does not move up to the fourth stage of terrorism, that is, the "blind" terrorism which in Algeria accompanied the insurrection. It denounces it and even executes those who are caught indulging in it, thereby signifying that it has taken deep enough root in an entire part of the population, that part where it finds itself like "a fish in water". That was evident in the Ayacucho region where tens of thousands of metis and Indians accompanied the coffin of a "victim of repression".

The Sendero arose first in Ayacucho. Here the founder of the movement, Abimael Guzman, called "Comrade Gonzalo", a former professor of philosophy and Kant specialist, became the head of personnel at the university where he recruited the first members of the nucleus of the future Sendero. His action was the culmination of the nth split among the Maoists.

The condemnation of "blind" terrorism seems to be a theoretical subtlety if one measures it against the thousands of "innocent" persons who have been assassinated. But the doctrine and the tactics remain in place. With the widely held trust in the inevitable extension of the movement, recourse to "blind" terrorism would be useless, especially as it would antagonize certain intellectual circles. Actually the latter are already frightened by the present "selective" terror and terrorism. They deplore their excesses, but do so rather meekly, for in many circumstances they endorse the analysis of the Sendero. We shall come back to this point.

In doctrinal terms justice thus meted out is not "blind" terrorism, for the "victims" were "dogs" who opposed the fulfilment of the revolution. To understand this concept properly, one needs to refer back to the Bolshevik Revolution and the Tcheka. Emulating Saint-Just, Dzerzhinsky said: "*The Tcheka does not judge; it strikes*". He also said that the Tcheka did not have to know if a citizen was innocent or guilty, nor even what his "opinions" were. His membership of a class defined his role, and as a consequence his fate. "*By the very fact that he reigns, Louis XVI is guilty*", wrote Saint-Just during the King's trial. By the simple fact that, *whether knowingly or not*, they serve the state or government policy, some peasants are guilty and must be struck down. Here is an example: if the Sendero gives the order to "starve the town", all those who henceforth do not limit themselves to self-sufficient farming or cattle breeding are guilty and must accordingly be punished. Conversely, in mid-November 1987, 17 peasants were killed because, under pressure from the "legitimate" authorities, they had abandoned the cultivation of coca in order to grow food crops. The Sendero wanted to maintain the production of coca because it shared in the proceeds of its sale. That is why the authorities refer to the followers of the Sendero as "narco-terrorists". Hence the terror unleashed against the peasants by the Sendero, though it appears "blind", is actually not so. It is *functional*. But who can see the difference? The extreme cruelty and violence of the criminal actions perpetrated by the Sendero victimize the stupefied populations. The latter no longer know which blows are the most to be feared: those struck by the armed forces – who have arrived to defend them – or those of the Sendero which are usually deadly. On this score the government, formed as a result of democratically held elections, is bitter. At the beginning of the 1980s, President Belaunde spoke of a "plot hatched by foreign hands". As a matter of fact, under the pretext that it denounces only state crimes, Amnesty International was more prompt to make public and denounce the "abuses" of the armed forces than to publish an account of the crimes committed by Sendero, which were more numerous and far more cruel and bloody.

Wherever it has not established itself as a genuine power or even as a counter-power, that is, beyond the Ayacucho zone and a part of the sierra on the south, the Sendero maintains its agitation by means of spectacular acts. These are some of its favoured psychological weapons: cutting telephone lines, plunging a city in darkness by blowing up a power station or network, as in Lima. Even though President Garcia is an energetic, popular man the democratic system seems to be terribly vulnerable, particularly powerless, in spite of the military operations conducted in the mountains. In Lima one is surprised to see that, instead of effectively protecting public services, the police forces have transformed their stations into blockhouses in an attempt to protect themselves. In the interior of the country, the army or the civil guards sometimes avoid spending the night in their posts or other official quarters. Instead they prefer to sleep in the open, feeling themselves to be in greater safety. Moreover the attempt to increase the number of beneficiaries of the agrarian reform has created many problems for the government. For henceforth the beneficiaries run the risk of becoming victims of Sendero, in the same way as the fellahs who benefited from the Soustelle reforms were hit by the FLN.

But the analogy ends there. Peru is not in the true sense a colonial society. Certainly the society comprises, on one side, Indians and, on the other, genuine Creoles and others. But, placed at the top of the pyramid of power and wealth, these Creoles have suffered a lot by the reforms implemented by the military – the Peruvian "revolution" of the seventies – and today their hegemony and their legitimacy are shaken and increasingly being called into question by the rise of the *mestizos*, people of mixed race, who denounce them for the flight of their capital to Miami, financial scandals and "legal" corruption. On the other hand the *mestizos*, who constitute the majority of the population, do to a great extent manage the affairs of the country being increasingly represented in the administration, the army, the universities, the tourist enterprises, the medical profession. In the country they have taken advantage of the agrarian reform. They speak Spanish, dress in the European style, in short, they have become "creolized". That is why they are spoken of as a "Creole society", that wants to pass for a Western society, even if the genuinely Creole "aristocracy" has cut itself off and prefers to live in Miami rather than in Lima, while still parroting the phrase "in Peru, we are all *mestizos*". Peru's mixed-race population is socially and ethnically quite diversified. The fraction of that society which is not fully integrated or rather which has not, in the sierra, benefited from the agrarian reform, constitutes the ground most favourable to the action of the Luminous Path, in addition to the growing slum population which has been driven away from the sierra by poverty.

In Ayacucho, one of the poorest provinces of Peru, at the centre of the territories aflame with insurrection, there exists a combination of opposing forces similar to what obtained, a century and a half earlier, at the time of the struggle for independence. Then the Indians, allied to the Spaniards, had fought against the Creole revolt. Today they seem to be the "objective" allies of the integrated Creoles and *mestizos*, but against the revolt of the Sendero with its following of "marginalized" *mestizos*.

This simplified analysis of the Sendero rebellion shows at least that is not a native movement, even if some of its theoretical framework, derived from Mariategui, has roots in native tradition and even flatters it. Besides the natives are flattered by everybody: the governing authorities, the opposition, the intellectuals, the pressure groups. It is fashionable to refer to Tupac Amaru, the last Inca rebel. Federico Garcia's film *Tupac Amaru* (1983) is screened in theatres filled to capacity in Lima and in Cuzco for either a *mestizo* or an Indian audience. In the film the last Inca, after a last Indian revolt, is finally defeated in 1781, due to the treachery of a Spaniard. This is film director's licence, for Tupac Amaru's defeat was due to other causes, in particular the divisions among the Indians who were no more united then than they are today. Their history did not begin with the arrival of the Spaniards; some of their present divisions are the legacy of a very ancient situation. In Peru, the characteristic nature of the conflict derives from a stratification which is difficult to discern. But the selection of this story reveals the feeling of guilt of Peruvian intellectuals and artists who, as Creoles or as creolized *mestizos*, have written the record of the conquest and of its consequences. In some ways their analyses have fed the expectations implied in the programmes of those revolutionary organizations whose activities for a long time remained merely verbal. By taking to action, and in such a bloody way, and by providing little or no explanation of its actions, the Sendero Luminoso has them with their backs to the wall.

Liberation theologies are another form of revolutionary movement. They thrive in Indian America; they were revived by Vatican II and by the Medellin Conference of 1968. Their proponents want to confront the institutional violence of which millions of paupers are the victims. As secular Christians or as members of the Church they deem this violence to be unbearable. Their participation in the political struggle has become more active since Castro's ideology fell into discredit, and since the violent death of Salvador Allende in Chile sounded the death knell of other forms of social reform. In Nicaragua, the Sandinista revolution had close links with Christians and the Church placed itself on the side of the oppressed, as it did in Guatemala. Yet a section of the senior clergy, with the support of John-Paul II, questions this revolutionary activism, which divides Catholics and favours the action of Protestant sects who, linked to the United States and well financed, engage in daily, effective social work, in a process of rallying and neutralizing the populations. One even hears talk of a "war of the Churches" in some Central American countries.

10

LIBERATION OR
DECOLONIZATION

Decolonization, the "change of sovereignty", was not due solely to peoples' struggles for liberation. As early as the sixteenth century, during the first wave of European expansion to the Americas, there were movements in the mother countries against slavery and the slave trade. Together with others, Voltaire asked: "What do the colonies profit us?" Such questioning and criticism had very limited effects.

Indirectly the rivalries among the powers also helped peoples and nations to loosen the hold upon them of the colonizing states. That was the case with Siam and China in the nineteenth century. But, they also had other secondary effects which took a long time to be felt.

In the twentieth century, one finds the same factors at work, though in different forms. But, after 1945, the pressure of the two Great Powers did contribute to bring colonization to an end. In this context the Suez crisis (1956) played a big role.

Lastly, the implosion of 1989–91 in the former USSR constitutes one of the features of the crisis that overtook the regime – though it is questionable if the consequences of this crisis have fulfilled the expectations of the non-Russian populations.

The role played by the movements of resistance to colonial domination has varied according to the different periods of history. Independence movements were vigorous at the time of the conquest, as much in black Africa, for example, as in Vietnam. Sometimes they quietened down later as a result the policies enacted by the conquerors, or as a result of the effects of evangelization. Then, subsequently, they reasserted themselves with renewed power, especially after the end of the Second World War, when a second colonial occupation became the order of the day, an occupation which was more concerned with profits and sought greater control of all the aspects of the agricultural production. This dramatic change was particularly evident in tropical countries: Kenya, Malaysia.

In French North Africa great was the political disappointment of the Arabs who felt they had been shabbily rewarded for the loyalty they had shown during the two wars. Their nationalism was rekindled, though some might have believed it had been on its way out. Actually it had never been completely extinguished. From 1945 on the colonists' opposition to any type of reform revived it.

At the same time, colonizers, especially the English, came to rely on social groups which had existed before their arrival, or on new ones which they had fostered, and on their good will. If these groups resisted, defaulted or rebelled, ultimately the colonial power found itself disarmed. This was a process which developed, by stages, in India, perhaps even, for France, in Morocco and Tunisia, and culminated in violence in Malaysia and Kenya. There is no need to mention the case of territories where – as in Algeria – the very idea of a native participation in the direction of the country was not entertained.

However, left to themselves, the liberation movements were rarely able to defeat the occupier militarily, though such was the case in Burma, Vietnam and Kenya. The military inferiority of the colonized was far too great, especially in black Africa, and the conclusion of a military confrontation could prove to be fatal.

There is another feature of liberation movements that is worth mentioning: their internal divisions, especially betweem collaborators, those who opposed collaboration, and those who tried to steer a middle course. A further characteristic feature consists in the oppressed being oppressors in their turn – in the USSR the Georgians maintained their hold over the Abkhaz – to the extent that divisions among the colonized peoples could be stronger than their unity in the face of the colonizer: for example, the Muslims and non-Muslims of Nigeria and of Sudan, the Azeris and the Armenians in their confrontation with the Russians.

Finally, in some cases, the metropolitan policy was able to delay or channel the rise of nationalism: the British set up the West Indian Federation, the South Arabian Federation, and France organized the French Union.

Conversely the outcome of colonization influenced the mother countries themselves, and not only with regard to colonial issues. Very early, during the conflict with the American colonists, Burke and Locke had become aware of the adverse effect of colonial domination on the democratic tradition of the English. Much later, during the Third Republic the colonial question became the pretext for political divisions in France: it led to the sacralization of the republican system, to the rallying together of the monarchists. Moreover, for their part, the colonial peoples or those who were fated to experience European domination did not fail to notice that their resistance had triggered a revolution in Russia in 1905 and, in France, a coup in 1958, the creation of the OAS and the putsch staged by the generals. Moreover Salazar confided to Pierre Messmer, a minister in De Gaulle's government, that his regime would collapse if the Portuguese empire fell (personal communication to Marc Ferro).

The point of view of the intellectuals: were the colonies profitable?

It is worth asking whether or not imperialism was a profitable venture. It is a question the enormous scope of which still preoccupies the minds of politicians and historians. Thinking minds raised this question very early; but it became crucial only in the twentieth century.

The first inkling was given by the British experiment with free trade on the eve of the First World War. Up to the middle of the nineteenth century the structure of trade between the mother country and the colonies remained that of mercantilist times, of the Navigation Acts. Customs preferences lasted till then. But then a marked change took place. Britain had become highly industrialized; she sold her manufactured goods in exchange for raw materials. India topped the list, accounting for a third of all colonial trade: she exported drugs, dyes and luxuries. The main commodities were Indian indigo, sugar from the West Indies, and wood from Canada. In return the Empire receives one third of British exports. But these exports reached a state of stagnation (F. Crouzet, 1964, pp. 290ff).

The turnaround first came about as a result of Britain's growing need for food products as a result of the conversion of the country to industrialization and of its demographic growth (from 21 million in 1851 to 41 million in 1911). In addition to these needs, Britain had to be supplied with rubber, later with oil. The settlement colonies – like Canada, Australia and New Zealand – also had a large share of this trade: they contributed wheat, meat, and so on. But two new developments intervened to accelerate the change in the structure of trade: the lowering of maritime freightages (by from 50 to 75 percent) resulting from the use of steamships and the building of railways which spearheaded the British colonization of Canada, Australia and of India. A massive investment of British capital made the construction of the railways possible: 60 percent of the capital collected in London between 1865 and 1894 was diverted to that effect. Still it was the local entrepreneurs who ensured the development of the production: the main function of British capital was to lay down the groundwork for economic take-off and growth.

It goes without saying that the export of capital was carried out to the detriment of investments in Britain itself. But that enabled the new countries, especially the dominions, to develop and to buy British goods. The crack in this system of trade occurred when Canada began to receive its equipment supplies from the United States.

The settlement colonies were the ones to benefit most from this new development. The share of the Empire in British imports went from 1 percent to 25 percent for meat, from 0.5 to 48 percent for wheat. But it went down for sugar, especially sugar from the West Indies, because of competition with European beet sugar; for coffee because Brazil got a larger share than Ceylon (Sri Lanka); for indigo, eliminated by chemical inventions. Overall, between 1854 and 1913, the Empire's share of total imports scarcely increased, from 22 to 25 percent. But a turnaround occurred at the expense of the former possessions. Accordingly the share of imports from the Empire showed proportionately little increase in relation to imports originating from other places, though its worth had quadrupled. On the other hand, the value of exports to the Empire had increased eightfold.

The important feature of this system of trade is that imperial commerce grew, even though the exports of capital abroad decreased. If the share of the Empire went down during periods of general prosperity (for example, 1868–72), it increased during depressions, thus acting like a safety valve.

Especially in Canada, the progress of foreign competition in imperial markets was real, from the moment when the imports from the Empire no longer consisted, as they did earlier, mainly of the textiles, but of equipment goods, which happened as soon as colonial countries had railways. Electrical equipment, machines and automobiles came most often exclusively from Britain. On the other hand if the dominions sold foodstuffs and raw materials, the dividends they brought in went also in part back to Britain.

Thanks to this system Britain found herself at the centre of a global network of multilateral transactions and settlements, whereas previously these had been simply segmental. The first partnership between Britain and her colonies had culminated in a serious crisis, that is, American independence. But the second partnership ensured the hegemony of the City and accordingly guaranteed imperial self-sufficiency, that is, the Empire's autonomy with regard to the rest of the world.

It is partly illusory to see a correlation between economic progress and the policy of territorial expansion. True, at the time of Disraeli or of Chamberlain, they were synchronous phases. But, in the final reckoning, what mattered most was the Empire's role as a relay, which did so much to assure the world dominance of the English economy. After all, with the exception of South Africa, the territories which were annexed during the time of expansionist hysteria were almost all areas devoid of any particular economic interest. Psychological motivations were more powerful than mere economic ones.

However the situation underwent a complete reversal with the Great War, and still more with the Crash of 1929. To withstand the depression and resist foreign competition, attempts to give shape to the dreams of imperial isolation were made, especially after the Ottawa accords. The aim of these dreams was imperial self-sufficiency. But soon the self-insufficiency of the Empire became the cause of the economic decline of Britain. As a matter of fact Britain followed a policy which was doomed to failure when she persisted in depending on her strictly colonial Empire, at a time when the Empire of the Dominions was increasingly becoming more and more independent. It had become impossible for Great Britain to "shut herself up within such a closed system" (A. Siegfried). The decline was hastened by the ordeal of the Second World War.

In 1939 Great Britain still engaged in an "inter-nations" commerce comparable with that of the United States and had an industrial base as highly developed as that of Germany. At any rate, London was the best place for the export of capital. The all-out mobilization required by four years of war transformed the country which even became the debtor of its imperial possessions. For instance, India which not long before had been a debtor, henceforth had a credit of one billion pounds sterling. Furthermore the cold war and the conflicts in the Middle East continued to burden the budget while industrial competitors, Italy, Germany and Japan, could rebuild their economy without being hampered with these burdens. According to Hugh Dalton, Chancellor of the Exchequer, the economic and financial crisis of the end of the forties was a major factor in the disengagement of Great Britain from India, Burma, Ceylon (Sri Lanka), and Palestine. Economic weakness and the cost of military operations liable to slow down the nationalist movements further hastened many a departure after 1960.

Elsewhere these difficulties had a cumulative effect, by a sort of inverse process. It became imperative to turn towards the tropical colonies particularly in order to obtain raw materials or finished products – so that they need not be paid for in dollars. This led to strict control over the production of some of these countries, especially Malaysia with its rubber, black Africa also. That policy became known as the "second colonial occupation". Associated with the sterling zone, these countries were tied to the British economy with the result that that they became grouped with countries like Australia, South Africa and India which till then had economic links only with London. But Britain had to pay the price of conceding them local powers which rendered them semi-independent. Malaysia, Nigeria and Ghana were on their way to independence from the middle fifties on, without this process being directly attributed to the weakness of the notion of suzerainty. Its consequences were "oblique".

Whatever may have been the reservations linked to the decision by Great Britain to join in the reconstruction of Europe in 1961, it nevertheless indicates a relative disengagement from the Empire, despite "imperial preference" continuing to be the dogma and the law of the British government. From 1950 to 1970 Great Britain's trade with her Empire went from half to a quarter of the totality of her trade. There was a global reorientation, a sort of economic disengagement which testified to a relative lack of interest in an outmoded system of relations. Its place was taken by an interplay of more dynamic connections with European,

American or Japanese partners. And thus came to an end a global world system of which Great Britain had been the mainspring.

The new situation therefore did not require the maintenance of the overseas dependencies in the straitjacket of the old political system. The multinationals could henceforth profitably substitute themselves for it.

In France the economic aspect of the colonial problem is more drastically analysed, in terms of the "cost" which the Empire represented. Questions were raised as to whether up to 1930 the Empire had been a "good bargain": in 1913, for its conquest, it had cost per year 20 percent of the current expenses of the state; its preservation and its management accounted for nearly 7 percent of these same current expenses, that is, the expenses for police, officials, and so on. It was a time when the Banque d'Indochine was making profits at the rate of 69 percent, the mines of Ouagla made profits at the rate of 120 percent. From 1913 to 1929 the Empire became the first commercial partner and the biggest financial trader. It was a financial burden on the State; it yielded big returns to the private sector.

Yet the 1929 Crash ushered in a process that started to separate the mother country from the Empire. This was, in the first instance, due to the decline of the industries which had their best outlet in the colonies: textiles, agribusiness. It was also due to an inversion of the pattern: during the glory days when colonial imperialism coexisted harmoniously with a dynamic economy, public opinion more or less ignored the colonial experience; it rallied round to it later on, at the very moment when a part of the business world was moving away from it. But had the burden really been shed?

For its part the State was embarked on a policy of sacrifices. For example, in North Africa, from 1948 to 1951, direct metropolitan financial aid increased fourfold. During the same period 15 percent of French investment went overseas, reaching 20 percent in 1955. Jacques Marseille has computed that 9 percent of the revenue paid by French taxpayers went on expenses incurred overseas. But "far from exhibiting the scope of this financial effort, it seems on the contrary that the French administration went out of its way to hide it" (pp. 93–153). Such practices fed the growing misunderstanding between native elites and French representatives: according to one of the latter the "moral" benefits were not equal to the sacrifices freely made. The fact is that most of the time the populations were not aware of these sacrifices, considering that in North Africa, for example, most of the benefits of these efforts went to the colonists, to the officials themselves, above all to the companies. Naturally the whole population shared in some of that beneficence. But that share could not be assessed. On the other hand, the standard of living of the colonists rose, over three generations, higher than that of the Arabs, higher even that that of the metropolitan French. How could such an advantage be measured?

Simultaneously the portion of the colonial imports coming from the mother country had risen from 27 percent in 1938 to 44 percent in 1952. In France 450,000 people worked for the overseas market. One of the arguments of the defenders of the Empire was precisely that its loss would trigger a tidal wave of unemployment.

Overall the financial groups maintained, in relation to the colonial problem, a cautious waiting attitude. A few rare groups may have been in favour of independence: like the Walker group, the mines of Zellidja, allied to the Morgan bank. But most of the big groups remained neutral, while the middle- and small-sized groups, like the majority of the colonists, were generally opposed to independence.

The latter, in chorus with all those who were left from the "colonial party", denounced the defeatism of the mother country. According to Gabriel Puaux, member of the Central Committee of Overseas France, this criticism did not refer only to Communists or anti-colonialists, but to "defeatists" of every kind. The metropolitan administration also had its defeatists who deemed that the colonial burden was too onerous: they feared that the mother country would reduce its own investment at home.

This was the argument which became known as "cartierism", a theory which, unlikely as it seems, was enunciated in *Paris-Match*, which popularized it. Others – Pierre Moussa, Raymond Aron – had already made similar statements; but these did not receive any publicity.

Raymond Cartier's idea was that neither Switzerland nor Sweden, themselves stable and prosperous countries, had ever had a colony; and Holland, which did not have an Empire any more, had subsequently become richer than it ever was in the past. "[Holland] lost her colonies in the worst conditions, when it was taken for granted that her existence depended on the East Indies, a collection of treasures, oil, rubber, rice, tea, coffee, tin, coprah, spices . . . After only a few years she has acquired more prosperity and well-being than ever before. She would not be in the same situation today if, instead of modernizing her factories and reclaiming the Zuiderzee, she had to build railways in Java, to cover Sumatra with dams, to pay family allowances to the polygamous men of Borneo."

The waste observed by Raymond Cartier during an investigation in black Africa lay at the source of those formulas which became instant hits: "It would have perhaps been better to establish an Office of the Loire than an Office of the Niger, to build in Nevers the super-hospital of Lomé, and in Tarbes the Lycée of Bobo-Dioulasso."

Georges Bidault denounced those who, in France, had "an accountant's vision". Nevertheless he made it clear that, with regard to Algeria, Saharan oil would tilt the scale in favour of the beneficiary.

311

The identity of the nation and the role of the dependencies

France

A host of political groups opposed those who believed that the greatness of France would survive economic withdrawal and lay in the preservation of her moral role. They opposed the "abandonment", the "decline" of the nation. Since the defeat of 1940, even a little earlier, since the colonial exhibition of 1931, they had seen the Empire as the arena which would enable France to rediscover her greatness. What was a necessity for Pétain was equally a necessity for De Gaulle who, at Brazzaville, promised reforms, but to be carried out within a republican framework. Moreover it was during the decades 1930 to 1950 that films and writings poured out in praise of French colonization and of its achievements. As late as 1954 François Mitterrand stated that "from Flanders to the Congo there is the law, a single nation, a single parliament".

During the Cold War the defence of national integrity was presented as part of the struggle against "the Soviet threat", against Communism, an attitude forged in the fire of the Indochinese war, for Ho Chi Minh was an associate of the Comintern prior to 1943, and had always belonged to the Communist Party. Consequently in defending her Empire, France was able to pose as the guardian of the West and of its civilization. When the colonial revolt broke out in the Maghreb, the defence of France was presented also as the preservation of republican order in the face of world revolution. That is what the military leaders thought; they did not want to "sell France off". But certain politicians, like Jacques Soustelle, for example, displayed a blend of the reformist with the counter-revolutionary and the Jacobin. Soustelle knew very well that in Algeria France had neither done her duty nor introduced the reforms which would have given legitimacy to her presence. He also claimed justice for the Arabs, as did Albert Camus: "When a Frenchman of Algeria is called Pierre, he has a claim on our affection because he has always belonged to us; when he is called Antonio, he has a double claim, because he has chosen to live among us; when he is called Rachid, he has a triple claim, for we have dragged him along a difficult and dangerous path." But as soon as the Arabs refused to acknowledge his justice, Soustelle believed that they were being manipulated, first by the USSR and Communism, and afterwards by Nasser.

Those were the views which were generally entertained by the Right, as much by political leaders like Georges Bidault, as by writers, though with some shades of difference, such as the novelist Jacques Laurent, or the historian Raoul Girardet. Soon, this resistance movement was joined *nolens volens* by leaders who were dragged along by the cycle of war and of repression, leaders who ranged from Martineau-Deplat to Mitterrand, including even the socialists Guy Mollet and Robert Lacoste, at least as regards Algeria. As a result this political orientation in France prevailed over the facts.

With De Gaulle, the decolonizing act sprang from the power of the Republic. But it was not anti-colonialism that initiated this change. Change came from the struggles for liberation, in Algeria especially. Nor does black Africa owe any heavy debt to anti-colonialism. But it is certain that here, thanks to Gaston Deferre and to De Gaulle, a work of decolonization was accomplished.

Great Britain

The pride of being the masters of a vast empire did exist, but the attitude in the mother country varied, depending on whether the territories had white populations or not. Two views of the British Empire existed: first, that of Lord Curzon who made India into the jewel in the crown; second, that of Lord Milner who envisaged a Commonwealth populated only by whites (which implied concern neither for the Indians of Canada, nor for the aborigines of Australia, nor for the Maoris of New Zealand). Thus violent reactions to the anti-British movements occurred particularly when the subjects of Her Majesty were directly concerned: in Cyprus, in Gibraltar, in Kenya, in Rhodesia, or in the Malvinas-Falklands.

Besides the loss of prestige of the House of Lords, the democratization process of the post-war period, the institution of the Welfare State in particular, have devalued the virtues which the Empire represented. Sentimentality has replaced virility, the Empire has become a charitable enterprise as well as a source of income. The turnaround has been total.

For genuine social democracy, with the institution of the Welfare State, was incompatible with imperialism. Only economic withdrawal, with the savings that it generated, made the Welfare State possible. Many people in Britain revived an old idea and assumed as a certainty that *the Empire had provided the ruling class with the foundation which had enabled it to perpetuate itself in power.* Moreover since the beginning of the nineteenth century the heirs of Cobden, even of Gladstone, were convinced that wars were henceforth the legacy of imperialist rivalries. Thus the Labour Party made its difference felt over the colonial question when, after the Second World War, it made concessions to the national movements in India and in Palestine in 1947–48. It is true that it had no choice. Later it proclaimed that it was not hostile to the Empire but to the "adventurist" policy embodied by Anthony Eden during the Suez Crisis, and that it favoured a Commonwealth which would perpetuate the greatness of Great Britain without compromising her bonds with the coloured peoples. The difficult moment came with the Central African crisis at the beginning of the sixties when white racism in Rhodesia called for a semi-disengagement which

313

proved to be difficult to put into practice. Additionally the unilateral proclamation of independence by the Smith government was opposed by the Labour Party which thereby earned the condemnation of the British in the rest of the Commonwealth.

The Conservatives, in power from 1951 to 1964, had had to endure the most humiliating defeats. The first was the "departure" from Australia and from New Zealand, as a result of an alliance with the United States from which Great Britain was excluded (the Anzus pact of 1951). It was a delayed effect of the strategic choice made by Churchill during the Second World War, when the defence of Singapore was given priority over that of Australia, for which the Australians never forgave him. The other defeats were the Mau-Mau uprising in Kenya (1952); the creation of the Central African Federation; the Suez fiasco (1956) and the termination of the British presence in the Middle East coinciding with the fall of King Faisal in Iraq (1958); the independence of Malaysia and of Ghana, of Sierra Leone, of Tanganyika (1957–61), then of the West Indies (1962). In Suez, egged on by Lord Amery, Anthony Eden was led to intervene against Nasser: he lost the battle which ended with Harold Macmillan recognizing Egyptian ownership of the canal.

Henceforth the Conservatives had to bow to the necessity of disengagement with the difference that, in contrast with the Labour Party, they were never suspected of having tried to liquidate the Empire.

In the case of Great Britain, as in that of France, external pressures were not wanting in speeding up the process that led to disengagement and to decolonization. During the Second World War the United States, independently of the role played by Japan, had added its voice to the threats that faced the Empire by openly denouncing the policies followed in India by Stafford Cripps and Churchill "where they were perpetuating the colonial system". It is true that the riots which followed the arrest in 1942 of Gandhi owed nothing to the Americans. But, for the first time, the British Government saw its powerful ally formulate a criticism, a challenge, a threat. The Americans assumed they were totally innocent of any imperialist vocation and scarcely imagined that their policy in Latin America was a variation of indirect colonialism. Nevertheless they preached morality to the colonial powers: it was a way to attempt to substitute themselves for them. That is what occurred in the aftermath of the Suez crisis.

French domination equally had to confront the same external threat as did its rival, which, during the war, had tried to take over from it in the Levant and in Madagascar. Defeated France was indeed vulnerable, and in her Empire too. But Bourguiba, the Sultan of Morocco and Ferhat Abbas had taken the same decision as did Ho Chi Minh: opposition to the fascist threat and subsequent reliance on the Americans, in order to extract hoped for concessions from France. In November 1942 Murphy

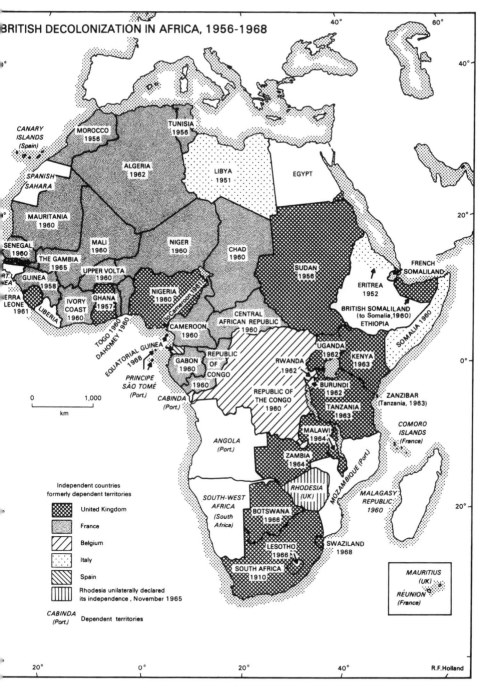

BRITISH DECOLONIZATION IN AFRICA, 1956-1968

40°   60°

40°

CANARY
ISLANDS
(Spain)

MOROCCO
1956

TUNISIA
1956

ALGERIA
1962

LIBYA
1951

EGYPT

SPANISH
SAHARA

20°

MAURITANIA
1960

SENEGAL
1960

THE GAMBIA
1965

MALI
1960

NIGER
1960

CHAD
1960

SUDAN
1956

FRENCH
SOMALILAND

RT./
NEA
GUINEA
1958

UPPER VOLTA
1960

ERITREA
1952

SIERRA
LEONE
1961

IVORY
COAST
1960

GHANA
1957

NIGERIA
1960

(to Cameroon 1961)

BRITISH SOMALILAND
(to Somalia,1960)

LIBERIA

CENTRAL
AFRICAN REPUBLIC
1960

ETHIOPIA

TOGO 1960

CAMEROON
1960

DAHOMEY 1960

EQUATORIAL GUINEA
1968

GABON
1960

REPUBLIC
OF
CONGO

RWANDA
1962

UGANDA
1962

KENYA
1963

SOMALIA 1960

PRINCIPE
SÃO TOMÉ
(Port.)

0   1,000

km

CABINDA
(Port.)

1960

REPUBLIC OF
THE CONGO
1960

BURUNDI
1962

TANZANIA
1963

ZANZIBAR
(Tanzania, 1963)

ANGOLA
(Port.)

MALAWI
1964

COMORO
ISLANDS
(France)

ZAMBIA
1964

MOZAMBIQUE (Port.)

0°

Independent countries
formerly dependent territories

United Kingdom

France

Belgium

Italy

Spain

Rhodesia unilaterally declared
its independence , November 1965

CABINDA
(Port.)   Dependent territories

SOUTH-WEST
AFRICA
(South
Africa)

RHODESIA
(UK)

BOTSWANA
1966

LESOTHO
1966

SWAZILAND
1968

SOUTH AFRICA
1910

MALAGASY
REPUBLIC
1960

20°

MAURITIUS
(UK)

RÉUNION
(France)

20°   0°   20°   40°   R.F.Holland

Source: A. N. Porter, *Atlas of British Overseas Expansion*, Routledge, 1994

had talks with Ferhat Abbas, just as Roosevelt had with the Sultan of Morocco. But, more concerned with winning the war, the Americans merely committed themselves to words. The colonists discerned correctly that their future was being threatened. Accordingly, at least in Morocco, they did not hesitate to attribute to the action of the Americans the events of 1950–52.

In Algeria, the colonists attributed it to the action of the Soviets to Communism. But then no one could foresee that Americans and Russians were to join hands, at Suez.

The international context: Suez and the twilight of empires

Three things led to the disappearance of the empires: the demands of the colonized peoples; the calling into question, in the mother country, of the advantages of expansion; lastly external pressure, stemming from rivals or new emergent powers that presented a challenge.

The rising power of the United States and the USSR, and the assertion of Arab nationalism thus came together, during the Suez Crisis, to signal the decline of the French and British empires, which was already in an advanced stage, but then became irreversible.

It is moreover paradoxical that, while the centuries old rivalry between France and England had promoted their rise to power and contributed to the development of their empires, their joining together for the first time on a colonial issue led to their collapse.

At the beginning of the fifties the Cold War was at its height. No longer having its hands tied in Korea, the United States was on the verge of intervening in Vietnam. Claiming to have been duped in the Yalta agreements, the Americans found that after China the Middle East was about to swing to the East, to Communism. The alarm bell had rung in Iran where Mossadeq had nationalized the oil industry. The Shah was restored to his throne, but in 1954 the USSR and Syria signed an agreement for the sale of arms, indicating that the USSR was moving towards the "warm seas" and the oil zones of the East.

The American leaders were swayed by the Riga spirit, that is, they were influenced by Balts opposed to the Yalta accord. They evinced an unconditional distrust of Soviet expansionism. Led by John Foster Dulles, they worked out the policy of containment aimed at surrounding the USSR, and Communist China, with a network of military alliances, backed up by a range of bases under American control. The aim was to stop the forward march of Soviet expansionism, which has already won control of Eastern Europe, North Korea and China, and of the Communist parties which were active in Iran (Tudeh), in Egypt, in Indonesia. In the West this role devolved upon NATO, in the Far East on SEATO, in the Middle East on the Baghdad Pact.

From then on adherence to this pact, the spirit in which countries participate in it, constitute the criterion for the American government's evaluation of its partners. For example, the rejection in 1954 by the French National Assembly of the treaty for the defence of the European community gave rise in the United States to a lasting mistrust of France. The effects were felt in the Suez crisis. In the Middle East the Americans relied on the British to win the agreement of Iraq and of Jordan. They themselves negotiated the adhesion to that pact, which was then called MEDO (Middle East Defence Organization) of Iran, Turkey and Egypt.

Dulles also met with Nasser. The political climate was favourable as the Egyptian military had built up contacts in the United States in anticipation of their putsch against King Farouk who tilted towards England. But when Dulles evoked the need for the "free world" to unite against the USSR, Nasser replied that "for him, the solidarity of the free world connotes imperialism and domination". He would only join the MEDO "once the English had left" (Heikal, H. *Les Documents du Caire*, Paris, 1973, pp. 9–43).

For the Americans the test was adhesion to the MEDO. The test for Nasser was the supply of arms, to drive away the British or wage war against Israel. With Dulles vacillating over the supply of arms, Nasser placed his order with the Soviets, *via* the Chinese. So as not to provoke the Americans the Russians had the order fulfilled by Czechoslovakia. The era of bid and counter-bid had started.

"They supply them with arms, we shall offer them prosperity", was Dulles' reaction, referring to Nasser's dream project, the construction of the great Aswan Dam. It represented a huge cost: one billion dollars. The World Bank allocated 200 million in hard currency, Britain and the United States 70 million each. It was still below the projected outlay even if the IBRD increased its participation. But the conditions imposed by the World Bank implied a sort of control over the expenditure of the Egyptian state which unfortunately recalled the 1880s when, as a result of its indebtedness, Egypt was forced to accept the suzerainty of France and of Britain, subsequently of England alone. Nasser rejected these conditions, despite the efforts of Eugene Black, the director of the IBRD. Then he repeated his action of the preceding years and asked for Russian help. At the same time he launched himself in a series of gestures "unfriendly" to the United States: recognition of Communist China, military pact with Syria. Dulles thought that a clash with Egypt would have no serious impact on the supply of oil to the West. Badgered by the Chinese lobby close to Chiang Kai-shek and the Jewish lobby favourable to Israel, careful not to offend the rest of the Arab world, while preserving the trust of the British who thought that the concessions made by the IBRD were improper, on 19 July 1956 Dulles cancelled the loan and justified it on the ground of the untrustworthiness of the Egyptian debtors. Nasser was surprised by

317

the "insulting" manner of the cancellation more than by the cancellation itself, which he expected, and which was followed by that of the British.

Two days later Nasser responded to this humiliation by announcing that, to finance the Aswan Dam, he was nationalizing the Suez Canal Company. Suez was to pay for Aswan.

This coup was aimed at Britain, more than at the Americans. But Nasser was not aware that France too identified herself with Suez. For the help which Egypt was bringing to the FLN this thunderous nationalization provided the Guy Mollet government with an unexpected pretext to intervene. The speech announcing the nationalization actually had a provocative tenor: "I began by finding in Eugene Black another Ferdinand de Lesseps, and my mind took me back to that time when Egypt, with 11 percent of the shares, committed itself to provide 120,000 workers, in order to complete works which cost us 8 million pounds . . . The Egyptian Company which was then created to serve Egyptian interest brought to England 100 million dollars of which we received only 3 million . . . We shall take back our rights, for the canal is the property of Egypt . . . " And, to the ovations of the crowd, Nasser ended his speech with a loud burst of laughter (*L'Economiste égyptien*, 29 July 1956).

La Voix des Arabes, an outfit supplied by the CIA, transmitted this burst of laughter to the Maghreb, to Paris, to London where it provoked anger.

The Britain of Anthony Eden was not reconciled to playing second fiddle to the United States. The twilight of the Empire was evident to one and all and, starting in 1947, the evacuation from Egypt had become the very symbol of that decline. The British believed they had twice "defended" Egypt and the Suez Canal: in 1917 against the Turks, in 1942 against Rommel and the Italians. The argument of the British was that Egypt had never been free since the time of the Pharaohs: it had been successively occupied by the Greeks, the Romans, the Byzantines, the Arabs, the Turks, the French. They captured it in order to defend it (cf. Valentine Chirol, *The Egyptian Problem*). But during the Second World War, the Egyptians felt they could dispense with that "protection", as was demonstrated by the noisy demonstrations that greeted the victories of Rommel in 1941. As a result the British deemed, once the war was over, that they had to evacuate Egypt. But, after their departure from Cairo in 1947, they obtained a concession whereby Ismailia and the Canal Zone could be militarily reoccupied to forestall an external threat against Turkey or the Arab world. This was aimed against the USSR, but it also appeared as a pretext.

Even though the evacuation had been carried out well within the agreed deadline, the relationship the British had with Generals Neguib and Nasser, who had come to power after the putsch in July 1952, very quickly deteriorated. In Suez and in Egypt the British wanted to continue playing the role of privileged patrons and to keep Egypt in their game plan. They looked down upon the new leaders, whom they did not control, as upstarts. They hoped to discredit them and to make them pass for dictators as they had suppressed the political parties: the WAFD in particular, the Communist Party. Further they were persecuting the Muslim Brotherhood – which had actually tried to assassinate Nasser. The ill will generated by the Aswan project was a feature of this policy. In fact the English felt that their evacuation of Egypt had been a retreat enforced under constraint, not the result of an agreement concluded with a partner. For their part Neguib and Nasser stepped up their hostile gestures against the allies of England, especially Iraq and the "insolent festivities celebrating the departure of the last English soldier" only added to the fury of the former occupiers.

At any rate Britain immediately reacted by recognizing Sudanese independence. The procedure went through no delay; it bore no comparison with the procrastinations which London manifested towards India, Egypt or Malaysia. The intention of the British was transparent. It was to cut the umbilical cord that bound Egypt to Sudan for, by a clever use of the procedure of self-determination, Nasser would have liked to maintain a sort of Sudano-Egyptian condominium, that is, to return to a past when Sudan had supplied "land for the Egyptian colonists, soldiers for their army, security for the water of the Nile". That is, Sudan would have become a dependency again, as in the days of Ismail.

The celebration of Sudanese independence, the commemoration of the heroic death of Gordon Pasha – so many demonstrations which exasperated the Anglo-Egyptian conflict. Like many members of the military, Nasser maintained links in Sudan. Accordingly he tried by all means to delay the date of the independence, seeking the help of pro-Egyptian sects like the Ansars and the Khatimas. But he could not overtly proclaim the colonialist ambition of Egypt at the very moment when, in confronting the "imperialist" West, he wanted to pose as the eulogist of the right of nations to dispose of their own destiny.

"Why do you oppose the Baghdad pact?", Eden asked Nasser when he met him. "Because it divides the Arab world", Nasser replied. The successor of Churchill was unwilling to grasp that the Egyptian Colonel's project consisted in regrouping the Arab countries, then the Islamic peoples, and ultimately the African continent. It seemed a crazy scheme and the combination of an expansionist urge with intransigence and anti-democratic policies made Nasser look like a "new Hitler" to Eden and other Western leaders. First, the British minister could not conceive that it was possible to have any policy other than to join the West or the Middle East. Secondly, he assumed that the heart of the Arab world lay in Iraq, not in Egypt, and he relied on Bagdad to rebuild its unity, for his benefit. Nor could Eden see that to ask Egypt to emulate Turkey or Iran – which had adhered to the pact – represented an insult to a country which had freed itself from the Turks and considered the Persians as rivals in the Arab world.

That is how the Bagdad pact "divided" the Arab world. On one side, was Iraq, linked with the enemy, or treacherous Turkish or Persian rivals. On the other side, was Egypt, allied to the truly Arab countries, Syria and Yemen, without the intervention of a foreign power. To that end Egypt had had to get rid of those who collaborated with the British, by toppling King Farouk and the WAFD, something which Noury Said could not do in Baghdad. Nor could the King of Jordan do so while he had by his side his army commander Glubb Pasha, an arabized Englishman. Only Ibn Saud of Arabia, with his oil and his control over the Holy Places could *also* represent the Arab world. But Nasser and his free officers represented a new Arab world of the intellectual or military middle class, not the old world of burnouses and of feudalism. The new stood against the old, which explains the attraction which the Nasser revolution exerted on the Syrian or Iraqi lower middle classes, so well expressed in the film *Les Murs*. Consequently, with the rising popularity of Nasser whose fame swelled with every Western affront, King Hussein of Jordan refused to join the pact which Bagdad had just signed with Ankara. At the same time Yemen signed a pact of mutual assistance with Egypt. Indeed for the British Nasser was the Number One enemy. Nasser knew it and he got ready to face reprisals for the nationalization of the Suez Canal. He was expecting France to join in. But he was surprised by the intervention of Israel.

In his *Bloc-Notes*, François Mauriac wrote: "When the last British soldier left the Canal Zone, some Frenchmen gloated and said: 'Ha, ha, the British too!' Just as there were Englishmen in the Colonial Office who rubbed their hands with satisfaction on reading the news coming from Algeria . . . But the departure of the last Englishman from Suez is a big defeat for France . . . and all the blows which we are receiving in North Africa strike at the British too" (p. 405).

Twenty-five years later, did François Mitterrand remember Mauriac's judgement when he became the first to express his endorsement of Great Britain's action in the Falklands crisis?

Whatever may be the case, François Mauriac was right. The mission of Christian Pineau was designed to thumb the nose at the British when he called on Nehru and then on Nasser. He spoke nice words to Syria which was under threat from Iraq led by Noury Saïd, and he tried to win the good offices of Nasser in the Algerian situation, but in a spirit of friendship. Twenty years later Christian Pineau acknowledged the limitations of his mission when he said: "In fact I had not established a close link between the policy to be adopted in the Arab countries and the Algerian question." Like Eden he too was unaware of the Arabo-Islamic renaissance and persisted in his thinking of the West-East relationship, in seeing the problem within the old colonial perspective. In Paris it was well known, ever since the discoveries of Soustelle in the Nemencha that Nasser had links with the "rebels". But it all seemed to be normal and Pineau accepted "the word of honour of Nasser who assured him that he did not have FLN cadres on his territory". He mentioned it in the Parliament.

The testimony of Nasser is interesting because it shows that Pineau, no more than Eden, could understand him: "He tried to reach an agreement with me for a solution of the Algerian problem. But I told him that I was not responsible for the Algerian revolution . . . Only the Algerians had started it; it emerged from within. I have not promised him not to help the Algerians. I told him: 'It is our responsibility to help our Arab brothers everywhere.' He asked me about the military training of the Algerians, about sending Egyptians to Algeria. I replied there were no Egyptians who were fighting with the Algerians . . . that there were no Algerians receiving training at that time" (March 1956).

A few days later, with the resumption of this training, French intelligence took delight in making this information public and in exposing Pineau to ridicule, for which he did not forgive Nasser. Moreover, at the time when Robert Lacoste, who had replaced Soustelle, announced the arrival of 100,000 men in Algeria and the "last quarter hour" of the "rebels", *The Voice of the Arabs* broadcast information which represented Nasser as the defender of the Algerian cause. This news has a massive impact at a time when the majority of the Algerian Muslims were still lacking in self-assurance, when the values of integration still appealed to a large number, when even the goals of the FLN were not known. The association of the FLN struggle with Islamo-Arab cause acted like a leaven, like a lever, raising the masses to new heights of fervour. The news of an Egyptian landing in Collo in August 1955 showed to what extent myth had become a part of the situation. The Arabs believed in it. So did Soustelle who in Philippeville had mistaken the eulogists of independence for Egyptian propagandists.

The goal of the French leaders was to sever the umbilical cord with the Arab and Islamic world. They believed that once Nasser was struck down, the insurrection would be quickly eliminated. And what a new affront to France when, in July 1956, Nasser nationalized Suez, "a French master-piece", inaugurated by Empress Eugénie, associated with the name of Ferdinand de Lesseps. *Le Monde* had this headline: "A challenge". *Le Quotidien* proclaimed: "He has acted like Hitler, he shall perish like Hitler." And it added: "The canal must be reoccupied."

The fact is that France relied on Israel to accomplish this task.

Assuredly Nasser did not expect that to happen. He himself wrote about it after the event. For, after his alliance with Syria and with Jordan, espe-cially after the departure of the British, he could not assess the extent to which Israel had become apprehensive of being encircled, of being attacked from the south bereft of the protective buffer of the British forces. Additionally Nasser thought that the British would never accept Israel's help, as that would be the surest way to alienate the Arab world. Indeed the British did not want an alliance with Israel. When the war actually started they even proposed bombing Tel Aviv as a subterfuge to mask their collusion with Jerusalem, something which Israel refused. But London had to yield and accept this alliance under pressure from Paris which, after having supplied Israel with arms to compensate for the supplies made to Nasser by the "Czechs", deemed that in the face of the common enemy Israel could serve as a rearguard ally. France laid this down as a condition for her intervening on the side of the British.

"Without the intervention of France and the assurance of England, the war in Sinai would certainly never have broken out", says Shimon Peres. He negotiated the arms supplies and later the conventions of Sèvres, which were concluded with Bourgès-Maunoury, Pineau, Eden and Selwyn Lloyd (October 1956) (cf. Abel, Thomas. *Comment Israël fut sauvé*, 1978).

Behind these accords loomed the shadow of Munich.

In Paris, many people thought that Nasser was the source of the difficulties which France was then experiencing in Algeria. For others he was only a pawn on the Soviet chessboard. For others still he was a new Hitler whose expansionist power had to be nipped in the bud. After all those capitulations – in Indo-China, in Tunisia, in Morocco – and, in an earlier time, those of the Anschluss, of the remilitarization of the Rhineland, there was no question of surrender, no going back to before 1939. In this pattern Israel, facing Hitler, played the role of little Czechoslovakia. Eden did not think otherwise: for twenty years he had been marked by a Rhineland complex and saw Nasser's hand everywhere, from the dismissal of Glubb Pasha in Jordan (which was true) to the Mau-Mau rebellion in Kenya (which was not true).

Above all Nasser struck at the sensitive spot of Great Britain; one third of her ships plied through the Canal. There was a threat to oil supplies. Like Churchill, Eden did not want Britain to become "a new Holland". Despite the risks of an intervention, supported by Israel, he would intervene.

Military action was thereupon envisaged. For the moment it appeared impossible. With its nuclear arsenal and its forces specially trained and equiped to serve in the colonies, Britain could not muster an *ad hoc* corps for this type of contingency. Nor could France, as she was mired in Algeria. The bitter memory of the failed parachute attack on Arnhem, in September 1944, paralysed the initiatives. In Great Britain Eden was inhibited by the reserve of the Labour Party which wanted to act only with the approval of the United Nations. On the contrary, France was urged to act by everybody with the exception of the Communists and of those who belonged to the circle of Mendès France. For a socialist government the question boiled down to dissociating the interests of the country from those of the shareholders of Suez, so as to have a reasonable pretext justifying the elimination of Nasser. The same Robert Lacoste who said that in Algeria the victorious fight against the fellaghas had reached "its last quarter hour", also said "that the war in Algeria would be inconclusive if Nasser triumphed in this crisis which he has himself brought about".

This mood lasted for a short while because, against all hope, Eisenhower informed Eden, and Dulles told Pineau, that other ways had to be sought to force Nasser to toe the line: the United States would see to that happening. For the United States it was simply a matter of the free passage of ships, dissociating the nationalization from its context. They held that Nasser "had the right to nationalize the Company". At the same time, while the French and the English recalled their pilots – to show the inability of the Egyptians to run the piloting of ships through the Canal by themselves – Dulles set up an "Association of the Users of the Canal". Such a development deprived the French and the English of their ability to act, since it promised not to act by using force.

Nasser began to wonder what the American attitude meant. Dulles made it plain by elucidating that "he refused to identify the policy of his country with the defence of the interests of the former powers".

This affront recalled to London the words of Roosevelt on the occasion of the riots in India in 1942 and of Gandhi's arrest. This led the British government to think the unthinkable: collaboration with Israel, which France had been handling for a long time. That was how in secret the Sèvres conventions were concluded.

It was a weighty decision on the part of Israel. But "such an opportunity would never recur". The idea was to let Israel attack Egypt, then to intervene to save the peace. In this way, in the view of the Arabs, the Western powers would not be "tarnished" by collaborating with Israel. Ben Gurion and Shimon Peres yielded to this humiliating proposition because it "ensured the security of Israel". As for France and Britain, "they would recover their influence in the East". The idea was to win the war without waging it, by letting the Israelis take the initiative, while the large Franco-British armada would only be left with taking over the task.

According to plan the Israelis invaded the Sinai on 29 October 1956. Taken by surprise the Egyptians took to flight. As had been decided, Dayan's tanks stopped at Akaba. As had been decided the English air force moved into position and so did the French support. A double ultimatum was sent and Israel complied. What was not foreseen was that Nasser would don the garb of a martyr, attacked by Israel. For, in the eyes of the Arab world the Anglo-French did not want to appear to back the Jewish State and their landing was planned for 6 November 1956. This delay proved to be fateful, for the entire United Nations was stirred up by the Arab States, and Dulles had a resolution passed against this intervention. On the 5th, Bulganin in his turn sent a threatening "Note" to Guy Mollet, to Eden, to Ben Gurion, to say that the USSR was ready to use all the modern forms of destructive weapons if the expedition were not brought to an end.

Meanwhile the Anglo-French troops had landed; they were progressing towards Suez. But they had to stop, with London and Paris yielding to the injunctions of the U.N., of Washington and of Moscow.

This disaster of the first magnitude, a real "diplomatic Dien Bien Phu", brought discredit to those who were responsible for it. Eden was the first to go; he resigned and abandoned politics. Then it was the turn of Guy Mollet, who tried to recall the positive aspects of the adventure: he had saved Israel.

In fact, even though they were bitter about having been stopped on the way to success, the Israelis felt some gratitude towards France for an operation which contributed to the survival of their state which was viewed to have been under a threat.

To Great Britain the 1956 crisis showed that from then on she had lost her great power status and could no longer act without the support of the United States. In confirmation of this collapse the British troops left Bagdad following the fall of Noury Said in July 1958. Besides this defeat loosened the bonds which London had maintained with its former imperial possessions, in particular India under the leadership of Nehru who had sternly denounced the return of offensive "colonialism". Above all in the Arab world the fall of Great Britain was indicated by the adoption by a certain number of countries of the "Eisenhower doctrine", which assured them of American assistance "in case of a threat coming from a power under the control of Moscow and of the Communists". This was aimed at Syria, which was friendly to Nasser, equipped by the USSR and had designs on Lebanon. This was a significant turnaround for a year earlier it was Iraq that threatened to absorb Syria.

Thus it was Suez that marked the end of the colonial regime of Great Britain in the Arab world.

The contest had decisive and paradoxical consequences for France and for the Algerian national movement. Independently of the resentment felt by the military who, after the defeats of Indo-China, of Morocco, of Tunisia, begrudged the regime for not knowing or daring to act to the bitter end in Suez (it quickly became known that Bulganin could not put his threats into practice and they were used to mask the intervention in Budapest); and independently of the part played by that failure in the fall of the Fourth Republic, it had immediate consequences in Algeria, where Nasser's victory inflamed the Muslim masses as he moved rapidly to internationalize the problem. Most of the Arab and Asian countries had rallied to the Algerian cause. Only Lebanon stood apart.

But it was a paradox that the victory of Nasser generated mistrust in the sensitive patriotism of the FLN leaders who feared lest Egypt would, this time too decisively, intervene in their affairs. An operation of disengagement followed as well as a *maghrebization of the Algerian problem*:

more precisely, it was the transfer to North Africa of the centre of gravity of Algerian actions. Hence Tunis became the seat of the Provisional Government of the Algerian Republic, with the result that the relationship between Bourguiba and France worsened. In actuality, because of Suez the Lacoste-Bourgès-Mollet line of policy-making culminated in a "maghrebization of the war", while the Mendès-Savary-Deferre alternative would have opted for a "maghrebization of the peace" by setting up a federation of the three North African states to counterbalance, in the West, the influence of Egypt and of the Arab League.

Above all Suez actually led to the emergence of the Third World. It had, in particular at Bandung, already given notice that it was a separate, independent entity, but mainly in order to take advantage of the rivalry between the two world powers. This was a concern which gained primacy over the need to affirm its identity and the legitimacy of its specific development. For the participants in the Bandung Conference disposed of limited means, except the threat of shifting from one camp to the other – a policy which the East and the West called "bargaining".

The first new thing to come out of the Suez crisis was that from then on the deprived nations possessed an asset: the canal, which had been taken by force from the West. Soon they had a second: oil, which Mossadeq had been unable to wrest completely from the great powers.

But more important still is the fact that, far from straying away towards Communism, as a certain determinist vision of history had predisposed them, the Islamic countries were on the contrary turning away from it, as much as, if not more than, from the Western model. Not only were they asserting their Islamic and national calling (Arab, Algerian), but they showed that a society can produce a history which belongs specifically to it and a history which identifies itself with that of a community, Islam. The world had seen in Nasser the guide and the hero of this regeneration. However, the unity of the Arab world, which was speeded up by the union of Egypt and Syria, failed to achieve its purpose, in spite of Suez and the establishment of the United Arab Republic. Egypt could never be a unifier like Piedmont or Prussia. Can it be that the Arab world has a feeling of solidarity in its relationship with others, rather than in an identity specific to it? It found it in the war against Iran, which is a Muslim country. But it was divided during the war against Iraq. The time for Arab unity seems to be gone forever.

The Suez crisis brought about also a stiffening of the attitude of the Algerian French, as well as of the military: a consequence which led to the coup of 13 May 1958,[1] while spreading the Algerian problem over the whole of North Africa. In the face of the turn taken by the colonized peoples' struggles for freedom, De Gaulle's attitude was uncertain. It was not known even to those who were close to him. In Great Britain the decolonization had destabilized the Conservatives; Anthony Eden had resigned.

When one compares the reactions and the careers of Churchill and of De Gaulle, one finds that they shed light on what became, subsequent to 1958, a policy of decolonization initiated by the mother country. In Algeria it came about as the result of a war. But the situation was different in French or English black Africa and in the other parts of the British Empire, where negotiation prevailed over armed struggle. The mother countries contributed to this process, so strong had been their reaction to the events in the Near East. It was as if Europe had stepped aside. Henceforth the two Great Powers ruled the world, and the Third World was coming into its own.

Churchill and De Gaulle in the face of decolonization

"I did not become His Majesty's Prime Minister to preside over the liquidation of the Empire", Churchill said during the Second World War. For the Empire was his glory and ever since *The River War*, his first great text on colonization, written in 1899, he had done nothing but condemn the excesses of patriotism, jingoism, though he was supposed to be a Tory. During the Boer War, he denounced the firebrands like Kitchener, even while the war was on. Yet his perception of India was always that of an old imperialist. "On seeing what has happened in Ireland, and what goes on in Egypt, one cannot blame those who ask for concessions in the distant possessions . . . But, in India, Great Britain must remain a real power." Actually Irwin and Baldwin wanted to concede dominion status in order to keep India better. Churchill thought that such a project was a wild dream, that concessions should not be made. Later he realized that the appeasers in India were the very ones who were also the appeasers with Hitler. He was a romantic against the realists who, in the India Defence League, joined Rudyard Kipling in organizing those characters – the "Colonel Blimps" who were the butt of ridicule in literature – who were intent on forming the UBI (Union of Britian and India). He fought the India Bill, not so much for political reasons, but because the Empire represented the history of his country, and above all of his youth. He thought that at a time when the danger of Hitler's militarism was on the rise, and when nationalism was spreading everywhere, the granting of dominion status to India by men like Baldwin and Hoare would lead to concessions which would weaken the country. But, in the Conservative Party, Churchill got only 356 out of 838 votes. His excessive language on several occasions contributed to the decline of his relationship with India. "It is alarming and also nauseating to see Mr. Gandhi, a seditious Middle Temple lawyer, now posing as a fakir of a type well known in the East, striding half naked up the steps of the Vice-Regal palace, while he is still organizing and conducting a defiant campaign of civil disobedience, to parley on equal terms with the representative of the King-Emperor" (23 February 1931).[2]

Yet, after the vote on the India Act (1935) Churchill changed his attitude towards Gandhi. He appreciated the Harijan strikes (conducted with the collaboration of Muslims) as an indication of the nobility of the Indian leader's views. But he exploded when, after the United States entered the war, Roosevelt opines that the Atlantic Charter should also apply to India. The pressure was so great that Churchill, with bad grace, sent Stafford Cripps with proposals which were rejected. But they gained time. Still Churchill understood that one day India would have to be granted independence. He himself organized the Simla conference to get ready for the inevitable.

His task was fulfilled by the Labour Party which succeeded him.

But he had strongly opposed the idea of granting dominion status while the war was still on. He said as much to Tej Bahadur Sapru, a moderate of the Congress Party. In his war cabinet no one dared broach the subject: Winston Churchill was himself a sort of "one man Indian Defence League" in his own government. At Yalta he was resolutely opposed to Roosevelt's proposal of the ancient colonies becoming mandated territories of the future United Nations. Churchill retorted: "I do not agree with a single word of the President". Under no circumstances would he tolerate forty or fifty nations poking their nose in the affairs of the British Empire. He would not budge an inch on this question. "What would you say if the Crimea were to be internationalized to serve as a summer residence?" he asked Stalin. When Roosevelt observed that India, like the United States between 1783 and 1789, could gradually elect her representatives and become a democracy, he replied that neither the problems nor the times could be compared. Did this mean that he did not believe that the Indians could practise democracy, or were his words those of a senile man (Lord Amery) who wanted to preserve the "India of nostalgia"? On 20 December 1946, Lord Attlee who had succeeded him, spoke of the future of Burma "which had to decide on its own fate either within, or outside, the Commonwealth", Winston Churchill, now the Leader of the Opposition, rose and said:

> We have held Burma since 1885. We have followed its affairs with attention. My father was responsible for the annexation of Burma ... We defended them as well as we could against the Japanese invasion, but we were not successful. It was only after a tremendous campaign of three years of heavy fighting that the Japanese were driven out, and the country was liberated from the invaders' hands ... This evil process, which has been attended by disasters of which at present we are only on the threshold, and which will to a large extent occupy or dominate the mind and attention of the present Parliament in the months and years to come, is now quite needlessly extended to Burma. I cannot see why this should be done, unless it

is to try to induce the Burmese representatives to come over here and discuss this matter with us. This haste is appalling. "Scuttle" is the only word that can be applied . . . We are seeing in home affairs the unseemly rush of legislation, disorganizing our national life and impeding our recovery, legislation thrust upon Paliament at breakneck speed . . . He [i.e. Prime Minister Clement Attlee] has in fact shorn Burma away from the British Crown by what is being done. That, at least, is a matter of which notice should be taken, if it be only passing notice, even in this period when we are getting so accustomed and indurated to the process of the decline and fall of the British Empire.

One does not find the same consistency in De Gaulle. His pronouncement on the Empire suffered a sea change in the face of a new situation, the Algerian war, where he finds himself to be the main player. Those who brought him to power – Jacques Soustelle more than any other – relied on his past actions to imagine that he would repeat them. They were mistaken and, like the pieds-noirs or others, believed that he had betrayed them. On the other hand, De Gaulle's *Mémoires* reconstruct history in such a way that it establishes a continuity between his views and his reactions to the event.

During the war De Gaulle and Churchill were openly in league with each other. Against the Americans they formed a common front on the colonial question. Undoubtedly events in Syria had roused the old antagonism between the two countries,[2] which nearly ended with a split. But it was only a tragic "episode". In reality the Soviet ambassador in Algiers, Alexandre Bogomolov, reached an unambiguous diagnosis, in a correspondence with Stalin, dated 19 January 1944: "It is evident that De Gaulle is getting rid little by little of the Giraudists . . . that the English (not the Americans) will send arms to the Resistance and that there is *a basic Anglo-French agreement* [Bogomolov's italics] in North Africa as well as in the Middle East. Churchill supports De Gaulle against the Americans so that the past misunderstandings will be forgotten . . . Consequently the Anglo-Saxons are certainly often in league against Soviet Union, but *not on the colonial problems* in which Great Britain seeks an alliance with France against the Americans. De Gaulle understands this very well and he fully supports England against the Americans (quoted in Ferro, 1987).

If the speech at Brazzaville (30 January 1944) marks a milestone, it is because it was delivered in the presence of Africans and it dealt with the problem of the status of the colonies. Its contents, however, are vague: "to exercise French sovereignty on new foundations". It did not even refer to belonging to the Empire. That was taken for granted. With hindsight, one finds that De Gaulle used that speech as a charter for the future. Indeed it was a novel gesture, as was the ordinance of December 1943 which enlarged the number of Algerian Muslims who would enjoy full citizenship rights, a development which the colonists had to accept with bad grace. Again it was De Gaulle who decided to bring 63 overseas deputies to the Constituent Assembly, out of 522 members, 25 of whom represented the colonies. Among them were Houphouët-Boigny (Ivory Coast), Léopold S. Senghor (Senegal), J. Raseta (Madagascar), Aimé Césaire (Martinique); and 11 representatives of the UDMA of Ferhat Abbas to the second Constituent Assembly. However De Gaulle did not disapprove of the Sétif incident: he only blamed Yves Chataigneau. If, in Indo-China, he shows his sympathy for Jean Sainteny and for Leclerc, it was nonetheless Admiral d'Argenlieu who was his man on the spot. Yet the latter was the man who broke off from Ho Chi Minh.

During the time spent in the wilderness, from 1947 to 1958, the foundation of the RPF (Rassemblement du Peuple Français) seems to have had as its origin the need for France to have recourse to an alternative, in case the decline of the Empire proceeded at a faster pace, and its placement under American supervision. On more than one occasion De Gaulle outlined his conception of the French Union, and every time he indicated his preference for an evolution towards internal autonomy. But he strongly reaffirmed the need to preserve Algeria as French: it was the "environment of uncertainty" of the 1947 status which shocked him, so much so that he "succumbed to overstatement". It is difficult to accept those statements in the *Mémoires*, written after 1960, where the General seems to suggest that it would have been better to allow the situation to evolve towards the formation of an Algerian State. There is nothing to confirm this in his utterances of that period.

After having declared and reiterated that, in Indo-China, the French were engaged in the same fight as the Americans' in Korea, against Communism, De Gaulle, in 1954, believed that it was necessary to deal with the enemy and he did not disapprove of the agreements signed by Pierre Mendès France at Geneva. As regards North Africa, that is, Tunisia and Morocco, he opted for a policy of association, punishing those guilty of crimes unworthy of France. He did not speak of abandonment. But he thought that the good solutions were beyond the reach of the "present regime".

Churchill had expressed and repeated the same opinion. That is, on the French side, what Michel Debré and Jacques Soustelle thought while taking part in the coup of 13 May 1958. At this moment, however, De Gaulle told the pieds-noirs: "I have understood you." They knew no more than others how the General would act. They were at the same time cautious, worried, and confident. De Gaulle criticized the previous governments not for their abandonment – except of the bases in Morocco, but for the absence of any policies on their part. What would his be?

By saying straight away that only one category of inhabitants lived in Algeria, "fully-fledged French citizens having the same rights and the same duties", De Gaulle was not announcing the declaration of 16 September

1959, as indicated in his *Mémoires*, he was actually reformulating the idea of integration, except that it was not clear whether or not France and Algeria formed one entity, that is, with 100 Algerian deputies in Paris. The pieds-noirs who were shouting "Soustelle, Soustelle" understood De Gaulle well. But by speaking of 10 million French in Algeria, he reverted to the immersion of the pieds-noirs in an Arab majority. The speech at Mostaganem – "Long live French Algeria" – maintained the ambiguity. But whenever he evoked the Algerian personality, since he associated Algeria *and* France, the choice was clear even if it was not explicitly spelled out. The words carried weight and, after having spoken of self-determination, he finally, in 1960, called for the Algerian Republic and for Algerian Algeria. He broke with Jacques Soustelle, with the Algerian French: "the softness of the oil lamps, the splendour of the sailing ships". As the call to "the peace of the brave" did not have an immediate effect, the General indirectly pointed to the path he intends to follow by allowing Mali – Senegal and Sudan – to accede to independence (June 1960).

Watching the haggard faces of the colonists who, on the huge white ship anchored in the harbour of Batavia, in 1947, were leaving the Dutch East Indies for good, few could have guessed that they foretold the fate of the French of Algeria fifteen years later.

Still a few had a premonition of the coming tragedy: for example, Albert Camus, half-Algerian, half-Oranian, who said that "between justice and his mother", he would choose his mother. For him justice meant the rights of the Arabs scoffed at by the colonists and by the French administration. He was one of the first to come to their defence and for this his fellow-citizens bore him a grudge. But he could not stomach the Algerian crisis culminating in the forced departure of the colonists, of his mother – indeed, he could not accept it. His statement drew the anger of the intellectuals, of Jean-Paul Sartre first among them, who scorned him for not having "a sense of history" (1957).

De Gaulle had this sense of history and he knew that Algerian independence was inevitable. It is a moot question whether he anticipated the consequences for the French in Algeria. At any rate, the nationalists of the FLN had let everyone believe, during the years 1950–56, that in an independent Algeria all the French would have rights equal to those of the other inhabitants of the country. It seems that, at the Soummam conference, a change was made on that point. The OAS widened the gulf which separated the two communities, with the Algerians doing nothing to bridge it.

Always prompt – and rightly so – to denounce torture, the metropolitan French never had a word to condemn terrorism. It was thought that terrorism was the answer to colonial terror – so much the worse for the victims of that terrorism.

De Gaulle had initiated a process for the end of the war. As the military operations had not ended, far from it, with a Dien Bien Phu, he had established contact with Si Salah, then with the FLN. To hasten the conclusion of the deal, he used the term "Algerian Republic", announced a referendum on self-determination, in which the "yes" won by 75 percent of the votes cast, 69 percent in Algeria where the large cities voted "no". Bidault and Soustelle had left De Gaulle (8 January 1961).

It is then that General Salan, with Generals Challe, Jouhaud and Zeller, thought the right moment had come to organize a coup with the underhand support of the OAS (Organisation de l'Armée Secrète), undoubtedly created on the initiative of Robert Martel, Lagaillarde and Susini, the men of the day of the barricades. De Gaulle ordered a call-up; the putsch failed. But the OAS survived as a terrorist organization which kills "whomever it wants to, whenever it wants to, wherever it wants to". During the summer of terror and counter-terror the number of victims and incidents multiplied: the autumn of 1961 became for some of the French of Algeria – whom the OAS had not assassinated – a time of hope. They hoped for the failure of the negotiations that had started in Evian. Then began a series of attacks which spread to the mother country: more than 100 in January–February 1962 in France; more than 800 in Algeria, due in part to the FLN, in part to the OAS, in part to the anti-OAS.

To the ceasefire and the Evian agreements of March 1962, which recognized the independence of Algeria and were approved by a referendum, the OAS responded with terror and scorched earth, controlling Bab-el-Oued and making of it a sort of Fort Chabrol and burning the library of Algiers. Yet, despite its orders and the intensification of the fighting, the exodus had started as soon as the putsch failed, Challe and Salan were arrested, and Soustelle and Bidault disappeared. The exodus of the pieds-noirs was at its height in April and May 1962, while the army, in order to cover their departure, abandoned part of the harkis to their tragic fate. Another part was brought back to the mother country. On the *Chanzy* and the *Ville d'Oran* the repatriated settlers sang the refrain of Edith Piaf: "Non, je ne regrette rien" ("No, I have no regrets") before Enrico Macias sang of the nostalgia of "his lost country".

De Gaulle and the decolonization of black Africa

As early as 1956, during the Suez crisis, De Gaulle had told the crown prince of Morocco, Moulay Hassan: "Algeria will be independent, whether we like it or not. But it is a question how to bring it about." "It will be long, there will be some rough stuff, a lot of it", he had told Jean Amrouche. And there was. And arduous was the path that led to the Evian agreements, as was later the struggle against the new putsch of the generals. Had General Challe, in 1962, called upon the pied-noir civilians, the crisis would have been more tragic. But he did not want to follow General Salan in that direction and the OAS was smashed.

Mitterrand and Deferre: two precursors

In black Africa decolonization was carried out more easily. De Gaulle could accomplish it, without any real bloodshed, because the predecessors had already initiated the process. In some way the pioneer in the mother country was François Mitterrand who, at the Ministry of Overseas France, put into practice the principle *ad augusta per angusta*. On one hand, he managed to establish close links with the leaders of the *Rassemblement Démocratique Africain* (African Democratization Union) of Houphouët-Boigny by separating him from his friends, the fellow-travellers of the Communist Party, like Arboussier. On the other hand, as the Minister of Overseas France, he conducted a policy "up to the point of no-return thanks to the indifference of metropolitan circles and to general ignorance". It is true that in black Africa bringing about a representative or pseudo-representative political existence did not clash with the power of the colonists, who rarely settled. "The understanding of the UDSR, the political sense which it manifests, and the trust which it shows in us have decided the course of events in French black Africa", said Houphouët-Boigny (1955). Accordingly the African leaders of black Africa collaborated on equal terms with the metropolitan political parties, which was not the case with Algeria. The UDSR was not the only example, since the SFIO also collaborated closely with the rival party of the RDA, the *Indépendants d'Outre-mer* (Overseas Independents) of Léopold Sédar Senghor, who enunciated the idea of an African Federal Republic. But the SFIO was much less adventurous. In Parliament it was strong and the African deputies were less important to it than to the UDSR.

It was during the quiet lull of 6 February 1956, in Algiers, that Gaston Deferre, a socialist, gave expression to the philosophy of a policy which proved to be a success. "Too often, beyond the seas, the French have given the impression that they are not able to act at the right time, and we have been the hostage of events ... If, in black Africa, we succeed in *getting ahead* [my italics] of them, we shall be able to reestablish in this country an environment of trust and concord."

That was the blueprint, the plan of which had been elaborated by Pierre-Henri Teitgen. Deferre saw to its adoption "knowing that the populations of black Africa are following attentively the events in North Africa". The reform granted universal suffrage and a single electoral college to all the territories of black Africa and of Madagascar. It provided for the creation of elected government councils the members of which would be "ministers", and for extended powers for the elected territoritial assemblies. In this way the powers of the governors-general were reduced

332

and the legislative power of each territory increased. Senghor described this project as a "balkanization". For Houphouët-Boigny it was "walking before running". For the Africans it was a phase, but they were divided on the form of independence and the nature of the bonds which would unite them among themselves and to France.

Gaston Deferre had called for a "restoration" of the climate of trust. Among the African leaders some were anxious and reserved in view of the uprising and the harsh repression in Madagascar, the exile of the Sultan of Morocco, the emergence of the fellaghas in Tunisia and later in Algeria. They were also apprehensive, within their own ranks, of the cultural gap being too wide between, on one side, the political elites motivated by ideologies and integrated with French partisan conflicts, and, on the other side, the protest ethnic movements, independent and uncontrolled, recalling the characteristic situation that prevailed in the Portuguese colonies. For their resolve to remain within the French cultural zone was unambiguous. They testified to it by merely paying lip service to the Panafrican movement. The black elites were intensely active in the area of French political life, but they were equally impatient to enhance their power within their own territory, before anyone could, as in Guinea, denounce the "complicity" between certain party leaders and the traditional chiefs.

On the other hand, the United Nations had begun to express its reservations about French colonial policies. At first it did so in regard to the territories under supervision: Togo and Cameroon. Togo became an independent republic, then in association with France. But, in 1958, Togo again appealed to the U.N. which called upon the Government of Félix Gaillard to accept the principle of a popular vote to resolve the question of independence. This was decided by a vote in September 1958. Independence was for 1960. The effect of these events was that they did not culminate in the reunion of the Ewés of former British Togo and those of former French Togo, as had been demanded by the leaders of the country such as, for example, Sylvanus Olympio.

The reunification of the two parts of Cameroon posed the same problem. While the north of the country wanted to associate itself with Nigeria, the south wanted to have a union with the "French" Cameroon. The vote of the populations, under the aegis of the U.N., made this solution possible. However, in "French" Cameroon the protest movement against the supervising power was more violent than in the rest of black Africa. In 1955, the existence of 84 political parties testified to the entrenchment of the political stakes in a population comprising a number of ethnic groups the formal unity of which had been brought about by the occupier. As early as 1948, political life had been dominated by one party, the UPC (Union des Peuples du Cameroun). It was a revolutionary party, closely allied to the Communists, but at the same time tied to the anti-colonialist circles of

Cairo. The UPC displayed its nationalist impatience by means of the violent riots of 1955 which, following the banning of the UPC, gave rise to terrorism and armed conflicts which lasted till 1960. In her confrontation with the UPC of V. M. Nyobé, France relied on the moderate parties led by a Muslim from the north, Amadou Ahijo. He succeeded in obtaining U.N. help for an end of French supervision. But France connived in his success. The outcome was that, paradoxically, independence was viewed by the UPC and a part of the population as a sort of betrayal. And it rekindled the civil struggles from the very day of its proclamation.

As can be seen, with the exception of the prolonged guerilla war waged by the UPC in Cameroon, decolonization in francophone black Africa proceeded by means of negotiation, with the U.N. or nationalist movements taking the initiative. It is noteworthy that before situations became irreversible, French politicians were able to take appropriate action or bring forth, on the spot, forces hostile to a violent separation, for instance, Ahijo in Cameroon.

Accordingly surprise greeted De Gaulle when he offered the Africans and the Malagasies the choice between a free association and secession. But earlier the ground had been sufficiently well prepared for him to take the risk. Actually he showed towards black Africa an affection stemming perhaps from the time of Brazzaville – which got a chilling response in Algiers – and out of 810 speeches delivered during the period 1940–69, 246 or 30 percent refer to black Africa. "We are proceeding towards an immense community of associated peoples": he kept on repeating this expression which could offend neither Senghor nor Houphouët-Boigny. It was a vaguer concept than that of a federation. "It is a historical vehicle to move from one age to another." "France likes large concessions which bring a return", he said in a further reference to black Africa.

De Gaulle did not choose a roundabout way to implement this policy: he did not encounter the same obstacles as in Algeria. Besides he was dealing with negotiators who did not have the same resentment against France as the Arabs had.

On 28 Septembre 1958, the vote on the Community produced 7,471,000 yes votes, and 1,120,000 no votes, of which 636,000 were from Guinea. Sékou Touré had rejected a choice being "granted" to him. He had replied with a "No", with the result that the Community comprised, beside France, 12 States with internal autonomy. But, even before the common institutions had started to function, some states were already forming new groups – Senegal and Sudan formed the Federation of Mali – which demanded independence a year after having accepted to join the Community. Others followed suit, in spite of the resistance of Houphouët-Boigny who preferred a lasting Franco-African community. "They are leaving, they are leaving", said De Gaulle. He let them go.

The Belgian Congo and the Gold Coast: a contrast

The shock wave of Suez had a direct impact on the events in the Middle East and in the Maghreb. While it also had a stimulating effect on the black African movements, it did not prompt them in all circumstances to provide unflinching help to the FLN. Despite the appeals the FLN made to them, the black African movements were distrustful of Arab Islam. But the shock wave showed Europeans that a new era had begun.

It was startlingly so for the Belgians who, in Congo, had been till then living in total ignorance of that decolonization process which did not seem to concern them. They could afford to do so for the country had been calm from 1945 to 1959, and the number of residents had risen from 35,000 to 115,000. Further, their sanitary policy being a good example of their achievements, the Belgians were convinced that they were the best of all colonizers. Again, the schools, well maintained by the Church, were proliferating and most of the time acted as the instruments of social progress. But the teaching was for the most part of a religious nature and few Africans attended universities in Belgium. Forced labour had given place to patronage. The number of cadres, known as "evolved ones", was fast rising in the towns, the Belgian administration attempted to control the phenomenon by instituting a "civil merit" card. To obtain this card became the main objective of the educated population. That is why a certain torpor apparently prevailed in the country when the urban riots of January 1959 broke out. The Belgians were unprepared for this eventuality. But it led them, in view of the events occurring elsewhere in the world, to bring the colonial system to an immediate end. "Belgium intends to transform the Congo into a democratic country capable of exercising the prerogatives of sovereignty and of deciding on its own the particulars of its independence." The surprise was total; so was the turnaround. Neither the rest of the world, nor the Africans anticipated such a total break away from the past. A political chasm had opened in front of partners who had not been prepared to bridge it.

In the French or English possessions of Africa decolonization benefited the native military – the main beneficiaries – the officials and the political leaders. But nothing of the sort occurred in the Congo where the Belgians continued to rule from Brussels over a country which was moving towards independence. Only the Church had managed to dissociate itself from the former colonial power. By 1960 there was no longer a state, nor anything else in its place. A concatenation of conflicts started, accompanied by unheard-of violence, directed first against the Belgian officers. The era of violence persisted through several wars between the Kasavubu government and the Prime Minister, Patrice Lumumba, a revolutionary Marxist; and later by the secession of Katanga which became a separate State under the aegis of Moïse Tshombé.

The way was open to an internationalization of the conflict.

For the Belgians the nightmare crisis of 1959 was indeed the "exit from a fairy story".

The contrast with the independence of the Gold Coast (Ghana) is enlightening for anyone who watches the newsreels which show the celebrations of 1957. In a festive atmosphere, that night, African statesmen and elegant black and British ladies danced the biguine, while in the distance dugouts illuminated *a giorno* floated off Accra, to the rhythm of wild music. The word "Liberty" resounded like a leitmotiv and pictures of Nkrumah and of the Queen of England stood side by side, illuminated.

The Colonial Office had remembered the lesson learnt in India, in Indonesia, in Vietnam. Scarcely had he arrived in the Gold Coast than Arden Clarke, the Governor, had Nkrumah out of prison and allowed him to win the elections. What an example that was! It may be conceded that the British officers of the Colonial Office had a weakness for the nationalist movements of West Africa. Their leaders had studied and done well at Oxford or in the United States; they took part in the mainly anglophone Panafrican movement and seemed to be closer to the British tradition than the white South Africans of Johannesburg or even of the Cape, who criticized the policies of London, which they deemed to be too much in favour of the emancipation of the blacks. Rightly or wrongly the British looked with greater suspicion upon the movements of East Africa, a region closer to the Arab world, where the conflicts among blacks, Indians and whites seemed to be unsurmountable. They too had to be resolved for the British retreat in the Middle East placed Africa in the front line. Stafford Cripps had observed that "the future of the sterling zone henceforth depends on Africa's ability to develop itself".

It was in East Africa that the contradiction appeared to be most glaring. On one hand, there were the demands of a reactivated economic development – which has been called the new colonization – associated with the globalization of markets and requiring, as a corollary, a penetration of the colonial system up to the furthest hinterland and the most distant villages. On the other hand, there was the ill disciplined will to transfer the direct or indirect administration to a budding representative system. But, at that level, the traditional chiefs and the new leaders, merchants, teachers, representatives of excluded ethnic groups, began to oppose one another. In Uganda, in Tanganyika and in Kenya these contradictions generated a nationalism and a vigilance on the part of the conflicting groups which placed their constituents under close watch. In view of the different ethnic groups increasingly asserting their representativeness and of the colonist lobby which started organizing itself, London came to the conclusion that to move forward too slowly was worse than making haste. Nevertheless four years separate the independence of Tanganyika, and six years that of Kenya, from that of Ghana (1957).

1960 had been the year of Africa. The British had been successful in their decolonization in the west of Africa. But their failure in the east was evident. Here the British had vacillated between their two policies: either to keep the white minority in power, even if they numbered only a handful; or to transfer power to the natives, even if they "do not know" or do not want to use the institutional instruments bequeathed to them by the colonizer.

Still it was independent Africa which impelled the black and Indian movements of South Africa, in particular the ANC (African National Congress) of Nelson Mandela. Founded in 1912, this movement had had to endure an increasingly bloody repression by South African governments, especially after 1947. By 1974 President Vorster had completed the institutionalization of the racist system of apartheid, the fundamentals of which had been explicitly borrowed from Nazi theories, in which the Afrikaners had found the justification for their actions. As the ruling party since 1948, the National Christian Party could accordingly enact laws while putting into practice a policy of exclusion the symbol of which was the internal passport, the prohibition of mixed marriages.

Black and Indian resistance stiffened under the influence of the books of Frantz Fanon and of the Black Panthers' writings and actions in the United States. Relying on the same argument the idea of an armed insurrection began to grow given that, to the non-violence advocated by the Church, the government responded by means of repression. The Soweto massacre of 1976 represented one of the more dramatic moments of this confrontation. However, the very powerful white unions which had for a long time been anti-black as well as anti-employers, were evolving along a line more favourable to the union idea of the defence of the deprived.

The United Nations' condemnation of the politics of apartheid, the exclusion of South Africa from the U.N., its leaving the Commonwealth, were the several ordeals which prompted an increasing number of whites to join the ranks of the liberals, who at that time were still few in number. It was also observed that in Zimbabwe black power had been able to protect the interests of the whites. However, the blacks were divided among themselves, with the Zulus denouncing the hegemony of the Xhosa and that of the ANC.

Thereupon President De Klerk decided that there was a need to change the politics of the day. He freed Nelson Mandela who had been imprisoned for more than twenty years. This set into motion a process which, in 1994, culminated in the organization of free elections for all, on the basis of one man, one vote. They brought in a black majority and the assurance of participating in the government of the country.

The former USSR: an implosion more than an explosion

There did exist, within the USSR, national movements bent on separation, particularly in the Baltic republics, but also in Ukraine, in Armenia and in Georgia. But during the time of Brezhnev, then of Andropov, even of Chernenko, everyone thought the idea of independence was simply a dream. That was an expression which the Balts used while under Gorbachev the liberalization of the Soviet state was already under way.

According to Gorbachev a Union Treaty was to initiate a process of decolonization, a scheme which gave wings to the nationalist movements roused by the free elections of 1989. While the "reformers" opposed the "traditionalists" – they were also called the *Narodnyi Front* and the *Intern Front* – the Armenians shouting "Karabakh, Karabakh" ushered in the resurgence of ethno-nationalist aspirations which had been assumed to be outmoded or suppressed.

From that time on a vast nationalist movement swept across the Soviet Empire from one end to the other. Gorbachev found himself in the classic situation of the Head of State who, in order to perpetuate and preserve the cohesion of the entire empire, is forced to make concessions to those who are most pugnacious. To prevent a conservative coup, Gorbachev acted like De Gaulle who had entrusted the army to Salan, or Kerenski who entrusted it to Kornilov: he filled his government with traditionalists in order to better control them. They were the ones who staged the coup.

The important point is that Boris Yeltsin succeeded in turning the situation around. His goal was certainly to substitute himself, as the President of Russia, for the President of the USSR. But his tactic resulted in decolonizing the USSR and causing it to disappear. In actuality, by proclaiming the sovereignty of Russia within the USSR, then by getting out of it after dissolving the Communist Party, he gave the different republics their *de facto* freedom. The republics followed suit with each of them transforming the structures of the USSR into an empty shell and leading its president to resign. Then Russia invited the independent republics to associate themselves with her. Some did, some did not. Thus was born the CIS (Commonwealth of Independent States), without Georgia (which joined in 1993), and without the Baltic Republics. At the same time, within the Federation of Russia, the movement which had been launched led some Republics – Tatar, Chechen – to reconsider their bonds with Moscow.

On the whole, however, the "centrifugal" movement was initiated by the centre. It was an unprecedented event in history.

Shaken as if by an earthquake the USSR was fractured. Yet, from 1993 on, it seemed that the cracks were being filled and some of the ancestral bonds were being sealed anew.

The expression "putsch" does not apply to the conservative coup of 1991 since the plot was hatched by civil or military leaders who represented the system and were in fact in charge of its administration. But after the failure of that coup the situation in the CIS and in the other states raised many questions. Following the break-up of the USSR and the disintegration of the Communist Party which used to cement its organization, common characteristics nevertheless outlasted the old unity insofar as none of the present republics is free from certain general phenomena such as the breakdown of the economic infrastructure. This situation extends even to the Baltic states. These phenomena include the permanence of the political establishment, with 30 to 90 percent of the personnel remaining active, depending on whether they are located close to or far away from Moscow: a feature which makes all the difference between this and most of the former popular democracies. The network of power structures and of intra- or trans-republican complicities also survives. Specific situations have arisen where there have been interethnic conflicts – in Moldavia, in the Caucasus, in the Baltic States, in Central Asia. Moscow deemed these to be dangerous to the extent that the recall of the Russian army to the Republic of Russia became a priority. Yet even as late as 1992 Moscow was finding plenty of reasons to delay this repatriation from the different popular democracies, in order to perpetuate the myth of a military presence in Eastern Europe. The same action could follow in the Kurile Islands.

Behind the struggle for power between Yeltsin and the Parliament, in the Republic of Russia, other conflicts often spill over the frontiers of the states born of the former USSR. At times they strengthen the return to an individual identity, at other times they neutralize it. This is due to several, often paradoxical, facts which deserve to be itemized in order to assess their effects.

To understand how they function we shall, contrary to custom, proceed from the periphery to the centre (cf. Ferro, *Les Origines de la Perestroika*, Ramsay, 1990, pp. 107ff).

The first proposition The Muslim republics were self-governing before the proclamation of their independence. That is, when Gorbachev arrived on the scene, the leaders of Uzbekistan were Uzbeks, those of Azerbaijan were Azeris, and so on. Gorbachev was surprised that the security forces did not intervene to stop the massacres of the Armenians. He was told that "Azeris were not going to shoot at Azeris in order to protect Armenians". The security forces in Azerbaijan were "Azeri" rather than "Soviet". Another example: hardly had Gorbachev replaced an opponent of perestroika in Alma-Alta in Kazakhstan than riots broke out. Gorbachev did not realize that the opponent was a Kazakh and his replacement Russian. In other words the republics were gradually becoming independent. That was true also of Armenia and of Georgia.

The second proposition Independence did not necessarily imply a will to separation on the part of the Muslim republics. They did not specifically want separation in the same way as, for example, Tunisia or Morocco did, when during the 1950s, in conjunction with Paris, they organized their separation in stages. On the contrary, in Central Asia there was a sort of *inverted separatism*, that is, the leaders of the republics strove to exert a pressure *on* the central institutions of the former USSR. For example, Pavlov, Minister of Finance – he took part in the 1991 coup – entertained close links with the Uzbek State apparatus and its mafia.

Given these conditions it is not surprising that, during the conflict which opposed Gorbachev to Yeltsin, in the year preceding the coup, the leaders of the republics sided with Gorbachev. They were against Yeltsin because, with the proclamation of Russian sovereignty he was actually setting in motion a process which would culminate in the separation of every republic. And that would entail the republics losing the advantages possessed at the Centre. Nor is it surprising that, on the whole, the republics or at least their bureaucracies supported the leaders of the coup.

The third proposition In Russia perestroika was perceived as a policy of openness to freedom. But in the Muslim republics it was felt as a danger for the future of the traditional social relations which, in some way, Communism had perpetuated: the President of the Soviet was often a former khan, etc. Moreover with glasnost Moscow was "uzbekanizing" the underworld traffic. Under the pretext that the opium poppy was being cultivated in Uzbekistan, Islam as a whole was criticized as soon as it staked its claims for mosques, while the central power openly flirted with the Orthodox Church. Any claim made in an Islamic country was viewed as a sign of a possible allegiance to Iran. Such an attitude on the part of the Russians resulted in the development of an Islamic political movement and all sorts of variations of a political Islam, the different types of which have reinforced the identity of each republic in relation to its neighbour. This process covers the Shi'ite fundamentalism prevailing in Tajikistan and the seemingly secular Islam of Azerbaijan, not to mention Sunni or other variations. The strengthening of the identity of each republic acts simultaneously against the reunification of "Turkestan", as well as against the absorption of the entire Islamic area by its great neighbours: Turkey, Iran or Pakistan. It may be further stressed that the *tempo* of the Islamic Revolution in Iran or elsewhere, and that of the crisis agitating the Soviet Republics did not coincide. Without any doubt, this staggering of political developments has averted the irreversible drift of Soviet Islam towards these three countries.

The fourth proposition The republics lying on the southern perimeter find themselves in a post-colonial situation, in the sense that the withdrawal of the Russians preceded the proclamation of independence by a long way. The exodus of the Russians continues apace, without any drama: in different circumstances it would have been called a *successful decolonization*. Then some of the Republics have kept "their" Russians or called upon new Russian "advisers" to aid them. Only Kazakhstan offers a different picture: here the Russians are as numerous as the Kazakhs, the responsibilities are, at all levels, equally divided and thus arises a situation which creates permanent inter-ethnic conflicts.

Conversely, in some republics which have become independent, especially in the Caucasus, the ethnic conflicts between Armenians and Turks-Azeris have resurfaced, with greater violence than before the Russian or Soviet era. And here we find an original situation. In their concern to liberate themselves from the Russians, the Georgians were not aware that they were exercising a sort of colonial power over the Abkhaz. Thus we are back in a pre-, not a post-colonial situation, with the Russian once again acting as arbiters in disputes breaking out on their borders.

The fifth proposition The observations made about the Muslim or Caucasian republics take on a particular significance when one notes that in *Russian* Siberia one comes across the same kind of phenomena. At the Siberian meeting held at Krasnoyarsk, in the spring of 1992, one delegate said "we are not going to separate from Russia, but from its government". Another delegate stressed that the meeting was viewed as a means of exerting pressure *on* Moscow. These are two characteristic features: on the one hand, the heads of the administration, the representatives of Moscow, were absent from the meeting. This signified a growing conflict between the central authority and the representative institutions. But, above all, it was out of fear of being associated with the "separatists" that the *national* Republics of Siberia (Republics of Tuva, Yakut and Buryat) explained and justified their absence. The Evenks emphasized that they intended to proceed from territorial autonomy to national autonomy, but this within a Russian, not a Siberian, framework.

When set against the second proposition, these facts make it quite plain that, in the spirit of the demands which were made, the national problem does not necessarily contain an ethnic component, nor does it seek a solution in separation while harbouring ulterior motives. For example, among the Balts the will to separate was the prime mover of the Lithuanians. At the beginning of perestroika the Estonians were violently anti-Russian and yet did not dare formulate their willingness to separate. Yet very quietly and globally this separatist will swept along all the Balts, the Georgians, the Ukrainians, even the Armenians. In short, separatism swayed the Christians, while elsewhere the trend was less apparent. On the other hand, within Russia the Republic of the Tatars wants to be sovereign, that is, its leaders, whether Tatar or Russian, want full freedom to dispose of their resources as they wish. In Siberia the same claim is made by Russians and Yakuts or Buryats.

Within the CIS it is therefore the question of hostility to the concentration of power and the problem of centralization at all levels of decision-making which are the common parameter of all the national or colonial situations. In a certain way one witnesses the return of the old antagonism which has always existed between, on one hand, the central power identified, at the time of the Communist Party, with its administration and, on the other hand, the representative institutions, whether the zemstvos prior to 1917, or the Soviets, afterwards. However, neither the zemstvos, nor the Soviets were ever able to go beyond the competence of a reduced local administration, whatever the competence of the elected representatives (zemstvo), or their real representation (soviet). As is well known, the history of the USSR can be explained, from 1917 onwards, by an absorption of the powers at ground level – the expression of a direct democracy – by the power at the top – which eulogizes and practises democratic centralism. In 1988 Gorbachev wanted to infuse new life in the Soviets, that is, to give back to the representative organs their rights and abilities. In 1993–94 Yeltsin eliminated them. What does this contradiction mean?

The real problem is that at both the top and at the bottom there is an igorance of the sharing of power. For example, Yeltsin has undertaken to appoint representatives of the president in the territories and regions – the *namestnik*, the emissary – while the governor is also appointed by Moscow. Consequently no real local autonomous administration exists. The Mayor of St Petersburg, Sobchak, does not hesitate to say that these Soviets are useless, because they are powerless. "In fact their only capacity is to scuttle the decisions". To simplify: in 1917, the local Soviets were illiterate or uncultured, but the elected members had all the power. Today they comprise educated and competent individuals, but they have no juridical or other capacity, except that of *countering* the power at the centre.

Accordingly the elected representatives at the base of the pyramid dream of being able to legislate, execute, judge. But they too know nothing about sharing power. In the face of the powerlessness of the base, the centre legislates and also executes. The problems of identity only constitute a *mobile variable* of the problem of power. That is our **sixth proposition**.

The problem of the conflict between the central authority and representative power at the base – yesterday, the soviets and tomorrow some other – comprehends many other problems, which would be extinguished if the local institutions were recognized as genuine executive powers. Till now the composition of the local authorities has gone through the least change since the days of perestroika and of the coup of 1991. But today the system of local powers serves as the backbone of the opposition and of identity-based separatism, of opposition to reforms. Eighty percent of the presidents of the former Soviets come from the Party apparatus. They could be eliminated after the bloody trial of strength which occurred in September 1993 between Yeltsin and the Parliament.

A strange development! The nomenklatura tries to avenge itself by moving through the channels of representative power for the sake of the interests of the citizens in their own region. This provokes an identity reaction and at times an anti-centralist nationalism. Hence Yeltsin must make concessions to the opponents of the free market, to the very ones who only yesterday were bent on shooting Gorbachev down. Yeltsin thus puts into practice the policies of his fallen rival and predecessor.

These propositions do clearly indicate that the return to identity, or the birth of a nation, linked most often to ethnic or ethno-linguistic or even religious considerations, can be associated with genuinely governmental, or political, or simply ideological considerations, whether these cut across the preceding ones or not. In Chechenia and in Omsk, in Murmansk or in Kuban, the tendency towards autonomy cuts across all the relevant particulars, independently of the ethnic composition of the populations in question.

All this would suggest that a nation is a permanent and at the same time a transitory formation.

11

DECOLONIZATION
HALTED

The liberated peoples thought that "a new order would rise from the ruins" and that the instability arising from their struggles for freedom would cease. But "the violence of the soldiers and of the officers, the heroes of victory, their pride, their lust for power culminated in a militarization of power whose victims happened to be the urbanized classes . . .". "Even though this movement terminated in a relative democratization of the local political system . . . , the inequalities of the past made room for others, ensuring at the same time the promotion of a few . . ." On the whole the regimes that were instituted were such "that they cast discredit upon those who had advocated change, upon the elites and the urban middle classes who had generated the political awareness that finally led to independence".

This diagnosis may seem to have been taken straight from René Dumont's *L'Afrique noire est mal partie* (1962). It is not. The diagnosis explains what happened a century earlier in Latin America, in the aftermath of the wars of independence. Its author is the Argentinian historian Tulio Halperin-Donghi. It may be observed that both colonist independence and the freedom movements of colonized peoples have brought about similar results, at least in the *short term*. In fact some of these features can be seen in many other countries besides those of black Africa, countries which became independent after the middle of the twentieth century.

One of the reasons for this similarity is that the independence movements of the nineteenth and twentieth centuries were overtaken by the perverted continuance of pre-colonial relationships, at the same time as they collided with a wider movement which has not ceased getting stronger.

Certain features of pre-colonial history come back, though they have been altered by the experience of colonization. In Upper Peru pre-conquest conflicts have reappeared: the conquest may be said to have "preserved" them. The same pattern has been seen in Vietnam which, scarcely after it won its independence, tried to seize Laos and Cambodia. This situation obtains also in the Caucasus where conflicts have survived

344

the Russian and the Soviet conquests. Other examples occur in South and in Central Africa.

Often old conflicts have been aggravated by the establishment of frontiers which stride across ancient relational structures, particularly in the whole of black Africa.

But more significant still is the resurgence of situations which, during its time, colonialism helped to modify or to exacerbate, though it may have seemed at the time that those old conflicts had been for ever exorcized. This is illustrated by a good example, provided in Jean-Pierre Chrétien's ethno-historical studies, relative to Burundi and Rwanda, where the bloody conflicts between Hutus and Tutsis were resumed in 1992. The division stems from a difference between the clans that preceded the arrival of the Europeans. But the bloody expression of the opposition between these groups and categories appeared only during the fifties and sixties. "The increasing importance of the ethnic factor in the constitution of political support gave rise to a chain of apparently uncontrollable discriminatory acts of violence and of fear. The colonial event lies between these two moments: that of the old experience of a difference and that of a racially determined conflict."

From European hegemony to American hegemony

In the nineteenth century this wider movement was the Industrial Revolution, of which Great Britian was the driving force. She effortlessly displaced Spain and Portugal in South America in order to sell her industrial products and to control the commercial networks. The new states ran into debt to acquire the marvels of British production and the British were satisfied with simply doing business. Thus a sort of new colonial pact got under way: it linked the interests of the European industrialists to the local leading classes. But soon the former had gained control over the economy of the country. Great Britain was actually the ruling power in Peru and in Argentina; German capitalists secured the coffee trade in Guatemala; American companies took possession of the sugar-cane lands in Cuba. Soon it was the turn of the low lands of Central America to be penetrated: controlled by Boston the banana empire took shape. In Haiti and in San Domingo, the American lender recovered his money by means of his control over the customs which yielded the bulk of the state revenue.

Between 1870 and 1910 one finds a situation and its attendant procedures similar to those obtaining in Egypt or in Tunisia.

The "Venezuelan crisis" in 1902 signalled the passage, in America, from the European to the United States hegemony. On behalf of all the creditors of Venezuela Theodore Roosevelt led an armed crusade against the debtors. He launched his campaign at the same time as the expedition led by Wilhelm II against the Boxers. The American intervention was justified in terms of the Monroe doctrine, but above all, like the German expedition, it took its stand on moral principles. Because the United States went about things in a different way from Europe.

In "Latin" America the British had not imparted a moral or ideological tone to their economic domination. Granted, they averred they were acting in the name of civilization in Africa or elsewhere, but not in "Latin" America. Here they conducted business, as usual, and they were satisfied with concrete advantages. Tulio Halperin-Donghi has correctly diagnosed that, on the contrary, the Americans wanted to export their original puritanism, this discipline of political virtue which was at the foundation of their independence and of their revolution. The "Yankees" wanted to lead the South Americans to a "healthy" management of their business. But what to the South Americans appeared like hypocritical cunning, designed to control their budget and their country, was actually something more than a mere tactic. It was a real strategy.

In other words, educational moralism was used to justify very evident material advantages, but its main goal was to perpetuate a relationship of domination. The master remains always the master.

In the name of principles, of the big stick policy, of the Monroe doctrine, Theodore Roosevelt had "liberated" Cuba (and the Philippines) from Spanish domination. In the name of their "security" the Americans from that time on controlled Central America and Panama: a policy which has lasted throughout the entire twentieth century – military intervention in Haiti in 1915, in Guatemala at the end of the Second World War, support for the landing in the Bay of Pigs against Castro's Cuba, a host of interventions in the politics of the small States of the banana empire during the sixties and seventies of the twentieth century, then against the Sandinista Revolution in Nicaragua. Noam Chomsky has correctly demonstrated that there is a correlation between the amount of the funds handed over by the State Department or by the CIA to Latin American governments and the crimes committed in these countries against human rights, especially since 1976, when Latin America again opened its door to foreign, more particularly North American, investors. This direct or indirect help has always been available in the name of the struggle "for democracy", against "subversion", and according to the principles of moral rectitude which American policies claim to represent.

In actuality, this American practice has not been limited only to the states of Hispanic America. It was also directed, after their accession to independence in the 1960s, at states under surveillance which had to be kept away from Communism, such as South Korea and Indonesia. In Vietnam this policy was the cause of one of the most cruel wars in history. Unable to drop an atom bomb on an ally of the USSR, and driven by public opinion, Nixon decided to withdraw (1973).

As for the "aid" which accompanied this policy, it has resulted in the enrichment of the richest of the leaders of the poorest countries, and in the impoverishment of the poorest of the inhabitants of these countries.

From post-colonial relations to multinational imperialism

Should one speak of a neo-colonialism or a neo-imperialism in the independent Afro-Asian world of the 1950s and 1960s? Perhaps both, depending on the particular case.

From the nineteenth century on, black Africa, like Latin America, experienced a type of class colonization. In 1961, Assalé, the Prime Minister of Cameroon, was told by a mayor that "the masses had the feeling that national sovereignty had created a privileged class which is alienated from them" (quoted in René Dumont, *L'Afrique noire est mal partie*). That is precisely what the Algerians were saying in 1993, with this difference, that in Algeria the elites who took over from the colonists do not govern the country which, both for them and for the masses, is being run by the military and by the FLN-state. "So we have not stopped being occupied . . ."

In black Africa, as someone wrote, administration is the main industry. In Dahomey, it absorbed 64 percent of the 1970 budget. Gabon had one deputy for every 6,000 inhabitants; in France there is one deputy for 100,000. In Gabon an entire life's work is not equivalent to two months' salary of a member of parliament. The figures for this degeneration may be multiplied in relation to the hopes arising from liberation. In other countries this decline was coupled with the poverty caused by the expenditure on armaments: in Iraq, for example, this has hindered the improvement of the standard of living of sections of the population. The case of Iraq serves only as an example: military expenditures have contributed to the collapse of the standard of living of entire populations. However the original colonial countries have to a great extent contributed to this state of affairs for the benefit of their own industries – those of France and of Great Britain – which have accordingly enjoyed "thirty glorious years" after decolonization. Such was the first form taken by neo-colonialism, perpetuating the privileged links between Europe and its former colonies. The second form consists of the institutionalization of the connivance between the new leaders of the colonies and the political or financial circles in the colonial countries.

Mongo Beti has made an attempt to understand how the repercussions of this corruption reached as far as his village, in the heart of a "devastated" Cameroon. He wonders if it is all the fault of the Africans. Is it an old or a new problem? Unless it results from those agreements made in due form which guaranteed to France and Great Britain certain advantages or monopolies – for example, the oil of the Sahara – while the former colonies bought too many tractors or increased their production of coffee, instead of developing their food crops. Such agreements testify to the survival of a sort of colonial pact.

Lastly, as a perverse effect of the colonial period, the adoption of the untouchability of frontiers instituted in the past is the cause of tragic conflicts following the independence of countries particularly in black Africa: Nigeria, Chad, Cameroon.

An inverse aspect of this type of relations bequeathed by the past has been the recourse by the colonial countries to *the industrial reserve army of the countries of the Third World*. The importation of migrant workers, which had begun in the 1930s, experienced a dramatic boom with the onset of decolonization in the 1960s. Especially in France, the power of the protest movement of the metropolitan workers was making the employers' success and the maintenance of their rate of profit less secure. At the same time a growing number of French were becoming more and more reluctant to perform tiresome jobs. Against this background the then governments of De Gaulle–Pompidou made it possible for a growing mass of migrants to move into the country. At first the latter were young and unmarried and consequently were cost-effective for management. The influx of these workers made it possible to alleviate the situation in the labour market and to rebuild an industrial reserve army more flexible than the national manpower. At the beginning of the 1970s the skilled workers were 23.1 percent Tunisians, 18 percent Moroccans, 15.9 percent Algerians, 9.5 percent blacks from the former French Africa (see P. Souyri, *La Dynamique du capitalisme au XX siécle*, p. 226). Thus *a colonial type situation in the mother country itself* was created where the French appropriated to themselves the white collar jobs, the higher-level positions, and so on. Gradually with the entrenchment of the immigrants from the overseas territories, families sprung up, grew, multiplied. Consequently the national budget swelled while at the outset the presence of this proletariat was an assurance only of financial advantages.

The return effect of colonization is felt also in Great Britain where Indians and Pakistanis, as well as the immigrants from the West Indies, have substituted themselves for the English proletariat in a number of sectors of productivity, for instance, the railways. But the immigrant elites have also penetrated the medical profession and other services of the Welfare State. This pattern obtains also in the Russian Republic where Koreans perform lowly jobs in the province of the Soviet Far East: they constitute a clandestine sub-proletariat deprived of rights.

The effects of post-colonialism and of neo-imperialism overlapped in the face of the rise of American hegemonism when, in the aftermath of the Second World War and during the decolonization process, the United States replaced the Europeans in the periphery of their former zones of domination: Saudi Arabia, Iran, West Indies. At the same time the new independent states tried to assert economic authority over the resources of their soil and sub-soil still under the control of trusts. The policy of nationalization adopted at that time has sparked a series of conflicts which, as an indirect consequence, have shaken the global economy, for example, the oil crisis of 1973.

With their inability to continue importing a henceforth "burdensome" manpower from the Third World, the leaders of the Western economies have displaced part of their activities towards the *human reserves of the periphery*. In view of the high salaries payable in their own country, the Americans set the example by building a growing number of factories in former colonies like the Philippines and Singapore, as well as in South Korea, Mexico, Nigeria. The Japanese were the first to imitate them in Taiwan, Hong Kong and Singapore; then the Germans did likewise, especially in Latin America, and finally the English and the French. Little by little the former colonizing countries indirectly benefited from the labour of this proletariat of the periphery, from that displacement, while a part of the active population of the developed countries become idle or unproductive.

But therein lies the difference between, on one hand, the African States which have not taken advantage of their independence and, on the other hand, some Latin American or Asian countries which have, on the contrary, been successful in compelling investors to cede an increasing proportion of their profits to the local governments or managerial classes. At the right time they have been able to hitch themselves on to the globalization process of the economy, to take part in it and even, as in Singapore and in Taiwan, to share in its management, on a footing equal to that of the great economic powers. Today, Malaysia imports foreign workers.

Consequently the differentiation that has occurred between this and that former colony since independence and, likewise, the problems inherited by the mother countries cannot be explained simply in terms of bilateral, neo-colonial relations, or even of neo-imperialism, but indeed by more general phenomena which, like the industrialization of the nineteenth century, have collided with decolonization.

As early as 1965 Nkrumah wrote: "The essence of neo-colonialism consists of the fact that a state which is in theory independent and endowed with all the attributes of sovereignty actually has its policies directed from outside." This opinion is the first definition provided by the head of a sovereign state who saw clearly that, from a certain point, the former imperialist powers no longer had any interest in controlling the former colonies "from inside", but were very interested in "helping" them to develop, and to replacing a visible presence by the invisible government of the big banks: the International Monetary Fund, World Bank, and so on. That is neo-imperialism, rather than neo-colonialism. Though with the globalization of the economy this term is no longer adequate. Nor is the expression "imperialism of the multinational firms", for it does not fully explain the interference of these interests with those of the states. Would it not be better to speak of "*multinational imperialism*"?

Aspects and effects of the unification of the world

One of the leading features of colonization was to set in motion the process of the unification of the world and, within this framework, to have widened the distance between the colonizing powers and the others. In 1967, at the time of decolonization, Josue de Castro's diagnosis elucidated this trait in regard to the exchange rates. Paul Bairoch confirmed it twenty-five years later.[1]

Colonization was indeed a standardizing process. But standardization did not necessarily occur as a result of the encounters between civilizations. It happened in the Americas, in Mexico and particularly in Peru, even though a part of the population was left out. However, in Africa, the integration process came rather late, though the structures of annexation had been established as early as in the sixteenth to eighteenth centuries. It was only after the 1880s, or rather in the period 1900–30, that it became operative and it only became unbearable after the "second" colonization, that of the 1950s. That was an evolutionary process that took place in Angola as well as in East Africa. In India, the process of the economic unification of the world reached the hinterland of the country only in the 1930s, starting from the cities built on the coast, and an entire section of society had to overcome the challenge posed by the widening of gaps. This cultural, even political process of unification has elicited strong resistances within the country, as it has in some parts of the Islamic world of today.

But it is the Far East which has responded to the challenge of decolonization and of imperialism in the most original way: by going beyond its precepts, while holding on to some of the forms of its own modernity which is not necessarily of the Western type. The crossroads of Java had already established a sort of "multinational system", before the arrival of the Europeans.

The status and the evolution of languages are revealing. First phase: in the colony, the Frenchman, the Englishman, the Spaniard only learn the native language in order to command better. Second phase: they hesitate to teach the natives the metropolitan culture in order not to run the risk of awakening them. Third phase: Anglo-Saxons, French, Russians and particularly the Soviets develop the teaching of their own language in order to perpetuate their technical, economic, political or cultural advantage. The end of the twentieth century is marked by a fourth phase; the Americans in their turn must learn the Japanese language in order not to be excluded from the subsidiary companies which Japanese industry has installed in the United States.

*

While there existed in the sixteenth century several world economies – China, the West, the Islamo-Turkish world – unification has proceeded irreversibly and today there exist scarcely any endorheic zones outside the system.

First phenomenon: between the sixteenth and the twentieth centuries, the unification of the world grew faster. During the generations which preceded the First World War distances were shortened at a faster rate than ever in the past; the world had never seemed so small. European trade and expansion strengthened the bonds between the East and the West. The consequences of this unification could not be foreseen. They did not have an impact simply on the colonies.

Accordingly even in Europe new authorities sprang up beside the traditional and well defined ones like the monarch, the priest, the law, the boss, the family, the officer. The new ones were anonymous and uncontrollable. Some which were linked to expansion and caused prices to suddenly soar or fall, ruined traditional agriculture, or altered fashions and styles, such as gastronomic tastes, sartorial or decorative styles, forms of entertainment. Essentially European, the changes and technological innovations nullified inventions almost as soon as they appeared, or they brought about the death of old traditional crafts.

All this in the name of progress, of science, of freedom.

But today, ever since the end of "decolonization", these phenomena have penetrated the most distant corners of the nerve centres of the world. Such cataclysms have smitten the plateaus of the Andes as well as those of black Africa. They see themselves ruined by the unification of markets which has paid no heed to the liberation of the formerly colonized peoples or to the aspiration of others to a political or cultural autonomy. Nothing has changed, whether the new master is the colonizer, or Wall Street, or Brussels, or the gold standard.

One can compare the results.

At the beginning of the twentieth century the majority of Europeans did not understand how the economy functioned. They still nurse this ignorance, but they are aware of it. In this incomprehensible world everyone has tried to escape from the curse which has fallen on them. The towns and villages of Europe at the end of the nineteenth century and at the beginning of the twentieth century too witnessed a return to religion: this movement is represented in France by Charles Péguy, in Russia by Vladimir Soloviev, and by others in other places. But not all could find a solace in religion. The proliferation of the popular press all over Europe at the beginning of this century testifies to this need for escape. Others chose alcohol, or suicide: it is not a matter of coincidence that Durkheim wrote a book on suicide in 1902.

Those were the *first signs of the loss of points of reference*. But a large number of people came up with a different reaction, as if all of a sudden, in the form of a collective or individual rebellion, so that emigration and revolution became two phenomena which are corollary and mutually connected (it has not been sufficiently demonstrated) and provided an answer to ill-fortune. Thus Russia and Italy were simultaneously the fatherlands of Bakunin and of Malatesta, countries of large-scale emigration, and the birthplaces of two answers to the crisis of this century, war: Communism and Fascism.

But, since the end of the colonies, what do we see?

In the midst of the uncertainties of our time and in the face of the inability of leaders to exert full control over the working of the economy or the functioning of society, we are witnessing again a return of mysticism, an attraction for the irrational in Western societies, as is proved by the success of foreign religious movements. Among the young, drug addiction has taken over from the alcohol of our forbears. Collective moments too have surfaced when emigration and revolt come together, as a reaction to the failure of decolonization, witness the rebirth of fundamentalist Islam in the Arab, or Turkish, or Iranian world.

Linked to the first, the second phenomenon does not concern individuals, but *nations*, states, ethnic groups. At the beginning of the twentieth century the progressive geographical concentration of industrial activities and the development of capitalism determined *general* economic phenomena unknown during the pre-industrial age. For example, the conditions governing the whole of agriculture were modified by the liberal laws of 1846. Subsequently coffee production in Brazil during the inter-war years and sugar production in Cuba after 1959 were all of a sudden crippled.

Then followed the collapse of the prices of agricultural products and of raw materials, the rise in interest rates initiated by the Central Bank of the United States, the debt crisis, which since 1982 has resulted in an inverse transfer of resources, the former colonies transferring to the rich countries more financial resources than they receive. International trade has rarely impoverished entire countries, but it has ruined the traditionally producing social strata, whether the respective country was independent or not.

Nowadays African countries find themselves completely ruined by specialization, so that, first in Europe then, today, in a large number of countries, each nation or each state has the feeling of being surrounded by enemies who have designs on its prosperity, even on its very existence. These feelings are exacerbated as soon as a society, by means of violence, transgresses the international practices which are designed to keep it down: the USSR in 1917, Germany after 1933, Egypt after Suez, Cuba in 1959, Iran under Khomeini.

Accordingly national sentiment has become one of the forms of the collective reaction of societies facing the phenomena arising from the, above all economic, unification of the world. The movement of nationalities is a variation of this sentiment: it is not only linked to religious or national oppression. One understands this feature better if one associates the patriotism of nations, in the twentieth century, to the resurgence of regionalism. This phenomenon can be seen in action in the Russian Empire, from the Tsarist period when, with the development of the railways, Russian colonists settled along the rail tracks, thus provoking resistance movements not only among those who never considered themselves Russians – Finns, Tatars, Georgians, but also among the Ukrainians, the Mordvins, the Maris.

Today one can see that between the obligation, for the Ukrainians, to speak Russian and the prohibition, for French school children, against speaking in patois, there is only a difference in degree, a form of resistance to the state centralization. The resurgence of Provençal or Breton regionalism in 1877, the persistence of the southern problem in Italy or even the Sicilian question, are phenomena of the same nature. It is a patriotism indeed, but it is dissociated from the present time.

Today the regionalist phenomenon – which for a long time seemed to have been buried – is resurfacing and spreading, not only in Corsica, in Wallonia, in the Spanish Basque region, where the presence of democracy deprives violence of any justification. It is manifesting itself beyond the bounds of little Europe, in those countries which have freed themselves from colonial oppression, or simply from those which exerted economic domination over them. The upsurge of regional entities occurs wherever the construction of a strong state, legitimized by the necessity of protection, has intimidated whole communities, micro-nations or nations which are rediscovering their identity: the Kurds since the time of Ataturk, the Kabyles of Algeria, the Sahraouis, and the myriad nations of India which will not tolerate the monopoly exercised by the Congress Party, in the name of Indianness.

Consequently one sees a centrifugal movement as the answer of minorities to institutional centralism, itself an answer to the threat which the external world presents to every state, to every community.

Institutional and bureaucratic standardization has gone hand in hand with the development of the state. In the West it dates from the sixteenth century, from the French Revolution or from the technocratic age. This phenomenon has taken the form of a multiplicity of social groups which have widened the area of the central authority, successively the clergy, the military, the officials, the cadres, even scholars and other experts. Their promotion extends the social distance between the centre and the periphery. Consequently those who are not integrated with the system are rejected to the exterior. This rejection affects those who are excluded, all the other collective victims, the "hinterland" as well as entire regions and proletarian nations, and even the developed countries ever since the bureaucracy has become supranational. By the end of the nineteenth century the peasant of the Cévennes saw, above the epaulettes of his officer, the face of his former master. Today the power is no longer that of the sub-prefect or of the deputy; it belongs to the Brussels Commission. *The citizen who has lost his points of reference, has also lost his refuge.* However, this penomenon equally affects all the new states which have been born or have reappeared since the end of the colonial period. The westernization of the world, linked to colonization, has culminated in a standardization of institutions, beginning with the forms of "representative democracy" and ending with those of dictatorship. The same administrative shifts can be seen in Africa and in South-East Asia.

At international conferences it is not the "proletarian" nations which have the least number of experts. Their political staff is equivalent to that of the other countries: little Barbados has its deputies, its ambassadors, its train of former ministers.

Cultural unification – like material unification – also tends towards standardization. But in this case it often concerns the consequences of what has been called the "Columbian exchange" between America and Europe. It relates to the food or other products which have crossed the Atlantic in one direction or the other – the turkey, corn, the horse – or have moved from one civilization to another – tea, coffee, tobacco – each of them often being identified with the new fashion.

Standardization is present in a few other areas. The most widespread one is dance, for in this area the conquering movement has proceeded from black Americas. In his often repressed desire for the Black Venus the white man welcomed negro dances, but by extending the distance between them and him. The first was the *lundu*, a Bantu erotic dance, adopted by the mulatto men and women of the eighteenth century. Then came those who were crazy about the tango of the blacks of Buenos Aires, a hybrid dance, with its faint reminiscence of the sexual act. It had become a sort of national dance in Argentina before reaching Europe and the United States. Then came the Brazilian samba, which gradually became a white dance, like the rumba, softened in relation to its African origins, and so on (cf. Paudrat, J.-L.).

While negro music – with jazz among others – has also spread over the entire world, African art has had a rather difficult itinerary. "Strange idols", people said in the sixteenth century, on bringing statuettes from Africa; "primitive art" was the term used at the time of the first Great Exhibition, following a mission by Pierre Savorgnan de Brazza in 1886. It attracted 30,000 visitors. But it was held in the Orangerie of the Jardin des Plantes, an annex of the Museum of Natural History, which consequently defined its status. Again in Paris, on the occasion of the World Exhibition of 1889, the organizers set about popularizing the colonial idea. Naturally there were collectors who appreciated the refinement of that statuary. But the publications related to the artefacts are mainly written by geographers, ethnologists, anthropologists.

Around 1905 Vlaminck and Gauguin, together with Matisse and Apollinaire, were the great discoverers of African sculpture. Carl Einstein published the first texts on their aesthetics which has had such an influence on modern art. "Official" recognition occurred in 1912, in an article in *Gil Blas* on negro "art", about which Jean Cocteau wrote, in 1917, "that it is not related to the beguiling flashes of childhood, of madness, but to the noblest styles of human civilization".

What is noteworthy is that from then on the rupture was more serious than at the time of Flaubert's *Salammbo* or of the orientalism of Loti or of Delacroix. A whole civilization was being questioned rather than an attempt made to amuse indifferent minds. The revolution went further still when, in the painting derived from the voodoo tradition, the aesthetics were based less on the forms than on the symbols. In pictures the organization of space corresponds to a magical logic, as for example, in those of Hervé Telemaque or Hector Hyppolite.

The recognition of this art brought about its participation in the process of cultural unification: in this case, though, it was protected from any drift towards standardization. This situation obtains also in the subsequent development of African cinema which, while using Western techniques (as does the Indian cinema), has nevertheless preserved its aesthetic identity.

Another phenomenon deserves mention. The struggles for freedom, the conquest of independence have not in any way extinguished the different processes of unification set up since the sixteenth century. This unification has been described in the economic area and standardization has in the same way invaded the nature of the political systems. It may be true that these states are self-governing, but they no longer control the functioning of their society and of production. Consequently the partial cancellation of the expected results of those struggles for independence is further aggravated by another phenomenon which generates reactions: the standardization of information and of the media.

In the West it is well known because it places itself in the foreground of daily life. The process of standardization is well under way both in the print media, with Springer, Hersant, Murdoch, and in television. The important point is that televised information becomes standardized independently of those who control the media, by virtue of the use of satellites, an effect *superadded* to the effects of concentration. Accordingly it has been observed that out of a hundred "subjects" filmed and distributed by the different channels (BBC, TF1, RAI, CBS) the number of common images has not stopped growing in a characteristic fashion for the past ten years, while the ability of each channel to produce independent images/ information has been correspondingly diminished, except as regards local incidents and brief news items. The same images appear on the television whether one is in London, or in Cairo, or in Lima. So one can speak of standardization. And one can imagine the protests of the non-producers in the Third World, that is, mostly the formerly colonized peoples, all those who do not own the right to the word, to the image.

Local radios and video films do not have the means to broadcast a genuine counter-information.

Yet there does exist a counter-analysis which is carried out at other levels. Without doubt it is one of the paradoxes of our time that it can be all the more vibrant the further standardization becomes more deeply entrenched.

The verification of this phenomenon occurs in a particular area, in historical analysis. It is central because it determines the interpretation of our time and safeguards the identity of nations and of ethnic groups.

For example, in the USSR, where history was for a long time at the service of power and the Party was supposed to embody its meaning and its progression, opponents and dissidents constructed a counter-analysis of the USSR. In some way their action was like an act of *smuggling*. This counter-history had very few takers in the USSR itself, because there was no institution to provide it with protection. That is why in Poland, at a time when *Solidarnocz* thought it would survive, one of its first projects was to rewrite history. Such a gesture recalls that of the Socialists of the last century, such as Mehring or Jaurès, who rethought history in terms of the class struggle in order to confront the official history.

But it was the former colonized peoples who not long ago gave a similar example of calling official history into question: the griots in black Africa, ulemas and marabouts in Islamic countries have fought a battle against the prevailing modes of information and history, first on the ground of facts and narration, and afterwards on that of values by calling into question those which gave legitimacy to the colonial conquest. In the United States the blacks undertook this task as early as 1974. And, today, again in the United States, the Indians are emulating them, as are the Catalans in Spain, the proponents of the Oc language in France, or the women's movements nearly everywhere.

For a long time oral tradition and later the cinema have been the most effective means to broadcast this counter-information. In North Africa as in South America (especially Columbia) in the 1960s, the transistor played this role of counter-media against the radios owned only by the well-to-do people of the cities, that is, the colonizers. It is today worth mentioning video versions of works like *Document sur le travail forcé en USSR* (Latvia, 1976), *The Black Hills Are Not for Sale* (U.S.A., 1974), *Un jour de grève aux usines Wonder* (France, 1968) to grasp fully that each society produces its own counter-history in contra-distinction to the standardization of historical knowledge. The cinema offers a host of other examples: from *Ceddo* which denounces the domination of Islam in Senegal (it controls knowledge and power) to *Tupac Amaru*, in Peru, which presents the Inca point of view on the Spanish conquest.

The process of standardization itself seems to be the fragmentation of visions of the world through an ethnocentric return pioneered by the colonized peoples. One can witness the expansion of this phenomenon in the Caucasus and in the Balkans.

The *last phenomenon* which marks the post-colonial period is undoubtedly the loss of faith in the Future of Science. The diminution of this faith, which prevailed in the last century, occurs correlatively with the process of calling the "progress" of history and the merits of colonization into question.

More than science as such, it was actually its applications that mesmerized public opinion: the railway, the telegraph, vaccines, etc. They seduced India and Japan. But, in Europe, behind these inventions there was always mathematics, with the result that the laws of statistics took over from Montesquieu's *Esprit des Lois.* At the beginning of the twentieth century, political programmes claimed to base themselves on a scientific interpretation of the world: the "scientific" socialism of Marx, the "scientific" anarchism of Kropotkin, and so on. It is noteworthy that independently of their "opinions" and of their ideology, Lenin, Schacht and F. D. Roosevelt would have read and annotated the works of Keynes. Only Japan produced its own autonomous scheme of development. Indeed, in the West, in the twentieth century, it seems that in lieu of the sword or of the speech, it is the diagram and the graph which hold sway. Though it is true that after the Great War "they will not catch us again" became the expression of a general resolve.

That is how the technocrats seized power in the East and in the West. They are all scholars and politicians who, in the days of Stalin, even claimed to have rebuilt the old alliance between the social sciences and the natural sciences (in 1949). The Knowledge of the Party was the summation of all types of knowledge and, in the USSR, it soon asserted its authority not only over economics and politics, but even over art and linguistics. And this knowledge even shifted from competence for the social body to competence for the human body, since it could decide who was mentally healthy or not. In the 1930s Nazi power in Germany could also decide, in the name of genetic science, who should live and who should not. Those "biological soldiers", those "psychiatrist-physicians", responsible for the tragedies which everyone now knows about, contributed to the discredit of all those systems of the Absolute, the certainties of which are flawless and always built on scholarship. The culture of the formerly colonized peoples suddenly appeared to be more generous and was consequently reaffirmed.

Medicine has always been the apology of the scientific power, a little like the Pasteur Institute was the alibi of French colonization. Scientific power has often been able to act in the name of the human body, of good health. Chemist-physicians and physician-chemists have, however, concealed many inventions used for ends other than increasing human happiness. At the beginning of the twentieth century, no one questioned the authority of the doctor and of the scientist. But today the situation is different: in the first instance, because with the democratization of health care, at least in the West, the medical practitioner has forfeited a major part of his symbolic power. But it has also been observed that, in the name of the same scientific knowledge, he could favour abortion in India and denounce it in Christian countries; that the same ailment does not require the same therapy for a black and for an Italian, for a Japanese in San Francisco and for an Irishman in Boston. And what place should be given to acupuncture in the midst of this scientific knowledge? Is science dogmatic, does it have a religion, an ideology, or does the doctor use this knowledge at his own convenience?

Doubt thus emerges: the power of science and its wisdom are denounced in the same way as is the power of tyrants.

Against the background of these transformations, one notes the emergence of alternative ideologies which offer an open or ambiguous opposition to them. The first that deserves mention is ecology which has become the Bible for those who do not want a Bible: it therefore has no theoretician. At the same time it fights the technocratic unification of the economy, the standardization of culture, and wants to belong neither to the Left nor to the Right. In the USSR it tries to be nationalistic, as in Estonia where in its attack on pollution it really takes aim at the state with its centre in Moscow. It is traditionalist in view of its glorification of the Russian nature polluted by industry (Rasputin), leftist in its struggle against the state, and so on. It is the same elsewhere; but the features of its ambiguities are less clear, if one may say so.

The other ideology on the rise is fundamentalism, which regenerates nationalism in its most conservative sense, as in Georgia for example: its success can be attributed to the emergence of deprived minorities, especially in Iran and in Morocco. For the rest, and as in the Islamic countries, Catholic and Jewish fundamentalism is also rising up against the great changes of the twentieth century.

The convergence of ecology and of fundamentalism with the phenomena which are in the process of growth, like the economic and cultural unification, has brought forth three types of conflicts which had more or less disappeared, or had been stifled, during the times of the triumphant ideologies and of the Moloch-State. How should they be defined?

- The territorial conflicts break out again wherever recent historical evolution has occurred more slowly than elsewhere: traditional conflicts have been revived in such places (Armenians/Azeris, Rumanians/Hungarians, Persians/Arabs). The law of blood, of the race, has gained the upper hand.

- Wherever economic evolution has fostered a situation of the "colonial" type within the same society, the revolt takes a violent turn, money being the thing at stake, poverty being the wages (Quebec, Sicily, Corsica, Morocco, Peru, Iran before Khomeini, urban ghettos in France, in Brazil). The colour of the insurgents' flag varies according to the faith, the identity, the class struggle.
- Wherever the Welfare State prevails, with progress in education and openness to the world, the peoples who consider themselves to be culturally superior do not tolerate being dependent. The Balts or the Slovenes are characteristic examples of this socio-political situation. The movement of rebellion is activated by the cultural level: it is demonstrated by the small number of mixed marriages (between Estonians and Russians, between Slovenes and Serbs).

The last examples illustrate the integration of the colonial with the national problem. Do they constitute a single entity?

There remain the mentalities.

The discourse of most colonizers is replete with *the myth of the "lazy" native*. In the 1880s the Russians proved to be an exception to the rule: they judged "themselves lazier than the Kazakhs..." (Y. Levada). But earlier they too thought like the others.

In succession, the Spaniards, the Dutch, the English, etc. have defined those necessarily negative traits in regard to the Filipinos, the Javanese, the Hindus – before the French or others took over from them, in regard to the blacks or the Arabs, "those arrant lazybones".

In a letter to one of his friends, in 1720, the friar Gaspar de San Augustin was the first to describe the thirty negative traits of the Filipinos. "One cannot trust them, for they are lazy and ever ready to go for a walk ... they are ungrateful and never return the money which they have borrowed ... Their laziness is such that they never close the doors which they open, they leave the tools where they have been working without storing them back in their proper place. They spend the advance of their wages and then do not come back. They enter the convent without warning, pry about everywhere and steal all they can find, break the chairs by their way of sitting on them, they always go to sleep between two chores ..."

A century later J. Siberg, the Governor-General of the East Indies, constructed a theory of native laziness to justify his resistance to the liberal reforms of Hogendorp who advocated putting an end to forced labour, to wages paid in kind. Siberg explained: "There are six reasons why this should not be done: 1) The Javanese are too lazy to work more land than they need to survive. 2) Forced labour at least compels them to work more.

3) With the liberalization of the economy in a capitalistic system, they would leave their work whenever they had money and would come back to it only afterwards . . . 5) It is the Chinese or the Europeans who will buy it at a low price. 6) If Hogendorp's reforms are adopted how will the Javanese notables accept them?" (1802).

This model argument can be encountered almost everywhere.

Whether this "laziness" is a form of resistance to colonization, or whether it is simply social, the fact is that it assumes a variety of forms and can change in substance whenever the general conditions are altered. But today colonization, in the narrow sense of the word, has come to an end, the unification and the standardization of mentalities culminate in a standardized vision of "morality". The media of the formerly colonized countries have adopted it as have others.

Accordingly, in 1971, the main Malay political party published *Revolusi mental*, "Mental Revolution", a collective work with contributions from fourteen authors, whose writings had been coordinated by a former Minister of Information. It described the society of that country by listing the traits of the population: it had been perverted by colonization, the Malays were irresponsible, lazy, fatalistic, defeatist, led by passion more than by reason: they did not persevere, they did not keep their word, they wanted wealth but without doing anything to obtain it; in short, the picture was still gloomier than that drawn by the colonizer. And, in contrast, the book stressed the qualities "of the Japanese, the Americans, the Germans, the Jews, the Chinese". It endorsed the diagnosis of Governor Clifford who averred that in Malaysia wealth is not produced by the Malays. But *Revolusi mental* showed that, without the participation of the Malays, no development would have been possible.

In summary, the model implicitly referred to by this work was not that of the *Droit à la paresse* ('Right to Laziness') (1880) of Paul Lafargue – who was black, West Indian and Jewish – but that of Rockfeller or of the Chinese millionaires. It attributed the responsibility for this "inferiority" of the Malays solely to historical conditions.

Of course.

This would mean that the mental standardization of the world, under the sign of King Money, goes beyond the scope of this history, colliding and conflicting with it beyond colonization and its "end".

CHRONOLOGY

1413	*Imago Mundi* of Pierre d'Ailly.
1417	The Chinese in east Africa.
1418	Henry the Navigator organizes his first voyage.
1419	The Portuguese in Madeira.
1420	Invention of the caravel.
1433	Last Chinese expedition in Mozambique.
1437	Portuguese disaster in Tangiers.
1445	Cape Verde. First Portuguese slaves.
1455	First African spices in Portugal.
1462	Ahmad ibn Madjid's sea treaty.
1465	Russians in Siberia.
	The Portuguese in the Gulf of Guinea.
	The first extensive developments of the black slave trade.
1466–1472	Nikitin, the Russian, in India.
1479	Treaty of Alcaçovas on the Atlantic islands between Spain and Portugal.
1485	Christopher Columbus in Spain.
1485–1488	Diego Cam and Bartolomeo Diaz at the Cape.
1492	Martin Behaim's globe.
	Christopher Columbus in the Caribbean Isles (West Indies).
1493	*Inter Caetera* Bull (Portugal-Spain).
1494	Treaty of Tordesillas (division of the world) for the Far East.
1496	John Cabot in Labrador.
1498	Vasco da Gama in Calicut.
1500	Discovery of Brazil.
1505–1515	Almeida and Albuquerque build the Portuguese Empire.
1508–1511	Discovery of Porto Rico and Jamaica.
1510	Albuquerque captures Goa and massacres the Muslim population.
1511–1515	Diego Velasquez in Cuba. Establishment of Havana.
c. 1518	Kabir and the attempted Hindu-Muslim merger.

1519–1521	Hernan Cortez in Mexico.
1521–1530	The Portuguese in Brazil.
1524	Monopoly of Seville.
1529	Treaty of Saragossa. Division of the Far East (Spain-Portugal).
1531–1534	Francesco Pizarro conquers the Inca Empire.
1532	Foundation of Sao Paolo.
1535	Extensive Arabo-Muslim slave trade throughout the Sahara. Foundation of Lima.
1535–1538	De Quesada conquers Columbia.
1536	Foundation of Buenos Aires.
1541	Foundation of Santiago in Chile.
1546	Foundation of Potosi.
1549	Francis Xavier in Japan.
1557	The Portuguese in Macao.
1560	Foundation of Caracas.
1562	John Hawkins deals in the slave trade.
1565	Foundation of Rio de Janeiro.
1574	The Portuguese in Angola.
1578	Battle of Alcazarquivir.
1581	First black slaves in America.
1584	Sir Walter Raleigh in Virginia.
1588	Defeat of the Invincible Armada.
1600	Foundation of the English East India Company.
1602	Foundation of the Dutch East India Company.
1605	The English in Barbados.
1608	Samuel de Champlain in Quebec.
1609	The Dutch seize Ceylon (Sri Lanka) from the Portuguese.
1619	The Dutch in Batavia.
1620	Odyssey of the *Mayflower*.
1621	Dutch Company of the West Indies.
1624	The Dutch in Taiwan.
1624–1654	Wars between the Portuguese and the Dutch over Brazil.
1625–1664	The French in the West Indies.
1626	Foundation of New Amsterdam (1664: New York).
1632	The Russians in Yakutsk.
1635	The French in Guadaloupe, Martinique, Dominica.
1637	The French in Senegal.
1641	The Dutch take Malacca.
1642	Foundation of Montreal.
1643	The Dutch in Curaçao.
1652	Foundation of the Cape by the Dutch.
1652–1674	Anglo-Dutch wars.

1655	The English in Jamaica.
1660	The French in Port-au-Prince.
1664	Colbert sets up the East India Company.
1674	Foundation of Manaos.
1682	Cavelier de la Salle in Louisiana.
1688–1698	War of the League of Augsburg.
1690	The English in the Bahamas.
1697	Ryswick. France receives Haiti.
1702–1703	Spanish war of succession.
1704	Condemnation of the Jesuits who take part in the Chinese rites.
1713	Anglo-Spanish treaty of Asiento.
	Treaty of Utrecht.
1721	Foundation of Mahé (1723: Yanaon).
1729	Massacre of the Natchez.
1739	Anglo-Spanish conflict in the Americas.
1741	Admiral Anson's voyage.
1744	Joseph François Dupleix in India.
1751	Victories of Robert Clive in India.
1755	The first batches of "voluntary" migrants to Siberia.
1756–1763	The Seven Years' War.
1759	James Wolfe takes Quebec.
1763	Treaty of Paris.
1764–1792	The British in Lucknow. Conquest of Mysore.
1764	Spanish expedition to drive the English from the Falklands (Malvinas).
1765	Creole rebellions in Mexico.
1768–1774	Russo-Turkish war.
1769	Portugal gives up the possession of Mazagan (Morocco).
1776–1783	American war of Independence.
1778	Beginning of the Kaffir wars.
1783	Treaty of Versailles.
1785–1789	Mgr. (Bishop) Migneau de Behaine in Annam.
1787	Foundation of the Society of the Friends of the Blacks.
1788	Arrival of the first convicts in Botany Bay (Sydney).
1793	Lord Cornwallis establishes The Permanent Settlement in India.
1798	Battle of Aboukir.
1801	The British assert their suzerainty over the Nizam of Hyderabad.
1804	Independence of Haiti.
1805	Battle of Trafalgar.

	Mehemet Ali proclaims himself as the Pasha of Egypt.
1806	Francisco Miranda's separatist coup in Venezuela.
1807	Beginning of the conflict in the Kurile Islands.
	Abolition of the black slave trade thanks to William Wilberforce.
1810	Wave of rebellions in Latin America: first Mexico.
	The British seize the Ile de France (Mauritius) in the Indian Ocean.
1812	Shaka, King of the Zulus, organizes the state and the army.
1815	Conference of Vienna. The British at the Cape.
1816	Anglo-Ashanti war.
1817	War of the United States and the Seminole Indians.
1819	The British in Singapore.
1821	San Martin and Simon Bolivar: independence of Spanish America.
1822	Champollion deciphers the hieroglyphics.
	Anti-Dutch revolts in Java.
	Independence of Brazil.
1823	Beginning of the "balkanization" of Latin America.
	Foundation of Liberia by the American Society of Colonization.
1824	First Anglo-Burmese war.
1825	Egypt conquers Sudan.
1826	The British in the Gold Coast.
1828	Treaty of Turkmen Chai: the Russians in Erevan and Nakhichevan.
1830	The French in Algeria.
	The Indian Removal Act which drives the Sioux to the west of the Mississipi.
1833	Abolition of the monopoly of the East India Company.
1836	Independence of Texas.
1837	Revolt of the French Canadians.
1838	Beginning of the conflict between the Maronites and the Druze in Lebanon.
1839	First Jewish settlement villages in Palestine.
	First Anglo-Afghan war.
1840	British sovereignty over New Zealand.
	Beginning of the Opium war: Britain against China.
1841	Annam annexes Cambodia. Vietnamization of the country.
1842	The French in Tahiti and in the Marquesas Islands.
	The British in Hong Kong.
1843	The British in Natal.
1847	Independence of Liberia.
1848	Abolition of slavery, brought about by Victor Schoelcher.

	Fall of Constantine and the end of Ottoman resistance in Algeria.
1849	Britain annexes Punjab.
1852	Creation of the convict prison in Cayenne Island.
1853	Annexation of New Caledonia.
	Holy war against the animists by El Haj Omar.
1854	The question of the use of the Holy Places launches the Crimean war.
	Britain recognizes the independence of the Orange state.
	Louis Faidherbe governor of Senegal.
	First use of quinine against malaria.
1857	The Indian Mutiny (now called by independent India "The First War of Independence").
1858	Expedition of the Scot David Livingstone in east Africa.
1859	Indonesia: division of Timor between the Netherlands and Portugal.
1861	Beginning of the War of Secession.
1863	French protectorate in Cambodia.
1865	First black Anglican bishop in Nigeria.
1867	Creation of the Canadian confederation.
	French expedition in Mexico.
1868	The Emperor of Japan assumes power: beginning of the Meiji era.
	Occupation of Cochin-China by the French.
1869	Inauguration of the Suez Canal.
1870	The Crémieux decree which naturalizes the Jews of Algeria.
1871	Rebellion in Kabylia.
1876	The Japanese force a friendship treaty upon Korea.
	The Egyptian state goes bankrupt.
1877	King Leopold of Belgium establishes the International African Association.
	Prime Minister Disraeli orders the annexation of Transvaal and of Orange.
1880	Kurdish rebellion against the Ottoman state.
1881	Boer victory over the British at Majuba Hill.
	French protectorate in Tunisia: treaty of Bardo.
1882	Savorgnan de Brazza signs the treaty of Makoko.
1883	Annam recognizes the French protectorate.
1884	The Germans in Namibia, in Togo, in Cameroon.
	The Berlin Conference: division of black Africa.
	First black newspaper in South Africa: *Imvo Zabatshundu* (Voice of the People).
1885	India: formation of the Congress Party.
	French Protectorate in Madagascar.

1886	Foundation of Johannesburg.
1888	Abolition of slavery in Brazil.
	José Rizal establishes the Filipino independence movement.
1889	Tanganyika, German colony.
1890	Birth of the Armenian independence movements.
1891	Division of Borneo between the British and the Dutch.
1892	French Protectorate in Dahomey.
1893	The United States annex the Hawaiian Islands.
	The Spanish occupy Mellila.
	Cecil Rhodes: Prime Minister of the Cape.
1895	China-Japan: Treaty of Shimonoseki.
1896	Defeat of the Italians at Adoua in Ethiopia.
1898	Spanish-American war: independence of Cuba, Puerto Rico and the Philippines become American possessions.
	The Crisis of Fashoda.
1899	Beginning of the Anglo-Boer war.
1901	The Boxer rebellion in China. European intervention.
1902	Macedonian uprising.
1904	Russo-Japanese war.
	The British in Lhassa.
	The Hereros rise against the Germans.
1905	Kaiser Wilhelm II in Morocco.
	China: foundation of the Kuo-min-tang.
	Russia-Japan: Treaty of Portsmouth.
	Japan in Korea.
1906	Morocco: the conference of Algesiras.
	Laperrine in the Sahara.
1907	Foundation of Cairo University.
	The Congo becomes a Belgian colony.
	Anglo-Russian agreement on the zones of influence in Persia (Iran) and in Afghanistan.
1908	Uprising of the Young Turks.
1909	Creation of the Anglo-Persian Oil Company.
1910	China reoccupies Tibet.
	Creation of the FEA (French Equatorial Africa) and of the South African Union.
	Foundation of the Pasteur Institute in Algiers.
1911	The *Panther* gunboat incident at Agadir.
	The Italians in Tripolitania.
1912	W. E. B. Du Bois develops the concept of Panafricanism.
	French protectorate in Morocco.
1914	The Senegalese B. Diagne: first black member of the Assembly.

1914–1918	First World War
1915	Massacre of Armenians in Turkey.
1916	Mobilization of the Arabs against the Ottomans.
	Sykes-Picot agreements.
1917	Balfour Declaration in favour of a Jewish homeland in Palestine.
	Russia: Lenin proclaims the right to self-determination.
1918	The fourteen points of President Wilson of the United States.
1919	Birth of the Comintern and of the communist parties.
	Syria proclaims its independence.
1920	Treaty of Sèvres.
	Baku Conference of the Peoples of the East.
1921	Abd el-Krim's insurrection.
	Mahatma Gandhi begins his campaign of civil disobedience.
	The International Labour Office (Geneva) condemns forced labour.
1924	"Rogue decrees" in Tunisia.
1929	Ubanghi-Shari: revolt of the Upper-Sangha.
	Black Friday in Wall Street.
1930	Birth of the Indochinese Communist Party, and of the Filipino Communist Party.
	Fall in the prices of raw materials, in the tropical countries.
1931	Paris: Colonial Exhibition.
	"Manchuria incident".
1933	First conference of the Muslim Brotherhood in Cairo.
1934	Foundation of the Neo-Destour.
1935	Beginning of the Ethiopian war.
1939–1945	Second World War.
1941	Atlantic Charter.
	Crisis in Syria and in Lebanon.
1943	The Japanese proclaim the independence of the Philippines, of Burma.
	Foundation of the Istiqlal (Morocco).
1944	Brazzaville conference.
1945	Foundation of the Arab League.
	Proclamation of the independence of Vietnam, of Indonesia.
1946	Beginning of the war in Indo-China.
	Intensification of apartheid in South Africa.
1947	Independence of India and of Pakistan.
1948	Assassination of Mahatma Gandhi.
	Recognition of the State of Israel.
1949	The Communists come to power in China.
	The Netherlands recognize the independence of Indonesia and France does the same for Vietnam.

1950–1953	Beginning of the war in Korea.
1951	Mossadeq nationalizes the Iran oil industry.
1952	Putsch by free officers in Egypt: Neguib-Nasser.
	Mau-Mau insurrection in Kenya.
	Gold Coast: Nkrumah, Prime Minister.
	Crisis in Tunisia and in Morocco (1952–1955).
1954	Dien Bien Phu: end of the war in Indo-China; the Geneva accords.
	Outbreak of the Algerian insurrection.
	Philippines: the Huk insurrection.
1955	The Bagdad Pact.
	Bandung conference.
	Agreements of La Celle-Saint-Cloud (Morocco).
1956	The Suez Crisis.
	Independence of Tunisia and of Morocco.
	Rhodesia-Nyasaland federation.
1957	Independence of Ghana.
	Riots in Belgian Congo.
1958	Foundation of the United Arab Republic (Syria-Egypt-Yemen).
	Pan-Arab revolt in Lebanon.
	Algeria: revolt of the French army.
	Accra: first conference of the independent States of Africa (Ethiopia, Ghana, UAR, Libya, etc.).
	Dissolution of French West Africa. Independence of Guinea.
1959	Revolt of Amilcar Cabral in Portuguese Guinea.
	Nationalist disturbances in black Africa.
1960	Year of the independence of African countries.
	Civil war in the former Belgian Congo (1960–1965).
1961	Uprising in Angola.
	End of the war in Algeria.
	India takes possession again of the Portuguese possessions (Goa, Diu).
	Independence of Southern Rhodesia and of South Africa.
1962	Independence of Trinidad-Tabago.
	Secession of Katanga.
	Algerian independence.
1963	Collapse of the Organization of African Unity (OAU) in Addis-Ababa.
	Birth of Malaysia.
	Saudi-Arabia: abolition of slavery.
	Independence of Kenya, Zanzibar.
1964	Nelson Mandela is arrested.

	First conference of the PLO (Palestine Liberation Organization). Mozambique: consitution of Frelimo and general insurrection.
1965	Independence of Rhodesia. End of the Mandate of South Africa on South West Africa (Namibia).
1967	Six-day war. Nigeria: Biafran war.
1968–1973	Vietnam war.
1970	The Khmers Rouges (Red Khmers) in Cambodia. Death of Nasser.
1973	Independence of Bangladesh, which separates from Pakistan. The Yom Kippur war. Beginning of terrorism in Palestine.
1974	Independence of Guinea-Bissau.
1975	The Lomé accords on cooperation between Europe, Africa and the West Indies. Independence of Angola. "Green" march towards western Sahara. Independence of Surinam. Beginning of the civil war in Lebanon.
1976	Portugal: the Carnation revolution.
1978	Camp David talks: Egypt-Israel.
1979	Vietnam invades Cambodia. Invasion of Afghanistan. Islamic revolution in Iran. "Decolonization" of Rhodesia.
1980	Beginning of the Iran-Iraq war.
1982	War in the Falklands (Malvinas).
1984	War of Lebanon.
1985	Struggle against apartheid in South Africa.
1986	Law on the status of New Caledonia.
1990	Dislocation of the USSR.
1991–1993	Formation of the CIS (Commonwealth of Independent States). Abolition of Communist rule in Eastern Europe and in Russia. Disintegration of Yugoslavia. Wars in the Caucasus.
1994	End of apartheid in South Africa. Beginning of Palestinian independence.

FILMOGRAPHIC SELECTION

(A): archival and edited films
(D): documentaries and reports
(F): fiction
The numbers between brackets indicate the chapters to which these films refer.

Adieu, Colonies. 1970. Henri de Turenne, director. France. (A) (9)
African Queen, The. 1951. John Huston, director. United States. (F) (4)
Algérie en flammes, L'. 1958. René Vautier, director. France. (A) (9)
Algérie 1954. La révolte d'un colonisé. 1970. Marie-Louise Derrien and Marc Ferro, directors. France. (A) (9)
Apartheid. 1993. Jean-Michel Meurice, director. France. (A) (4)
Appel du silence, L'. 1936. Léon Poirier, director. France. (D) (3)
Atlandide, L'. 1921. Jacques Feyder, director. France. (F) (3)
Aube. 1960. Omar Khlibi, director. Tunisia. (F) (4)
Avoir vingt ans dans les Aurès. 1972. René Vautier, director. France. (F) (9)
Babatou et les Trois Conseils. 1975. Jean Rouch, director. France. (D) (5)
Bandera, La. 1935. Jean Duvivier, director. France. (F) (5)
Bataille d'Alger, La. 1966. Gillo Pontecorvo, director. Italy–Algeria. (F) (9)
Black Hills Are Not For Sale, The. 1978. Sandra Osawa, director. United States. (D) (6)
Bled, Le. 1929. Jean Renoir, director. France. (F) (6)
Bourrasque. 1935. René Vilon, director. France. (F) (4)
Ceddo. 1977. Sembene Ousmane, director. Senegal. (F) (6)
Charge of the Light Brigade, The. 1936. Michael Curtiz, director. United States. (F) (5)
Chronique des années de braise. 1975. Mohammed Lakhdar-Hamina, director. Algeria. (F) (9)
Come back Africa. 1959. Lionel Rogosin, director. South Africa. (F) (4)
Crabe-Tambour, Le. 1977. Pierre Schoendoerffer, director. France. (F) (9)
Dix-septième Parallèle. 1967. Joris Ivens, director. France. (D) (9)

Escadron Blanc, L'. 1934. Joseph Peyre and A. Genina, directors. Italy. (F) (3)

Fond de l'Air est rouge, Le. 1934. Josephy Peyre and A. Genina, directors. Italy. (F) (3)

Four Feathers. 1939. Alexandre Korda, director. United States. (F) (4)

Française chez les guerriers du Yémen, Une. 1964. Troeller and G. Deffarge, directors. France. (D) (8)

Gandhi. 1985. Richard Attenborough, director. Great Britain. (F) (9)

Goha. 1958. Jacques Baratier, director. France. (F) (4)

Guerre d'Algérie, La. 1972. Yves Corrière and Philippe Monnier, director. France. (A) (9)

Guerre de pacification en Azazonie, La. Yves Billon, director. France. (D) (4)

Guerre sans nom, La. 1992. Bertrand Tavernier and Patrick Rotman, directors. France. (D) (9)

Gunga Din. 1939. George Stevens, director. Great Britain. (F) (5)

Heure des brasiers, L'. 1973. F. Solanas, director. Argentine Republic. (D) (11)

Histoire de la médicine, Une. 1980.Claude de Givrey, directors. France. (D) (4)

Indonésie appelle, L'. 1946. Joris Ivens, director. France. (D) (8)

Itto. 1934. Jean Benoît-Levy, director. France. (F) (4)

King Solomon's Mines. 1950. Andrew Marton and Compton Bennett, directors. United States. (F) (4)

Lawrence of Arabia. 1962. David Lean, director. Great Britain. (F) (3)

Lives of a Bengal Lancer. 1935. Henry Hathaway, director. United States. (F) (4)

Maison du Maltais, La. 1938. Pierre Chenal, director. France. (F) (4)

Maîtres fous. 1968. Jean Rouch, director. France. (D) (6)

Mandat, Le. 1968. Ousmane Sembéné, director. Senegal. (F) (6)

Mémoire fertile. 1982. Michel Khleifi, director. Palestine. (F) (8)

Non, ou la vaine gloire de commander. 1971. Manoel de Oliveria, director. Portugal. (F) (1)

Nouba des femmes du mont Chenoua, La. 1978. Assia Djebar, director. Algeria. (D) (6)

Pépé le Moko. 1938. Jean Duvivier, director. France. (F) (4)

Premier Maître, Le. 1963. Andrei Mikhalkov-Kontchalovski. CIS. (F) (4)

Roman d'un spahi, Le. 1935. M. Bernheim, director. France. (F) (4)

Sang du condor, Le. 1969. Jorge Sandjines, director. Bolivia. (F) (11)

Serment du bois caïman, Le. 1993. Charles Najman, director. France. (D) (4)

Si, les cavaliers. 1982. Bakabé Mahamane, director. Nigeria. (F) (6)

Sucre amer. 1964. Yann Lemasson, director. France. (D) (8)

Tempest over Asia. 1928. Vsevolod Poudoukine, director. CIS. (F) (4)

Terre en transes. 1967. Glauber Rocha, director. Brazil. (F) (11)

Tupac Amaru. 1981. Federico Garcia, director. Peru. (F) (6)

Vent des Aurès, Le. 1967. Temfik Farès and Mohammed Lakhdar-Hamina, directors. Algeria. (F) (6)

Vietnam, année du cochon. 1969. E. de Antonio, director. France. (A) (9)

Visitors, The. 1969. Elia Kazan, director. United States. (F) (11)

Zulu. 1963. Cyril Enfield, director. United States. (F) (3)

NOTES

PREFACE

1 For another similarity revealed in films, see p. 167.

1 COLONIZATION OR IMPERIALISM

1 The Battle of Poitiers (732) is scarcely mentioned in the Arab chronicles of Egypt. It makes it appearance in historiography only later.
2 See pp. 171–6.

4 A NEW RACE OF SOCIETIES

1 Between 1600 and 1900, the Atlantic slave trade affected about 11.5 million persons: 1.8 million in the seventeenth century, 6.1 million in the eighteenth century, 3.3 million in the nineteenth century. Starting earlier the (Arab) Saharan slave trade affected about 4 million persons: 900,000 persons before 1600 and later, 700,000 in the seventeenth century, 700,000 in the eighteenth, 1.8 million in the nineteenth century. Cf. C. Coquery-Vidrovitch, 1992, p. 33.
2 See pp. 187–8.
3 Likewise, in South Chile, the Mapuche Indians are in the process of using legal means to recover their lands.

5 ROSE-COLOURED LEGEND AND PITCH-BLACK LEGEND

1 Annabella in *La Bandera*, Dalio in "*L'Esclave Blanche*, Le Vigan in *L'Occident*, etc. This characteristic can be seen elsewhere. In *The Good Earth* (1937) the Americans have Paul Muni and Luise Rainer play the roles of the two main Chinese characters.
2 This corresponds to the Nazi anti-semitism. Either Süss the Jew remains a Jew and he is contemptible; or he modernizes himself and he is not to be trusted.
3 See pp. 274–5.
4 In Vietnam, colonization contributed to the breaking up of the traditional family, which led to the emancipation of the young women, particularly during the war.
5 It must also be stressed that, after having derided the colonialist claim that France, prior to 1900, was providing Cambodia with "protection" against the

designs of Vietnam, the anti-colonialists failed to raise their voice when, after acceding to independence, Vietnam tried to reannex Cambodia during the seventies of the twentieth century.

6 THE VISION OF THE VANQUISHED

1 Cf. in C. A. Bayly (op. cit.) a list of Indian monographs on colonial India, for the 1945–79 period. I prefer to rely on the work of Claude Markovits, which has been analysed below.

7 THE MOVEMENTS FOR COLONIST-INDEPENDENCE

1 What the FLN calls the beginning of the insurrection, on 2 November 1954, was actually a series of about ten attacks. As of that date the term "fellaghas" was still being used in regard to the rebels of Tunisia.

8 LEAVEN AND LEVERS

1 In October 1935 Maurice Thorez announced his commitment to the defence of the Algerian people. But it actually consisted of his association with the national Algerian "bourgeois" reformists, like Ferhat Abbas who, at the time of the "class against class" struggle, was denounced as a counter-revolutionary. But, for Thorez, it was only a matter of bringing the Algerians together with the French people, for fear of an absorption by Italian or German fascism. Ten years later, it was in the name of the struggle against absorption by American imperialism that the PCF (French Communist Party) and the PCA (Algerian Communist Party) addressed themselves to the PPA (Algerian Popular Party) of Messali.
2 In the United States the Black Panthers followed the teachings of Malcolm X and believed that the blacks were treated like colonized people. They did not want to be "blacks", but revolutionaries. They followed the example of Cabral, of Che Guevara (during the years 1960–70).

9 INDEPENDENCE OR REVOLUTION

1 De Gaulle had left the government. During my conversations with Jean Sainteny, for the making of the film *Indochine 45*, in 1965, I did not feel that De Gaulle had a very clear vision of the policy to be adopted in Indo-China. Was he more in favour of d'Argenlieu than of Leclerc and Sainteny?
2 See p. 118 for the Englishman's vision of the Hindus and the Muslims in India.
3 The same hardening of attitude is evident in the behaviour of the French delegation, which broke off all relations with the UNEF.
4 See pp. 231–8 above.

10 LIBERATION OR DECOLONIZATION

1 See pp. 231–8.
2 From the speech delivered on 23 February 1931 to the Council of the West Essex

Conservative Association (cf. Martin Gilbert *Winston Churchill*, Vol. V, Heinemann, London, 1976, p. 390).

11 DECOLONIZATION HALTED

1 In 1954 a jeep could be bought with 14 bags of coffee; in 1962 it required 39. What is the rate today?

BIBLIOGRAPHY

Abd el Krim et la République du Rif (Proceedings of the International Colloquium on Historial and Sociological Studies, 18–20 January 1973). 1976. Paris: François Masperso.

Abd el-Malek, Anouar. 1970. *La pensée politique arabe contemporaine*. Paris: Éditions du Seuil.

Ageron, Charles-Robert. 1973. *Politiques coloniales au Maghreb*. Paris: Presses Universitaires de France.

——. 1990. *L'histoire de l'Algérie contemporaine, 1830–1988*. Paris: Presses Universitaires de France.

——. 1990. Les colonies devant l'opinion publique française, 1919–1939. *Revue française d'histoire d'outre-mer* 77, 286: 31–73.

——. 1991. *La décolonisation française*. Paris: Armand Colin Éditeur.

Ageron, Charles-Robert and Michel Marc, eds. 1992. *L'Afrique noire française à l'heure de l'indépendance*. Paris: Centre National de Recherche Scientifique.

Alatas, Syed Hussein. 1970. Religion and modernization in South East Asia. *Archives européennes de sociologie* 11, 2: 265–96.

——. 1977. *The myth of the lazy native. A study of the image of the Malays, Filipinos and Javanese from the 16th to the 20th century and its function in the ideology of colonial capitalism*. London: Frank Cass.

Alberro, Solange. 1992. *Les Espagnols dans le Mexique colonial. Histoire d'une acculturation*. Paris: Armand Colin Éditeur.

Albertini, Rudolf von. 1976. *Europäische Kolonialherrschaft, 1880–1940*. Zurich: Atlantis Verlag.

——. 1966. *Dekolonisation. Die Diskussion über Verwaltung und Zukunft der Kolonien, 1919–1960*. Cologne: Westdeutcher Verlag.

Aldrich, Robert. 1990. *The French presence in the South Pacific, 1842–1940*. Honolulu: University of Hawaii Press.

Amin, Samir. 1976. *Impérialisme et sous-développement en Afrique*. Paris: Éditions Anthropos.

Amselle, Jean-Loup. 1990. *Logiques métisses. Anthropologie de l'identité en Afrique et ailleurs*. Paris: Éditions Payot.

Ansprenger, Franz. 1989. *The dissolution of the colonial empires*. London: Routledge.

Arendt, Hannah. 1951. *Imperialism*. New York: Harcourt.

Ashe, Geoffrey. 1968. *Gandhi. A study in revolution*. London: Heinemann.

Aubin, Jean. 1976. L'ambassade du prêtre Jean à D. Mauvel. *Mare Luso-Indicum* 1–56.

Augé, Marc. 1982. *Génie du paganisme*. Paris: Éditions Gallimard.

Bailyn, Bernard. 1967. *The ideological origins of the American revolution*. Cambridge: Belknap Press of Harvard University Press.

Bairoch, P. 1980. Le bilan économique du colonialisme. In L. Blussé, H. L. Wesseling and G. D. Winius, eds., *History and underdevelopment*, 29–42. Leiden: Leiden University Centre for the History of Europe Expansion.

Balandier, Georges. 1963. *Sociologie actuelle de l'Afrique noire. Dynamique sociale en Afrique centrale.* Paris: Presses Universitaires de France.

Ballhatchet, Kenneth. 1980. *Race, sex and class under the Raj. Imperial attitudes and policies and their critics, 1793–1905.* London: Weidenfeld and Nicolson.

Barnadas, Joseph M. 1984. The Catholic Church in colonial Spanish America. In Leslie Bethell, ed., *The Cambridge history of Latin America*, vol. 1, pp. 511–40. 11 vols. Cambridge: Cambridge University Press.

Bastide, Roger. 1967. *Les Amériques noires. Les civilisations africaines dans le nouveau monde.* Paris: Payot.

Bataillon, Marcel. 1967. Les colons du Pérou contre Charles V. Analyse du movement pizarriste, 1544–1548. *Annales* 22, 3: 479–94.

Bataillon, Marcel and André Saint-Lu. 1971. *Las Casas et la défense des Indiens.* Paris: Julliard.

Baumont, Maurice. 1949. *L'essor industriel et l'impérialisme colonial, 1878–1904.* Paris: Presses Universitaires de France.

Bayly, Christopher A. 1975. *The local roots of Indian politics. Allahabad, 1880–1920.* Oxford: Oxford University Press.

——. 1979. English-language historiography on British expansion in India and Indian reactions since 1945. In P. C. Emmer and H. L. Wesseling, eds., *Reappraisals in overseas history*, pp. 21–54. Leiden: Leiden University Centre for the History of European Expansion.

Benassar, Bartolome. 1985. *Histoire des espagnols.* 2 vols. Paris: Laffont.

Benassar, Bartolome and Lucile. 1991. *1492, un monde nouveau?* Paris: Perrin.

Bender, Gerald J. 1978. *Angola under the Portuguese. The myth and the reality.* Berkeley: University of California Press.

Bennigsen, Alexandre. 1974. *Russes et Chinois avant 1917.* Paris: Flammarion.

Bennigsen, Alexandre and Chantal Quelquejay. 1960. *Les mouvements nationaux chez les musulmans de Russie. Le 'sultangalievisme' au Tatarstan.* Paris: Mouton.

Bénot, Yves. 1987. *La révolution française et la fin des colonies. Essai.* Paris: Éditions La Découverte.

——. 1992. *La démence coloniale sous Napoléon. Essai.* Paris: Éditions La Découverte.

Bernand, Carmen and Serge Gruzinski. 1991–1993. *Histoire du nouveau monde.* 2 vols. Paris: Librairie Arthème Fayard.

Berque, Augustin. 1974. La chaîne culturelle d'une colonisation: les paysans japonais à Hokkaidô. *Annales* 29, 6: 1425–49.

Bessis, Sophie, ed. 1992. Finalement, pillons-nous vraiment le tiers-monde? *Panoramiques.*

Bethell, Leslie, ed. 1984–96. *The Cambridge history of Latin America.* 11 vols. Cambridge: Cambridge University Press.

Beti, Mongo. 1993. *La France contre l'Afrique. Retour au Cameroun.* Paris: Éditions La Découverte.

Beyssade, Pierre. 1968. *La ligue arabe.* Paris: Éditions Planète.

Bidwell, Robin. 1973. *Marocco under colonial rule. French administration of tribal areas, 1912–1956.* London: Frank Cass.

Blanchard, Pascal and Armelle Chatelia, eds. 1993. *Images et colonies. Nature, discours et influence de l'inconographie coloniale liée à la propagande coloniale et à la représentation des Africains et de l'Afrique en France, de 1920 aux indépendances.* Paris: ACHAC.

Blum, Alain. 1994. *Naître, vivre et mourir en URSS, 1917–1991.* Paris: Plon.

Blussé, Léonard, H. L. Wesseling and G. D. Winius, eds. 1980. *History and underdevelopment.* Leiden: Leiden University Centre for the History of Europe Expansion.

Bobrie, François. 1976. Finances publique et conquête coloniale: le coût budgétaire de l'expansion française entre 1850 à 1913. *Annales ESC* 6: 1225–44.

Bocanegra, Guadalupe and José A. Ortiz, eds. 1993. *Les 500 années de l'Amérique Latine, 1492–1992. L'Amérique Latine et l'Europe face à l'histoire.* Montreuil: Éditions Page et Image.

Botte, Roger. 1991. Les rapports Nord-Sud: la traite négrière et le Fuuta Jaloo à la fin du XVIIIe siècle. *Annales ESC* 6: 1411–35.

Bouchon, Denise. 1991. *Flux et relux, 1815–1962.* Volume 1 of *Histoire de la colonisation française.* Paris: Librairie Arthème Fayard.

Bouchon, Geneviève. 1973. Les Musulmans de Kerala à l'époque de la découverte portugaise. *Mare Luso-Indicum* 2: 3–59.

———. 1975. *Mamale de Canandor. Un adversaire de l'Inde Portugaise, 1507–1528.* Geneva: Droz.

———. 1976. Le premier voyage de Lopo Soares en Inde, 1504–1505. *Mare Luso-Indicum* 3: 57–84.

———. 1987. *L'Asie du Sud à l'époque des Grandes découvertes.* London: Variorum Reprints.

Boughedir, Ferid. 1985. Panorama des cinemas de Maghreb. *Cinemaction* 43, 1, 59–71.

Boulanger, Pierre. 1975. *Le cinéma colonial. De 'l'Atlantide' à 'Lawrence d'Arabie'.* Paris: Éditions Seghers.

Bourdieu, Pierre, Alain Darbel, Jean-Paul Rivet and Claude Seibel. 1958. *Travail et travailleurs en Algérie.* Paris: Presses Universitaires de France.

Bourges, Hervé and Claude Wauthier. 1979. *Les cinquante Afriques.* 2 vols. Paris: Éditions du Seuil.

Boxer, C. R. 1975. *Mary and misogyny. Women in Iberian expansion overseas, 1415–1815. Some facts, fancies and personalities.* London: Duckworth.

Braudel, Fernand. 1949. *La Méditerranée et le monde méditerranéen à l'époque de Philippe II.* Paris: Armand Colin Éditeur.

———. 1979. *Civilisation matérielle, économie et capitalisme, XVe–XVIIIe siècle.* 3 vols. Paris: Armand Colin Éditeur.

Bromberger, Merry and Serge. 1959. *Les 13 complots du 13 mai. Ou la délivrance de Gulliver.* Paris: Librairie Arthème Fayard.

Brunschwig, Henri. 1960. *Mythes et réalités de l'impérialisme colonial français, 1871–1914.* Paris: Armand Colin Éditeur.

———. 1963. *L'avènement de l'Afrique noire, du XIXe siècle à nos jours.* Paris: Armand Colin Éditeur.

———. 1971. *Le partage de l'Afrique noire.* Paris: Flammarion.

Cahen, Michel, ed. 1989. *"Vilas" et "Cidades". Bourgs et villes en Afrique lusophone.* Paris: Éditions L'Harmattan.

Cain, P. J. and A. G. Hopkins. 1993. *British imperialism.* 2 vols. London: Longman.

Carlier, Omar. 1995. *Entre nation et jihad. Histoire sociale des radicalismes algériens.* Paris: Presses Fondation Sciences Sociales.

Carré, Olivier and Gérard Michaud. 1983. *Les frères musulmans. Egypte et Syrie, 1928–1982.* Paris: Gallimard/Julliard.

Carrère d'Encausse, Hélène. 1966. *Réforme et révolution chez les musulmans de l'Empire russe, Bukhara, 1867–1924.* Paris: Presses de la Fondation Nationale des Sciences Politiques.

Cerkasov, P. P. 1985. *Padensie Francuzkogo Kolonjalhogo Imperii.* Moscow: Nauka.

Cervenka, Zdenek. 1977. *The unfinished quest for unity? Africa and the OUA.* New York: Africana Publishing.

Césaire, Aimé. 1955. *Discours sur le colonialisme.* Paris: Présence Africaine.

Chaffard, Georges. 1965. *Les carnets secrets de la décolonisation.* Paris: Calmann-Lévy.

Chandeigne, Michel, ed. 1990. *Lisbonne hors les murs. 1415–1580, l'invention du monde par les navigateurs portugais.* Paris: Éditions Autrement.

Charmley, John. 1993. *Churchill, the end of glory. A political biography.* London: Hodder and Stoughton.

Charnay, Jean-Paul, ed. 1965. *De l'impérialisme à la colonisation.* Paris: Éditions de Minuit.

Chaunu, Pierre (with collaboration from Huguette Chaunu). 1977. *Séville et l'Amérique aux XVIe et XVIIe siècles.* Paris: Flammarion.

Chauvelot, Robert. 1931. *En Indochine. Aquarelles de Hubert Robert.* Grenoble: Arthaud.

Chesneaux, Jean. 1965. L'implantation géographique des intérêts coloniaux au Viet-nam et ses rapports avec l'économie traditionnelle. In Jean-Paul Charnay, ed., *De l'impérialisme à la colonisation,* pp. 101–17. Paris: Éditions de Minuit.

——. 1971. *Une lecture politique de Jules Verne.* Paris: François Maspero.

Chevaldonné, François. 1984. Notes sur le cinéma colonial en AFN: naissance et fonctionnement d'un code. In Sylvie Dallet, ed., *Guerres révolutionnaires, histoire et cinéma.* Paris: Éditions L'Harmattan.

Chirol, Valentin. 1921. *The Egyptian problem.* London: Macmillan.

Chomsky, Noam and Edward S. Herman. 1979. *The political economy of human rights.* 2 vols. Volume 1, Boston: South End Press; Volume 2, Montreal: Black Rose Books.

Chrétien, Jean-Pierre. 1970. Une révolte au Burundi en 1934. *Annales ESC* 6: 1678–1717.

——. 1993. *Burundi, l'histoire retrouvée. 25 ans de métier d'historien en Afrique.* Paris: Éditions Karthala.

Clastres, Hélène. 1985. Introduction. In Yves d'Evreux, *Voyage au nord du Brésil fait en 1613 et 1614,* pp. 9–21. Paris: Payot.

Cohen, Jean. 1955. Colonialisme et racisme en Algérie. *Les temps modernes* 11, 1, 119: 580–90.

Coles, Paul. 1968. *The Ottoman impact on Europe.* London: Thames and Hudson.

Colley, Linda. 1992. *Britons. Forging the nation, 1707–1837.* New Haven: Yale University Press.

Colonna, Fanny. 1975. *Instituteurs algériens, 1883–1939.* Paris: Presses de la Fondation Nationale des Sciences Politiques.

Comarmond, Patrice de and Claude Duchet, eds. 1969. *Racisme et société.* Paris: François Maspero.

Coquery-Vidrovitch, Catherine. 1992. *Afrique noire. Permanences et ruptures.* Paris: Éditions L'Harmattan.

—— (with collaboration from Odile Goerg), ed. 1992. *L'Afrique occidentale au temps des Français. Colonisateurs et colonisés,* c. 1860–1960. Paris: Éditions La Découverte.

Coquin, François-Xavier. 1969. *La Sibérie. Peuplement et immigration paysanne au XIXe siècle.* Paris: Institut d'Études Slaves.

Corm, Georges. 1989. *L'Europe et l'Orient de la balkanisation à la libanisation. Histoire d'une modernité inaccomplie.* Paris: Éditions La Découverte.

Cornevin, Marianne. 1979. *L'apartheid. Pouvoir et falsification historique.* Paris: UNESCO.

Crosby, Alfred W. 1972. *The Columbian exchange. Biological and cultural consequences of 1492.* Westport, Connecticut: Greenwood Press.

Crouzet, François. 1964. Commerce et empire: l'expérience Britannique de libre-echange a la Première Guerre mondiale. *Annales ESC* 2: 281–310.

Curtin, Philip. 1975. *Economic change in precolonial Africa. Senegambia in the era of the slave trade.* Madison: University of Wisconsin Press.

Dallet, Sylvie, ed. 1984. *Guerres révolutionnaires, histoire et cinéma*. Paris: Éditions L'Harmattan.

Darwin, John. 1991. *The end of the British Empire. The historical debate*. Oxford: Basil Blackwell.

Davidson, Alastair. 1991. *The invisible state. The formation of the Australian state, 1788–1901*. Cambridge: Cambridge University Press.

de Queiroz Mattoso, Katia. 1993. Les marques de l'esclavage Africain. In Hélène Rivière d'Arc, ed., *L'Amérique du Sud aux XIXᵉ et XXᵉ siècles. Héritages et territoires*, pp. 63–84. Paris: Armand Colin Éditeur.

Debasch, Yvon. 1961. Le marronage: essai sur la désertion de l'esclave antillais. *Année sociologique* 12 (3rd series): 1–112.

——. 1962. La société coloniale contre le marronage. *Année sociologique* 13 (3rd series): 117–96.

Décolonisation comparées (Colloquium Aix-en-Provence). 1993. Aix-en-Provence: University of Provence and IHTP.

Decraene, Philippe. 1959. *Le panafricanisme*. Paris: Presses Universitaires de France.

Degregori, Carlos Ivan. 1986. Sendero luminoso: los hondos y mortales desencuentros. In Eduardo Ballón, ed., *Movimientos sociales y crisis*. Lima.

del Boca, Angelo. 1976. *Gli Italiani in Africa Orientale*. 4 vols. Bari: Laterza.

der Thiam, Iba. 1993. Histoire de la revendication d'indépendance. In Charles-Robert Ageron and Marc Michel, eds., *L'Afrique noire française. L'heure des indépendances*, pp. 663–88. Paris: Centre National de Recherche Scientifique.

Devillers, Philippe. 1952. *Histoire du Viêt-Nam de 1940 à 1952*. Paris: Éditions du Seuil.

Dmytryshyn, Basil. 1990. Russian expansion to the Pacific, 1580–1700. A historiographical review. *Siberica*.

Dower, John W. 1986. *War without mercy. Race and power in the Pacific war*. New York: Pantheon Books.

Dresch, J. 1946. Lyautey. In Charles-André Julien, ed., *Les techniciens de la colonisation, XIXᵉ et XXᵉ siècles*, pp. 133–56. Paris: Presses Universitaires de France.

Dreyfus, Simone. 1992. Les Réseaux politiques indigènes en Guyane occidentale et leurs transformations aux XVIIᵉ–XVIIIᵉ siècles. *L'Homme* 122–124, 2–4: 75–99.

Dubois, Colette. 1993. L'Italie: cas atypique d'une puissance européenne en Afrique. *Matériaux pour l'histoire de notre temps* 32–33: 10–14.

Duchet, Michèle. 1971. *Anthropologie et histoire au siècle des lumières. Buffon, Voltaire, Rousseau, Helvétius, Diderot*. Paris: François Maspero.

—— and Claude. 1956. Un problème politique: la scolarisation de l'Algérie. *Les temps modernes* 11, 2, 123: 1387–1426.

Dumont, René. 1962. *L'Afrique noire est mal partie*. Paris: Éditions du Seuil.

Duverger, Christian. 1987. *La conversion des indiens de Nouvelle-Espagne*. Paris: Éditions du Seuil.

Elgey, Georgette. 1993. *Histoire de la IVᵉ République*. 3 vols. Paris: Librairie Arthème Fayard.

Elliott, J. H. 1984. The Spanish conquest and settlement of America. In Leslie Bethell, ed., *The Cambridge history of Latin America*, vol. 1, pp. 149–206. 11 vols. Cambridge: University of Cambridge Press.

——. 1984. Spain and America in the sixteenth and seventeenth centuries. In Leslie Bethell, ed., *The Cambridge history of Latin America*, vol. 1, pp. 287–340. 11 vols. Cambridge: University of Cambridge Press.

Elkin, Adolphus Peter. 1938. *The Australian aborigines. How to understand them*. Sydney: Angus and Robertson.

Emmer, P. C. and H. L. Wesseling, eds. 1979. *Reappraisals in overseas history*. Leiden: Leiden University Centre for the History of European Expansion.

Erikson, Erik H. 1969. *Gandhi's truth. On the origins of militant nonviolence.* New York: W. W. Norton.

Fabre, Michel, ed. 1970. *Esclaves et planteurs dans le Sud américain au XIXᵉ siècle.* Paris: Julliard.

Fall, Bernard B. 1964. *The two Vietnams. A political and military analysis.* New York: Praeger.

Fanon, Frantz. 1952. *Peau noire, masques blancs.* Paris: Éditions du Seuil.

——. 1961. *Les damnés de la terre.* Paris: François Maspero.

Favier, Jean. 1991. *Les grandes découvertes, d'Alexandre à Magellan.* Paris: Librairie Arthème Fayard.

Favre, Henri. 1972. Pérou, sentier lumineux et horizons obscurs. *Problèmes d'Amérique Latine.*

Femme dans les sociétés coloniale, La. 1984. *Études et documents* 19.

Ferro, Marc. 1967–76. *La révolution de 1917.* 2 vols. Paris: Aubier Montaigne.

——. 1992. *Comment on raconte l'histoire aux enfants à travers le monde entier.* Paris: Payot.

——. 1987. *L'histoire sous surveillance. Science et conscience de l'histoire.* Paris: Gallimard.

Fischer, Georges. 1966. *Le Parti travailliste et la decolonisation de l'Inde.* Paris: François Maspero.

Forest, A. and Tsuboï Yoshiharu (with collaboration from Yoshiaki Ishizawa and Jacques Gernet), eds. 1988. *Catholicisme et sociétés Asiatiques.* Paris: L'Harmattan.

Fourcade, Marie. 1994. Les dénommées "tribus criminelles" de l'Inde Britannique. Violence coloniale, violence traditionnelle. *Purusartha* 16: 187–211.

Fourniau, Charles. 1983. Les contacts franco-vietnamiens en Annam et au Tonkin de 1885 à 1896. PhD dissertation, University of Provence, Aix-en-Provenance.

Freyre, Gilberto. 1952. *Maîtres et esclaves. La formation de la société brésilienne* (translated from the Portuguese by Roger Bastide). Paris: Éditions Gallimard.

Friend, Theodor. 1988. *The blue-eyed enemy. Japan against the West in Java and Luzon, 1942–1945.* Princeton: Princeton University Press.

Gaikwad, V. R. 1967. *The Anglo-Indians. A study in the problems and processes involved in emotional and cultural integration.* London: Asia Publishing House.

Gallo, Max. 1967. *L'affaire d'Éthiopie.* Paris: Éditions du Centurion.

Gammer, Moshe. 1992. Was General Klüge-von-Klugenau Shamil's Desmichels? *Cahiers du monde Russe et Soviétique* 33, 2–3: 207–22.

Gandhi, M. K. 1927. *An Autobiography or the Story of my Experiments with Truth.* Ahmedabad: Navajivan.

Ganiage, Jean. 1959. *Les origines du protectorat français en Tunisie, 1861–1881.* Paris: Presses Universitaires de France.

—— (with collaboration from Jean Martin). 1994. *Histoire contemporaine du Maghreb.* Paris: Librairie Arthème Fayard.

Garsoïan, Nina. 1982. Le royaume du Nord (Section 1 of L'indépendance retrouvée: royaume du Nord et royaume du Sud, IXᵉ–XIᵉ siècle). In Gerard Dedeyan, ed., *Histoire des Arméniens,* pp. 215–47. Toulouse: Privat.

Gautier, Arlette. 1985. *Les soeurs de solitude. La condition féminine dans l'esclave aux Antilles du XVIIᵉ au XIXᵉ siècle.* Paris: Éditions Caribéennes.

Gautier, Emile-Félix. 1939. *L'Afrique blanche.* Paris: Librairie Arthème Fayard.

Geiss, Imanuel. 1968. *Panafrikanismus.* Europäische Verlagsanstalt.

Gellner, Ernest. 1970. Pouvoir politique et fonction religieuse dans l'Islam marocain. *Annales* 25, 3: 699–713.

Gernet, Jacques. 1982. *Chine et Christianisme. Action et réaction.* Paris: Éditions Gallimard.

——. 1988. Problèmes d'acclimatation du Christianisme dans la Chine du XVIIᵉ siècle. In A. Forest and Tsuboï Yoshiharu (with collarboration from Yoshiaki

Ishizawa and Jacques Gernet), eds., *Catholicisme et sociétés asiatiques*, pp. 35–47. Paris: L'Harmattan.

Girardet, Raoul. 1972. *L'idée coloniale en France de 1871 à 1962*. Paris: La Table Ronde.

Giraud, François. 1986. Viol et société coloniale: le cas de la Nouvelle-Espagne au XVIIIᵉ siècle. *Annales* 41, 3: 625–37.

Girault, René (with collaboration from Robert Frank and Jacques Thobie). 1979–93. *Histoire des relations internationales contemporaines*. 3 vols. Paris: Masson.

Godement, François. 1993. *La renaissance de l'Asie*. Paris: Odile Jacob.

Godinho, Vitorino de Magalhaes. 1969. L'économie de l'empire portugais au XVᵉ et XVIᵉ siècles. Paris: SEVPEN.

——. 1990. Les découvertes, XVᵉ, XVIᵉ: une révolution des mentalités. Paris: Autrement.

Goitein, S. D. 1954. From the Mediterranean to India. Documents on the trade to India, South Arabia, and East Africa from the eleventh and twelfth century. *Speculum* 29, 2, 1: 181–97.

Gollwitzer, Heinz. 1969. *Europe in the age of imperialism, 1880–1914*. London: Thames and Hudson.

Gong, Gerrit W. 1984. *The standard of "civilization" in international society*. Oxford: Clarendon Press.

Gourou, Pierre. 1966. *Les pays tropicaux. Principes d'une géographie humaine et économique*. Paris: Presses Universitaires de France.

Greenberger, Allen J. 1969. *The British image of India. A study in the literature of imperialism, 1880–1960*. London: Oxford University Press.

Gruzinski, Serge. 1988. *La colonisation de l'imaginaire. Sociétés indigènes et occidentalisation dans le Mexique espagnol, XVIᵉ–XVIIIᵉ siècle*. Paris: Éditions Gallimard.

Guillebaud, Jean-Claude. 1976. *Les confettis de l'empire*. Paris: Éditions du Seuil.

Hagège, Claude. 1992. *Le souffle de la langue. Voies et destins des parlers d'Europe*. Paris: Odile Jacob.

Halévy, Élie. 1912–1947. *Histoire du peuple anglais au XIXᵉ siècle*. 6 vols. Paris: Hachette Littérature.

Halperin-Donghi, Tulio. 1969. *Historia contemporánea de América Latina*. Madrid: Alianza Editorial.

Hammond, Thomas T. (with collaboration from Robert Farrell), ed. 1975. *The anatomy of communist takeovers*. New Haven: Yale University Press.

Hamnett, Brian R. 1971. *Politics and trade in southern Mexico, 1750–1821*. Cambridge: Cambridge University Press.

Hamoumou, Mohamed. 1993. *Et ils sont devenus harkis*. Paris: Fayard.

Harbi, Mohammed, ed. 1981. *Les archives de la révolution algérienne*. Paris: Éditions Jeune Afrique.

Hargreaves, John D. 1988. *Decolonization in Africa*. London: Longman.

Harrison, J. B. 1961. Five Portuguese historians. In C. H. Philips, ed., *Historians of India, Pakistan and Ceylon*, pp. 155–69. London: Oxford University Press

Hauser, Henri and Augustin Renaudet. 1929. *Les débuts de l'âge moderne. La renaissance et la réforme*. Paris: Librairie Félix Alcan.

Heers, Jacques. 1981. *Christophe Colomb*. Paris: Hachette.

Hennebelle, Guy and Catherine Ruelle. 1980. *Cinéastes d'Afrique noire, cin'action*.

Hobsbawn, Eric. 1987. *The age of empire, 1875–1914*. London: Weidenfeld & Nicolson.

Hodeir, Catherine and Michel Pierre. 1991. *L'exposition coloniale*. Bruxelles: Complexe.

Holland, Robert. 1985. *European decolonization 1918–1981. An introduction survey*. London.

Hourani, Albert. 1991. *A history of the Arab peoples*. Cambridge, MA: Harvard University Press.

Hughes, Robert. 1987. *The fatal shore*. New York: Knopf.

Huttenback, Henry R., ed. 1990. *Soviet nationality policies. Ruling ethnic groups in the URSS*. London: Mansell.

Ienaga, Saburo. 1978. *The Pacific War, 1931–1945. A critical perspective on Japan's role in World War II* (translated from the Japanese by Frank Baldwia). New York: Pantheon Books.

Jaulin, Robert. 1970. *La paix blanche. Introduction à l'ethnocide*. Paris: Éditions du Seuil.

——, ed. 1972. *L'éthnocide à travers les Amériques*. Paris: Librairie Arthème Fayard.

Julien, Charles-André, ed. 1946. *Les techniciens de la colonisation, XIXe et XXe siècles*. Paris: Presses Universitaires de France.

——. 1946. Bugeaud. In *Les techniciens de la colonisation, XIXe et XXe siècles*, pp. 55–74. Paris: Presses Universitaires de France.

——, ed. 1949. *Les politiques d'expansion impérialiste*. Paris: Presses Universitaires de France.

——. 1952. *L'Afrique du nord en marche. Nationalismes musulmans et souveraineté française*. Paris: René Julliard.

Julliard, Jacques. 1968. *La IVe République, 1947–1958*. Paris: Calmann-Lévy.

Kabou, Axelle. 1991. *Et si l'Afrique refusait le développement?* Paris: L'Harmattan.

Kalfon, P. and J. Leenhart. 1992. *Les Amériques Latines en France*. Paris: Gallimard.

Kappeler, Andreas. 1994. *La Russie: empire multi-ethnique*. Paris: Institut d'Études Slaves-Irenise.

Kaspi, André. 1976. *L'indépendance américaine, 1763–1789*. Paris: Éditions Gallimard/Julliard.

Kato, Echi. 1988. Adaptation et élimination: comment le Christianisme a-t-il été reçu au Japon. In A. Forest and Tsuboï Yoshiharu (with collaboration from Yoshiaki Ishizawa and Jacques Gernet), eds., *Catholicisme et sociétés asiatiques*, pp. 79–105. Paris: L'Harmattan.

Kniebiehler, Yvonne and Régine Goutalier. 1987. Femmes et colonisation. *Rapport terminal au ministère des relations extérieures et de la coopération: Études et documents*. Aix-en-Provence: Institut d'Histoire des Pays d'Outre-Mer.

Kolarz, Walter. 1952. *Russia and her colonies*. London: George Philip.

Kurz, B. G. and E. I. Kypy. 1928. *Otnosenie Mezdu Russkix i Kitajskix*. Moscow: Taskent.

Lacouture, Jean. 1967. *Hô Chi Minh*. Paris: Éditions du Seuil.

Lacouture, Jean and Simonne. 1956. *L'Égypte en movement*. Paris: Éditions du Seuil.

Lagana, Marc. 1990. *Le Parti colonial français. Éléments d'histoire*. Sillery: Presses de l'Université du Québec.

Landes, David S. 1958. *Bankers and pashas. International finance and economic imperialism in Egypt*. Toronto: Heinemann.

Lanternari, Vittorio. 1960. *Movimenti religiosi di libertà e di salvezza dei popoli oppressi*. Milan: Feltrinelli.

Laqueur, Walter. 1956. *Communism and nationalism in the Middle East*. London: Routledge.

Laran, Michel and Jean Saussay, eds. 1975. *La Russie ancienne, IXe–XVIIe siècles*. Paris: Masson.

Laroui, Abdallah. 1970. *L'histoire du Maghreb. Un essai de synthèse*. Paris: François Maspero.

——. 1977. *Les origines sociales et culturelles du nationalisme marocain, 1830–1912*. Paris: François Maspero.

Lavrin, Asunción. 1984. Women in Spanish American colonial society. In Leslie Bethell, ed., *The Cambridge history of Latin America*, vol. 2, pp. 321–55. 11 vols. Cambridge: University of Cambridge Press.

Lê, Thanh Khôi. 1954. *Le Viêt-Nam, histoire et civilisation*. Paris: Éditions de Minuit.

Lesure, Michel. 1972. *Lépante*. Paris: Julliard.

——. 1978. La France et le Caucase à l'époque de Chamil, à la lumière des dépêches des consuls français. *Cahiers du monde Russe et Soviétique* 19, 1–2: 5–65.

Lévi-Strauss, Claude. 1991. *Histoire de lynx*. Paris: Plon.

Lewis, Bernard. 1971. *Race and color in Islam*. New York: Harper.

——. 1982. *The Muslim discovery of Europe*. New York: W. W. Norton.

——. 1991. Watan. *Journal of contemporary history* 26, 3–4: 523–33.

Lichtheim, George. 1971. *Imperialism*. New York: Praeger.

Lombard, Denys. 1990. *Le carrefour Javanais. Essai d'histoire globale*. 3 vols. Paris: Éditions de l'École des Hautes Études en Sciences Sociales.

Low, D. A. 1991. *Eclipse of empire*. Cambridge: Cambridge University Press.

Lyons, Maryinez. 1988. Sleeping sickness, colonial medicine and imperialism: some connections in the Belgian Congo. In Roy MacLeod and Milton Lewis, eds., *Disease, medicine and empire. Perspectives on Western medicine and the experience of European expansion*, pp. 242–56. London: Routledge.

MacLeod, Roy and Milton Lewis, eds. 1988. *Disease, medicine, and empire. Perspectives on Western medicine and the experience of European expansion*. London: Routledge.

Madjarian, Grégoire. 1977. *La question coloniale et la politique du Parti communiste français, 1944–1947. Crise de l'impérialisme colonial et movement ouvrier*. Paris: François Maspero.

Mahn-Lot, Marianne. 1970. *La découverte de l'Amérique*. Paris: Flammarion.

Maitra, Kiran. 1991. *Roy, Comintern and Marxism in India*. Calcutta: Darbar Prakashan.

Malowist, Marian. 1962. Un essai d'histoire comparée: les movements d'expansion en Europe aux XVᵉ et XVIe siècles. *Annales ESC* 5: 923–29.

Manchester, William. 1983–88. *The last lion. Winston Spencer Churchill*. 2 vols. Boston: Littel, Brown and Company.

Mandouze, André. 1965. *La révolution algérienne par les textes*. Paris: François Maspero.

Mannoni, Octave. 1950. *Psychologie de la colonisation*. Paris: Éditions du Seuil.

Mantran, Robert, ed. 1989. *Histoire de l'Empire ottoman*. Paris: Fayard.

Marcovich, Anne. 1988. French colonial medicine and colonial rule: Algeria and Indochina. In Roy MacLeod and Milton Lewis, eds., *Disease, medicine, and empire. Perspectives on Western medicine and the experience of European expansion*, pp. 103–119. London: Routledge.

Margarido, Alfredo. 1971. La décolonisation. In Marc Ferro, ed., *L'histoire de 1871 à 1971: les idées, les problèmes*, vol. 1, pp. 144–77. 2 vols. Paris: Centre d'Étude et de Promotion de la Lecture.

——. 1974a. La réciprocité dans un mouvement paysan du sud du Brésil. *Annales* 29, 6: 1338–45.

——. 1974b. Review of *Peau noire, masques blancs* by Frantz Fanon. *Annales* 29, 2: 297–302.

Markovits, Claude. 1982. L'Inde coloniale: nationalisme et histoire. *Annales ESC* 4: 648–68.

——, ed. 1994. *Histoire de l'Inde moderne, 1480–1950*. Paris: Librairie Arthème Fayard.

Marks, Shula and Neil Andersson. 1988. Typhus and social control: South Africa, 1917–1950. In Roy MacLeod and Milton Lewis, eds., *Disease, medicine, and empire*.

Perspectives on Western medicine and the experience of European expansion, pp. 257–84. London: Routledge.

Marr, David G. 1971. *Vietnamese anticolonialism, 1885–1925*. Berkeley: University of California Press.

Marseille, Jacques. 1984. *Empire colonial et capitalisme français. Histoire d'un divorce*. Paris: Albin Michel.

Mascarenhas, Joao de Carvalho. 1993. *Esclave à Alger. Récit de captivité de Joao Mascarenhas, 1621–1626* (translated from the Portuguese by Paul Teyssier). Paris: Éditions Chandeigne.

Maskin, M. N. 1981. *Francuskie socialisty i demokraty i kolonialinyi vopros, 1830–1871*. Moscow: Nauka.

Maspero, François. 1993. *L'honneur de Saint-Arnaud*. Paris: Plon.

Mauro, F. 1991. Voyages de découvertes et premières colonisations: les comportements Portugais et Français comparés. Paper presented at the Colloquium on "Descobrimentos e Encontros de Culturas Historia y Memoria, p. sec. XV–XIX" held at Lisbon.

M'Bokolo, Elikia (with collaboration from Sophie Le Callennec, Thierno Bah, Jean Copans, Locha Mateso and Lelo Nzuzi). 1992. *Afrique noire. Histoire et civilisations, XIXᵉ et XXᵉ siècles*. Paris: Hatier.

Merle, Marcel, ed. 1969. *L'anticolonialisme européen de Las Casas à Karl Marx*. Paris: Armand Colin Éditeur.

Meyer, Jean A. 1973. *La révolution mexicaine, 1910–1940*. Paris: Calmann-Lévy.

———. 1990. *L'Europe et la conquête du monde, XVIe–XVIIIᵉ siècle*. Paris: Armand Colin Éditeur.

———, Jean Tarrade, Annie Rey-Goldzeigner and Jacques Thobie. 1991. *Histoire de la France coloniale, 1914*. Vol. 1. Paris: Armand Colin Éditeur.

Michel, Marc. 1993. *Décolonisation et emergence du Tiers-Monde*. Paris: Hachette.

Miège, Jean-Louis. 1973. *Expansion européenne et décolonisation de 1870 à nos jours*. Paris: Presses Universitaires de France.

Moquin, Wayne (with Charles van Doren), eds. 1971. *A documentary history of the Mexican-Americans*. New York: Praeger.

Morazé, Charles. 1957. *Les bourgeois conquérants, XIXᵉ siècle*. Paris: Armand Colin Éditeur.

Mormanne, Thierry. 1992. *Le problème des Kouriles: pour un retour à Saint-Pétersbourg*. Cipangu.

Mörner, Magnus. 1967. *Race mixture in the history of Latin America*. Boston: Little, Brown and Company.

Morris-Jones, W. H. and Georges Fisher, eds. 1980. *Decolonization and after. The British and French experience*. London: Frank Cass.

Mouradian, Claire. 1990. *De Staline à Gorbatchev. Histoire d'une république soviétique: l'Arménie*. Paris: Éditions Ramsay.

Mus, Paul. 1952. *Viêt-nam. Sociologie d'une guerre*. Paris: Éditions du Seuil.

Mutwa, Credo Vusa'mazula. 1969. *My people, my Africa*. New York: John Day.

Myrdal, Gunnar. 1968. *Asian drama. An inquiry into the poverty of nations*. 3 vols. New York: Twentieth Century Fund.

Naraghi, Ehsan. 1992. *Enseignement et changements sociaux en Iran du VIIᵉ au XXᵉ siècle. Islam et laicité, leçons d'une expérience seculaire*. Paris: Éditions de la Maison des Sciences de l'Homme.

Nehru, Jawaharlal. 1952. *Ma vie et mes prisons*. Paris: Denoël.

Neil, Bruce. 1975. *Portugal. The last empire*. New York: John Wiley.

Ninomiya, Hiroyuki. 1990. L'époque moderne. In Francine Herail, Jean Esmein, François Macé, Hiroyuki Ninomiya and Pierre Souyri, *Histoire du Japon*, pp. 301–424. Le Coteau: Éditions Horvath.

Nkrumah, Kwane. 1965. *Neo-colonialism. The last stage of imperialism.* London: Nelson.

Nolde, Boris. 1952–53. *La formation de l'Empire russe. Études, notes et documents.* 2 vols. Paris: Institut d'Études Slaves.

Nora, Pierre. 1961. *Les français d'Algérie.* Paris: Julliard.

Nouschi, André. 1962. *La naissance du nationalisme Algérien.* Paris: Éditions de Minuit.

Ortiz, José A. 1993. La conquete des pays du Rio de la Plata. In Guadalupe Bocanegra and José A. Ortiz, eds., *Les 500 années de l'Amérique latine, 1492–1992. L'Amérique latine et l'Europe face à l'histoire,* pp. 73–77. Montreuil: Éditions Page et Image.

Panikkar, K. M. 1947. *A survey of Indian history.* London: Meridan Books.

——. 1953. *Asia and Western dominance. A survey of the Vasco Da Gama epoch of Asian history, 1498–1945.* London: George Allen & Unwin.

Park, Mungo. 1815. *Travels in the interior districts of Africa. Performed in the years 1795, 1796 and 1797. With an account of a subsequent mission to that country in 1805.* 2 vols. London: John Murray.

Paton, Alan. 1948. *Cry, the beloved country.* New York: Charles Scribner.

Paudrat, Jean-Louis 1984. From Africa. In William Rubin, ed., *"Primitivism" in 20th century art. Affinity of the tribal and the modern,* vol. 1, pp. 125–75. 2 vols. New York: Museum of Modern Art.

Payne, Robert. 1969. *The life and death of Mahatma Gandhi.* New York: E. P. Dutton.

Pearson, M. N. 1987. *The Portuguese in India.* Cambridge: Cambridge University Press.

Pelissier, René. 1979. *Le naufrage des caravelles. Études sur la fin de l'Empire portugais, 1961–1975.* Montamets: Éditions Pelissier.

Person, Yves. 1968. *Samori. Une révolution dyula.* 3 vols. Dakar: Institut Fondamental d'Afrique Noire.

Pierre, Michel. 1982. *Terre de la grande punition. La Guyane.* Paris: Ramsay.

Pipes, Richard. 1957. *The formation of the Soviet Union. Communism and nationalism, 1917–1923.* Cambridge, MA: Harvard University Press.

Platonov, S. F. Inozemci na russkom severe XVIe–XVIIIe. In, *Ocerki po istorii Kolonizacii severa i Sibiri,* pp. 5–17. Petrograd.

Pluchon, Pierre. 1991. *Le premier empire colonial, des origines à 1815.* Volume 2 of *Histoire de la colonisation française.* Paris: Librairie Arthème Fayard.

Pouchepadass, Jacques. 1975. *L'Inde au XXe siècle.* Paris: Presses Universitaires de France.

—— and Henri Stern, eds. 1991. De la royauté à l'état anthropologie et histoire du politique dans le monde indien. *Purusartha* 13.

Preiswerk, Roy and Dominique Perrot. 1975. *Ethnocentrisme et histoire. L'Afrique, l'Amérique indienne et l'Asie dans les manuels occidentaux.* Paris: Éditions Anthropos.

Priollaud, Nicole, ed. 1983. *La France colonisatrice.* Paris: Lina Levi Sylvie Messinger.

Prunier, Gérard. 1992. L'Égypte et le Soudan 1820–1885: Empire tardif ou proto-colonisation en Afrique Orientale. *Hérodote* 65/66, 2/3, 169–90.

Quested, R. K. I. 1968. *The expansion of Russia in East Asia, 1857–1860.* Kuala Lumpur: University of Malaya Press.

Ramasubban, Radhika. 1988. Imperial health in British India, 1857–1900. In Roy MacLeod and Milton Lewis, eds., *Disease, medicine, and empire. Perspectives on Western medicine and the experience of European expansion,* pp. 38–60. London: Routledge.

Ramos, Guerreiro. 1957. *Sociologia crítica Brasileira.* Rio de Janeiro.

Randles, W. G. L. 1969. De la traite à la colonisation: les Portugais en Angola. *Annales* 24, 2: 289–304.

——. 1975. Échanges de marchandises et échanges de dieux ou chassé-croisé culturel entre Européens et Bantu. *Annales ESC* 4: 635–53.

Raulin, Henri. 1962. Psychologie du paysan des tropiques. *Études rurales* 2, 7: 59–82.

Raymond, André. 1989. Les provinces arabes, XVIe siècle–XVIIIe siècle. In Robert Mantran, ed., *Histoire de l'Empire ottoman*, pp. 341–420. Paris: Fayard.

——. 1993. *Le caire*. Paris: Fayard.

Rémond, René. 1974. *Introduction à l'histoire de notre temps*. 3 vols. Paris: Éditions du Seuil.

Richards, Jeffrey. 1973. *Visions of yesterday*. London: Routledge.

Ridley, Hugh. 1983. *Images of imperial role*. London: Croom Helm.

Rioux, Jean-Pierre, ed. 1990. *La guerre d'Algérie et les français*. Paris: Librairie Arthème Fayard.

—— and Jean-François Sirinelli, eds. 1991. *La guerre d'Algérie et les intellectuels français*. Bruxelles: Éditions Complexe.

Rivet, Daniel. 1976. Le commandement français et ses réactions vis-à-vis du movement rifain, 1924–1926. In, *Abd el-Krim et la République du Rif*, pp. 101–36. Paris: François Maspero.

Rivière d'Arc, Hélène, ed. 1993. *L'Amérique du Sud aux XIXe et XXe siècles. Héritages et territoires*. Paris: Armand Colin Éditeur.

Rizzi, Bruno. 1939. *La bureaucratisation du monde*. Paris: Published by the Author.

Rodinson, Maxime. 1971. Racisme, xénophobie, ethnisme. In Marc Ferro, ed., *L'histoire de 1811 à 1971: les idées, les problèmes*, vol. 1, pp. 392–411. 2 vols. Paris: Centre d'Étude et de Promotion de la Lecture.

——. 1972. *Marxisme et monde musulman*. Paris: Éditions du Seuil.

——. 1993. *L'Islam. Politique et croyance*. Paris: Librairie Arthème Fayard.

Romano, Ruggiero. 1972. *Les mécanismes de la conquête coloniale. Les conquistadores*. Paris: Flammarion.

Rose, Deborah Bird. 1991. *Hidden histoires. Black stories from Victoria river downs, Humbert river and Wave Hill stations*. Canberra: Aboriginal Studies Press.

Rossiiskie. 1990. *Putesestvenniki v. indii, XIX^r–XX^r v*. Moscow: Grvl

Rouet, Jeanine. 1973. Des puritans aux Yankees: l'évolution. *Annales ESC* 5: 1131–42.

Rowbotham, Sheila. 1972. *Women, resistance and revolution. A history of women and revolution in the modern world*. London: Penguin.

Sarinov, J. 1955. *La lutte des travailleurs du Tadjikistan pour le renforcement du pouvoir Soviétique pendant la période d'activité du Comité Révolutionnaire de la République de Tadjikistan, 1924–1926*. 2 vols. Stalinabad: IANTSSR.

Saul, S. B. 1960. *Studies in British overseas trade, 1870–1914*. Liverpool: Liverpool University Press.

Schram, Stuart. 1965. *Le marxisme et l'Asie, 1853–1964*. Paris: Armand Colin Éditeur.

Schreuder, D. M. 1980. *The scramble for Southern Africa, 1877–1895. The politics of partition reappraised*. Cambridge: Cambridge University Press.

Schumpeter, Joseph. 1941. Zur soziologie der imperialism. *Archiv für sozialwissenschaft und social politik* 46: 1–39 and 275–310.

Seton-Watson, Hugh N. 1977. *Nations and states. An enquiry into the origins of nations and the politics of nationalism*. London: Methuen.

Sicroff, Albert A. 1960. *Les controverses des statuts de "pureté de sang" en Espagne du XVe au XVIIe siècle*. Paris: Librairie Marcel Didier.

Siegfried, André. 1931. *La crise britannique au XXe siècle*. Paris: Armand Colin Éditeur.

——. 1946. A. Wakefield. In Charles André Julien, ed., *Les techniciens de la colonisation, XIXe et XXe siècles*, pp. 175–194. Paris: Presses Universitaires de France.

Singer, Barnett. 1991. Lyautey: an interpretation of the Man and French imperialism. *Journal of contemporary history* 26, 1: 131–57.

Sivan, Emmanuel. Modern Arab historiography of the crusades. *Asian and African studies* 8: 109–149.

Slavin, D. H. 1991. The French Left and the Rif War, 1924–25: racism and the limits of internationalism. *Journal of contemporary history* 26, 1: 5–32.

Socialisme et barbarie 28 and 29. 1959. Un algérien ranconte sa vie.

Soinbaclv, T. J. 1962. K Voprosy o prisoedinenii srednego juza k Rossii. In, *Voprosy istorii Kazakhstana i vostocnogo Turkestana*, pp. 41–60.

Soustelle, Jacques. 1963. *Aimée et souffrante. Algérie.* Paris: Librairie Plon.

Souyri, Pierre. 1983. *La dynamique du capitalisme au XX⁰ siècle.* Paris: Payot.

Souyri, Pierre-François. 1995. *Une forme originale de domination coloniale. Les Japonais et le Hokkaido avant l'époque Meiji.* Mélanges offerts à Marc Ferro. Paris: Irenise.

Spear, Percival. 1932. *The Nabobs. A study of the social life of the English in eighteenth century India.* London: Oxford University Press.

———. 1965. *The Oxford history of modern India, 1740–1947.* Oxford: Clarendon Press.

Spring, Derek W. 1979, Russian imperialism in Asia in 1914. *Cahiers du monde russe et soviétique* 20, 3–4: 305–322.

Stengers, Jean. 1989. *Congo. Mythes et réalités.* Louvain: Duculot.

Stora, Benjamin. 1986. *Messali Hadj. Pionnier du nationalisme algérien, 1898–1974.* Paris: Éditions L'Harmattan.

———. 1993. *Histoire de la guerre d'Algérie, 1954–1962.* Paris: Éditions La Découverte.

Szyliowicz, Joseph S. 1973. *Education and modernization in the Middle East.* Ithaca: Cornell University Press.

Tardits, Claude. 1962–63. Réflexions sur le problème de la scolarisation des filles au Dahomey. *Cahiers d'études africaines* 3, 10: 266–88.

Tawney, Richard Henry. 1926. *Religion and the rise of capitalism. A historical study.* London: John Murray.

Taylor, William B. 1972. *Landlord and peasant in colonial Oaxaca.* Stanford: Stanford University Press.

———. 1979. *Drinking, homicide & rebellion in colonial Mexican villages.* Stanford: Stanford University Press.

Ter, Minassian Anahide. 1973. Le movement révolutionnaire Arménien, 1890–1903. *Cahiers du monde Russe et Soviétique* 14, 3–4: 536–607.

Terray, Emmanuel. 1977. Asante au XIX⁰ siècle. *Annales ESC* 2: 311–25.

Thobie, Jacques. 1982. *La France impériale, 1880–1914.* Paris: Éditions Megrelis.

———. 1985. *Ali et les 40 voleurs. Impérialismes et Moyen-Orient de 1914 à nos jours.* Paris: Messidor/Temps Actuels.

———, Gilbert Meynier, Catherine Coquery-Vidrovitch, Charles-Robert Ageron. 1990. *Histoire de la France coloniale, 1914–1990.* Vol. 2. Paris: Armand Colin Éditeur.

Thornton, John. 1992. *Africa and Africans in the making of the Atlantic world, 1400–1680.* Cambridge: Cambridge University Press.

Thrupp, Sylvia. 1962. Millennian dreams in action: essays in comparative study. *Comparative studies in society and history* 11–31.

Todorov, Tzvetan. 1982. *La conquête de l'Amérique. La question de l'autre.* Paris: Éditions du Seuil.

Touchard, Jean. 1978. *Le gaullisme, 1940–1969.* Paris: Éditions du Seuil.

Trigger, Bruce G. 1985. *Natives and newcomers. Canada's "heroic age" reconsidered.* Montreal: McGill-Queen's University Press.

Valensi, Lucette. 1969. *Le Maghreb avant la prise d'Alger, 1790–1830.* Paris: Flammarion.

———. 1977. *Fellahs tunisiens. L'économie rurale et la vie des campagnes aux 18⁰ et 19⁰ siècles.* Paris: Mouton.

——. 1992. *Fables de la mémoire. La glorieuse bataille des trois rois.* Paris: Éditions du Seuil.

Van Onselen, Charles. 1992. Paternalisme et violence dans les fermes du Transvaal de 1900 à 1950. *Annales ESC* 1: 5–34.

Veinstein, Gilles. 1989. L'empire dans sa grandeur, XVIe siècle. In Robert Mantran, ed., *Histoire de l'Empire Ottoman,* pp. 159–227. Paris: Fayard.

Vergès, Jacques. 1968. *De la stratégie judiciaire.* Paris: Éditions du Seuil.

Vernadsky, George, ed. 1972. *A source book for Russian history from early times to 1917.* 3 vols. New Haven: Yale University Press.

Vidal, Denis, Gilles Tarabout and Eric Meyer, eds. 1994. Violences et non-violences en Inde. *Purusartha* 16.

Vidal-Naquet, Pierre. 1972. *La torture dans la République. Essai d'histoire et de politique contemporaines, 1954–1962.* Paris: Éditions du Minuit.

Vigié, Marc. 1993. *Dupleix.* Paris: Fayard.

Vincent, Bernard. 1991. *1492 "l'année admirable".* Paris: Aubier.

Viollis, Andrée. 1948. *L'Afrique du Sud, cette inconnue.* Paris: Hachette.

Wachtel, Nathan. 1967. La vision des vaincus. La conquête Espagnole dans le foklore indigène. *Annales ESC* 3: 554–85.

——. 1990. *Le retour des ancêtres. Les indiens Urus de Bolivie, XXe–XVIe siècle. Essai d'histoire régressive.* Paris: Éditions Gallimard.

Wallerstein, Immanuel. 1974–1989. *The modern world-system.* 3 vols. New York: Academic Press.

Wandjuk, Marika. 1977. *The aboriginal children's history of Australia.* Melbourne.

Weber, Eugen J. 1976. *Peasants into Frenchmen. The modernization of rural France, 1870–1914.* Stanford: Stanford University Press.

Werth, Alexander. 1956. *France, 1940–1955.* London: Robert Hale.

Westermann, Diedrich. 1943. *Autobiographies d'Africains* (translated from the German by L. Homburger). Paris: Payot.

Wieviorka, Michel. 1988. *Sociétés et terrorisme.* Paris: Fayard.

Wilks, Ivor. 1975. *Asante in the nineteenth century. The structure and evolution of a political order.* Cambridge: Cambridge University Press.

Williams, Eric. 1970. *From Columbus to Castro. The history of the Caribbean, 1492–1969.* London: Harper & Row.

Winock, Michel. 1978. *La République se meurt. Chronique 1956–1958.* Paris: Éditions du Seuil.

Wish, Harvey, ed. 1964. *Slavery in the South. First-hand accounts of the ante-bellum American Southland from northern and southern whites, Negroes, and foreing observers.* New York: Farrar, Straus.

Wobeser, Gisela von. 1983. *La formación de la hacienda en la época colonial. El uso de la tierra y el agua.* Mexico: UNAM.

Woeikof, A. 1914. *Le Turkestan Russe.* Paris: Armand Colin Éditeur.

Wood, Gordon S. 1969. *The creation of the American Republic, 1776–1787.* Chapel Hill: University of North Carolina Press.

Wray, Harold. 1971. *Changes and continuity in Japanese image of the Kokutai and attitudes toward the outside world.* Honolulu: University of Hawaii Press.

Yacine, Kateb. 1956. *Nedjma.* Paris: Éditions du Seuil.

Yazawa, Toshihiko. 1988. Une analyse des persécutions du Catholicisme en Chine. In A. Forest and Tsuboï Yoshiharu (with collaboration from Yoshiaki Ishizawa and Jacques Gernet), eds, *Catholicism et sociétés Asiatiques,* pp. 31–47. Paris: L'Harmattan and Tokyo: Sophia University Press.

Zorgbibe, Charles. 1993. *L'après-guerre froide dans le monde.* Paris: Presses Universitaires de France.

INDEX